Artificial Intelligence Illuminated

Ben Coppin

JONES AND BARTLETT PUBLISHERS

Sudbury, Massachusetts

BOSTON   TORONTO   LONDON   SINGAPORE

World Headquarters

Jones and Bartlett Publishers
40 Tall Pine Drive
Sudbury, MA 01776
978-443-5000
info@jbpub.com
www.jbpub.com

Jones and Bartlett Publishers
Canada
2406 Nikanna Road
Mississauga, ON L5C 2W6
CANADA

Jones and Bartlett Publishers
International
Barb House, Barb Mews
London W6 7PA
UK

Cover image © Photodisc

Library of Congress Cataloging-in-Publication Data
Coppin, Ben.
    Artificial intelligence illuminated / by Ben Coppin.--1st ed.
        p. cm.
Includes bibliographical references and index.
    ISBN 0-7637-3230-3
    1. Artificial intelligence.   I. Title.
    Q335.C586 2004
    006.3--dc22

                              2003020604

Acquisitions Editor: Stephen Solomon
Production Manager: Amy Rose
Marketing Manager: Matthew Bennett
Editorial Assistant: Caroline Senay
Manufacturing Buyer: Therese Bräuer
Cover Design: Kristin E. Ohlin
Text Design: Kristin E. Ohlin
Composition: Northeast Compositors
Technical Artist: George Nichols
Printing and Binding: Malloy, Inc.
Cover Printing: Malloy, Inc.

Printed in the United States of America
08 07 06 05   10 9 8 7 6 5 4 3 2

For Erin

Preface

Who Should Read This Book

This book is intended for students of computer science at the college level, or students of other subjects that cover Artificial Intelligence. It also is intended to be an interesting and relevant introduction to the subject for other students or individuals who simply have an interest in the subject.

The book assumes very little knowledge of computer science, but does assume some familiarity with basic concepts of algorithms and computer systems. Data structures such as trees, graphs, and stacks are explained briefly in this book, but if you do not already have some familiarity with these concepts, you should probably seek out a suitable book on algorithms or data structures.

It would be an advantage to have some experience in a programming language such as C++ or Java, or one of the languages commonly used in Artificial Intelligence research, such as PROLOG and LISP, but this experience is neither necessary nor assumed.

Many of the chapters include practical exercises that require the reader to develop an algorithm or program in a programming language of his or her choice. Most readers should have no difficulty with these exercises. However, if any reader does not have the necessary skills he or she simply should describe in words (or in pseudocode) how his or her programs work, giving as much detail as possible.

How to Read This Book

This book can be read in several ways. Some readers will choose to read the chapters through in order from Chapter 1 through Chapter 21. Any chapter that uses material which is presented in another chapter gives a clear reference to that chapter, and readers following the book from start to finish should not need to jump forward at any point, as the chapter dependencies tend to work in a forward direction.

Another perfectly reasonable way to use this book is as a reference. When a reader needs to know more about a particular subject, he or she can pick up this book and select the appropriate chapter or chapters, and can be illuminated on the subject (at least, that is the author's intent!)

Chapter 12 contains a diagram that shows how the dependencies between chapters work (Section 12.6.2). This diagram shows, for example, that if a reader wants to read Chapter 8, it would be a good idea to already have read Chapter 7.

This book is divided into six parts, each of which is further divided into a number of chapters. The chapters are laid out as follows:

Part 1: Introduction to Artificial Intelligence

Chapter 1: A Brief History of Artificial Intelligence

Chapter 2: Uses and Limitations

Chapter 3: Knowledge Representation

Part 2: Search

Chapter 4: Search Methodologies

Chapter 5: Advanced Search

Chapter 6: Game Playing

Part 3: Logic

Chapter 7: Propositional and Predicate Logic

Chapter 8: Inference and Resolution for Problem Solving

Chapter 9: Rules and Expert Systems

Each chapter includes an introduction that explains what the chapter covers, a summary of the chapter, some exercises and review questions, and some suggestions for further reading. There is a complete bibliography at the back of the book.

This book also has a glossary, which includes a brief definition of most of the important terms used in this book. When a new term is introduced in the text it is highlighted in **bold**, and most of these words are included in the glossary. The only such terms that are not included in the glossary are the ones that are defined in the text, but that are not used elsewhere in the book.

The use of third person pronouns is always a contentious issue for authors of text books, and this author has chosen to use he and she interchangeably. In some cases the word "he" is used, and in other cases "she." This is not intended to follow any particular pattern, or to make any representations about the genders, but simply is in the interests of balance.

The first few chapters of this book provide introductory material, explaining the nature of Artificial Intelligence and providing a historical background, as well as describing some of the connections with other disciplines. Some readers will prefer to skip these chapters, but it is advisable to at least glance through Chapter 3 to ensure that you are familiar with the concepts of that chapter, as they are vital to the understanding of most of the rest of the book.

Acknowledgments

Although I wrote this book single-handedly, it was not without help. I would like to thank, in chronological order, Frank Abelson; Neil Salkind and everyone at Studio B; Michael Stranz, Caroline Senay, Stephen Solomon, and Tracey Chapman at Jones & Bartlett; also a number of people who read chapters of the book: Martin Charlesworth, Patrick Coyle, Peter and Petra Farrell, Robert Kealey, Geoffrey Price, Nick Pycraft, Chris Swannack, Edwin Young, my parents, Tony and Frances, and of course Erin—better late than never.

Thanks also to:

The MIT Press for the excerpt from 'Learning in Multiagent Systems' by Sandip Sen and Gerhard Weiss, © 2001, The MIT Press.

The MIT Press for the excerpt from 'Adaptation in Natural and Artificial Systems' by John H. Holland, © 1992, The MIT Press.

The MIT Press for the excerpt from 'The Artificial Life Roots of Artificial Intelligence' by Luc Steels, © 1994, the Massachusetts Institute of Technology.

The IEEE for the excerpt from 'Steps Towards Artificial Intelligence' by Marvin Minsky, © 2001, IEEE.

I have attempted to contact the copyright holders of all copyrighted quotes used in this book. If I have used any quotes without permission, then this was inadvertent, and I apologize. I will take all measures possible to rectify the situation in future printings of the book.

Contents

Introduction to Artificial Intelligence

Introduction to Part 1

Part 1 is divided into three chapters.

CHAPTER 1

A Brief History of Artificial Intelligence

This chapter provides a brief overview of the history of the study of Artificial Intelligence. It also provides background from philosophy, psychology, biology, and linguistics and explains how these subjects have contributed to the subject.

CHAPTER 2

Uses and Limitations

The second chapter discusses the prevalence of Artificial Intelligence in our world today, at the beginning of the 21st century. It also looks at the limitations of Artificial Intelligence and discusses some of the arguments against the principle of strong AI, which claims that a machine that can behave in an intelligent way is actually capable of having mental states, much like a human being.

CHAPTER 3

Knowledge Representation

This chapter introduces an idea that is used throughout this book: knowledge representation. It explains why representation is so important and why it is vital to choose the right representation to solve a problem.

It also explains some common representational methods used in Artificial Intelligence, such as frames, semantic nets, and search trees, which are used more extensively in Chapters 4 and 5.

This chapter also provides a number of example problems and explains how to use the representational methods introduced to solve the problems.

CHAPTER 1

A Brief History of Artificial Intelligence

What is all knowledge too but recorded experience, and a product of history; of which, therefore, reasoning and belief, no less than action and passion, are essential materials?

—Thomas Carlyle, *Critical and Miscellaneous Essays*

History is Philosophy from Examples.

—Dionysius, *Ars Rhetorica*

Science is built upon facts, as a house is built of stones; but an accumulation of facts is no more a science than a heap of stones is a house.

—Henri Poincaré, *Science and Hypothesis*

You seek for knowledge and wisdom as I once did; and I ardently hope that the gratification of your wishes may not be a serpent to sting you, as mine has been.

—Mary Shelley, Frankenstein

1.1 Introduction

Although Artificial Intelligence is one of the newest fields of intellectual research, its foundations began thousands of years ago. In studying Artificial Intelligence, it is useful to have an understanding of the background of a number of other subjects, primarily philosophy, linguistics, psychology, and biology.

This chapter will present a selected history of the thinking and research that led up to the present state of what we now call Artificial Intelligence.

In this chapter, we will look at the contributions made by philosophy, linguistics, psychology, and biology to Artificial Intelligence. We will also look at the difference between the claims made by proponents of weak AI (AI is a commonly used abbreviation for Artificial Intelligence) compared with those who support strong AI, as well as look at the difference between strong methods and weak methods in Artificial Intelligence.

We will begin by looking at Artificial Intelligence itself and trying to find a definition for the subject.

1.2   What Is Artificial Intelligence?

Perhaps a better starting point would be to ask, "What is intelligence?" This is a complex question with no well-defined answer that has puzzled biologists, psychologists, and philosophers for centuries. In Chapter 13 we pose a similar question when we ask, "What is life?" in order to help us understand what Artificial Life, a branch of Artificial Intelligence, is.

One could certainly define intelligence by the properties it exhibits: an ability to deal with new situations; the ability to solve problems, to answer questions, to devise plans, and so on. It is perhaps harder to define the difference between the intelligence exhibited by humans and that exhibited by dolphins or apes.

For now we will confine ourselves, then, to the somewhat simpler question that is posed by the title of this section: What Is Artificial Intelligence?

A simple definition might be as follows:

Artificial intelligence is the study of systems that act in a way that to any observer would appear to be intelligent.

This definition is fine, but in fact it does not cover the whole of Artificial Intelligence. In many cases, Artificial Intelligence techniques are used to solve relatively simple problems or complex problems that are internal to more complex systems. For example, the search techniques described in Chapter 4 are rarely used to provide a robot with the ability to find its way out of a maze, but are frequently used for much more prosaic problems.

This may lead us to another definition of Artificial Intelligence, as follows:

Artificial Intelligence involves using methods based on the intelligent behavior of humans and other animals to solve complex problems.

Hence, in Chapter 20, we look at systems that are able to "understand" human speech, or at least are able to extract some meaning from human utterances, and carry out actions based on those utterances. Such systems may not be designed to behave in an intelligent way, but simply to provide some useful function. The methods they use, however, are based on the intelligent behavior of humans.

This distinction is brought into sharper contrast when we look at the difference between so-called **strong AI** and **weak AI**.

The followers of strong AI believe that by giving a computer program sufficient processing power, and by providing it with enough intelligence, one can create a computer that can literally think and is conscious in the same way that a human is conscious.

Many philosophers and Artificial Intelligence researchers consider this view to be false, and even ludicrous. The possibility of creating a robot with emotions and real consciousness is one that is often explored in the realms of science fiction but is rarely considered to be a goal of Artificial Intelligence.

Weak AI, in contrast, is simply the view that intelligent behavior can be modeled and used by computers to solve complex problems. This point of view argues that just because a computer behaves intelligently does not prove that it is actually intelligent in the way that a human is. We will examine this argument in more detail in Chapter 2, when we look at the Chinese Room thought experiment and the arguments around it.

1.3   Strong Methods and Weak Methods

We have discussed the difference between the claims of weak AI and strong AI. This difference is not to be confused with the difference between **strong methods** and **weak methods**.

Weak methods in Artificial Intelligence use systems such as logic, automated reasoning, and other general structures that can be applied to a wide range of problems but that do not necessarily incorporate any real knowledge about the world of the problem that is being solved.

In contrast, strong method problem solving depends on a system being given a great deal of knowledge about its world and the problems that it might encounter. Strong method problem solving depends on the weak methods because a system with knowledge is useless without some methodology for handling that knowledge.

Hence, the production systems we will examine in Chapter 9 are based on the weak method expert system shells but use strong method rules to encode their knowledge.

The earliest research in Artificial Intelligence focused on weak methods. Newell and Simon's General Problem Solver (GPS), which is discussed in Chapter 15, was an attempt to use weak methods to build a system that could solve a wide range of general problems. That this approach ultimately failed led to a realization that more was needed than simple representations and algorithms to make Artificial Intelligence work: knowledge was the key ingredient.

A great number of the subjects covered in this book are weak methods. This does not mean that they are not worth studying, or even that they are not useful. In many situations, weak methods are ideal for solving problems. However, the addition of knowledge is almost always essential to build systems that are able to deal intelligently with new problems; if our aim is to build systems that appear to behave intelligently, then strong methods are certainly essential.

1.4   From Aristotle to Babbage

In Chapter 7 of this book, we present the propositional and predicate logics. These systems for logical reasoning are based on the logic invented by Aristotle, a philosopher from ancient Greece, who lived from 384 to 322 B.C. and who studied under Plato during that time. The writings of Aristotle (on this and many other subjects) have formed the basis for a great deal of our modern scientific thinking.

From the point of view of Artificial Intelligence, the most interesting aspect of Aristotle's work is his study of logic. He invented the idea of the **syllogism**, which he defined as follows:

> "A discourse in which certain things having been stated, something else follows of necessity from their being so."

Aristotle's logic was developed and expanded on by later philosophers, mathematicians, and logicians. The first real steps in the study of logic after Aristotle took place in the 12th century, when Peter Abelard (who lived from 1079 to 1142 A.D.) wrote *Dialectica*, a treatise on logic. In the following centuries, more work was carried out, but the greatest developments were made in the last few centuries.

In the late 17th to early 18th centuries, Gottfried Leibniz, the German mathematician and philosopher who along with Isaac Newton had a part in the invention of the calculus used by mathematicians today, invented the idea of developing a formal mathematical language for reasoning. His universal language would allow us to express with great precision problems of all kinds, and then go about solving them. Leibniz did not succeed in creating this universal language, but his work provided the basis for the propositional and predicate logics that are so important to Artificial Intelligence research today.

In the 19th century, George Boole, an English mathematician, who lived from 1815 to 1864, developed Boolean algebra, the logical system we still use as part of propositional and predicate logics. Boolean algebra is widely used by electronics engineers in developing logical gates for silicon chips and is also used by computer scientists. Boolean algebra provides a language for expressing concepts such as "A is true" and "A is true but B is false."

Around the same time that Boole was inventing his algebra, Charles Babbage invented the world's first computer—the Analytic Engine. He didn't ever manage to build the computer, but his designs were later used to build a working model. The designs of computers in the 20th century didn't bear much resemblance to Babbage's computer, but they certainly owed a great deal to it.

Babbage's idea of a digital computer remained a dream until around the middle of the 20th century. By the 1950s, a number of working computers had been built. Unlike Babbage's mechanical engines, these computers were electronic. The very first electromechanical computers were soon replaced by computers based on vacuum tubes.

1.5   Alan Turing and the 1950s

One of the great figures in the history of Artificial Intelligence is Alan Turing. During World War II, Turing famously worked in Bletchley Park, helping to solve the Germans' codes. After the war, he began to work on the idea of the possibility of building a computer that could think. His paper published in 1950, *Computing Machinery & Intelligence*, was one of the first papers to be written on this subject.

The **Turing test** was designed by Turing as a way to judge the success or otherwise of an attempt to produce a thinking computer. More specifically, it was based on the idea that if a person who interrogated the computer could not tell if it was a human or a computer, then to all intents and purposes, Turing said, it is intelligent.

The test is designed as follows:

The interrogator is given access to two individuals, one of whom is a human and the other of whom is a computer. The interrogator can ask the two individuals questions, but cannot directly interact with them. Probably the questions are entered into a computer via a keyboard, and the responses appear on the computer screen.

The human is intended to attempt to help the interrogator, but if the computer is really intelligent enough, it should be able to fool the interrogator into being uncertain about which is the computer and which is the human.

The human can give answers such as "I'm the human—the other one is the computer," but of course, so can the computer. The real way in which the human proves his or her humanity is by giving complex answers that a computer could not be expected to comprehend. Of course, the inventors of the truly intelligent computer program would have given their program the ability to anticipate all such complexities.

Turing's test has resulted in a number of computer programs (such as Weizenbaum's ELIZA, designed in 1965) that were designed to mimic human conversation. Of course, this in itself is not a particularly useful function, but the attempt has led to improvements in understanding of areas such as natural language processing. To date, no program has passed the Turing test, although cash prizes are regularly offered to the inventor of the first computer program to do so.

Later in the 1950s computer programs began to be developed that could play games such as checkers and chess (see Chapter 6), and also the first work was carried out into developing computer programs that could understand human language (Chapter 20).

A great deal of work at this stage was done in computer translation. It was, indeed, widely believed that computers could eventually be programmed to translate accurately from one human language to another. It has since been found that the task of machine translation is actually an extremely difficult one, and not one that has yet been completely solved. This subject is discussed in more detail in Chapter 20.

In 1956, the term **Artificial Intelligence** was first used by John McCarthy at a conference in Dartmouth College, in Hanover, New Hampshire.

In 1957, Newell and Simon invented the idea of the GPS, whose purpose was, as the name suggests, to solve almost any logical problem. The program used a methodology known as means ends analysis, which is based on the idea of determining what needs to be done and then working out a way to do it. This works well enough for simple problems, but AI researchers soon realized that this kind of method could not be applied in such a general way—the GPS could solve some fairly specific problems for which it was ideally suited, but its name was really a misnomer.

At this time there was a great deal of optimism about Artificial Intelligence. Predictions that with hindsight appear rash were widespread. Many commentators were predicting that it would be only a few years before computers could be designed that would be at least as intelligent as real human beings and able to perform such tasks as beating the world champion at chess, translating from Russian into English, and navigating a car through a busy street. Some success has been made in the past 50 years with these problems and other similar ones, but no one has yet designed a computer that anyone would describe reasonably as being intelligent.

In 1958, McCarthy invented the LISP programming language, which is still widely used today in Artificial Intelligence research.

1.6   The 1960s to the 1990s

Since the 1950s, a great deal of the original optimism has gone out of Artificial Intelligence and has been replaced with a degree of realism.

The aim of the study of Artificial Intelligence is no longer to create a robot as intelligent as a human, but rather to use algorithms, heuristics, and methodologies based on the ways in which the human brain solves problems. Hence, systems have been designed such as Thomas Evans' **Analogy** and Melanie Mitchell's **Copycat Architecture**, which were designed to be able to solve problems that involve analogies. Mitchell's Copycat, for example, can solve problems such as "ABC is to CBA as DEF is to ???."

The ability to solve problems of this kind does not represent intelligence, but the development of systems that can solve such problems is the mainstay of Artificial Intelligence research and arguably an extremely useful step along the way to producing more and more useful computer software systems.

In Chapter 2, we will discuss the subject of whether a computer program can really be "intelligent."

In the most recent decades, the study of Artificial Intelligence has flourished. Areas of particular importance include the following:

- machine learning
- multi-agent systems
- artificial life
- computer vision
- planning
- playing games (chess in particular)

In Chapter 2, we will look at the prevalence of Artificial Intelligence in the world today. This prevalence has more than justified the work of the past 50 years.

1.7   Philosophy

The philosophy of great thinkers, from Plato to Descartes and to Daniel Dennett, has had a great deal of influence on the modern study of Artificial Intelligence.

The influence of Aristotle has already been mentioned, but it has been argued (Dreyfus, 1972) that the history of Artificial Intelligence begins when Plato wrote that his teacher Socrates said, "I want to know what is characteristic of piety which makes all actions pious. . . that I may have it to turn to, and to use as a standard whereby to judge your actions and those of other men."

Socrates was claiming that an algorithm could be defined that described the behavior of humans and determined whether a person's behavior was good or bad.

This leads us to a fundamental question that has been asked by philosophers and students of Artificial Intelligence for many years: Is there more to the mind than simply a collection of neurons? Or, to put it another way, if each neuron in the human brain was replaced by an equivalent computational device, would the resultant be the same person? Would it indeed be capable of intelligent thought?

This kind of question is regularly debated by modern philosophers such as Daniel Dennett, and while the answer is far from clear, it is an instructive debate to follow, and its implications for Artificial Intelligence are enormous.

In the 17th century, the great philosopher René Descartes was a strong believer in **dualism**, the idea that the universe consists of two entirely separate things: mind and matter. Descartes's view was that the mind (or soul) was entirely separate from the physical body and not constrained by it in any way.

Importantly, Descartes did not believe that this dualism extended to animals. In other words, in his view a cat or a dog is simply a machine: a highly complex machine, but a machine nonetheless. This view gives hope to the proponents of Artificial Intelligence who believe that by simply putting enough computing power together and programming it in the correct way, a machine could be made to behave in the same way as an animal, or even a human being.

1.8 Linguistics

The study of human language has a vital role to play in Artificial Intelligence. As is discussed in some detail in Chapter 20, compared with computer languages such as Java and LISP, human languages are extraordinarily complex and are full of pitfalls that almost seem designed to trap anyone (human or computer) inexperienced in the use of the language.

This complexity, combined with a sense of optimism, may well have been part of the reason that natural language processing was such a popular research area in the early days of Artificial Intelligence.

Some of the optimism surrounding Natural Language Processing came from the writings of Noam Chomsky, who in the 1950s proposed his theory of Syntactic Structures, which was a formal theory of the structure of human language. His theory also attempted to provide a structure for human knowledge, based on the knowledge of language.

This idea of knowledge representation is at the very core of Artificial Intelligence and is a recurring theme throughout this book.

Almost all of the techniques described in this book depend on a formal method of representation for knowledge that enables a computer to use information from the world, or concerning the problems it is to solve, without necessarily needing to understand that knowledge.

There is a close relationship between linguistics and Artificial Intelligence, and the two fields join together in the study of natural language processing, which is discussed in some detail in Chapter 20.

1.9   Human Psychology and Biology

Some of the techniques, such as search algorithms, described in this book do not clearly map onto any specific biological or psychological function of human beings. On the other hand, many of them do. For example, McCulloch and Pitts's electronic neurons, which are used today to build neural networks, are directly based on the way in which neurons in the human brain function.

In a similar way, much research in Artificial Intelligence has been related to **cognitive psychology**, which is based on the idea that the human brain uses knowledge or information that it is capable of processing in order to solve problems, make decisions, draw conclusions, and carry out other intelligent acts.

This form of psychology was in contrast to behaviorism, which prevailed for much of the first half of the 20th century. Behaviorism relates behavior directly to stimuli, without taking into account knowledge or information that might be contained in the brain. This is the kind of psychology that Pavlov was demonstrating in his famous experiment with dogs.

Psychology is certainly useful to the study of Artificial Intelligence in one respect: it helps to answer the important question, "What is intelligence?" As we have seen already, this is a difficult question to answer, but in studying it, psychologists give us a great deal of information that is useful in forming the ideas behind Artificial Intelligence.

1.10   AI Programming Languages

A number of programming languages exist that are used to build Artificial Intelligence systems. General programming languages such as C++ and Java are often used because these are the languages with which most computer scientists have experience. There also exist two programming languages that have features that make them particularly useful for programming Artificial Intelligence projects—PROLOG and LISP.

We will now provide a brief overview of these two languages and explain how they are used in Artificial Intelligence research. Of course, a number of other programming languages exist that are also widely used for Artificial Intelligence, but we will focus on PROLOG and LISP because these are certainly the most widely used and the ones on which there is the widest range of relevant literature.

1.10.1 PROLOG

PROLOG (PROgramming in LOGic) is a language designed to enable programmers to build a database of **facts** and **rules**, and then to have the system answer questions by a process of logical deduction using the facts and rules in the database.

Facts entered into a PROLOG database might look as follows:

```
tasty (cheese).
made_from (cheese, milk).
contains (milk, calcium).
```

These facts can be expressed as the following English statements:

> Cheese is tasty.
>
> Cheese is made from milk.
>
> Milk contains calcium.

We can also specify rules in a similar way, which express relationships between objects and also provide the instructions that the PROLOG theorem prover will use to answer queries. The following is an example of a rule in PROLOG:

```
contains (X, Y) :- made_from (X, Z), contains (Z, Y).
```

This rule is made up of two main parts, separated by the symbol ":-".

The rule thus takes the form:

```
B :- A
```

which means "if A is true, then B is true," or "A implies B."

Hence, the rule given above can be translated as "If X is made from Z and Z contains Y then X contains Y."

In Chapters 7, 8, and 9, we make a great deal of use of rules of this kind.

Having entered the three facts and one rule given above, the user might want to ask the system a question:

```
?- contains (cheese, calcium).
```

Using a process known as resolution (which is described in detail in Chapter 8), the PROLOG system is able to use the rule and the facts to determine that because cheese is made from milk, and because milk contains calcium, therefore cheese does contain calcium. It thus responds:

```
yes
```

It would also be possible to ask the system to name everything that contains calcium:

```
?- contains (X, calcium)
```

The system will use the same rules and facts to deduce that milk and cheese both contain calcium, and so will respond:

```
X=milk.
X=cheese.
```

This has been a very simple example, but it should serve to illustrate how PROLOG works. Far more complex databases of facts and rules are routinely built using PROLOG, and in some cases simple databases are built that are able to solve complex mathematical problems.

PROLOG is not an efficient programming language, and so for many problems a language such as C++ would be more appropriate. In cases where logical deduction is all that is required, and the interactive nature of the PROLOG interface is suitable, then PROLOG is the clear choice. PROLOG provides a way for programmers to manipulate data in the form of rules and facts without needing to select algorithms or methodologies for handling those data.

1.10.2 LISP

LISP (LISt Programming) is a language that more closely resembles the imperative programming languages such as C++ and Pascal than does PROLOG. As its name suggests, LISP is based around handling of lists of data. A list in LISP is contained within brackets, such as:

[A B C]

This is a list of three items. LISP uses lists to represent data, but also to represent programs. Hence, a program in LISP can be treated as data. This introduces the possibility of writing self-modifying programs in LISP, and as we see in Chapter 13, it also allows us to use evolutionary techniques to "evolve" better LISP programs.

LISP is a far more complex language syntactically than PROLOG, and so we will not present any detail on its syntax here. It provides the usual kinds of mechanisms that other programming languages provide, such as assignment, looping, evaluating functions, and conditional control (if. . . then. . .). It also provides a great deal of list manipulation functions, such as car and cdr, which are used to return the first entry in a list and all the entries except for the first entry, respectively.

1.11　Chapter Summary

- Intelligence is difficult to define, and as a result Artificial Intelligence is also hard to define.

- One definition of Artificial Intelligence is:

  Artificial intelligence is the study of systems that act in a way that to any observer would appear to be intelligent.

- Proponents of strong AI believe that a computer that behaves in an intelligent way is capable of possessing mental states and, therefore, of being truly conscious and intelligent in the same way that humans are.

- Weak AI is a less controversial idea—that computers can be programmed to behave in intelligent ways in order to solve specific problems. This book is concerned with the methods of weak AI.

- Weak and strong AI are not to be confused with weak and strong methods.

- Weak methods are those that do not rely on any knowledge or understanding of the world and the problems being solved. Most of the techniques described in this book are weak methods.

- Strong methods are those that use knowledge about the world and about the problem being solved. The strong method approach is essential for solving many complex real world problems using Artificial Intelligence.

- In studying Artificial Intelligence, it is extremely useful to understand the background of philosophy, linguistics, biology, and psychology.

- Philosophers, from Plato and Aristotle to Searle and Dennett, have asked questions and provided opinions concerning the nature of intelligence and the ability to define it in a way that would enable us to program a computer with real intelligence.

- The 1950s were a time of great optimism in Artificial Intelligence and also a time of great progress in the field.

- Turing's test is a way to determine if a computer is truly intelligent, by seeing if it could fool a human in conversation into thinking that it too was human. It is widely believed today that even if a computer could pass the Turing test, it would still not truly be conscious or intelligent in the way that humans are.

- In 1956 the term Artificial Intelligence was coined by John McCarthy.

- Since the 1950s, the study of Artificial Intelligence has been flavored with a great deal more realism. The progress in recent years has been phenomenal.

1.12   Review Questions

1.1 What is intelligence?

1.2 What is Artificial Intelligence? What do you hope to learn by reading this book?

1.3 Is Artificial Intelligence a branch of computer science or an alternative to computer science?

1.4 Why is Artificial Intelligence a worthwhile subject to study?

1.5 Explain the difference between strong and weak methods in Artificial Intelligence. Explain how this dichotomy differs from the difference between strong and weak AI.

1.6 Why are PROLOG and LISP so well suited to Artificial Intelligence research? Do you think languages such as C++ and Java could also be used for such research?

1.7 What do you think led mankind to embark upon the study of Artificial Intelligence? Which fields of study particularly fed into it?

What human desires did the study of Artificial Intelligence seek to satisfy?

1.8 When did Artificial Intelligence first begin to be studied? Your answer should be more detailed than a simple date.

1.13 Further Reading

Crevier (1999) gives a fascinating history of the subject of Artificial Intelligence.

Throughout this book, details are given of other books that can be referenced to learn more about the material covered herein. The following books are general Artificial Intelligence texts that cover almost all of the topics covered by this book and also provide excellent introductions to the subject as a whole.

Each of these books takes a different approach to the material, and it is worth selecting the text that best fits your personal preferences in studying this subject.

For example, Russell and Norvig present the material in terms of intelligent agents. Winston explains his material with a great deal of examples but tends not to go into a great deal of detail, while Luger goes into greater depth, but with fewer examples. Schalkoff gives a good coverage of Artificial Intelligence using examples in PROLOG and LISP; it also therefore serves as a useful text in those languages.

Computation & Intelligence, edited by George Luger, contains a number of extremely important papers collected from the whole history of Artificial Intelligence. It includes papers by such pioneers of the subject as Alan Turing, Marvin Minsky, John McCarthy, Allen Newell, and Herbert Simon.

The Handbook of Artificial Intelligence, edited by A. Barr and E. Feigenbaum (1989 – William Kaufman)

The Essence of Artificial Intelligence, by Alison Cawsey (1998 – Prentice Hall)

Introduction to Artificial Intelligence, by Eugene Charniak and Drew McDermott (1985 – Addison Wesley; out of print)

The Computational Brain, by Patricia S. Churchland and Terrence J. Sejnowski (1992 – The MIT Press)

AI: The Tumultuous History of the Search for Artificial Intelligence, by Daniel Crevier (1999 – Basic Books)

Understanding Artificial Intelligence (Science Made Accessible), compiled by Sandy Fritz (2002 – Warner Books)

The Anatomy of Programming Languages, by Alice E. Fischer and Frances S. Grodzinsky (1993 – Prentice Hall)

Introduction to Artificial Intelligence, by Philip C. Jackson (1985 – Dover Publications)

AI Application Programming, by M. Tim Jones (2003 – Charles River Media)

Artificial Intelligence: Structures and Strategies for Complex Problem-Solving, by George F. Luger (2002 – Addison Wesley)

Computation & Intelligence: Collected Readings, edited by George F. Luger (1995 – The AAAI Press / The MIT Press)

Artificial Intelligence: A Guide to Intelligent Systems, by Michael Negnevitsky (2002 – Addison Wesley)

Artificial Intelligence: A New Synthesis, by N.J. Nilsson (1998 – Morgan Kauffman)

Artificial Intelligence: A Modern Approach, by Stuart Russell and Peter Norvig (1995 – Prentice Hall)

The Emperor's New Mind: Concerning Computers, Minds, and the Laws of Physics, by Roger Penrose (1989 – Oxford University Press)

Understanding Intelligence, by Rolf Pfeiffer and Christian Scheier (2000 – The MIT Press)

Artificial Intelligence: An Engineering Approach, by Robert J. Schalkoff (1990 – McGraw Hill)

The Encyclopedia of Artificial Intelligence, edited by S.C. Shapiro (1992 - Wiley)

Artificial Intelligence, by Patrick Henry Winston (1992 – Addison Wesley)

CHAPTER 2

Uses and Limitations

The limits of my language mean the limits of my world.

 —Ludwig Wittgenstein, *Tractatus Logico-Philosophicus*

Why, sometimes I've believed as many as six impossible things before breakfast.

 —Lewis Carroll, *Through the Looking Glass*

Who hath put wisdom in the inward parts? Or who hath given understanding to the heart?

 —*The Book of Job*, Chapter 38, Verse 36

2.1 Introduction

As was explained in Chapter 1, the early history of Artificial Intelligence was filled with a great deal of optimism—optimism that today seems at best to have been unfounded. In this chapter, we look at some of the arguments against strong AI (the belief that a computer is capable of having mental states) and also look at the prevalence of Artificial Intelligence today and explain why it has become such a vital area of study.

We will also look at the extent to which the Artificial Intelligence community has been successful so far in achieving the goals that were believed to be possible decades ago. In particular, we will look at whether the computer HAL in the science fiction film *2001: A Space Odyssey* is a possibility with today's technologies.

We will also look at the prevalence of Artificial Intelligence, and how it is used in the world today, the 21st century.

2.2 The Chinese Room

We will start by examining philosophical objections to strong AI, in particular the Chinese Room argument of John Searle.

The American philosopher John Searle has argued strongly against the proponents of strong AI who believe that a computer that behaves sufficiently intelligently could in fact be intelligent and have consciousness, or mental states, in much the same way that a human does.

One example of this is that it is possible using data structures called **scripts** (see Chapter 17) to produce a system that can be given a story (for example, a story about a man having dinner in a restaurant) and then answer questions (some of which involve a degree of subtlety) about the story. Proponents of strong AI would claim that systems that can extend this ability to deal with arbitrary stories and other problems would be intelligent.

Searle's Chinese Room experiment was based on this idea and is described as follows:

An English-speaking human is placed inside a room. This human does not speak any language other than English and in particular has no ability to read, speak, or understand Chinese.

Inside the room with the human are a set of cards, upon which are printed Chinese symbols, and a set of instructions that are written in English.

A story, in Chinese, is fed into the room through a slot, along with a set of questions about the story. By following the instructions that he has, the human is able to construct answers to the questions from the cards with Chinese symbols and pass them back out through the slot to the questioner.

If the system were set up properly, the answers to the questions would be sufficient that the questioner would believe that the room (or the person inside the room) truly understood the story, the questions, and the answers it gave.

Searle's argument is now a simple one. The man in the room does not understand Chinese. The pieces of card do not understand Chinese. The room itself does not understand Chinese, and yet the system as a whole is able to exhibit properties that lead an observer to believe that the system (or some part of it) does understand Chinese.

In other words, running a computer program that behaves in an intelligent way does not necessarily produce understanding, consciousness, or real intelligence.

This argument clearly contrasts with Turing's view that a computer system that could fool a human into thinking it was human too would actually be intelligent.

One response to Searle's Chinese Room argument, the Systems Reply, claims that although the human in the room does not understand Chinese, the room itself does. In other words, the combination of the room, the human, the cards with Chinese characters, and the instructions form a system that in some sense is capable of understanding Chinese stories. There have been a great number of other objections to Searle's argument, and the debate continues.

There are other objections to the ideas of strong AI. The **Halting Problem** and Gödel's incompleteness theorem tell us that there are some functions that a computer cannot be programmed to compute, and as a result, it would seem to be impossible to program a computer to perform all the computations needed for real consciousness. This is a difficult argument, and one potential response to it is to claim that the human brain is in fact a computer, and that although it must also be limited by the Halting Problem, it is still capable of intelligence.

This claim that the human brain is a computer is an interesting one. Upon it is based the idea of neural networks. By combining the processing power of individual neurons, we are able to produce artificial neural networks that are capable of solving extremely complex problems, such as recognizing faces. Proponents of strong AI might argue that such successes are steps along the way to producing an electronic human being, whereas objectors would point out that this is simply a way to solve one small set of problems—not only does it not solve the whole range of problems that humans are capable of, but it also does not in any way exhibit anything approaching consciousness.

2.3   HAL—Fantasy or Reality?

One of the most famous fictional accounts of Artificial Intelligence comes in the film *2001: A Space Odyssey*, based on the story by Arthur C. Clarke.

One of the main characters in the film is HAL, a Heuristically programmed ALgorithmic computer. In the film, HAL behaves, speaks, and interacts with humans in much the same way that a human would (albeit in a disembodied form). In fact, this humanity is taken to extremes by the fact that HAL eventually goes mad.

In the film, HAL played chess, worked out what people were saying by reading their lips, and engaged in conversation with other humans. How many of these tasks are computers capable of today?

We shall see in Chapter 6 that there has been a great deal of success with developing computers that can play chess. In 1997, a computer, Deep Blue, beat the chess world champion Garry Kasparov. As we discuss in Chapter 6, this was not the end of supremacy at chess for mankind, however. The victory was not a particularly convincing one and has not been repeated. Chess-playing computers are certainly capable of beating most human chess players, but those who predicted that chess computers would be vastly superior to even the best human players by now were clearly wrong.

In some games, such as Go, the best computers in the world are able to play only at the level of a reasonably accomplished amateur human player. The game is so complex that even the best heuristics and Artificial Intelligence techniques are not able to empower a computer with the ability to come close to matching the capabilities of the best human players.

In Chapter 20, we look at techniques that are used to enable computers to understand human language and in theory to enable them to engage in conversation. Clearly no computer program has yet been designed that is able to pass the Turing test and engage fully in conversation in such a way that would be indistinguishable from a human, and there is no sign that any such program will be designed in the near future.

The ability to interpret spoken words by examining the movement of lips is one that only a few humans have. It combines a number of complex problems: first, the visual problem of identifying sounds from the shape of lips. In Chapter 21, we will see how computers can be programmed to interpret visual information in the same kinds of ways that humans do. Interpreting the shape of human lips would probably not be impossible, and it is likely that a neural network could be trained to solve such a problem. The next problem is to combine the sounds together into words—again, not a difficult problem given a suitably large lexicon of words. Finally, HAL would have needed to be able to interpret and understand the words in the same way that he would have done when listening to spoken words.

HAL, as portrayed in the film, did have some capabilities that Artificial Intelligence has given to computers today, but it is certainly not the case that computers exist with the breadth of capabilities and in particular the ability to communicate in so human a manner. Finally, the likelihood of a computer becoming insane is a rather remote one, although it is of course possible that a malfunction of some kind could cause a computer to exhibit properties not unlike insanity!

Artificial Intelligence has been widely represented in other films. The Stephen Spielberg film AI: Artificial Intelligence is a good example. In this film, a couple buy a robotic boy to replace their lost son. The audience's sympathies are for the boy who feels emotions and is clearly as intelligent (if not more so) as a human being. This is strong AI, and while it may be the ultimate goal of some Artificial Intelligence research, even the most optimistic proponents of strong AI would agree that it is not likely to be achieved in the next century.

2.4 AI in the 21st Century

Artificial Intelligence is all around us. The techniques described in this book are used in a staggering array of machines and systems that we use every day. Fuzzy logic, for example, is widely used in washing machines, cars, and elevator control mechanisms. (Note that no one would claim that as a result those machines were intelligent, or anything like it! They are simply using techniques that enable them to behave in a more intelligent way than a simpler control mechanism would allow.)

Intelligent agents, which are described in Chapter 19, are widely used. For example, there are agents that help us to solve problems while using our computers and agents that traverse the Internet, helping us to find documents that might be of interest. The physical embodiment of agents, robots, are also becoming more widely used. Robots are used to explore the oceans and other worlds, being able to travel in environments inhospitable to humans. It is still not the case, as was once predicted, that robots are widely used by households, for example, to carry shopping items or to play with children, although the AIBO robotic dog produced by Sony and other similar toys are a step in this direction.

Expert systems are used by doctors to help with symptoms that are hard to diagnose or to prescribe treatments in cases where even human experts have difficulty.

Artificial Intelligence systems are used in a wide range of industries, from helping travel agents select suitable holidays to enabling factories to schedule machines.

Artificial Intelligence is particularly useful in situations where traditional methods would be too slow. Combinatorial problems, such as scheduling teachers and pupils to classrooms, are not well solved by traditional computer science techniques. In such cases, the heuristics and techniques provided by Artificial Intelligence can provide excellent solutions.

Many computer games have been designed based on Artificial Intelligence. In order to provide more realistic play, the computer game *Republic: The Revolution,* launched in 2003, contained a million individual Artificial Intelligences, each capable of interacting with the world and with the player of the game, as well as capable of being manipulated by the player.

It is likely that Artificial Intelligence will become more prevalent in our society. And whether or not we eventually create an Artificial Intelligence that is truly intelligent, we are likely to find computers, machines, and other objects appearing to become more intelligent—at least in terms of the way they behave.

2.5   Chapter Summary

- The Chinese Room argument is a thought experiment designed by John Searle, which is designed to refute strong AI.

- The computer HAL, as described in the film *2001: A Space Odyssey,* is not strictly possible using today's technology, but many of its capabilities are not entirely unrealistic today.

- The computer program, Deep Blue, beat world chess champion Garry Kasparov in a six-game chess match in 1997. This feat has not been repeated, and it does not yet represent the end of human supremacy at this game.

- Artificial Intelligence is all around us and is widely used in industry, computer games, cars, and other devices, as well as being a valuable tool used in many computer software programs.

2.6   Review Questions

2.1   Explain the difference between strong AI and weak AI. Which of the two do you think this book will be about? Why?

2.2 Are there any tasks that a human can do that you think a computer could never be programmed to do? Why?

2.3 What kinds of problems that humans find difficult do you think computers are particularly well suited to solve? Are there any such problems that you know of that computers cannot currently solve but which you believe computers will one day be able to solve? What advances in technology or understanding are necessary before those problems can be solved?

2.4 Explain the Chinese Room argument, and present some of the arguments against it, and the counter-arguments. Which do you find most convincing? How does this affect your view on the overall worth of the study of Artificial Intelligence?

2.5 If a computer passed the Turing Test, what would that prove? What conditions would you want to be sure had been observed in setting up the test?

2.6 If you replaced each of the neurons in your brain one by one with electronic neurons (take on trust for now that electronic neurons are possible), what do you think would be the effect? How would your perceptions of the world change during the process? At the end of the process, would you still be you? Would you still be conscious? Would you still be capable of having mental states and emotions? (Note: there are no right answers to these questions. The purpose in asking them is to make you think about them and hopefully to inspire you to read more about the subject.)

2.7 Further Reading

The works of Dreyfus and Dennett provide a great introduction to the philosophical arguments surrounding strong AI. The opposing view can be found thoroughly explored in Kurzweil's works, among others. The original Chinese Room argument can be found in Searle (1980).

A number of other books give good coverage of the popularity of Artificial Intelligence in the modern world. Challoner (2002) is probably too basic for most readers but does provide an entertaining introduction to the subject that would make a good introduction for a younger relative who was interested in learning more about the subject.

Cambrian Intelligence: The Early History of the New AI, by Rodney A. Brooks (1999 – MIT Press)

Artificial Intelligence, by Jack Challoner (2002 – Dorling Kindersley, Essential Science)

The Turing Test and the Frame Problem: AI's Mistaken Understanding of Intelligence, by Larry J. Crockett (1994 – Intellect)

Brainstorms: Philosophical Essays on Mind and Psychology, by Daniel Dennett (1978 – Bradford)

Consciousness Explained, by Daniel Dennett (1992 – Little, Brown & Co.)

What Computers Still Can't Do, by Hubert L. Dreyfus (1999 – The MIT Press)

Artificial Intelligence: The Very Idea, by J. Haugeland (1985 – The MIT Press)

The Age of Spiritual Machines, by Ray Kurzweil (1999 – Viking Penguin)

The Society of Mind, by Marvin Minsky (1988 – Simon & Schuster)

Robot: Mere Machine to Transcendent Mind, by Hans P. Moravec (2000 – Oxford University Press)

Views into the Chinese Room: New Essays on Searle and Artificial Intelligence, edited by John Preston and Mark Bishop (2002 – Oxford University Press)

Are We Spiritual Machines?: Ray Kurzweil vs. the Critics of Strong A.I., edited by Jay W. Richards (2002 – Discovery Institute)

The Turing Test: The Elusive Standard of Artificial Intelligence, edited by James H. Moor (2003 – Kluwer Academic Publishers)

Minds, Brains, and Programs, by John R. Searle (1980 – in *The Behavioral and Brain Sciences*, vol. 3, Cambridge University Press)

Minds, Brains and Science, by John R. Searle (1986 – Harvard University Press)

In the Mind of the Machine: The Breakthrough in Artificial Intelligence, by Kevin Warwick (1998 – Random House)

Arguing A. I.: The Battle for Twenty-First Century Science, by Sam Williams (2002 – Random House)

CHAPTER 3

Knowledge Representation

If, for a given problem, we have a means of checking a proposed solution, then we can solve the problem by testing all possible answers. But this always takes much too long to be of practical interest. Any device that can reduce this search may be of value.

—Marvin Minsky, *Steps Toward Artificial Intelligence*

Study is like the heaven's glorious sun,
That will not be deep-search'd with saucy looks;
Small have continual plodders ever won,
Save base authority from others' books.
These earthly godfathers of Heaven's lights
That give a name to every fixed star,
Have no more profit of their shining nights
Than those that walk and wot not what they are.

—William Shakespeare, *Love's Labours Lost*

Better the rudest work that tells a story or records a fact, than the richest without meaning.

—John Ruskin, *Seven Lamps of Architecture*

3.1 Introduction

Throughout this book we will be discussing representations. The reason for this is that in order for a computer to solve a problem that relates to the real world, it first needs some way to represent the real world internally. In dealing with that internal representation, the computer is then able to solve problems.

This chapter introduces a number of representations that are used elsewhere in this book, such as semantic nets, goal trees, and search trees, and explains why these representations provide such a powerful way to solve a wide range of problems.

This chapter also introduces frames and the way in which inheritance can be used to provide a powerful representational system.

This chapter is illustrated with a number of problems and suitable representations that can be used to solve those problems.

3.2   The Need for a Good Representation

As we will see elsewhere in this book, the representation that is used to represent a problem is very important. In other words, the way in which the computer represents a problem, the variables it uses, and the operators it applies to those variables can make the difference between an efficient algorithm and an algorithm that doesn't work at all. This is true of all Artificial Intelligence problems, and as we see in the following chapters, it is vital for search.

Imagine that you are looking for a contact lens that you dropped on a football field. You will probably use some knowledge about where you were on the field to help you look for it. If you spent time in only half of the field, you do not need to waste time looking in the other half.

Now let us suppose that you are having a computer search the field for the contact lens, and let us further suppose that the computer has access to an omniscient oracle that will answer questions about the field and can accurately identify whether the contact lens is in a particular spot.

Now we must choose a representation for the computer to use so that it can formulate the correct questions to ask.

One representation might be to have the computer divide the field into four equal squares and ask the oracle for each square, "Is the lens in this square?" This will identify the location on the field of the lens but will not really be very helpful to you because you will still have a large area to search once you find which quarter of the field the lens is in.

Another representation might be for the computer to have a grid containing a representation of every atom contained in the field. For each atom, the computer could ask its oracle, "Is the lens in contact with this atom?"

This would give a very accurate answer indeed, but would be an extremely inefficient way of finding the lens. Even an extremely powerful computer would take a very long time indeed to locate the lens.

Perhaps a better representation would be to divide the field up into a grid where each square is one foot by one foot and to eliminate all the squares from the grid that you know are nowhere near where you were when you lost the lens. This representation would be much more helpful.

In fact, the representations we have described for the contact lens problem are all really the same representation, but at different levels of granularity. The more difficult problem is to determine the data structure that will be used to represent the problem we are exploring. As we will see throughout this book, there are a wide range of representations used in Artificial Intelligence.

When applying Artificial Intelligence to search problems, a useful, efficient, and meaningful representation is essential. In other words, the representation should be such that the computer does not waste too much time on pointless computations, it should be such that the representation really does relate to the problem that is being solved, and it should provide a means by which the computer can actually solve the problem.

In this chapter, we look at a number of representations that are used in search, and in particular we will look at search trees, which are used throughout this part of the book.

3.3 Semantic Nets

The semantic net is a commonly used representation in Artificial Intelligence. A semantic net is a **graph** consisting of **nodes** that are connected by **edges**. The nodes represent objects, and the links between nodes represent relationships between those objects. The links are usually labeled to indicate the nature of the relationship.

A simple example of a semantic net is shown in Figure 3.1.

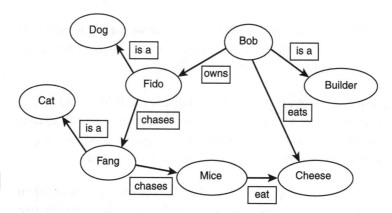

Figure 3.1

A simple semantic net

Note that in this semantic net, the links are arrows, meaning that they have a direction. In this way, we can tell from the diagram that Fido chases Fang, not that Fang chases Fido. It may be that Fang does chase Fido as well, but this information is not presented in this diagram.

Semantic nets provide a very intuitive way to represent knowledge about objects and the relationships that exist between those objects. The data in semantic nets can be reasoned about in order to produce systems that have knowledge about a particular domain. Semantic nets do have limitations, such as the inability to represent negations: "Fido is not a cat." As we see in Chapter 7, this kind of fact can be expressed easily in first-order predicate logic and can also be managed by rule-based systems.

Note that in our semantic net we have represented some specific individuals, such as Fang, Bob, and Fido, and have also represented some general classes of things, such as cats and dogs. The specific objects are generally referred to as **instances** of a particular **class**. Fido is an instance of the class dog. Bob is an instance of the class Builder.

It is a little unclear from Figure 3.1 whether cheese is a class or an instance of a class. This information would need to be derived by the system that is manipulating the semantic net in some way. For example, the system might have a rule that says "any object that does not have an 'is-a' relationship to a class is considered to represent a class of objects." Rules such as this must be applied with caution and must be remembered when building a semantic net.

An important feature of semantic nets is that they convey meaning. That is to say, the relationship between nodes and edges in the net conveys information about some real-world situation. A good example of a semantic net is a family tree diagram. Usually, nodes in these diagrams represent people, and there are edges that represent parental relationships, as well as relationships by marriage.

Each node in a semantic net has a label that identifies what the node represents. Edges are also labeled. Edges represent connections or relationships between nodes. In the case of searching a dictionary for a page that contains a particular word, each node might represent a single page, and each edge would represent a way of getting from one page to another.

The particular choice of semantic net representation for a problem will have great bearing on how the problem is solved. A simple representation for searching for a word in a dictionary would be to have the nodes arranged in a chain with one connection from the first node to the second, and then from the second to the third, and so on. Clearly, any method that attempts to search this graph will be fairly inefficient because it means visiting each node in turn until the desired node is found. This is equivalent to flicking through the pages of the dictionary in order until the desired page is found.

As we see in Section 3.7, representing the dictionary by a different data structure can give much more efficient ways of searching.

3.4 Inheritance

Inheritance is a relationship that can be particularly useful in AI and in programming. The idea of inheritance is one that is easily understood intuitively. For example, if we say that all mammals give birth to live babies, and we also say that all dogs are mammals, and that Fido is a dog, then we can conclude that Fido gives birth to live mammals. Of course, this particular piece of reasoning does not take into account the fact that Fido might be male, or if Fido is female, might be too young or too old to give birth.

So, inheritance allows us to specify properties of a **superclass** and then to define a **subclass**, which inherits the properties of the superclass. In our example, mammals are the superclass of dogs and Fido. Dogs are the subclass of mammals and the superclass of Fido.

If you have programmed with an object-oriented programming language such as C++ or Java, then you will be familiar with the concept of inheritance and will appreciate its power. Object-oriented programming is discussed further in Section 3.6.

As has been shown, although inheritance is a useful way to express generalities about a class of objects, in some cases we need to express exceptions to those generalities (such as, "Male animals do not give birth" or "Female dogs below the age of six months do not give birth"). In such cases, we say that the **default value** has been **overridden** in the subclass.

As we will see, it is usually useful to be able to express in our chosen representation which values can be overridden and which cannot.

3.5   Frames

Frame-based representation is a development of semantic nets and allows us to express the idea of inheritance.

As with semantic nets, a **frame system** consists of a set of frames (or nodes), which are connected together by relations. Each **frame** describes either an instance (an **instance frame**) or a class (a **class frame**).

Thus far, we have said that instances are "objects" without really saying what an object is. In this context, an object can be a physical object, but it does not have to be. An object can be a property (such as a color or a shape), or it can be a place, or a situation, or a feeling. This idea of objects is the same that is used in object-oriented programming languages, such as C++ and Java. Frames are thus an object-oriented representation that can be used to build expert systems. Object-oriented programming is further discussed in Section 3.6.

Each frame has one or more **slots**, which are assigned **slot values**. This is the way in which the frame system network is built up. Rather than simply having links between frames, each relationship is expressed by a value being placed in a slot. For example, the semantic net in Figure 3.1 might be represented by the following frames:

Frame Name	Slot	Slot Value
Bob	is a	Builder
	owns	Fido
	eats	Cheese
Fido	is a	Dog
	chases	Fang
Fang	is a	Cat
	chases	Mice
Mice	eat	Cheese
Cheese		
Builder		
Dog		
Cat		

We can also represent this frame system in a diagrammatic form using representations such as those shown in Figure 3.2.

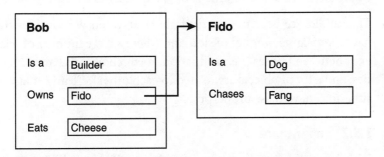

Figure 3.2
Partial representation for a frame system for the semantic net shown in Figure 3.1

When we say, "Fido is a dog," we really mean, "Fido is an instance of the class dog," or "Fido is a member of the class of dogs." Hence, the "is-a" relationship is very important in frame-based representations because it enables us to express membership of classes. This relationship is also known as **generalization** because referring to the class of mammals is more general than referring to the class of dogs, and referring to the class of dogs is more general than referring to Fido.

It is also useful to be able to talk about one object being a part of another object. For example, Fido has a tail, and so the tail is part of Fido. This relationship is known as **aggregation** because Fido can be considered an aggregate of dog parts.

Other relationships are known as **association**. An example of such a relationship is the "chases" relationship. This explains how Fido and Fang are related or associated with each other. Note that association relationships have meaning in two directions. The fact that Fido chases Fang means that Fang is chased by Fido, so we are really expressing two relationships in one association.

3.5.1   Why Are Frames Useful?

Frames can be used as a data structure by Expert Systems, which are discussed in more detail in Chapter 9.

The main advantage of using frame-based systems for expert systems over the rule-based approach is that all the information about a particular object is stored in one place. In a rule-based system, information about Fido might be stored in a number of otherwise unrelated rules, and so if Fido changes, or a deduction needs to be made about Fido, time may be wasted examining irrelevant rules and facts in the system, whereas with the frame system, the Fido frame could be quickly examined.

This difference becomes particularly clear when we consider frames that have a very large number of slots and where a large number of relationships exist between frames (i.e., a situation in which objects have a lot of properties, and a lot of objects are related to each other). Clearly, many real-world situations have these properties.

3.5.2   Inheritance

We might extend our frame system with the following additional information:

> Dogs chase cats
>
> Cats chase mice

In expressing these pieces of information, we now do not need to state explicitly that Fido chases Fang or that Fang chases mice. In this case, we can inherit this information because Fang is an instance of the class Cats, and Fido is an instance of the class Dogs.

We might also add the following additional information:

Mammals breathe

Dogs are mammals

Cats are mammals

Hence, we have now created a new superclass, mammals, of which dogs and cats are subclasses. In this way, we do not need to express explicitly that cats and dogs breathe because we can inherit this information. Similarly, we do not need to express explicitly that Fido and Fang breathe—they are instances of the classes Dogs and Cats, and therefore they inherit from those classes' superclasses.

Now let us add the following fact:

Mammals have four legs

Of course, this is not true, because humans do not have four legs, for example. In a frame-based system, we can express that this fact is the **default value** and that it may be overridden. Let us imagine that in fact Fido has had an unfortunate accident and now has only three legs. This information might be expressed as follows:

Frame Name	Slot	Slot Value
Mammal	*number of legs	four
Dog	subclass	Mammal
Cat	subclass	Mammal
Fido	is a	Dog
	number of legs	three
Fang	is a	Cat

Here we have used an asterisk (*) to indicate that the value for the "number of legs" slot for the Mammal class is a default value and can be overridden, as has been done for Fido.

3.5.3 Slots as Frames

It is also possible to express a range of values that a slot can take—for example, the number of legs slot might be allowed a number between 1 and 4 (although, for the insects class, it might be allowed 6).

One way to express this kind of restriction is by allowing slots to be frames. In other words, the number of legs slot can be represented as a frame, which includes information about what range of values it can take:

Frame Name	Slot	Slot Value
Number of legs	minimum value	1
	maximum value	4

In this way, we can also express more complex ideas about slots, such as the **inverse** of a slot (e.g., the "chases" slot has an inverse, which is the "chased by" slot). We can also place further limitations on a slot, such as to specify whether or not it can take multiple values (e.g., the "number of legs" slot should probably only take one value, whereas the "eats" slot should be allowed to take many values).

3.5.4   Multiple Inheritance

It is possible for a frame to inherit properties from more than one other frame. In other words, a class can be a subclass of two superclasses, and an object can be an instance of more than one class. This is known as **multiple inheritance**.

For example, we might add the following frames to our system:

Frame Name	Slot	Slot Value
Human	Subclass	Mammal
	Number of legs	two
Builder	Builds	houses
Bob	is a	Human

From this, we can see that Bob is a human, as well as being a builder. Hence, we can inherit the following information about Bob:

He has two legs

He builds houses

In some cases, we will encounter **conflicts**, where multiple inheritance leads us to conclude contradictory information about a frame. For example, let us consider the following simple frame system:

Frame Name	Slot	Slot Value
Cheese	is	smelly
Thing wrapped in foil	is	not smelly
Cheddar	is a	Cheese
	is a	Thing wrapped in foil

(Note: the slot "is" might be more accurately named "has property." We have named it "is" to make the example clearer.)

Here we can see that cheddar is a type of cheese and that it comes wrapped in foil. Cheddar should inherit its smelliness from the Cheese class, but it also inherits nonsmelliness from the Thing wrapped in foil class. In this case, we need a mechanism to decide which features to inherit from which superclasses. One simple method is to simply say that conflicts are resolved by the order in which they appear. So if a fact is established by inheritance, and then that fact is contradicted by inheritance, the first fact is kept because it appeared first, and the contradiction is discarded.

This is clearly rather arbitrary, and it would almost certainly be better to build the frame system such that conflicts of this kind cannot occur.

Multiple inheritance is a key feature of most object-oriented programming languages. This is discussed in more detail in Section 3.6.

3.5.5 Procedures

In object-oriented programming languages such as C++ or Java, classes (and hence objects) have **methods** associated with them. This is also true with frames. Frames have methods associated with them, which are called **procedures**. Procedures associated with frames are also called **procedural attachments**.

A procedure is a set of instructions associated with a frame that can be executed on request. For example, a **slot reader** procedure might return the value of a particular slot within the frame. Another procedure might insert a value into a slot (a **slot writer**). Another important procedure is the **instance constructor**, which creates an instance of a class.

Such procedures are called when needed and so are called **WHEN-NEEDED procedures**. Other procedures can be set up that are called automatically when something changes.

3.5.6   Demons

A **demon** is a particular type of procedure that is run automatically whenever a particular value changes or when a particular event occurs.

Some demons act when a particular value is read. In other words, they are called automatically when the user of the system, or the system itself, wants to know what value is placed in a particular slot. Such demons are called **WHEN-READ procedures**. In this way, complex calculations can be made that calculate a value to return to the user, rather than simply giving back static data that are contained within the slot. This could be useful, for example, in a large financial system with a large number of slots because it would mean that the system would not necessarily need to calculate every value for every slot. It would need to calculate some values only when they were requested.

WHEN-CHANGED procedures (also known as **WHEN-WRITTEN procedures**) are run automatically when the value of a slot is changed. This type of function can be particularly useful, for example, for ensuring that the values assigned to a slot fit within a set of constraints. For example, in our example above, a WHEN-WRITTEN procedure might run to ensure that the "number of legs" slot never has a value greater than 4 or less than 1. If a value of 7 is entered, a system message might be produced, telling the user that he or she has entered an incorrect value and that he or she should enter a different value.

3.5.7   Implementation

With the addition of procedures and demons, a frame system becomes a very powerful tool for reasoning about objects and relationships. The system has **procedural semantics** as opposed to **declarative semantics**, which means that the order in which things occur affects the results that the system produces. In some cases, this can cause problems and can make it harder to understand how the system will behave in a given situation.

This lack of clarity is usually compensated for by the level of flexibility allowed by demons and the other features that frame systems possess.

Frame systems can be implemented by a very simple algorithm if we do not allow multiple inheritance. The following algorithm allows us to find the value of a slot S, for a frame F. In this algorithm definition, we will use the notation **F[S]** to indicate the value of slot S in frame F. We also use the notation **instance (F1, F2)** to indicate that frame F1 is an instance of frame F2 and **subclass (F1, F2)** to indicate that frame F1 is a subclass of frame F2.

```
Function find_slot_value (S, F)
{
    if F[S] == V            // if the slot contains
        then return V       // a value, return it.
    else if instance (F, F')
        then return find_slot_value (S, F')
    else if subclass (F, F_S)
        then return find_slot_value (S, F_S)
    else return FAILURE;
}
```

In other words, the slot value of a frame F will either be contained within that frame, or a superclass of F, or another frame of which F is an instance. If none of these provides a value, then the algorithm fails.

Clearly, frames could also be represented in an object-oriented programming language such as C++ or Java.

A frame-based expert system can be implemented in a similar way to the rule-based systems, which we examine in Chapter 9. To answer questions about an object, the system can simply examine that object's slots or the slots of classes of which the object is an instance or a subclass.

If the system needs additional information to proceed, it can ask the user questions in order to fill in additional information. In the same way as with rule-based systems, WHEN-CHANGED procedures can be set up that monitor the values of slots, and when a particular set of values is identified, this can be used by the system to derive a conclusion and thus recommend an action or deliver an explanation for something.

3.5.8   Combining Frames with Rules

It is possible to combine frames with rules, and, in fact, many frame-based expert systems use rules in much the same way that rule-based systems do, with the addition of **pattern matching** clauses, which are used to identify values that match a set of conditions from all the frames in the system.

Typically, a frame-based system with rules will use rules to try to derive conclusions, and in some cases where it cannot find a value for a particular slot, a WHEN-NEEDED procedure will run to determine the value for that slot. If no value is found from that procedure, then the user will be asked to supply a value.

3.5.9   Representational Adequacy

We can represent the kinds of relationships that we can describe with frames in first-order predicate logic. For example:

$\forall x \; Dog(x) \; \rightarrow \; Mammal(x)$

First-order predicate logic is discussed in detail in Chapter 7. For now, you simply need to know how to read that expression. It is read as follows:

> "For all x's, if x is a dog, then x is a mammal."

This can be rendered in more natural English as:

> "All dogs are mammals."

In fact, we can also express this relationship by the introduction of a new symbol, which more closely mirrors the meaning encompassed by the idea of inheritance:

$$Dog \xrightarrow{\text{subset}} Mammal$$

Almost anything that can be expressed using frames can be expressed using first-order predicate logic (FPOL). The same is not true in reverse. For example, it is not easy to represent negativity ("Fido is not a cat") or quantification ("there is a cat that has only one leg"). We say that FOPL has greater **representational adequacy** than frame-based representations.

In fact, frame-based representations do have some aspects that cannot be easily represented in FOPL. The most significant of these is the idea of exceptions, or overriding default values.

Allowing exceptions to override default values for slots means that the frame-based system is not monotonic (monotonicity is discussed in Chapter 7). In other words, conclusions can be changed by adding new facts to the system.

In this section, we have discussed three main representational methods: logic, rules, and frames (or semantic nets). Each of these has advantages and disadvantages, and each is preferable over the others in different situations. The important thing is that in solving a particular problem, the correct representation must be chosen.

3.6 Object-Oriented Programming

We now briefly explore some of the ideas used in object-oriented programming, and, in particular, we see how they relate to some of the ideas we have seen in Sections 3.4 and 3.5 on inheritance and frames.

Two of the best-known object-oriented programming languages are Java and C++. These two languages use a similar syntax to define classes and objects that are instantiations of those classes.

A typical class in these languages might be defined as:

```
class animal
{
        animal ();
        Eye *eyes;
        Leg *legs;
        Head head;
        Tail tail;
}
```

This defines a class called animal that has a number of fields, which are the various body parts. It also has a **constructor**, which is a function that is called when an instantiation of the class is called. Classes can have other functions too, and these functions are equivalent to the procedures we saw in Section 3.5.5.

We can create an instance of the class animal as follows:

```
animal an_animal = new animal ();
```

This creates an instance of the class animal. The instance, which is an object, is called "an_animal". In creating it, the constructor animal () is called.

We can also create a subclass of animal:

```
Class dog : animal
{
     bark ();
}
```

Here we have created a subclass of animal called dog. Dog has inherited all of the properties of animal and also has a new function of its own called bark ().

In some object-oriented programming languages, it is possible to use multiple inheritance. This means that one class inherits properties from more than one parent class. While C++ does allow multiple inheritance, Java, which itself inherited many features from C++, does not allow multiple inheritance. This is because multiple inheritance was seen by the developers of Java as an "unclean" idea—one that creates unnecessarily complicated object-oriented structures. Additionally, it is always possible to achieve the same results using single inheritance as it is with multiple inheritance.

Object-oriented programming languages such as Java and C++ use the principles that were invented for the frames structure. There are also object-oriented programming languages such as IBM's APL2 that use a frame-based structure.

The ideas explored in Sections 3.4 and 3.5 of this book are thus very relevant to object-oriented programming, as well as being an important part of Artificial Intelligence research.

3.7   Search Spaces

Many problems in Artificial Intelligence can be represented as search spaces. In simple terms, a search space is a representation of the set of possible choices in a given problem, one or more of which are the solution to the problem.

For example, attempting to find a particular word in a dictionary with 100 pages, a search space will consist of each of the 100 pages. The page that is being searched for is called a goal, and it can be identified by seeing

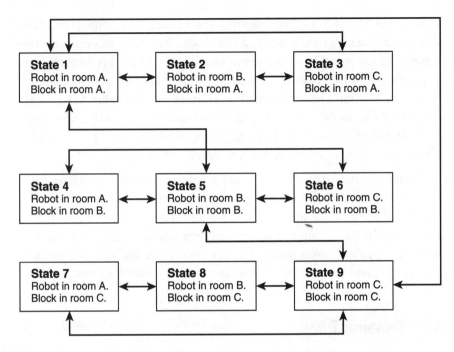

Figure 3.3
A simple state-space diagram

whether the word we are looking for is on the page or not. (In fact, this identification might be a search problem in itself, but for this example we will assume that this is a simple, atomic action.)

The aim of most search procedures is to identify one or more goals and, usually, to identify one or more paths to those goals (often the shortest path, or path with least cost).

Because a search space consists of a set of states, connected by paths that represent actions, they are also known as **state spaces**. Many search problems can be represented by a state space, where the aim is to start with the world in one state and to end with the world in another, more desirable state. In the missionaries and cannibals problem that is discussed later in this chapter, the start state has all missionaries and cannibals on one side of the river, and the goal state has them on the other side. The state space for the problem consists of all possible states in between.

Figure 3.3 shows a very simple state-space diagram for a robot that lives in an environment with three rooms (room A, room B, and room C) and with a block that he can move from room to room. Each state consists of a possible arrangement of the robot and the block. Hence, for example, in state 1, both the robot and the block are in room A. Note that this diagram does not explain how the robot gets from one room to another or how the block is moved. This kind of representation assumes that the robot has a representation of a number of **actions** that it can take. To determine how to get from one state to another state, the robot needs to use a process called **planning**, which is covered in detail in Part 5 of this book.

In Figure 3.3, the arrows between states represent **state transitions**. Note that there are not transitions between every pair of states. For example, it is not possible to go from state 1 to state 4 without going through state 5. This is because the block cannot move on its own and can only be moved to a room if the robot moves there. Hence, a state-space diagram is a valuable way to represent the possible actions that can be taken in a given state and thus to represent the possible solutions to a problem.

3.8 Semantic Trees

A **semantic tree** is a kind of semantic net that has the following properties:

- Each node (except for the root node, described below) has exactly one **predecessor** (parent) and one or more **successors** (children). In the semantic tree in Figure 3.4, node A is the predecessor of node B: node A connects by one edge to node B and comes before it in the tree. The successors of node B, nodes D and E, connect directly (by one edge each) to node B and come after it in the tree. We can write these relationships as: succ (B) = D and pred (B) = A.

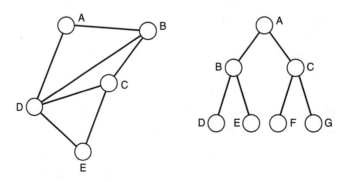

Figure 3.4

A semantic net and a semantic tree

The nonsymmetric nature of this relationship means that a semantic tree is a **directed** graph. By contrast, **nondirected graphs** are ones where there is no difference between an arc from A to B and an arc from B to A.

- One node has no predecessors. This node is called the **root node**. In general, when searching a semantic tree, we start at the root node. This is because the root node typically represents a starting point of the problem. For example, when we look at game trees in Chapter 6, we will see that the game tree for a game of chess represents all the possible moves of the game, starting from the initial position in which neither player has made a move. This initial position corresponds to the root node in the game tree.

- Some nodes have no successors. These nodes are called **leaf nodes**. One or more leaf nodes are called **goal nodes**. These are the nodes that represent a state where the search has succeeded.

- Apart from leaf nodes, all nodes have one or more successors. Apart from the root node, all nodes have exactly one predecessor.

- An **ancestor** of a node is a node further up the tree in some path. A **descendent** comes after a node in a path in the tree.

A **path** is a route through the semantic tree, which may consist of just one node (a path of length 0). A path of length 1 consists of a node, a branch that leads from that node, and the successor node to which that branch leads. A path that leads from the root node to a goal node is called a **complete path**. A path that leads from the root node to a leaf node that is not a goal node is called a **partial path**.

When comparing semantic nets and semantic trees visually, one of the most obvious differences is that semantic nets can contain cycles, but semantic trees cannot. A **cycle** is a path through the net that visits the same node more than once. Figure 3.4 shows a semantic net and a semantic tree. In the semantic net, the path A, B, C, D, A . . . is a cycle.

In semantic trees, an edge that connects two nodes is called a **branch**. If a node has n successors, that node is said to have a **branching factor** of n. A tree is often said to have a branching factor of n if the average branching factor of all the nodes in the tree is n.

The root node of a tree is said to be at level 0, and the successors of the root node are at level 1. Successors of nodes at level n are at level $n + 1$.

3.9 Search Trees

Searching a semantic net involves traversing the net systematically (or in some cases, not so systematically), examining nodes, looking for a goal node. Clearly following a cyclic path through the net is pointless because following A,B,C,D,A will not lead to any solution that could not be reached just by starting from A. We can represent the possible paths through a semantic net as a **search tree**, which is a type of semantic tree.

The search tree shown in Figure 3.5 represents the possible paths through the semantic net shown in Figure 3.4. Each node in the tree represents a path, with successive layers in the tree representing longer and longer paths. Note that we do not include cyclical paths, which means that some branches in the search tree end on leaf nodes that are not goal nodes. Also note that we label each node in the search tree with a single letter, which

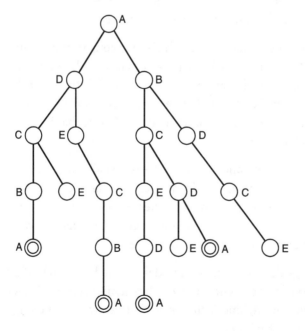

Figure 3.5

A search tree representation for the semantic net in Figure 3.4.

represents the path from the root node to that node in the semantic net in Figure 3.4.

Hence, searching for a node in a search tree corresponds to searching for a complete path in a semantic net.

3.9.1 Example 1: Missionaries and Cannibals

The Missionaries and Cannibals problem is a well-known problem that is often used to illustrate AI techniques. The problem is as follows:

Three missionaries and three cannibals are on one side of a river, with a canoe. They all want to get to the other side of the river. The canoe can only hold one or two people at a time. At no time should there be more cannibals than missionaries on either side of the river, as this would probably result in the missionaries being eaten.

To solve this problem, we need to use a suitable representation.

First of all, we can consider a state in the solving of the problem to consist of a certain number of cannibals and a certain number of missionaries on each side of the river, with the boat on one side or the other. We could represent this, for example, as

  3, 3, 1   0, 0, 0

The left-hand set of numbers represents the number of cannibals, missionaries, and canoes on one side of the river, and the right-hand side represents what is on the other side.

Because the number that is on one side is entirely dependent on the number that is on the other side, we can in fact just show how many of each are on the finishing side, meaning that the starting state is represented as

  0, 0, 0

and the goal state is

  3, 3, 1

An example of a state that must be avoided is

  2, 1, 1

Here, there are two cannibals, one canoe, and just one missionary on the other side of the river. This missionary will probably not last very long.

To get from one state to another, we need to apply an operator. The operators that we have available are the following:

1. Move one cannibal to the other side

2. Move two cannibals to the other side

3. Move one missionary to the other side

4. Move two missionaries to the other side

5. Move one cannibal and one missionary to the other side

So if we apply operator 5 to the state represented by 1, 1, 0, then we would result in state 2, 2, 1. One cannibal, one missionary, and the canoe have now moved over to the other side. Applying operator 3 to this state would lead to an illegal state: 2, 1, 0.

We consider rules such as this to be **constraints**, which limit the possible operators that can be applied in each state. If we design our representation correctly, the constraints are built in, meaning we do not ever need to examine illegal states.

We need to have a test that can identify if we have reached the goal state—3, 3, 1.

We will consider the cost of the path that is chosen to be the number of steps that are taken, or the number of times an operator is applied. In some cases, as we will see later, it is desirable to find a solution that minimizes cost.

The first three levels of the search tree for the missionaries and cannibals problem is shown in Figure 3.6 (arcs are marked with which operator has been applied).

Now, by extending this tree to include all possible paths, and the states those paths lead to, a solution can be found. A solution to the problem would be represented as a path from the root node to a goal node.

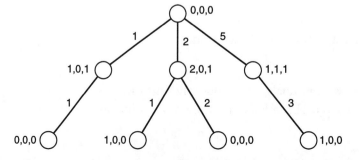

Figure 3.6

A partial search tree for the missionaries and cannibals problem

This tree represents the presence of a cycle in the search space. Note that the use of search trees to represent the search space means that our representation never contains any cycles, even when a cyclical path is being followed through the search space.

By applying operator 1 (moving one cannibal to the other side) as the first action, and then applying the same operator again, we return to the start state. This is a perfectly valid way to try to solve the problem, but not a very efficient one.

3.9.2 Improving the Representation

A more effective representation for the problem would be one that did not include any cycles. Figure 3.7 is an extended version of the search tree for the problem that omits cycles and includes goal nodes.

Note that in this tree, we have omitted most repeated states. For example, from the state 1,0,0, operator 2 is the only one shown. In fact, operators 1 and 3 can also be applied, leading to states 2,0,1 and 1,1,1 respectively. Neither of these transitions is shown because those states have already appeared in the tree.

As well as avoiding cycles, we have thus removed suboptimal paths from the tree. If a path of length 2 reaches a particular state, s, and another path of length 3 also reaches that state, it is not worth pursuing the longer path because it cannot possibly lead to a shorter path to the goal node than the first path.

Hence, the two paths that can be followed in the tree in Figure 3.7 to the goal node are the shortest routes (the paths with the least cost) to the goal, but they are by no means the only paths. Many longer paths also exist.

By choosing a suitable representation, we are thus able to improve the efficiency of our search method. Of course, in actual implementations, things may not be so simple. To produce the search tree without repeated states, a memory is required that can store states in order to avoid revisiting them. It is likely that for most problems this memory requirement is a worthwhile tradeoff for the saving in time, particularly if the search space being explored has many repeated states and cycles.

Solving the Missionaries and Cannibals problem involves **searching** the search tree. As we will see, search is an extremely useful method for solving problems and is widely used in Artificial Intelligence.

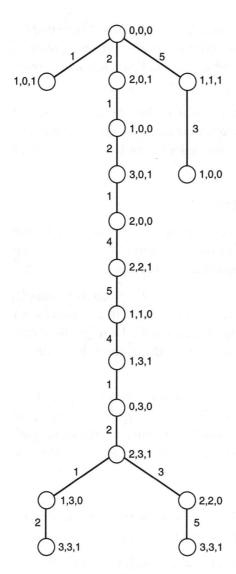

Figure 3.7
Search tree without cycles

3.9.3   Example 2: The Traveling Salesman

The Traveling Salesman problem is another classic problem in Artificial Intelligence and is **NP-Complete**, meaning that for large instances of the problem, it can be very difficult for a computer program to solve in a reasonable period of time. A problem is defined as being in the class P if it can be solved in polynomial time. This means that as the size of the problem increases, the time it will take a deterministic computer to solve the problem will increase by some polynomial function of the size. Problems that are NP can be solved nondeterministically in polynomial time. This means that if a possible solution to the problem is presented to the computer, it will be able to determine whether it is a solution or not in polynomial time. The hardest NP problems are termed NP-Complete. It was shown by Stephen Cook that a particular group of problems could be transformed into the satisfiability problem (see Chapter 16). These problems are defined as being NP-Complete. This means that if one can solve the satisfiability problem (for which solutions certainly do exist), then one can solve any NP-Complete problem. It also means that NP-Complete problems take a great deal of computation to solve.

The Traveling Salesman problem is defined as follows:

A salesman must visit each of a set of cities and then return home. The aim of the problem is to find the shortest path that lets the salesman visit each city.

Let us imagine that our salesman is touring the following American cities:

A   Atlanta

B   Boston

C   Chicago

D   Dallas

E   El Paso

Our salesman lives in Atlanta and must visit all of the other four cities before returning home. Let us imagine that our salesman is traveling by plane and that the cost of each flight is directly proportional to distance being traveled and that direct flights are possible between any pair of cities.

Hence, the distances can be shown on a graph as in Figure 3.8.

(Note: The distances shown are not intended to accurately represent the true locations of these cities but have been approximated for the purposes of this illustration.)

The graph in Figure 3.8 shows the relationships between the cities. We could use this graph to attempt to solve the problem. Certainly, we can use it to find possible paths: One possible path is A,B,C,E,D,A, which has a length of 4500 miles.

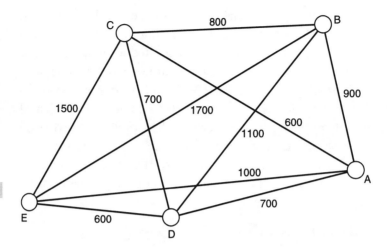

Figure 3.8

Simplified map showing Traveling Salesman problem with five cities

To solve the problem using search, a different representation would be needed, based on this graph. Figure 3.9 shows a part of the search tree that represents the possible paths through the search space in this problem. Each node is marked with a letter that represents the city that has been reached by the path up to that point. Hence, in fact, each node represents the path from city A to the city named at that node. The root node of the graph thus represents the path of length 0, which consists simply of the city A. As with the previous example, cyclical paths have been excluded from the tree, but unlike the tree for the missionaries and cannibals problem, the tree does allow repeated states. This is because in this problem each state must be visited once, and so a complete path must include all states. In the Missionaries and Cannibals problem, the aim was to reach a particular state by the shortest path that could be found. Hence, including a path such as A,B,C,D where a path A,D had already been found would be wasteful because it could not possibly lead to a shorter path than A,D. With the Traveling Salesman problem, this does not apply, and we need to examine every possible path that includes each node once, with the start node at the beginning and the end.

Figure 3.9 is only a part of the search tree, but it shows two complete paths: A,B,C,D,E,A and A,B,C,E,D,A. The total path costs of these two paths are 4000 miles and 4500 miles, respectively.

In total there will be $(n - 1)!$ possible paths for a Traveling Salesman problem with n cities. This is because we are constrained in our starting city

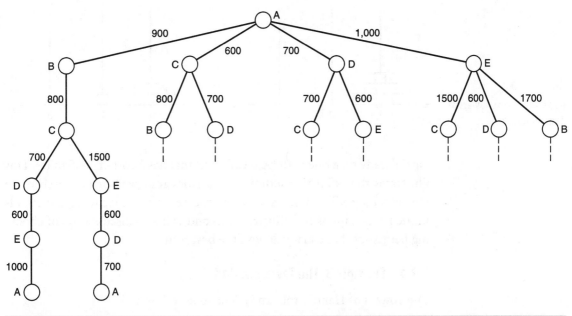

Figure 3.9

Partial search tree for Traveling Salesman problem with five cities

and, thereafter, have a choice of any combination of $(n - 1)$ cities. In problems with small numbers of cities, such as 5 or even 10, this means that the complete search tree can be evaluated by a computer program without much difficulty; but if the problem consists of 40 cities, there would be 40! paths, which is roughly 10^{48}, a ludicrously large number. As we see in the next chapter, methods that try to examine all of these paths are called **brute-force search** methods. To solve search problems with large trees, knowledge about the problem needs to be applied in the form of **heuristics**, which enable us to find more efficient ways to solve the problem. A heuristic is a rule or piece of information that is used to make search or another problem-solving method more effective or more efficient. The use of heuristics for search is explained in more detail in Chapters 4 and 5.

For example, a heuristic search approach to solving the Traveling Salesman problem might be: rather than examining every possible path, we simply extend the path by moving to the city closest to our current position that has not yet been examined. This is called the **nearest neighbor heuristic**. In our example above, this would lead to the path A,C,D,E,B,A, which has a total cost of 4500 miles. This is certainly not the best possible path, as we

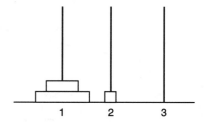

Figure 3.10

Two states in the Towers of Hanoi problem

have already seen one path (A,B,C,D,E,A) that has a cost of 4000 miles. This illustrates the point that although heuristics may well make search more efficient, they will not necessarily give the best results. We will see methods in the next chapters that illustrate this and will also discuss ways of choosing heuristics that usually do give the best result.

3.9.4   Example 3: The Towers of Hanoi

The Towers of Hanoi problem is defined as follows:

We have three pegs and a number of disks of different sizes. The aim is to move from the starting state where all the disks are on the first peg, in size order (smallest at the top) to the goal state where all the pegs are on the third peg, also in size order. We are allowed to move one disk at a time, as long as there are no disks on top of it, and as long as we do not move it on top of a peg that is smaller than it.

Figure 3.10 shows the start state and a state after one disk has been moved from peg 1 to peg 2 for a Towers of Hanoi problem with three disks.

Now that we know what our start state and goal state look like, we need to come up with a set of operators:

Op1	Move disk from peg 1 to peg 2
Op2	Move disk from peg 1 to peg 3
Op3	Move disk from peg 2 to peg 1
Op4	Move disk from peg 2 to peg 3
Op5	Move disk from peg 3 to peg 1
Op6	Move disk from peg 3 to peg 2

We also need a way to represent each state. For this example, we will use vectors of numbers where 1 represents the smallest peg and 3 the largest

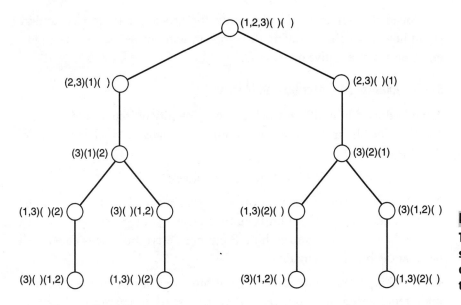

Figure 3.11

The first five levels of the search tree for the Towers of Hanoi problem with three disks

peg. The first vector represents the first peg, and so on. Hence, the starting state is represented as

(1,2,3) () ()

The second state shown in figure 3.10 is represented as

(2,3) (1) ()

and the goal state is

() () (1,2,3)

The first few levels of the search tree for the Towers of Hanoi problem with three disks is shown in Figure 3.11. Again, we have ignored cyclical paths. In fact, with the Towers of Hanoi problem, at each step, we can always choose to reverse the previous action. For example, having applied operator Op1 to get from the start state to (2,3) (1) (), we can now apply operator Op3, which reverses this move and brings us back to the start state. Clearly, this behavior will always lead to a cycle, and so we ignore such choices in our representation.

As we see later in this book, search is not the only way to identify solutions to problems like the Towers of Hanoi. A search method would find a solution by examining every possible set of actions until a path was found that led from the start state to the goal state. A more intelligent system might be developed that understood more about the problem and, in fact, understood how to go about solving the problem without necessarily having to examine any alternative paths at all.

3.9.5   Example 4: Describe and Match

A method used in Artificial Intelligence to identify objects is to describe it and then search for the same description in a database, which will identify the object.

An example of Describe and Match is as follows:

Alice is looking out of her window and can see a bird in the garden. She does not know much about birds but has a friend, Bob, who does. She calls Bob and describes the bird to him. From her description, he is able to tell her that the bird is a penguin.

We could represent Bob's knowledge of birds in a search tree, where each node represents a question, and an arc represents an answer to the question. A path through the tree describes various features of a bird, and a leaf node identifies the bird that is being described.

Hence, Describe and Match enables us to use search in combination with knowledge to answer questions about the world.

A portion of the search tree Bob used to identify the penguin outside Alice's window is shown in Figure 3.12.

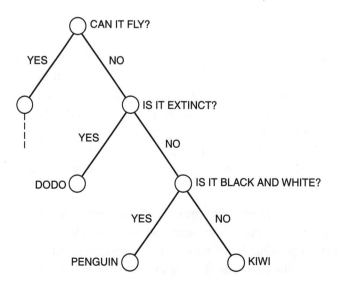

Figure 3.12

Search tree representation used with Describe and Match to identify a penguin

First, the question at the top of the tree, in the root node, is asked. The answer determines which branch to follow from the root node. In this case, if the answer is "yes," the left-hand branch is taken (this branch is not shown in the diagram). If the answer is "no," then the right-hand branch is taken, which leads to the next question—"Is it extinct?"

If the answer to this question is "yes," then a leaf node is reached, which gives us the answer: the bird is a dodo. If the answer is "no," then we move on to the next question. The process continues until the algorithm reaches a leaf node, which it must eventually do because each step moves one level down the tree, and the tree does not have an infinite number of levels.

This kind of tree is called a **decision tree**, and we learn more about them in Chapter 10, where we see how they are used in machine learning.

3.10 Combinatorial Explosion

The search tree for a Traveling Salesman problem becomes unmanageably large as the number of cities increases. Many problems have the property that as the number of individual items being considered increases, the number of possible paths in the search tree increases **exponentially**, meaning that as the problem gets larger, it becomes more and more unreasonable to expect a computer program to be able to solve it. This problem is known as **combinatorial explosion** because the amount of work that a program needs to do to solve the problem seems to grow at an explosive rate, due to the possible combinations it must consider.

3.11 Problem Reduction

In many cases we find that a complex problem can be most effectively solved by breaking it down into several smaller problems. If we solve all of those smaller **subproblems**, then we have solved the main problem. This approach to problem solving is often referred to as **goal reduction** because it involves considering the ultimate goal of solving the problem in a way that involves generating subgoals for that goal.

For example, to solve the Towers of Hanoi problem with n disks, it turns out that the first step is to solve the smaller problem with $n - 1$ disks.

Figure 3.13

The starting state of the Towers of Hanoi problem with four disks

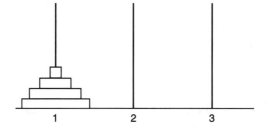

Figure 3.14

Towers of Hanoi problem of size 4 reduced to a problem of size 3 by first moving the largest disk from peg 1 to peg 3

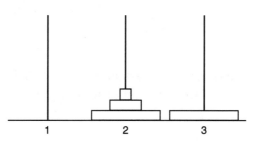

For example, let us examine the Towers of Hanoi with four disks, whose starting state is shown in Figure 3.13.

To solve this problem, the first step is to move the largest block from peg 1 to peg 3. This will then leave a Towers of Hanoi problem of size 3, as shown in Figure 3.14, where the aim is to move the disks from peg 2 to peg 3. Because the disk that is on peg 3 is the largest disk, any other disk can be placed on top of it, and because it is in its final position, it can effectively be ignored.

In this way, a Towers of Hanoi problem of any size n can be solved by first moving the largest disk to peg 3, and then applying the Towers of Hanoi solution to the remaining disks, but swapping peg 1 and peg 2.

The method for moving the largest disk is not difficult and is left as an exercise.

3.12   Goal Trees

A **goal tree** (also called an **and-or tree**) is a form of semantic tree used to represent problems that can be broken down in this way. We say that the solution to the problem is the **goal**, and each individual step along the way is a **subgoal**. In the case of the Towers of Hanoi, moving the largest disk to peg 3 is a subgoal.

Each node in a goal tree represents a subgoal, and that node's children are the subgoals of that goal. Some goals can be achieved only by solving **all** of

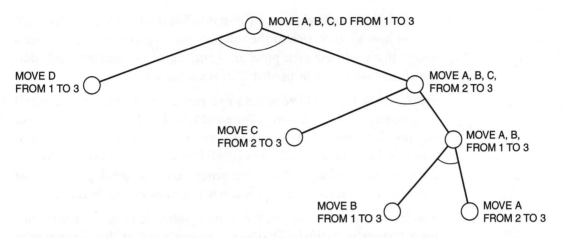

Figure 3.15

Goal tree for Towers of Hanoi problem with four disks

its subgoals. Such nodes on the goal tree are **and-nodes,** which represent **and-goals.**

In other cases, a goal can be achieved by achieving *any one* of its subgoals. Such goals are **or-goals** and are represented on the goal tree by **or-nodes.**

Goal trees are drawn in the same way as search trees and other semantic trees. An and-node is shown by drawing an arc across the arcs that join it to its subgoals (children). Or-nodes are not marked in this way. The main difference between goal trees and normal search trees is that in order to solve a problem using a goal tree, a number of subproblems (in some cases, all subproblems) must be solved for the main problem to be solved. Hence, leaf nodes are called **success nodes** rather than goal nodes because each leaf node represents success at a small part of the problem.

Success nodes are always and-nodes. Leaf nodes that are or-nodes are impossible to solve and are called **failure nodes.**

A goal tree for the Towers of Hanoi problem with four disks is shown in Figure 3.15. The root node represents the main goal, or **root goal,** of the problem, which is to move all four disks from peg 1 to peg 3. In this tree, we have represented the four disks as A,B,C, and D, where A is the smallest disk, and D is the largest. The pegs are numbered from 1 to 3. All of the nodes in this tree are and-nodes. This is true of most problems where there is only one reasonable solution.

Figure 3.15 is somewhat of an oversimplification because it does not explain how to solve each of the subgoals that is presented. To produce a system that could solve the problem, a larger goal tree that included additional subgoals would be needed. This is left as an exercise.

Breaking down the problem in this way is extremely advantageous because it can be easily extended to solving Towers of Hanoi problems of all sizes. Once we know how to solve the Towers of Hanoi with three disks, we then know how to solve it for four disks. Hence, we also know how to solve it for five disks, six disks, and so on. Computer programs can be developed easily that can solve the Towers of Hanoi problem with enormous numbers of disks.

Another reason that reducing problems to subgoals in this way is of such great interest in Artificial Intelligence research is that this is the way in which humans often go about solving problems. If you want to cook a fancy dinner for your friends, you probably have a number of subgoals to solve first:

- find a recipe
- go to the supermarket
- buy ingredients
- cook dinner
- set the table

And so on. Solving the problem in this way is very logical for humans because it treats a potentially complex problem as a set of smaller, simpler problems. Humans work very well in this way, and in many cases computers do too.

One area in which goal trees are often used is computer security. A **threat tree** represents the possible threats to a computer system, such as a computerized banking system. If the goal is "steal Edwin's money from the bank," you can (guess **or** convince me to divulge my PIN) **and** (steal **or** copy my card) and so on. The threat tree thus represents the possible paths an attacker of the system might take and enables security experts to determine the weaknesses in the system.

3.12.1   Top Down or Bottom Up?

There are two main approaches to breaking down a problem into subgoals—**top down** and **bottom up**.

A top-down approach involves first breaking down the main problem into smaller goals and then recursively breaking down those goals into smaller goals, and so on, until leaf nodes, or success nodes, are reached, which can be solved.

A bottom-up approach involves first determining all of the subgoals that are necessary to solve the entire problem, and then starting by solving the success nodes, and working up until the complete solution is found. As we see elsewhere in this book, both of these approaches are valid, and the correct approach should be taken for each problem.

Again, humans often think in these terms.

Businesses often look at solving problems either from the top down or from the bottom up. Solving a business problem from the top down means looking at the global picture and working out what subgoals are needed to change that big picture in a satisfactory way. This often means passing those subgoals onto middle managers, who are given the task of solving them. Each middle manager will then break the problem down into smaller subproblems, each of which will be passed down the chain to subordinates. In this way, the overall problem is solved without the senior management ever needing to know how it was actually solved. Individual staff members solve their small problems without ever knowing how that impacts on the overall business.

A bottom-up approach to solving business problems would mean looking at individual problems within the organization and fixing those. Computer systems might need upgrading, and certain departments might need to work longer hours. The theory behind this approach is that if all the individual units within the business are functioning well, then the business as a whole will be functioning well.

3.12.2 Uses of Goal Trees

We can use **goal-driven search** to search through a goal tree. As we describe elsewhere in this book, this can be used to solve a number of problems in Artificial Intelligence.

3.12.3 Example 1: Map Coloring

Map-coloring problems can be represented by goal trees. For example, Figure 3.16 shows a goal tree that can be used to represent the map-coloring

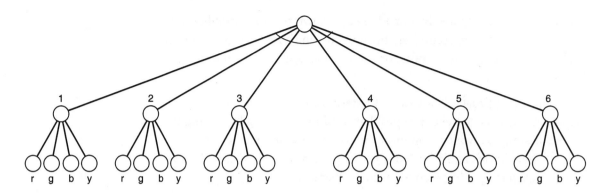

Figure 3.16

Goal tree representing a map-coloring problem with six countries and four colors

problem for six countries with four colors. The tree has just two levels. The top level consists of a single and-node, which represents the fact that all countries must be colored. The next level has an or-node for each country, representing the choice of colors that can be applied.

Of course, this tree alone does not represent the entire problem. **Constraints** must be applied that specify that no two adjacent countries may have the same color. Solving the tree while applying these constraints solves the map-coloring problem. In fact, to apply a search method to this problem, the goal tree must be redrawn as a search tree because search methods generally are not able to deal with and-nodes.

This can be done by redrawing the tree as a search tree, where paths through the tree represent **plans** rather than goals. Plans are discussed in more detail in Part 5 of this book. A plan consists of steps that can be taken to solve the overall problem. A search tree can thus be devised where nodes represent partial plans. The root node has no plan at all, and leaf nodes represent complete plans.

A part of the search tree for the map-coloring problem with six countries and four colors is shown in Figure 3.17.

One of the search methods described in Chapter 4 or 5 can be applied to this search tree to find a solution. This may not be the most efficient way to solve the map-coloring problem, though.

3.12.4   Example 2: Proving Theorems

As will be explained in Part 3 of this book, goal trees can be used to represent theorems that are to be proved. The root goal is the theorem that is to

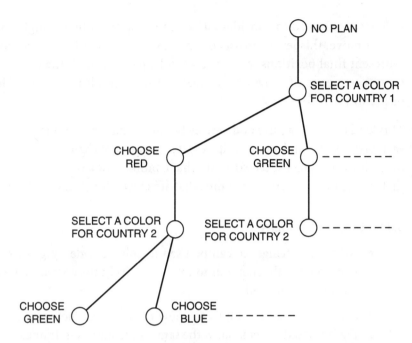

Figure 3.17
Partial search tree for map-coloring problem with six countries and four colors

be proved. It is an or-node because there may be several ways to prove the theorem. The next level down consists of and-nodes, which are lemmas that are to be proven. Each of these lemmas again may have several ways to be proved so, therefore, is an or-node. The leaf-nodes of the tree represent axioms that do not need to be proved.

3.12.5   Example 3: Parsing Sentences

As is described in Chapter 20, a **parser** is a tool that can be used to analyze the structure of a sentence in the English language (or any other human language). Sentences can be broken down into phrases, and phrases can be broken down into nouns, verbs, adjectives, and so on. Clearly, this is ideally suited to being represented by goal trees.

3.12.6   Example 4: Games

Game trees, which are described in more detail in Chapter 6, are goal trees that are used to represent the choices made by players when playing two-player games, such as chess, checkers, and Go. The root node of a game tree represents the current position, and this is an or-node because I must choose one move to make. The next level down in the game tree represents the possible choices my opponent might make, and because I need to consider all possible responses that I might make to that move, this level consists of and-nodes. Eventually, the leaf nodes represent final positions in the game, and a path through the tree represents a sequence of moves from start to finish, resulting in a win, loss, or a draw.

This kind of tree is a **pure and-or tree** because it has an or-node at the top, each or-node has and-nodes as its direct successors, and each and-node has or-nodes as its direct successors. Another condition of a pure and-or tree is that it does not have any constraints that affect which choices can be made.

3.13   Chapter Summary

- Artificial Intelligence can be used to solve a wide range of problems, but for the methods to work effectively, the correct representation must be used.

- Semantic nets use graphs to show relationships between objects. Frame-based systems show the same information in frames.

- Frame-based systems allow for inheritance, whereby one frame can inherit features from another.

- Frames often have procedures associated with them that enable a system to carry out actions on the basis of data within the frames.

- Search trees are a type of semantic tree. Search methods (several of which are described in Chapters 4 and 5) are applied to search trees, with the aim of finding a goal.

- Describe and Match is a method that can be used to identify an object by searching a tree that represents knowledge about the universe of objects that are being considered.

- Problems such as the Towers of Hanoi problem can be solved effectively by breaking them down into smaller subproblems, thus reducing an overall goal to a set of subgoals.

- Goal trees (or and-or trees) are an effective representation for problems that can be broken down in this way.

- Data-driven search (forward chaining) works from a start state toward a goal. Goal-driven search (backward chaining) works in the other direction, starting from the goal.

3.14 Review Questions

3.1 Why are representations so important in Artificial Intelligence? What risks are inherent in using the wrong representation?

3.2 Explain the connection between frames and object-oriented structures in programming languages, such as Java and C++.

3.3 Explain the relationship between graphs, semantic nets, semantic trees, search spaces, and search trees.

3.4 Explain why goal trees are so useful to artificial intelligence research. Give illustrations of how they are used.

3.5 Explain the connection between decision trees and the Describe and Match algorithm. How efficient do you think this algorithm is? Can you think of any ways to improve it?

3.6 Explain the problem of combinatorial explosion. What impact does this have on the methods we use for solving large problems using search?

3.7 Explain why removing cycles from a search tree is a good idea.

3.8 Explain how and-or trees can be used to represent games. What limitations do you think a system that uses game trees to play chess might face? Would it face different limitations if it played tic-tac-toe? Or poker?

3.9 What is the difference between a top-down approach to solving a problem and a bottom-up approach? In what kinds of situations might each be more appropriate?

3.15 Exercises

3.10 Convert the following information into:

a) a semantic net

b) a frame-based representation

A Ford is a type of car. Bob owns two cars. Bob parks his car at home. His house is in California, which is a state. Sacramento is the state capital of California. Cars drive on the freeway, such as Route 101 and Highway 81.

3.11 Design a decision tree that enables you to identify an item from a category in which you are interested (e.g., cars, animals, pop singers, films, etc.).

3.12 Devise your own representation for the Missionaries and Cannibals problem and implement it either with pen and paper or in the programming language of your choice. Use it to solve the problem. How efficient is your representation compared with that used in Section 3.9.1 of this book? Does it come up with the same answer? Which approach is easier for an observer to quickly grasp? Which would you say is the better representation overall, and why?

3.13 Design a suitable representation and draw the complete search tree for the following problem:

A farmer is on one side of a river and wishes to cross the river with a wolf, a chicken, and a bag of grain. He can take only one item at a time in his boat with him. He can't leave the chicken alone with the grain, or it will eat the grain, and he can't leave the wolf alone with the chicken, or the wolf will eat the chicken. How does he get all three safely across to the other side?

3.14 Write a program using the programming language of your choice to implement the representation you designed for Review Question 3.3. Have your program solve the problem, and have it show on the screen how it reaches the solution. Does it find the best possible solution? Does it find it as quickly as it might?

3.15 Write a program that solves either

a) the Towers of Hanoi problem with up to 1000 disks, or,

b) the Traveling Salesman problem with up to 10 cities.

You may need to wait until you have read about some of the search techniques described in Chapter 4 before you can write this program. For now, you can design a suitable representation and implement a suitable data structure for the problem in the language of your choice.

3.16   Further Reading

All Artificial Intelligence textbooks deal with the subject of representation. A particularly good description in terms of search for problem solving is found in Russell and Norvig (1995).

Winston (1993) provides a good description in terms of semantics.

Dromey (1982) provides an excellent description of the development of an algorithm for the Towers of Hanoi problem by problem reduction.

And-or trees and their uses are particularly well described by Luger (2002) and Charniak and McDermott (1985).

Frames were introduced by Marvin Minsky in his 1975 paper, *A framework for Representing Knowledge*.

Knowledge Representation, Reasoning and Declarative Problem Solving, by Chitta Baral (2003 – Cambridge University Press)

How to Solve it by Computer, by R.G. Dromey (1982 – out of print)

Knowledge Representation and Defeasible Reasoning (Studies in Cognitive Systems, Vol 5), edited by Ronald P. Loui and Greg N. Carlson (1990 – Kluwer Academic Publishers)

A Framework for Representing Knowledge, by Marvin Minsky (1975 – in *Computation & Intelligence – Collected Readings*, edited by George F. Luger, The MIT Press)

Knowledge Representation: Logical, Philosophical, and Computational Foundations, by John F. Sowa and David Dietz (1999 – Brooks Cole)

Search

Introduction to Part 2

Part 2 is divided into three chapters.

Search Methodologies

Chapter 4 introduces a number of search methods, including depth-first search and breadth-first search. Metrics are presented that enable analysis of search methods and provide a way to determine which search methods are most suitable for particular problems.

This chapter also introduces the idea of heuristics for search and presents a number of methods, such as best-first search, that use heuristics to improve the performance of search methods.

Advanced Search

Chapter 5 introduces a number of more complex search methods. In particular, it explains the way that search can be used to solve combinatorial optimization problems using local search and presents a number of local search methods, such as simulated annealing and tabu search. The chapter also explains how search can be run in parallel and discusses some of the complications that this introduces.

Game Playing

Chapter 6

This chapter explains the relationship between search and games, such as chess, checkers, and tic-tac-toe. It explains the Minimax algorithm and how alpha–beta pruning can be used to make it more efficient. It explains some of the more advanced techniques used in modern game-playing computers and discusses why computers are currently unable to beat humans at games such as Go.

CHAPTER 4

Search Methodologies

Research is the process of going up alleys to see if they are blind.

—Marston Bates

When a thing is funny, search it carefully for a hidden truth.

—George Bernard Shaw

If we do not find anything pleasant, at least we shall find something new.

—Voltaire, *Candide*

Everyone that asketh receiveth; and he that seeketh findeth.

—*The Gospel according to St Matthew*, Chapter 7, Verse 8

4.1 Introduction

In Chapter 3, we introduced search trees and other methods and representations that are used for solving problems using Artificial Intelligence techniques such as search. In Chapter 4, we introduce a number of methods that can be used to search, and we discuss how effective they are in different situations. Depth-first search and breadth-first search are the best-known and widest-used search methods, and in this chapter we examine why this is and how they are implemented. We also look at a number of properties of search methods, including optimality and completeness, that can be used to determine how useful a search method will be for solving a particular problem.

The methods that are described in this chapter and Chapter 5 impact on almost every aspect of Artificial Intelligence. Because of the serial nature in which computers tend to operate, search is a necessity to determine solutions to an enormous range of problems.

This chapter starts by discussing **blind** search methods and moves on to examine search methods that are more **informed**—these search methods use **heuristics** to examine a search space more efficiently.

4.2   Problem Solving as Search

Problem solving is an important aspect of Artificial Intelligence. A problem can be considered to consist of a **goal** and a set of actions that can be taken to lead to the goal. At any given time, we consider the **state** of the **search space** to represent where we have reached as a result of the actions we have applied so far.

For example, consider the problem of looking for a contact lens on a football field. The **initial state** is how we start out, which is to say we know that the lens is somewhere on the field, but we don't know where. If we use the representation where we examine the field in units of one square foot, then our first action might be to examine the square in the top-left corner of the field. If we do not find the lens there, we could consider the state now to be that we have examined the top-left square and have not found the lens. After a number of actions, the state might be that we have examined 500 squares, and we have now just found the lens in the last square we examined. This is a **goal state** because it satisfies the goal that we had of finding a contact lens.

Search is a method that can be used by computers to examine a problem space like this in order to find a goal. Often, we want to find the goal as quickly as possible or without using too many resources. A problem space can also be considered to be a **search space** because in order to solve the problem, we will search the space for a goal state. We will continue to use the term **search space** to describe this concept.

In this chapter, we will look at a number of methods for examining a search space. These methods are called **search methods**.

4.3   Data-Driven or Goal-Driven Search

There are two main approaches to searching a search tree, which roughly correspond to the top-down and bottom-up approaches discussed in Section 3.12.1. **Data-driven search** starts from an initial state and uses actions that are allowed to move forward until a goal is reached. This approach is also known as **forward chaining**.

Alternatively, search can start at the goal and work back toward a start state, by seeing what moves could have led to the goal state. This is **goal-driven search**, also known as **backward chaining**.

Most of the search methods we will examine in this chapter and Chapter 5 are data-driven search: they start from an initial state (the root node in the search tree) and work toward the goal node.

In many circumstances, goal-driven search is preferable to data driven-search, but for most of this part of the book, when we refer to "search," we are talking about data-driven search.

Goal-driven search and data-driven search will end up producing the same results, but depending on the nature of the problem being solved, in some cases one can run more efficiently than the other—in particular, in some situations one method will involve examining more states than the other.

Goal-driven search is particularly useful in situations in which the goal can be clearly specified (for example, a theorem that is to be proved or finding an exit from a maze). It is also clearly the best choice in situations such as medical diagnosis where the goal (the condition to be diagnosed) is known, but the rest of the data (in this case, the causes of the condition) need to be found.

Data-driven search is most useful when the initial data are provided, and it is not clear what the goal is. For example, a system that analyzes astronomical data and thus makes deductions about the nature of stars and planets would receive a great deal of data, but it would not necessarily be given any direct goals. Rather, it would be expected to analyze the data and determine conclusions of its own. This kind of system has a huge number of possible goals that it might locate. In this case, data-driven search is most appropriate.

It is interesting to consider a maze that has been designed to be traversed from a start point in order to reach a particular end point. It is nearly always far easier to start from the end point and work back toward the start point. This is because a number of dead end paths have been set up from the start (data) point, and only one path has been set up to the end (goal) point. As a result, working back from the goal to the start has only one possible path.

4.4   Generate and Test

The simplest approach to search is called **Generate and Test**. This simply involves generating each node in the search space and testing it to see if it is a goal node. If it is, the search has succeeded and need not carry on. Otherwise, the procedure moves on to the next node.

This is the simplest form of **brute-force search** (also called **exhaustive search**), so called because it assumes no additional knowledge other than how to traverse the search tree and how to identify leaf nodes and goal nodes, and it will ultimately examine every node in the tree until it finds a goal.

To successfully operate, Generate and Test needs to have a suitable **Generator**, which should satisfy three properties:

1. It must be complete: In other words, it must generate every possible solution; otherwise it might miss a suitable solution.

2. It must be nonredundant: This means that it should not generate the same solution twice.

3. It must be well informed: This means that it should only propose suitable solutions and should not examine possible solutions that do not match the search space.

The Generate and Test method can be successfully applied to a number of problems and indeed is the manner in which people often solve problems where there is no additional information about how to reach a solution. For example, if you know that a friend lives on a particular road, but you do not know which house, a Generate and Test approach might be necessary; this would involve ringing the doorbell of each house in turn until you found your friend. Similarly, Generate and Test can be used to find solutions to combinatorial problems such as the eight queens problem that is introduced in Chapter 5.

Generate and Test is also sometimes referred to as a **blind** search technique because of the way in which the search tree is searched without using any information about the search space.

More systematic examples of brute-force search are presented in this chapter, in particular, depth-first search and breadth-first search.

More "intelligent" (or **informed**) search techniques are explored later in this chapter.

4.5 Depth-First Search

A commonly used search algorithm is **depth-first search**. Depth-first search is so called because it follows each path to its greatest depth before moving on to the next path. The principle behind the depth-first approach is illustrated in Figure 4.1. Assuming that we start from the left side and work toward the right, depth-first search involves working all the way down the left-most path in the tree until a leaf node is reached. If this is a goal state, the search is complete, and success is reported.

If the leaf node does not represent a goal state, search backtracks up to the next highest node that has an unexplored path. In Figure 4.1, after examining node G and discovering that it is not a leaf node, search will backtrack to node D and explore its other children. In this case, it only has one other child, which is H. Once this node has been examined, search backtracks to the next unexpanded node, which is A, because B has no unexplored children.

This process continues until either all the nodes have been examined, in which case the search has failed, or until a goal state has been reached, in which case the search has succeeded. In Figure 4.1, search stops at node J, which is the goal node. As a result, nodes F, K, and L are never examined.

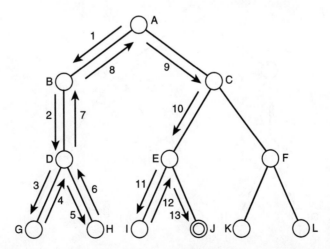

Figure 4.1
Illustrating depth-first search

Depth-first search uses a method called **chronological backtracking** to move back up the search tree once a dead end has been found. Chronological backtracking is so called because it undoes choices in reverse order of the time the decisions were originally made. We will see later in this chapter that **nonchronological backtracking**, where choices are undone in a more structured order, can be helpful in solving certain problems.

Depth-first search is an example of **brute-force search**, or **exhaustive search**.

Depth-first search is often used by computers for search problems such as locating files on a disk, or by search engines for **spidering** the Internet.

As anyone who has used the *find* operation on their computer will know, depth-first search can run into problems. In particular, if a branch of the search tree is extremely large, or even infinite, then the search algorithm will spend an inordinate amount of time examining that branch, which might never lead to a goal state.

4.6   Breadth-First Search

An alternative to depth-first search is breadth-first search. As its name suggests, this approach involves traversing a tree by breadth rather than by depth. As can be seen from Figure 4.2, the breadth-first algorithm starts by examining all nodes one level (sometimes called one **ply**) down from the root node.

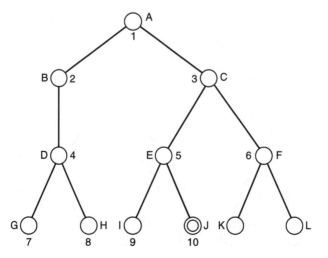

Figure 4.2

Illustrating breadth-first search. The numbers indicate the order in which the nodes are examined.

Table 4.1   Comparison of depth-first and breadth-first search

Scenario	Depth first	Breadth first
Some paths are extremely long, or even infinite	Performs badly	Performs well
All paths are of similar length	Performs well	Performs well
All paths are of similar length, and all paths lead to a goal state	Performs well	Wasteful of time and memory
High branching factor	Performance depends on other factors	Performs poorly

If a goal state is reached here, success is reported. Otherwise, search continues by expanding paths from all the nodes in the current level down to the next level. In this way, search continues examining nodes in a particular level, reporting success when a goal node is found, and reporting failure if all nodes have been examined and no goal node has been found.

Breadth-first search is a far better method to use in situations where the tree may have very deep paths, and particularly where the goal node is in a shallower part of the tree. Unfortunately, it does not perform so well where the branching factor of the tree is extremely high, such as when examining **game trees** for games like Go or Chess (see Chapter 6 for more details on game trees).

Breadth-first search is a poor idea in trees where all paths lead to a goal node with similar length paths. In situations such as this, depth-first search would perform far better because it would identify a goal node when it reached the bottom of the first path it examined.

The comparative advantages of depth-first and breadth-first search are tabulated in Table 4.1.

As will be seen in the next section, depth-first search is usually simpler to implement than breadth-first search, and it usually requires less memory usage because it only needs to store information about the path it is currently exploring, whereas breadth-first search needs to store information about all paths that reach the current depth. This is one of the main reasons that depth-first search is used so widely to solve everyday computer problems.

The problem of infinite paths can be avoided in depth-first search by applying a **depth threshold**. This means that paths will be considered to have terminated when they reach a specified depth. This has the disadvantage that some goal states (or, in some cases, the only goal state) might be missed but ensures that all branches of the search tree will be explored in reasonable time. As is seen in Chapter 6, this technique is often used when examining **game trees**.

4.7   Properties of Search Methods

As we see in this chapter, different search methods perform in different ways. There are several important properties that search methods should have in order to be most useful.

In particular, we will look at the following properties:

- complexity
- completeness
- optimality
- admissibility
- irrevocability

In the following sections, we will explain what each of these properties means and why they are useful. We will continue to refer to many of these properties (in particular, completeness and complexity) as we examine a number of search methods in this chapter and in Chapter 5.

4.7.1   Complexity

In discussing a search method, it is useful to describe how efficient that method is, over time and space. The **time complexity** of a method is related to the length of time that the method would take to find a goal state. The **space complexity** is related to the amount of memory that the method needs to use.

It is normal to use Big-O notation to describe the complexity of a method. For example, breadth-first search has a time complexity of $O(b^d)$, where b is the branching factor of the tree, and d is the depth of the goal node in the tree.

Depth-first search is very efficient in space because it only needs to store information about the path it is currently examining, but it is not efficient in time because it can end up examining very deep branches of the tree.

Clearly, complexity is an important property to understand about a search method. A search method that is very inefficient may perform reasonably well for a small test problem, but when faced with a large real-world problem, it might take an unacceptably long period of time. As we will see, there can be a great deal of difference between the performance of two search methods, and selecting the one that performs the most efficiently in a particular situation can be very important.

This complexity must often be weighed against the adequacy of the solution generated by the method. A very fast search method might not always find the best solution, whereas, for example, a search method that examines every possible solution will guarantee to find the best solution, but it will be very inefficient.

4.7.2   Completeness

A search method is described as being **complete** if it is guaranteed to find a goal state if one exists. Breadth-first search is complete, but depth-first search is not because it may explore a path of infinite length and never find a goal node that exists on another path.

Completeness is usually a desirable property because running a search method that never finds a solution is not often helpful. On the other hand, it can be the case (as when searching a game tree, when playing a game, for example) that searching the entire search tree is not necessary, or simply not possible, in which case a method that searches *enough* of the tree might be good enough.

A method that is not complete has the disadvantage that it cannot necessarily be believed if it reports that no solution exists.

4.7.3   Optimality

A search method is **optimal** if it is guaranteed to find the best solution that exists. In other words, it will find the path to a goal state that involves taking the least number of steps.

This does not mean that the search method itself is efficient—it might take a great deal of time for an optimal search method to identify the optimal solution—but once it has found the solution, it is guaranteed to be the best one. This is fine if the process of searching for a solution is less time consuming than actually implementing the solution. On the other hand, in some cases implementing the solution once it has been found is very simple, in which case it would be more beneficial to run a faster search method, and not worry about whether it found the optimal solution or not.

Breadth-first search is an optimal search method, but depth-first search is not. Depth-first search returns the first solution it happens to find, which may be the worst solution that exists. Because breadth-first search examines all nodes at a given depth before moving on to the next depth, if it finds a solution, there cannot be another solution before it in the search tree.

In some cases, the word *optimal* is used to describe an algorithm that finds a solution in the quickest possible time, in which case the concept of **admissibility** is used in place of optimality. An algorithm is then defined as **admissible** if it is guaranteed to find the best solution.

4.7.4   Irrevocability

Methods that use backtracking are described as tentative. Methods that do not use backtracking, and which therefore examine just one path, are described as irrevocable. Depth-first search is an example of tentative search. In Section 4.13 we look at hill climbing, a search method that is irrevocable.

Irrevocable search methods will often find suboptimal solutions to problems because they tend to be fooled by local optima—solutions that look good locally but are less favorable when compared with other solutions elsewhere in the search space.

4.8   Why Humans Use Depth-First Search

Both depth-first and breadth-first search are easy to implement, although depth-first search is somewhat easier. It is also somewhat easier for humans to understand because it much more closely relates to the natural way in which humans search for things, as we see in the following two examples.

4.8.1 Example 1: Traversing a Maze

When traversing a maze, most people will wander randomly, hoping they will eventually find the exit (Figure 4.3). This approach will usually be successful eventually but is not the most rational and often leads to what we call "going round in circles." This problem, of course, relates to search spaces that contain loops, and it can be avoided by converting the search space into a search tree.

An alternative method that many people know for traversing a maze is to start with your hand on the left side of the maze (or the right side, if you prefer) and to follow the maze around, always keeping your left hand on the left edge of the maze wall. In this way, you are guaranteed to find the exit. As can be seen in Figure 4.3, this is because this technique corresponds exactly to depth-first search.

In Figure 4.3, certain special points in the maze have been labeled:

- A is the entrance to the maze.
- M is the exit from the maze.
- C, E, F, G, H, J, L, and N are dead ends.
- B, D, I, and K are points in the maze where a choice can be made as to which direction to go next.

In following the maze by running one's hand along the left edge, the following path would be taken:

A, B, E, F, C, D, G, H, I, J, K, L, M

You should be able to see that following the search tree using depth-first search takes the same path. This is only the case because the nodes of the search tree have been ordered correctly. The ordering has been chosen so that each node has its left-most child first and its right-most child last. Using a different ordering would cause depth-first search to follow a different path through the maze.

4.8.2 Example 2: Searching for a Gift

When looking for a Christmas present for a relative in a number of shops, each of which has several floors, and where each floor has several departments, depth-first search might be a natural, if rather simplistic, approach.

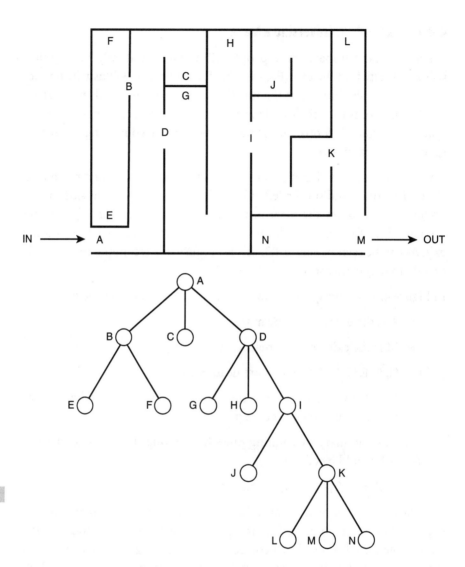

Figure 4.3

A maze and a search tree representation of the maze.

This would involve visiting each floor in the first building before moving on to the next building. A breadth-first approach would mean examining the first department in each shop, and then going back to examine the second department in each shop, and so on. This way does not make sense due to the spatial relationship between the departments, floors, and shops. For a computer, either approach would work equally well as long as a representation was used where moving from one building to another did not take any computation time.

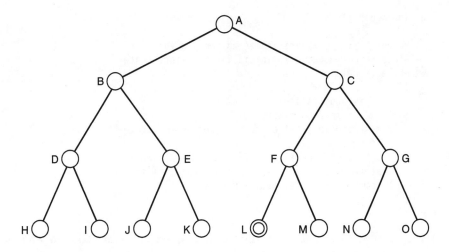

Figure 4.4

A simple search tree with fifteen nodes. The tree has a branching factor of two and a depth of three.

In both of the examples above, it can be seen that using breadth-first search, although a perfectly reasonable approach for a computer system, would be rather strange for a human. This is probably because with depth-first search, the approach is to explore each path fully before moving onto another path, whereas with breadth-first search, the approach involves revisiting and extending particular paths many times.

Despite this, implementations in software of both algorithms are nearly identical, at least when expressed in pseudocode.

4.9   Implementing Depth-First and Breadth-First Search

A pseudocode implementation of depth-first search is given below.

The variable **state** represents the current state at any given point in the algorithm, and **queue** is a data structure that stores a number of states, in a form that allows insertion and removal from either end. In this algorithm, we always insert at the front and remove from the front, which as we will see later on means that depth-first search can be easily implemented using a stack.

In this implementation, we have used the function **successors (state)**, which simply returns all successors of a given state.

```
Function depth ()
{
    queue = [];      // initialize an empty queue
    state = root_node;   // initialize the start state
    while (true)
    {
        if is_goal (state)
            then return SUCCESS
        else add_to_front_of_queue (successors (state));
        if queue == []
            then report FAILURE;
        state = queue [0]; // state = first item in queue
        remove_first_item_from (queue);
    }
}
```

Table 4.2 shows the states that the variables **queue** and **state** take on when running the depth-first search algorithm over a simple search tree, as shown in Figure 4.3.

In fact, depth-first search can be readily implemented on most computer systems using a **stack**, which is simply a "last in first out" queue (sometimes called a LIFO). In this way, a recursive version of the algorithm given above can be used, as follows. Because this function is recursive, it needs to be called with an argument:

```
recursive_depth (root_node);
```

The function is defined as follows:

```
Function recursive_depth (state)
{
    if is_goal (state)
        then return SUCCESS
    else
    {
        remove_from_stack (state);
        add_to_stack (successors (state))
    }
    while (stack != [])
    {
        if recursive_depth (stack [0]) == SUCCESS
            then return SUCCESS;
        remove_first_item_from (stack);
    }
    return FAILURE;
}
```

If you run through this algorithm on paper (or in a programming language such as C++ or LISP), you will find that it follows the tree in the same way as the previous algorithm, **depth**.

Table 4.2   Analysis of depth-first search of tree shown in Figure 4.5

Step	State	Queue	Notes
1	A	(empty)	The queue starts out empty, and the initial state is the root node, which is A.
2	A	B,C	The successors of A are added to the queue.
3	B	C	
4	B	D,E,C	The successors of the current state, B, are added to the front of the queue.
5	D	E,C	
6	D	H,I,E,C	
7	H	I,E,C	H has no successors, so no new nodes are added to the queue.
8	I	E,C	Similarly, I has no successors.
9	E	C	
10	E	J,K,C	
11	J	K,C	Again, J has no successors.
12	K	C	K has no successors. Now we have explored the entire branch below B, which means we backtrack up to C.
13	C	(empty)	The queue is empty, but we are not at the point in the algorithm where this would mean failing because we are about to add successors of C to the queue.
14	C	F,G	
15	F	G	
16	F	L,M,G	
17	L	M,G	SUCCESS: the algorithm ends because a goal node has been located. In this case, it is the only goal node, but the algorithm does not know that and does not know how many nodes were left to explore.

As was mentioned previously, depth-first search and breadth-first search can be implemented very similarly. The following is a pseudocode of a non-recursive implementation of breadth-first search, which should be compared with the implementation above of depth-first search:

```
Function breadth ()
{
    queue = [];        // initialize an empty queue
    state = root_node;   // initialize the start state
    while (true)
{
        if is_goal (state)
            then return SUCCESS
        else add_to_back_of_queue (successors (state));
        if queue == []
            then report FAILURE;
        state = queue [0]; // state = first item in queue
        remove_first_item_from (queue);
    }
}
```

Notice that the only difference between depth and breadth is that where depth adds successor states to the front of the queue, breadth adds them to the back of the queue. So when applied to the search tree in Figure 4.4, breadth will follow a rather different path from depth, as is shown in Table 4.3.

You will notice that in this particular case, depth-first search found the goal in two fewer steps than breadth-first search. As has been suggested, depth-first search will often find the goal quicker than breadth-first search if all leaf nodes are the same depth below the root node. However, in search trees where there is a very large subtree that does not contain a goal, breadth-first search will nearly always perform better than depth-first search.

Another important factor to note is that the queue gets much longer when using breadth-first search. For large trees, and in particular for trees with high branching factors, this can make a significant difference because the depth-first search algorithm will never require a queue longer than the maximum depth of the tree, whereas breadth-first search in the worst case will need a queue equal to the number of nodes at the level of the tree with the most nodes (eight in a tree of depth three with branching factor of two, as in Figure 4.3). Hence, we say that depth-first search is usually more memory efficient than breadth-first search.

Table 4.3   Analysis of breadth-first search of tree shown in Figure 4.4

Step	State	Queue	Notes
1	A	(empty)	The queue starts out empty, and the initial state is the root node, which is A.
2	A	B,C	The two descendents of A are added to the queue.
3	B	C	
4	B	C,D,E	The two descendents of the current state, B, are added to the back of the queue.
5	C	D,E	
6	C	D,E,F,G	
7	D	E,F,G	
8	D	E,F,G,H,I	
9	E	F,G,H,I	
10	E	F,G,H,I,J,K	
11	F	G,H,I,J,K	
12	F	G,H,I,J,K,L,M	
13	G	H,I,J,K,L,M	
14	G	H,I,J,K,L,M,N,O	
15	H	I,J,K,L,M,N,O	H has no successors, so we have nothing to add to the queue in this state, or in fact for any subsequent states.
16	I	J,K,L,M,N,O	
17	J	K,L,M,N,O	
18	K	L,M,N,O	
19	L	M,N,O	SUCCESS: A goal state has been reached.

As we have seen, however, depth-first search is neither optimal nor complete, whereas breadth-first search is both. This means that depth-first search may not find the best solution and, in fact, may not ever find a solution at all. In contrast, breadth-first search will always find the best solution.

4.10   Example: Web Spidering

An example of the importance of choosing the right search strategy can be seen in spidering the world wide web. The assumption is made that the majority of the web is connected, meaning that it is possible to get from one page to another by following a finite number of links, where a link connects two pages together.

Some parts of the Internet have a very high branching factor, with many pages containing hundreds of links to other pages. On average though, the branching factor is reasonably low, and so it seems that breadth-first search might be a sensible approach to spidering. In practice, however, the search tree that represents the connected part of the Internet is huge, and searching it by pure breadth-first search would involve a prohibitive storage requirement. Depth-first search would also not be practical because some paths might have almost infinite depth, particularly given that some pages on the Internet are generated automatically at the time they are accessed.

Hence, Internet spiders must use a combination of approaches, with a particular emphasis placed on web pages that change frequently and pages that are considered by some metric to be "important." Another important aspect of search engines is their ability to search in parallel. We discuss this concept in more detail in Chapter 5.

4.11   Depth-First Iterative Deepening

Depth-First Iterative Deepening, or DFID (also called Iterative Deepening Search or IDS), is an exhaustive search technique that combines depth-first with breadth-first search. The DFID algorithm involves repeatedly carrying out depth-first searches on the tree, starting with a depth-first search limited to a depth of one, then a depth-first search of depth two, and so on, until a goal node is found.

This is an algorithm that appears to be somewhat wasteful in terms of the number of steps that are required to find a solution. However, it has the advantage of combining the efficiency of memory use of depth-first search with the advantage that branches of the search tree that are infinite or extremely large will not sidetrack the search.

It also shares the advantage of breadth-first search that it will always find the path that involves the fewest steps through the tree (although, as we will see, not necessarily the *best* path).

Although it appears that DFID would be an extremely inefficient way to search a tree, it turns out to be almost as efficient as depth-first or breadth-first search. This can be seen from the fact that for most trees, the majority of nodes are in the deepest level, meaning that all three approaches spend most of their time examining these nodes.

For a tree of depth d and with a branching factor of b, the total number of nodes is

> 1 root node
>
> b nodes in the first layer
>
> b^2 nodes in the second layer
>
> ...
>
> b^n nodes in the nth layer

Hence, the total number of nodes is

$$1 + b + b^2 + b^3 + \ldots + b^d$$

which is a **geometric progression** equal to

$$\frac{1 - b^{d+1}}{1 - b}$$

For example, for a tree of depth 2 with a branching factor of 2, there are

$$\frac{1 - 8}{1 - 2} = 7 \text{ nodes}$$

Using depth-first or breadth-first search, this means that the total number of nodes to be examined is seven.

Using DFID, nodes must be examined more than once, resulting in the following progression:

$$(d + 1) + b(d) + b^2 (d - 1) + b^3(d - 2) + \ldots + b^d$$

Hence, DFID has a time complexity of $O(b^d)$. It has the memory efficiency of depth-first search because it only ever needs to store information about the current path. Hence, its space complexity is $O(bd)$.

In the case of the tree with depth of 2 and branching factor of 2, this means examining the following number of nodes:

$$(3 + 1) + 3 \times 2 + 4 \times 2 = 18$$

Hence, for a small tree, DFID is far more inefficient in time than depth-first or breadth-first search.

However, if we compare the time needed for a larger tree with depth of 4 and branching factor of 10, the tree has the following number of nodes:

$$\frac{1 - 10^5}{1 - 10} = 11,111 \text{ nodes}$$

DFID will examine the following number of nodes:

$$(4 + 1) + 10 \times 4 + 100 \times 3 + 1,000 \times 2 + 10,000 = 12,345 \text{ nodes}$$

Hence, as the tree gets larger, we see that the majority of the nodes to be examined (in this case, 10,000 out of 12,345) are in the last row, which needs to be examined only once in either case.

Like breadth-first search, DFID is optimal and complete. Because it also has good space efficiency, it is an extremely good search method to use where the search space may be very large and where the depth of the goal node is not known.

4.12 Using Heuristics for Search

Depth-first and breadth-first search were described as brute-force search methods. This is because they do not employ any special knowledge of the search trees they are examining but simply examine every node in order until they happen upon the goal. This can be likened to the human being who is traversing a maze by running a hand along the left side of the maze wall.

In some cases, this is the best that can be done because there is no additional information available that can be used to direct the search any better.

Often, however, such information does exist and can be used. Take the example of looking for a suitable Christmas gift. Very few people would simply walk into each shop as they came across it, looking in each department in turn until they happened upon a present. Most people would go straight to the shop that they considered to be most likely to have a suitable gift. If no gift was found in that shop, they would then proceed to the shop they considered to be the next most likely to have a suitable gift.

This kind of information is called a **heuristic**, and humans use them all the time to solve all kinds of problems. Computers can also use heuristics, and in many problems heuristics can reduce an otherwise impossible problem to a relatively simple one.

A **heuristic evaluation function** is a function that when applied to a node gives a value that represents a good estimate of the distance of the node from the goal. For two nodes m and n, and a heuristic function f, if $f(m) < f(n)$, then it should be the case that m is more likely to be on an **optimal path** to the goal node than n. In other words, the lower the heuristic value of a node, the more likely it is that it is on an optimal path to a goal and the more sensible it is for a search method to examine that node.

The following sections provide details of a number of search methods that use heuristics and are thus thought of as **heuristic search methods**, or **heuristically informed search methods**.

Typically, the heuristic used in search is one that provides an estimate of the distance from any given node to a goal node. This estimate may or may not be accurate, but it should at least provide better results than pure guesswork.

4.12.1   Informed and Uninformed Methods

A search method or heuristic is **informed** if it uses additional information about nodes that have not yet been explored to decide which nodes to examine next. If a method is not informed, it is **uninformed**, or **blind**. In other words, search methods that use heuristics are informed, and those that do not are blind.

Best-first search is an example of informed search, whereas breadth-first and depth-first search are uninformed or blind.

A heuristic h is said to be **more informed** than another heuristic, j, if $h(\text{node}) \leq j(\text{node})$ for all nodes in the search space. (In fact, in order for h

to be more informed than j, there must be some node where $h(\text{node}) <$ $j(\text{node})$. Otherwise they are as informed as each other.)

The more informed a search method is, the more efficiently it will search.

4.12.2   Choosing a Good Heuristic

Some heuristics are better than others, and the better (more informed) the heuristic is, the fewer nodes it needs to examine in the search tree to find a solution. Hence, like choosing the right representation, choosing the right heuristic can make a significant difference in our ability to solve a problem.

In choosing heuristics, we usually consider that a heuristic that reduces the number of nodes that need to be examined in the search tree is a good heuristic. It is also important to consider the efficiency of running the heuristic itself. In other words, if it takes an hour to compute a heuristic value for a given state, the fact that doing so saves a few minutes of total search time is irrelevant. For most of this section, we will assume that heuristic functions we choose are extremely simple to calculate and so do not impact on the overall efficiency of the search algorithm.

4.12.3   The 8-puzzle

To illustrate the way in which heuristics are developed, we will use the 8-puzzle, as illustrated in Figure 4.5.

The puzzle consists of a 3×3 grid, with the numbers 1 through 8 on tiles within the grid and one blank square. Tiles can be slid about within the grid, but a tile can only be moved into the empty square if it is adjacent to the empty square. The start state of the puzzle is a random configuration, and the goal state is as shown in the second picture in Figure 4.5, where the

Figure 4.5

The 8-puzzle, start state and goal state

7	6	
4	3	1
2	5	8

1	2	3
8		4
7	6	5

numbers go from 1 to 8 clockwise around the empty middle square, with 1 in the top left.

Typically, it takes about 20 moves to get from a random start state to the goal state, so the search tree has a depth of around 20. The branching factor depends on where the blank square is. If it is in the middle of the grid, the branching factor is 4; if it is on an edge, the branching factor is 3, and if it is in a corner, the branching factor is 2. Hence, the average branching factor of the search tree is 3.

So, an exhaustive search of the search tree would need to examine around 3^{20} states, which is around 3.5 billion. Because there are only 9! or 362,880 possible states, the search tree could clearly be cut down significantly by avoiding repeated states.

It is useful to find ways to reduce the search tree further, in order to devise a way to solve the problem efficiently. A heuristic would help us to do this, by telling us approximately how many moves a given state is from the goal state. We will examine a number of possible heuristics that could be used with the 8-puzzle.

To be useful, our heuristic must never overestimate the cost of changing from a given state to the goal state. Such a heuristic is defined as being **admissible**. As we will see, in many search methods it is essential that the heuristics we use are admissible.

The first heuristic we consider is to count how many tiles are in the wrong place. We will call this heuristic, $h_1(node)$. In the case of the first state shown in Figure 4.5, h_1 (node) = 8 because all the tiles are in the wrong place. However, this is misleading because we could imagine a state with a heuristic value of 8 but where each tile could be moved to its correct place in one move. This heuristic is clearly admissible because if a tile is in the wrong place, it must be moved at least once.

An improved heuristic, h_2, takes into account how far each tile had to move to get to its correct state. This is achieved by summing the **Manhattan distances** of each tile from its correct position. (Manhattan distance is the sum of the horizontal and vertical moves that need to be made to get from one position to another, named after the grid system of roads used in Manhattan.)

For the first state in Figure 4.5, this heuristic would provide a value of

$$h_2 \text{ (node)} = 2 + 2 + 2 + 2 + 3 + 3 + 1 + 3 = 18$$

Clearly, this is still an admissible heuristic because in order to solve the puzzle, each tile must be moved one square at a time from where it starts to where it is in the goal state.

It is worth noting that h_2 (node) $\geq h_1$ (node) for any node. This means that h_2 **dominates** h_1, which means that a search method using heuristic h_2 will always perform more efficiently than the same search method using h_1. This is because h_2 is more informed than h_1. Although a heuristic must never overestimate the cost, it is always better to choose the heuristic that gives the highest possible underestimate of cost. The ideal heuristic would thus be one that gave exactly accurate costs every time.

This efficiency is best understood in terms of the **effective branching factor**, b^*, of a search.

If a search method expands n nodes in solving a particular problem, and the goal node is at depth d, then b^* is the branching factor of a **uniform tree** that contains n nodes. Heuristics that give a lower effective branching factor perform better. A search method running with h_2 has a lower effective branching factor than the same search method running with h_1 in solving the 8-puzzle.

A third heuristic function, h_3, takes into account the fact that there is extra difficulty involved if two tiles have to move past each other because tiles cannot jump over each other. This heuristic uses a function k(node), which is equal to the number of direct swaps that need to be made between adjacent tiles to move them into the correct sequence.

$$h_3 \text{ (node)} = h_2 \text{ (node)} + (2 \times k(\text{node}))$$

Because k(node) must be at least 0, h_3 (node) must be greater than h_2 (node), meaning that h_3 is a more informed heuristic than h_2.

The heuristic functions h_1, h_2, and h_3 are all admissible, meaning that using the **A*** algorithm (see Section 4.16.1) with any of these heuristics would guarantee to find the quickest solution to the puzzle.

There are a number of possible ways to generate useful heuristic functions. Functions like h_1 and h_2 can be generated by **relaxing** the 8-puzzle problem. A **relaxed problem** is a version of a problem that has fewer **constraints**. For example, a relaxed version of the 8-puzzle might be that a tile can be moved to an adjacent square regardless of whether that square is empty or not. In that case, h_2 (node) would be exactly equal to the number of moves needed to get from a node to the goal node.

If the problem were relaxed further, we might say that a tile could move to any square, even if that square is not adjacent to the square it is starting from. In this case, h_1 (node) exactly equals the number of moves needed to get from a node to the goal node.

Hence, using an exact cost function for a relaxed version of a problem is often a good way to generate a heuristic cost function for the main problem.

It is clear that h_3 is the best heuristic function to use of the three we generated because it dominates both h_1 and h_2. In some cases, a number of heuristic functions may exist, none of which dominates the others. In that case, a new heuristic can be generated from the heuristics $h_1 \ldots h_n$, as follows:

$$h(node) = \max (h_1 [node], h_2 [node], \ldots, h_n [node])$$

Because all of h_1 to h_n is admissible, $h(node)$ must also be admissible. The heuristic function h dominates all of the heuristics $h_1 \ldots h_n$ and so is clearly the best one to use.

As we see in Chapter 6, another way to find a heuristic is to take advantage of features of the problem that is being modeled by the search tree. For example, in the case of playing checkers, computers are able to use heuristics such as the fact that a player with more kings on the board is likely to win against a player with fewer kings.

4.12.4 Monotonicity

A search method is described as **monotone** if it always reaches a given node by the shortest possible path.

So, a search method that reaches a given node at different depths in the search tree is not monotone. A monotone search method must be admissible, provided there is only one goal state.

A **monotonic** heuristic is a heuristic that has this property.

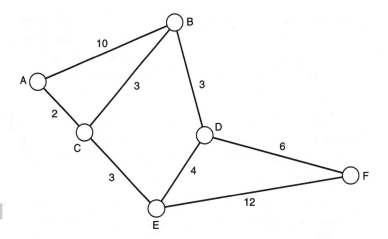

Figure 4.6

Map of five cities

An **admissible heuristic** is a heuristic that never overestimates the true distance of a node from the goal. A monotonic heuristic is also admissible, assuming there is only one goal state.

4.12.5   Example: The Modified Traveling Salesman Problem

It is usual when examining heuristic search methods to relate the search problem to a real-world situation in order to derive suitable heuristics. For this explanation, we will use the example of finding the best route between two cities, a variation of the **Traveling Salesman problem**, as shown in Figure 4.6.

In this diagram, each node represents a town, and the vertices between nodes represent roads that join towns together. A is the starting node, and F is the goal node. Each vertex is labeled with a distance, which shows how long that road is. Clearly the diagram is not drawn to scale.

The aim of this problem is to find the shortest possible path from city A to city F. This is different from the traditional Traveling Salesman problem, in which the problem is to find a way to travel around a group of cities and finally arrive back at the starting city.

We can represent the search space of the map in Figure 4.6 as a search tree by showing each possible path as a leaf node in the tree. In doing so, we need to be careful to remove repetitions of paths, or loops, because those would add redundancy to the graph and make searching it inefficient. The tree for this search space is shown in Figure 4.7.

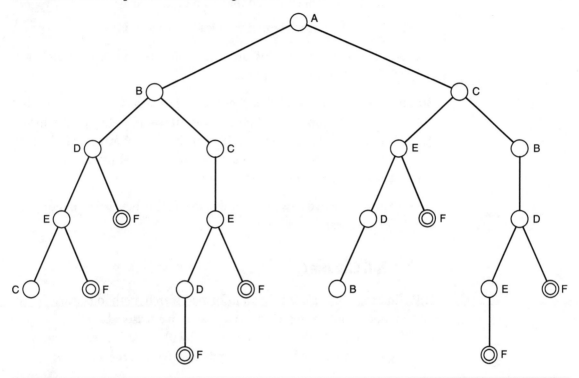

Figure 4.7

Search tree for map in Figure 4.6

You will notice that this tree has nine leaf nodes, seven of which are goal nodes. Two of the paths lead to cyclical paths and so are abandoned. There are seven distinct paths that successfully lead from A to F. These seven paths can be traced from the tree as follows:

1   A,B,D,E,F

2   A,B,D,F

3   A,B,C,E,D,F

4   A,B,C,E,F

5   A,C,E,F

6   A,C,B,D,E,F

7   A,C,B,D,F

The two cyclical paths are as follows:

1   A,B,D,E,C (which would then lead on to A or B)

2   A,C,E,D,B (which would then lead on to A or C)

A depth-first approach to this problem would provide path number 1, A,B,D,E,F, which has a total distance of 29.

Breadth-first search always produces the path that has the least steps, but not necessarily the shortest path. In this case, it would yield path 2, which is A,B,D,F and which has a length of 19. This is much shorter than the path produced by depth-first search but is not the shortest path (the shortest path is path 5, A,C,E,F, which has a length of 17).

Now we introduce two new search methods that use heuristics to more efficiently identify search solutions.

4.13   Hill Climbing

Hill climbing is an example of an **informed** search method because it uses information about the search space to search in a reasonably efficient manner. If you try to climb a mountain in fog with an altimeter but no map, you might use the hill climbing Generate and Test approach:

Check the height 1 foot away from your current location in each direction: north, south, east, and west.

As soon as you find a position where the height is higher than your current position, move to that location and restart the algorithm.

If all directions lead lower than your current position, then you stop and assume you have reached the summit. As we see later, this might not necessarily always be true.

In examining a search tree, hill climbing will move to the first successor node that is "better" than the current node—in other words, the first node that it comes across with a heuristic value lower than that of the current node.

4.13.1   Steepest Ascent Hill Climbing

Steepest ascent hill climbing is similar to hill climbing, except that rather than moving to the first position you find that is higher than the current

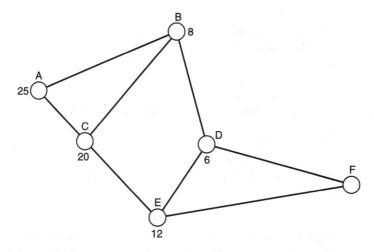

Figure 4.8
The map of five cities
where the straight-line
distance from each city to
the goal city (F) is shown

position, you always check around you in all four directions and choose the position that is highest.

Steepest ascent hill climbing can also be thought of as a variation on depth-first search, which uses information about how far each node is from the goal node to choose which path to follow next at any given point.

For this method, we apply a heuristic to the search tree shown in Figure 4.7, which is the straight-line distance from each town to the goal town. We are using this heuristic to approximate the actual distance from each town to the goal, which will of course be longer than the straight-line distance.

In Figure 4.8, we can see the same search problem as presented in Figure 4.6, but instead of noting the lengths of vertices, we note how far each city is (using a straight-line measurement) from the goal, city F.

Now hill climbing proceeds as with depth-first search, but at each step, the new nodes to be added to the queue are sorted into order of distance from the goal. Note that the only difference between this implementation and that given for depth-first search is that in hill climbing the successors of state are sorted according to their distance from the goal before being added to the queue:

```
Function hill ()
{
    queue = [];      // initialize an empty queue
    state = root_node;   // initialize the start state
    while (true)
```

```
{
    if is_goal (state)
        then return SUCCESS
    else
    {
        sort (successors (state));
        add_to_front_of_queue (successors (state));
    }
    if queue == []
        then report FAILURE;
    state = queue [0]; // state = first item in queue
    remove_first_item_from (queue);
}
```

This algorithm thus searches the tree in a depth-first manner, at each step choosing paths that appear to be most likely to lead to the goal.

The steps taken by a hill-climbing algorithm in solving the preceding problem are shown in Table 4.4:

Table 4.4   Analysis of hill climbing

Step	State	Queue	Notes
1	A	(empty)	The queue starts out empty, and the initial state is the root node, which is A.
2	A	B,C	The successors of A are sorted and placed on the queue. B is placed before C on the queue because it is closer to the goal state, F.
3	B	C	
4	B	D,C,C	
5	D	C,C	
6	D	F,E,C,C	F is placed first on the queue because it is closest to the goal. In fact, it is the goal, as will be discovered in the next step.
7	F	E,C,C	SUCCESS: Path is reported as A,B,D,F.

In this case, hill climbing has produced the same path as breadth-first search, which is the path with the least steps, but not the shortest path. In many cases though, using this heuristic enables hill climbing to identify shorter paths than would be identified by depth-first or breadth-first search. Hill climbing uses heuristics to identify paths efficiently but does not necessarily identify the best path.

If we ran the searches from right to left, instead of from left to right (or ordered the search tree the other way around), then we would find that breadth-first search would produce a different path: A,C,E,F (which is in fact the shortest path), but hill climbing would still produce the same path, A,B,D,F. In other words, the particular ordering of nodes used affects which result is produced by breadth-first and depth-first search but does not affect hill climbing in the same way. This can clearly be a useful property.

4.13.2 Foothills, Plateaus, and Ridges

Although we have been talking about using search techniques to traverse search trees, they can also be used to solve search problems that are represented in different ways. In particular, we often represent a search problem as a three-dimensional space, where the x- and y-axes are used to represent variables and the z-axis (or height) is used to represent the outcome.

The goal is usually to maximize the outcome, and so search methods in these cases are aiming to find the highest point in the space.

Many such search spaces can be successfully traversed using hill climbing and other heuristically informed search methods. Some search spaces, however, will present particular difficulties for these techniques.

In particular, hill climbing can be fooled by **foothills**, **plateaus**, and **ridges**. Figure 4.9 has three illustrations, showing foothills, a plateau, and a ridge. This figure shows the search space represented as a three-dimensional terrain. In this kind of terrain, the aim of search is to find the x and y values that give the highest possible value of z—in other words, the highest point in the terrain. This is another way of looking at traditional search: search is normally aiming to maximize some function, which in this case is shown as the height of the terrain, but is traditionally a function that details the distance of a node from the goal node.

Foothills are often called **local maxima** by mathematicians. A local maximum is a part of the search space that appears to be preferable to the parts around it, but which is in fact just a foothill of a larger hill. Hill-climbing

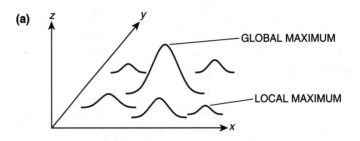

(a)

GLOBAL MAXIMUM

LOCAL MAXIMUM

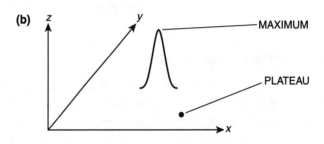

(b)

MAXIMUM

PLATEAU

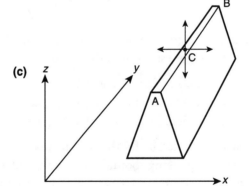

(c)

Figure 4.9

(a) FOOTHILLS

(b) PLATEAU

(c) RIDGE

techniques will reach this peak, where a more sophisticated technique might move on from there to look for the **global maximum**. Figure 4.9 (a) shows a search space that has a single global maximum surrounded by a number of foothills, or local maxima. Many search methods would reach the top of one of these foothills and, because there was nowhere higher nearby, would conclude that this was the best solution to the problem.

Later in this chapter and in Chapter 5, we see methods such as simulated annealing that are good at avoiding being trapped by local maxima.

A plateau is a region in a search space where all the values are the same. In this case, although there may well be a suitable maximum value somewhere nearby, there is no indication from the local terrain of which direction to go to find it. Hill climbing does not perform well in this situation. Figure 4.9 (b) shows a search space that consists of just one peak surrounded by a plateau. A hill-climbing search method could well find itself stuck in the plateau with no clear indication of where to go to find a good solution.

The final problem for hill climbing is presented by ridges. A ridge is a long, thin region of high land with low land on either side. When looking in one of the four directions, north, south, east, and west from the ridge, a hill-climbing algorithm would determine that any point on the top of the ridge was a maximum because the hill falls away in those four directions. The correct direction is a very narrow one that leads up the top of the ridge, but identifying this direction using hill climbing could be very tricky.

Figure 4.9 (c) shows a ridge. The point marked A is lower than the point marked B, which is the global maximum. When a hill-climbing method finds itself at point C, it might find it hard to get from there to B. The arrows on point C show that in moving north, south, east, or west, the method would find itself at a lower point. The correct direction is up the ridge.

4.14   Best-First Search

Best-first search employs a heuristic in a similar manner to hill climbing. The difference is that with best-first search, the entire queue is sorted after new paths have been added to it, rather than adding a set of sorted paths.

In practical terms, this means that best-first search follows the best path available from the current (partially developed) tree, rather than always following a depth-first style approach.

```
Function best ()
{
    queue = [];      // initialize an empty queue
    state = root_node;   // initialize the start state
    while (true)
    {
        if is_goal (state)
            then return SUCCESS
        else
```

```
    {
        add_to_front_of_queue (successors (state));
        sort (queue);
    }
    if queue == []
        then report FAILURE;
    state = queue [0]; // state = first item in queue
    remove_first_item_from (queue);
    }
}
```

The path taken through the search tree shown in Figure 4.7 is shown in Table 4.5.

Table 4.5   Analysis of best-first search of tree shown in Figure 4.4

Step	State	Queue	Notes
1	A	(empty)	The queue starts out empty, and the initial state is the root node, which is A.
2	A	B,C	The successors of the current state, B and C, are placed in the queue.
	A	B,C	The queue is sorted, leaving B in front of C because it is closer to the goal state, F.
3	B	C	
4	B	D,C,C	The children of node B are added to the front of the queue.
5	B	D,C,C	The queue is sorted, leaving D at the front because it is closer to the goal node than C.
6	D	C,C	Note that although the queue appears to contain the same node twice, this is just an artifact of the way the search tree was constructed. In fact, those two nodes are distinct and represent different paths on our search tree.
7	D	E,F,C,C	The children of D are added to the front of the queue.
8	D	F,E,C,C	The queue is sorted, moving F to the front.
9	F	E,C,C	SUCCESS: Path is reported as A,B,D,F.

It can be seen that, in this case, best-first search happens to produce the same path as hill climbing and breadth-first search, although the queue is ordered differently during the process. As with hill climbing, best-first search will tend to provide a shorter path than depth first or breadth first, but not necessarily the shortest path.

4.15   Beam Search

Beam search is a form of breadth-first search that employs a heuristic, as seen with hill climbing and best-first search. Beam search works using a threshold so that only the best few paths are followed downward at each level. This method is very efficient in memory usage and would be particularly useful for exploring a search space that had a very high branching factor (such as in game trees for games, such as Go or Chess). It has the disadvantage of not exhaustively searching the entire tree and so may fail to ever find a goal node.

In this implementation, the function call select_best_paths   (queue,   n) removes all but the best n paths from the queue.

```
Function beam ()
{
    queue = [];      // initialize an empty queue
    state = root_node;   // initialize the start state
    while (true)
    {
        if is_goal (state)
            then return SUCCESS
        else
        {
            add_to_back_of_queue (successors (state));
            select_best_paths (queue, n);
        }
        if queue == []
            then report FAILURE;
        state = queue [0]; // state = first item in queue
        remove_first_item_from (queue);
    }
}
```

In this pseudocode, n is used to represent the width threshold, which is set at the beginning of the procedure.

Table 4.6   Analysis of beam search of tree shown in Figure 4.7

Step	State	Queue	Notes
1	A	(empty)	The queue starts out empty, and the initial state is the root node, which is A.
2	A	B,C	The two children of the current node are added to the back of the queue.
3	B	C	
4	B	C,D,C	The two children of B are added to the back of the queue.
5	B	D,C	All but the two best paths are discarded from the queue.
6	D	C	
7	D	C,E,F	The two children of the current node are added to the back of the queue.
8	D	E,F	At this step, C is removed from the queue because we only require the two best paths.
9	E	F	
10	E	F,C,F	The two children of E are added to the back of the queue.
11	E	F,F	The path that leads to C is discarded, in favor of the two better paths, both of which lead to F.
12	F	F	SUCCESS: Path is reported as A,B,D,E,F.

The interesting aspect of this method is the choice of how to define the "best" paths to include in the queue. Often, the path that involves the fewest steps is used or the path that has reached the point with the highest heuristic value (in other words, the path that got closest to the goal).

In Table 4.6, the value of state and queue are shown for the problem tree shown in Figure 4.7, using beam search with a threshold of 2 (in other words, only two paths are extended down from each level). For this implementation, we have used the heuristic value of each node to determine which path is the "best" path. So the "best" path will be the one that has reached the closest to a goal node so far.

4.16 Identifying Optimal Paths

Several methods exist that do identify the **optimal path** through a search tree. The optimal path is the one that has the lowest **cost** or involves traveling the shortest distance from start to goal node. The techniques described previously may find the optimal path by accident, but none of them are guaranteed to find it.

The simplest method for identifying the optimal path is called the **British Museum procedure**. This process involves examining every single path through the search tree and returning via the best path that was found. Because every path is examined, the optimal path must be found. This process is implemented as an extension of one of the exhaustive search techniques, such as depth-first or breadth-first search, but rather than stopping when a solution is found, the solution is stored and the process continues until all paths have been explored. If an alternative solution is found, its path is compared with the stored path, and if it has a lower cost, it replaces the stored path.

The following more sophisticated techniques for identifying optimal paths are outlined in this section:

- A*
- uniform cost search (Branch and Bound)
- greedy search

The British Museum procedure also has the property that it generates *all* solutions. Most of the search methods we look at in this book stop when they find a solution. In some cases, this will be the best solution, and in other cases it may even be the worst available solution (depth-first search will do this if the worst solution happens to be the left-most solution).

In some cases, it may be necessary to identify all possible solutions, in which case something like the British Museum procedure would be useful.

Assuming that none of the branches of the tree is infinitely deep, and that no level has an infinite branching factor, then it does not matter which approach is used (depth first or breadth first, for example) when running the British Museum procedure: because the goal is to visit every node, the order the nodes are visited probably does not matter.

4.16.1   A* Algorithms

A* algorithms are similar to best-first search but use a somewhat more complex heuristic to select a path through the tree. The best-first algorithm always extends paths that involve moving to the node that appears to be closest to the goal, but it does not take into account the cost of the path to that node so far.

The A* algorithm operates in the same manner as best-first search but uses the following function to evaluate nodes:

$$f(node) = g(node) + h(node)$$

$g(node)$ is the cost of the path so far leading up to the node, and $h(node)$ is an underestimate of the distance of the node from a goal state; f is called a **path-based evaluation function**. When operating A*, $f(node)$ is evaluated for successor nodes and paths extended using the nodes that have the *lowest* values of f.

If $h(node)$ is always an *underestimate* of the distance of a node to a goal node, then the A* algorithm is optimal: it is *guaranteed* to find the shortest path to a goal state. A* is described as being optimally efficient, in that in finding the path to the goal node, it will expand the fewest possible paths. Again, this property depends on $h(node)$ always being an underestimate.

Note that running the A* algorithm on the search tree shown in Figure 4.4 would not be guaranteed to find the shortest solution because the estimated values for $h(node)$ are not all underestimates. In other words, the heuristic that is being used is not admissible. If a nonadmissible heuristic for $h(node)$ is used, then the algorithm is called **A**.

A* is the name given to the algorithm where the $h(node)$ function is admissible. In other words, it is guaranteed to provide an underestimate of the true cost to the goal.

A* is optimal and complete. In other words, it is guaranteed to find a solution, and that solution is guaranteed to be the best solution.

A* is in fact only complete if the tree it is searching has a finite branching factor and does not contain a path of finite cost, which has an infinite number of nodes along it. Both of these conditions are likely to be met in all real-world situations, and so for simplicity we can state that A* is complete; although, to be more accurate:

A* is complete if the graph it is searching is **locally finite** (that is, it has a finite branching factor) and if every arc between two nodes in the graph has a non-zero cost.

That A* is optimal can be proved by considering a counter-example:

Imagine we are applying the A* algorithm to a graph with two goals, G1 and G2. The path cost of G1 is f1 and the path cost of G2 is f2, where f2 > f1. G1 is the goal with the lower cost, but let us imagine a scenario where the A* algorithm has reached G2 without having explored G1. In other words, we are imagining a scenario where the algorithm has not chosen the goal with the lesser cost.

If we consider a node, n, that is on an optimal path from the root node to G1, then because h is an admissible heuristic:

$$f1 \geq f(n)$$

The only reason the algorithm would not choose to expand n before it reaches G2 would be if

$$f(n) > f(G2)$$

Hence, by combining these two expressions together, we arrive at

$$f1 \geq f(G2)$$

Because G2 is a goal state, it must be the case that $h(G2) = 0$, and thus $f(G2) = g(G2)$. Thus we have

$$f1 \geq g(G2)$$

This, therefore, contradicts our original assumption that G2 had a higher path cost than G1, which proves that A* can only ever choose the least cost path to a goal.

It was mentioned that A* is similar to breadth-first search. In fact, breadth-first search can be considered to be a special case of A*, where h(node) is always 0, so $f(node) = g(node)$, and where every direct path between a node and its immediate successor has a cost of 1.

4.16.2   Uniform Cost Search

Uniform cost search (or **Branch and Bound**) is a variation on best-first search that uses the evaluation function g(node), which for a given node evaluates to the cost of the path leading to that node. In other words, this is an A* algorithm but where h(node) is set to zero. At each stage, the path that has the lowest cost so far is extended. In this way, the path that is generated is likely to be the path with the lowest overall cost, but this is not guaranteed. To find the best path, the algorithm needs to continue running after a solution is found, and if a preferable solution is found, it should be accepted in place of the earlier solution.

Uniform cost search is complete and is optimal, providing the cost of a path increases monotonically. In other words, if for every node m that has a successor n, it is true that $g(m) < g(n)$, then uniform cost is optimal. If it is possible for the cost of a node to be less than the cost of its parent, then uniform cost search may not find the best path.

Uniform cost search was invented by Dijkstra in 1959 and is also known as Dijkstra's algorithm.

4.16.3   Greedy Search

Greedy search is a variation of the A* algorithm, where g(node) is set to zero, so that only h(node) is used to evaluate suitable paths. In this way, the algorithm always selects the path that has the lowest heuristic value or estimated distance (or cost) to the goal.

Greedy search is an example of a best-first strategy.

Greedy-search methods tend to be reasonably efficient, although in the worst case, like depth-first search, it may never find a solution at all. Additionally, greedy search is not optimal and can be fooled into following extremely costly paths. This can happen if the first step on the shortest path toward the goal is longer than the first step along another path, as is shown in Figure 4.10.

4.16.4   Example: The Knapsack Problem

The knapsack problem is an interesting illustration of the use of greedy-search algorithms and their pitfalls. The **fractional knapsack problem** can be expressed as follows:

A man is packing items into his knapsack. He wants to take the most valuable items he can, but there is a limit on how much weight he can fit in his knapsack. Each item has a weight w_i and is worth v_i. He can only fit a total weight of W in his knapsack. The items that he wants to take are things that can be broken up and still retain their value (like flour or milk), and he is

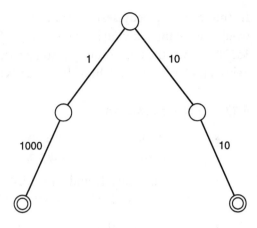

Figure 4.10

A search tree where a greedy-search method will not find the best solution

able to take fractions of items. Hence, the problem is called the *fractional* knapsack problem.

In solving this problem, a greedy-search algorithm provides the best solution.

The problem is solved by calculating the value per unit weight of each item: v_i/w_i, and then taking as much as he can carry of the item with the greatest value per unit weight. If he still has room, he moves on to the item with the next highest value per unit weight, and so on.

The **0-1 knapsack problem** is the same as the fractional knapsack problem, except that he cannot take parts of items. Each item is thus something like a television set or a laptop computer, which must be taken whole. In solving this problem, a greedy-search approach does not work, as can be seen from the following example:

Our man has a knapsack that lets him carry a total of 100 pounds. His items are:

     1 gold brick worth $1800 and weighing 50 pounds

     1 platinum brick worth $1500 and weighing 30 pounds

     1 laptop computer worth $2000 and weighing 50 pounds

Hence, we have four items, whose values of v and w are as follows:

$$v_1 = 1800 \qquad w_1 = 50 \qquad v_1/w_1 = 36$$
$$v_2 = 1500 \qquad w_2 = 30 \qquad v_2/w_2 = 50$$
$$v_3 = 2000 \qquad w_3 = 50 \qquad v_3/w_3 = 40$$

In this case, a greedy-search strategy would pick item 2 first, and then would take item 3, giving a total weight of 80 pounds, and a total value of $3500. In fact, the best solution is to take items 1 and 3 and to leave item 2 behind giving a total weight of 100 pounds and a total value of $3800.

4.17   Chapter Summary

- Generate and Test is an extremely simple example of a brute-force or exhaustive search technique.

- Depth-first search and breadth-first search are extremely commonly used and well understood exhaustive search methods.

- In analyzing search methods, it is important to examine the complexity (in time and space) of the method.

- A search method is complete if it will always find a solution if one exists. A search method is optimal (or admissible) if it always finds the best solution that exists.

- Depth-First Iterative Deepening (DFID) is a search method that has the low memory requirements of depth-first search and is optimal and complete, like breadth-first search.

- Heuristics can be used to make search methods more informed about the problem they are solving. A heuristic is a method that provides a better guess about the correct choice to make at any junction that would be achieved by random guessing.

- One heuristic is more informed than another heuristic if a search method that uses it needs to examine fewer nodes to reach a goal.

- Relaxing problems is one way to identify potentially useful heuristics.

- Hill climbing is a heuristic search method that involves continually moving from one potential solution to a better potential solution until no better solution can be found.

- Hill climbing has problems in search spaces that have foothills, plateaus, and ridges.

- A* is a heuristic search method that in most situations is optimal and complete. It uses the path evaluation function to choose suitable paths through the search space.

- Uniform cost search is similar to A* but uses a simpler evaluation function, which is based just on the cost of reaching the node so far.

- Greedy search involves always moving to the most immediately attractive position on the next step. It can be used to solve the fractional knapsack problem, but not the 1-0 knapsack problem.

4.18   Review Questions

4.1 Explain the idea behind Generate and Test. Why is this method described as being *exhaustive*?

4.2 Explain the differences and similarities between depth-first search and breadth-first search. Give examples of the kinds of problems where each would be appropriate.

4.3 Explain what is meant by the following terms in relation to search methods:

- complexity
- completeness
- optimality

4.4 What is the complexity (in space and in time) of the following search methods:

- depth-first search
- breadth-first search
- best-first search
- greedy search

4.5 What does it mean to say that a search method is monotonic? How desirable is this property? Which of the search methods described in this chapter is monotonic?

4.6 Explain why Depth-First Search Iterative Deepening is reasonably efficient. Why might it be preferable to use DFID rather than depth-first search?

4.7 Provide a definition of the word "heuristic." In what ways can heuristics be useful in search? Name three ways in which you use heuristics in your everyday life.

4.8 Explain the components of the path evaluation function f(node) used by A*. Do you think it is the best evaluation function that could be used? To what kinds of problems might it be best suited? And to what kinds of problems would it be worst suited?

4.9 Show that A* is optimal and complete in most circumstances.

4.10 Explain why a greedy method provides suboptimal solutions to the 0-1 knapsack problem but provides optimal solutions to the fractional knapsack problem. Could there be a search tree for which greedy search found optimal solutions?

4.11 What effect does the ordering of a search tree have on the efficiency of search? What effect does it have on the quality of the results? How would ordering affect the way that depth-first search or greedy search would perform when searching the search tree shown in Figure 4.10?

4.19 Exercises

4.12 Implement a data structure that represents search trees in a programming language of your choice. Have the program display the tree on the screen, and provide functions that can select nodes and display paths.

4.13 Implement depth-first search in your program. Implement breadth-first search. Build a search tree of depth 10 and with a branching factor of 2. Which of your search methods finds a goal the most quickly? Can you change the tree so that the other method finds the goal more quickly?

4.14 Add the concept of path cost to your implementation. Implement A*. Does it perform much better than depth-first or breadth-first search? How well does it do with the large tree you built in Exercise 4.8?

4.15 Implement a greedy-search algorithm. How well does it perform compared with the other methods you have implemented? Invent a 0-1 knapsack problem, and use your search tree implementation to model this problem. Can you model the fractional knapsack problem using a search tree?

4.16 Investigate the file search facility on your computer. Which type of search method do you think it uses? Why do you think this particular search method was chosen? What problems could this approach cause it? How well does it work when it is searching directories with large numbers of files in them?

4.20   Further Reading

Search is covered well by almost all artificial intelligence text books, although the approaches taken vary.

A detailed description and analysis of Dijkstra's algorithm (uniform cost search) can be found in Cormen et al. (2001). Books such as this that cover algorithms in more detail provide an interesting non-Artificial Intelligence perspective on the subject.

Marvin Minsky's 1961 paper, *Steps Toward Artificial Intelligence*, introduced the idea of hill climbing and discussed some of the difficulties faced by hill-climbing methods.

Allen Newell and Herbert A. Simon's 1976 paper, *Computer Science as Empirical Inquiry*, contains an excellent discussion of heuristic search for problem solving.

A good description of the way that Prolog uses depth-first search for unification is contained in Russell and Norvig (1995).

Introduction to Algorithms, by Thomas H. Cormen, Charles E. Leiserson, Ronald L. Rivest, and Clifford Stein (2001 – MIT Press)

Artificial Intelligence: Strategies, Applications, and Models Through Search, by Benedict Du Boulay and Christopher James Thornton (1999 – AMACOM)

Algorithmics: The Spirit of Computing, by David Harel (1987 – Addison Wesley)

Art of Computer Programming: Sorting and Searching, by Donald Knuth (1973 – Pearson Addison Wesley)

Steps Towards Artificial Intelligence, by Marvin Minsky (1961 – in *Computation & Intelligence—Collected Readings*, edited by George F. Luger, MIT Press)

Computer Science as Empirical Enquiry: Symbols and Search, by Allen Newell and Herbert A. Simon (1976 – in *Computation & Intelligence—Collected Readings*, edited by George F. Luger, MIT Press)

Algorithms, by Robert Sedgewick (1988 – Addison Wesley)

CHAPTER 5

Advanced Search

The difficult we do immediately. The impossible takes a little longer.

—US Armed Forces slogan

Had I been present at the Creation, I would have given some useful hints for the better ordering of the universe.

—Alfonso 'the wise', on studying the Ptolemaic system (13th century A.D.)

If we value the pursuit of knowledge, we must be free to follow wherever that search may lead us. The free mind is not a barking dog, to be tethered on a ten-foot chain.

—Adlai E. Stevenson Jr., speech at the University of Wisconsin, Madison, October 8, 1952

5.1 Introduction

In Chapter 4, we examined a range of methods that can be used to search a problem space. In Chapter 5, we introduce some more sophisticated methods.

First, we examine constraint satisfaction problems, such as the eight-queens problem, and search methods and heuristics that can be used to solve them.

We also discuss **local search methods**, such as simulated annealing, that attempt to find a solution to large **combinatorial problems** by moving from one possible solution to another that is a little better. We also introduce the idea of **parallel search**—using multiple processors (or multiple computers) to deal with a single search problem to solve it more quickly. Much of the material in this chapter is introductory in nature, and references are given to books and papers where more information can be learned on the methods.

5.2   Constraint Satisfaction Search

Search can be used to solve problems that are limited by constraints, such as the eight-queens problem. Such problems are often known as **Constraint Satisfaction Problems**, or **CSPs**.

In this problem, eight queens must be placed on a chess board in such a way that no two queens are on the same diagonal, row, or column. If we use traditional chess board notation, we mark the columns with letters from a to g and the rows with numbers from 1 to 8. So, a square can be referred to by a letter and a number, such as a4 or g7.

This kind of problem is known as a constraint satisfaction problem (CSP) because a solution must be found that satisfies the constraints.

In the case of the eight-queens problem, a search tree can be built that represents the possible positions of queens on the board.

One way to represent this is to have a tree that is 8-ply deep, with a branching factor of 64 for the first level, 63 for the next level, and so on, down to 57 for the eighth level.

A goal node in this tree is one that satisfies the constraints that no two queens can be on the same diagonal, row, or column.

An extremely simplistic approach to solving this problem would be to analyze every possible configuration until one was found that matched the constraints.

A more suitable approach to solving the eight-queens problem would be to use depth-first search on a search tree that represents the problem in the following manner:

The first branch from the root node would represent the first choice of a square for a queen. The next branch from these nodes would represent choices of where to place the second queen.

The first level would have a branching factor of 64 because there are 64 possible squares on which to place the first queen. The next level would have a

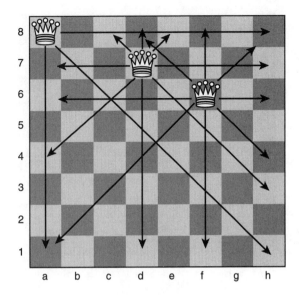

Figure 5.1

The eight-queens problem. Three queens have been placed so far.

somewhat lower branching factor because once a queen has been placed, the constraints can be used to determine possible squares upon which the next queen can be placed. The branching factor will decrease as the algorithm searches down the tree. At some point, the tree will terminate because the path being followed will lead to a position where no more queens can be placed on legal squares on the board, and there are still some queens remaining.

In fact, because each row and each column must contain exactly one queen, the branching factor can be significantly reduced by assuming that the first queen must be placed in row 1, the second in row 2, and so on. In this way, the first level will have a branching factor of 8 (a choice of eight squares on which the first queen can be placed), the next 7, the next 6, and so on.

In fact, the search tree can be further simplified as each queen placed on the board "uses up" a diagonal, meaning that the branching factor is only 5 or 6 after the first choice has been made, depending on whether the first queen is placed on an edge of the board (columns a or h) or not. The next level will have a branching factor of about 4, and the next may have a branching factor of just 2, as shown in Figure 5.1.

The arrows in Figure 5.1 show the squares to which each queen can move. Note that no queen can move to a square that is already occupied by another queen.

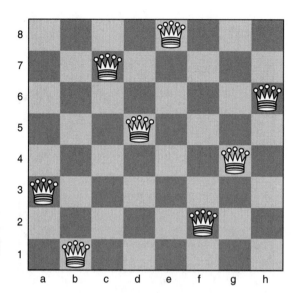

Figure 5.2

A solution to the eight-queens problem

In Figure 5.1, the first queen was placed in column a of row 8, leaving six choices for the next row. The second queen was placed in column d of row 7, leaving four choices for row 6. The third queen was placed in column f in row 6, leaving just two choices (column c or column h) for row 5.

Using knowledge like this about the problem that is being solved can help to significantly reduce the size of the search tree and thus improve the efficiency of the search solution.

A solution will be found when the algorithm reaches depth 8 and successfully places the final queen on a legal square on the board. A goal node would be a path containing eight squares such that no two squares shared a diagonal, row, or column.

One solution to the eight-queens problem is shown in Figure 5.2.

Note that in this solution, if we start by placing queens on squares e8, c7, h6, and then d5, once the fourth queen has been placed, there are only two choices for placing the fifth queen (b4 or g4). If b4 is chosen, then this leaves no squares that could be chosen for the final three queens to satisfy the constraints. If g4 is chosen for the fifth queen, as has been done in Figure 5.2, only one square is available for the sixth queen (a3), and the final two choices are similarly constrained. So, it can be seen that by applying the constraints appropriately, the search tree can be significantly reduced for this problem.

Using chronological backtracking in solving the eight-queens problem might not be the most efficient way to identify a solution because it will backtrack over moves that did not necessarily directly lead to an error, as well as ones that did. In this case, nonchronological backtracking, or **dependency-directed backtracking** (see Section 5.17) could be more useful because it could identify the steps earlier in the search tree that caused the problem further down the tree.

5.3   Forward Checking

In fact, backtracking can be augmented in solving problems like the eight-queens problem by using a method called **forward checking**. As each queen is placed on the board, a forward-checking mechanism is used to delete from the set of possible future choices any that have been rendered impossible by placing the queen on that square. For example, if a queen is placed on square a1, forward checking will remove all squares in row 1, all squares in column a, and also squares b2, c3, d4, e5, f6, g7, and h8. In this way, if placing a queen on the board results in removing all remaining squares, the system can immediately backtrack, without having to attempt to place any more queens. This can often significantly improve the performance of solutions for CSPs such as the eight-queens problem.

5.4   Most-Constrained Variables

A further improvement in performance can be achieved by using the **most-constrained variable** heuristic. At each stage of the search, this heuristic involves working with the variable that has the least possible number of valid choices. In the case of the eight-queens problem, this might be achieved by considering the problem to be one of assigning a value to eight variables, a through h. Assigning value 1 to variable a means placing a queen in square a1. To use the most constrained variable heuristic with this representation means that at each move we assign a value to the variable that has the least choices available to it. Hence, after assigning $a = 1, b = 3$, and $c = 5$, this leaves three choices for d, three choices for e, one choice for f, three choices for g, and three choices for h. Hence, our next move is to place a queen in column f.

This heuristic is perhaps more clearly understood in relation to the map-coloring problem. It makes sense that, in a situation where a particular country can be given only one color due to the colors that have been assigned to its neighbors, that country be colored next.

The **most-constraining variable** heuristic is similar in that it involves assigning a value next to the variable that places the greatest number of constraints on future variables.

The **least-constraining value** heuristic is perhaps more intuitive than the two already presented in this section. This heuristic involves assigning a value to a variable that leaves the greatest number of choices for other variables. This heuristic can be used to make n-queens problems with extremely large values of n quite solvable.

5.5   Example: Cryptographic Problems

The constraint satisfaction procedure is also a useful way to solve problems such as cryptographic problems. For example:

FORTY

+ TEN

+ TEN

SIXTY

Solution:

29786

+ 850

+ 850

31486

This cryptographic problem can be solved by using a Generate and Test method, applying the following constraints:

- Each letter represents exactly one number.
- No two letters represent the same number.

As explained in Chapter 4, Generate and Test is a brute-force method, which in this case involves cycling through all possible assignments of numbers to letters until a set is found that meets the constraints and solves the problem.

Without using constraints, the method would first start by attempting to assign 0 to all letters, resulting in the following sum:

00000
+ 000
+ 000
00000

Although this may appear to be a valid solution to the problem, it does not meet the constraints laid down that specify that each letter can be assigned only one number, and each number can be assigned only to one letter.

Hence, constraints are necessary simply to find the correct solution to the problem. They also enable us to reduce the size of the search tree. In this case, for example, it is not necessary to examine possible solutions where two letters have been assigned the same number, which dramatically reduces the possible solutions to be examined.

As we see in the next section, there are more efficient methods than Generate and Test to solve problems of this nature.

5.6 Heuristic Repair

Heuristics can be used to improve performance of solutions to constraint satisfaction problems. One way to do this is to use a **heuristic repair method**, which involves generating a possible solution (randomly, or using a heuristic to generate a position that is close to a solution) and then making changes that reduce the distance of the state from the goal.

In the case of the eight-queens problem, this could be done using the **min-conflicts** heuristic. To move from one state to another state that is likely to be closer to a solution using the min-conflicts heuristic, select one queen that **conflicts** with another queen (in other words, it is on the same row, column, or diagonal as another queen). Now move that queen to a square where it conflicts with as few queens as possible. Continue with another queen.

To see how this method would work, consider the starting position shown in Figure 5.3.

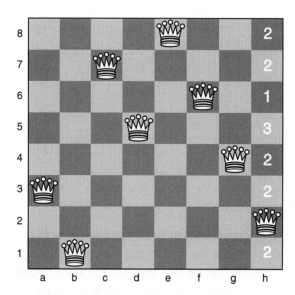

Figure 5.3

Almost a solution to the eight-queens problem

This starting position has been generated by placing the queens such that there are no conflicts on rows or columns. The only conflict here is that the queen in column 3 (on c7) is on a diagonal with the queen in column h (on h2).

To move toward a solution, we choose to move the queen that is on column h. We will only ever apply a move that keeps a queen on the same column because we already know that we need to have one queen on each column. Each square in column h has been marked with a number to show how many other queens that square conflicts with. Our first move will be to move the queen on column h up to row 6, where it will conflict only with one queen. Then we arrive at the position shown in Figure 5.4.

Because we have created a new conflict with the queen on row 6 (on f6), our next move must be to move this queen. In fact, we can move it to a square where it has zero conflicts. This means the problem has been solved, and there are no remaining conflicts.

This method can be used not only to solve the eight-queens problem but also has been successfully applied to the n-queens problem for extremely large values of n. It has been shown that, using this method, the 1,000,000-queens problem can be solved in an average of around 50 steps.

Solving the 1,000,000-queens problem using traditional search techniques would be impossible because it would involve searching a tree with a branching factor of 10^{12}.

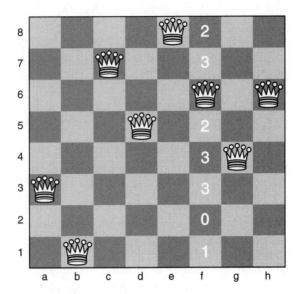

Figure 5.4

Almost a solution to the eight-queens problem; position after applying min-conflicts heuristic once to the position shown in Figure 5.3

5.7 Combinatorial Optimization Problems

Local search uses a range of techniques to solve large **combinatorial optimization problems**. A combinatorial optimization problem is simply a problem that can be expressed in terms of finding the best possible set of values for a group of variables.

An example of a combinatorial optimization problem is the eight-queens problem presented in Chapter 4. The variables in this case can be considered to be the eight queens, which can take on values that represent the squares on the board. The constraints of the problem make it harder than simply picking any eight values for the variables, and hence, as we have seen, it is useful to find ways to restrict the number of choices that are available for each queen to avoid the problem of combinatorial explosion.

Real-world combinatorial optimization problems include allocating teachers to classrooms, scheduling machines and workers in factories, and selecting the best routes for buses, taxis, and other vehicles. The traveling salesman problem is another such problem.

A relaxed optimization problem is a version of a problem where there are more possible solutions (the **feasible region** is larger), or where there are fewer constraints applied to the possible values that the variables can take. For example, a relaxed (and trivial) version of the eight-queens problem might be that the eight queens must be placed on the board so that no two queens are on the same row or column. As we see in Section 5.2, finding solutions to relaxed problems can help to develop heuristics for more complex problems.

5.8   Local Search and Metaheuristics

Local search methods work by starting from some initial configuration (usually random) and making small changes to the configuration until a state is reached from which no better state can be achieved. Hill climbing is a good example of a local search technique. Local search techniques, used in this way, suffer from the same problems as hill climbing and, in particular, are prone to finding local maxima that are not the best solution possible.

The methods used by local search techniques are known as **metaheuristics**. Examples of metaheuristics include simulated annealing (see Section 5.9), tabu search (see Section 5.8.3), genetic algorithms (see Chapter 14), ant colony optimization (see Section 5.8.4), and neural networks (see Chapter 11).

This kind of search method is also known as **local optimization** because it is attempting to optimize a set of values but will often find local maxima rather than a global maximum.

A local search technique applied to the problem of allocating teachers to classrooms would start from a random position and make small changes until a configuration was reached where no inappropriate allocations were made.

5.8.1   Exchanging Heuristics

The simplest form of local search is to use an **exchanging heuristic**. An exchanging heuristic moves from one state to another by exchanging one or more variables by giving them different values. We saw this in solving the eight-queens problem as heuristic repair. A **k-exchange** is considered to be a method where k variables have their values changed at each step. The heuristic repair method we applied to the eight-queens problem was 2-exchange.

A k-exchange can be used to solve the traveling salesman problem. A tour (a route through the cities that visits each city once, and returns to the start) is generated at random. Then, if we use 2-exchange, we remove two edges from the tour and substitute them for two other edges. If this produces a valid tour that is shorter than the previous one, we move on from here. Otherwise, we go back to the previous tour and try a different set of substitutions.

In fact, using $k = 2$ does not work well for the traveling salesman problem, whereas using $k = 3$ produces good results. Using larger numbers of k will give better and better results but will also require more and more iterations. Using $k = 3$ gives reasonable results and can be implemented efficiently. It does, of course, risk finding local maxima, as is often the case with local search methods.

5.8.2   Iterated Local Search

Iterated local search techniques attempt to overcome the problem of local maxima by running the optimization procedure repeatedly, from different initial states. If used with sufficient iterations, this kind of method will almost always find a global maximum.

The aim, of course, in running methods like this is to provide a very good solution without needing to exhaustively search the entire problem space. In problems such as the traveling salesman problem, where the search space grows extremely quickly as the number of cities increases, results can be generated that are good enough (i.e., a local maximum) without using many iterations, where a perfect solution would be impossible to find (or at least it would be impossible to guarantee a perfect solution— even one iteration of local search may happen upon the global maximum, of course!).

5.8.3   Tabu Search

Tabu search is a metaheuristic that uses a list of states that have already been visited to attempt to avoid repeating paths. The tabu search metaheuristic is used in combination with another heuristic and operates on the principle that it is worth going down a path that appears to be poor if it avoids following a path that has already been visited. In this way, tabu search is able to avoid local maxima.

To quote from the *www.tabusearch.net* website: "a bad strategic choice can yield more information than a good random choice."

5.8.4   Ant Colony Optimization

Foraging ants leave a trail of pheromones so that they can lead other ants to find the food that they have found. The trail of pheromones is renewed regularly, so that if another ant finds a better route, the pheromones along the old route will gradually fade, and the new, superior route will become the most popular choice.

The **ant colony optimization** (ACO) metaheuristic is based on this behavior. For example, when attempting to solve the traveling salesman problem, a set of "artificial ants" is sent out along the routes, leaving trails of "pheromones" that indicate how short the route they have taken is. Pheromones gradually fade, meaning that ants that follow later will take the route whose pheromones have been most recently updated, while attempting to follow the pheromones that indicate the shortest path. ACO has been successfully used to enable engineers to find the best way to route cables through a communications network. Because the "ants" are continually foraging through the network, this method is able to cope extremely well with changes in the environment, such as blockages and new routes.

We will learn more about Artificial Intelligence methods based on biological systems (**artificial life**) in Chapter 13.

5.9   Simulated Annealing

Annealing is a process of producing very strong glass or metal, which involves heating the material to a very high temperature and then allowing it to cool very slowly. In this way, the atoms are able to form the most stable structures, giving the material great strength.

Simulated annealing is a local search metaheuristic based on this method and is an extension of a process called **metropolis Monte Carlo simulation**.

Simulated annealing is applied to a multi-value combinatorial problem where values need to be chosen for many variables to produce a particular value for some global function, dependent on all the variables in the system. This value is thought of as the **energy of the system**, and in general the aim of simulated annealing is to find a minimum energy for a system.

Simple Monte Carlo simulation is a method of learning information (such as shape) about the shape of a search space. The process involves randomly selecting points within the search space. An example of its use is as follows:

A square is partially contained within a circle. Simple Monte Carlo simulation can be used to identify what proportion of the square is within the circle and what proportion is outside the circle. This is done by randomly sampling points within the square and checking which ones are within the circle and which are not.

Metropolis Monte Carlo simulation extends this simple method as follows: Rather than selecting new states from the search space at random, a new state is chosen by making a small change to the current state. If the new state means that the system as a whole has a lower energy than it did in the previous state, then it is accepted. If the energy is higher than for the previous state, then a probability is applied to determine whether the new state is accepted or not. This probability is called a **Boltzmann acceptance criterion** and is calculated as follows:

$$e^{(-dE/T)}$$

where T is the current **temperature** of the system, and dE is the increase in energy that has been produced by moving from the previous state to the new state. The temperature in this context refers to the percentage of steps that can be taken that lead to a rise in energy: At a higher temperature, more steps will be accepted that lead to a rise in energy than at low temperature.

To determine whether to move to a higher energy state or not, the probability $e^{(-dE/T)}$ is calculated, and a random number is generated between 0 and 1. If this random number is lower than the probability function, the new state is accepted. In cases where the increase in energy is very high, or the temperature is very low, this means that very few states will be accepted that involve an increase in energy, as $e^{(-dE/T)}$ approaches zero.

The fact that some steps are allowed that increase the energy of the system enables the process to escape from local minima, which means that simulated annealing often can be an extremely powerful method for solving complex problems with many local maxima.

Note: Some systems use $e^{(-dE/kT)}$ as the probability that the search will progress to a state with a higher energy, where k is Boltzmann's constant (Boltzmann's constant is approximately 1.3807×10^{-23} Joules per Kelvin).

Simulated annealing uses Monte Carlo simulation to identify the most stable state (the state with the lowest energy) for a system. This is done by running successive iterations of metropolis Monte Carlo simulation, using progressively lower temperatures. Hence, in successive iterations, fewer and fewer steps are allowed that lead to an overall increase in energy for the system.

A **cooling schedule** (or **annealing schedule**) is applied, which determines the manner in which the temperature will be lowered for successive iterations. Two popular cooling schedules are as follows:

$$T_{new} = T_{old} - dT$$
$$T_{new} = C \times T_{old} \text{ (where } C < 1.0)$$

The cooling schedule is extremely important, as is the choice of the number of steps of metropolis Monte Carlo simulation that are applied in each iteration. These help to determine whether the system will be trapped by local minima (known as **quenching**). The number of times the metropolis Monte Carlo simulation is applied per iteration is for later iterations.

Also important in determining the success of simulated annealing are the choice of the initial temperature of the system and the amount by which the temperature is decreased for each iteration. These values need to be chosen carefully according to the nature of the problem being solved.

When the temperature, T, has reached zero, the system is frozen, and if the simulated annealing process has been successful, it will have identified a minimum for the total energy of the system.

Simulated annealing has a number of practical applications in solving problems with large numbers of interdependent variables, such as circuit design. It has also been successfully applied to the traveling salesman problem.

5.9.1   Uses of Simulated Annealing

Simulated annealing was invented in 1983 by Kirkpatrick, Gelatt, and Vecchi. It was first used for placing VLSI[*] components on a circuit board.

Simulated annealing has also been used to solve the traveling salesman problem, although this approach has proved to be less efficient than using heuristic methods that know more about the problem. It has been used much more successfully in scheduling problems and other large combina-

---

[*]VLSI — Very Large-Scale Integration—a method used to get very large numbers of gates onto silicon chips.

torial problems where values need to be assigned to a large number of variables to maximize (or minimize) some function of those variables.

5.10 Genetic Algorithms for Search

Genetic algorithms are discussed in much more detail in Chapter 14. This section provides a brief overview of the ways in which genetic algorithms can be used to solve search problems but does not assume any detailed understanding of the mechanics of genetic algorithms.

Genetic algorithms involve finding solutions to complex problems using a method based on the process of evolution that we see in nature. In much the same way as nature evolves creatures that are best designed to suit their environments by selecting features that work (survival of the fittest), genetic algorithms work by combining potential solutions to a problem together in a way that tends to produce better solutions over successive generations. This is a form of local optimization, but where mutation and crossover are used to try to avoid local maxima.

As is explained in Chapter 14, genetic algorithms are usually used to identify optimal solutions to complex problems. This can clearly be easily mapped to search methods, which are aiming toward a similar goal. Genetic algorithms can thus be used to search for solutions to multi-value problems where the closeness of any attempted solution to the actual solution (**fitness**) can be readily evaluated.

In short, a **population** of possible solutions (**chromosomes**) is generated, and a fitness value for each chromosome is determined. This fitness is used to determine the likelihood that a given chromosome will survive to the next generation, or reproduce. Reproduction is done by applying **crossover** to two (or more) chromosomes, whereby features (**genes**) of each chromosome are combined together. Mutation is also applied, which involves making random changes to particular genes.

5.11 Real-Time A*

Real-time A* is a variation of A*, as presented in Chapter 4. Search continues on the basis of choosing paths that have minimum values of $f(node) = g(node) + h(node)$. However, $g(node)$ is the distance of the node from the current node, rather than from the root node. Hence, the algorithm will backtrack if the cost of doing so plus the estimated cost of solving the problem from the new node is less than the estimated cost of solving the problem from the current node.

Implementing real-time A* means maintaining a hash table of previously visited states with their h(node) values.

5.12   Iterative-Deepening A* (IDA*)

By combining iterative-deepening with A*, we produce an algorithm that is optimal and complete (like A*) and that has the low memory requirements of depth-first search.

IDA* is a form of iterative-deepening search where successive iterations impose a greater limit on f(node) rather than on the depth of a node.

IDA* performs well in problems where the heuristic value f(node) has relatively few possible values. For example, using the Manhattan distance as a heuristic in solving the eight-queens problem, the value of f(node) can only have values 1, 2, 3, or 4. In this case, the IDA* algorithm only needs to run through a maximum of four iterations, and it has a time complexity not dissimilar from that of A*, but with a significantly improved space complexity because it is effectively running depth-first search.

In cases such as the traveling salesman problem where the value of f(node) is different for every state, the IDA* method has to expand $1 + 2 + 3 + \ldots + n$ nodes $= O(n^2)$ where A* would expand n nodes.

5.13   Parallel Search

Many of the search methods that have been described in this book were developed in the 1960s, 1970s, and 1980s, when computers lacked the power, memory, and storage space that they have today. Many of the issues that were thus of concern when those algorithms were developed are no longer important.

Nowadays, computers have far more processing power and storage space and so are able to run algorithms, such as search, a great deal faster. As we see in Chapter 6, this has helped to lead to a great improvement in the ability of chess-playing computer programs. Another aspect of chess-playing computer programs is that they tend to run parallel search. The names of many of the best chess computers include the word *deep*: Deep Thought, Deep Blue, Deep Junior, and Deep Fritz, for example. The word *deep* means *parallel*.

The idea of parallel processing is that if a task can be broken down into a number of sub-tasks, where those sub-tasks do not need to be run sequentially, then they can be run in parallel, simultaneously on separate processors.

As with much of Artificial Intelligence, there is a good basis for this idea: the human brain. The human brain is **massively parallel**, which means that it is able to do millions of things simultaneously. Computers are much faster at raw processing than a human brain, but because the brain is able to do so many things simultaneously, it is able to operate at a much faster rate than a computer.

Applying this idea to search is clearly desirable because many search problems (such as playing chess) can be heavily time dependent.

One search method that can be simply parallelized is depth-first search. If we assume that we have two processors, we could simply divide the descendants of the root node in half and assign half of them to one processor and half to the other. The two processors would then run a series of depth-first searches on each of its nodes. The first processor to find a goal node would report success, and the whole computation would stop.

More complex search methods such as **alpha–beta pruning**, which is described in Chapter 6, are not so easy to implement in parallel. Alpha–beta pruning is a method that is used to eliminate portions of the search tree for playing games such as chess that can provide a great increase in performance. It has been shown that running alpha–beta pruning searches in parallel by simply dividing the search tree up between processors actually provides worse results than running it in serial (Fox et al. 1994).

To develop a parallel version of an algorithm such as alpha–beta pruning, more care needs to be taken in how the tasks are split up so that performance is not degraded.

One area where parallel search can be readily applied is in solving constraint satisfaction problems. In general, CSPs are not well solved by using brute-force search because this involves a combinatorial optimization problem. In situations where the search tree can be reduced somewhat, and no better method can be found than blind search, the performance of the search can be significantly improved by running it in a parallel fashion, by simply dividing the search tree between processors. In some cases, search problems can be divided between individual computers.

Of course, problems that can be solved using goal reduction are also often solved more efficiently using parallel search because the goal tree can be broken down into sub-goal trees, which can be worked on in parallel by separate processors.

When distributing work in this way, important concepts to consider are **task distribution** (deciding which task to give to which processor), **load balancing** (ensuring that all processors have enough work to do and that no single processor is overworked), and **tree ordering** (determining the correct order to process the search tree).

5.13.1 Task Distribution

Cook (1998) explores the process of implementing a parallel version of IDA* search.

One approach to distributing tasks for parallel implementations of IDA* was to use **parallel window search** (PWS). This involves searching the different depth-limited searches concurrently, rather than in series. For example, using three processors, the first processor might search with a depth limit of 1, the second with a depth limit of 2, and the third with a depth limit of 3. As soon as any processor completes a search, it is assigned a new search with a depth that is deeper than any currently running. Unfortunately, if there are too many processors (more than the number of iterations needed to find an optimal solution) the PWS method can be very inefficient because many processors will be idle for the entire search.

Another approach used by Cook was **distributed tree search** (DTS). First, a breadth-first search is carried out until there are as many leaf nodes available as there are processors. Then, each of these nodes is assigned to a processor for search. To ensure that this method is optimal, when a processor finishes an iteration, it must wait for all other processors to finish their iterations before starting another. This means that there will often be idle processors.

Cook's paper provides a very detailed analysis of both of these methods and their respective advantages and disadvantages.

In their paper *Randomized Parallel Algorithms for Backtrack Search and Branch-and-Bound Computation*, Richard Karp and Yanjun Zhang showed that distributing tasks between processors at random gives better results, particularly when running a variation of depth-first search called **backtracking search**. In backtracking search, when a node is discovered, the processor passes one of the children of that node to an idle processor, if one is available. The normal method of determining to which processor to pass this child node is fairly complex and can create a significant overhead. By passing the child nodes randomly, this overhead can be eliminated, and the search becomes much more efficient.

5.13.2   Tree Ordering

When running IDA* in parallel, the order of the tree can be very important. Since the search tree is expanded in depth-first order from left to right, if the optimal solution is on the left side of the tree, it will be found much more quickly than if it is on the right side. Clearly, if a way could be found to ensure that the optimal solution was always on the left side of the tree, then a search method would not be needed to find it. However, heuristics can be used to attempt to examine the tree in a way that will increase the likelihood of finding an optimal solution quickly. These heuristics operate in much the same way that the heuristics for best-first search and other serial informed search methods use.

5.13.3   Search Engines

Search engines are an excellent example of parallel search systems. One problem faced by search engines is the enormous size of the Internet (estimated to be many billions of pages and growing continually). To index a reasonable percentage of these pages, search engines need to run in parallel. Typically, search engines run their indexing on a number of indexing servers. Pages or websites are distributed among the servers by a scheduling process. Clearly, as well as getting the schedule right, it is important that the search engines are able to communicate with each other. For example, if two search engines both come across the same page, they need to be able to decide which one will search that page. Instead of crawling independently like this, some search engine spiders simply have a list of links that they need to crawl. When a spider finds a page, it indexes the page and extracts all the links from it. The spider places these links into a central database and carries on with its own list of links. A central scheduling system then decides how to distribute the links in the central database to the servers. In this way, no two servers will ever duplicate work.

5.14   Bidirectional Search

Bidirectional search (also known as **wave search**, due to the wave-like nature in which paths are followed through the search space) is applied when searching for the best path between a start node and a known goal node. This is somewhat different from most of the other search algorithms discussed in this part, where the goal node is not known, and the purpose of the algorithm is to find a path to a goal node without knowing where the goal node will be located in the tree.

Bidirectional search involves simultaneously spreading out paths in a breadth-first fashion from both the start and goal nodes.

This requires that a predecessor function be available for each node, as well as the successor function, so that paths can be extended backward from the goal node.

As soon as the two paths meet, a complete path has been generated that begins at the start node, goes through the point where the two paths met, and ends at the goal node. This path is guaranteed to be the shortest path (or rather, the path involving the fewest steps).

5.15   Nondeterministic Search

Nondeterministic search is a combination of depth-first and breadth-first search, which avoids the problems of both but does not necessarily have the advantages of either.

When running a nondeterministic search, new paths are added to the queue at random positions. In the following pseudo-code implementation, the function call add_randomly_to_queue (successors (state)) adds the successors of state to random positions in the queue:

```
Function random ()
{
    queue = [];      // initialize an empty queue
    state = root_node;   // initialize the start state
    while (true)
```

```
    {
        if is_goal (state)
            then return SUCCESS
        else add_randomly_to_queue (successors (state));
        if queue == []
            then report FAILURE;
        state = queue [0]; // state = first item in queue
        remove_first_item_from (queue);
    }
}
```

This method is useful in cases where very little information is available about the search space—for example, in a situation where there may be extremely long, or even infinite, paths and may also be an extremely large branching factor. In situations like that, depth-first search might end up stuck down an infinitely long path, and breadth-first search could be extremely inefficient in dealing with the large branching factor. A nondeterministic search will avoid these problems but will not necessarily find the best path.

Nondeterministic search can also be used in combination with other search techniques. For example, by applying a nondeterministic search when a maximum is found in hill climbing, the problems of local maxima (the foothill problem) can be avoided.

5.16   Island-Driven Search

Island-driven search assumes that an **island** exists roughly half way between the root node and a goal node. The method involves finding a path between the root node and the island, and a path between the island and a goal node. If no path exists that goes through the island, the method reverts to another search method that ignores the island.

This method is useful in situations where it is extremely likely that the island actually does lie on a path to the goal, for example, if we are trying to identify a route between Milan and Naples, given the knowledge that all roads lead to Rome.

5.17   Nonchronological Backtracking

Nonchronological backtracking, or dependency-directed backtracking, is an alternative to chronological backtracking, which we saw being used in search methods such as depth-first search.

Chronological backtracking operates as follows:

When a dead end in a tree is found (in other words, a leaf node that is not a goal node), move back up the search tree to the last point in the tree where a decision had to be made. Undo this decision, and all its consequences, and choose the next option at this junction instead.

In some cases, additional information is available about the search space that can help to backtrack in a more efficient manner, undoing decisions that are more likely to lead to success, rather than just undoing each decision in chronological order. In these cases, we use nonchronological backtracking, which is also known as dependency-directed backtracking.

It is particularly useful in solving constraint satisfaction problems, where backtracking can be applied by going back to the previous choice that caused a constraint to fail.

5.18 Chapter Summary

- Constraint satisfaction problems (CSPs) such as the eight-queens problem, can be solved using search.

- Methods such as forward checking and heuristics such as the most-constrained variable heuristic and min-conflicts make it possible to solve extremely large CSPs (such as the 1,000,000-queens problem).

- Large combinatorial optimization problems are best solved using local search methods.

- Local search methods (or metaheuristics) move from one potential solution to another by making small changes. When a local maximum is found, the search stops.

- Iterating the local search from different random starting configurations can avoid the problem of identifying local maxima and ignoring a global maximum.

- Local search methods include tabu search, ant colony optimization, and simulated annealing.

- Simulated annealing is based on the way in which metals are hardened by being heated up and then slowly cooled, so that the crystalline structure forms the strongest possible arrangement.

- Variations on A* such as real-time A* and iterative-deepening A* can provide enhanced performance.

- Parallel search methods can take advantage of modern parallel computers. Issues such as task distribution, load balancing, and tree ordering need to be considered.

5.19   Review Questions

5.1   Explain how search can be used to solve constraint satisfaction problems, such as the eight-queens problem. What difficulties arise when such problems become extremely large (e.g., the 1,000,000-queens problem)? What kinds of methods can be applied to solve such large problems efficiently?

5.2   Explain the idea behind the following heuristics:

- most-constrained variable

- most-constraining variable

- least-constraining variable

- min-conflicts

5.3   Why is local search more practical than depth-first search for solving large combinatorial optimization problems? Explain what a metaheuristic is and why it is useful.

5.4   How does iterated local search avoid the problem of local maxima? Why is this important?

5.5   Explain how ant colony optimization works. Why might it be useful for communications routing?

5.6   Describe in layman's terms the idea behind simulated annealing and why it works. What kinds of problems might it be useful for solving?

5.7   Explain the purpose of the temperature variable in simulated annealing. How effective would the method be without it?

5.8   Explain why IDA* might be used instead of A*. In what kinds of situations might it be less useful?

5.9 Explain the importance of the following principles when running parallel search methods:

- task distribution

- load balancing

- tree ordering

5.10 How do search engines make use of search? Research a few of the best known search engines, and try to find out what kind of search algorithms they use. How efficient do you think they are at searching? Could you implement them better?

5.20 Exercises

5.1 Write a program in a programming language of your choice for solving the *n*-queens problem. Run it with 8 queens, and then try it with 100 queens. How well does it perform? Could your program find a solution for 1,000,000 queens? If not, why not? If so, what optimizations have you used to make that possible?

5.2 Write a program that can solve arbitrary cryptographic problems. Add heuristics to your implementation to make it more efficient. What limitations does your program have?

5.3 Investigate tabu search. Write 1000 words explaining how it works and what sorts of problems it is best suited to solving.

5.4 Write a program that uses simulated annealing to solve the traveling salesman problem of arbitrary size. Do you think that simulated annealing is a good way to solve this problem? Explain your answer.

5.5 Implement a nondeterministic search algorithm. Build search trees for which it performs the following:

a. better than depth-first search

b. worse than depth-first search

c. better than breadth-first search

d. worse than breadth-first search

5.21   Further Reading

Most of the material covered in this chapter is covered well by the majority of Artificial Intelligence textbooks. Material on local search is relatively new, and not so well covered by the older textbooks.

Tabu Search by Glover and Laguna, the inventors of tabu search, provides a good insight into the tabu search metaheuristic.

The min-conflicts heuristic was invented by Gu in 1989. Further information on the method can be found in Minton (1992).

Pearl (1984) gives a good overview of search methods with a particular focus on heuristics.

Rayward-Smith et al. (1996) gives excellent coverage of heuristics and metaheuristics in particular.

Jansen (1997) reports on research that has been done using simulated annealing in information retrieval to select a suitable ordering of results to return to a user in response to a keyword text query.

Multiobjective Heuristic Search: An Introduction to Intelligent Search Methods for Multicriteria Optimization by Pallab Dasgupta, P. P. Chakrabarti, S. C. Desarkar (1999 - Friedrich Vieweg & Sohn)

Adaptive Parallel Iterative Deepening Search by Diane J. Cook and R. Craig Varnell (1998 – in *Journal of Artificial Intelligence Research,* Vol. 9, pp. 139–166)

Parallel Computing Works by G. C. Fox, R. D. Williams, and P. C. Messina (1994 – Morgan Kaufmann)

Tabu Search by Fred W. Glover, Manuel Laguna (1998 – Kluwer Academic Publishers)

Simulated Annealing for Query Results Ranking by B. J. Jansen (1997 – in ACM Computer Science Education Conference)

Learning to Solve Problems by Searching for Macro-Operators (Research Notes in Artificial Intelligence, Vol. 5) by Richard E. Korf (1985 – Longman Group United Kingdom)

Search by Richard E. Korf (1987 – in *Encyclopedia of Artificial Intelligence* edited by E. Shapiro – Wiley)

Learning Search Control Knowledge: An Explanation Based Approach by Stephen Minton (1988 – Kluwer Academic Publishers)

Minimizing Conflicts: A Heuristic Repair Method for Constraint Satisfaction and Scheduling Problems by S. Minton, M. D. Johnson, A. B. Philips, and P. Laird (1992 – *Artificial Intelligence*, Vol. 58)

How to Solve It: Modern Heuristics by Zbigniew Michalewicz and David B. Fogel (1999 – Springer Verlag)

Local Search for Planning and Scheduling: Ecai 2000 Workshop, Berlin, Germany, August 21, 2000: Revised Papers (Lecture Notes in Computer Science, 2148) edited by Alexander Nareyek (2001 – Springer Verlag)

Combinatorial Optimization: Algorithms and Complexity by Christos H. Papadimitriou and Kenneth Steiglitz (1998 – Dover Publications)

Heuristics: Intelligent Search Strategies for Computer Problem Solving by Judea Pearl (1984 – Addison Wesley)

Modern Heuristic Search Methods edited by V. J. Rayward-Smith, I. H. Osman, Colin R. Reeves, and G. D. Smith (1996 – John Wiley & Sons)

The Algorithm Design Manual by Steven S. Skiena (1997 – Telos)

Simulated Annealing: Theory and Applications by P. J. M. Van Laarhoven and E. H. L. Aarts (1987 - D. Reidel Publishing Company – Out of Print)

CHAPTER 6

Game Playing

After the other matches I felt hooked to be part of this competition because I believe it is very important for the game of chess and the human race as a whole. Now I hope to use my experience to help set new standards and also prove that human players are not hopeless.

—Garry Kasparov before his six-game chess match against Deep Junior

One hundred years from now, the idea that humans could still beat computers will seem quaint. It will be like men trying to race cars at the turn of the century. Who's better? Who cares? The technology is what matters. It's improving, and that's what counts.

—Professor Jonathan Schaeffer discussing Kasparov's chess match with Deep Junior

'The Game', said he, 'is never lost till won.'

—George Crabbe, *Gretna Green*

The Game's Afoot.

—William Shakespeare, *Henry V*

6.1 Introduction

One of the most interesting and well publicized areas of Artificial Intelligence research has been in the playing of games. With the success of Deep Blue in 1997, a landmark was reached: a computer program that could defeat the best chess player in the world.

Game-playing systems tend to rely heavily on the search techniques described in Chapters 4 and 5, in combination with a number of heuristics and often a detailed database of knowledge about the game.

This chapter explains the relationship between search and games such as chess, checkers, and backgammon. It explains the concepts of alpha–beta pruning and Minimax. It uses Chinook, a checkers-playing computer system, to explain some of the more advanced techniques used in modern game-playing computers and discusses why computers are currently unable to beat humans at games such as Go.

6.2 Game Trees

Many two-player games can be efficiently represented using trees, called **game trees**. A game tree is an instance of a tree in which the root node represents the state before any moves have been made, the nodes in the tree represent possible states of the game (or **positions**), and arcs in the tree represent moves.

It is usual to represent the two players' moves on alternate levels of the game tree, so that all edges leading from the root node to the first level represent possible moves for the first player, and edges from the first level to the second represent moves for the second player, and so on.

Leaf nodes in the tree represent final states, where the game has been won, lost, or drawn. In simple games, a goal node might represent a state in which the computer has won, but for more complex games such as chess and Go, the concept of a goal state is rarely of use.

One approach to playing a game might be for the computer to use a tree search algorithm such as depth-first or breadth-first search, looking for a goal state (i.e., a final state of the game where the computer has won). Unfortunately, this approach does not work because there is another intelligence involved in the game. We will consider this to be a rational, informed opponent who plays to win. Whether this opponent is human or another computer does not matter—or should not matter—but for the purposes of this section of the book, we will refer to the opponent as being human, to differentiate him or her from the computer.

Consider the game tree shown in Figure 6.1. This partial tree represents the game of tic-tac-toe, in which the computer is playing noughts, and the human opponent is playing crosses. The branching factor of the root node

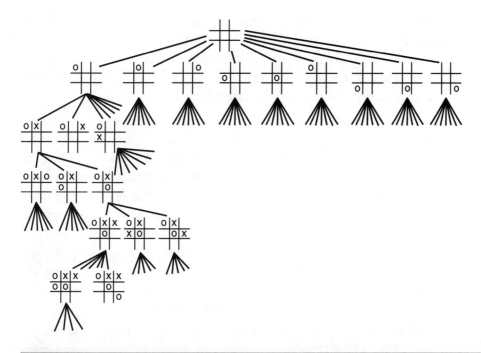

Figure 6.1

A partial game tree for the game tic-tac-toe

is 9 because there are nine squares in which the computer can place its first nought. The branching factor of the next level of the tree is 8, then 7 for the next level, and so on. The tree shown in Figure 6.1 is clearly just a part of that tree and has been pruned to enable it to fit comfortably on the page.

For a computer to use this tree to make decisions about moves in a game of tic-tac-toe, it needs to use an **evaluation function**, which enables it to decide whether a given position in the game is good or bad. If we use exhaustive search, then we only need a function that can recognize a win, a loss, and a draw. Then, the computer can treat "win" states as goal nodes and carry out search in the normal way.

6.2.1   Rationality, Zero Sum, and Other Assumptions

All the methods discussed in this chapter are designed for games with two players. In most of the games, there is no element of chance (in other words, no dice are thrown, or cards drawn), and the players have complete knowledge of the state of the game, which means that the players do not conceal information (apart from their strategies and plans) from their opponents. This sets games such as chess and Go aside from games such as poker, in which there is an element of chance, and it is also important that players conceal information from each other.

Most of the games we will consider in this chapter are **zero-sum games**, which means that if the overall score at the end of a game for each player can be 1 (a win), 0 (a draw), or −1 (a loss), then the total score for both players for any game must always be 0. In other words, if one player wins, the other must lose. The only other alternative is that both players draw. For this reason, we consider the search techniques that are discussed here to be **adversarial** methods because each player is not only trying to win but to cause the opponent to lose. In the algorithms such as Minimax and alpha–beta that are discussed later, it is important that the computer can assume that the opponent is rational and adversarial. In other words, the computer needs to assume that the opponent will play to win.

In discussing game trees, we use the concept of **ply**, which refers to the depth of the tree. In particular, we refer to the ply of lookahead. When a computer evaluates a game tree to ply 5, it is examining the tree to a depth of 5. The 4th ply in a game tree is the level at depth 4 below the root node.

Because the games we are talking about involve two players, sequential plies in the tree will alternately represent the two players. Hence, a game tree with a ply of 8 will represent a total of eight choices in the game, which corresponds to four moves for each player. It is usual to use the word *ply* to represent a single level of choice in the game tree, but for the word *move* to represent two such choices—one for each player.

6.2.2   Evaluation Functions

Evaluation functions (also known as **static evaluators** because they are used to evaluate a game from just one static position) are vital to most game-playing computer programs. This is because it is almost never possible to search the game tree fully due to its size. Hence, a search will rarely reach a leaf node in the tree at which the game is either won, lost, or drawn, which means that the software needs to be able to **cut off** search and evaluate the position of the board at that node. Hence, an evaluation function is used to examine a particular position of the board and estimate how well the computer is doing, or how likely it is to win from this position. Due to the enormous number of positions that must be evaluated in game playing, the evaluation function usually needs to be extremely efficient, to avoid slowing down game play.

One question is how the evaluation function will compare two positions. In other words, given positions A and B, what relative values will it give those positions? If A is a clearly better position than B, perhaps A should receive a much higher score than B. In general, as we will see elsewhere, to be successful, the evaluation function does not need to give values that linearly represent the quality of positions: To be effective, it just needs to give a higher score to a better position.

An evaluation function for a chess game might look at the number of pieces, taking into account the relative values of particular pieces, and might also look at pawn development, control over the center of the board, attack strength, and so on. Such evaluation functions can be extremely complex and, as we will see, are essential to building successful chess-playing software.

Evaluation functions are usually **weighted linear functions**, meaning that a number of different scores are determined for a given position and simply added together in a weighted fashion. So, a very simplistic evaluation function for chess might count the number of queens, the number of pawns, the number of bishops, and so on, and add them up using weights to indicate the relative values of those pieces:

q = number of queens

r = number of rooks

n = number of knights

b = number of bishops

p = number of pawns

$score = 9q + 5r + 3b + 3n + p$

If two computer programs were to compete with each other at a game such as checkers, and the two programs had equivalent processing capabilities and speeds, and used the same algorithms for examining the search tree, then the game would be decided by the quality of the programs' evaluation functions.

In general, the evaluation functions for game-playing programs do not need to be perfect but need to give a good way of comparing two positions to determine which is the better. Of course, in games as complex as chess and Go, this is not an easy question: two grandmasters will sometimes differ on the evaluation of a position.

As we will see, one way to develop an accurate evaluation function is to actually play games from each position and see who wins. If the play is perfect on both sides, then this will give a good indication of what the evaluation of the starting position should be.

This method has been used successfully for games such as checkers, but for games such as chess and Go, the number of possible positions is so huge that evaluating even a small proportion of them is not feasible. Hence, it is necessary to develop an evaluation function that is dynamic and is able to accurately evaluate positions it has never seen before.

6.2.3   Searching Game Trees

Even for the game of tic-tac-toe, a part of whose game tree is illustrated in Figure 6.1, it can be inefficient for the computer to exhaustively search the tree because it has a maximum depth of 9 and a maximum branching factor of 9, meaning there are approximately $9 \times 8 \times 7 \times \ldots \times 2 \times 1$ nodes in the tree, which means more than 350,000 nodes to examine. Actually, this is a very small game tree compared with the trees used in games like chess or Go, where there are many more possible moves at each step and the tree can potentially have infinite depth.

In fact, using exhaustive search on game trees is almost never a good idea for games with any degree of complexity. Typically, the tree will have very high branching factors (e.g., a game tree representing chess has an average branching factor of 38) and often will be very deep. Exhaustively searching such trees is just not possible using current computer technology, and so in this chapter, we will explore methods that are used to **prune** the game tree and heuristics that are used to evaluate positions.

There is another problem with using exhaustive search to find goal nodes in the game tree. When the computer has identified a goal state, it has simply identified that it *can* win the game, but this might not be the case because the opponent will be doing everything he or she can to stop the computer from winning. In other words, the computer can choose one arc in the game tree, but the opponent will choose the next one. It may be that depth-first search reveals a path to a leaf node where the computer wins, but the computer must also assume that the opponent will be attempting to choose a different path, where the computer loses.

So, as we see later in this chapter, the computer can use methods like depth-first or breadth-first search to identify the game tree, but more sophisticated methods need to be used to choose the correct moves.

6.3 Minimax

When evaluating game trees, it is usual to assume that the computer is attempting to maximize some score that the opponent is trying to minimize. Normally we would consider this score to be the result of the evaluation function for a given position, so we would usually have a high positive score mean a good position for the computer, a score of 0 mean a neutral position, and a high negative score mean a good position for the opponent.

The Minimax algorithm is used to choose good moves. It is assumed that a suitable static evaluation function is available, which is able to give an overall score to a given position. In applying Minimax, the static evaluator will only be used on leaf nodes, and the values of the leaf nodes will be filtered up through the tree, to pick out the best path that the computer can achieve.

This is done by assuming that the opponent will play **rationally** and will always play the move that is best for him or her, and thus worst for the computer. The principle behind Minimax is that a path through the tree is chosen by assuming that at its turn (a **max node**), the computer will choose the move that will give the highest eventual static evaluation, and that at the human opponent's turn (a **min node**), he or she will choose the move that will give the lowest static evaluation. So the computer's aim is to maximize the lowest possible score that can be achieved.

Figure 6.2 shows how Minimax works on a very simple game tree. Note that the best result that max can achieve is a score of 6. If max chooses the left branch as its first choice, then min will inevitably choose the right branch, which leaves max a choice of 1 or 3. In this case, max will choose a score of 3. If max starts by choosing the right branch, min will have a choice between a path that leads to a score of 7 or a path that leads to a score of 6. It will therefore choose the left branch, leaving max a choice between 2 and 6.

Figure 6.2 shows how Minimax can use depth-first search to traverse the game tree. The arrows start from the root node at the top and go down to the bottom of the left branch.

This leads to a max node, which will get a score of 5. The value 5 is therefore passed up to the parent of this max node. Following the right path from this min node leads to another max node, this time getting a score of

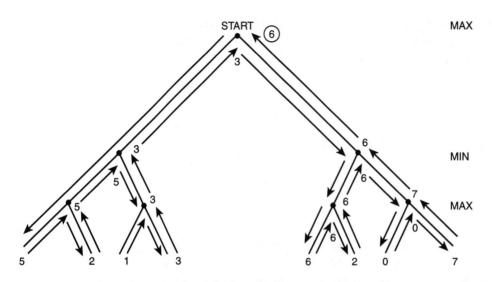

Figure 6.2
Illustrating how minimax works on a very simple game tree. The arrows show the order in which the nodes are examined by the algorithm, and the values that are passed through the tree.

3. This comes back up to the min node, which now chooses the minimum of 3 and 5, and selects 3. Eventually, having traversed the whole tree, the best result for max comes back up to the root node: 6.

The Minimax function provides a best available score for a given node as follows:

```
Function minimax (current_node)
{
    if is_leaf (current_node)
        then return static_evaluation (current_node);
    if is_min_node (current_node)
        then return min (minimax (children_of
        (current_node)));
    if is_max_node (current_node)
        then return max (minimax (children_of
        (current_node)));
    // this point will never be reached since
    // every node must be a leaf node, a min node or a
    // max node.
}
```

This is a recursive function because to evaluate the scores for the children of the current node, the Minimax algorithm must be applied recursively to those children until a leaf node is reached.

Minimax can also be performed nonrecursively, starting at the leaf nodes and working systematically up the tree, in a reverse breadth-first search.

6.3.1 Bounded Lookahead

Minimax, as we have defined it, is a very simple algorithm and is unsuitable for use in many games, such as chess or Go, where the game tree is extremely large. The problem is that in order to run Minimax, the entire game tree must be examined, and for games such as chess, this is not possible due to the potential depth of the tree and the large branching factor.

In such cases, **bounded lookahead** is very commonly used and can be combined with Minimax. The idea of bounded lookahead is that the search tree is only examined to a particular depth. All nodes at this depth are considered to be leaf nodes and are evaluated using a static evaluation function. This corresponds well to the way in which a human plays chess. Even the greatest grandmasters are not able to look forward to see every possible move that will occur in a game. Chess players look forward a few moves, and good chess players may look forward a dozen or more moves. They are looking for a move that leads to as favorable a position as they can find and are using their own static evaluator to determine which positions are the most favorable.

Hence, the Minimax algorithm with bounded lookahead is defined as follows:

```
Function bounded_minimax (current_node, max_depth)
{
    if is_leaf (current_node)
        then return static_evaluation (current_node);
    if depth_of (current_node) == max_depth
        then return static_evaluation (current_node);
    if is_min_node (current_node)
        then return min (minimax (children_of
        (current_node)));
    if is_max_node (current_node)
        then return max (minimax (children_of
        (current_node)));
    // this point will never be reached since
    // every node must be a leaf node, a min node or a
    // max node.
}
```

Figure 6.3

Chess position with black to move

In fact, it is not necessarily sensible to apply a fixed cut-off point for search. The reason for this can be seen from the chess position shown in Figure 6.3. If bounded Minimax search cut off search at this node, it might consider the position to be reasonably even because the two players have the same pieces, which are roughly equally well developed. In fact, although it is black's turn to move, white will almost certainly take black's queen after this move, meaning that the position is extremely strong for white.

This problem must be avoided if a computer program is to play chess or any other game successfully. One way to avoid the problem is to only cut off search at positions that are deemed to be quiescent. A quiescent position is one where the next move is unlikely to cause a large change in the relative positions of the two players. So, a position where a piece can be captured without a corresponding recapture is not quiescent.

Another problem with bounded Minimax search is the **horizon problem**. This problem involves an extremely long sequence of moves that clearly lead to a strong advantage for one player, but where the sequence of moves, although potentially obvious to a human player, takes more moves than is allowed by the bounded search. Hence, the significant end of the sequence has been pushed over the horizon. This was a particular problem for **Chinook**, the checkers-playing program that we learn more about in Section 6.5.

There is no universal solution to the horizon problem, but one method to minimize its effects is to always search a few ply deeper when a position is found that appears to be particularly good. The **singular-extension heuristic** is defined as follows: if a static evaluation of a move is much better than that of other moves being evaluated, continue searching.

6.4 Alpha–Beta Pruning

Bounded lookahead can help to make smaller the part of the game tree that needs to be examined. In some cases, it is extremely useful to be able to **prune** sections of the game tree. Using alpha–beta pruning, it is possible to remove sections of the game tree that are not worth examining, to make searching for a good move more efficient.

The principle behind alpha–beta pruning is that if a move is determined to be worse than another move that has already been examined, then further examining the possible consequences of that worse move is pointless.

Consider the partial game tree in Figure 6.4.

This very simple game tree has five leaf nodes. The top arc represents a choice by the computer, and so is a **maximizing level** (in other words, the top node is a max node). After calculating the static evaluation function for the first four leaf nodes, it becomes unnecessary to evaluate the score for the fifth. The reason for this can be understood as follows:

In choosing the left-hand path from the root node, it is possible to achieve a score of 3 or 5. Because this level is a minimizing level, the opponent can be expected to choose the move that leads to a score of 3. So, by choosing the left-hand arc from the root node, the computer can achieve a score of 3.

By choosing the right-hand arc, the computer can achieve a score of 7 or 1, or a mystery value. Because the opponent is aiming to minimize the score,

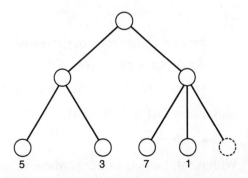

Figure 6.4

A partial game tree

he or she could choose the position with a score of 1, which is worse than the value the computer could achieve by choosing the left-hand path. So, the value of the rightmost leaf node doesn't matter—the computer must not choose the right-hand arc because it definitely leads to a score of **at best** 1 (assuming the opponent does not irrationally choose the 7 option).

6.4.1   The Effectiveness of Alpha–Beta Pruning

In this contrived example, alpha–beta pruning removes only one leaf node from the tree, but in larger game trees, it can result in fairly valuable reductions in tree size. However, as Winston (1993) showed, it will not necessarily remove large portions of a game tree. In fact, in the worst case, alpha–beta pruning will not prune any searches from the game tree, but even in this case it will compute the same result as Minimax and will not perform any less efficiently.

The alpha–beta pruning method provides its best performance when the game tree is arranged such that the best choice at each level is the first one (i.e., the left-most choice) to be examined by the algorithm. With such a game tree, a Minimax algorithm using alpha–beta cut-off will examine a game tree to double the depth that a Minimax algorithm without alpha–beta pruning would examine in the same number of steps.

This can be shown as follows:

If a game tree is arranged optimally, then the number of nodes that must be examined to find the best move using alpha–beta pruning can be derived as follows:

$$S = \begin{cases} 2b^{d/2} - 1 & \text{if } d \text{ is even} \\ b^{(d+1)/2} + b^{(d-1)/2} - 1 & \text{if } d \text{ is odd} \end{cases}$$

where

b = branching factor of game tree

d = depth of game tree

s = number of nodes that must be examined

This means that approximately

$s = 2b^{d/2}$

Without alpha–beta pruning, where all nodes must be examined:

$s = b^d$

Hence, we can consider that using alpha–beta pruning reduces the effective branching factor from b to $\sqrt{b}$, meaning that in a fixed period of time, Minimax with alpha–beta pruning can look twice as far in the game tree as Minimax without pruning.

This represents a significant improvement—for example, in chess it reduces the effective branching factor from around 38 to around 6—but it must be remembered that this assumes that the game tree is arranged optimally (such that the best choice is always the left-most choice). In reality, it might provide far less improvement.

It was found that in implementing the Deep Blue chess computer (see Section 6.6), use of the alpha–beta method did in fact reduce the average branching factor of the chess game tree from 38 to around 6.

6.4.2 Implementation

The alpha-beta pruning algorithm is implemented as follows:

- The game tree is traversed in depth-first order. At each non-leaf node a value is stored. For max nodes, this value is called alpha, and for min nodes, the value is beta.

- An alpha value is the maximum (best) value found so far in the max node's descendants.

- A beta value is minimum (best) value found so far in the min node's descendants.

In the following pseudo-code implementation, we use the function call `beta_value_of (min_ancestor_of (current_node))`, which returns the beta value of some min node ancestor of the current node to see how it compares with the alpha value of the current node. Similarly, `alpha_value_of (max_ancestor_of (current_node))` returns the alpha value of some max node ancestor of the current node in order that it be compared with the beta value of the current node.

```
Function alpha_beta (current_node)
{
    if is_leaf (current_node)
        then return static_evaluation (current_node);
    if is_max_node (current_node) and
        alpha_value_of (current_node) >=
        beta_value_of (min_ancestor_of (current_node))
    then cut_off_search_below (current_node);
```

```
    if is_min_node (current_node) and
       beta_value_of (current_node) <=
       alpha_value_of (max_ancestor_of (current_node))
    then cut_off_search_below (current_node);
}
```

To avoid searching back up the tree for ancestor values, values are propagated down the tree as follows:

- For each max node, the minimum beta value for all its min node ancestors is stored as beta.

- For each min node, the maximum alpha value for all its max node ancestors is stored as alpha.

- Hence, each non-leaf node will have a beta value *and* an alpha value stored.

- Initially, the root node is assigned an alpha value of negative infinity and a beta value of infinity.

So, the alpha_beta function can be modified as follows. In the following pseudo-code implementation, the variable children is used to represent all of the children of the current node, so the following line:

```
alpha = max (alpha, alpha_beta (children, alpha, beta));
```

means that alpha is set to the greatest of the current value of alpha, and the values of the current node's children, calculated by recursively calling alpha_beta.

```
Function alpha_beta (current_node, alpha, beta)
{
    if is_root_node (current_node)
    then
    {
        alpha = -infinity
        beta = infinity
    }
    if is_leaf (current_node)
    then return static_evaluation (current_node);
    if is_max_node (current_node)
    then
    {
        alpha = max (alpha, alpha_beta (children, alpha, beta));
        if alpha >= beta
        then cut_off_search_below (current_node);
    }
```

```
if is_min_node (current_node)
then
{
    beta = min (beta, alpha_beta (children, alpha, beta));
    if beta <= alpha
    then cut_off_search_below (current_node);
}
}
```

To see how alpha–beta pruning works in practice, let us examine the game tree shown in Figure 6.5.

The non-leaf nodes in the tree are labeled from a to g, and the leaf nodes have scores assigned to them by static evaluation: a is a max node; b and c are min nodes; and d, e, f, and g are max nodes.

Following the tree by depth-first search, the first step is to follow the path a,b,d and then to the three children of d. This gives an alpha value for d of 3. This is passed up to b, which now has a beta value of 3, and an alpha value that has been passed down from a of negative infinity.

Now, the first child of e is examined and has a score of 4. In this case, clearly there is no need to examine the other children of e because the minimizing choice at node b will definitely do worse by choosing e rather than d. So cut-off is applied here, and the nodes with scores of 5 and 7 are never examined.

The full analysis of the tree is shown in Table 6.1, which shows how the scores move through the tree from step to step of the process.

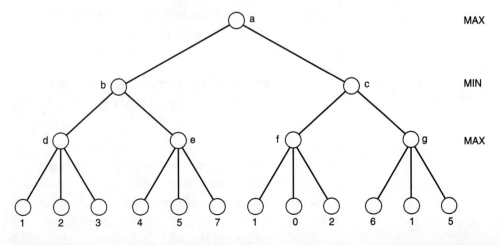

Figure 6.5

A simple game tree

TABLE 6.1   Analysis of alpha–beta pruning for the game tree in Figure 6.5

Step	Node	Alpha	Beta	Notes
1	a	$-\infty$	∞	Alpha starts as $-\infty$ and beta starts as ∞.
2	b	$-\infty$	∞	
3	d	$-\infty$	∞	
4	d	1	∞	
5	d	2	∞	
6	d	3	∞	At this stage, we have examined the three children of d and have obtained an alpha value of 3, which is passed back up to node b.
7	b	$-\infty$	3	At this min node, we can clearly achieve a score of 3 or better (lower). Now we need to examine the children of e to see if we can get a lower score.
8	e	$-\infty$	3	
9	e	4	3	CUT-OFF. A score of 4 can be obtained from the first child of e. Min clearly will do better to choose d rather than e because if he chooses e, max can get at least 4, which is worse for min than 3. Hence, we can now ignore the other children of e.
10	a	3	∞	The value of 3 has been passed back up to the root node, a. Hence, max now knows that he can score at least 3. He now needs to see if he can do better.
11	c	3	∞	
12	f	3	∞	We now examine the three children of f and find that none of them is better than 3. So, we pass back a value of 3 to c.
13	c	3	3	CUT-OFF. Max has already found that by taking the left-hand branch, he can achieve a score of 3. Now it seems that if he chooses the right-hand branch, min can choose f, which will mean he can only achieve a score of 2. So cut-off can now occur because there is no need to examine g or its children.

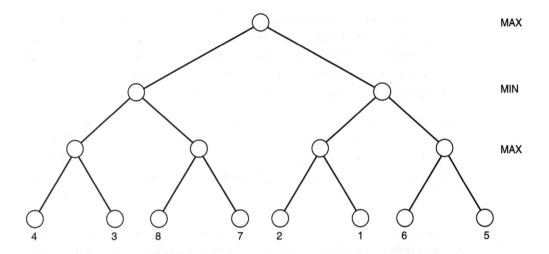

Figure 6.6

A game tree optimized for alpha–beta search

Hence, out of the 12 leaf nodes in the tree, the algorithm has needed to examine only 7 to conclude that the best move for max to make is b, in which case min will choose d and max will choose the right hand node, ending with a static evaluation of 3.

At this stage, we can easily see that this is the right answer because if max chooses c, then min will clearly choose f, resulting in max being able to achieve a score of only 2.

An ideal tree for alpha–beta pruning is shown in Figure 6.6.

In this case, the Minimax algorithm with alpha–beta cut-off will need to examine only five of the eight leaf nodes.

6.5 Checkers

The game of checkers (or draughts[1]) has proved to be an excellent challenge for the methods of Artificial Intelligence and one that has been met with a reasonable degree of success.

---

[1]Draughts is another name for the common variety of checkers, which is played on an 8×8 board. International checkers is another variety, which is played on a 10×10 board.

In his paper of 1959, *Some Studies in Machine Learning Using the Game of Checkers*, Arthur Samuel described a computer system that could play checkers to a reasonable level, using Minimax with alpha–beta pruning. This system used a weighted linear function of a variety of heuristics that measured how strong a particular position was.

If a particular strategy was played and found to lose, the system would adjust its weights to avoid making such a mistake in the future. In this way, by playing many games it was able to learn to play checkers to a fairly high level. Samuel's system was a significant milestone in the Artificial Intelligence research. Unfortunately, it was widely reported by the media that Samuel's system had solved the game of checkers and was able to beat a top-ranked human player. Neither of these claims was true, but it caused the Artificial Intelligence community to believe that there was nothing more to be learned about checkers, and so until Chinook, very little further research was done on the game.

6.5.1   Chinook

Chinook is a checkers-playing computer that was developed by a team led by Dr. Jonathan Schaeffer of the University of Alberta in Canada.

Chinook uses Minimax search with alpha–beta pruning. It also applies iterative deepening (see Section 4.11) and a number of heuristics to maximize the efficiency of the search and to minimize the size of the game tree that the program needs to examine for each move. Chinook also has a database of endgames consisting of hundreds of billions of possible positions. Such a database would not be practical in chess, due to the enormous number of possible positions, but is possible with checkers because there are fewer legal squares on the board (32 instead of 64), fewer piece types (2 as opposed to 6), and a smaller average branching factor (8 compared with 38).

Chinook also has a large amount of knowledge about the game and built-in heuristics to help it evaluate positions and choose better moves.

On average, Chinook examines the game tree to a depth of 20 ply and is able to examine around 1000 positions per second per MIPS (millions of instructions per second) of processing power.

In 1990, Chinook was beaten by the world champion checkers player, Marion Tinsley, by a margin of 7.5 to 6.5. Tinsley had been world champion for 40 years and is commonly recognized as the greatest checkers player of all time.

In 1992, Tinsley beat Chinook in the World Checkers Championship. Forty games were played; Chinook won two and Tinsley won four. Thirty-three games were drawn. This was the first World Championship match of any game in which a computer had taken part. In a rematch in 1994, Tinsley and Chinook played six games, all of which were drawn, after which Tinsley resigned due to ill health, surrendering the world championship title to Chinook. Sadly, Marion Tinsley succumbed to cancer in 1995 before a further rematch could be played. Chinook did beat Don Lafferty, who was then the world's second-best human player, in 1995 to retain the title. The current world champion, Ron King, has been beaten many times by Chinook, but never in a championship match.

The version of Chinook that played in 1994 was a significantly more powerful player (running on a much more powerful computer and using more sophisticated algorithms). One might imagine that with increasing computer power, a checkers computer could be developed that would "solve" the game of checkers—that is, a computer program that could examine the entire game tree for checkers and determine the outcome before a game was started. This is a difficult challenge and one that does not seem likely to be achieved in the near future. The main problem is that as the depth of analysis increases, the improvement in play increases less than linearly, meaning that a much deeper analysis is needed to provide small improvements (compare with chess—Section 6.6). Additionally, although the complete game tree for checkers would be vastly smaller than that for chess, it would still be extremely large (around 10^{20} possible moves to examine).

6.5.2 Chinook's Databases

One of the secrets of Chinook's success at playing checkers lies in its databases of endgame positions and opening moves. Chinook uses the **opening book** of a commercial checkers program, Colossus. This book had been developed over years, mainly from the published literature on the game. Chinook spent a number of months examining each position in the book to a depth of at least 19 ply to ensure that the opening moves were correct.

This process was also used to identify unusual opening moves that might surprise an experienced player such as Tinsley.

In fact, to make Chinook play more imaginatively, the developers chose to avoid the use of the opening book in most situations. Instead, they built an anti-book that contains moves that Chinook should avoid, and in most other cases, Chinook uses search to decide on good moves to make. Schaeffer and his team have found that this actually tends to lead to better play than following the opening book.

The main power of Chinook lies in its databases of endgame positions. In 1992, Chinook's database contained an evaluation (win, lose, or draw) for every possible position involving seven pieces—around 40 billion positions.

By 1994, the databases had been extended to cover all positions involving eight pieces—another 440 billion positions.

In most games, within a few moves from the start, Chinook's search has reached a position stored in its database, meaning that it can usually determine the outcome of a game within 10 moves of the start. Most possible games lead to a draw, but Chinook has been programmed to look for draws that involve complicated strategies that the opponent is likely to miss. Hence, in evaluating the game tree, Chinook does not give all draws a score of zero, but gives them a score depending on how likely it is that the opponent will make a mistake and lose the game.

6.5.3 Chinook's Evaluation Function

Chinook uses a linear weighted static evaluation function, based on a number of heuristics. These heuristics include piece count, king count, balance (the distribution of pieces between the left and right sides of the board), the number of trapped kings, and so on.

Chinook divides the game up into four phases, which are identified by the number of pieces left on the board.

Phase	Number of pieces
1	20–24
2	14–19
3	10–13
4	less than 10

Chinook has different sets of weights for its 25 heuristic values for each phase of the game, so that, for example, it places more importance on kings in later phases of the game than in the first phase.

6.5.4 Forward Pruning

Another technique used by Chinook, and other game-playing systems, is forward pruning. The idea behind forward pruning is that if a line of play (i.e., a path through the game tree) is being examined in which a number of pieces are lost without any way to recapture, then examination of the path is terminated and the tree is pruned at this point.

Hence, unlike alpha–beta pruning, no static evaluation is needed. It is possible, but unlikely, that such pruning could miss a useful strategy, but this is less likely with checkers than with chess, where sacrifices of important pieces can often lead to a win.

6.5.5 Limitations of Minimax

Schaeffer's work with Chinook has revealed some serious limitations with alpha–beta search.

In some cases, Minimax with alpha–beta pruning might show that a number of different paths lead to a draw. As was mentioned in the previous section, some draws can be harder to achieve than others. In particular, one position might lead to a draw no matter what moves a player makes, whereas another position might lead to a draw only if a player makes the correct choice on each move for 40 moves. Clearly the latter draw is much harder to achieve. Chinook was programmed to take advantage of this, after it drew a game that it could probably have won because it chose a draw that was easy for its opponent to achieve and neglected a draw that looked very much like a win to most human players.

Similarly, in one game against Marion Tinsley, Chinook discovered a long, complicated win for Tinsley, and made a sacrifice to try to avoid this. As a result, it lost the game easily. In fact, it is quite possible that Tinsley would have missed the win without the sacrifice.

A modified version of Minimax would take advantage of the difficulty of particular paths through the game tree, as well as the final outcome.

6.5.6 Blondie 24

In 2000, a new kind of checkers program was developed, called Blondie 24. Unlike Chinook, Blondie 24 does not have any knowledge of the game (other than the basic rules) built in. The program, developed by Dr. David Fogel of Natural Selection Inc. based in San Diego, uses evolutionary techniques (described in Chapter 13) to develop neural networks (see Chapter 11) that can learn how to play checkers, and how to win.

In fact, Blondie uses standard Minimax evaluation to search the game tree. The evolutionary method was used to develop the static evaluation function.

The static evaluation function is evaluated by neural networks that were developed by starting with programs that would play the game randomly and breeding together the ones that played the most successfully. Repeating this over many generations, and allowing random mutations, led to the final version of the software, which proved able to beat many human players. This program is not nearly at the level of Chinook, which currently is the checkers world champion, but it does represent a fascinating example of a combination of artificial life techniques with Artificial Intelligence, generating a solution that performs extremely well, without ever having had any help from humans.

6.6 Chess

One of the best-known applications of Artificial Intelligence is the development of computer programs that can play chess against human players. Chess programs typically use Minimax algorithms with alpha–beta pruning and are almost always programmed with large libraries of opening moves (similar to the databases used in Chinook for endgame moves).

It has been shown that there is a more or less linear relationship between the depth to which a program can examine the game tree for chess and its skill in playing the game. In other words, a system that is able to examine the tree to 12 ply is likely to beat a system that can only examine the tree to 10 ply (see Newborn 2002, pages 291–294). As mentioned in Section 6.5, this is not true for checkers, where a law of diminishing returns applies. In fact, Schaeffer (1991) claims that this relationship is the same for chess and checkers, but that the relationship is more or less linear up to a depth of around 15, tailing off after this. Because the best chess programs tend to analyze to a depth of around 12, they have not yet reached the nonlinear stage of the graph.

As a result of this relationship, great advances in the ability of computers to play chess have been made simply as a result of improvement in speed of computers and in the use of parallel computing techniques.

In 1997, a chess-playing computer system developed by IBM called Deep Blue beat world champion Garry Kasparov, who is generally considered to be the strongest chess player of all time. The final score after six games was 3.5 to 2.5. Kasparov won one game, Deep Blue won two, and three were drawn.

In 2002, Vladimir Kramnik, one of the highest-ranking chess players in the world, played a match against a German computer program, Deep Fritz. The eight-game match ended in a draw. There are a number of other chess computers that can play at a comparable level, and at the time of writing this book, the competition between human and computer chess players is very close. In January 2003, Garry Kasparov played a six-game match against Deep Junior, an Israeli computer program. The match ended in a draw, with Kasparov and Deep Junior each winning one game, and the other four games being drawn.

It is certainly not the case as it is with games such as Othello and checkers that the best computers are unbeatable by humans, and neither is it the case as with Go or bridge that computers cannot beat the best humans.

It seems likely that given the linear relationship between depth of search and quality of play that with the improvement in computer power, it will soon be the case that the best computers are unbeatable by even the very best human players.

6.7 Go

Go is an ancient Japanese game, which is considered by many to be the final frontier for research in game-playing computers. It is certainly more complex than chess: Go is played on a 19×19 board, with far greater freedom of choice in playing most moves than chess, resulting in an enormous branching factor (on average around 360, compared with around 38 for chess).

It has thus been impossible to develop a system that searches the game tree for Go in the same way as for chess or checkers. Systems have been developed that play Go, but the best of these can compete only at the level of a weak club player. None have shown any possibility yet of approaching the level of the best human players. Methods usually involve extremely **selective** search—using constraints to eliminate many options at each stage of the game tree. Some success has also been had with pattern recognition techniques.

A Taiwanese business man offered one million dollars to the first person who could write a computer program that could beat a professional Go player. Although the business man died in 1997, his bet looks as though it will remain safe for a while yet.

6.7.1   Go-Moku

Go-moku is a far simpler version of Go, usually played on a 15×15 board. This game is often used for teaching and illustrating Artificial Intelligence because it is fairly simple. Alternate players place stones on the board, and the first player to place five stones in a row wins the game.

Go-Moku belongs to a group of games including Connect-4 and tic-tac-toe (noughts and crosses) that have been **solved**. That is to say, the complete game tree has been evaluated such that the outcome of the game can be determined from the start. Assuming both players play correctly, the player who starts the game will always win.

6.8   Othello (Reversi)

Othello is a simpler game than chess, and typical Othello computer programs can now examine the search tree to a depth of around 50 ply. The best human players are now unable to beat this level of play. In 1997, the human world champion Takeshi Murakami of Japan was beaten 6–0 by an American Othello computer program, developed by Michael Buro, called Logistello.

6.9   Games of Chance

Unlike the games we have considered so far, many games involve an element of chance—often introduced by a dice roll or a draw of cards. With the exception of simple games like Chutes and Ladders and Ludo, most games of chance still involve a reasonable degree of skill because the chance element merely restricts the choices that can be made.

Games such as backgammon, scrabble, and bridge are popular games that involve chance. Computer programs have been developed that can play backgammon and Scrabble at a level where they can beat all but the best human players in the world. Bridge is rather more complex, with its bidding system presenting real problems for Artificial Intelligence system developers. Bridge systems have been developed that can play at an intermediate level but are not yet close to playing at the level of the best human players.

6.9.1 Expectiminimax

Expectiminimax is a version of the Minimax algorithm that has been extended to take into account the probability of each successor node being reached. In games that involve the throw of a single die, the successor nodes at each ply will all have equal probabilities (one-sixth), but in more complex games, the probabilities are not so straightforward. For example, in backgammon, where two dice are rolled for each move (or rather, for each ply in the game tree), the likelihood of achieving a double (1 and 1, 2 and 2, 3 and 3, 4 and 4, 5 and 5, or 6 and 6) is 1 in 36, whereas the likelihood of rolling any other pair is 1 in 18.

Rather than giving each position in the game tree a particular Minimax value, the Expectiminimax algorithm, which is described in more detail in Russell and Norvig (1995) assigns an **expected value** to each node, which is the average value that could be obtained on the node, taking into account the probabilities of each possible outcome.

6.10 Chapter Summary

- Game trees can be used to represent two-player games.

- Searching game trees is very hard for all but the simplest games.

- Minimax is an algorithm that identifies the best move to make in a two-player game with perfect knowledge, assuming the entire tree can be examined.

- When the entire tree cannot be examined, a static evaluator is needed that can assign a score to any given position according to how well each player is doing and how likely each player is to win the game from that position.

- Alpha–beta pruning enables Minimax to run more efficiently because it removes unnecessary branches from the game tree.

- In the best case, alpha–beta pruning enables Minimax to search the game tree to double the depth that it would be able to search without pruning.

- Games such as Go-moku and tic-tac-toe have been solved, meaning that the result of a game is known from the start.

- Computers are able to beat the best players in the world at games such as Othello and checkers.

- Computers cannot compete with humans at games such as Go and bridge.

- Although Deep Blue beat Garry Kasparov at chess in 1997, computers and humans are fairly evenly matched at chess at the moment.

6.11 Review Questions

6.1 Discuss the current state of the art of game-playing computer systems in relation to the following games: chess, checkers, Go, bridge, Othello, tic-tac-toe. What advances are likely in the near future? Do you believe there are any fundamental limitations?

6.2 Discuss the approach you would take to building a system for playing Scrabble or another word game of the sort. What limitations does your system have? How likely do you think it is that your system would be able to beat the best human players in the world?

6.3 What problems did the developers of Chinook face? What new techniques did they add to simple Minimax with alpha–beta pruning? Would these techniques extend well to other games?

6.4 Explain why the alpha–beta procedure will always generate the same answer as Minimax without pruning. Why is it useful?

6.5 Show the steps that would be taken in running the Minimax algorithm on the game tree in Figure 6.7. Now run through the same tree using alpha–beta pruning. How do the two compare?

6.6 Why might it be particularly difficult to program a computer to successfully play card games like bridge or poker? What sort of algorithms might you use to play these games?

6.7 What does it mean to say that a game has been *solved*? How likely is it that games like Go and chess will ever be solved? Is it always the

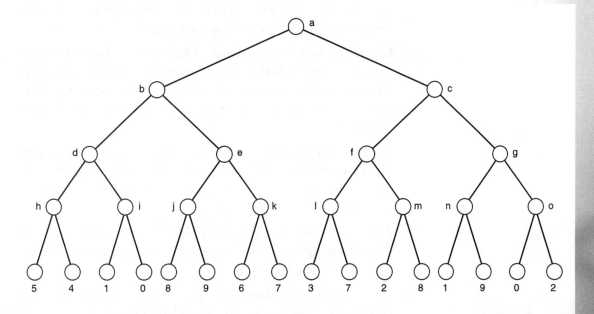

Figure 6.7

Game tree for question 6.5

case that the player who goes first will win a game that has been
solved? Even if both players play correctly?

6.8   Most commercially available chess programs for home users are
designed to play at a range of levels from beginner up to grand-
master. Consider the additional difficulties involved in programming a computer to play suboptimally. Would alpha–beta pruning
still be appropriate? What methods might a programmer use to
program the computer to play over such a range of abilities?

6.12   Exercises

6.1   For a game tree of depth d, and branching factor b, show that iterative deepening does not increase by a great deal the number of
static evaluations needed to examine the tree.

6.2   Write an algorithm in pseudo-code, or a programming language of
your choice, that evaluates a position in tic-tac-toe. Your static

evaluator should give 0 for a drawn position, 1 for a won position for crosses, −1 for won position for noughts.

6.3 Extend the algorithm you designed for Exercise 6.2 so that it is able to evaluate positions that are nonterminal—in other words, positions where the game has not yet finished. Your score should be positive for an advantage to crosses, and negative for an advantage to noughts.

6.4 Implement a Minimax algorithm using your static evaluator for tic-tac-toe, and write a simple program that plays the game. Have the program output how many nodes in the game tree it had to examine as well as its choice of move.

6.5 Add alpha–beta pruning to your program, and see what difference (if any) it makes to the number of nodes the program has to examine when playing a game.

6.6 Implement an Expectiminimax algorithm for a game of chance (you might use backgammon, or another dice game).

6.7 Is it possible to add alpha–beta pruning to your Expectiminimax program? If so, do so. If not, can you find another way of pruning the tree that improves the performance of the program? How can you tell if it is improving the performance?

6.13 Further Reading

There is a great deal of fascinating literature on the subject of game playing using Artificial Intelligence. The Chinook website is well worth visiting and contains a great deal of insight into the way game-playing systems are developed and improved. It can be found using any search engine.

Arthur Samuel's articles on his checkers-playing system are also worth reading.

A number of books and articles have been published on the subject of Deep Blue and other chess computers. Monty Newborn's book does not contain a great deal of computer science but does make a fascinating read, particularly for anyone interested in the game of chess.

Blondie 24: Playing at the Edge of AI by David B. Fogel (2001 – Morgan Kaufmann)

Behind Deep Blue: Building the Computer That Defeated the World Chess Champion by Feng-Hsiung Hsu (2002 – Princeton University Press)

An analysis of alpha beta pruning, by Donald Knuth and R. W. Moore (1975 - in Artificial Intelligence, Vol. 6(4), pp. 293–326)

Deep Blue: An Artificial Intelligence Milestone by Monty Newborn (2003 – Springer Verlag)

Kasparov Versus Deep Blue: Computer Chess Comes of Age by Monty Newborn (1997 – Springer Verlag)

Kasparov and Deep Blue by Bruce Pandolfini (1997 – Fireside)

Some Studies in Machine Learning Using the Game of Checkers by Arthur Samuel (1959–in *Computation & Intelligence – Collected Readings* edited by George F. Luger - MIT Press)

One Jump Ahead: Challenging Human Supremacy in Checkers by Jonathan Schaeffer (1997 – Springer Verlag)

A Re-examination of Brute-force Search by Jonathan Schaeffer, Paul Lu, Duane Szafron, and Robert Lake (1993 – in *Games: Planning and Learning*, AAAI 1993 Fall Symposium, Report FS9302, pp. 51–58)

A World Championship Caliber Checkers Program by Jonathan Schaeffer, Joseph Culberson, Norman Treloar, Brent Knight, Paul Lu, and Duane Szafron – (1992 – in *Artificial Intelligence*, Vol. 53(2–3), pp. 273–290)

Knowledge Representation and Automated Reasoning

Introduction to Part 3

Part 3 is divided into three chapters:

CHAPTER 7

Propositional and Predicate Logic

In Chapter 7, the basic concepts behind propositional calculus and predicate calculus are introduced. Truth tables and the ideas behind proofs by deduction are explained. The concept of tautology is introduced, as is satisfiability and logical equivalence.

Properties of logical systems such as soundness, completeness, and decidability are discussed. Logical systems other than those of classical logic are briefly introduced.

CHAPTER 8

Inference and Resolution for Problem Solving

In Chapter 8, we introduce in detail the ideas behind proof by refutation and resolution for automated theorem proving. The chapter explains the steps needed to automate resolution, including: converting expressions to conjunctive normal form, Skolemization, and unification. The use of resolution and Horn Clauses in Prolog is discussed, as are other practical applications of resolution, such as for solving combinatorial search problems.

CHAPTER 9

Rules and Expert Systems

Chapter 9 discusses how rules and frames are used to build expert systems and discusses the practicalities of implementing such systems. Methods such as forward and backward chaining and conflict resolution are discussed, as is the Rete Algorithm for a more efficient rule-based approach.

The ideas behind inheritance and multiple inheritance are discussed in relation to frames, and the relationship between frames and object-oriented programming languages such as C++ and Java is explored.

CHAPTER 7

Propositional and Predicate Logic

If, dear Reader, you will faithfully observe these Rules, and so give my little book a really fair trial, I promise you, most confidently, that you will find Symbolic Logic to be one of the most, if not the most, fascinating of mental recreations!

—Lewis Carroll, from the Introduction to Symbolic Logic

If it was so, it might be; and if it were so, it would be: but as it isn't, it ain't. That's logic.

—Lewis Carroll, from *Through The Looking Glass*

Of science and logic he chatters
As fine and as fast as he can;
Though I am no judge of such matters,
I'm sure he's a talented man.

—Winthrop Mackworth Praed, from *The Talented Man*

7.1 Introduction

In this chapter, we introduce propositional calculus and first-order predicate calculus, the languages of logic. We introduce methods that can be used to carry out deductions and prove whether or not a conclusion follows from a set of premises.

We introduce the ideas of logical equivalence, tautologies, and satisfiability. This chapter also discusses some important properties of logical systems, including soundness, completeness, monotonicity, and decidability.

This chapter assumes no previous knowledge of logic, so readers who are already familiar with the ideas of propositional logic and the predicate calculus may wish to skim this chapter.

7.2 What Is Logic?

Logic is concerned with reasoning and the validity of arguments. In general, in logic, we are not concerned with the *truth* of statements, but rather with their **validity**. That is to say, although the following argument is clearly logical, it is not something that we would consider to be true:

>All lemons are blue
>
>Mary is a lemon
>
>Therefore, Mary is blue

This set of statements is considered to be **valid** because the conclusion (Mary is blue) follows logically from the other two statements, which we often call the **premises**.

The reason that validity and truth can be separated in this way is simple: a piece of a reasoning is considered to be valid if its conclusion is true in cases where its premises are also true. Hence, a valid set of statements such as the ones above can give a false conclusion, provided one or more of the premises are also false.

We can say: *a piece of reasoning is valid if it leads to a true conclusion in every situation where the premises are true.*

Logic is concerned with **truth values**. The possible truth values are true and false. These can be considered to be the fundamental units of logic, and almost all logic is ultimately concerned with these truth values.

7.3 Why Logic Is Used in Artificial Intelligence

Logic is widely used in computer science, and particularly in Artificial Intelligence. Logic is widely used as a representational method for Artificial Intelligence. Unlike some other representations (such as **frames**, which are described in detail in Chapter 3), logic allows us to easily reason about negatives (such as, "this book is not red") and disjunctions ("or"—such as, "He's either a soldier or a sailor").

Logic is also often used as a representational method for communicating concepts and theories within the Artificial Intelligence community. In addition, logic is used to represent language in systems that are able to understand and analyze human language.

As we will see, one of the main weaknesses of traditional logic is its inability to deal with **uncertainty**. Logical statements must be expressed in terms of truth or falsehood—it is not possible to reason, in classical logic, about possibilities. We will see different versions of logic such as **modal logics** that provide some ability to reason about possibilities, and also probabilistic methods and fuzzy logic that provide much more rigorous ways to reason in uncertain situations.

7.4   Logical Operators

In reasoning about truth values, we need to use a number of **operators**, which can be applied to truth values. We are familiar with several of these operators from everyday language:

> I like apples **and** oranges.
>
> You can have an ice cream **or** a cake.
>
> **If** you come from France, **then** you speak French.
>
> I am **not** stupid!

Here we see the four most basic logical operators being used in everyday language. The operators are:

- and

- or

- not

- if . . . then . . . (usually called **implies**)

These operators work more or less as we expect them to. One important point to note is that *or* is slightly different from the way we usually use it. In the sentence, "You can have an icecream or a cake," the mother is usually suggesting to her child that he can only have one of the items, but not both. This is referred to as an **exclusive-or** in logic because the case where both are allowed is excluded. The version of *or* that is used in logic is called **inclusive-or** and allows the case with both options.

The operators are usually written using the following symbols, although other symbols are sometimes used, according to the context:

and $\quad\wedge$

or $\quad\vee$

not $\quad\neg$

implies $\quad\rightarrow$

iff $\quad\leftrightarrow$

Iff is an abbreviation that is commonly used to mean "if and only if." We see later that this is a stronger form of implies that holds true if one thing implies another, and also the second thing implies the first.

For example, "you can have an ice-cream if and only if you eat your dinner." It may not be immediately apparent why this is different from "you can have an icecream if you eat your dinner." This is because most mothers really mean *iff* when they use *if* in this way.

7.5   Translating between English and Logic Notation

To use logic, it is first necessary to convert facts and rules about the real world into logical expressions using the logical operators described in Section 7.4. Without a reasonable amount of experience at this translation, it can seem quite a daunting task in some cases.

Let us examine some examples.

First, we will consider the simple operators, $\wedge$, $\vee$, and $\neg$.

Sentences that use the word *and* in English to express more than one concept, all of which is true at once, can be easily translated into logic using the AND operator, $\wedge$. For example:

"It is raining and it is Tuesday."

might be expressed as:

$R \wedge T$

Where R means "it is raining" and T means "it is Tuesday." Note that we have been fairly arbitrary in our choice of these terms. This is all right, as long as the terms are chosen in such a way that they represent the problem adequately. For example, if it is not necessary to discuss where it is raining, R is probably enough. If we need to write expressions such as "it is raining in New York" or "it is raining heavily" or even "it rained for 30 minutes on Thursday," then R will probably not suffice.

To express more complex concepts like these, we usually use predicates. Hence, for example, we might translate "it is raining in New York" as:

$N(R)$

We might equally well choose to write it as:

$R(N)$

This depends on whether we consider the rain to be a property of New York, or vice versa. In other words, when we write $N(R)$, we are saying that a property of the rain is that it is in New York, whereas with $R(N)$ we are saying that a property of New York is that it is raining.

Which we use depends on the problem we are solving. It is likely that if we are solving a problem about New York, we would use $R(N)$, whereas if we are solving a problem about the location of various types of weather, we might use $N(R)$.

Let us return now to the logical operators. The expression "it is raining in New York, and I'm either getting sick or just very tired" can be expressed as follows:

$R(N) \land (S(I) \lor T(I))$

Here we have used both the $\land$ operator, and the $\lor$ operator to express a collection of statements. The statement can be broken down into two sections, which is indicated by the use of parentheses. The section in the parentheses is $S(I) \lor T(I)$, which means "I'm either getting sick OR I'm very tired". This expression is "AND'ed" with the part outside the parentheses, which is $R(N)$.

Finally, the $\neg$ operator is applied exactly as you would expect—to express negation. For example,

It is not raining in New York,

might be expressed as

$\neg R(N)$

It is important to get the $\neg$ in the right place. For example: "I'm either not well or just very tired" would be translated as

$\neg W(I) \lor T(I)$

The position of the ¬ here indicates that it is bound to $W(I)$ and does not play any role in affecting $T(I)$. This idea of **precedence** is explained further in Section 7.7.

Now let us see how the → operator is used. Often when dealing with logic we are discussing rules, which express concepts such as "if it is raining then I will get wet."

This sentence might be translated into logic as

$$R \to W(I)$$

This is read "R implies $W(I)$" or "IF R THEN $W(I)$". By replacing the symbols R and $W(I)$ with their respective English language equivalents, we can see that this sentence can be read as

"raining implies I'll get wet"

or   "IF it's raining THEN I'll get wet."

Implication can be used to express much more complex concepts than this. For example, "Whenever he eats sandwiches that have pickles in them, he ends up either asleep at his desk or singing loud songs" might be translated as

$$S(y) \land E(x, y) \land P(y) \to A(x) \lor (S(x, z) \land L(z))$$

Here we have used the following symbol translations:

$S(y)$ means that y is a sandwich.

$E(x, y)$ means that x (the man) eats y (the sandwich).

$P(y)$ means that y (the sandwich) has pickles in it.

$A(x)$ means that x ends up asleep at his desk.

$S(x, z)$ means that x (the man) sings z (songs).

$L(z)$ means that z (the songs) are loud.

In fact, there are better ways to express this kind of sentence, as we will see when we examine the quantifiers ∃ and ∀ in Section 7.13.

The important thing to realize is that the choice of variables and predicates is important, but that you can choose any variables and predicates that map well to your problem and that help you to solve the problem. For example, in the example we have just looked at, we could perfectly well have used instead

$$S \to A \lor L$$

where S means "he eats a sandwich which has pickles in it," A means "he ends up asleep at his desk," and L means "he sings loud songs."

The choice of granularity is important, but there is no right or wrong way to make this choice. In this simpler logical expression, we have chosen to express a simple relationship between three variables, which makes sense if those variables are all that we care about—in other words, we don't need to know anything else about the sandwich, or the songs, or the man, and the facts we examine are simply whether or not he eats a sandwich with pickles, sleeps at his desk, and sings loud songs. The first translation we gave is more appropriate if we need to examine these concepts in more detail and reason more deeply about the entities involved.

Note that we have thus far tended to use single letters to represent logical variables. It is also perfectly acceptable to use longer variable names, and thus to write expressions such as the following:

$$\text{Fish}(x) \wedge \text{living}(x) \rightarrow \text{has\_scales}(x)$$

This kind of notation is obviously more useful when writing logical expressions that are intended to be read by humans but when manipulated by a computer do not add any value.

7.6 Truth Tables

We can use **variables** to represent possible truth values, in much the same way that variables are used in algebra to represent possible numerical values. We can then apply logical operators to these variables and can reason about the way in which they behave.

It is usual to represent the behavior of these logical operators using **truth tables**. A truth table shows the possible values that can be generated by applying an operator to truth values.

7.6.1 Not

First of all, we will look at the truth table for not, $\neg$.

Not is a **unary** operator, which means it is applied only to one variable. Its behavior is very simple:

$\neg$ true is equal to false

$\neg$ false is equal to true

If variable A has value *true*, then $\neg A$ has value *false.*

If variable B has value *false*, then $\neg B$ has value *true.*

These can be represented by a truth table,

A	$\neg$ A
true	false
false	true

7.6.2 And

Now, let us examine the truth table for our first **binary** operator—one which acts on two variables:

A	B	A $\wedge$ B
false	false	false
false	true	false
true	false	false
true	true	true

$\wedge$ is also called the **conjunctive operator**. $A \wedge B$ is the **conjunction** of A and B.

You can see that the only entry in the truth table for which $A \wedge B$ is *true* is the one where A is *true* **and** B is *true*. If A is *false*, or if B is *false*, then $A \wedge B$ is *false*. If both A and B are *false*, then $A \wedge B$ is also *false*.

What do A and B mean? They can represent any statement, or **proposition**, that can take on a truth value. For example, A might represent "It's sunny," and B might represent "It's warm outside." In this case, $A \wedge B$ would mean "It is sunny **and** it's warm outside," which clearly is true only if the two component parts are true (i.e., if it is true that it is sunny and it is true that it is warm outside).

7.6.3 Or

The truth table for the *or* operator, $\vee$, should need little explanation.

A	B	A $\vee$ B
false	false	false
false	true	true
true	false	true
true	true	true

∨ is also called the **disjunctive operator**. $A \lor B$ is the **disjunction** of A and B.

Clearly $A \lor B$ is true for any situation except when both A and B are *false*. If A is *true*, or if B is *true*, or if both A and B are *true*, $A \lor B$ is true.

You should notice that this table represents the inclusive-or operator. A table to represent exclusive-or would have *false* in the final row. In other words, while $A \lor B$ is *true* if A and B are both *true*, A EOR B (A exclusive-or B) is *false* if A and B are both *true*.

You may also notice a pleasing symmetry between the truth tables for ∧ and ∨. This will become useful later, as will a number of other symmetrical relationships.

7.6.4   Implies

The truth table for *implies* ($\rightarrow$) is a little less intuitive.

A	B	$A \rightarrow B$
false	false	true
false	true	true
true	false	false
true	true	true

(This form of implication is also known as **material implication**.)

In the statement $A \rightarrow B$, A is the **antecedent**, and B is the **consequent**.

The bottom two lines of the table should be obvious. If A is *true* and B is *true*, then $A \rightarrow B$ seems to be a reasonable thing to believe. For example, if A means "you live in France" and B means "You speak French," then $A \rightarrow B$ corresponds to the statement "if you live in France, then you speak French." Clearly, this statement is true ($A \rightarrow B$ is *true*) if I live in France and I speak French (A is *true* and B is *true*).

Similarly, if I live in France, but I don't speak French (A is *true*, but B is *false*), then it is clear that $A \rightarrow B$ is not *true*.

The situations where A is *false* are a little less clear. If I do not live in France (A is not *true*), then the truth table tells us that regardless of whether I speak French or not (the value of B), the statement $A \rightarrow B$ is *true*.

$A \rightarrow B$ is usually read as "A implies B" but can also be read as "If A then B" or "If A is true then B is true." Hence, if A is *false*, the statement is not really saying anything about the value of B, so B is free to take on any value (as long as it is *true* or *false*, of course!).

This can lead to some statements being valid that might at first glance appear absurd. All of the following statements are valid:

$$5^2 = 25 \rightarrow 4 = 4 \qquad (\text{true} \rightarrow \text{true})$$
$$9 \times 9 = 123 \rightarrow 8 > 3 \quad (\text{false} \rightarrow \text{true})$$
$$52 = 25 \rightarrow 0 = 2 \qquad (\text{false} \rightarrow \text{false})$$

In fact, in the second and third examples, the consequent could be given *any* meaning, and the statement would still be true. For example, the following statement is valid:

$$52 = 25 \rightarrow \text{Logic is weird}$$

Notice that when looking at simple logical statements like these, there does not need to be any real-world relationship between the antecedent and the consequent. For logic to be useful, though, we tend to want the relationships being expressed to be meaningful as well as being logically true.

7.6.5   iff

The truth table for *iff* (if and only if {$\leftrightarrow$}) is as follows:

A	B	A $\leftrightarrow$ B
false	false	true
false	true	false
true	false	false
true	true	true

It can be seen that $A \leftrightarrow B$ is *true* as long as A and B have the same value. In other words, if one is *true* and the other *false*, then $A \leftrightarrow B$ is *false*. Otherwise, if A and B have the same value, $A \leftrightarrow B$ is *true*.

7.7   Complex Truth Tables

Truth tables are not limited to showing the values for single operators. For example, a truth table can be used to display the possible values for $A \wedge (B \vee C)$.

A	B	C	A ∧ (B ∨ C)
false	false	false	false
false	false	true	false
false	true	false	false
false	true	true	false
true	false	false	false
true	false	true	true
true	true	false	true
true	true	true	true

Note that for two variables, the truth table has four lines, and for three variables, it has eight. In general, a truth table for n variables will have 2^n lines.

The use of brackets in this expression is important. $A \wedge (B \vee C)$ is not the same as $(A \wedge B) \vee C$.

To avoid ambiguity, the logical operators are assigned precedence, as with mathematical operators. The order of precedence that is used is as follows:

$\neg, \wedge, \vee, \rightarrow, \leftrightarrow$

Hence, in a statement such as

$\neg A \vee \neg B \wedge C$

the $\neg$ operator has the greatest precedence, meaning that it is most closely tied to its symbols. $\wedge$ has a greater precedence than $\vee$, which means that the sentence above can be expressed as

$(\neg A) \vee ((\neg B) \wedge C)$

Similarly, when we write

$\neg A \vee B$

this is the same as

$(\neg A) \vee B$

rather than

$\neg(A \vee B)$

In general, it is a good idea to use brackets whenever an expression might otherwise be ambiguous.

7.8   Tautology

Consider the following truth table:

A	A $\lor \neg$ A
false	true
true	true

This truth table has a property that we have not seen before: the value of the expression $A \lor \neg A$ is *true* regardless of the value of A. An expression like this that is always *true* is called a **tautology**.

If A is a tautology, we write:

$$\models A$$

Tautologies may seem like rather uninteresting entities, but in fact they are extremely useful for logic, as we see later.

A logical expression that is a tautology is often described as being **valid**. A valid expression is defined as being one that is true under any **interpretation**. In other words, no matter what meanings and values we assign to the variables in a valid expression, it will still be true. For example, the following sentences are all valid:

If wibble is true, then wibble is true.

Either wibble is true, or wibble is not true.

In the language of logic, we can replace *wibble* with the symbol A, in which case these two statements can be rewritten as

$$A \rightarrow A$$
$$A \lor \neg A$$

If an expression is *false* in any interpretation, it is described as being **contradictory**. The following expressions are contradictory:

$$A \land \neg A$$
$$(A \lor \neg A) \rightarrow (A \land \neg A)$$

It doesn't matter what *A* means in these expressions, the result cannot be *true*.

Some expressions are **satisfiable**, but not valid. This means that they are true under some interpretation, but not under all interpretations. The following expressions are satisfiable:

A ∨ B

(A ∧ B ∨ ¬ C) → (D ∧ E)

A contradictory expression is clearly not satisfiable and so is described as being **unsatisfiable**.

7.9   Equivalence

Consider the following two expressions:

A ∧ B

B ∧ A

It should be fairly clear that these two expressions will always have the same value for a given pair of values for *A* and B. In other words, we say that the first expression is **logically equivalent** to the second expression. We write this as

A ∧ B ≡ B ∧ A

This means that the ∧ operator is **commutative**.

Note that this is not the same as implication:

A ∧ B → B ∧ A

although this second statement is also true. The difference is that if for two expressions *e1* and *e2*:

e1 ≡ e2

then *e1* will always have the same value as *e2* for a given set of variables. On the other hand, as we have seen, *e1* → *e2* is *true* if *e1* is *false* and *e2* is *true*.

There are a number of logical equivalences that are extremely useful. The following is a list of a few of the most common:

A ∨ A ≡ A

A ∧ A ≡ A

A ∧ (B ∧ C) ≡ (A ∧ B) ∧ C   (∧ is **associative**)

$$A \lor (B \lor C) \equiv (A \lor B) \lor C \qquad (\lor \text{ is } \mathbf{associative})$$
$$A \land (B \lor C) \equiv (A \land B) \lor (A \land C) \quad (\land \text{ is } \mathbf{distributive} \text{ over } \lor)$$
$$A \land (A \lor B) \equiv A$$
$$A \lor (A \land B) \equiv A$$
$$A \land \text{true} \equiv A$$
$$A \land \text{false} \equiv \text{false}$$
$$A \lor \text{true} \equiv \text{true}$$
$$A \lor \text{false} \equiv A$$

All of these equivalences can be proved by drawing up the truth tables for each side of the equivalence and seeing if the two tables are the same. You may want to try this to satisfy yourself that all of the equivalences are correct, particularly for some of the less intuitive ones.

The following is a very important equivalence:

$$A \to B \equiv \neg A \lor B$$

You can verify this by checking the truth tables. The reason that this is useful is that it means we do not need to use the $\to$ symbol at all—we can replace it with a combination of $\neg$ and $\lor$. Similarly, the following equivalences mean we do not need to use $\land$ or $\leftrightarrow$:

$$A \land B \equiv \neg(\neg A \lor \neg B)$$
$$A \leftrightarrow B \equiv \neg(\neg(\neg A \lor B) \lor \neg (\neg B \lor A))$$

In fact, *any* binary logical operator can be expressed using $\neg$ and $\lor$. This is a fact that is employed in electronic circuits, where *nor* gates, based on an operator called *nor*, are used. *Nor* is represented by $\downarrow$, and is defined as follows:

$$A \downarrow B \equiv \neg(A \lor B)$$

Finally, the following equivalences are known as **DeMorgan's Laws** and will be used later in this chapter:

$$A \land B \equiv \neg(\neg A \lor \neg B)$$
$$A \lor B \equiv \neg(\neg A \land \neg B)$$

By using these and other equivalences, logical expressions can be **simplified**. For example,

$$(C \land D) \lor ((C \land D) \land E)$$

can be simplified using the following rule:

$$A \lor (A \land B) \equiv A$$

hence,

$$(C \land D) \lor ((C \land D) \land E) \equiv C \land D$$

In this way, it is possible to eliminate subexpressions that do not contribute to the overall value of the expression.

7.10   Propositional Logic

There are a number of possible systems of logic. The system we have been examining so far in this chapter is called **propositional logic**. The language that is used to express propositional logic is called the **propositional calculus** (although in practice, many people use the expressions *logic* and *calculus* interchangeably in this context).

A logical system can be defined in terms of its syntax (the alphabet of symbols and how they can be combined), its semantics (what the symbols mean), and a set of rules of **deduction** that enable us to derive one expression from a set of other expressions and thus make arguments and proofs.

7.10.1   Syntax

We have already examined the syntax of propositional calculus. The alphabet of symbols, Σ is defined as follows

$$\Sigma = \{\text{true}, \text{false}, \neg, \rightarrow, (,), \land, \lor, \leftrightarrow, p_1, p_2, p_3, \ldots, p_n, \ldots\}$$

Here we have used **set notation** to define the possible values that are contained within the alphabet Σ. Note that we allow an infinite number of **proposition letters**, or **propositional symbols**, $p_1, p_2, p_3, \ldots$, and so on. More usually, we will represent these by capital letters P, Q, R, and so on, although if we need to represent a very large number of them, we will use the subscript notation (e.g., p_1).

An expression is referred to as a **well-formed formula** (often abbreviated as wff) or a **sentence** if it is constructed correctly, according to the rules of the syntax of propositional calculus, which are defined as follows. In these rules, we use *A*, *B*, *C* to represent sentences. In other words, we define a sentence recursively, in terms of other sentences. The following are well-formed sentences:

P, Q, R. . .

true, false

(A)

¬A

A ∧ B

A ∨ B

A → B

A ↔ B

Hence, we can see that the following is an example of a wff:

$$P \wedge Q \vee (B \wedge \neg C) \to A \wedge B \vee D \wedge (\neg E)$$

This is not to make any claims about the validity or otherwise of the expression, simply that it is allowed within the syntax of propositional calculus.

7.10.2 Semantics

The semantics of the operators of propositional calculus can be defined in terms of truth tables. As we have seen, the meaning of $P \wedge Q$ is defined as "*true* when *P* is *true* and *Q* is also *true*."

The meaning of symbols such as *P* and *Q* is arbitrary and could be ignored altogether if we were reasoning about pure logic. In other words, reasoning about sentences such as $P \vee Q \wedge \neg R$ is possible without considering what *P*, *Q*, and *R mean*.

Because we are using logic as a representational method for artificial intelligence, however, it is often the case that when using propositional logic, the meanings of these symbols are very important. The beauty of this representation is that it is possible for a computer to reason about them in a very general way, without needing to know much about the real world.

In other words, if we tell a computer, "I like ice cream, and I like chocolate," it might represent this statement as $A \wedge B$, which it could then use to reason with, and, as we will see, it can use this to make deductions.

7.11 Deduction

If we have a set of assumptions $\{A_1, A_2, \ldots, A_n\}$, and from those assumptions we are able to derive a conclusion, C, then we say that we have **deduced** C from the assumptions, which is written

$$\{A_1, A_2, \ldots, A_n\} \vdash C$$

If C can be concluded without any assumptions, then we write

$$\vdash C$$

To derive a conclusion from a set of assumptions, we apply a set of **inference rules**. To distinguish an inference rule from a sentence, we often write $A \vdash B$ as follows:

$$\frac{A}{B}$$

Some of the most useful inference rules for propositional logic are as follows. In these rules, A, B, and C stand for any logical expressions.

7.11.1 ∧-Introduction

$$\frac{A \quad B}{A \wedge B}$$

This rule is very straightforward. It says: Given A and B, we can deduce $A \wedge B$. This follows from the definition of $\wedge$.

7.11.2 ∧-Elimination

$$\frac{A \wedge B}{A}$$

Similarly,

$$\frac{A \wedge B}{B}$$

These rules say that given $A \wedge B$, we can deduce A and we can also deduce B separately. Again, these follow from the definition of $\wedge$.

7.11.3   Or-Introduction

$$\frac{A}{A \vee B}$$

$$\frac{B}{A \vee B}$$

These rules say that from A we can deduce the disjunction of A with *any* expression. For example, from the statement "I like logic," we can deduce expressions such as "I like logic or I like cheese," "I like logic or I do not like logic," "I like logic or fish can sing," "I like logic or $2 + 2 = 123$," and so on. This follows because *true* $\vee$ B is *true* for any value of B.

7.11.4 $\rightarrow$ Elimination

This rule is usually known as **modus ponens** and is one of the most commonly used rules in logical deduction. It is expressed as follows:

$$\frac{A \quad A \rightarrow B}{B}$$

In other words, if A is *true* and A implies B is *true*, then we know that B is *true*.

For example, if we replace A with "it is raining" and B with "I need an umbrella," then we produce the following:

> It is raining. If it's raining, I need an umbrella. Therefore, I need an umbrella.

This kind of reasoning is clearly valid.

7.11.5   Reductio Ad Absurdum

We need to introduce a new notation for this rule:

$$\frac{\begin{array}{c} \neg A \\ \vdots \\ \bot \end{array}}{A}$$

The symbol $\bot$ is called **falsum,** which is used to indicate an absurdity, or a contradiction. For example, $\bot$ can be deduced from $A \wedge \neg A$.

The reductio ad absurdum rule simply says that if we assume that A is *false* ($\neg A$) and this leads to a contradiction ($\bot$), then we can deduce that A is *true*. This is known as **proof by contradiction**.

As we will see, this is an extremely powerful concept and is widely used in logical systems.

7.11.6   → Introduction

$$A$$
$$\vdots$$
$$C$$
$$\overline{A \rightarrow C}$$

This rule shows that if in carrying out a proof we start from an assumption A and derive a conclusion C, then we can conclude that $A \rightarrow C$.

7.11.7   ¬¬ Elimination

$$\frac{\neg\neg A}{A}$$

This rule states that if we have a sentence that is negated twice, we can conclude the sentence itself, without the negation. Clearly, this rule follows from the definition of $\neg$.

7.11.8   Example 1

To carry out a proof that one set of sentences follows logically from another, we selectively apply the rules presented above to the assumptions until we arrive at the conclusions.

For example, it would be useful to prove the following:

$$\{A, \neg A\} \vdash \bot$$

In other words, if we start from the set of assumptions A and $\neg A$, we can conclude falsum.

First, note that

$$\neg A \equiv A \rightarrow \bot$$

This can be seen by comparing the truth tables for $\neg A$ and for $A \rightarrow \bot$.

Hence, we can take as our set of assumptions

$$\{A, A \rightarrow \perp\}$$

Thus, our proof using modus ponens (the $\rightarrow$ ELIMINATION rule presented in Section 7.11.2) is as follows:

$$\frac{A \quad A \rightarrow \perp}{\perp}$$

7.11.9   Example 2

Let us prove the following:

$$\{A \wedge B\} \vdash A \vee B$$

The proof is as follows:

$$\frac{\dfrac{A \wedge B}{A}}{A \vee B} \quad \begin{array}{l} \text{assumption} \\ \text{by } \wedge \text{ elimination} \\ \text{by } \vee \text{ introduction} \end{array}$$

7.11.10   Example 3

We will use reductio ad absurdum to prove the following:

$$\vdash (\neg A \rightarrow B) \rightarrow (\neg B \rightarrow A)$$

The usual method for carrying out such proofs is based on the idea that in order to prove something of the form $A \rightarrow B$, it is a good idea to start by assuming A.

We will start with two assumptions: $\neg A$ and $(\neg A \rightarrow B)$. After the first step, which uses modus ponens, on our original assumptions to prove B, we introduce a new assumption, which is $\neg B$. The proof is as follows:

$$\frac{\dfrac{\dfrac{\dfrac{\dfrac{\dfrac{\neg A \quad \neg A \rightarrow B}{B \quad \neg B}}{B \quad B \rightarrow \perp}}{\perp}}{A}}{\neg B \rightarrow A}}{(\neg A \rightarrow B) \rightarrow (\neg B \rightarrow A)} \quad \begin{array}{l} \text{assumptions} \\ \text{modus ponens} \\ \text{rewriting } \neg B \\ \text{modus ponens} \\ \text{reductio ad absurdum} \\ \rightarrow \text{introduction} \\ \rightarrow \text{introduction} \end{array}$$

In carrying out this proof, we have used the relationship between ¬B and B → ⊥ as we did in Example 1. We have also used reductio absurdum to show that if we start by assuming ¬A, we end up with a contradiction (⊥), and therefore our initial assumption, ¬A, was *false*. Hence, A must be true.

7.11.11   Example 4

Let us now aim to prove the following:

$$\vdash (A \rightarrow B) \rightarrow ((B \rightarrow C) \rightarrow ((C \rightarrow D) \rightarrow (A \rightarrow D)))$$

To prove this, we will need to make a series of assumptions. We will start by making two assumptions, A and A → B. Hence, our proof is as follows:

$\underline{A \quad A \rightarrow B}$	assumptions
$\underline{B \quad\; B \rightarrow C}$	modus ponens
$\underline{C \quad C \rightarrow D}$	modus ponens
$\underline{D}$	modus ponens
$\underline{A \rightarrow D}$	→ introduction
$\underline{(C \rightarrow D) \rightarrow (A \rightarrow D)}$	→ introduction
$\underline{(B \rightarrow C) \rightarrow ((C \rightarrow D) \rightarrow (A \rightarrow D))}$	→ introduction
$(A \rightarrow B) \rightarrow ((B \rightarrow C) \rightarrow ((C \rightarrow D) \rightarrow (A \rightarrow D)))$	→ introduction

7.12   The Deduction Theorem

A useful rule known as the **deduction theorem** provides us with a way to make propositional logic proofs easier. The rule is as follows:

if $A \bigcup \{B\} \vdash C$ then $A \vdash (B \rightarrow C)$

Here A is a set of wff's, which makes up our assumptions. Note that this rule is *true* even if A is the empty set. $A \bigcup \{B\}$ means the **union** of the set A with the set consisting of one element, B.

The rule also holds in reverse:

if $A \vdash (B \rightarrow C)$ then $A \bigcup \{B\} \vdash C$

Let us see an example of a proof using the deduction theorem.

Our aim is to prove the following:

$$\{A \rightarrow B\} \vdash A \rightarrow (C \rightarrow B)$$

Recall the axiom that was presented earlier:

$$A \rightarrow (B \rightarrow A)$$

Because propositional logic is monotonic (see Section 7.18), we can add in an additional assumption, that A is *true*:

$$A$$

Now, by applying modus ponens to this assumption and our hypothesis, $A \rightarrow B$, we arrive at

$$B$$

We can now apply our axiom

$$B \rightarrow (C \rightarrow B)$$

And by modus ponens on the above two lines, we get

$$C \rightarrow B$$

Hence, we have shown that

$$\{A \rightarrow B\} \bigcup A \vdash (C \rightarrow B)$$

And, therefore, by the deduction theorem

$$\{A \rightarrow B\} \vdash A \rightarrow (C \rightarrow B)$$

7.13   Predicate Calculus

7.13.1   Syntax

Predicate calculus allows us to reason about properties of objects and relationships between objects. In propositional calculus, we could express the English statement "I like cheese" by A. This enables us to create constructs such as $\neg A$, which means "I do not like cheese," but it does not allow us to extract any information about the cheese, or me, or other things that I like.

In predicate calculus, we use **predicates** to express properties of objects. So the sentence "I like cheese" might be expressed as

$$L(me, cheese)$$

where L is a predicate that represents the idea of "liking." Note that as well as expressing a property of *me*, this statement also expresses a relationship between *me* and *cheese*. This can be useful, as we will see, in describing environments for robots and other **agents**. For example, a simple agent may be concerned with the location of various blocks, and a statement about the world might be

$$T(A,B)$$

which could mean: Block *A* is on top of Block *B*.

Thus far we have expressed ideas about specific objects. It is also possible to make more general statements using the predicate calculus. For example, to express the idea that everyone likes cheese, we might say

$$(\forall x)(P(x) \rightarrow L(x, C))$$

The symbol $\forall$ is read "for all," so the statement above could be read as "for every *x* it is true that if property *P* holds for *x*, then the relationship *L* holds between *x* and *C*," or in plainer English: "every *x* that is a person likes cheese." (Here we are interpreting $P(x)$ as meaning "*x* is a person" or, more precisely, "*x* has property *P*.")

Note that we have used brackets rather carefully in the statement above. This statement can also be written with fewer brackets:

$$\forall x\, P(x) \rightarrow L(x, C)$$

$\forall$ is called the **universal quantifier.**

The quantifier $\exists$ can be used to express the notion that some values do have a certain property, but not necessarily all of them:

$$(\exists x)(L(x,C))$$

This statement can be read "there exists an *x* such that *x* likes cheese." This does not make any claims about the possible values of *x*, so *x* could be a person, or a dog, or an item of furniture. When we use the **existential quantifier** in this way, we are simply saying that there is *at least one* value of *x* for which $L(x,C)$ holds.

Note, therefore, that the following is true:

$$(\forall x)(L(x,C)) \rightarrow (\exists x)(L(x,C))$$

but the following is not:

$$(\exists x)(L(x,C)) \rightarrow (\forall x)(L(x,C))$$

7.13.2   Relationships between $\forall$ and $\exists$

It is also possible to combine the universal and existential quantifiers, such as in the following statement:

$$(\forall x)\ (\exists y)\ (L(x,y))$$

This statement can be read "for all x, there exists a y such that L holds for x and y," which we might interpret as "everyone likes something."

A useful relationship exists between $\forall$ and $\exists$. Consider the statement "not everyone likes cheese." We could write this as

$$\neg(\forall x)(P(x) \rightarrow L(x,C)) \tag{1}$$

As we have already seen, $A \rightarrow B$ is equivalent to $\neg A \vee B$. Using DeMorgan's laws, we can see that this is equivalent to $\neg(A \wedge \neg B)$. Hence, the statement (1) above, can be rewritten:

$$\neg(\forall x)\neg(P(x) \wedge \neg L(x,C)) \tag{2}$$

This can be read as "It is not true that for all x the following is not true: x is a person and x does not like cheese." If you examine this rather convoluted sentence carefully, you will see that it is in fact the same as "there exists an x such that x is a person and x does not like cheese." Hence we can rewrite it as

$$(\exists x)(P(x) \wedge \neg L(x,C)) \tag{3}$$

In making this transition from statement (2) to statement (3), we have utilized the following equivalence:

$$\exists x \equiv \neg(\forall x)\neg$$

In an expression of the form $(\forall x)(P(x,\ y))$, the variable x is said to be **bound**, whereas y is said to be **free**. This can be understood as meaning that the variable y could be replaced by any other variable because it is free, and the expression would still have the same meaning, whereas if the variable x were to be replaced by some other variable in $P(x,y)$, then the meaning of the expression would be changed:

$$(\forall x)(P(y,\ z))$$

is not equivalent to $(\forall x)(P(x,\ y))$, whereas $(\forall x)(P(x,\ z))$ is. Note that a variable can occur both bound and free in an expression, as in

$$(\forall x)(P(x,y,z) \rightarrow (\exists y)(Q(y,z)))$$

In this expression, x is bound throughout, and z is free throughout; y is free in its first occurrence but is bound in $(\exists y)(Q(y,z))$. (Note that both occurrences of y are bound here.)

Making this kind of change is known as **substitution**. Substitution is allowed of any free variable for another free variable.

7.13.3   Functions

In much the same way that **functions** can be used in mathematics, we can express an object that relates to another object in a specific way using functions. For example, to represent the statement "my mother likes cheese," we might use

   L(m(me),cheese)

Here the function $m(x)$ means the mother of x. Functions can take more than one argument, and in general a function with n arguments is represented as

   $f(x_1, x_2, x_3, \ldots, x_n)$

7.14   First-Order Predicate Logic

The type of predicate calculus that we have been referring to is also called **first-order predicate logic (FOPL)**. A first-order logic is one in which the quantifiers $\forall$ and $\exists$ can be applied to objects or **terms**, but not to predicates or functions. So we can define the syntax of FOPL as follows. First, we define a term:

   A constant is a term.

   A variable is a term.

   $f(x_1, x_2, x_3, \ldots, x_n)$ is a term if $x_1, x_2, x_3, \ldots, x_n$ are all terms.

Anything that does not meet the above description cannot be a term. For example, the following is not a term: $\forall x\, P(x)$. This kind of construction we call a sentence or a well-formed formula (wff), which is defined as follows. In these definitions, P is a predicate, $x_1, x_2, x_3, \ldots, x_n$ are terms, and A,B are wff's. The following are the acceptable forms for wff's:

   $P(x_1, x_2, x_3, \ldots, x_n)$

   $\neg A$

   $A \wedge B$

   $A \vee B$

   $A \rightarrow B$

   $A \leftrightarrow B$

   $(\forall x)A$

   $(\exists x)A$

An **atomic formula** is a wff of the form $P(x_1, x_2, x_3, \ldots, x_n)$.

Higher order logics exist in which quantifiers can be applied to predicates and functions, and where the following expression is an example of a wff:

$$(\forall P)(\exists x)P(x)$$

In this book, we will stick with first-order logics, in which quantifiers can only be applied to variables, not predicates or functions.

7.15   Soundness

We have seen that a logical system such as propositional logic consists of a syntax, a semantics, and a set of rules of deduction. A logical system also has a set of fundamental truths, which are known as axioms. The axioms are the basic rules that are known to be true and from which all other **theorems** within the system can be proved.

An axiom of propositional logic, for example, is

$$A \rightarrow (B \rightarrow A)$$

A theorem of a logical system is a statement that can be proved by applying the rules of deduction to the axioms in the system.

If A is a theorem, then we write

$$\vdash A$$

A logical system is described as being **sound** if every theorem is logically valid, or a tautology.

It can be proved by induction that both propositional logic and FOPL are sound.

7.16   Completeness

A logical system is **complete** if every tautology is a theorem—in other words, if every valid statement in the logic can be proved by applying the rules of deduction to the axioms. Both propositional logic and FOPL are complete. The proofs that these systems are complete are rather complex.

7.17   Decidability

A logical system is decidable if it is possible to produce an algorithm that will determine whether any wff is a theorem. In other words, if a logical system is decidable, then a computer can be used to determine whether logical expressions in that system are valid or not.

We can prove that propositional logic is decidable by using the fact that it is complete. Thanks to the completeness of propositional logic, we can prove that a wff A is a theorem by showing that it is a tautology. To show if a wff is a tautology, we simply need to draw up a truth table for that wff and show that all the lines have *true* as the result. This can clearly be done algorithmically because we know that a truth table for n values has 2^n lines and is therefore finite, for a finite number of variables.

FOPL, on the other hand, is not decidable. This is due to the fact that it is not possible to develop an algorithm that will determine whether an arbitrary wff in FOPL is logically valid.

7.18   Monotonicity

A logical system is described as being monotonic if a valid proof in the system cannot be made invalid by adding additional premises or assumptions. In other words, if we find that we can prove a conclusion C by applying rules of deduction to a premise B with assumptions A, then adding additional assumptions A' and B' will not stop us from being able to deduce C.

Both propositional logic and FOPL are monotonic. Elsewhere in this book, we learn about probability theory, which is not a monotonic system.

Monotonicity of a logical system can be expressed as follows:

If we can prove {A, B} ⊢ C,

then we can also prove: {A, B, A', B'} ⊢ C.

Note that A' and B' can be anything, including ¬A and ¬B. In other words, even adding contradictory assumptions does not stop us from making the proof in a monotonic system. In fact, it turns out that adding contradictory assumptions allows us to prove *anything*, including invalid conclusions.

This makes sense if we recall the line in the truth table for →, which shows that *false* → *true*. By adding a contradictory assumption, we make our assumptions *false* and can thus prove any conclusion.

7.19   Abduction and Inductive Reasoning

The kind of reasoning that we have seen so far in this chapter has been **deductive reasoning**, which in general is based on the use of modus ponens and the other deductive rules of reasoning. This kind of reasoning assumes that we are dealing with certainties and does not allow us to reason about things of which we are not certain. As we see elsewhere in this book, there is another kind of reasoning, **inductive reasoning**, which does not have the same logical basis but can be extremely powerful for dealing with situations in which we lack certainty.

Strangely, another form of reasoning, **abduction**, is based on a common fallacy, which can be expressed as

$$\frac{B \quad A \rightarrow B}{A}$$

Note that abduction is very similar to modus ponens but is not logically sound. A typical example of using this rule might be "When Jack is sick, he doesn't come to work. Jack is not at work today. Therefore Jack is sick."

In fact, Jack may be having a holiday, or attending a funeral, or it may be Sunday or Christmas Day.

Given that this type of reasoning is invalid, why are we discussing it here? It turns out that although abduction does not provide a logically sound model for reasoning, it does provide a model that works reasonably well in the real world because it allows us to observe a phenomenon and propose a possible explanation or cause for that phenomenon without complete knowledge. Abductive reasoning is discussed in more detail in Chapter 17.

Inductive reasoning enables us to make predictions about what will happen, based on what has happened in the past. Humans use inductive reasoning all the time without realizing it. In fact, our entire lives are based around inductive reasoning, for example, "the sun came up yesterday and the day before, and every day I know about before that, so it will come up again tomorrow." It's possible it won't, but it seems fairly unlikely. This kind of reasoning becomes more powerful when we apply probabilities to it, as in "I've noticed that nearly every bird I see is a swallow. Therefore, it's quite likely that that bird is a swallow."

As we will see, these kinds of reasoning are extremely useful for dealing with uncertainty and are the basis of most of the learning techniques used in Artificial Intelligence.

7.20   Modal Logics and Possible Worlds

The forms of logic that we have dealt with so far deal with facts and properties of objects that are either true or false. In these **classical logics**, we do not consider the possibility that things change or that things might not always be as they are now.

Modal logics are an extension of classical logic that allow us to reason about possibilities and certainties. In other words, using a modal logic, we can express ideas such as "although the sky is usually blue, it isn't always" (for example, at night). In this way, we can reason about possible worlds. A possible world is a universe or scenario that could logically come about.

The following statements may not be true in our world, but they are possible, in the sense that they are not illogical, and could be true in a possible world:

> Trees are all blue.
>
> Dogs can fly.
>
> People have no legs.

It is possible that some of these statements will become true in the future, or even that they were true in the past. It is also possible to imagine an alternative universe in which these statements are true now. The following statements, on the other hand, cannot be true in any possible world:

> $A \land \neg A$
>
> $(x > y) \land (y > z) \land (z > x)$

The first of these illustrates the **law of the excluded middle**, which simply states that a fact must be either true or false: it cannot be both true and false. It also cannot be the case that a fact is neither true nor false. This is a law of classical logic, and as we see in Chapter 18, it is possible to have a logical system without the law of the excluded middle, and in which a fact can be both true *and* false.

The second statement cannot be true by the laws of mathematics. We are not interested in possible worlds in which the laws of logic and mathematics do not hold.

A statement that may be true or false, depending on the situation, is called **contingent**. A statement that must always have the same truth value, regardless of which possible world we consider, is **noncontingent**. Hence, the following statements are contingent:

A ∧ B

A ∨ B

I like ice cream.

The sky is blue.

The following statements are noncontingent:

A ∨ ¬A

A ∧ ¬A

If you like all ice cream, then you like this ice cream.

Clearly, a noncontingent statement can be either true or false, but the fact that it is noncontingent means it will always have that same truth value.

If a statement A is contingent, then we say that *A* is **possibly** true, which is written

◇A

If A is noncontingent, then it is **necessarily** true, which is written

□A

7.20.1   Reasoning in Modal Logic

It is not possible to draw up a truth table for the operators ◇ and □. (Consider the four possible truth tables for unary operators—it should be clear that none of these matches these operators.) It is possible, however, to reason about them.

The following rules are examples of the axioms that can be used to reason in this kind of modal logic:

□A → ◇A

□¬A → ¬◇A

◇A → ¬□A

Although truth tables cannot be drawn up to prove these rules, you should be able to reason about them using your understanding of the meaning of the □ and ◇ operators.

Modal logic, and other nonclassical logics, are discussed in Chapter 17.

7.21   Dealing with Change

As we have seen, classical logics do not deal well with change. They assume that if an object has a property, then it will always have that property and always has had it. Of course, this is not true of very many things in the real world, and a logical system that allows things to change is needed. The situation and event calculi are covered in more detail in Chapters 17 and 19.

7.22   Chapter Summary

- Logic is primarily concerned with the logical validity of statements, rather than with truth.

- Logic is widely used in Artificial Intelligence as a representational method.

- Abduction and inductive reasoning are good at dealing with uncertainty, unlike classical logic.

- The main operators of propositional logic are $\wedge$, $\vee$, $\neg$, $\rightarrow$, and $\leftrightarrow$ (and, or, not, implies, and iff).

- The behavior of these logical operators can be expressed in truth tables. Truth tables can also be used to solve complex problems.

- Propositional logic deals with simple propositions such as "I like cheese." First-order predicate logic allows us to reason about more complex statements such as "All people who eat cheese like cats," using the quantifiers $\forall$ and $\exists$ ("for all", and "there exists").

- A statement that is always true in any situation is called a tautology. $A \vee \neg A$ is an example of a tautology.

- Two statements are logically equivalent if they have the same truth tables.

- First-order predicate logic is sound and complete, but not decidable. Propositional logic is sound, complete, and decidable.

- Modal logics allow us to reason about certainty.

7.23   Review Questions

7.1   Explain the meanings of the following terms in the context of logic:

    a.   truth

    b.   validity

    c.   equivalent

    d.   uncertainty

    e.   tautology

    f.   satisfiable

    g.   sound

    h.   complete

    i.   decidable

    j.   modal logic

7.2 "Inductive reasoning is a reasonable way to think about everyday life, but it does not provide the logical structure that propositional logic does." Discuss.

7.3 Explain what is meant by the following: "Classical logics are not good at dealing with uncertainty."

7.4 Explain why the addition of the quantifiers $\forall$ and $\exists$ makes predicate calculus so powerful.

7.5 Explain the rule of modus ponens. Explain how it is used in everyday life.

7.6 Explain in layman's terms what the law of the excluded middle means. What difficulties might you encounter in logical deduction if you ignored the law of the excluded middle?

7.7 Assume the law of the excluded middle is not true, and use this to prove the equality $1 = 0$.

7.8 What does it mean to say that a logic is monotonic? Is propositional logic monotonic? What complexities do you think nonmonotonicity would add to the process of logical deduction? Would modus ponens still hold in a nonmonotonic logic?

7.24 Exercises

7.1 Translate the following sentences into logical statements, using either propositional or predicate logic as appropriate:

    a.   I like apples and pears.

    b.   When I eat apples and pears, I usually like to have a walk.

    c.   Every apple that I have ever eaten has been delicious.

    d.   The fact that some pears are not delicious will not stop me eating them.

e.   I can only eat an apple if I have first eaten a pear, and I can only eat a pear if I eat an apple immediately afterward.

f.   There exists a book that includes details of every book.

g.   There exists somewhere in the world a book that lists every single person who doesn't appear in any other book.

h.   If you haven't read the book that lists all other books, then you haven't read any book, unless you've read the book that lists books that do not exist, in which case you've read every book.

7.2   Draw a truth table for the following expression:

$\neg A \wedge (A \vee B) \wedge (B \vee C)$

7.3   (Hard) Prove that propositional logic and first-order predicate logic are sound and complete.

7.4   Write expressions in propositional calculus to represent the following statements:

a.   If you go to Mexico, you will be far away.

b.   I cannot hear you when you are far away.

c.   When I can't hear you, I forget what you look like.

d.   If I come to Mexico, and I don't know what you look like, I won't be able to find you.

e.   Therefore, if you go to Mexico, and I follow you, I won't be able to find you.

Prove whether the conclusion follows from the premises or not.

7.5   Write expressions in first-order predicate logic to represent the following statements, and prove whether the conclusion follows from the premises or not:

a.   All dancers love to dance.

b.   Everyone who sings and plays an instrument loves to dance.

c.   Therefore, all dancers sing and play an instrument.

7.6   Prove the following:

a. $\vdash A \rightarrow A$

b. $\vdash ((\neg A \rightarrow \neg B) \rightarrow A) \rightarrow ((\neg B \rightarrow \neg A) \rightarrow \neg B)$

c. $\vdash (\neg\neg\neg A \rightarrow \neg\neg\neg B) \rightarrow (\neg A \rightarrow \neg B)$

7.25   Further Reading

Most textbooks on Artificial Intelligence provide good coverage of logic. An excellent, short introduction to logic that provides more detail on most of the subject than has been provided here is Kelly (1997). Lewis Carroll's work, though over 100 years old, still makes for an interesting and relevant read on the subject of logic and reasoning, although his approach was rather different from that usually found today.

The idea of abduction was introduced by C. S. Peirce, in his 1878 paper *How to Make Our Ideas Clear*, published in *Popular Science Monthly*.

Francis Bacon introduced the idea of inductive reasoning in 1620. His writings on the subject can be found in *The New Organon, and Related Writings*, published in 1960.

Francis Bacon: The New Organon by Francis Bacon, edited by Lisa Jardine and Michael Silverthorne (2002 – Cambridge University Press)

Propositional Logic: Deduction and Algorithms by Hans Kleine Büning and Theodor Lettmann (1999 – Cambridge University Press)

Symbolic Logic and *Game of Logic* by Lewis Carroll (published in one volume – 1958 – Dover Books).

Predicate Logic: The Semantic Foundations of Logic by Richard L. Epstein (2000 – Wadsworth Publishing)

Propositional Logics: The Semantic Foundations of Logic by Richard L. Epstein (2000 – Wadsworth Publishing)

The Essence of Logic by John Kelly (1997 – Prentice Hall)

Introduction to Logic: Propositional Logic by Howard Pospesel (1999 – Prentice Hall)

Logic for Computer Science by Steve Reeves and Michael Clarke (1993 – Addison Wesley)

Logical Forms: An Introduction to Philosophical Logic by Mark Sainsbury (1991 – Blackwell)

Logic and Prolog by Richard Spencer-Smith (1991 – Harvester Wheatsheaf)

CHAPTER 8

Inference and Resolution for Problem Solving

Early work in theorem proving programs for quantified logics culminated in 1965 with Alan Robinson's development of machine-oriented formulation of first-order logic called Resolution (Robinson, 1965). There followed an immensely productive period of exploration of resolution-based theorem-proving.

—Alan Newell, *The Knowledge Level*

When you have eliminated the impossible, whatever remains, no matter how improbable, must be the truth.

—Sir Arthur Conan Doyle, *The Sign of Four*

At thirty a man suspects himself a fool;
Knows it at forty, and reforms his plan;
At fifty chides his infamous delay,
Pushes his prudent purpose to resolve;
In all the magnanimity of thought
Resolves; and re-resolves; then dies the same.

—Edward Young, *Night Thoughts*

8.1   Introduction

This chapter introduces the main ideas behind automated reasoning, or theorem proving. The method of resolution is discussed in some detail because it pertains to both propositional logic and first-order predicate logic (FOPL).

To explain resolution, ideas such as unification, normal forms, and Herbrand universes are introduced. This chapter is somewhat more advanced than Chapter 7 and assumes an understanding of propositional calculus and first-order predicate calculus.

This chapter also briefly explains how PROLOG uses resolution to process data and to provide solutions to problems. In fact, resolution is fundamental to the way that PROLOG works. Resolution is an important part of Artificial Intelligence research and provides a common method for systems to reason logically and to prove theorems in an automated manner. This has advantages over other theorem-proving methods that depend more on intuition and experience and are thus best applied by humans. In this chapter, we show how resolution can be entirely automated and an algorithm generated for using resolution to prove theorems.

The representational methods discussed in this chapter and Chapter 7 provide a powerful tool for reasoning logically and, in particular, for enabling computer systems to automatically reason about a database of facts. This representational method, though, is not suitable for all problems, and in many situations it is entirely inadequate.

In particular, predicate logic does not have a mechanism for dealing with change or with time. We will discuss a number of alternative representations in Chapters 17 and 18 that overcome some of these difficulties. As we see in these chapters, and in Chapter 19, intelligent agents and other Artificial Intelligence systems often need to reason about events, situations, and other time-based factors. The logic we are looking at here is better suited to static environments, which is certainly appropriate for solving a number of problems.

8.2   Resolution in Propositional Logic

In Chapter 7, we introduced a method of deductive reasoning in order to make proofs in predicate and propositional logic. It is not clear how this process might be automated because at each stage an amount of initiative was required to choose the right next step. We now introduce a proof method, **resolution**, which can be automated because it involves a fixed set of steps. Before we examine resolution, we must introduce some key ideas.

8.2.1   Normal Forms

A sentence or well-formed formula (wff) is in **conjunctive normal form** if it is of the following form:

$$A_1 \wedge A_2 \wedge A_3 \wedge \ldots \wedge A_n$$

where each **clause**, A_i, is of the form

$B_1 \lor B_2 \lor B_3 \lor \ldots \lor B_n$

Each B_i is a **literal**, where a literal is a basic symbol of propositional logic. In fact, a literal can be more accurately defined as an atom or an atom that is negated, where an atom is one of the basic object symbols in propositional logic. Hence, in the following expression:

$A \land B \lor (\neg C \land D)$

A is an atom, as are B, C, and D. The literals are A, B, $\neg C$, and D.

So, an expression is in conjunctive normal form (often written CNF) if it consists of a set of *or* phrases *and*ed together, such as:

$A \land (B \lor C) \land (\neg A \lor \neg B \lor \neg C \lor D)$

Trivially, a literal is also in CNF.

A sentence is in **disjunctive normal form** (DNF) if it consists of a set of *and* phrases *or*ed together, as in

$A \lor (B \land C) \lor (\neg A \land \neg B \land \neg C \land D)$

Any wff can be converted to CNF by using the following equivalences, which we have encountered previously:

1. $A \leftrightarrow B \equiv (A \rightarrow B) \land (B \rightarrow A)$

2. $A \rightarrow B \equiv \neg A \lor B$

3. $\neg(A \land B) \equiv \neg A \lor \neg B$

4. $\neg(A \lor B) \equiv \neg A \land \neg B$

5. $\neg\neg A \equiv A$

6. $A \lor (B \land C) \equiv (A \lor B) \land (A \lor C)$

For example, we will convert $(A \rightarrow B) \rightarrow C$ to CNF:

$(A \rightarrow B) \rightarrow C$	
$\neg(A \rightarrow B) \lor C$	(2)
$\neg(\neg A \lor B) \lor C$	(3)
$(A \land \neg B) \lor C$	(4)
$(A \lor C) \land (\neg B \lor C)$	(6)

A further example follows:

$A \leftrightarrow (B \wedge C)$

$(A \rightarrow (B \wedge C)) \wedge ((B \wedge C) \rightarrow A)$ \hfill (1)

$(\neg A \vee (B \wedge C)) \wedge (\neg (B \wedge C) \vee A)$ \hfill (2)

$(\neg A \vee (B \wedge C)) \wedge (\neg B \vee \neg C \vee A)$ \hfill (3)

$(\neg A \vee B) \wedge (\neg A \vee C) \wedge (\neg B \vee \neg C \vee A)$ \hfill (6)

Note that this process can be automated, as the equivalences can always be applied in the order they were listed, replacing symbols and constructions as they are encountered. As we will see, this is a useful fact: **an algorithm can be expressed that will convert any wff into CNF.**

Having converted a wff into CNF, we can now express it as a set of clauses. So our expression above

$$(\neg A \vee B) \wedge (\neg A \vee C) \wedge (\neg B \vee \neg C \vee A)$$

would be represented in clause form as

$$\{(\neg A, B), (\neg A, C), (\neg B, \neg C, A)\}$$

8.2.2 The Resolution Rule

Now we introduce a new rule to sit alongside the rules presented in Section 7.10, which is called the resolution rule:

$$\frac{A \vee B \qquad \neg B \vee C}{A \vee C}$$

This rule is not as immediately obvious as the rules in Section 7.10, but it does prove to be extremely useful. It can also be written as follows:

$$\frac{\neg A \rightarrow B \qquad B \rightarrow C}{\neg A \rightarrow C}$$

In this form, the rule can be seen to be saying that implication is transitive, or in other words, if A implies B and B implies C, then A implies C.

This can be applied to wff's in clause form, as follows:

If a wff contains a clause that contains literal L and another clause that contains literal $\neg L$, then these two clauses can be combined together, and L and $\neg L$ can be removed from those clauses. For example,

$$\{(A, B), (\neg B, C)\}$$

can be resolved to give

$$\{(A, C)\}$$

Similarly,

$$\{(A, B, C), D, (\neg A, D, E), (\neg D, F)\}$$

can be resolved to give

$$\{(B, C, D, E), D, (\neg D, F)\}$$

which can be further resolved to give either

$$\{(B, C, D, E), F\}$$

or

$$\{(B, C, E, F), D\}$$

Note that at the first step, we also had a choice and could have resolved to

$$\{(A, B, C), D, (\neg A, E, F)\}$$

which can be further resolved to give

$$\{(B, C, E, F), D\}$$

Now, if wff P resolves to give wff Q, we write

$$P \models Q$$

For example, we can resolve $(A \lor B) \land (\neg A \lor C) \land (\neg B \lor C)$ as follows:

$$\{(A, B), (\neg A, C), (\neg B, C)\}$$

$$\{(B, C), (\neg B, C)\}$$

$$\{C\}$$

We can express this as

$$(A \lor B) \land (\neg A \lor C) \land (\neg B \lor C) \models C$$

If we resolve two clauses, we produce the **resolvent** of those clauses. The resolvent is a logical consequence of the two clauses.

8.2.3   Resolution Refutation

Now let us resolve the following clauses:

$$\{(\neg A, B), (\neg A, \neg B, C), A, \neg C\}$$

We begin by resolving the first clause with the second clause, thus eliminating B and $\neg B$:

$\{(\neg A, C), A, \neg C\}$

$\{C, \neg C\}$

$\bot$

The fact that this resolution has resulted in falsum means that the original clauses were inconsistent. We have **refuted** the original clauses, using **resolution refutation**. We can write

$\{(\neg A, B), (\neg A, \neg B, C), A, \neg C\} \models \bot$

The idea behind resolution refutation is explained in more detail in Section 8.2.4.

8.2.4   Proof by Refutation

Proof by refutation (also known as **proof by contradiction**), as used in resolution refutation, is a powerful method for solving problems. For example, let us imagine that we want to determine whether the following logical argument is valid:

If it rains and I don't have an umbrella, then I will get wet.

It is raining, and I don't have an umbrella.

Therefore, I will get wet.

We can rewrite this in propositional calculus as follows:

$(A \wedge \neg B) \rightarrow C$

$A \wedge \neg B$

$\therefore C$

To prove this by refutation, we first negate the conclusion and convert the expressions into clause form. The first expression is the only one that is not already in CNF, so first we convert this to CNF as follows:

$(A \wedge \neg B) \rightarrow C$

$\equiv \neg(A \wedge \neg B) \vee C$

$\equiv \neg A \vee B \vee C$

Now, to prove that our conclusion is valid, we need to show that

$$\{(\neg A, B, C), A, \neg B, \neg C\} \models \bot$$

We resolve these clauses as follows:

$$\{(B, C), \neg B, \neg C\}$$

$$\{C, \neg C\}$$

$$\bot$$

Hence, in showing that by negating our conclusion we lead to a contradiction, we have shown that our original conclusion must have been true.

If this process leads to a situation where some clauses are unresolved, and falsum cannot be reached, we have shown that the clauses with the negated conclusion are *not* contradictory and that therefore the original conclusion was not valid.

Because following resolution explanations in this way can be confusing, it is often preferable to present a resolution proof in the form of a tree, where pairs of resolved clauses are connected together, as shown in the following proof:

$$A \rightarrow B$$

$$B \rightarrow C$$

$$C \rightarrow D$$

$$D \rightarrow E \vee F$$

$$\therefore A \rightarrow F$$

First we negate the conclusion, to give: $\neg(A \rightarrow F)$. Next we convert to clause form:

$$D \rightarrow E \vee F$$

$$\equiv \neg D \vee (E \vee F)$$

and

$$\neg(A \rightarrow F)$$

$$\equiv \neg(\neg A \vee F)$$

$$\equiv A \wedge \neg F$$

So, our clauses are

$$\{(\neg A, B), (\neg B, C), (\neg C, D), (\neg D, E, F), A, \neg F)\}$$

Our proof in tree form is as follows:

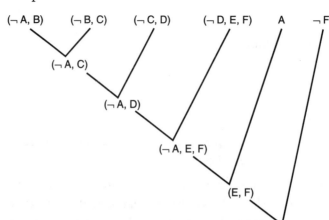

We have not been able to reach falsum because we are left with a single clause {E}, which cannot be resolved with anything. Hence, we can conclude that our original conclusion was not valid. You can prove this for yourself using a truth table.

8.3   Applications of Resolution

Clearly, resolution can be used to automate the process of proving whether a conclusion can be derived in a valid way from a set of premises or not. This is certainly useful, but resolution is not limited in its applications to just proving logical arguments.

A **combinatorial search problem** is a problem where there are a number of variables, each of which can be assigned a particular value. For example, a jigsaw puzzle can be seen as a problem where each piece is represented by a variable, and the position that each piece is placed in is the value assigned to that variable. Of course, the point of the puzzle is that there is only one correct way to place the pieces, so correspondingly, there would only be one set of assignments of values to variables that would be correct. We have already examined combinatorial search problems and seen ways to solve them in Chapter 5. Although resolution cannot help us to solve such problems, it can help by telling us whether a solution exists or not.

An example of a combinatorial search problem is the **three-coloring problem**: Given a map, is it possible to color the countries using three colors such that no two countries that are next to each other have the same color?

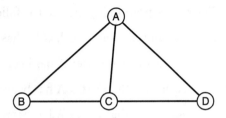

Figure 8.1
A graph representing a
three-coloring problem

A slightly more general version of the three-coloring problem for maps is to represent the countries in the three-coloring problem as nodes on a **graph**, as in Figure 8.1. The problem now is to assign values from a set of three possible values to each of the nodes in the graph, such that no two nodes that are joined by an edge have been assigned the same value.

For example, in the graph in Figure 8.1, the following assignments would be a suitable three-coloring:

   A = red

   B = green

   C = blue

   D = green

Note that in the graph shown in Figure 8.2, no suitable three-coloring exists.

Also note that some graphs do not represent maps of countries, as in the case of a graph with five nodes where every pair of nodes is connected by an edge. However, any map of countries can be represented by a graph, and solving the three-coloring problem for that graph is equivalent to solving the three-coloring problem for the map.

The three-coloring problem for graphs can be solved using resolution and propositional logic, by representing the graph as a set of clauses and determining whether the clauses can be satisfied.

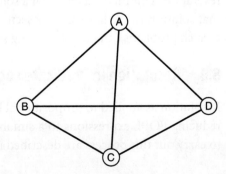

Figure 8.2
Graph that cannot be
three-colored

The representation is generated as follows:

First we can represent which color has been assigned to a vertex, as follows:

A_r means that vertex A has been colored red.

A_g means that vertex A has been colored green.

A_b means that vertex A has been colored blue.

And so on for all vertices.

Hence, for each vertex, we can generate the following set of clauses to represent that it must be given a color, but cannot be given more than one color:

$A_r \lor A_g \lor A_b$

$\neg A_r \lor \neg A_g \quad (\equiv A_r \rightarrow \neg A_g)$

$\neg A_g \lor \neg A_b$

$\neg A_b \lor \neg A_r$

Similarly, for each edge, we can represent the fact that the two nodes at either end of the edge must have different colors:

If (A,B) is an edge, then:

$\neg A_r \lor \neg B_r$

$\neg A_b \lor \neg B_b$

$\neg A_g \lor \neg B_g$

Now, if we $\land$ these sets of clauses together, and apply resolution to the result, we can see if the set is satisfiable. If so, then a three-coloring solution does exist for the graph. If not, then it does not.

In the same way, any instance of a combinatorial search problem can be represented as a set of clauses, and their satisfiability can be tested using resolution. This method tells us if a solution exists but does not tell us what that solution is. We have already seen in Part 2 of this book how solutions to such problems can be found using search.

8.4 Resolution in Predicate Logic

Resolution as applied to propositional logic can also be applied to FOPL by reducing FOPL expressions to a suitable normal form. The methods used to carry out this process are described in the following sections.

8.5   Normal Forms for Predicate Logic

To apply resolution to FOPL expressions, we first need to deal with the presence of the quantifiers $\forall$ and $\exists$. The method that is used is to move these quantifiers to the beginning of the expression, resulting in an expression that is in **prenex normal form**.

In converting a wff to prenex normal form, we use the same rules as we used to convert a wff to CNF:

1. $A \leftrightarrow B \equiv (A \rightarrow B) \wedge (B \rightarrow A)$

2. $A \rightarrow B \equiv \neg A \vee B$

3. $\neg(A \wedge B) \equiv \neg A \vee \neg B$

4. $\neg(A \vee B) \equiv \neg A \wedge \neg B$

5. $\neg\neg A \equiv A$

6. $A \vee (B \wedge C) \equiv (A \vee B) \wedge (A \vee C)$

In addition, we use the following rules to move the quantifiers to the front:

7. $\neg(\forall x)A(x) \equiv (\exists x)\neg A(x)$

8. $\neg(\exists x)A(x) \equiv (\forall x)\neg A(x)$

9. $(\forall x)A(x) \wedge B \equiv (\forall x)(A(x) \wedge B)$

10. $(\forall x)A(x) \vee B \equiv (\forall x)(A(x) \vee B)$

11. $(\exists x)A(x) \wedge B \equiv (\exists x)(A(x) \wedge B)$

12. $(\exists x)A(x) \vee B \equiv (\exists x)(A(x) \vee B)$

13. $(\forall x)A(x) \wedge (\forall y)B(y) \equiv (\forall x)(\forall y)(A(x) \wedge B(y))$

14. $(\forall x)A(x) \wedge (\exists y)B(y) \equiv (\forall x)(\exists y)(A(x) \wedge B(y))$

15. $(\exists x)A(x) \wedge (\forall y)B(y) \equiv (\exists x)(\forall y)(A(x) \wedge B(y))$

16. $(\exists x)A(x) \wedge (\exists y)B(y) \equiv (\exists x)(\exists y)(A(x) \wedge B(y))$

Note that rules 9, 10, 11, and 12 can be used only if x does not occur in B.

Let us briefly examine why some of these rules make logical sense. Rule 7, for example, can be stated in layman's terms as "if it is not true that all x's have property A, then there must exist some x for which A is not true." This is clearly valid.

Similarly, rule 8 states "if there does not exist an x for which A is true, then A is not true for any x."

Rules 9 through 12 take advantage of the fact that x is not present in B. Hence, if B is true, then it is also true for all x:

$$B \rightarrow \forall x B$$

provided x is not free in B.

Rules 13 through 16 similarly take advantage of the fact that x is not present in $B(y)$ and that y is not present in $A(x)$.

A further set of rules (17–20) can be generated by replacing $\land$ with $\lor$ in rules 13 through 16.

For example, let us convert the following wff to prenex normal form:

$$(\forall x)(A(x) \rightarrow B(x)) \rightarrow (\exists y)(A(y) \land B(y))$$

$$\neg(\forall x)(A(x) \rightarrow B(x)) \lor (\exists y)(A(y) \land B(y)) \tag{2}$$

$$\neg(\forall x)(\neg A(x) \lor B(x)) \lor (\exists y)(A(y) \land B(y)) \tag{2}$$

$$(\exists x)\neg(\neg A(x) \lor B(x)) \lor (\exists y)(A(y) \land B(y)) \tag{7}$$

$$(\exists x)(\neg\neg A(x) \land \neg B(x)) \lor (\exists y)(A(y) \land B(y)) \tag{4}$$

$$(\exists x)(A(x) \land \neg B(x)) \lor (\exists y)(A(y) \land B(y)) \tag{5}$$

$$(\exists x)(\exists y)((A(x) \land \neg B(x)) \lor (A(y) \land B(y))) \tag{19}$$

$$(\exists x)(\exists y)(((A(x) \lor A(y)) \land (\neg B(x) \lor A(y)) \land (A(x) \lor B(y)) \land (\neg B(x) \lor B(y)))) \tag{6}$$

8.6 Skolemization

Before resolution can be carried out on a wff, we need to eliminate all the existential quantifiers, $\exists$, from the wff.

This is done by replacing a variable that is existentially quantified by a constant, as in the following case:

$$\exists(x) \, P(x)$$

would be converted to

$$P(c)$$

where c is a constant *that has not been used elsewhere in the wff.* Although $P(c)$ is not logically equivalent to $\exists(x)\ P(x)$, we are able to make this substitution in the process of resolution because we are interested in seeing whether a solution exists. If there exists some x for which $P(x)$ holds, then we may as well select such an x and name it c. This process is called **skolemization**, and the variable c is called a **skolem constant**.

The variable c can be thought of as an example of a suitable value for x. It is extremely important that c not appear anywhere else in the expression because that would create a conflict. Imagine, for example, replacing x with b in the following expression:

$$\exists x(x \vee b)$$

This would leave us with

$$b \vee b$$

which reduces to

$$b$$

This clearly is not the same expression, and, in fact, it should be skolemized using a different constant, such as:

$$c \vee b$$

Skolemization must proceed slightly differently in cases where the $\exists$ follows a $\forall$ quantifier, as in the following example:

$$(\forall x)(\exists y)(P(x,y))$$

In this case, rather than replacing y with a skolem constant, we must replace it with a **skolem function**, such as in the following:

$$(\forall x)(P(x,f(x)))$$

Note that the skolem function is a function of the variable that is universally quantified, in this case, x.

Having removed the existential quantifiers in this way, the wff is said to be in **skolem normal form**, and has been **skolemized.**

8.6.1 Example of Skolemization

The following expression

$$(\forall x)(\exists y)(\forall z)(P(x) \wedge Q(y,\ z))$$

would be skolemized as follows:

$$(\forall x)(\forall z)(P(x) \wedge Q(f(x), z)$$

Note that *y* has been replaced by *f(x)* because $\exists y$ occurred *after* $\forall x$.

8.6.2   Second Example of Skolemization

The following expression:

$$(\forall w)(\forall x)(\exists y)(\forall z)(P(x) \wedge Q(w, y, z))$$

would be skolemized as follows:

$$(\forall w)(\forall x)(\forall z)(P(x) \wedge Q(w, f(w,x), z)$$

Here *y* has been replaced by a function of both *w* and *x*: f(w,x) because $\exists y$ occurred after $\forall w$ and $\forall x$.

To proceed with resolution, this wff must now be represented as set of clauses. To do this, we first drop the universal quantifiers. Hence, our expression above will be represented as the following set of two clauses:

$$\{(P(x)), (Q(w, f(w,x), z))\}$$

8.6.3   Unification

To carry out resolution on wff's in FOPL, we need to carry out one final stage, which is to make **substitutions**.

For example, if we had the following set of clauses:

$$\{(P(w,x)), (\neg P(y,z))\}$$

It seems clear that we should be able to resolve *P* with ¬*P*, but they are not currently identical because they have different arguments. These clauses can be resolved by making a **substitution**. We will replace *w* with *y* and *x* with *z*, to result in the following clauses:

$$\{(P(y,z)), (\neg P(y,z))\}$$

These can now clearly be resolved to give falsum.

The substitution that was made here can be written as

$$\{y/w, z/x\}$$

In this case, it was easy to see which substitution to make, but with more complex clauses, it can be harder. A formal process exists for determining how to make these substitutions, which of course means the process can be automated.

In general, we use the symbol σ to indicate a substitution, and we can write

$\sigma = \{y/w, z/x\}$

$A = P(w,x)$

$B = \neg P(y,z)$

$A\sigma = P(y,z)$

$B\sigma = \neg P(y,z)$

In general, if a substitution can be applied to a set of clauses $\{A, B, C, \ldots\}$ such that

$A\sigma = B\sigma = C\sigma = \ldots$

Then σ is called a **unifier** for the set $\{A, B, C, \ldots\}$.

In some cases, more than one substitution needs to be applied to produce a form that can be resolved. The operator, o, can be applied to two substitutions to provide the **composition** of those two substitutions, which produces a third substitution that is effectively the same as applying both substitutions.

Let us take two substitutions $\sigma 1$ and $\sigma 2$, defined as follows:

$\sigma 1 = \{a_1/x_1, a_2/x_2, \ldots, a_m/x_m\}$

$\sigma 2 = \{b_1/y_1, b_2/y_2, \ldots, b_n/y_n\}$

Now we define the composition of these two substitutions as follows:

$\sigma 1 \text{ o } \sigma 2 = \{a_1\sigma 2/x_1, a_2\sigma 2/x_2, \ldots, a_n\sigma 2/x_n, b_1/y_1, b_2/y_2, \ldots, b_n/y_n\}$

Certain elements on the composite set can be eliminated:

If $y_i = x_j$ then b_i/y_i can be eliminated.

If $a_i\sigma 2 = x_i$ then $a_i\sigma 2/x_i$ can be eliminated.

For example, let us form the composition of the following two substitutions:

$\sigma 1 = \{a/x, x/y, f(a)/z\}$

$\sigma 2 = \{y/x, f(z)/y\}$

$\sigma 1 \text{ o } \sigma 2 = \{a\sigma 2/x, x\sigma 2/y, f(a)\sigma 2/z, y/x, f(z)/y\}$

$\qquad\qquad = \{a/x, y/y, f(a)/z, y/x, f(z)/y\}$

$\qquad\qquad = \{a/x, f(a)/z, f(z)/y\}$

Notice that y/y is removed because this is a form of $a_i\sigma2 = x_i$ and that y/x is removed because this matches the elimination rule where $y_i = x_j$.

Now let us find $\sigma2 \text{ o } \sigma1$:

$$\sigma1 = \{a/x, x/y, f(a)/z\}$$

$$\sigma2 = \{y/x, f(z)/y\}$$

$$\sigma2 \text{ o } \sigma1 = \{y\sigma1/x, f(z)\sigma1/y, a/x, x/y, f(a)/z\}$$

$$= \{x/x, f(f(a))/y, a/x, x/y, f(a)/z\}$$

$$= \{f(f(a))/y, f(a)/z\}$$

Hence, the o operator is not commutative, as $\sigma1 \text{ o } \sigma2 \neq \sigma2 \text{ o } \sigma1$.

Some rules determine the way in which unifiers can be applied:

1. A constant, such as a, cannot be replaced by a variable.

2. A variable x cannot be replaced by a term that contains x.

Hence, for example, the following substitutions are not valid unifiers:

$$\{P(x)/x\}$$

$$\{x/a\}$$

8.6.4   Most General Unifiers

A unifier u_1 is called a **most general unifier** for a set $S = \{A, B, C, \dots\}$ if any other unifier u_2 can be expressed as the composition of u_1 with some other substitution (i.e., $u_2 = u_1 \text{ o } u_3$).

A most general unifier (**mgu**) is a unique unifier that provides the most general set of substitutions to unify a set of clauses. By most general, we mean where possible variables are used in place of constants because constants are specific and variables are general.

8.6.5   Unification Algorithm

To automate the process of resolution in FOPL, we need an algorithm for generating a most general unifier, in order to put clauses in a form that can be resolved.

The unification algorithm is expressed as follows:

To unify a set of clauses, S_0:

> Initialize: $\sigma_0 = \{\}$
>
> > $i = 0$

> Loop: If S_i has only one element, terminate and report that σ_i is the mgu for S_0.
>
> If S_i has more than one element, find the **disagreement** set D_i of S_i (i.e., the substitutions that need to be made).
>
> If D_i contains a variable x and a term t where x is not contained within t, then we say:
>
> > $\sigma_{i+1} = \sigma_i \circ \{t/x\}$
> >
> > $S_{i+1} = S_i \{t/x\}$
>
> Increment i, and repeat the loop.

8.6.6 Unification Example

Let us find the mgu for the following set of clauses:

> $S_0 = \{P(a, x, y, z), P(x, y, z, w)\}$

(a is a constant, and x, y, z are variables).

We initialize $\sigma_0 = \{\}$ and $i = 0$.

Now we proceed as follows:

> $D_0 = \{a,x\}$
>
> $\sigma_1 = \sigma_0 \circ \{a/x\} = \{a/x\}$
>
> $S_1 = S_0 \{a/x\} = \{P(a, a, y, z), P(a, y, z, w)\}$
>
> $D_1 = \{a,y\}$
>
> $\sigma_2 = \{a/x\} \circ \{a/y\} = \{a/x, a/y\}$
>
> $S_2 = S_1 \{a/x, a/y\} = \{P(a, a, a, z), P(a, a, z, w)\}$
>
> $D_2 = \{a, z\}$
>
> $\sigma_3 = \{a/x, a/y\} \circ \{a/z\} = \{a/x, a/y, a/z\}$
>
> $S_3 = S_2 \{a/x, a/y, a/z\} = \{P(a, a, a, a), P(a, a, a, w)\}$

$$D_3 = \{a, w\}$$

$$\sigma_4 = \{a/x, a/y, a/z\} \text{ o } \{a/w\} = \{a/x, a/y, a/z, a/w\}$$

$$S_4 = S_3 \{a/x, a/y, a/z, a/w\} = \{P(a, a, a, a), P(a, a, a, a)\}$$

$$= \{P(a, a, a, a)\}$$

Now we stop because S_4 has just one element, and we have found a mgu, σ_4, which is $\{a/x, a/y, a/z, a/w\}$.

The following is also a unifier of S_0:

$$\sigma_5 = \{x/a, x/y, x/z, x/w\}$$

However, this is not a mgu because we can find another substitution σ_6 such that the composition $\sigma_5 \text{ o } \sigma_6$ gives the mgu, σ_4:

$$\{x/a, x/y, x/z, x/w\} \text{ o } \{a/x\}$$

gives

$$\{x\{a/x\}/a, x\{a/x\}/y, x\{a/x\}/z, x\{a/x\}/w\}$$

which in turn leads to

$$\{a/a, a/x, a/y, a/z, a/w\}$$

We can eliminate a/a, which gives us

$$\{a/x, a/y, a/z, a/w\}$$

which is the mgu σ_4. because σ_4 is a mgu, we could find another substitution σ_x for any other unifier σ_u, such that $\sigma_u \text{ o } \sigma_x = \sigma_4$.

8.7   Resolution Algorithm

Now we have all the tools we need to produce an automated system for generating proofs using resolution on FOPL expressions. Given a set of assumptions and a conclusion, we can prove whether the assumption logically follows from the assumptions as follows:

- First, negate the conclusion and add it to the list of assumptions.

- Now convert the assumptions into prenex normal form.

- Next, skolemize the resulting expression.

- Now convert the expression into a set of clauses.

Now we resolve the clauses using the following method:

If our clauses are $\{A, B, C, \ldots\}$ and A has a literal L_A and B has a literal L_B such that L_A and $\neg L_B$ have a mgu σ, then we can resolve A and B to give the resolvent of these clauses, which is:

$$(A\sigma - L_A\sigma) \bigcup (B\sigma - L_B\sigma)$$

where $\cup$ is the set union operator, and $-$ is the set difference operator. For example, in resolving the following clauses:

$$\{A(x,y), B(f(y)), C(x, y, z)\}$$

$$\{A(f(x), z), \neg B(z), C(f(a), b, z)\}$$

we note that $B(f(y))$ and $B(z)$ have a mgu that is $\{f(y)/z\}$. Hence, we apply this unifier to the two clauses to give:

$$\{A(x,y), B(f(y)), C(x, y, z)\}\{f(y)/z\} - B(f(y))\{f(y)/z\}$$

$$\bigcup (A(f(x), z), \neg B(z), C(f(a), b, z)) - \neg B(z)\{f(y)/z\}$$

$$= \{A(x,y), C(x, y, z)\} \cup \{A(f(x), z), C(f(a), b, z)\}$$

$$= \{A(x,y), C(x, y, z), A(f(x), z), C(f(a), b, z)\}$$

In this way, we have removed the two literals $\neg B(z)$ and $B(f(y))$, and by continuing this process until no further literals can be resolved, a set of clauses can be tested for contradiction. Note that each stage of this process can be expressed as an algorithm, and so the process of resolution can be used by computers to prove the validity of deductions in FOPL.

8.8   Horn Clauses and PROLOG

A **Horn clause**, or **Horn sentence**, is a clause that has, at most, one positive literal. Hence, the following Horn clause takes the following form:

$$A \vee \neg B \vee \neg C \vee \neg D \vee \neg E \ldots$$

where $A, B, C, D, E,$ and so on are positive literals.

This Horn clause can also be written as an implication:

$$B \wedge C \wedge D \wedge E \rightarrow A$$

In the programming language PROLOG, this would be written in reverse, with the conclusion on the left, as follows:

$$A :- B, C, D, E$$

Horn clauses can take three forms. The type we have seen above, where there is one positive literal, and one or more negative literals is called a **rule relation**.

A clause with no negative literals is called a **fact**:

   A :–

Finally, a clause with no positive literal is called a **goal**, or a **headless clause**:

   :– B, C, D, E

Unfortunately, not all expressions can be represented as Horn clauses (e.g., $A \lor B$). However, this representation does have the benefit of efficiency, and it also means that if a set of clauses has a contradiction, then resolution by **depth-first search** (see Chapter 4) is guaranteed to result in the empty clause

   :–

thus proving the original assertion.

A program in PROLOG consists of a set of Horn clauses. PROLOG applies unification and resolution to attempt to derive conclusions from a set of rules that are defined in the language.

In fact, the programmer is able to define **rules** and **facts**, and to set up a goal that the PROLOG system must attempt to prove, using unification and resolution.

Rules and their uses in programming are briefly mentioned in Chapter 3 and are examined in more detail in Chapter 9.

The rule for resolution in PROLOG can be expressed as follows:

$$\frac{D :– A, B, \ldots \qquad G:– D, E, \ldots}{G :– A, B, E, \ldots}$$

Hence, for example, a PROLOG programmer might start by establishing the following facts:

   speaks (Bob, French).

   spoken_in (French, France).

   located_in (Task1, France).

Next, the programmer writes a rule:

   assign_task (X, P) :– located_in (X, C),

                          spoken_in (L, C),

                          speaks (P, L)

Finally, the goal is set up:

>   assign_task (Task1, Bob)

This is simply asking, should Task1 be assigned to Bob?

First, the system needs to use unification to be able to carry out resolution.

Clearly, our goal could be resolved with the rule if we made the following substitution:

>   {Task1 / X, Bob / P}

After applying this substitution and resolution, we are left with a new goal:

>   :—   located_in (Task1, C),
>
>   spoken_in (L, C),
>
>   speaks (Bob, L)

Now we apply a further substitution:

>   {France / C, French / L}

which enables us to resolve this new goal with the three established facts to result in the empty clause:

>   :—

Hence, the goal has been proved.

8.9   Herbrand Universes

For a set of clauses, S, the **Herbrand universe**, H_S, is defined as being the set of constants that are contained within S, and the set of functions in S applied to those constants. These constants and functions are known as **ground terms** because they do not contain variables.

For example,

>   S is {{A(x), B(y, a), C(z)}, {D(x, a, b), ¬E(y, c, b)}}

then H_S, the Herbrand universe of S, is defined as follows:

> H_S = {a, b, c}

Because there are no functions in S, the Herbrand universe consists just of the constants in S, which are a, b, and c.

A further example follows:

   S is {{A(x), B(y, a), C(z)}, {D(x, a, b), ¬E(y, f(x, y))}}

In this case, where S contains a function, the Herbrand universe is infinite:

   H_S = {a, b, c, f(a, a), f(a, b), f (b, a), f(b, b), f(f(a), a), f(f(a), f(a)) . . . }

In the following case, S contains no functions or constants:

   S is {{A(x), B(y, z), C(z)}, {D(x, y, z), ¬E(y, x)}}

In such cases, we define the Herbrand universe to contain the constant a:

   H_S = {a}

A **ground instance** of a clause in S is a version of that clause in which any variables it contains have been replaced by ground terms from H_S.

For instance, given the following definition of S:

   S is {{A(x), B(y, a), C(z)}, {D(x, a, b), ¬E(y, c, b)}}

a ground instance of the first clause could be

   {A(a), B(b, a), C(a)}

Another ground instance of the same clause is

   {A(c), B(a, a), C(c)}

8.9.1 The Herbrand Base

The **Herbrand base** of S, $H_S(S)$, is defined as the set of **ground atoms** that can be obtained by replacing variables in S by members of H_S. A ground atom is a formula that contains no variables, only ground terms.

For example,

   S is {{A(x), B(y, a), C(z)}, {D(x, a, b), ¬E(y, c, b)}}

then

   H_S = {a, b, c}

and

   $H_S(S)$ = {{A(a), B(a, a), C(a), D(a, a, b), ¬E(a, c, b),

   A(b), B(b, a), C(b), D(b, a, b), ¬E(b, c, b),

   . . . }

In this case, where there are no functions in S, the Herbrand base is finite (although it will consist of a large number of clauses). As with the Herbrand universe, if the clauses contain functions, then the Herbrand base will be infinite.

8.9.2 Herbrand Interpretations

A **Herbrand interpretation** for S is defined as a set of assignments of true and false to the elements of the Herbrand base, $H_S(S)$.

For example,

S is $\{\{A(x, y), B(a, x)\}, \{\neg C(z, a), D(a, z)\}$

$H_S = \{a\}$

$H_S(S) = \{A(a, a), B(a, a), C(a, a), D(a, a)\}$

Then two possible Herbrand interpretations of S are

$\{\neg A(a, a), B(a, a), C(a, a), D(a, a)\}$

$\{A(a, a), \neg B(a, a), C(a, a), \neg D(a, a)\}$

In the first interpretation, all the elements of $H_S(S)$ have been assigned the value *true*, apart from $A(a, a)$, which has been assigned *false*. In general, if we assign a value *true* to A, we write A, and if we assign the value *false* to A, we write $\neg A$. In the second interpretation, the second and fourth elements of $H_S(S)$ have been assigned the value *false*, and the first and third have been assigned the value *true*.

For this set, S, there will be 16 possible Herbrand interpretations because there are four elements in the Herbrand base. In general, if there are n elements in the Herbrand base, there will be 2^n Herbrand interpretations.

Now we come back to the idea of satisfiability. In some cases, a given Herbrand interpretation of a set S will be set to **satisfy** S.

Let us use our previous example again:

S is $\{\{A(x, y), B(a, x)\}, \{\neg C(z, a), D(a, z)\}$

We presented two Herbrand interpretations for this S:

$\{\neg A(a, a), B(a, a), C(a, a), D(a, a)\}$

$\{A(a, a), \neg B(a, a), C(a, a), \neg D(a, a)\}$

Now we say that a given interpretation for S satisfies S if the assignments from the interpretation make each clause in S true.

For example, replacing the variables in S with the constants from the Herbrand universe, we get the following:

$$\{\{A(a, a), B(a, a)\}, \{\neg C(a, a), D(a, a)\}$$

Now, if we use the first interpretation where $A(a, a)$ was the only element that had been assigned the value *false*, we see that the clauses become

$$\{\{false, true\}, \{false, true\}\}$$

Now, recall that clauses are a set of conjunctions of disjunctions, and so we can rewrite this as

$$(false \lor true) \land (false \lor true)$$

which clearly is true. Hence, this interpretation satisfies S.

Using the second interpretation, the clauses become

$$\{\{true, false\}, \{false, false\}\}$$

which is not true. So the second interpretation does not satisfy S.

It can be shown that if no Herbrand interpretation exists for a set of clauses S that satisfies S, then S is not satisfiable. This is, in fact, the basis for resolution because it can further be shown that if a set of clauses is unsatisfiable, then resolving that set of clauses will lead to falsum.

8.9.3   Example

We have seen that the satisfiability of a set of clauses can be proved or disproved by examining the Herbrand interpretations for the set. We now present an example:

$$S = \{\{\neg A(y, a), B(y)\}, \{\neg B(x)\}, \{B(a), A(x, a)\}\}$$

Then we can define the Herbrand universe as

$$H_S = \{a\}$$

Next, we define the Herbrand base:

$$H_S(S) = \{A(a, a), B(a)\}$$

Thus, there are four possible Herbrand interpretations for S:

1. $\{A(a, a), B(a)\}$
2. $\{A(a, a), \neg B(a)\}$
3. $\{\neg A(a, a), B(a)\}$
4. $\{\neg A(a, a), \neg B(a)\}$

You should be able to see that none of these interpretations satisfies S. Hence, we have proved that S is unsatisfiable.

8.10   Resolution for Problem Solving

Although it seems complex, resolution is made up a series of simple steps. Because each of those steps can be readily automated, resolution is widely used. As has already been explained, PROLOG systems use resolution to solve problems.

Let us now see how resolution can be used to solve a simple logic problem.

Consider the following set of premises:

1.   Some children will eat any food.
2.   No children will eat food that is green.
3.   All children like food made by Cadbury's.

We now wish to prove that the following conclusion follows from these premises:

No food made by Cadbury's is green.

First, we need to represent the premises and the conclusion in predicate calculus. We will use the following symbols:

$C(x)$ means "x is a child."

$F(x)$ means "x is food."

$L(x, y)$ means "x likes y."

$G(x)$ means "x is green."

$M(x, y)$ means "x makes y."

c means "Cadbury's."

So our premises can be represented as:

1. $(\exists x)(C(x) \wedge (\forall y)(F(y) \rightarrow L(x,y)))$

2. $(\forall x)(C(x) \rightarrow (\forall y)((F(y) \wedge G(y)) \rightarrow \neg L(x,y)))$

3. $(\forall x)((F(x) \wedge M(c,x)) \rightarrow (\forall y)(C(y) \rightarrow L(y,x)))$

Our conclusion can be represented as follows:

$(\forall x)((F(x) \wedge M(c,x)) \rightarrow \neg G(x))$

First, we must negate the conclusion and add it to the set of premises, which means we must now prove that the following expression cannot be satisfied:

$(\exists x)(C(x) \wedge (\forall y)(F(y) \rightarrow L(x,y)))$

$\wedge (\forall x)(C(x) \rightarrow (\forall y)((F(y) \wedge G(y)) \rightarrow \neg L(x,y)))$

$\wedge (\forall x)((F(x) \wedge M(c,x)) \rightarrow (\forall y)(C(y) \rightarrow L(y,x)))$

$\wedge \neg ((\forall x)((F(x) \wedge M(c,x)) \rightarrow \neg G(x)))$

We will convert this into a set of clauses, starting with expression 1:

$(\exists x)(C(x) \wedge (\forall y)(F(y) \rightarrow L(x,y)))$

$\rightarrow$ must be eliminated first:

$(\exists x)(C(x) \wedge (\forall y)(\neg F(y) \vee L(x,y)))$

Next, we bring the quantifiers to the front of the expression:

$(\exists x)(\forall y)(C(x) \wedge (\neg F(y) \vee L(x,y)))$

Now we skolemize this expression, to eliminate the existential quantifier:

$(\forall y)(C(a) \wedge (\neg F(y) \vee L(a,y)))$

This can be expressed as the following clauses:

$\{C(a)\}, \{\neg F(y), L(a,y)\}$

Next, we deal with expression 2 in the same way:

$(\forall x)(C(x) \rightarrow (\forall y)((F(y) \wedge G(y)) \rightarrow \neg L(x,y)))$

$\rightarrow$ is eliminated first:

$(\forall x)(\neg C(x) \vee (\forall y)(\neg (F(y) \wedge G(y)) \vee \neg L(x,y)))$

Now DeMorgan's law is applied:

$$(\forall x)(\neg C(x) \vee (\forall y)(\neg F(y) \vee \neg G(y) \vee \neg L(x,y)))$$

Quantifiers are moved to the front:

$$(\forall x)(\forall y)(\neg C(x) \vee \neg F(y) \vee \neg G(y) \vee \neg L(x,y))$$

This can be written as the following single clause:

$$\{\neg C(x), \neg F(y), \neg(G(y), \neg L(x,y)\}$$

Now, for expression 3:

$$(\forall x)((F(x) \wedge M(c,x)) \rightarrow (\forall y)(C(y) \rightarrow L(y,x)))$$

We first eliminate →:

$$(\forall x)(\neg(F(x) \wedge M(c,x)) \vee (\forall y)(\neg C(y) \vee L(y,x)))$$

Next, we apply DeMorgan's law:

$$(\forall x)(\neg F(x) \vee \neg M(c,x) \vee (\forall y)(\neg C(y) \vee L(y,x)))$$

Now we bring the quantifiers to the front of the expression:

$$(\forall x)(\forall y)(\neg F(x) \vee \neg M(c,x) \vee \neg C(y) \vee L(y,x))$$

This can be expressed as the following single clause:

$$\{\neg F(x), \neg M(c,x), \neg C(y), L(y,x)\}$$

Now we deal with the conclusion, which has been negated:

$$\neg(\forall x)((F(x) \wedge M(c,x)) \rightarrow \neg G(x))$$

First, we eliminate →:

$$\neg(\forall x)(\neg(F(x) \wedge M(c,x)) \vee \neg G(x))$$

Now we apply the quantifier equivalence to move the ¬ from the front of the expression:

$$(\exists x)\neg(\neg(F(x) \wedge M(c,x)) \vee \neg G(x))$$

DeMorgan's law can now be applied:

$$(\exists x)(\neg\neg(F(x) \wedge M(c,x)) \wedge \neg\neg G(x))$$

We can now remove ¬¬:

$$(\exists x)(F(x) \wedge M(c,x) \wedge G(x))$$

This expression is now skolemized:

$$F(b) \wedge M(c,b) \wedge G(b))$$

This can be expressed as the following set of clauses:

$$\{\{F(b)\}, \{M(c,b)\}, \{G(b)\}\}$$

Now we have arrived at a set of clauses, upon which resolution can be applied. The clauses we have are the following:

1. $\{C(a)\}$
2. $\{\neg F(y), L(a,y)\}$
3. $\{\neg C(x), \neg F(y), \neg(G(y), \neg L(x,y)\}$
4. $\{\neg F(x), \neg M(c,x), \neg C(y), L(y,x)\}$
5. $\{F(b)\}$
6. $\{M(c,b)\}$
7. $\{G(b)\}$

We now apply resolution as follows:

First, we unify lines 1 and 3 using $\{a/x\}$ and resolve these two, to give

8. $\{\neg F(y), \neg(G(y), \neg L(a,y)\}$

Similarly, the unifier $\{b/y\}$ can be applied to lines 2 and 5, which are then resolved to give

9. $\{L(a,b)\}$

Now we apply $\{b/y\}$ to resolve line 5 with line 8 to give

10. $\{\neg(G(b), \neg L(a,b)\}$

Now lines 9 and 10 can be resolved to give

11. $\{\neg(G(b)\}$

Finally, line 7 can be resolved with line 11 to give

12. $\perp$

Hence, we have proven that the set of clauses derived from the premises 1, 2, and 3, and the negation of the conclusion, are unsatisfiable. Thus we have successfully proved that the conclusion does indeed follow from the premises, and so the argument is a valid one.

8.11   Chapter Summary

- Any well-formed formula (wff) can be expressed in conjunctive normal form (CNF) or disjunctive normal form (DNF). An expression in CNF is a conjunction of disjunctions, and an expression in DNF is a disjunction of conjunctions.

- An algorithm can be generated that will convert any wff into CNF.

- The resolution rule says that if you know $(A \lor B)$ and you know $(\neg B \lor C)$, then you can eliminate the instances of B from these two expressions, to produce $(A \lor C)$.

- By negating a conclusion, and proving that the resultant set of expressions is unsatisfiable, one can prove that an argument is valid. Such reasoning is called proof by refutation (or proof by contradiction). The traditional method for using resolution is to prove arguments valid by refutation.

- Any combinatorial problem can be represented as a set of clauses, and the existence of a solution to the problem can be determined using resolution on those clauses.

- To apply resolution in first-order predicate logic, an expression needs to be first converted to prenex normal form (where the quantifiers are at the beginning) and then skolemized, which involves removing variables that are existentially quantified by replacing them with constants and functions.

- Unification involves using a unifier to resolve two similar clauses that do not have the same variables. An algorithm can be generated to unify any sets of clauses that can be unified.

- A unifier u_1 is a most general unifier if any other unifier, u_2, can be expressed as the composition of u_1 with another unifier, u_3: $u_2 = u_1 \circ u_3$.

- Resolution can be applied to a set of clauses that have been skolemized. This process can be automated because each step can be expressed algorithmically.

- A Horn clause is one with, at most, one positive literal. PROLOG uses resolution on Horn clauses to solve problems.

- If no Herbrand interpretation exists for a set of clauses that satisfies that set, then the clauses are not satisfiable.

8.12   Review Questions

8.1   Explain the concept of proof by refutation.

8.2   Explain how and to what extent combinatorial problems can be solved using resolution.

8.3   Explain what is meant by prenex normal form and skolem normal form.

8.4   Explain each step of the algorithm for resolution in first-order predicate logic.

8.5   Explain the following terms:

- Herbrand universe
- Herbrand base
- Herbrand interpretation

8.13   Exercises

8.1   Convert the following expression to CNF and to DNF:

$$A \vee (B \wedge C) \vee (D \wedge E \wedge \neg (A \vee B))$$

8.2   Convert the following expressions to a set of clauses:

$$(\forall x)(P(x) \rightarrow (A(x) \wedge B(x) \vee \neg C(x, a))$$

$$(\exists y)(Q(y, a) \wedge ((\forall z) A(z) \rightarrow \neg B(y))).$$

8.3   Prove that the resolution rule is valid.

8.4   Generate the full set of clauses for the map-coloring graph in Figure 8.1. Resolve these clauses to prove that a three-coloring solution does exist for the graph.

8.5   Use resolution to determine whether the following is valid:

$$(((\forall x)(A (x) \rightarrow B(x))) \wedge (\neg B(x))) \rightarrow \neg A(x)$$

8.6   Use resolution to determine whether the following is valid:

$$(\forall x)(\exists y) (((A (x) \wedge B(y)) \rightarrow (A (y) \wedge B(x))) \rightarrow (A(x) \rightarrow B(x)))$$

8.7   Use resolution to prove that the following logical argument, devised by Lewis Carroll, is valid:

No shark ever doubts that it is well fitted out

A fish, that cannot dance a minuet, is contemptible

No fish is quite certain that it is well fitted out, unless it has three rows of teeth

All fishes, except sharks, are kind to children

No heavy fish can dance a minuet

A fish with three rows of teeth is not to be despised

Conclusion:

No heavy fish is unkind to children

8.14 Further Reading

Resolution is covered by most of the standard Artificial Intelligence texts, but you may need to look in the specialized books such as Chang and Lee (1973) to find deeper coverage of the subject. Reeves (1990) provides a good introduction to resolution.

A Resolution Principle for a Logic With Restricted Quantifiers by H. J. Burckert (1992 – Springer Verlag)

The Resolution Calculus by Alexander Leitsch (1997 – Springer Verlag)

Automated Theorem Proving: A Logical Basis by Donald W. Loveland (1978 – Elsevier Science – out of print)

Automated Theorem Proving: Theory and Practice by Monty Newborn (2001 – Springer Verlag)

Logic, Form and Function: The Mechanization of Deductive Reasoning by John Alan Robinson (1980 – Elsevier Science)

Using Sophisticated Models in Resolution Theorem Proving (Lecture Notes in Computer Science, Vol. 90) by David M. Sandford (1981 – Springer Verlag)

Resolution Proof Systems: An Algebraic Theory (Automated Reasoning Series, Vol. 4) by Zbigniew Stachniak (1996 – Kluwer Academic Publishers)

Symbolic Logic and Mechanical Theorem Proving by Chin-Liang Chang and Richard Char-Tung Lee (1973 – Academic Press)

CHAPTER 9

Rules and Expert Systems

Any problem that can be solved by your in-house expert in a 10–30 minute telephone call can be developed as an expert system.

— M. Firebaugh, *Artificial Intelligence: A Knowledge-Based Approach*

'Rule Forty-two. All persons more than a mile high to leave the court.'
'That's not a regular rule: you invented it just now.'
'It's the oldest rule in the book,' said the King.
'Then it ought to be number one,' said Alice.

— Lewis Carroll, *Alice's Adventures in Wonderland*

These so-called expert systems were often right, in the specific areas for which they had been built, but they were extremely brittle. Given even a simple problem just slightly beyond their expertise, they would usually get a wrong answer. Ask a medical program about a rusty old car, and it might blithely diagnose measles.

— Douglas B. Lenat, *Programming Artificial Intelligence*

9.1 Introduction

In this chapter, we introduce the ideas behind production systems, or expert systems, and explain how they can be built using rule-based systems, frames, or a combination of the two.

This chapter explains techniques such as forward and backward chaining, conflict resolution, and the Rete algorithm. It also explains the architecture of an expert system and describes the roles of the individuals who are involved in designing, building, and using expert systems.

9.2   Rules for Knowledge Representation

One way to represent knowledge is by using rules that express what must happen or what does happen when certain conditions are met. Rules are usually expressed in the form of IF . . . THEN . . . statements, such as:

> IF A THEN B

This can be considered to have a similar logical meaning as the following:

> $A \rightarrow B$

As we saw in Chapter 7, A is called the antecedent and B is the consequent in this statement. In expressing rules, the consequent usually takes the form of an **action** or a **conclusion**. In other words, the purpose of a rule is usually to tell a system (such as an **expert system**) what to do in certain circumstances, or what conclusions to draw from a set of inputs about the current situation.

In general, a rule can have more than one antecedent, usually combined either by AND or by OR (logically the same as the operators $\wedge$ and $\vee$ we saw in Chapter 7). Similarly, a rule may have more than one consequent, which usually suggests that there are multiple actions to be taken.

In general, the antecedent of a rule compares an **object** with a possible **value**, using an **operator**. For example, suitable antecedents in a rule might be

> IF $x > 3$
>
> IF name is "Bob"
>
> IF weather is cold

Here, the objects being considered are x, name, and weather; the operators are ">" and "is", and the values are 3, "Bob," and cold. Note that an object is not necessarily an object in the real-world sense—the weather is not a real-world object, but rather a state or condition of the world. An object in this sense is simply a variable that represents some physical object or state in the real world.

An example of a rule might be

IF name is "Bob"

AND weather is cold

THEN tell Bob 'Wear a coat'

This is an example of a **recommendation** rule, which takes a set of inputs and gives advice as a result. The conclusion of the rule is actually an action, and the action takes the form of a recommendation to Bob that he should wear a coat. In some cases, the rules provide more definite actions such as "move left" or "close door," in which case the rules are being used to represent **directives**.

Rules can also be used to represent relations such as:

IF temperature is below 0

THEN weather is cold

9.3   Rule-Based Systems

Rule-based systems or **production systems** are computer systems that use rules to provide recommendations or diagnoses, or to determine a course of action in a particular situation or to solve a particular problem.

A rule-based system consists of a number of components:

- a database of rules (also called a **knowledge base**)
- a database of facts
- an **interpreter**, or **inference engine**

In a rule-based system, the knowledge base consists of a set of rules that represent the knowledge that the system has. The database of facts represents inputs to the system that are used to derive conclusions, or to cause actions.

The interpreter, or inference engine, is the part of the system that controls the process of deriving conclusions. It uses the rules and facts, and combines them together to draw conclusions.

As we will see, these conclusions are often derived using deduction, although there are other possible approaches. Using deduction to reach a conclusion from a set of antecedents is called **forward chaining**. An alternative method, **backward chaining**, starts from a conclusion and tries to show it by following a logical path backward from the conclusion to a set of antecedents that are in the database of facts.

9.3.1   Forward Chaining

Forward chaining employs the same deduction method that we saw in Chapter 7. In other words, the system starts from a set of facts, and a set of rules, and tries to find a way of using those rules and facts to deduce a conclusion or come up with a suitable course of action.

This is known as **data-driven reasoning** because the reasoning starts from a set of data and ends up at the goal, which is the conclusion.

When applying forward chaining, the first step is to take the facts in the fact database and see if any combination of these matches all the antecedents of one of the rules in the rule database. When all the antecedents of a rule are matched by facts in the database, then this rule is **triggered**. Usually, when a rule is triggered, it is then **fired**, which means its conclusion is added to the facts database. If the conclusion of the rule that has fired is an action or a recommendation, then the system may cause that action to take place or the recommendation to be made.

For example, consider the following set of rules that is used to control an elevator in a three-story building:

Rule 1

IF on first floor and button is pressed on first floor

THEN open door

Rule 2

IF	on first floor
AND	button is pressed on second floor
THEN	go to second floor

Rule 3

IF	on first floor
AND	button is pressed on third floor
THEN	go to third floor

Rule 4

| IF | on second floor |
| AND | button is pressed on first floor |

AND	already going to third floor
THEN	remember to go to first floor later

This represents just a subset of the rules that would be needed, but we can use it to illustrate how forward chaining works.

Let us imagine that we start with the following facts in our database:

Fact 1

At first floor

Fact 2

Button pressed on third floor

Fact 3

Today is Tuesday

Now the system examines the rules and finds that Facts 1 and 2 match the antecedents of Rule 3. Hence, Rule 3 fires, and its conclusion

Go to third floor

is added to the database of facts. Presumably, this results in the elevator heading toward the third floor. Note that Fact 3 was ignored altogether because it did not match the antecedents of any of the rules.

Now let us imagine that the elevator is on its way to the third floor and has reached the second floor, when the button is pressed on the first floor. The fact

Button pressed on first floor

Is now added to the database, which results in Rule 4 firing. Now let us imagine that later in the day the facts database contains the following information:

Fact 1

At first floor

Fact 2

Button pressed on second floor

Fact 3

Button pressed on third floor

In this case, two rules are triggered—Rules 2 and 3. In such cases where there is more than one possible conclusion, **conflict resolution** needs to be applied to decide which rule to fire.

9.3.2   Conflict Resolution

In a situation where more than one conclusion can be deduced from a set of facts, there are a number of possible ways to decide which rule to fire (i.e., which conclusion to use or which course of action to take).

For example, consider the following set of rules:

IF it is cold

THEN wear a coat

IF it is cold

THEN stay at home

IF it is cold

THEN turn on the heat

If there is a single fact in the fact database, which is "it is cold," then clearly there are three conclusions that can be derived. In some cases, it might be fine to follow all three conclusions, but in many cases the conclusions are incompatible (for example, when prescribing medicines to patients).

In one conflict resolution method, rules are given priority levels, and when a conflict occurs, the rule that has the highest priority is fired, as in the following example:

IF patient has pain

THEN prescribe painkillers priority 10

IF patient has chest pain

THEN treat for heart disease priority 100

Here, it is clear that treating possible heart problems is more important than just curing the pain.

An alternative method is the **longest-matching strategy**. This method involves firing the conclusion that was derived from the longest rule. For example:

IF patient has pain

THEN prescribe painkiller

IF patient has chest pain

AND patient is over 60

AND patient has history of heart conditions

THEN take to emergency room

Here, if all the antecedents of the second rule match, then this rule's conclusion should be fired rather than the conclusion of the first rule because it is a more specific match.

A further method for conflict resolution is to fire the rule that has matched the facts most recently added to the database.

In each case, it may be that the system fires one rule and then stops (as in medical diagnosis), but in many cases, the system simply needs to choose a suitable ordering for the rules (as when controlling an elevator) because each rule that matches the facts needs to be fired at some point.

9.3.3   Meta Rules

In designing an expert system, it is necessary to select the conflict resolution method that will be used, and quite possibly it will be necessary to use different methods to resolve different types of conflicts. For example, in some situations it may make most sense to use the method that involves firing the most recently added rules. This method makes most sense in situations in which the timeliness of data is important. It might be, for example, that as research in a particular field of medicine develops, new rules are added to the system that contradict some of the older rules. It might make most sense for the system to assume that these newer rules are more accurate than the older rules.

It might also be the case, however, that the new rules have been added by an expert whose opinion is less trusted than that of the expert who added the earlier rules. In this case, it clearly makes more sense to allow the earlier rules priority.

This kind of knowledge is called **meta knowledge**—knowledge about knowledge. The rules that define how conflict resolution will be used, and how other aspects of the system itself will run, are called **meta rules**.

The knowledge engineer who builds the expert system is responsible for building appropriate meta knowledge into the system (such as "expert A is to be trusted more than expert B" or "any rule that involves drug X is not to be trusted as much as rules that do not involve X").

Meta rules are treated by the expert system as if they were ordinary rules but are given greater priority than the normal rules that make up the expert system. In this way, the meta rules are able to override the normal rules, if necessary, and are certainly able to control the conflict resolution process.

9.3.4   Backward Chaining

Forward chaining applies a set of rules and facts to deduce whatever conclusions can be derived, which is useful when a set of facts are present, but you do not know what conclusions you are trying to prove. In some cases, forward chaining can be inefficient because it may end up proving a number of conclusions that are not currently interesting. In such cases, where a single specific conclusion is to be proved, **backward chaining** is more appropriate.

In backward chaining, we start from a conclusion, which is the **hypothesis** we wish to prove, and we aim to show how that conclusion can be reached from the rules and facts in the database.

The conclusion we are aiming to prove is called a **goal**, and so reasoning in this way is known as **goal-driven reasoning**.

As we see in Chapter 16, backward chaining is often used in formulating plans. A plan is a sequence of actions that a program (such as an intelligent agent) decides to take to solve a particular problem. Backward chaining can make the process of formulating a plan more efficient than forward chaining.

Backward chaining in this way starts with the goal state, which is the set of conditions the agent wishes to achieve in carrying out its plan. It now examines this state and sees what actions could lead to it. For example, if the goal state involves a block being on a table, then one possible action would be to place that block on the table. This action might not be possible from the start state, and so further actions need to be added before this action in order to reach it from the start state. In this way, a plan can be formulated starting from the goal and working back toward the start state.

The benefit in this method is particularly clear in situations where the first state allows a very large number of possible actions. In this kind of situation, it can be very inefficient to attempt to formulate a plan using forward chaining because it involves examining every possible action, without paying any attention to which action might be the best one to lead to the goal state. Backward chaining ensures that each action that is taken is one that will definitely lead to the goal, and in many cases this will make the planning process far more efficient.

9.3.5 Comparing Forward and Backward Chaining

Let us use an example to compare forward and backward chaining. In this case, we will revert to our use of symbols for logical statements, in order to clarify the explanation, but we could equally well be using rules about elevators or the weather.

Rules:

```
Rule 1      A ∧ B → C
Rule 2      A → D
Rule 3      C ∧ D → E
Rule 4      B ∧ E ∧ F → G
Rule 5      A ∧ E → H
Rule 6      D ∧ E ∧ H → I
```

Facts:

```
Fact 1   A
Fact 2   B
Fact 3   F
```

Goal:

Our goal is to prove H.

First let us use forward chaining. As our conflict resolution strategy, we will fire rules in the order they appear in the database, starting from Rule 1.

In the initial state, Rules 1 and 2 are both triggered. We will start by firing Rule 1, which means we add C to our fact database. Next, Rule 2 is fired, meaning we add D to our fact database.

We now have the facts A, B, C, D, F, but we have not yet reached our goal, which is G.

Now Rule 3 is triggered and fired, meaning that fact E is added to the database. As a result, Rules 4 and 5 are triggered. Rule 4 is fired first, resulting in Fact G being added to the database, and then Rule 5 is fired, and Fact H is added to the database. We have now proved our goal and do not need to go on any further.

This deduction is presented in the following table:

Facts	Rules triggered	Rule fired
A, B, F	1, 2	1
A, B, C, F	2	2
A, B, C, D, F	3	3
A, B, C, D, E, F	4, 5	4
A, B, C, D, E, F, G	5	5
A, B, C, D, E, F, G, H	6	STOP

Now we will consider the same problem using backward chaining. To do so, we will use a goals database in addition to the rule and fact databases. In this case, the goals database starts with just the conclusion, H, which we want to prove. We will now see which rules would need to fire to lead to this conclusion. Rule 5 is the only one that has H as a conclusion, so to prove H, we must prove the antecedents of Rule 5, which are A and E.

Fact A is already in the database, so we only need to prove the other antecedent, E. Therefore, E is added to the goal database. Once we have proved E, we now know that this is sufficient to prove H, so we can remove H from the goals database.

So now we attempt to prove Fact E. Rule 3 has E as its conclusion, so to prove E, we must prove the antecedents of Rule 3, which are C and D. Neither of these facts is in the fact database, so we need to prove both of them. They are both therefore added to the goals database. D is the conclusion of Rule 2 and Rule 2's antecedent, A, is already in the fact database, so we can conclude D and add it to the fact database.

Similarly, C is the conclusion of Rule 1, and Rule 1's antecedents, A and B, are both in the fact database. So, we have now proved all the goals in the goal database and have therefore proved H and can stop.

This process is represented in the table below:

Facts	Goals	Matching rules
A, B, F	H	5
A, B, F	E	3
A, B, F	C, D	1
A, B, C, F	D	2
A, B, C, D, F		STOP

In this case, backward chaining needed to use one fewer rule. If the rule data-base had had a large number of other rules that had A, B, and F as their antecedents, then forward chaining might well have been even more inefficient.

In many situations, forward chaining is more appropriate, particularly in a situation where a set of facts is available, but the conclusion is not already known.

In general, backward chaining is appropriate in cases where there are few possible conclusions (or even just one) and many possible facts, not very many of which are necessarily relevant to the conclusion. Forward chaining is more appropriate when there are many possible conclusions.

The way in which forward or backward chaining is usually chosen is to consider which way an expert would solve the problem. This is particularly appropriate because rule-based reasoning is often used in **expert systems**.

9.4   Rule-Based Expert Systems

An expert system is one designed to model the behavior of an expert in some field, such as medicine or geology. Rule-based expert systems are designed to be able to use the same rules that the expert would use to draw conclusions from a set of facts that are presented to the system.

9.4.1   The People Involved in an Expert System

The design, development, and use of expert systems involves a number of people. The **end-user** of the system is the person who has the need for the system. In the case of a medical diagnosis system, this may be a doctor, or it may be an individual who has a complaint that they wish to diagnose.

The **knowledge engineer** is the person who designs the rules for the system, based on either observing the expert at work or by asking the expert questions about how he or she works.

The **domain expert** is very important to the design of an expert system. In the case of a medical diagnosis system, the expert needs to be able to explain to the knowledge engineer how he or she goes about diagnosing illnesses.

9.4.2   Architecture of an Expert System

A typical expert system architecture is shown in Figure 9.1.

The knowledge base contains the specific domain knowledge that is used by an expert to derive conclusions from facts. In the case of a rule-based expert system, this domain knowledge is expressed in the form of a series of rules.

The explanation system provides information to the user about how the inference engine arrived at its conclusions. This can often be essential, particularly if the advice being given is of a critical nature, such as with a medical diagnosis system. If the system has used faulty reasoning to arrive at its

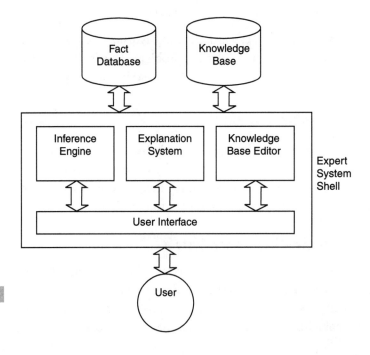

Figure 9.1

Architecture of an expert system

conclusions, then the user may be able to see this by examining the data given by the explanation system.

The fact database contains the case-specific data that are to be used in a particular case to derive a conclusion. In the case of a medical expert system, this would contain information that had been obtained about the patient's condition.

The user of the expert system interfaces with it through a user interface, which provides access to the inference engine, the explanation system, and the knowledge-base editor. The inference engine is the part of the system that uses the rules and facts to derive conclusions. The inference engine will use forward chaining, backward chaining, or a combination of the two to make inferences from the data that are available to it.

The knowledge-base editor allows the user to edit the information that is contained in the knowledge base. The knowledge-base editor is not usually made available to the end user of the system but is used by the knowledge engineer or the expert to provide and update the knowledge that is contained within the system.

9.4.3   The Expert System Shell

Note that in Figure 9.1, the parts of the expert system that do not contain domain-specific or case-specific information are contained within the **expert system shell**. This shell is a general toolkit that can be used to build a number of different expert systems, depending on which knowledge base is added to the shell.

An example of such a shell is CLIPS (C Language Integrated Production System), which is described in more detail in Section 9.4. Other examples in common use include OPS5, ART, JESS, and Eclipse.

9.4.4   The Rete Algorithm

One potential problem with expert systems is the number of comparisons that need to be made between rules and facts in the database. In some cases, where there are hundreds or even thousands of rules, running comparisons against each rule can be impractical.

The **Rete Algorithm** is an efficient method for solving this problem and is used by a number of expert system tools, including OPS5 and Eclipse.

The **Rete** is a directed, acyclic, rooted graph (or a **search tree**, which was discussed in great detail in Chapters 3 and 4).

Each path from the root node to a leaf in the tree represents the left-hand side of a rule. Each node stores details of which facts have been matched by the rules at that point in the path.

As facts are changed, the new facts are propagated through the Rete from the root node to the leaves, changing the information stored at nodes appropriately. This could mean adding a new fact, or changing information about an old fact, or deleting an old fact.

In this way, the system only needs to test each new fact against the rules, and only against those rules to which the new fact is relevant, instead of checking each fact against each rule.

The Rete algorithm depends on the principle that in general, when using forward chaining in expert systems, the values of objects change relatively infrequently, meaning that relatively few changes need to be made to the Rete. In such cases, the Rete algorithm can provide a significant improvement in performance over other methods, although it is less efficient in cases where objects are continually changing.

9.4.5   Knowledge Engineering

Knowledge engineering is a vital part of the development of any expert system. The knowledge engineer does not need to have expert domain knowledge but does need to know how to convert such expertise into the rules that the system will use, preferably in an efficient manner. Hence, the knowledge engineer's main task is communicating with the expert, in order to understand fully how the expert goes about evaluating evidence and what methods he or she uses to derive conclusions.

Having built up a good understanding of the rules the expert uses to draw conclusions, the knowledge engineer must encode these rules in the expert system shell language that is being used for the task.

In some cases, the knowledge engineer will have freedom to choose the most appropriate expert system shell for the task. In other cases, this decision will have already been made, and the knowledge engineer must work with what he is given.

9.5   CLIPS (C Language Integrated Production System)

CLIPS is a freely available expert system shell that has been implemented in C. It provides a language for expressing rules and mainly uses forward chaining to derive conclusions from a set of facts and rules.

The notation used by CLIPS is very similar to that used by LISP. The following is an example of a rule specified using CLIPS:

```
(defrule birthday
  (firstname ?r1 John)
  (surname ?r1 Smith)
  (haircolor ?r1 Red)
  =>
  (assert (is-boss ?r1)))
```

?r1 is used to represent a variable, which in this case is a person. *Assert* is used to add facts to the database, and in this case the rule is used to draw a conclusion from three facts about the person: If the person has the first name John, has the surname Smith, and has red hair, then he is the boss.

This can be tried in the following way:

```
(assert (firstname x John))
(assert (surname x Smith))
(assert (haircolor x Red))
(run)
```

At this point, the command (facts) can be entered to see the facts that are contained in the database:

```
CLIPS>  (facts)
f-0   (firstname x John)
f-1   (surname x Smith)
f-2   (haircolor x Red)
f-3   (is-boss x)
```

So CLIPS has taken the three facts that were entered into the system and used the rule to draw a conclusion, which is that *x* is the boss. Although this is a simple example, CLIPS, like other expert system shells, can be used to build extremely sophisticated and powerful tools.

For example, MYCIN is a well-known medical expert system that was developed at Stanford University in 1984. MYCIN was designed to assist doctors to prescribe antimicrobial drugs for blood infections. In this way, experts in antimicrobial drugs are able to provide their expertise to other doctors who are not so expert in that field. By asking the doctor a series of questions, MYCIN is able to recommend a course of treatment for the patient. Importantly, MYCIN is also able to explain to the doctor which rules fired and therefore is able to explain why it produced the diagnosis and recommended treatment that it did.

MYCIN has proved successful: for example, it has been proven to be able to provide more accurate diagnoses of meningitis in patients than most doctors.

MYCIN was developed using LISP, and its rules are expressed as LISP expressions. The following is an example of the kind of rule used by MYCIN, translated into English:

```
IF the infection is primary-bacteria
AND the site of the culture is one of the sterile sites
AND the suspected portal of entry is the gastrointestinal tract
THEN there is suggestive evidence (0.7) that infection is bacteroid
```

In Chapter 17, we learn more about how MYCIN uses **certainty factors** to aid its diagnosis process.

The following is a very simple example of a CLIPS session where rules are defined to operate an elevator:

```
CLIPS>  (defrule rule1
(elevator ?floor_now)
(button ?floor_now)
=>
(assert (open_door)))
CLIPS>  (defrule rule2
(elevator ?floor_now)
(button ?other_floor)
=>
(assert (goto ?other_floor)))
CLIPS>  (assert (elevator floor1))
==> f-0 (elevator floor1)
<Fact-0>
CLIPS>  (assert (button floor3))
==> f-1 (button floor3)
<Fact-1>
<CLIPS>  (run)
==>f-2  (goto floor3)
```

The segments in **bold** are inputs by the knowledge engineer, and the plain text sections are CLIPS.

Note that **?floor_now** is an example of a variable within CLIPS, which means that any object can match it for the rule to trigger and fire. In our example, the first rule simply says: If the elevator is on a floor, and the button is pressed on the same floor, then open the door. The second rule says: If the elevator is on one floor, and the button is pressed on a different floor, then go to that floor.

After the rules, two facts are inserted into the database. The first fact says that the elevator is on floor 1, and the second fact says that the button has been pressed on floor 3.

When the *(run)* command is issued to the system, it inserts a new fact into the database, which is a command to the elevator to go to floor 3.

9.6   Backward Chaining in Rule-Based Expert Systems

A common method for building expert systems is to use a rule-based system with backward chaining. Typically, a user enters a set of facts into the system, and the system tries to see if it can prove any of the possible hypotheses using these facts. In some cases, it will need additional facts, in which case the expert system will often ask the user questions, to ascertain facts that could enable further rules to fire.

The algorithm is applied as follows:

To prove a conclusion, we must prove a set of hypotheses, one of which is the conclusion. For each hypothesis, H:

> If H is in the facts database, it is proved.

> Otherwise, if H can be determined by asking a question, then enter the user's answer in the facts database. Hence, it can be determined whether H is true or false, according to the user's answer.

> Otherwise, find a rule whose conclusion is H. Now apply this algorithm to try to prove this rule's antecedents.

> If none of the above applies, we have failed to prove H.

Typically, backward chaining is used in combination with forward chaining. Whenever a new fact is added to the database, forward chaining is applied to see if any further facts can be derived. Backward chaining is then used to try to prove each possible hypothesis.

Let us imagine a simple medical expert system that is designed to diagnose and treat patients' diseases. The rules might be as follows:

> Rule 1:   If headache then prescribe painkiller

Rule 2:   If headache and sore throat and coughing then diagnose flu

Rule 3:   If tired and headache then diagnose glandular fever

Rule 4:   If tired and sore throat then diagnose tonsillitis

Rule 5:   If tired then diagnose stress

Now we might imagine a session between the user (the patient) and the expert system as follows:

Patient: I have a headache

System: I suggest you take a painkiller. Do you have a sore throat?

Patient: Yes, I do.

System: Have you been coughing?

Patient: No, why do you ask?

System: If you had a headache and a sore throat and had been coughing, I would have concluded you might have flu. It doesn't sound as though you have flu. Have you been feeling tired recently?

Patient: Yes, I have.

System: It sounds as though you may have glandular fever or tonsillitis.

This was a rather simplistic example, but it illustrates the way that the system uses forward chaining to derive new facts and asks questions in order to carry out its backward chaining analysis. For example, having been told that the patient has a headache, the system first applies forward chaining with Rule 1 and, as a result, adds "prescribe painkiller" to its database of facts. This fact has an action, or a recommendation, associated with it, and so the system advises the patient that she should take a painkiller.

Next, the system tries to see if it can prove any other hypotheses. The possible hypotheses are flu, tonsillitis, glandular fever, and stress. First, the system uses backward chaining to try to prove the hypothesis that the patient has the flu.

To prove this hypothesis, the antecedents of Rule 2 must be proved: that the patient has a headache and a sore throat and has been coughing. The patient has already said that she has a headache, so this fact is already in the fact database. Next, the system must establish whether the patient has a sore throat. She says that she does, so this fact is added to the fact database.

She has not been coughing, though, so the system concludes that she does not have flu.

At this point also note that the patient asks why the system asked the last question. The system is able to use its explanation facility to provide an explanation for why it asked the question and what conclusion it was able to draw from the answer.

Finally, the patient says that she has been feeling tired, and as a result of this fact being added to the database, Rules 3, 4, and 5 are all triggered. In this case, conflict resolution has been applied in a rather simplistic way, such that Rules 3 and 4 both fire, but 5 does not. In a real medical expert system, it is likely that further questions would be asked, and more sophisticated rules applied to decide which condition the patient really had.

9.7 CYC

CYC is an example of a frame-based representational system of knowledge, which is, in a way, the opposite of an expert system. Whereas an expert system has detailed knowledge of a very narrow domain, the developers of CYC have fed it information on over 100,000 different concepts from all fields of human knowledge. CYC also has information of over 1,000,000 different pieces of "common sense" knowledge about those concepts. The system has over 4000 different *types* of links that can exist between concepts, such as inheritance, and the "is–a" relationship that we have already looked at.

The idea behind CYC was that humans function in the world mainly on the basis of a large base of knowledge built up over our lifetimes and our ancestors' lifetimes. By giving CYC access to this knowledge, and the ability to reason about it, they felt they would be able to come up with a system with common sense. Ultimately, they predict, the system will be built into word processors. Then word processors will not just correct your spelling and grammar, but will also point out inconsistencies in your document. For example, if you promise to discuss a particular subject later in your document, and then forget to do so, the system will point this out to you. They also predict that search engines and other information retrieval systems (see Chapter 20) will be able to find documents even though they do not contain any of the words you entered as your query.

CYC's knowledge is segmented into hundreds of different contexts to avoid the problem of many pieces of knowledge in the system contradicting each other. In this way, CYC is able to know facts about Dracula and to reason about him, while also knowing that Dracula does not really exist.

CYC is able to understand analogies, and even to discover new analogies for itself, by examining the similarities in structure and content between different frames and groups of frames. CYC's developers claim, for example, that it discovered an analogy between the concept of "family" and the concept of "country."

9.8 Chapter Summary

- IF . . . THEN . . . rules can be used to represent knowledge about objects.

- Rule-based systems, or production systems, use rules to attempt to derive diagnoses or to provide instructions.

- Rule systems can work using forward chaining, backward chaining, or both. Forward chaining works from a set of initial facts, and works toward a conclusion. Backward chaining starts with a hypothesis and tries to prove it using the facts and rules that are available.

- Conflict resolution methods are used to determine what to do when more than one solution is provided by a rule-based system.

- Knowledge from a domain expert is translated by a knowledge engineer into a form suitable for an expert system, which is then able to help an end-user solve problems that would normally require a human expert.

- In many cases, expert systems use backward chaining and ask questions of the end user to attempt to prove a hypothesis.

- Expert systems are usually built on an expert system shell (such as CLIPS), which provides a generic toolkit for building expert systems.

- The Rete algorithm provides an efficient method for chaining in rule-based systems where there are many rules and where facts do not change frequently.

- Semantic nets and frame-based systems are also used as the basis for expert systems.

- CYC is a system built with knowledge of over 100,000 objects and is able to make complex deductions about the real world.

9.9   Review Questions

9.1   Explain why expert systems are so called.

9.2   Explain the difference between forward chaining and backward chaining. Explain the advantages and disadvantages of each method.

9.3   Explain the various methods of conflict resolution that can be used in rule-based expert systems. For each of these, give an example of a scenario where using it would *not* give the correct result.

9.4   What is the purpose of meta rules? Would an expert system have any advantages if it knew the difference between meta rules and normal rules?

9.5   Describe the architecture of an expert system, and describe the roles of the various people involved in it.

9.6   What is the purpose of the Rete algorithm? Describe how it works.

9.7   Explain the relationships between rules, logic, semantic nets, and frames. Give an example of a situation where you might use each of them. Which system has the greatest representational adequacy? Which has the least? Why?

9.10   Exercises

9.1   Extend the CLIPS rules given in Section 9.5 to produce a more useful system for running an elevator on a building with five floors.

9.2   Implement a rule-based or frame-based expert system shell in the programming language of your choice. Implement an expert system in your expert system shell to solve problems in an area in which you have expertise (for example, solving computer science problems, or identifying films or songs).

9.11   Further Reading

Negnevitsky (2002) provides an excellent overview of rule- and frame-based expert systems.

For a more detailed description of the Rete algorithm, see *Rete: A Fast Algorithm for the Many Pattern / Many Object Pattern Match Problem* by C. L. Forgy from *Artificial Intelligence,* Vol. 19, pp. 17–37, 1982.

Winston (1993) also covers the Rete algorithm.

A brief description of the CYC expert system, and some of the difficulties faced in building it can be found in Douglas B. Lenat's article, *Programming Artificial Intelligence,* which was first published in *Scientific American* in September 1995 and can also be found in Fritz (2002).

Deeper coverage of CYC can be found in Lenat and Guha (1990).

Discussion of productions systems and an example of an expert system implementation in PROLOG can be found in *Logic and Prolog* by Richard Spencer-Smith (1991).

An interesting discussion of some of the limitations of MYCIN can be found in McCarthy (1983). In particular, he points out that the system is not aware of its own limitations and so is liable to make confident recommendations that are potentially dangerous.

Fundamentals of Expert System Technology: Principles and Concepts by Samuel J. Biondo (1990 – Intellect)

Rule-Based Expert Systems: The MYCIN Experiments of the Stanford Heuristic Programming Project by B. G. Buchanan and E. H. Shortliffe (1984 – Addison Wesley)

Prolog Programming for Students: With Expert Systems and Artificial Intelligence Topics by David Callear (2001 – Continuum)

Artificial Intelligence: A Knowledge-Based Approach by Morris W. Firebaugh (1988 – Boyd & Fraser Publishing Company – out of print)

Understanding Artificial Intelligence (Science Made Accessible) compiled by Sandy Fritz (2002 – Warner Books)

Expert Systems: Principles and Programming by Joseph C. Giarratano (1998 – Brooks Cole)

Managing Uncertainty in Expert Systems by Jerzy W. Grzymala-Busse (1991 – Kluwer Academic Publishers)

Expert Systems: Artificial Intelligence in Business by Paul Harmon (1985 – John Wiley & Sons – out of print)

Introduction to Expert Systems by Peter Jackson (1999 – Addison Wesley)

Knowledge Acquisition for Expert Systems: A Practical Handbook by Alison L. Kidd (1987 – Plenum Publishing Corporation)

Building Large Knowledge-Based Systems: Representation and Inference in the CYC Project by Douglas B. Lenat and R. V. Guha (1990 – Addison Wesley)

The Logic of Knowledge Bases by Hector J. Levesque and Gerhard Lakemeyer (2001 – MIT Press)

Some Expert Systems Need Common Sense by John McCarthy (1983 – in *Computer Culture: The Scientific, Intellectual and Social Impact of the Computer* edited by Heinz Pagels, Vol. 426)

Building Expert Systems in Prolog by Dennis Merritt (1995 – Springer Verlag)

Artificial Intelligence: A Guide to Intelligent Systems by Michael Negnevitsky (2002 – Addison Wesley)

Computer Based Medical Consultations: Mycin by Edward Shortliffe (1976 – Elsevier Science, out of print)

Logic and Prolog by Richard Spencer-Smith (1991 – Harvester Wheatsheaf)

Managing Expert Systems edited by Efraim Turban and Jay Liebowitz (1992 – Idea Group Publishing)

Machine Learning

Introduction to Part 4

Part 4 is divided into five chapters:

CHAPTER 10 — Introduction to Machine Learning

This chapter introduces a number of techniques for machine learning, such as ID3 for learning decision trees, version spaces, and the nearest neighbor algorithm. It also introduces the ideas behind neural networks, which are covered in more detail in Chapter 11.

This chapter explains the idea of inductive bias and why it is important in machine learning.

CHAPTER 11 — Neural Networks

This chapter expands on the ideas introduced in Chapter 10 and gives a more detailed coverage of neural networks. It explains the relationship between artificial neurons and biological neurons, and introduces perceptions. The chapter then explains multilayer networks and introduces backpropagation as a way to train multilayer networks. It also introduces recurrent networks, such as Hopfield networks.

This chapter explains unsupervised neural networks (such as Kohonen maps) as well as supervised ones.

Finally, this chapter briefly introduces the idea of evolving neural networks, combining ideas from this chapter with ideas from Chapters 13 and 14.

CHAPTER 10

Introduction to Machine Learning

O, what learning is!

—William Shakespeare, *Romeo and Juliet*

Much learning doth make thee mad.

—The Acts of the Apostles, Chapter 26, Verse 24

Whence is thy learning? Hath thy toil

O'er books consumed the midnight oil?

—John Gay, *Fables*

Learning and intelligence are intimately related to each other. It is usually agreed that a system capable of learning deserves to be called intelligent; and conversely, a system being considered as intelligent is, among other things, usually expected to be able to learn. Learning always has to do with the self-improvement of future behaviour based on past experience.

—Sandip Sen and Gerhard Weiss, *Learning in Multiagent Systems*

10.1   Introduction

Machine learning is an extremely important part of Artificial Intelligence. This chapter provides a brief overview of some of the main methods and ideas that are used in machine learning and also provides a very brief introduction to neural networks, which are covered in more detail in Chapter 11.

In this chapter, concept learning methods are explored, which are able to generalize from a set of training data to be able to correctly classify data that has not been seen before. Decision-tree learning is examined, and the ID3 algorithm is explained.

10.2   Training

In most learning problems, the task is to learn to classify inputs according to a finite (or sometimes infinite) set of classifications. Typically, a learning system is provided with a set of training data, which have been classified by hand. The system then attempts to learn from these training data how to classify the same data (usually a relatively easy task) and also how to classify new data that it has not seen.

Learning to classify unseen data clearly assumes that there is some relationship between the data and the classifications—in other words, some function f can be generated such that if a piece of data x belongs in classification y, then

$$f(x) = y$$

For example, if the equality function were used, the learning task would be relatively simple because each datum would be classified as itself. Clearly most real-world problems are not so simple, and producing a function that approximates the correct mapping is one of the main challenges of machine learning.

In fact, in most learning problems, the input data consist of more than one variable.

For example, let us consider a system that is to learn how to evaluate static chess positions.

First, we will consider a number of variables:

x_1: Number of white pieces on the board

x_2: Number of black pieces on the board

x_3: Number of black pieces threatened by white pieces

x_4: Number of white pieces threatened by black pieces

x_5: Can white checkmate on the next go?

x_6: Can black checkmate on the next go?

x_7: Number of different moves white can make

x_8: Number of different moves black can make

Clearly, this is an oversimplification because a real chess system would need to use a much more complex set of variables to evaluate a position.

Note that the variables are not all of the same type: most of the variables are numeric, but two of them are Boolean (can each side achieve checkmate on the next go). Many learning problems will involve data of a number of different types.

The evaluation of each position is to be calculated as a high positive in the event that white has the better position and a high negative if black has the better position. A value of 0 indicates a level position, and a score of ± 100 indicates that one side has won the game, or is about to win.

It seems probable that a simple linear weighted function of these variables will suffice: We will write our evaluation function f as follows:

$$f(x_1, x_2, x_3, x_4, x_5, x_6, x_7, x_8) =$$

$$w_1x_1 + w_2x_2 + w_3x_3 + w_4x_4 + w_5x_5 + w_6x_6 + w_7x_7 + w_8x_8$$

where w_1 to w_8 are the weights associated with the eight variables. The aim of the system is to determine suitable values for these weights, based on the training data that are provided.

An item of training data might be

$$f(10, 2, 1, 0, \text{true}, \text{false}, 10, 1) = 100$$

This suggests that the position described by the training data is a definite win for white.

Clearly, there are an extraordinarily large number of possible sets of training data for this function, and it may not even be the case that a suitable function exists for this representation. A superior representation, for which a suitable function certainly exists, would be to map the positions of all 32 pieces to the 64 squares on the board. In this case, a system could certainly be trained to determine whether any given position was better for white or for black, but the enormous number of possible input data makes the problem somewhat harder.

In Chapter 11, we see how artificial neural networks can be used to provide extremely accurate mappings from input data to classifications for problems such as this.

In this chapter, we will look at methods that are primarily used to learn somewhat simpler mappings, although these methods can certainly be extended to work with more complex sets of data.

10.3   Rote Learning

The simplest way for a computer to learn from experience is simply to learn by **rote**. Training involves storing each piece of training data and its classification. Thereafter, a new item of data is classified by looking to see if it is stored in memory. If it is, then the classification that was stored with that item is returned. Otherwise, the method fails.

Hence, a rote learner is able to classify only data that it has already seen, and no attempt is made to approximate the mapping function, which is a major weakness.

10.4   Learning Concepts

We will now look at a number of methods that can be used to learn concepts. **Concept learning** involves determining a mapping from a set of input variables to a Boolean value.

The methods described here are known as **inductive-learning methods**. These methods are based on the principle that if a function is found that correctly maps a large set of training data to classifications, then it will also correctly map unseen data. In doing so, a learner is able to **generalize** from a set of training data.

To illustrate these methods, we will use a simple toy problem, as follows:

Our learning task will be to determine whether driving in a particular manner in particular road conditions is safe or not. We will use the following attributes:

Attribute	Possible values
Speed	slow, medium, fast
Weather	wind, rain, snow, sun
Distance from car in front	10ft, 20ft, 30ft, 40ft, 50ft, 60ft
Units of alcohol driver has drunk	0, 1, 2, 3, 4, 5
Time of day	morning, afternoon, evening, night
Temperature	cold, warm, hot

We will consider a **hypothesis** to be a vector of values for these attributes. A possible hypothesis is

h_1 = <slow, wind, 30ft, 0, evening, cold>

We also want to represent in a hypothesis that we do not care what value an attribute takes. This is represented by "?", as in the following hypothesis:

h_2 = <fast, rain, 10ft, 2, ?, ?>

h_2 represents the hypothesis that driving quickly in rainy weather, close to the car in front after having drunk two units of alcohol is safe, regardless of the time of day or the temperature. Clearly, this hypothesis is untrue and would be considered by the learner to be a **negative training example**.

In other cases, we need to represent a hypothesis that no value of a particular attribute will provide a positive example. We write this as "∅", as in the following hypothesis:

h_3 = <fast, rain, 10ft, 2, ∅, ∅>

h_3 states the opposite of h_2—that driving quickly in rainy weather, close to the car in front after having drunk two units of alcohol cannot be safe, regardless of the time of day or the temperature.

The task of the concept learner is to examine a set of positive and negative training data and to use these to determine a hypothesis that matches all the training data, and which can then be used to classify instances that have not previously been seen.

Concept learning can be thought of as search through a search space that consists of all possible hypotheses, where the goal is the hypothesis that most closely represents the correct mapping.

10.5   General-to-Specific Ordering

Consider the following two hypotheses:

$$h_g = <?, ?, ?, ?, ?, ?>$$

$$h_s = <\emptyset, \emptyset, \emptyset, \emptyset, \emptyset, \emptyset>$$

h_g is the hypothesis that it is safe to drive regardless of the conditions—this is the **most general hypothesis**.

h_s is the **most specific hypothesis**, which states that it is never safe to drive, under any circumstances.

These hypotheses represent two extremes, and clearly a useful hypothesis that accurately represents the mapping from attribute values to a Boolean value will be somewhere in between these two.

One method for concept learning is based on the idea that a **partial order** exists over the space of hypotheses. This partial order is represented by the relationship "more general than":

$$\geq_g$$

We write

$$h_1 \geq_g h_2$$

which states that h_1 is more general than (or as general as) h_2. Similarly, we could write

$$h_1 >_g h_2$$

in the case where h_1 is certainly more general than h_2.

$\geq_g$ defines a partial order over the hypothesis space, rather than a total order, because some hypotheses are neither more specific nor more general than other hypotheses. For example, consider the following hypotheses:

$$h_1 = <?, ?, ?, ?, evening, cold>$$

$$h_2 = <medium, snow, ?, ?, ?, ?>$$

We cannot express any relationship between h_1 and h_2 in terms of generality.

One hypothesis is more general than (or equally general as) another hypothesis if every instance that is matched by the second hypothesis is also matched by the first hypothesis.

For example,

$$<\text{slow}, ?, ?, ?, ?, ?> \geq_g <\text{slow}, ?, ?, ?, ?, \text{cold}>$$

It should be clear that a more general hypothesis matches more instances than a less general hypothesis.

10.5.1   A Simple Learning Algorithm

The following algorithm uses the general-to-specific ordering of hypotheses to search the hypothesis space for a suitable hypothesis. The method is as follows:

Start with the most specific hypothesis. In our example above, this would be $<\varnothing, \varnothing, \varnothing, \varnothing, \varnothing, \varnothing, \varnothing, \varnothing>$.

Now, for each positive training example, determine whether each attribute in the example is matched by the current hypothesis. If it is not, replace the attributes in the hypothesis with the next more general value that does match.

For example, let us consider the following set of positive training data:

   <slow, wind, 30ft, 0, evening, cold>

   <slow, rain, 20ft, 0, evening, warm>

   <slow, snow, 30ft, 0, afternoon, cold>

First, let us compare the first item of training data with the current hypothesis, which is $<\varnothing, \varnothing, \varnothing, \varnothing, \varnothing, \varnothing, \varnothing, \varnothing>$. Clearly, none of the attributes are matched by this hypothesis. The next most general value for each attribute than $\varnothing$ that matches the training data is the value contained in the training data. So we replace our hypothesis with the following hypothesis:

   <slow, wind, 30ft, 0, evening, cold>

Clearly, the hypothesis $<?, ?, ?, ?, ?, ?, ?, ?>$ would have been more general than the initial hypothesis, but the method we are using is to select the *next more general* value for each attribute. In this way, we move from a hypothesis that is too specific to one that is general enough to match all the training data.

We will now consider the second item of training data:

   <slow, rain, 20ft, 0, evening, warm>

Now we compare each attribute value with the corresponding value in our current hypothesis. Where the values match, we do not need to make any change. Where they do not match, we need to replace the value with "?" so that the hypothesis matches both items of training data. Hence, our new hypothesis is

<slow, ?, ?, 0, evening, ?>

By comparing with our final item of training data, we arrive at the following hypothesis:

<slow, ?, ?, 0, ?, ?>

This hypothesis states that it is only safe to drive if one drives slowly and has not drunk any alcohol, and that this is true regardless of the road or weather conditions.

This hypothesis is **consistent** with the training examples, which means that it maps each of them to the correct classification.

This algorithm will generate the most specific hypothesis that matches all of the training data. There are a number of problems with this algorithm: first of all, it may not be desirable to identify the most specific hypothesis—it may be that the most general hypothesis that matches the training data provides a better solution. Secondly, the most specific hypothesis identified by the algorithm may not be the only solution— there may be other most specific hypotheses that match the data, one of which may be a preferable solution. Additionally, this algorithm does not make any use of negative examples. As we will see, most useful learning methods are able to make use of negative as well as positive training examples.

Finally, the method does not deal well with inconsistent or incorrect training data. In real-world problems, an ability to deal with such errors is vital, as we see later in this part of the book.

10.6 Version Spaces

Given a set of training examples (positive and negative), the set of hypotheses that correctly map each of the training examples to its classification is called the **version space**.

One method for learning from a set of data is thus to start from a complete version space that contains all hypotheses and systematically remove all the hypotheses that do not correctly classify each training example. Although this method might work well on small problems, for problems of any reasonable size, the task of enumerating all hypotheses would be impractical.

10.7   Candidate Elimination

We now explore another method that uses version spaces to learn. The aim of these methods is to identify a single hypothesis, if possible, that correctly describes the problem. The more training data that are available, the fewer hypotheses are contained in the version space. If all the training data have been used, and the version space contains just a single hypothesis, then this matches all the training data and should also match unseen data.

The **candidate elimination** learning method operates in a similar manner to the simple algorithm presented in Section 10.5.1. Unlike the earlier simple method, the candidate elimination method stores not just a single hypothesis, but two sets of hypotheses. In addition to maintaining a set of most specific hypotheses that match the training data, this method also maintains a set of hypotheses that starts out as a set with the single item $<?, ?, ?, ?, ?, ?, ?, ?>$ and ends up being a set of the most general hypotheses that match all the training data. This algorithm is thus able to make use of negative training data as well as positive training data.

The method operates as follows: Two sets are maintained of hypotheses, h_s and h_g: h_s is initialized as $\{<\varnothing, \varnothing, \varnothing, \varnothing, \varnothing, \varnothing, \varnothing, \varnothing>\}$ and h_g is initialized as $\{<?, ?, ?, ?, ?, ?, ?, ?>\}$.

When a positive training example is encountered, it is compared with the hypotheses contained in h_g. If any of these hypotheses does not match the training example, it is removed from h_g. The positive training data are then compared with the hypotheses contained in h_s. If one of these hypotheses does not match the training data, it is replaced by the set of slightly more general hypotheses that are consistent with the data, and such that there is at least one hypothesis in h_g that is more general.

This method is applied in reverse for negative training data. By applying this method to each item of training data, the sets h_g and h_s move closer to each other and eventually between them contain the full version space of hypotheses that match all the training data.

10.8   Inductive Bias

All learning methods have an *inductive bias*. Inductive bias refers to the restrictions that are imposed by the assumptions made in the learning method. For example, in the above discussions we have been assuming that the solution to the problem of road safety can be expressed as a conjunction of a set of eight concepts. This does not allow for more complex expressions that cannot be expressed as a conjunction. This inductive bias means that there are some potential solutions that we cannot explore, and which are, therefore, not contained within the version space we examine.

This may seem like an unfortunate limitation, but in fact inductive bias is essential for learning. In order to have an unbiased learner, the version space would have to contain every possible hypothesis that could possibly be expressed. This would impose a severe limitation: the solution that the learner produced could never be any more general than the complete set of training data. In other words, it would be able to classify data that it had previously seen (as the rote learner could) but would be unable to generalize in order to classify new, unseen data.

The inductive bias of the candidate elimination algorithm is that it is only able to classify a new piece of data if all the hypotheses contained within its version space give the data the same classification. Hence, the inductive bias does impose a limitation on the learning method.

In the 14th century, William of Occam proposed his famous "**Occam's razor**," which simply states that it is best to choose the simplest hypothesis to explain any phenomenon. We can consider this to be a form of inductive bias, which states that the best hypothesis to fit a set of training data is the simplest hypothesis. We will see later how this inductive bias can be useful in learning decision trees.

10.9   Decision-Tree Induction

In Chapter 3, we see a tree that was used to determine which species a particular bird belonged to, based on various observed features of the bird. A variation of this kind of tree, where the leaf nodes are all Boolean values is

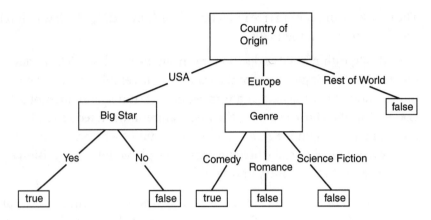

Figure 10.1

A simple decision tree for determining whether or not a film will be a box-office success

called a **decision tree**. A decision tree takes in a set of attribute values and outputs a Boolean decision.

An example of a decision tree is shown in Figure 10.1. This decision tree can be used to determine whether or not a given film will be a success at the box office.

To use the decision tree, we start at the top and apply the question to the film. If the film is made in the United States, we move down the first branch of the tree; if it is made in Europe the second; and if elsewhere then we explore the third branch. The final boxes represent the Boolean value, true or false, which expresses whether a film is a success or not.

According to this extremely simplistic (and possibly somewhat contentious) decision tree, a film can only be a box-office success if it is made in the United States and has a big star, or if it is a European comedy.

Whereas version spaces are able to represent expressions that consist solely of conjunctions, decision trees can represent more complex expressions, involving disjunctions and conjunctions. For example, the decision tree in Figure 10.1 represents the following expression:

```
((Country = USA) ∧ (Big Star = yes)) ∨ ((Country = Europe) ∧
(Genre = comedy))
```

Decision-tree induction (or decision-tree learning) involves using a set of training data to generate a decision tree that correctly classifies the training data. If the learning has worked, this decision tree will then correctly classify new input data as well.

The best-known decision tree induction algorithm is ID3, which was developed by Quinlan in the 1980s.

The ID3 algorithm builds a decision tree from the top down. The nodes are selected by choosing features of the training data set that provide the most information about the data and turning those features into questions. For example, in the above example, the first feature to be noted might be that the country of origin is a significant determinant of whether a film will be a success or not. Hence, the first question to be placed into the decision tree is "what is the film's country of origin?".

The most important feature of ID3 is how the features are chosen. It would be possible to produce a decision tree by selecting the features in an arbitrary order, but this would not necessarily produce the most efficient decision tree. The ID3 algorithm finds the shortest possible decision tree that correctly classifies the training data.

10.9.1   Information Gain

The method used by ID3 to determine which features to use at each stage of the decision tree is to select, at each stage, the feature that provides the greatest **information gain**. Information gain is defined as the reduction in entropy. The entropy of a set of training data, S, is defined as

$$H(S) = -p_1 \log_2 p_1 - p_0 \log_2 p_0$$

where p_1 is defined as the proportion of the training data that includes positive examples, and p_0 is defined as the proportion that includes negative examples. The entropy of S is zero when all the examples are positive, or when all the examples are negative. The entropy reaches its maximum value of 1 when exactly half of the examples are positive and half are negative.

The information gain of a particular feature tells us how closely that feature represents the entire target function, and so at each stage, the feature that gives the highest information gain is chosen to turn into a question.

10.9.2 Example

We will start with the training data given below:

Film	Country of origin	Big star	Genre	Success
Film 1	United States	yes	Science Fiction	true
Film 2	United States	no	Comedy	false
Film 3	United States	yes	Comedy	true
Film 4	Europe	no	Comedy	true
Film 5	Europe	yes	Science fiction	false
Film 6	Europe	yes	Romance	false
Film 7	Rest of World	yes	Comedy	false
Film 8	Rest of World	no	Science fiction	false
Film 9	Europe	yes	Comedy	true
Film 10	United States	yes	Comedy	true

We will now calculate the information gain for the three different attributes of the films, to select which one to use at the top of the tree.

First, let us calculate the information gain of the attribute "country of origin." Our collection of training data consists of five positive examples and five negative examples, so currently it has an entropy value of 1.

Four of the training data are from the United States, four from Europe, and the remaining two from the rest of the world.

The information gain of this attribute is the reduction in entropy that it brings to the data. This can be calculated as follows:

First, we calculate the entropy of each subset of the training data as broken up by this attribute. In other words, we calculate the entropy of the items that are from the United States, the entropy of the items from Europe, and the entropy of the items from the rest of the world.

Of the films from the United States, three were successes and one was not. Hence, the entropy of this attribute is

$$H(USA) = -(3/4) \log_2 (3/4) - (1/4) \log_2 (1/4)$$

$$= 0.311 + 0.5$$

$$= 0.811$$

Similarly, we calculate the entropies of the other two subsets as divided by this attribute:

$$H(Europe) = 1$$

(since half of the European films were successes, and half were not).

$$H(Rest\ of\ world) = 0$$

(since none of these films were successes).

The total information gain is now defined as the original entropy of the set minus the weighted sum of these entropies, where the weight applied to each entropy value is the proportion of the training data that fell into that category. For example, four-tenths of the training data were from the United States, so the weight applied to H(USA) is $4/10 = 0.4$.

The information gain is defined as:

$$Gain = 1 - (0.4 \times 0.811) - (0.4 \times 1) - (0.2 \times 0)$$

$$= 1 - 0.3244 - 0.4 - 0$$

$$= 0.2756$$

Hence, at this stage, the information gain for the "country of origin" attribute is 0.2756.

For the "Big star" attribute

$$H(yes) = 0.9852$$

$$H(no) = 1$$

so, the information gain for this attribute is

$$\text{Gain} = 1 - (0.7 \times 0.9852) - (0.3 \times 1)$$

$$= 1 - 0.68964 - 0.3$$

$$= 0.01$$

For the "Genre" attribute

$$H(\text{science fiction}) = 0.918296$$

$$H(\text{comedy}) = 0.918296$$

$$H(\text{romance}) = 0$$

(note that we treat $0 \times \log_2 0$ as 0)

hence, the information gain for this attribute is

$$\text{Gain} = 1 - (0.3 \times 0.918296) - (0.6 \times 0.918296) - (0.1 \times 0)$$

$$= 1 - 0.2754888 - 0.5509776 - 0$$

$$= 0.17$$

Hence, at this stage, the category "Country of origin" provides the greatest entropy gain and so is placed at the top of the decision tree. This method is then applied recursively to the sub-branches of the tree, examining the entropy gain achieved by subdividing the training data further.

10.9.3 Inductive Bias of ID3

ID3's inductive bias is that it tends to produce the shortest decision tree that will correctly classify all of the training data. This fits very well with Occam's razor, which was briefly introduced in Section 10.8. It is not the case that Occam's razor can be applied in all situations to provide the optimal solution: it is, however, the case that ID3 tends to produce adequate results. Additionally, a smaller decision tree is clearly easier for humans to understand, which in some circumstances can be very useful, for example if the need arises to debug the learner and find out why it makes a mistake on a particular piece of unseen data.

10.10   The Problem of Overfitting

In some situations, decision trees (and other learning methods) can run into the problem of overfitting. Overfitting usually occurs when there is noise in the training data, or when the training data do not adequately represent the entire space of possible data. In such situations, it can be possible for one decision tree to correctly classify all the training data, but to perform less well at classifying unseen data than some other decision tree that performs poorly at classifying the training data. In other words, if the training data do not adequately and accurately represent the entire data set, the decision tree that is learned from it may not match unseen data.

This problem does not just apply to decision trees, but also to other learning methods. It can best be understood by examining the illustration in Figure 10.2.

In the first diagram in Figure 10.2, black dots are positive training data, and white dots are negative training data. The two lines represent two hypotheses that have been developed to distinguish the training data. The thin line is a relatively simple hypothesis, which incorrectly classifies some of the training data—it should have all positive examples below it and all negative examples above it. The thicker line correctly classifies all the training data, using a more complex hypothesis, which is somewhat warped by noise in the data. In the next diagram, the thin line is shown to map reasonably effectively the full set of data. It does make some errors, but it reasonably

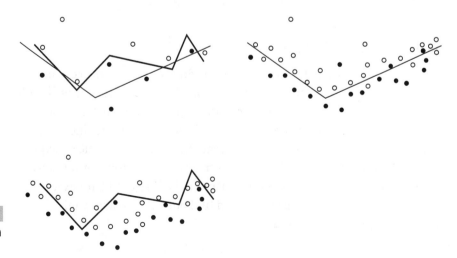

Figure 10.2

Illustration of the problem of overfitting

closely represents the trend in the data. The third diagram, however, shows that the more complex solution does not at all represent the full set of data. This hypothesis has been overfitted to the training data, allowing itself to be warped by noise in the training data.

Overfitting is, perhaps, a good illustration of why Occam's razor can sometimes be a useful inductive bias: selecting a complex solution to accommodate all of the training data can be a bad idea when the training data contain errors.

10.11   The Nearest Neighbor Algorithm

The **nearest neighbor algorithm** is an example of instance-based learning. Instance-based learning methods do not attempt to generalize from training data to produce a hypothesis to match all input data, instead, they store the training data and use these data to determine a classification for each new piece of data as it is encountered.

The nearest neighbor algorithm operates in situations where each instance can be defined by an n-dimensional vector, where n is the number of attributes used to describe each instance, and where the classifications are discrete numerical values. The training data are stored, and when a new instance is encountered it is compared with the training data to find its nearest neighbors. This is done by computing the Euclidean distance between the instances in n-dimensional space. In two-dimensional space, for example, the distance between $<x_1, y_1>$ and $<x_2, y_2>$ is

$$\sqrt{\left((x_1 - x_2)^2 + (y_1 - y_2)^2\right)}$$

Typically, the nearest neighbor algorithm obtains the classifications of the nearest k neighbors to the instance that is to be classified and assigns it the classification that is most commonly returned by those neighbors.

An alternative approach is to weight the contribution of each of the neighbors according to how far it is from the instance that is to be classified. In this way, it is possible to allow every instance of training data to contribute to the classification of a new instance. When used in this way, the algorithm is known as **Shepard's method** (see Shepard 1968).

Unlike decision-tree learning, the nearest neighbor algorithm performs very well with noisy input data. Its inductive bias is to assume that instances that are close to each other in terms of Euclidean distance will have similar classifications. In some cases, this can be an erroneous assumption; for example, in a situation where 10 attributes are used to define each instance, but only 3 of those attributes play any part in determining the classification of the instance. In this situation, instances can be very far apart from each other in 10-dimensional space and yet have the same classification. This problem can be avoided to some extent by neglecting to include unimportant attributes from the calculations.

10.12   Learning Neural Networks

An **artificial neural network** is a network of simple processing nodes, which is roughly modeled on the human brain. The human brain is a massively parallel computation device, which achieves its power through the enormous connectivity between its **neurons**. Each neuron is a very simple device that can either fire or not fire, but by combining billions of these neurons together, the brain is able to achieve levels of complexity as yet unattainable by machines.

The word artificial is often used to describe neural networks to differentiate them from the biological neural networks that make up the human brain, but in this book we shall simply refer to them as neural networks because it should be clear from the context which type of network we are referring to.

Neural networks consist of a number of nodes, each of which can be thought of as representing a neuron. Typically, these neurons are arranged into layers, and the neurons from one layer are connected to the neurons in the two layers on either side of it.

Typically, the network is arranged such that one layer is the input layer, which receives inputs that are to be classified. These inputs cause some of the neurons in the input layer to fire, and these neurons in turn pass signals to the neurons to which they are connected, some of which also fire, and so on. In this way, a complex pattern of firings is arranged throughout the network, with the final result being that some neurons in the final output layer fire.

The connections between neurons are weighted, and by modifying these weights, the neural network can be arranged to perform extremely complex classification tasks such as handwriting analysis and face recognition.

As we see in Chapter 11 where we discuss them in more detail, neural networks have a number of advantages over other learning methods. Many of these advantages derive from features of the human brain. For example, neural networks are extremely **robust**, both to errors in any training data and to damage that may be caused to the network itself.

10.13 Supervised Learning

Supervised learning networks learn by being presented with preclassified training data. The techniques we have discussed so far in this chapter use forms of supervised learning. Neural networks that use supervised learning learn by modifying the weights of the connections within their networks to more accurately classify the training data. In this way, neural networks are able to generalize extremely accurately in many situations from a set of training data to the full set of possible inputs.

One of the most commonly used methods for supervised learning is back-propagation, which will be discussed in Chapter 11.

10.14 Unsupervised Learning

Unsupervised learning methods learn without any human intervention. A good example of an unsupervised learning network is a **Kohonen map**. A Kohonen map is a neural network that is able to learn to classify a set of input data without being told what the classifications are and without being given any training data. This method is particularly useful in situations where data need to be classified, or clustered, into a set of classifications but where the classifications are not known in advance.

For example, given a set of documents retrieved from the Internet (perhaps by an intelligent information agent), a Kohonen map could cluster similar documents together and automatically provide an indication of the distinct subjects that are covered by the documents.

Another method for unsupervised learning in neural networks was proposed by Donald Hebb in 1949 and is known as Hebbian learning. Hebbian learning is based on the idea that if two neurons in a neural network are connected together, and they fire at the same time when a particular input is given to the network, then the connection between those two neurons should be strengthened. It seems likely that something not dissimilar from Hebbian learning takes place in the human brain when learning occurs (Edelman 1987).

10.15   Reinforcement Learning

Classifier systems, which are discussed in Chapter 13, use a form of **reinforcement learning**. A system that uses reinforcement learning is given a positive reinforcement when it performs correctly and a negative reinforcement when it performs incorrectly. For example, a robotic agent might learn by reinforcement learning how to pick up an object. When it successfully picks up the object, it will receive a positive reinforcement.

The information that is provided to the learning system when it performs its task correctly does not tell it *why* or *how* it performed it correctly, simply that it did.

Some neural networks learn by reinforcement. The main difficulty with such methods is the problem of **credit assignment**. The classifier systems (which are discussed in Chapter 13) use a **bucket brigade algorithm** for deciding how to assign credit (or blame) to the individual components of the system. Similar methods are used with neural networks to determine to which neurons to give credit when the network performs correctly and which to blame when it does not.

10.16   Chapter Summary

- Many learning methods use some form of training to learn to generalize from a set of preclassified training data to be able to correctly classify unseen data.

- Rote learning involves simply memorizing the classifications of training data. A rote learning system is not able to generalize and so is only able to classify data it has seen before.

- A general-to-specific ordering of hypotheses can be used to learn to generalize from a set of training data to a hypothesis that matches all input data. This is known as concept learning.

- A version space, which consists of all possible hypotheses that match a given set of training data, can be used to generalize from those training data to learn to classify unseen data.

- Candidate elimination is a method that uses the general-to-specific ordering to produce a set of hypotheses that represent the entire version space for a problem.

- The inductive bias of a learning method is the assumptions it makes about the possible hypotheses that can be used. A learning system with no inductive bias is not capable of generalizing beyond the training data it is given.

- Decision-tree induction can be used to learn a decision tree that will correctly classify a set of input data. The inductive bias of decision-tree induction is to prefer shorter trees.

- The problem of overfitting occurs when there is noise in the training data that causes a learning method to develop a hypothesis that correctly matches the training data but does not perform well on other input data.

- The nearest neighbor algorithm simply memorizes the classifications of the training data, and when presented with a new piece of data gives the majority answer given by the closest neighbors to this piece of data in n-dimensional space.

- Neural networks are based on biological networks of neurons contained within the human brain.

- Supervised learning methods learn from manually classified training data.

- Unsupervised learning methods such as Kohonen maps learn without any manual intervention.

- A system that uses reinforcement learning is given a positive reinforcement when it performs correctly. Credit and blame assignment are important features of such methods.

10.17   Review Questions

10.1   Explain the idea behind learning by generalization.

10.2   What is meant by inductive bias? Is it a good thing? What is the inductive bias of the ID3 algorithm?

10.3   Explain how candidate elimination uses version spaces to learn.

10.4   Explain how a system can learn by building decision trees, using the ID3 algorithm.

10.5   How does the nearest neighbor algorithm work?

10.6   Explain the problem of overfitting and how it can be avoided.

10.7 Explain the differences and similarities between the following three types of learning methods:

supervised

unsupervised

reinforcement

10.18   Exercises

10.1 Use the ID3 algorithm to build the full decision tree for the data set given in Section 10.9.2.

10.2 Implement the nearest neighbor algorithm in the programming language of your choice. The algorithm should work with vectors of up to 10 integer values and allow up to 10 integer classifications. By mapping each value to a number, use your program to learn from the training data given in Section 10.9.2. Have your program now classify the following films:

Film	Country of origin	Big star	Genre
Film 11	United States	no	Science fiction
Film 12	United States	yes	Romance
Film 13	United States	no	Romance
Film 14	Europe	no	Science fiction
Film 15	Rest of world	no	Romance

Comment on the results.

10.19   Further Reading

Mitchell (1997) provides an excellent coverage of many aspects of machine learning. An excellent background from a biological perspective is provided by Pfeifer and Scheier (1999). Winston (1992) developed many of the concepts that are used today in machine learning.

Further references on neural networks are given in the Further Reading section of Chapter 11 of this book.

Learning from Data: Concepts, Theory, and Methods by Vladimir Cherkassky and Filip Mulier (1998 – Wiley Interscience)

Neural Darwinism: The Theory of Neuronal Group Selection by Gerald M. Edelman (1990 – Oxford University Press)

Learning and Soft Computing: Support Vector Machines, Neural Networks, and Fuzzy Logic Models (Complex Adaptive Systems) by Vojislav Kecman (2001 – MIT Press)

Machine Learning by Tom M. Mitchell (1997 – McGraw Hill)

Machine Learning: A Theoretical Approach by Balas K. Natarajan (1991 – Morgan Kaufmann)

Understanding Intelligence by Rolf Pfeifer and Christian Scheier (1999 – MIT Press)

Induction of Decision Trees by J. R. Quinlan (1986 – from *Machine Learning*, Vol. 1, pp. 81–106)

A Two Dimensional Interpolation Function for Irregularly Spaced Data by D. Shepard (1968 - *Proceedings of the 23rd National Conference of the ACM*, pp. 517–523)

Reinforcement Learning: An Introduction (Adaptive Computation and Machine Learning) by Richard S. Sutton and Andrew G. Barto (1998 – MIT Press)

Statistical Learning Theory by Vladimir N. Vapnik (1998 – Wiley Interscience)

An Introduction to Computational Learning Theory by Michael J. Kearns and Umesh V. Vazirani (1994 – MIT Press)

Learning and Generalization: With Applications to Neural Networks by Mathukumalli Vidyasagar (2002 – Springer Verlag)

CHAPTER 11

Neural Networks

Man, unlike any other thing organic or inorganic in the universe, grows beyond his work, walks up the stairs of his concepts, emerges ahead of his accomplishments.

—John Steinbeck, *The Grapes of Wrath*

Behind a pot of ferns the wagging clock
Tells me the hour's word, the neural meaning
Flies on the shafted disc, declaims the morning
And tells the windy weather in the cock.

—Dylan Thomas, *Especially When the October Wind*

His high pitched voice already stood out above the general murmur of well-behaved junior executives grooming themselves for promotion within the Bell corporation. Then he was suddenly heard to say: 'No, I'm not interested in developing a powerful brain. All I'm after is just a mediocre brain, something like the President of the American Telephone and Telegraph Company.'

—Alan Turing, quoted in *Alan Turing the Enigma of Intelligence* by A. Hodge

11.1 Introduction

This chapter introduces the relationship between biological neurons, which make up human brains, and artificial neurons, which are used in artificial neural networks. McCulloch and Pitts neurons are explained, and the capabilities and limitations of perceptrons are examined. Multilayer neural networks are explored, and the backpropagation algorithm for supervised learning in multilayer networks is explained. Recurrent networks, such as Hopfield networks and other bidirectional associative memories, are also explained. Unsupervised learning is explained through the use of Kohonen maps and Hebb's law.

Although the neural networks presented in this chapter are very simplistic, real-world networks can be extremely complex, consisting of hundreds or even thousands of neurons. Networks of this size can often appear like a "black box," in the sense that it is not clear why they behave in the way they do. In fact, the behavior of complex neural networks is often emergent.

11.2   Neurons

11.2.1   Biological Neurons

The human brain contains over ten billion **neurons**, each of which is connected, on average, to several thousand other neurons. These connections are known as **synapses**, and the human brain contains about 60 trillion such connections.

Neurons are in fact very simple processing elements. Each neuron contains a **soma**, which is the body of the neuron, an **axon**, and a number of **dendrites**. A simplified diagram of a biological neuron is shown in Figure 11.1.

The neuron receives inputs from other neurons along its dendrites, and when this input signal exceeds a certain threshold, the neuron "fires"—in

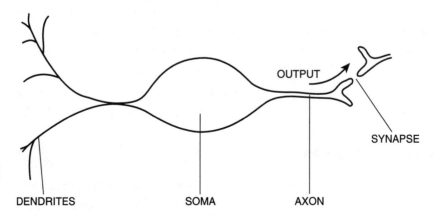

Figure 11.1

A neuron in the human brain

DENDRITES   SOMA   AXON

fact, a chemical reaction occurs, which causes an electrical pulse, known as an **action potential**, to be sent down the axon (the output of the neuron), toward synapses that connect the neuron to the dendrites of other neurons.

Although each neuron individually is extremely simple, this enormously complex network of neurons is able to process information at a great rate and of extraordinary complexity. The human brain far exceeds in terms of complexity any device created by man, or indeed, any naturally occurring object or structure in the universe, as far as we are aware today.

The human brain has a property known as **plasticity**, which means that neurons can change the nature and number of their connections to other neurons in response to events that occur. In this way, the brain is able to learn. As is explained in Chapter 10, the brain uses a form of credit assignment to strengthen the connections between neurons that lead to correct solutions to problems and weakens connections that lead to incorrect solutions. The strength of a connection, or synapse, determines how much influence it will have on the neurons to which it is connected, and so if a connection is weakened, it will play less of a role in subsequent computations.

11.2.2 Artificial Neurons

Artificial neural networks are modeled on the human brain and consist of a number of artificial neurons. Neurons in artificial neural networks tend to have fewer connections than biological neurons, and neural networks are all (currently) significantly smaller in terms of number of neurons than the human brain.

The neurons that we examine in this chapter were invented by McCulloch and Pitts (1943) and so are often referred to as McCulloch and Pitts neurons.

Each neuron (or **node**) in a neural network receives a number of inputs. A function called the **activation function** is applied to these input values, which results in the **activation level** of the neuron, which is the output value of the neuron. There are a number of possible functions that can be used in neurons. Some of the most commonly used activation functions are illustrated in Figure 11.2.

In Figure 11.2, the x-axis of each graph represents the input value to the neuron, and the y-axis represents the output, or the activation level, of the neuron.

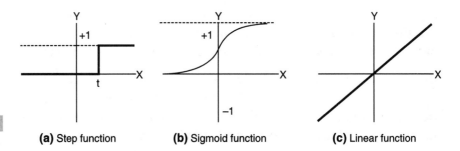

Figure 11.2

Three activation functions

(a) Step function   **(b)** Sigmoid function   **(c)** Linear function

One of the most commonly used functions is the step function, or **linear threshold** function. In using this function, the inputs to the neuron are summed (having each been multiplied by a weight), and this sum is compared with a threshold, t. If the sum is greater than the threshold, then the neuron fires and has an activation level of $+1$. Otherwise, it is inactive and has an activation level of zero. (In some networks, when the sum does not exceed the threshold, the activation level is considered to be -1 instead of 0).

Hence, the behavior of the neuron can be expressed as follows:

$$X = \sum_{i=1}^{n} w_i x_i$$

X is the weighted sum of the n inputs to the neuron, x_1 to x_n, where each input, x_n is multiplied by its corresponding weight w_n. For example, let us consider a simple neuron that has just two inputs. Each of these inputs has a weight associated with it, as follows:

$w_1 = 0.8$

$w_2 = 0.4$

The inputs to the neuron are $x1$ and $x2$:

$x_1 = 0.7$

$x_2 = 0.9$

So, the summed weight of these inputs is

$(0.8 \times 0.7) + (0.4 \times 0.9) = 0.92$

The activation level Y, is defined for this neuron as

$$Y = \begin{cases} +1 & \text{for } X > t \\ 0 & \text{for } X \leq t \end{cases}$$

Hence, if t is less than or equal to 0.92, then this neuron will fire with this particular set of inputs. Otherwise, it will have an activation level of zero.

A neuron that uses the linear activation function simply uses the weighted sum of its inputs as its activation level. The sigmoid function converts inputs from a range of $-\infty$ to $+\infty$ into an activation level in the range of 0 to +1.

A neural network consists of a set of neurons that are connected together. Later in this chapter we explore the ways in which neurons are usually connected together. The connections between neurons have weights associated with them, and each neuron passes its output on to the inputs of the neurons to which it is connected. This output depends on the application of the activation function to the inputs it receives. In this way, an input signal to the network is processed by the entire network and an output (or multiple outputs) produced. There is no central processing or control mechanism—the entire network is involved in every piece of computation that takes place.

The way in which neurons behave over time is particularly interesting. When an input is given to a neural network, the output does not appear immediately because it takes some finite period of time for signals to pass from one neuron to another. In artificial neural networks this time is usually very short, but in the human brain, neural connections are surprisingly slow. It is only the enormously parallel nature of the brain that enables it to calculate so quickly.

For neural networks to learn, the weight associated with each connection (equivalent to a synapse in the biological brain) can be changed in response to particular sets of inputs and events. As is mentioned in Chapter 10, Hebbian learning involves increasing the weight of a connection between two neurons if both neurons fire at the same time. We learn more about this later in the chapter.

11.3   Perceptrons

The perceptron, which was first proposed by Rosenblatt (1958), is a simple neuron that is used to classify its inputs into one of two categories.

The perceptron can have any number of inputs, which are sometimes arranged into a grid. This grid can be used to represent an image, or a field of vision, and so perceptrons can be used to carry out simple image classification or recognition tasks.

A perceptron uses a step function that returns +1 if the weighted sum of the inputs, X, is greater than a threshold, t, and -1 if X is less than or equal to t:

$$X = \sum_{i=1}^{n} w_i x_i$$

$$Y = \begin{cases} +1 & \text{for } X > t \\ 0 & \text{for } X \leq t \end{cases}$$

This function is often written as Step (X):

$$Step(X) = \begin{cases} +1 & \text{for } X > t \\ 0 & \text{for } X \leq t \end{cases}$$

in which case, the activation function for a perceptron can be written as

$$Y = Step\left(\sum_{i=0}^{n} w_i x_i \right)$$

Note that here we have allowed i to run from 0 instead of from 1. This means that we have introduced two new variables: w_0 and x_0. We define x_0 as 1, and w_0 as $-t$.

A single perceptron can be used to learn a classification task, where it receives an input and classifies it into one of two categories: 1 or 0. We can consider these to represent *true* and *false*, in which case the perceptron can learn to represent a Boolean operator, such as AND or OR.

The learning process for a perceptron is as follows:

First, random weights are assigned to the inputs. Typically, these weights will be chosen between -0.5 and $+0.5$.

Next, an item of training data is presented to the perceptron, and its output classification observed. If the output is incorrect, the weights are adjusted to try to more closely classify this input. In other words, if the perceptron incorrectly classifies a positive piece of training data as negative, then the weights need to be modified to increase the output for that set of inputs. This can be done by adding a positive value to the weight of an input that had a negative input value, and vice versa.

The formula for this modification, as proposed by Rosenblatt (Rosenblatt 1960) is as follows:

$$w_i \leftarrow w_i + (a \times x_i \times e)$$

where e is the error that was produced, and a is the **learning rate**, where $0 < a < 1$; e is defined as 0 if the output is correct, and otherwise it is positive if the output is too low and negative if the output is too high. In this way, if the output is too high, a decrease in weight is caused for an input that received a positive value. This rule is known as the **perceptron training rule**.

Once this modification to the weights has taken place, the next piece of training data is used in the same way. Once all the training data have been applied, the process starts again, until all the weights are correct and all errors are zero. Each iteration of this process is known as an **epoch**.

Let us examine a simple example: we will see how a perceptron can learn to represent the logical-OR function for two inputs. We will use a threshold of zero ($t = 0$) and a learning rate of 0.2.

First, the weight associated with each of the two inputs is initialized to a random value between -1 and $+1$:

$$w_1 = -0.2$$
$$w_2 = 0.4$$

Now, the first epoch is run through. The training data will consist of the four combinations of 1's and 0's possible with two inputs.

Hence, our first piece of training data is

$$x1 = 0$$
$$x2 = 0$$

and our expected output is $x1 \lor x2 = 0$.

We apply our formula for Y:

$$Y = Step\left(\sum_{i=0}^{n} w_i x_i\right)$$
$$= Step\big((0 \times -0.2) + (0 \times 0.4)\big)$$
$$= 0$$

Hence, the output Y is as expected, and the error, e, is therefore 0. So the weights do not change.

Now, for $x1 = 0$ and $x2 = 1$:

$$Y = \text{Step} \, ((0 \times -0.2) + (1 \times 0.4))$$
$$= \text{Step} \, (0.4)$$
$$= 1$$

Again, this is correct, and so the weights do not need to change.

For $x1 = 1$ and $x2 = 0$:

$$Y = \text{Step} \, ((1 \times -0.2) + (0 \times 0.4))$$
$$= \text{Step} \, (-0.2)$$
$$= 0$$

This is incorrect because $1 \vee 0 = 1$, so we should expect Y to be 1 for this set of inputs. Hence, the weights are adjusted.

We will use the perceptron training rule to assign new values to the weights:

$$w_i \leftarrow w_i + (a \times x_i \times e)$$

Our learning rate is 0.2, and in this case, the e is 1, so we will assign the following value to $w1$:

$$w1 = -0.2 + (0.2 \times 1 \times 1)$$
$$= -0.2 + (0.2)$$
$$= 0$$

We now use the same formula to assign a new value to $w2$:

$$w2 = 0.4 + (0.2 \times 0 \times 1)$$
$$= 0.4$$

Because $w2$ did not contribute to this error, it is not adjusted.

The final piece of training data is now used ($x_1 = 1$ and $x_2 = 1$):

$$Y = \text{Step} \, ((0 \times 1) + (0.4 \times 1))$$
$$= \text{Step} \, (0 + 0.4)$$
$$= \text{Step} \, (0.4)$$
$$= 1$$

This is correct, and so the weights are not adjusted.

This is the end of the first epoch, and at this point the method runs again and continues to repeat until all four pieces of training data are classified correctly.

Table 11.1   A sample run showing how the weights change for a simple perceptron when it learns to represent the logical OR function

Epoch	X1	X2	Expected Y	Actual Y	Error	w1	w2
1	0	0	0	0	0	−0.2	0.4
1	0	1	1	1	0	−0.2	0.4
1	**1**	**0**	**1**	**0**	**1**	**0**	**0.4**
1	1	1	1	1	0	0	0.4
2	0	0	0	0	0	0	0.4
2	0	1	1	1	0	0	0.4
2	**1**	**0**	**1**	**0**	**1**	**0.2**	**0.4**
2	1	1	1	1	0	0.2	0.4
3	0	0	0	0	0	0.2	0.4
3	0	1	1	1	0	0.2	0.4
3	1	0	1	1	0	0.2	0.4
3	1	1	1	1	0	0.2	0.4

Table 11.1 shows the complete sequence—it takes just three epochs for the perceptron to correctly learn to classify input values. Lines in which an error was made are marked in **bold.**

After just three epochs, the perceptron learns to correctly model the logical-OR function.

In the same way, a perceptron can be trained to model other logical functions such as AND, but there are some functions that cannot be modeled using a perceptron, such as exclusive OR.

The reason for this is that perceptrons can only learn to model functions that are **linearly separable.** A linearly separable function is one that can be drawn in a two-dimensional graph, and a single straight line can be drawn between the values so that inputs that are classified into one classification are on one side of the line, and inputs that are classified into the other are on the other side of the line. Figure 11.3 shows how such a line can be drawn for the OR function, but not for the exclusive-OR function. Four

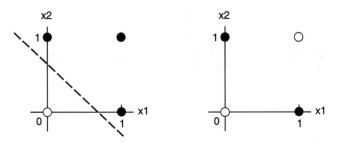

Figure 11.3

Illustrating the difference between a linearly separable function and one which is not

points are plotted on each graph, and a solid dot represents *true*, and a hollow dot represents a value of *false*. It should be clear that no dashed line could be drawn in the second case, for the exclusive OR function, that would separate solid dots from hollow ones.

The reason that a single perceptron can only model functions that are linearly separable can be seen by examining the following function:

$$X = \sum_{i=1}^{n} w_i x_i$$

$$Y = \begin{cases} +1 & for\ X > t \\ -1 & for\ X \leq t \end{cases}$$

Using these functions, we are effectively dividing the search space using a line for which $X = t$. Hence, in a perceptron with two inputs, the line that divides one class from the other is defined as follows:

$$w_1 x_1 + w_2 x_2 = t$$

The perceptron functions by identifying a set of values for w_i, which generates a suitable function. In cases where no such linear function exists, the perceptron cannot succeed.

11.4   Multilayer Neural Networks

Most real-world problems are not linearly separable, and so although perceptrons are an interesting model for studying the way in which artificial neurons can work, something more powerful is needed.

As has already been indicated, neural networks consist of a number of neurons that are connected together, usually arranged in layers.

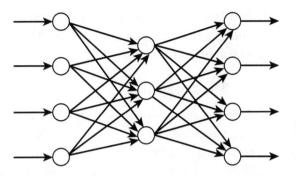

Figure 11.4
A simple three-layer feed-forward neural network

A single perceptron can be thought of as a single-layer perceptron. Multi-layer perceptrons are capable of modeling more complex functions, including ones that are not linearly separable, such as the exclusive-OR function.

To see that a multilayer network is capable of modeling a function that is not linearly separable, such as exclusive-OR, note that the functions NOR and NAND are both linearly separable and so can be represented by a single perceptron. By combining these functions together, all other Boolean functions can be generated. Hence, by combining single perceptrons in just two layers, any binary function of two inputs can be generated.

A typical architecture for a multilayer neural network is shown in Figure 11.4.

The network shown in Figure 11.4 is a **feed-forward network**, consisting of three layers.

The first layer is the **input layer**. Each node (or neuron) in this layer receives a single input signal. In fact, it is usually the case that the nodes in this layer are not neurons, but simply act to pass input signals on to the nodes in the next layer, which is in this case a **hidden layer**.

A network can have one or more hidden layers, which contain the neurons that do the real work. Note that each input signal is passed to each of the nodes in this layer and that the output of each node in this layer is passed to each node in the final layer, which is the **output layer**. The output layer carries out the final stage of processing and sends out output signals.

The network is called feed-forward because data are fed forward from the input nodes through to the output nodes. This is in contrast with **recurrent** networks, which we examine in Section 11.5, where some data are passed back from the output nodes to the input nodes.

A typical feed-forward neural network consists of an input layer, one or two hidden layers, and an output layer, and may have anywhere between 10 and 1000 neurons in each layer.

11.4.1 Backpropagation

Multilayer neural networks learn in much the same way as single percep-trons. The main difference is that in a multilayer network, each neuron has weights associated with its inputs, and so there are a far greater number of weights to be adjusted when an error is made with a piece of training data. Clearly, an important question is how to assign blame (or credit) to the var-ious weights. One method that is commonly used is **backpropagation.**

Rather than using the simple Step function that single perceptrons use, multilayer backpropagation networks usually use the sigmoid function, which is illustrated in Figure 11.2(b).

The sigmoid function is defined as follows:

$$\sigma(x) = \frac{1}{1 + e^{-x}}$$

This function is easy to differentiate because

$$\frac{d\sigma(x)}{dx} = \sigma(x) \cdot (1 - \sigma(x))$$

This is in contrast with the Step function used by perceptrons, which has no simple derivative.

As with the single perceptron, the backpropagation algorithm starts by ini-tializing the weights in the network to random values, which are usually set to small values, say in the range of -0.5 to 0.5. Alternatively, the weights can be normally distributed over the range from $-2.4/n$ to $2.4/n$, where n is the number of inputs to the input layer.

Each iteration of the algorithm involves first feeding data through the net-work from the inputs to the outputs. The next phase, which gives the algo-rithm its name, involves feeding errors back from the outputs to the inputs. These error values feed back through the network, making changes to the weights of nodes along the way. The algorithm repeats in this way until the outputs produced for the training data are sufficiently close to the desired values—in other words, until the error values are sufficiently small.

Because the sigmoid function cannot actually reach 0 or 1, it is usual to accept a value such as 0.9 as representing 1 and 0.1 as representing 0.

Now we shall see the formulae that are used to adjust the weights in the backpropagation algorithm. We will consider a network of three layers and will use i to represent nodes in the input layer, j to represent nodes in the hidden layer, and k to represent nodes in the output layer. Hence, for example, w_{ij} refers to the weight of a connection between a node in the input layer and a node in the hidden layer.

The function that is used to derive the output value for a node j in the network is as follows:

$$X_j = \sum_{i=1}^{n} x_i \cdot w_{ij} - \theta_j$$

$$Y_j = \frac{1}{1 + e^{-X_j}}$$

where n is the number of inputs to node j; w_{ij} is the weight of the connection between each node i and node j; θ_j is the threshold value being used for node j, which is set to a random value between 0 and 1; x_i is the input value for input node I; and y_j is the output value produced by node j.

Once the inputs have been fed through the network to produce outputs, an **error gradient** is calculated for each node k in the output layer.

The error signal for k is defined as the difference between the desired value and the actual value for that node:

$$e_k = d_k - y_k$$

d_k is the desired value for node k, and y_k is the actual value, in this iteration.

The error gradient for output node k is defined as the error value for this node multiplied by the derivative of the activation function:

$$\delta_k = \frac{\partial y_k}{\partial x_k} \cdot e_k$$

x_k is the weighted sum of the input values to the node k.

Because y is defined as a sigmoid function of x, we can use the formula that was given above for the derivative of the sigmoid function to obtain the following formula for the error gradient:

$$\delta_k = y_k \cdot (1 - y_k) \cdot e_k$$

Similarly, we calculate an error gradient for each node j in the hidden layer, as follows:

$$\delta_j = y_j \cdot (1 - y_j) \sum_{k=1}^{n} w_{jk} \delta_k$$

where n is the number of nodes in the output layer, and thus the number of outputs from each node in the hidden layer.

Now each weight in the network, w_{ij} or w_{jk}, is updated according to the following formula:

$$w_{ij} \leftarrow w_{ij} + \alpha \cdot x_i \cdot \delta_j$$

$$w_{jk} \leftarrow w_{jk} + \alpha \cdot y_j \cdot \delta_k$$

where x_i is the input value to input node i, and α is the learning rate, which is a positive number below 1, and which should not be too high.

This method is known as **gradient descent** because it involves following the steepest path down the surface that represents the error function to attempt to find the minimum in the error space, which represents the set of weights that provides the best performance of the network.

In fact, the iteration of the backpropagation algorithm is usually terminated when the sum of the squares of the errors of the output values for all training data in an epoch is less than some threshold, such as 0.001.

Note that this method assigns blame to individual nodes within the network by comparing the weights attached to each node with the error associated with that node. In the case of hidden nodes, there is no error value because there is no specific desired output value for these nodes. In this case, the weight of each connection between a hidden layer node and an output node is multiplied by the error of that output node to attempt to distribute the blame between the nodes in the hidden layer according to how much each one contributes to the error.

Unlike Hebbian learning, which is discussed in more detail in Section 11.6.3, backpropagation does not appear to occur in the human brain. Additionally, it is rather inefficient and tends to be too slow for use in solv-

ing real-world problems. With some simple problems it can take hundreds
or even thousands of epochs to reach a satisfactorily low level of error.

11.4.2   Improving the Performance of Backpropagation

A common method used to improve the performance of backpropagation
is to include **momentum** in the formula that is used to modify the weights.
The momentum takes into account the extent to which a particular weight
was changed on the previous iteration. We shall use t to represent the current iteration, and $t - 1$ to represent the previous iteration. Hence, we can
write our learning rules as follows:

$$\Delta w_{ij}(t) = \alpha \cdot x_i \cdot \delta_j + \beta \Delta w_{ij}(t-1)$$
$$\Delta w_{jk}(t) = \alpha \cdot y_j \cdot \delta_k + \beta \Delta w_{jk}(t-1)$$

$\Delta w_{ij}(t)$ is the amount that is added to the weight of the connection between
nodes i and j, w_{ij} at iteration t; β is the momentum value, which is a positive
number between 0 and 1. Typically, a fairly high value such as 0.95 is used.
If β is zero, this is the same as the backpropagation algorithm without
using momentum.

This rule, including the momentum value, is known as the **generalized
delta rule**.

The inclusion of the momentum value has the benefit of enabling the
backpropagation method to avoid local minima and also to move more
quickly through areas where the error space is not changing.

An alternative method of speeding up backpropagation is to use the **hyper-
bolic tangent** function, tanh, instead of the sigmoid function, which tends
to enable the network to converge on a solution in fewer iterations. The
tanh function is defined as:

$$tanh(x) = \frac{2a}{1 + e^{-bx}} - a$$

where a and b are constants, such as $a = 1.7$ and $b = 0.7$.

A final way to improve the performance of backpropagation is to vary the
value of the learning rate, α during the course of training the network. Two
heuristics proposed by R. A. Jacobs (1988) use the direction of change

(increase or decrease) of the sum of the square of the errors from one epoch to the next to determine the change in learning rate:

If for several epochs the sum of the square of the errors changes in the same direction, increase the learning rate.

1. If for several epochs the sum of the square of the errors changes in the same direction, increase the learning rate.

2. If the sum of the square of the errors alternates its change in direction over several epochs, decrease the learning rate.

By using these heuristics in combination with the generalized delta rule, the performance of the backpropagation algorithm can be significantly improved.

11.5   Recurrent Networks

The neural networks we have been studying so far are feed-forward networks. A feed-forward network is acyclic, in the sense that there are no cycles in the network, because data passes from the inputs to the outputs, and not vice versa,. Once a feed-forward network has been trained, its state is fixed and does not alter as new input data is presented to it. In other words, it does not have **memory**.

A recurrent network can have connections that go backward from output nodes to input nodes and, in fact, can have arbitrary connections between any nodes. In this way, a recurrent network's internal state can alter as sets of input data are presented to it, and it can be said to have a memory.

This is particularly useful in solving problems where the solution depends not just on the current inputs, but on all previous inputs. For example, recurrent networks could be used to predict the stock market price of a particular stock, based on all previous values, or it could be used to predict what the weather will be like tomorrow, based on what the weather has been.

Clearly, due to the lack of memory, feed-forward networks are not able to solve such tasks.

When learning, the recurrent network feeds its inputs through the network, including feeding data back from outputs to inputs, and repeats this process until the values of the outputs do not change. At this point, the network is said to be in a state of **equilibrium** or **stability**. For this reason, recurrent networks are also known as **attractor networks** because they are attracted to certain output values. The stable values of the network, which are also known as **fundamental memories**, are the output values used as the response to the inputs the network received.

Hence, a recurrent network can be considered to be a **memory**, which is able to learn a set of states—those that act as attractors for it. Once such a network has been trained, for any given input it will output the attractor that is closest to that input.

For example, a recurrent network can be used as an error-correcting network. If only a few possible inputs are considered "valid," the network can correct all other inputs to the closest valid input.

It is not always the case that a recurrent network will reach a stable state: some networks are **unstable**, which means they oscillate between different output values.

11.5.1   Hopfield Networks

In the 1980s, John Hopfield invented a form of recurrent network that has come to be known as a Hopfield network.

The activation function used by most Hopfield networks is the **sign activation** function, which is defined as:

$$Sign(X) = \begin{cases} +1 & for\ X > 0 \\ -1 & for\ X < 0 \end{cases}$$

Note that this definition does not provide a value for $Sign(0)$. This is because when a neuron that uses the sign activation function receives an input of 0, it stays in the same state—in other words, it continues to output 1 if it was outputting 1 in the previous iteration, and continues to output -1 if it was outputting -1.

When considering the operation of a Hopfield network, it is usual to use matrix arithmetic. The weights of the network are represented by a matrix, W, which is calculated as follows:

$$W = \sum_{i=1}^{N} X_i X_i^t - N\ \mathrm{I}$$

where each X_i is an input vector, representing the m input values to the network; X_i^t is the matrix transposition of X_i; **I** is the $m \times m$ identity matrix; N is the number of states (X_i) that are to be learned. The transposition of a matrix is simply one where the rows and columns are swapped. If

$$X_1 = \begin{bmatrix} 1 \\ -1 \\ 1 \end{bmatrix}$$

then the transposition of X_1 is

$$X_i^t = \begin{bmatrix} 1 & -1 & 1 \end{bmatrix}$$

The identity matrix, **I**, is a matrix with zeros in every row and column, but with 1s along the leading diagonal. For example,

$$I = \begin{bmatrix} 1 & 0 & 0 \\ 0 & 1 & 0 \\ 0 & 0 & 1 \end{bmatrix}$$

Now let us examine an example. We will imagine a single-layer Hopfield network with five nodes and three training inputs that are to be learned by the network. We will have our network learn the following three states:

$$X_1 = \begin{bmatrix} 1 \\ 1 \\ 1 \\ 1 \\ 1 \end{bmatrix} \quad X_2 = \begin{bmatrix} -1 \\ -1 \\ -1 \\ -1 \\ -1 \end{bmatrix} \quad X_3 = \begin{bmatrix} 1 \\ -1 \\ 1 \\ 1 \\ -1 \end{bmatrix}$$

We thus have three states (vectors) that are to be learned, each of which consists of five input values. The inputs can be either 1 or -1; similarly, the output values can be either 1 or -1, and so the output can be represented as a similar vector of five values, each of which is either 1 or -1.

The weight matrix is calculated as follows:

$$W = \sum_{i=1}^{3} X_i X_i^t - 3\,\mathbf{I}$$

$$= X_1 X_i^t + X_2 X_i^t + X_3 X_i^t - 3\,\mathbf{I}$$

$$= \begin{bmatrix} 1 \\ 1 \\ 1 \\ 1 \\ 1 \end{bmatrix} \begin{bmatrix} 1 & 1 & 1 & 1 & 1 \end{bmatrix} + \begin{bmatrix} -1 \\ -1 \\ -1 \\ -1 \\ -1 \end{bmatrix} \begin{bmatrix} -1 & -1 & -1 & -1 & -1 \end{bmatrix} +$$

$$\begin{bmatrix} 1 \\ -1 \\ 1 \\ 1 \\ -1 \end{bmatrix} \begin{bmatrix} 1 & -1 & 1 & 1 & -1 \end{bmatrix} - 3 \begin{bmatrix} 1 & 0 & 0 & 0 & 0 \\ 0 & 1 & 0 & 0 & 0 \\ 0 & 0 & 1 & 0 & 0 \\ 0 & 0 & 0 & 1 & 0 \\ 0 & 0 & 0 & 0 & 1 \end{bmatrix}$$

$$= \begin{bmatrix} 1 & 1 & 1 & 1 & 1 \\ 1 & 1 & 1 & 1 & 1 \\ 1 & 1 & 1 & 1 & 1 \\ 1 & 1 & 1 & 1 & 1 \\ 1 & 1 & 1 & 1 & 1 \end{bmatrix} + \begin{bmatrix} 1 & 1 & 1 & 1 & 1 \\ 1 & 1 & 1 & 1 & 1 \\ 1 & 1 & 1 & 1 & 1 \\ 1 & 1 & 1 & 1 & 1 \\ 1 & 1 & 1 & 1 & 1 \end{bmatrix} + \begin{bmatrix} 1 & -1 & 1 & 1 & -1 \\ -1 & 1 & -1 & -1 & 1 \\ 1 & -1 & 1 & 1 & -1 \\ 1 & -1 & 1 & 1 & -1 \\ -1 & 1 & -1 & -1 & 1 \end{bmatrix} -$$

$$\begin{bmatrix} 3 & 0 & 0 & 0 & 0 \\ 0 & 3 & 0 & 0 & 0 \\ 0 & 0 & 3 & 0 & 0 \\ 0 & 0 & 0 & 3 & 0 \\ 0 & 0 & 0 & 0 & 3 \end{bmatrix}$$

$$= \begin{bmatrix} 0 & 1 & 3 & 3 & 1 \\ 1 & 0 & 1 & 1 & 3 \\ 3 & 1 & 0 & 3 & 1 \\ 3 & 1 & 3 & 0 & 1 \\ 1 & 3 & 1 & 1 & 0 \end{bmatrix}$$

Note that the weight matrix has zeros along its leading diagonal. This means that each node in the network is not connected to itself (i.e., $w_{ii} = 0$ for all i). A further property of a Hopfield network is that the two connections between a pair of nodes have the same weight. In other words, $w_{ij} = w_{ji}$ for any nodes i and j.

The three training states used to produce the weight matrix will be stable states for the network. We can test this by determining the output vectors for each of them.

The output vector is defined by

$$Y_i = Sign(WX_i - \theta)$$

where θ is the threshold matrix, which contains the thresholds for each of the five inputs. We will assume that the thresholds are all set at zero.

$$Y_1 = Sign\left(\begin{bmatrix} 0 & 1 & 3 & 3 & 1 \\ 1 & 0 & 1 & 1 & 3 \\ 3 & 1 & 0 & 3 & 1 \\ 3 & 1 & 3 & 0 & 1 \\ 1 & 3 & 1 & 1 & 0 \end{bmatrix}\begin{bmatrix} 1 \\ 1 \\ 1 \\ 1 \\ 1 \end{bmatrix} - \begin{bmatrix} 0 \\ 0 \\ 0 \\ 0 \\ 0 \end{bmatrix}\right)$$

$$= Sign\begin{bmatrix} 8 \\ 6 \\ 8 \\ 8 \\ 6 \end{bmatrix}$$

$$= \begin{bmatrix} 1 \\ 1 \\ 1 \\ 1 \\ 1 \end{bmatrix} = X_1$$

Hence, the first input state is a stable state for the network. Similarly, we can show that $Y_2 = X_2$ and that $Y_3 = X_3$.

Now let us see how the network treats an input that is different from the training data. We will use

$$X_4 = \begin{bmatrix} 1 \\ 1 \\ -1 \\ 1 \\ 1 \end{bmatrix}$$

Note that this vector differs from X_1 in just one value, so we would expect the network to converge on X_1 when presented with this input.

$$Y_4 = Sign \left(\begin{bmatrix} 0 & 1 & 3 & 3 & 1 \\ 1 & 0 & 1 & 1 & 3 \\ 3 & 1 & 0 & 3 & 1 \\ 3 & 1 & 3 & 0 & 1 \\ 1 & 3 & 1 & 1 & 0 \end{bmatrix} \begin{bmatrix} 1 \\ 1 \\ -1 \\ 1 \\ 1 \end{bmatrix} - \begin{bmatrix} 0 \\ 0 \\ 0 \\ 0 \\ 0 \end{bmatrix} \right)$$

$$= Sign \begin{bmatrix} 2 \\ 4 \\ 8 \\ 2 \\ 4 \end{bmatrix}$$

$$= \begin{bmatrix} 1 \\ 1 \\ 1 \\ 1 \\ 1 \end{bmatrix} = X_1$$

Now we will try an input that is very different from the training data:

$$X_5 = \begin{bmatrix} -1 \\ 1 \\ -1 \\ 1 \\ 1 \end{bmatrix}$$

Let us apply the network to this input data:

$$Y_5 = Sign \left(\begin{bmatrix} 0 & 1 & 3 & 3 & 1 \\ 1 & 0 & 1 & 1 & 3 \\ 3 & 1 & 0 & 3 & 1 \\ 3 & 1 & 3 & 0 & 1 \\ 1 & 3 & 1 & 1 & 0 \end{bmatrix} \begin{bmatrix} -1 \\ 1 \\ -1 \\ 1 \\ 1 \end{bmatrix} - \begin{bmatrix} 0 \\ 0 \\ 0 \\ 0 \\ 0 \end{bmatrix} \right)$$

$$= Sign \begin{bmatrix} 2 \\ 2 \\ 2 \\ -4 \\ 2 \end{bmatrix} = \begin{bmatrix} 1 \\ 1 \\ 1 \\ -1 \\ 1 \end{bmatrix}$$

Because this is different from X_5 and is not one of the attractors, we need to apply the rule again:

$$Y_5 = Sign \left(\begin{bmatrix} 0 & 1 & 3 & 3 & 1 \\ 1 & 0 & 1 & 1 & 3 \\ 3 & 1 & 0 & 3 & 1 \\ 3 & 1 & 3 & 0 & 1 \\ 1 & 3 & 1 & 1 & 0 \end{bmatrix} \begin{bmatrix} 1 \\ 1 \\ 1 \\ -1 \\ 1 \end{bmatrix} - \begin{bmatrix} 0 \\ 0 \\ 0 \\ 0 \\ 0 \end{bmatrix} \right)$$

$$= Sign \begin{bmatrix} 2 \\ 4 \\ 2 \\ 8 \\ 4 \end{bmatrix} = \begin{bmatrix} 1 \\ 1 \\ 1 \\ 1 \\ 1 \end{bmatrix} = X_1$$

The use of the Hopfield network involves three stages. In the first stage, the network is trained to learn the set of attractor states. This can be thought of as a **storage** or **memorization** stage. This is done by setting the weights of the network according to the values given by the weights matrix, W, which is calculated as described above.

The second phase involves testing the network, by providing the attractor states as inputs, and checking that the outputs are identical. The final stage involves using the network, in which the network, in acting as a memory, is required to **retrieve** data from its memory.

In each case, the network will retrieve the attractor closest to the input that it is given. In this case, the nearest attractor is $X1$, which differs in just two inputs. The measure of distance that is usually used for such vectors is the **Hamming distance**. The Hamming distance measures the number of elements of the vectors that differ. The Hamming distance between two vectors, X and Y, is written $||X, Y||$.

For the vectors we have used

$$||X_1, X_4|| = 1$$

$$||X_1, X_5|| = 2$$

Hence, the Hopfield network is a memory that usually maps an input vector to the memorized vector whose Hamming distance from the input vector is least.

In fact, although a Hopfield network always converges on a stable state, it does not always converge on the state closest to the original input. No method has yet been found for ensuring that a Hopfield network will always converge on the closest state.

A Hopfield network is considered to be an **autoassociative memory**, which means that it is able to remember an item itself, or a similar item that might have been modified slightly, but it cannot use one piece of data to remember another. The human brain is fully associative, or **heteroassociative**, which means one item is able to cause the brain to recall an entirely different item. A piece of music or a smell will often cause us to remember an old memory: this is using the associative nature of memory. A Hopfield network is not capable of making such associations.

11.5.2   Bidirectional Associative Memories (BAMs)

A **Bidirectional Associative Memory**, or BAM, is a neural network first discussed by Bart Kosko (1988) that is similar in structure to the Hopfield network and which can be used to associate items from one set to items in another set.

The network consists of two layers of nodes, where each node in one layer is connected to every other node in the other layer—this means that the layers are **fully connected**. This is in contrast to the Hopfield network, which consists of just a single layer of neurons: in the Hopfield network, each neuron is connected to every other neuron within the same layer, whereas in the BAM, each neuron is connected just to neurons in the other layer, not to neurons in its own layer.

As with Hopfield networks, the weight matrix is calculated from the items that are to be learned. In this case, two sets of data are to be learned, so that when an item from set X is presented to the network, it will recall a corresponding item from set Y.

The weights matrix $\mathbf{W}$ is defined as:

$$\mathbf{W} = \sum_i^n \mathbf{X}_i \mathbf{Y}_i^t$$

The BAM uses a neuron with a sign activation function, which is also used by a Hopfield network.

When the network is given a vector X_i as an input, it will recall the corresponding vector Y_i, and similarly, when presented with Y_i, the network will recall X_i.

Let us examine a simple example:

$$X_1 = \begin{bmatrix} 1 \\ 1 \end{bmatrix} \quad X_2 = \begin{bmatrix} -1 \\ -1 \end{bmatrix}$$

$$Y_1 = \begin{bmatrix} 1 \\ 1 \\ 1 \end{bmatrix} \quad Y_2 = \begin{bmatrix} -1 \\ -1 \\ -1 \end{bmatrix}$$

We are using our network to learn two sets of vectors. The network has two layers: the input layer has two neurons, and the output layer has three neurons.

The weights matrix is calculated as follows:

$$\mathbf{W} = \begin{bmatrix} 1 \\ 1 \end{bmatrix} \begin{bmatrix} 1 & 1 & 1 \end{bmatrix} + \begin{bmatrix} -1 \\ -1 \end{bmatrix} \begin{bmatrix} -1 & -1 & -1 \end{bmatrix}$$

$$= \begin{bmatrix} 2 & 2 & 2 \\ 2 & 2 & 2 \end{bmatrix}$$

Now we will test the network. When presented with input X_1, the network will output the following vector:

$$Sign\left(W^t X_1\right)$$

If the network is functioning correctly, this should be equal to Y_1:

$$Sign\left(W^t X_1\right) = Sign\left(\begin{bmatrix} 2 & 2 \\ 2 & 2 \\ 2 & 2 \end{bmatrix}\begin{bmatrix} 1 \\ 1 \end{bmatrix}\right)$$

$$= Sign\begin{bmatrix} 4 \\ 4 \\ 4 \end{bmatrix}$$

$$= \begin{bmatrix} 1 \\ 1 \\ 1 \end{bmatrix} = Y_1$$

So the network has correctly recalled Y_1 when presented with X_1.

Similarly, the association should work in reverse: when presented with Y_1, the network should recall X_1:

$$Sign\left(WY_1\right)$$

$$= Sign\left(\begin{bmatrix} 2 & 2 & 2 \\ 2 & 2 & 2 \end{bmatrix}\begin{bmatrix} 1 \\ 1 \\ 1 \end{bmatrix}\right)$$

$$= Sign\begin{bmatrix} 6 \\ 6 \end{bmatrix} = \begin{bmatrix} 1 \\ 1 \end{bmatrix} = X_1$$

Note that in this case, we are using the output layer as if it were an input layer, and vice versa—hence, the network is **bidirectional**.

Like a Hopfield network, the BAM is guaranteed to produce a stable output for any given inputs and for any training data. In fact, a Hopfield network is a type of BAM, with the additional requirement that the weight matrix be square and that each neuron not have a connection to itself (or to its corresponding neuron in the other layer). BAMs are extremely useful neural networks, although their capabilities (and limitations) are not yet fully understood.

11.6 Unsupervised Learning Networks

The networks we have studied so far in this chapter use **supervised learning**: they are presented with preclassified training data before being asked to classify unseen data. We will now look at a number of methods that are used to enable neural networks to learn in an unsupervised manner.

11.6.1 Kohonen Maps

A **Kohonen map**, or **self-organizing feature map**, is a form of neural network invented by Kohonen in the 1980s. The Kohonen map uses the **winner-take-all algorithm**, which leads to a form of unsupervised learning known as **competitive learning**. The winner-take-all algorithm uses the principle that only one neuron provides the output of the network in response to a given input: the neuron that has the highest activation level. During learning, only connections to this neuron have their weights altered.

The purpose of a Kohonen map is to **cluster** input data into a number of clusters. For example, a Kohonen map could be used to cluster news stories into subject categories. A Kohonen map is not told what the categories are: it determines the most useful segmentation itself. Hence, a Kohonen map is particularly useful for clustering data where the clusters are not known in advance.

A Kohonen map has two layers: an input layer and a **cluster layer**, which serves as the output layer. Each input node is connected to every node in the cluster layer, and typically the nodes in the cluster layer are arranged in a grid formation, although this is not essential.

The method used to train a Kohonen map is as follows: Initially, all weights are set to small random values. The learning rate, α, is also set, usually to a small positive value.

An input vector is presented to the input layer of the map. This layer feeds the input data to the cluster layer. The neuron in the cluster layer that most closely matches the input data is declared the winner. This neuron provides the output classification of the map and also has its weights updated.

To determine which neuron wins, its weights are treated as a vector, and this vector is compared with the input vector. The neuron whose weight vector is closest to the input vector is the winner.

The Euclidean distance d_i from the input vector x of a neuron with weight vector w_i is calculated as follows:

$$d_i = \sqrt{\sum_{j=1}^{n} \left(w_{ij} - x_j \right)^2}$$

where n is the number of neurons in the input layer and hence the number of elements in the input vector.

For example, let us calculate the distance between the following two vectors:

$$w_i = \begin{bmatrix} 1 \\ 2 \\ -1 \end{bmatrix} \quad x = \begin{bmatrix} 3 \\ -1 \\ 2 \end{bmatrix}$$

$$\therefore d_i = \sqrt{(1-3)^2 + (2+1)^2 + (-1-2)^2}$$

$$= \sqrt{4+3+9}$$

$$= \sqrt{16}$$

$$= 4$$

So the Euclidean distance between these two vectors is 4.

The neuron for which d_i is the smallest is the winner, and this neuron has its weight vector updated as follows:

$$w_{ij} \leftarrow w_{ij} + \alpha \left(x_j - w_{ij} \right)$$

This adjustment moves the weight vector of the winning neuron closer to the input vector that caused it to win.

In fact, rather than just the winning neuron having its weights updated, a neighborhood of neurons around the winner are usually updated. The neighborhood is usually defined as a radius within the two-dimensional grid of neurons around the winning neuron.

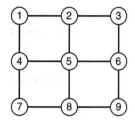

Figure 11.5

The cluster layer of a
simple Kohonen map

Typically, the radius decreases over time as the training data are examined, ending up fixed at a small value. Similarly, the learning rate is often reduced during the training phase.

This training phase usually terminates when the modification of weights becomes very small for all the cluster neurons. At this point, the network has extracted from the training data a set of clusters, where similar items are contained within the same cluster, and similar clusters are near to each other.

11.6.2   Kohonen Map Example

Let us examine a simplified example of a Kohonen map.

Our Kohonen map has just two inputs and nine cluster neurons, which are arranged into a 3×3 grid, as shown in Figure 11.5.

Figure 11.5 shows how the neurons are arranged in a grid. Each node in the cluster layer is connected to each of the two input nodes. The cluster layer nodes are not connected to each other. The grid shown in Figure 11.5 does not represent physical connection, but rather spatial proximity—node 1 is close to nodes 2 and 4. This spatial proximity of neurons is used to calculate the neighborhood set that is used to determine which weights to update during the training phase.

Note that this square arrangement is by no means necessary. The nodes are often arranged in a rectangular grid, but other shapes can be used equally successfully.

Because there are two input nodes in the network, we can represent each input as a position in two-dimensional space. Figure 11.6 shows the nine input values that are to be used to train this network.

In Figure 11.6, x_1 and x_2 are the two input values that are to be presented to the input layer, which contains two neurons.

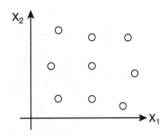

Figure 11.6

Training data for the Kohonen map shown in Figure 11.5

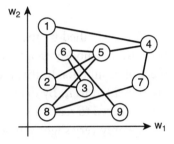

Figure 11.7

Initial weight vectors for the Kohonen map

Note that the training data have been selected randomly from the available space, such that they fill as much of the space as possible. In this way the data will be as representative as possible of all available input data, and so the Kohonen map will be able to cluster the input space optimally.

Because each neuron in the cluster layer has connections to the two input layer neurons, their weight vectors can be plotted in two-dimensional space. These weight vectors are initially set to random values, which are shown in Figure 11.7. The connections between nodes in Figure 11.7 represent spatial proximity again, as in Figure 11.5.

Because there are nine cluster nodes and nine pieces of training data, we expect the network to assign each neuron to one piece of training data. Most real Kohonen maps consist of far more neurons, and many more training data are usually used.

In our simple example, by running a number of iterations of the Kohonen map, the weight vectors are modified to those shown in Figure 11.8.

In this case, it is easy to see what the map has done: by modifying the weight vector of each neuron so that it closely resembles one training vector, the nodes have been modified so that each node will respond extremely well to one of the input data. When a new piece of input data is presented,

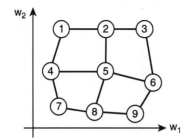

Figure 11.8

Weight vectors after training the Kohonen map

it will be classified by the node whose weight vector is closest to it. Additionally, that node's weight vector will be moved slightly toward the new piece of input data. In this way, the network continues to learn as new data are presented to it. By decreasing the learning rate over time, the network can be forced to reach a stable state where the weights no longer change, or change only very slightly, when presented with new input data.

This example illustrates the self-organizing nature of Kohonen maps. The space-filling shape shown in Figure 11.8 is typical of the behavior of these networks.

11.6.3   Hebbian Learning

Hebbian learning is based on Hebb's law, which was stated by D. O. Hebb in 1949. Hebb's law is stated as follows:

When an axon of cell A is near enough to excite a cell B and repeatedly or persistently takes part in firing it, some growth process or metabolic change takes place in one or both cells such that A's efficiency, as one of the cells firing B, is increased.

In terms of artificial neural networks, this rule can be restated as follows:

If two neurons that are connected to each other fire at the same time, the weight of the connection between those neurons is increased.

Conversely, if the neurons fire at different times, the weight of the connection between them is decreased.

Neural networks use Hebbian learning to learn without needing to be given preclassified training data.

Using Hebbian learning, the weight of a connection between neurons i and j is increased according to the following rule:

$$w_{ij} \leftarrow w_{ij} + \alpha \cdot y_i \cdot x_i$$

where α is the learning rate; x_i is the input to node i, and y_i is the output of node i (and thus the input contributed to node j by node i). This rule is known as the **activity product rule**.

By treating the weights of neuron i as a vector, $\mathbf{W}_i$, this rule can also be written as

$$\mathbf{W}_i \leftarrow \mathbf{W}_i + \alpha \cdot \mathbf{X}_i \cdot y_i$$

where $\mathbf{X}_i$ is the input vector to node i, and y_i is the output of node i.

The activity product rule does not allow for decreasing weights, which is required by Hebb's law. The rule can be modified to allow weights to be decreased by using a **forgetting factor**, ϕ, as follows:

$$w_{ij} \leftarrow w_{ij} + \alpha \cdot y_i \cdot x_i - \phi \cdot y_i \cdot w_{ij}$$

When ϕ is zero, the network cannot "forget," and the weights are always increased during learning. If ϕ were set to 1, the network would not be able to learn at all because it would forget everything. Usually a small value, such as between 0.01 and 0.1, is used as the forgetting factor.

Using Hebb's law, a neural network is able to learn to associate one input with another input. This can be thought of as analogous to the experiment conducted by Pavlov in which he rang a bell whenever he fed his dogs, which led the dogs to salivate whenever they heard a bell ring.

11.7   Evolving Neural Networks

The ideas that we cover in Chapter 14 on genetic algorithms can be applied to neural networks. Genetic algorithms can be used to evolve suitable starting weight vectors for a network. This is useful because the initial weight vector that is chosen for a network can significantly affect the ability of the network to solve a particular problem. Neural networks suffer from many of the problems faced by search methods presented in Part 2 of this book, such as falling into local minima. By repeatedly running a full training session on a neural network with different random starting weights, this problem can be avoided. Clearly, this problem can also be avoided by using evolutionary methods to select starting weight vectors.

Similarly, a genetic algorithm can be used to determine the connectivity of the network. In this way, the number of neurons and the connections between those neurons can be evolved to produce an optimal architecture.

11.8   Chapter Summary

- Biological neurons are the building blocks of the human brain. Each neuron has a number of inputs, and one output, which fires depending on the inputs.

- Artificial neurons are modeled on biological neurons and are used to build artificial neural networks. Artificial neurons often use a function such as a Step function to calculate their output based on the weighted sum of their inputs.

- A perceptron is a very simple neuron that can model problems that are linearly separable.

- Multilayer neural networks, using backpropagation, can solve problems that are not linearly separable.

- Recurrent networks, such as Hopfield networks, allow arbitrary connections between neurons within the network, which is particularly useful for modeling functions such as the value of the stock market, where the value at one point in time is dependent on previous values.

- Unsupervised neural networks, such as Kohonen maps, learn to classify without being presented any preclassified training data.

- Hebbian learning is an unsupervised learning technique based on the idea that if two neurons fire at the same time, then the connection between them should be strengthened.

11.9   Review Questions

11.1   Explain how the human brain uses neurons to learn. What are the similarities and differences between artificial neurons and biological neurons?

11.2   How likely do you think it is that a neural network of the complexity of the human brain will ever be built in software? In hardware?

11.3   Explain how the backpropagation algorithm is used. Why is momentum used with backpropagation?

11.4   Explain the limitations of a perceptron. What kind of problems can they solve? Give a real-world example.

11.5   Explain how Hopfield networks operate.

11.6   Explain the difference between supervised and unsupervised learning. When might each be most useful?

11.7   Explain what is meant by Hebbian learning. Why is forgetting important to Hebbian learning?

11.8   Explain in detail how a Kohonen map might be used to cluster a set of web documents in response to a user's keyword query.

11.9   What are the advantages and disadvantages of applying evolutionary techniques to neural networks? What could be the ultimate goal of such a combination?

11.10   Exercises

11.10   Run through the training process for a perceptron to calculate the binary AND function on three inputs.

11.11   Design a multilayer neural network with two inputs and one hidden layer that uses the backpropagation algorithm to learn to represent the logical exclusive-OR function for two inputs. Your network should have two nodes in the input layer, two in the hidden layer, and one in the output layer. Initialize the weights to random values, and run the algorithm (on paper) for three epochs. Comment on your results. Implement this network in the programming language of your choice. Run it until the sum of the squares of the errors is less than 0.001. How many epochs does the network take to learn the exclusive-OR function? Try to modify your program so that it learns the function in fewer epochs.

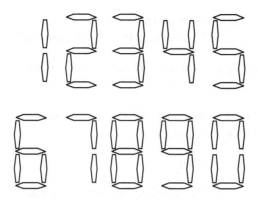

Figure 11.9
The 10 digits possible with
a seven-segment display

11.12 On paper, calculate the weight matrix for a Hopfield network that is to learn the following two input vectors:

$$X_1 = \begin{bmatrix} 1 \\ 1 \\ 1 \\ 1 \end{bmatrix} \quad X_2 = \begin{bmatrix} -1 \\ -1 \\ -1 \\ -1 \end{bmatrix}$$

Now calculate the behavior of the network when it is presented with X_1 as an input. How does it behave when it is presented with the following input?

$$X_3 = \begin{bmatrix} -1 \\ -1 \\ 1 \\ -1 \end{bmatrix}$$

11.14 Design and implement a neural network system for recognizing numbers. You could start by building a network to recognize the 10 possible digits represented in a seven-segment LED, as shown in Figure 11.9. If you are feeling ambitious, extend your algorithm to work with numbers displayed in a dot-matrix display of 8-by-8 dots. What problems do you encounter?

11.11 Further Reading

There are a number of excellent introductory texts on neural networks, as well as many more advanced ones. Introductions by Gurney (1997) and

Callan (1999) cover most of the material introduced in this chapter. For more advanced readings, consult the papers and books referenced below.

To learn more about evolutionary neural networks, consult Negnevitsky (2002) or Bäck et al. (1997).

The Handbook of Brain Theory and Neural Networks: Second Edition edited by Michael A. Arbib (2002 – MIT Press)

Handbook of Evolutionary Computation edited by T. Bäck, D. B. Fogel, and Z. Michalewicz (1997 – Institute of Physics Publishing)

Neural Networks for Pattern Recognition by Christopher M. Bishop (1996 – Oxford University Press)

Understanding 99% of Artificial Neural Networks: Introduction & Tricks by Marcelo Bosque (2002 – Writers Club Press)

The Essence of Neural Networks by Robert Callan (1999 – Prentice Hall)

Fundamentals of Neural Networks by Laurene V. Fausett (1994 – Prentice Hall)

An Introduction to Neural Networks by Kevin Gurney (1997 – UCL Press)

Neural Networks: A Comprehensive Foundation by Simon S. Haykin (1998 – Prentice Hall)

The Organisation of Behavior: A Neuropsychological Theory by D. O. Hebb (1949 – republished in 2002 by Lawrence Erlbaum Assoc.)

Increased Rates of Convergence Through Learning Rate Adaptation by R. A. Jacobs (1987 – in *Neural Networks*, Vol. 1, pp. 295–307).

Self-Organizing Maps by Teuvo Kohonen (2000 – Springer Verlag)

Bidirectional Associative Memories by Bart Kosko (1988 – in *IEEE Transactions Systems, Man & Cybernetics*, Vol. 18, pp. 49–60).

A Logical Calculus of the Ideas Immanent in Nervous Activity by W. S. McCulloch and W. Pitts (1943 – in *Bulletin of Mathematical Biophysics*, Vol. 5, pp. 115–137).

Perceptrons by Marvin Minsky and Seymour A. Papert (1969 – now available in an extended edition: *Perceptrons - Expanded Edition: An Introduction to Computational Geometry*. 1987 – MIT Press)

Machine Learning by Tom M. Mitchell (1997 – McGraw Hill)

Artificial Intelligence: A Guide to Intelligent Systems by Michael Negnevitsky (2002 – Addison Wesley)

Computational Explorations in Cognitive Neuroscience: Understanding the Mind by Simulating the Brain by Randall C. O'Reilly (Author) and Yuko Munakata (2000 – MIT Press)

Understanding Intelligence by Rolf Pfeifer and Christian Scheier (2000 – MIT Press)

The Perceptron: A Probabilistic Model for Information Storage and Organization in the Brain by F. Rosenblatt (1958 – in *Psychological Review*, Vol. 65, pp. 386–408)

CHAPTER 12

Probabilistic Reasoning and Bayesian Belief Networks

But to us, probability is the very guide of life.

—Joseph Butler, *The Analogy of Religion*

Probable Impossibilities are to be preferred to improbable possibilities.

—Aristotle, *Poetics*

Do not expect to arrive at certainty in every subject which you pursue. There are a hundred things wherein we mortals must be content with probability, where our best light and reasoning will reach no farther.

—Isaac Watts

12.1 Introduction

This chapter introduces the ideas behind probabilistic reasoning, and in particular Bayes' Theorem. Thomas Bayes was an English mathematician and theologian who lived from 1702 to 1761. His theorem is used extensively today in dealing with situations that lack certainty.

This chapter explains the relationship between probability theory and the logic that we saw in Part 3. It explains joint probability distributions and goes on to explain Bayes' theorem, using two examples.

This chapter explains how Bayesian belief networks can be built and used to learn from data about which certainty is lacking. Bayesian classifiers are also explained. The chapter also includes an introduction to the ideas behind collaborative filtering and explains how this increasingly popular technique relates to Bayesian reasoning.

12.2   Probabilistic Reasoning

In this section, we will present a brief introduction to probability theory and the notation that is used to express it. Probability theory is used to discuss events, categories, and hypotheses about which there is not 100% certainty.

The notation that we saw in Chapter 7 for making and analyzing logical statements does not function in situations that are lacking **certainty**.

For example, we might write

$A \rightarrow B$

which means that if A is true, then B is true. If we are unsure whether A is true, then we cannot make use of this expression. In many real-world situations, it is very useful to be able to talk about things that lack certainty. For example, what will the weather be like tomorrow? We might formulate a very simple hypothesis based on general observation, such as "it is sunny only 10% of the time, and rainy 70% of the time." We can use a notation similar to that used for predicate calculus to express such statements:

$P(S) = 0.1$
$P(R) = 0.7$

The first of these statements says that the probability of S ("it is sunny") is 0.1. The second says that the probability of R is 0.7. Probabilities are always expressed as real numbers between 0 and 1. A probability of 0 means "definitely not" and a probability of 1 means "definitely so." Hence, $P(S) = 1$ means that it is always sunny.

Many of the operators and notations that are used in prepositional logic can also be used in probabilistic notation. For example, $P(\neg S)$ means "the probability that it is not sunny"; $P(S \wedge R)$ means "the probability that it is both sunny and rainy."

$P(A \vee B)$, which means "the probability that either A is true or B is true," is defined by the following rule:

$$P(A \vee B) = P(A) + P(B) - P(A \wedge B)$$

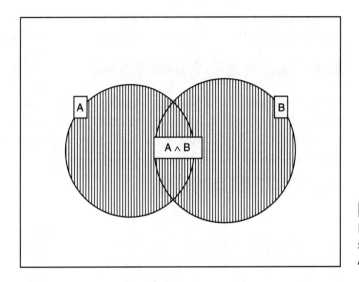

Figure 12.1

Illustrating the relation-ship between $A \wedge B$ and $A \vee B$

This rule can be seen to be true by examining the Venn diagram shown in Figure 12.1.

The notation $P(B|A)$ can be read as "the probability of B, given A." This is known as **conditional probability**—it is conditional on A. In other words, it states the probability that B is true, given that we already know that A is true.

$P(B|A)$ is defined by the following rule:

$$P(B|A) = \frac{P(B \wedge A)}{P(A)}$$

Of course, this rule cannot be used in cases where $P(A) = 0$.

For example, let us suppose that the likelihood that it is both sunny and rainy at the same time is 0.01. Then we can calculate the probability that it is rainy, given that it is sunny as follows:

$$P(R|S) = \frac{P(R \wedge S)}{P(S)}$$

$$= \frac{0.01}{0.1}$$

$$= 0.1$$

Note that the probability that it is sunny given that it is overcast—$P(S|R)$—is different from this: $0.01/0.7 = 0.14$; hence, $P(A|B) \neq P(B|A)$.

12.3   Joint Probability Distributions

A **joint probability distribution** (also known as a **joint**) can be used to represent the probabilities of combined statements, such as $A \wedge B$. For example, the following table shows a joint probability distribution of two variables, A and B:

	A	¬A
B	0.11	0.09
¬B	0.63	0.17

This shows, for example, that $P(A \wedge B) = 0.11$, and that $P(A \wedge \neg B) = 0.63$. By summing these two values, we can find $P(A) = 0.11 + 0.63 = 0.74$. Similarly, $P(B) = 0.11 + 0.09 = 0.2$.

We can use this table to determine the probability of any logical combination of A and B. For example, $P(A \vee B) = 0.11 + 0.09 + 0.63 = 0.83$. We could have obtained this result by noting that $P(\neg A \wedge \neg B) = 0.17$ and that $P(\neg A \wedge \neg B) = 1 - P(A \vee B) = 1 - 0.17 = 0.83$.

Similarly, we can determine conditional probabilities, such as $P(B|A)$ using the following rule:

$$P(B|A) = \frac{P(B \wedge A)}{P(A)}$$

In this case, $P(B \wedge A) = 0.11$ and $P(A) = 0.11 + 0.63 = 0.74$, so $P(B|A) = 0.11 / 0.74 = 0.15$.

Calculations like this are easy when we use a joint probability of just two variables. Real-world problems will often involve much greater numbers of variables, and in these cases, drawing up probability distribution tables is clearly much less straightforward.

12.4   Bayes' Theorem

Bayes' theorem can be used to calculate the probability that a certain event will occur or that a certain proposition is true, given that we already know a related piece of information.

The theorem is stated as follows:

$$P(B|A) = \frac{P(A|B) \cdot P(B)}{P(A)}$$

$P(B)$ is called the **prior probability** of B. $P(B|A)$, as well as being called the conditional probability, is also known as the **posterior probability** of B.

Let us briefly examine how Bayes' theorem is derived:

We can deduce a further equation from the rule given in Section 12.2 above. This rule is known as the **product rule**:

$$P(A \wedge B) = P(A|B)P(B)$$

Note that due to the commutativity of $\wedge$, we can also write

$$P(A \wedge B) = P(B|A)P(A)$$

Hence, we can deduce:

$$P(B|A)P(A) = P(A|B)P(B)$$

This can then be rearranged to give Bayes' theorem:

$$P(B|A) = \frac{P(A|B) \cdot P(B)}{P(A)}$$

12.4.1 Example: Medical Diagnosis

Let us examine a simple example to illustrate the use of Bayes' theorem for the purposes of medical diagnosis.

When one has a cold, one usually has a high temperature (let us say, 80% of the time). We can use A to denote "I have a high temperature" and B to denote "I have a cold." Therefore, we can write this statement of posterior probability as

$$P(A|B) = 0.8$$

Note that in this case, we are using A and B to represent pieces of data that could each either be a hypothesis or a piece of evidence. It is more likely that we would use A as a piece of evidence to help us prove or disprove the hypothesis, B, but it could work equally well the other way around (at least, mathematically speaking).

Now, let us suppose that we also know that at any one time around 1 in every 10,000 people has a cold, and that 1 in every 1000 people has a high temperature. We can write these prior probabilities as

$$P(A) = 0.001$$

$$P(B) = 0.0001$$

Now suppose that you have a high temperature. What is the likelihood that you have a cold? This can be calculated very simply by using Bayes' theorem:

$$P(B|A) = \frac{P(A|B) \cdot P(B)}{P(A)}$$

$$= \frac{0.8 \cdot 0.0001}{0.001}$$

$$= 0.008$$

Hence, we have shown that just because you have a high temperature does not necessarily make it very likely that you have a cold—in fact, the chances that you have a cold are just 8 in 1000.

Bayes' theorem can be extended to express a conditional probability involving more than two variables as follows:

$$P(H|E_1 \wedge \ldots \wedge E_n) = \frac{P(E_1 \wedge \ldots \wedge E_n|H) \cdot P(H)}{P(E_1 \wedge \ldots \wedge E_n)}$$

Provided the n pieces of evidence $E_1 \ldots E_n$ are independent of each other, given the hypothesis H,[1] then this can be rewritten as follows:

$$P(H|E_1 \wedge \ldots \wedge E_n) = \frac{P(E_1|H) \cdot \ldots \cdot P(E_n|H) \cdot P(H)}{P(E_1 \wedge \ldots \wedge E_n)}$$

12.4.2   Example: Witness Reliability

Let us examine a further example. In the city of Cambridge, there are two taxi companies. One taxi company uses yellow taxis, and the other uses white taxis. The yellow taxi company has 90 cars, and the white taxi company has just 10 cars.

A hit-and-run incident has been reported, and an eye witness has stated that she is certain that the car was a white taxi.

---

[1] In other words, if H is true, then the truth or otherwise of E_i should have no effect on the truth of E_j for any i and j.

So far, we have the following information:

$P(Y) = 0.9$ (the probability of any particular taxi being yellow)

$P(W) = 0.1$ (the probability of any particular taxi being white)

Let us further suppose that experts have asserted that given the foggy weather at the time of the incident, the witness had a 75% chance of correctly identifying the taxi.

Given that the lady has said that the taxi was white, what is the likelihood that she is right?

Let us denote by $P(C_W)$ the probability that the culprit was driving a white taxi and by $P(C_Y)$ the probability that it was a yellow car.

We will use $P(W_W)$ to denote the probability that the witness says she saw a white car and $P(W_Y)$ to denote that she says she saw a yellow car. (We assume the witness tells the truth!)

Now, if the witness really saw a yellow car, she would say that it was yellow 75% of the time, and if she says she saw a white car, she would say it was white 75% of the time. Hence, we now know the following:

$P(C_Y) = 0.9$

$P(C_W) = 0.1$

$P(W_W | C_W) = 0.75$

$P(W_Y | C_Y) = 0.75$

Hence, we can apply Bayes' theorem to find the probability, given that she is saying that the car was white, that she is correct:

$$P(C_W | W_W) = \frac{0.75 \cdot 0.1}{P(W_W)}$$

We now need to calculate $P(W_W)$—the prior probability that the lady would say she saw a white car.

Let us imagine that the lady is later shown a random sequence of 1000 cars. We expect 900 of these cars to be yellow and 100 of them to be white. The witness will misidentify 250 of the cars: Of the 900 yellow cars, she will incorrectly say that 225 are white. Of the 100 white cars, she will incorrectly say that 25 are yellow. Hence, in total, she will believe she sees 300 white cars—even though only 100 of them are really white. So, $P(W_W)$ is $300/1000 = 0.3$.

We can now complete our equation to find $P(C_W|W_W)$:

$$P(C_W|W_W) = \frac{0.75 \cdot 0.1}{0.3}$$
$$= 0.25$$

In other words, if the lady says that the car was white, the probability that it was in fact white is only 0.25—it is three times more likely that it was actually yellow!

In this example, Bayes' theorem takes into account the actual number of each color of taxi in the city. If the witness had said she saw a yellow taxi, it would be very likely that she was right—but this is likely anyway because there are so many more yellow taxis than white taxis. If the witness were a perfect observer who made no errors, then the probability $P(C_W|W_W)$ would, of course, be 1.

This example also helps to illustrate the fact that in many real-world situations we do have enough information to be able to use Bayes' theorem. It can look as though Bayes' theorem will apply only in contrived situations, but in fact it is usually the case that obtaining the data needed to use Bayes' theorem is easier than obtaining the posterior probability by other means. This is particularly true in cases where there are a large number of individuals being discussed.

12.4.3   Comparing Conditional Probabilities

In many situations, it can be useful to compare two probabilities. In particular, in making a diagnosis from a set of evidence, one will often have to choose from a number of possible hypotheses.

For example, let us extend the medical example given in Section 12.4.1. There we used A to represent the piece of evidence "I have a high temperature" and B to represent the hypothesis "I have a cold," where

$P(A) = 0.001$
$P(B) = 0.0001$

$P(A|B) = 0.8$

Let us further use C to represent the hypothesis "I have plague," where

$P(C) = 0.000000001$

$P(A|C) = 0.99$

In other words, it is highly unlikely for anyone to have plague, but if they do, they will almost certainly have a high temperature.

In this case, when carrying out a diagnosis of a patient that has a high temperature, it will be useful to determine which is the more likely hypothesis—B or C.

Bayes' theorem gives us the following:

$$P(B|A) = \frac{P(A|B) \cdot P(B)}{P(A)}$$

$$P(C|A) = \frac{P(A|C) \cdot P(C)}{P(A)}$$

Clearly, to find the more likely of B and C, given A, we can eliminate $P(A)$ from these equations and can determine the **relative likelihood** of B and C as follows:

$$\frac{P(B|A)}{P(C|A)} = \frac{P(A|B) \cdot P(B)}{P(A|C) \cdot P(C)}$$

$$= \frac{0.8 \cdot 0.001}{0.95 \cdot 0.000000001}$$

$$= 842,105$$

Hence, it is hundreds of thousands of times more likely given that a patient has a high temperature that he has a cold than that he has plague.

12.4.4 Normalization

Normalization is the process whereby the posterior probabilities of a pair of variables are divided by a fixed value to ensure that they sum to 1.

This can be done by considering the following two equations:

$$P(B|A) = \frac{P(A|B) \cdot P(B)}{P(A)}$$

$$P(\neg B|A) = \frac{P(A|\neg B) \cdot P(\neg B)}{P(A)}$$

Given that A is true, B must either be true or false, which means that $P(B|A)$ + $P(\neg B|A) = 1$.

Hence, we can add the two equations above to give

$$1 = \frac{P(A|B) \cdot P(B)}{P(A)} + \frac{P(A|\neg B) \cdot P(B)}{P(A)}$$

$$\therefore P(A) = P(A|B) \cdot P(B) + P(A|\neg B) \cdot P(\neg B)$$

Now we can replace $P(A)$ in the equation for Bayes' theorem, to give

$$P(B|A) = \frac{P(A|B) \cdot P(B)}{P(A|B) \cdot P(B) + P(A|\neg B) \cdot P(\neg B)}$$

Hence, it is possible to use Bayes' theorem to obtain the conditional probability $P(B|A)$ without needing to know or calculate $P(A)$, providing we can obtain $P(A|\neg B)$. [$P(\neg B)$ is simply $1 - P(B)$].

This equation is often written as follows:

$$P(B|A) = \alpha \cdot P(A|B) \cdot P(B)$$

where α represents the normalizing constant:

$$\alpha = \frac{1}{P(A|B) \cdot P(B) + P(A|\neg B) \cdot P(\neg B)}$$

Let us examine our diagnosis example again. The facts we have are as follows:

$$P(A) = 0.001$$
$$P(B) = 0.0001$$
$$P(A|B) = 0.8$$

Let us now suppose that $P(A|\neg B) = 0.00099$. This conditional probability states the likelihood that a person will have a high temperature if she does not have a cold ($\neg B$). We can now thus use the following equation to calculate $P(B|A)$:

$$P(B|A) = \frac{P(A|B) \cdot P(B)}{P(A|B) \cdot P(B) + P(A|\neg B) \cdot P(\neg B)}$$

$$= \frac{0.8 \cdot 0.0001}{0.8 \cdot 0.001 + 0.00099 \cdot 0.9999}$$

$$= \frac{0.00008}{0.001069901}$$

$$= 0.075$$

Similarly, we can calculate $P(\neg B|A)$:

$$P(\neg B|A) = \frac{P(A|\neg B) \cdot P(\neg B)}{P(A|\neg B) \cdot P(\neg B) + P(A|B) \cdot P(B)}$$

$$= \frac{0.00099 \cdot 0.9999}{0.00099 \cdot 0.9999 + 0.8 \cdot 0.0001}$$

$$= \frac{0.000989901}{0.001069901}$$

$$= 0.925$$

The net result of this normalization process has been to ensure that $P(B|A) + P(\neg B|A) = 1$. We could now carry out a similar process to calculate $P(C|A)$ and $P(\neg C|A)$, which would enable us to ensure that they also sum to 1.

12.5 Simple Bayesian Concept Learning

A very simple model for learning can be developed using Bayes' rule.

Throughout the above discussion we have been talking about probabilities of hypotheses or of specific pieces of evidence. To use probability theory in learning, it is useful to talk about the probability that some hypothesis is true, given a particular set of evidence. We can use the same notation for this, and write

$P(H|E)$

Hence, given a set of evidence, the learner can determine which hypothesis to believe in by identifying the posterior probability of each. Let us suppose that there are n possible hypotheses, $H_1 \ldots H_n$. Hence, for each H_i

$$P(H_i|E) = \frac{P(E|H_i) \cdot P(H_i)}{P(E)}$$

So the algorithm could calculate $P(H_i|E)$ for each possible hypothesis and select the one that has the highest probability. Similarly, the system could use this method to determine an action to take, where H_i is the hypothesis that the best action to take in the current situation is action A_i.

In fact, the formula above can be simplified in this situation: because $P(E)$ is **independent** of H_i, it will have the same value for each hypothesis. So because we are simply looking for the hypothesis with the maximum posterior probability, we can eliminate $P(E)$ from the calculation and simply aim to maximize the following value:

$$P(E|H_i) \cdot P(H_i)$$

In fact, if we assume that all hypotheses are equally likely, given no additional information (i.e., $P(H_i) = P(H_j)$ for any i and j), we can in fact reduce this further and simply choose the hypothesis for whom the value $P(E|H_i)$ is the highest. This value is known as the **likelihood** of the evidence E, given hypothesis H_i. Of course, by learning from observations what the prior probabilities are of each of the hypotheses, more accurate results can be obtained, but the simpler formula is more efficient in calculation time.

Recall the discussion from Chapter 7 of abduction and inductive reasoning. These are really a form of learning: by observing the events that occur, we are able to make reasonable guesses about future events, and these guesses can often guide our actions. For example, if a robot observed that every time it heard a particular noise, an enemy robot appeared, it might learn to hide when it heard that noise. In doing so, it is learning from experience and using Bayesian reasoning to decide upon the correct course of action. The robot is not using rules of logical deduction, such as modus ponens, which was explained in Chapter 7, but a rather more probabilistic form of reasoning, along the lines of "I have noticed in the past that when this noise occurs, an enemy appears. I have also noticed in the past that if I do not hide when an enemy appears, I get hurt by the enemy. Hence, I should probably hide when I hear the noise."

Humans use learning of this kind all the time, and it is essential for learning in situations in which there is very little certainty, such as the real world.

12.6   Bayesian Belief Networks

The concept of **dependence** is very important in probability theory. Two events, A and B, are **independent** if the likelihood of occurrence of A is entirely unrelated to whether or not B occurs.

For example, in tossing two coins, the likelihood that the first coin will come up heads and the likelihood that the second coin will come up heads are two independent probabilities because neither one depends on the other.

If A and B are independent, then the probability that A and B will both occur can be calculated very simply:

$$P(A \wedge B) = P(A).P(B)$$

We know that this equation does not hold if A depends on B because we have already seen the following equation:

$$P(B|A) = \frac{P(B \wedge A)}{P(A)}$$

By comparing these two equations, we can see that A and B are independent if $P(B|A) = P(B)$. In other words, the likelihood of B is unaffected by whether or not A occurs. B is independent of A. If B is dependent on A, then $P(B|A)$ will be different from $P(B)$.

These relationships can be expressed extremely succinctly in a belief network, such as the one shown in Figure 12.2.

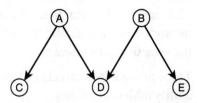

Figure 12.2
A simple belief network

A **Bayesian belief network** is an acyclic directed graph, where the nodes in the graph represent evidence or hypotheses, and where an arc that connects two nodes represents a dependence between those two nodes.

The belief network in Figure 12.2 contains five nodes that represent pieces of evidence (A and B) and three hypotheses (C, D, and E). The arcs between these nodes represent the interdependence of the hypotheses. According to this diagram, C and D are both dependent on A, and D and E are both dependent on B. Two nodes that do not have an arc between them are independent of each other. For example, B is independent of A.

Each node in the network has a set of probabilities associated with it, based on the values of the nodes on which it is dependent. Hence, A and B both have just prior probabilities, $P(A)$ and $P(B)$, because they are not dependent on any other nodes. C and E are each dependent on just one other node. Hence, for example, $P(C)$ must be represented in the two cases—A is true and A is false. $P(D)$ must be represented in four cases, depending on the values of A and B.

For example, the following conditional probabilities might be used in the network shown in Figure 12.2:

$P(A) = 0.1$

$P(B) = 0.7$

$P(C|A) = 0.2$

$P(C|\neg A) = 0.4$

$P(D|A \wedge B) = 0.5$

$P(D|A \wedge \neg B) = 0.4$

$P(D|\neg A \wedge B) = 0.2$

$P(D|\neg A \wedge \neg B) = 0.0001$

$P(E|B) = 0.2$

$P(E|\neg B) = 0.1$

The above list of probabilities, combined with the diagram shown in Figure 12.2, represent a complete (rather simple) Bayesian belief network. The network states beliefs about a set of hypotheses or pieces of evidence and the ways that they interact.

These probabilities can also be expressed in the form of **conditional probability tables**, as follows:

P(A)
0.1

P(B)
0.7

A	P(C)
true	0.2
false	0.4

B	P(E)
true	0.2
false	0.1

A	B	P(D)
true	true	0.5
true	false	0.4
false	true	0.2
false	false	0.0001

Compare these tables with the logical truth tables described in Chapter 7. In those tables, a logical value (*true* or *false*) was given for a variable that depended on the values of one or more other variables. Hence, a conditional probability table is very similar to a truth table, except that it expresses the probability of one variable, given the truth values of one or more other variables.

A joint probability can be calculated from the Bayesian belief network using the definition of conditional probability:

$$P(B|A) = \frac{P(B \wedge A)}{P(A)}$$

Hence,

$$P(A,B,C,D,E) = P(E|A,B,C,D) \cdot P(A,B,C,D)$$

We can apply this rule recursively to obtain

$$P(A,B,C,D,E) = P(E|A,B,C,D,) \cdot P(D|A,B,C,) \cdot P(C|A,B) \cdot P(B|A) \cdot P(A)$$

In fact, the nature of our belief network allows us to simplify this expression, and because we know that, for example, E is not dependent on A, C, or D, we can reduce $P(E|A,B,C,D)$ to $P(E|B)$.

$$P(A,B,C,D,E) = P(E|B) \cdot P(D|A,B) \cdot P(C|A) \cdot P(B) \cdot P(A)$$

We have now greatly reduced the complexity of the calculation needed to compute the joint probability. This has only been possible due to the way in which the nodes were ordered in the original expression. For example, if we used the same method blindly on the expression

P(E,D,C,B,A)

we would be left with the following expression:

$$P(E,D,C,B,A) = P(A|E,D,C,B) \cdot P(B|E,D,C) \cdot P(C|E,D) \cdot P(D|E) \cdot P(E)$$

This is not correct because E is dependent on B, and so we need to include P(E|B). Similarly, D is dependent on A and B, which is not reflected in this expression.

In other words, to calculate the joint probability, the nodes must be ordered in the expression in such a way that if a node X is dependent on another node Y, then X appears before Y in the joint. Hence, we could have used any ordering in which A and B appear before C, D, and E; B,A,E,D,C would have worked equally well, for example.

As a result of this, when constructing a Bayesian belief network, it is essential that the graph be constructed in the correct order—in other words, in an order such that the connections between nodes makes logical sense. This usually means starting with causes and then adding the events they cause, and then treating those events as causes, and adding any further events they cause.

The nature of Bayesian belief networks means that in general they are an efficient way of storing a joint probability distribution. The network does not store the conditional probability $P(X|Y)$ if X and Y are independent of each other, given the parents of X. In the network shown in Figure 12.2, for example, this means that $P(E|A)$ does not need to be stored.

12.6.1   Example: Life at College

Let us examine the simple Bayesian belief network shown in Figure 12.3.

In Figure 12.3, the five nodes represent the following statements:

C = that you will go to college

S = that you will study

P = that you will party

E = that you will be successful in your exams

F = that you will have fun

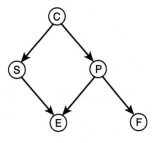

Figure 12.3
A Bayesian network to represent activities at college

This network shows us at a glance that if you go to college, this will affect the likelihood that you will study and the likelihood that you will party. Studying and partying affect your chances of exam success, and partying affects your chances of having fun.

To complete the Bayesian belief network, we need to include the conditional probability tables. Let us define these as follows:

P(C)
0.2

C	P(S)
true	0.8
false	0.2

C	P(P)
true	0.6
false	0.5

S	P	P(E)
true	true	0.6
true	false	0.9
false	true	0.1
false	false	0.2

P	P(F)
true	0.9
false	0.7

Note that according to this belief network there is a dependence between F and C, but because it is not a direct dependence, no information needs to be stored about it.

These conditional probability tables give us all the information we need to carry out any reasoning about this particular domain. For example, we can clearly obtain values such as $P(\neg C)$ by using the fact that

$$P(\neg C) = 1 - P(C) = 1 - 0.2 = 0.8.$$

We can use the network to determine conditional probabilities, such as $P(F|P)$ by observing that in the final table, if P is true, then $P(F) = 0.9$. Hence, $P(F|P) = 0.9$.

The joint probability distribution for this domain represents the entire state of the domain. We can represent such a state using the notation as used in the following example:

$$P(C = \text{true}, S = \text{true}, P = \text{false}, E = \text{true}, F = \text{false})$$

We can simplify this notation as follows:

$$P(C, S, \neg P, E, \neg F)$$

This represents the probability that you will go to college and that you will study and be successful in your exams, but will not party or have fun. This probability can be calculated using the following rule:

$$P(x_1, \ldots, x_n) = \prod_{i=1}^{n} P(x_i | E)$$

where E is the evidence on which each x_i is dependent—in other words, in the Bayesian belief network, E consists of the nodes that are parents of x_i. For example, using the network shown in Figure 12.3, we can calculate the following probability:

$$P(C, S, \neg P, E, \neg F) = P(C) \cdot P(S|C) \cdot P(\neg P|C) \cdot P(E|S \wedge \neg P) \cdot P(\neg F|\neg P)$$
$$= 0.2 \cdot 0.8 \cdot 0.4 \cdot 0.9 \cdot 0.3$$
$$= 0.01728$$

Hence, for S we need to include in the product $P(S|C)$ because S is only dependent on C, and C is true in the situation we are examining. Similarly, for E we need to include $P(E|S \wedge \neg P)$ because E is dependent on S and on P, and S is true and P is not true in the scenario.

We can also calculate more complex conditional probabilities. In fact, this is an extremely simple process, due to the way in which the belief network has been created. For example, let us look at the following conditional probability:

$$P(E|F \wedge \neg P \wedge S \wedge C)$$

This is the probability that you will have success in your exams if you have fun and study at college, but don't party.

The assumption behind the Bayesian belief network is that because there is no direct connection between E and C, E is independent of C, given S and P. In other words, if we wish to calculate the following:

$$P(E|C \wedge S \wedge P)$$

we can in fact drop C from this altogether, and simply obtain

$$P(E|S \wedge P) = 0.6$$

Similarly, the more complex conditional probability above can be simplified by dropping F and C to give

$$P(E|S \wedge \neg P) = 0.9$$

Hence, any calculation that we might need to make about this domain can be made simply using the conditional probability tables of the belief network.

Similarly, we can make diagnoses about your college life by determining posterior probabilities. For example, let us say that we know that you had fun and studied hard while at college and we know that you succeeded in your exams, but we want to know whether you partied or not.

Clearly, we know C, S, E, and F, but we do not know P. We need to determine the most likely value for P. Hence, we can compare the values of the following two expressions:

$$P(C \wedge S \wedge P \wedge E \wedge F) = P(C) \cdot P(S|C) \cdot P(P|C) \cdot P(E|S \wedge P) \cdot P(F|P)$$

$$= 0.2 \cdot 0.8 \cdot 0.6 \cdot 0.6 \cdot 0.9$$

$$= 0.05184$$

$$P(C \wedge S \wedge \neg P \wedge E \wedge F) = P(C) \cdot P(S|C) \cdot P(\neg P|C) \cdot P(E|S \wedge \neg P) \cdot P(F|\neg P)$$

$$= 0.2 \cdot 0.8 \cdot 0.4 \cdot 0.9 \cdot 0.7$$

$$= 0.04032$$

Hence, it is slightly more likely that you *did* party while at college than that you did not.

12.6.2   Example: Chapter Dependencies

We will now examine a simple example of a slightly unusual Bayesian network. Rather than each node representing a hypothesis or a piece of diagnostic information, each node in the Bayesian network shown in Figure 12.4 represents a chapter of this book. The arcs between nodes represent the dependencies between chapters. For example, the network shows that if you plan to read Chapter 8, which covers logical proof by resolution, it is a good idea to have read Chapter 7 on propositional and predicate logic first.

To see this as a more standard belief network, we can consider each node to represent the likelihood that you have read a given chapter and that a dependency from Chapter 8 to Chapter 7, for example, represents the fact that, if you have read Chapter 8, it is likely that you have also read Chapter 7. For this network to be useful to you in deciding which order to read the chapters, you can think of the dependencies as being advice about whether you should read a particular chapter before reading another.

12.7   The Noisy-V Function

Thus far, we have assumed that the probabilities contained with a joint probability distribution are unrelated to each other, in the sense that they have been determined by observing the way in which events occur. In some situations, it can be possible to use the fact that events in a Bayesian

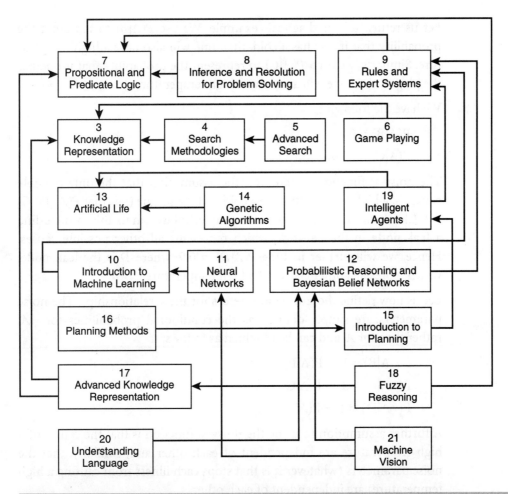

Figure 12.4

A Bayesian belief network that shows dependencies between chapters in this book

belief network are related to each other by some kind of mathematical or logical relation.

Clearly, logical relations such as ∧ and ∨, as defined in propositional logic, will not do because they do not provide a way to handle probabilities. **Fuzzy logic** (which is described in Chapter 18) could provide suitable relations. Another useful class of relations is **noisy logical relationships**.

Let us return to our diagnosis example. We use $P(A|B)$ to represent the probability that if one has a cold, then one will also have a high temperature. Similarly, we used $P(A|C)$ to represent the probability that if one has the plague, then one will also have a high temperature.

We have the following:

$$P(A|B) = 0.8$$
$$P(A|C) = 0.99$$

The noisy-$\vee$ function is based on the assumption that the only possible causes of a high temperature are a cold and the plague (i.e., that $P(A|B \vee C) = 1$. Clearly this is not true for our example, but we can fix this by including a **leak node** in the network, which represents all other possible causes. Hence, we will further include $P(A|D) = 0.9$, where D is the leak node, which represents other causes of a high temperature.

Let us now define the **noise parameters** for these relationships. The noise parameters are simply defined as the conditional probabilities for $\neg A$, rather than for A, and can be obtained as follows:

$$P(\neg A|B) = 1 - P(A|B) = 0.2$$
$$P(\neg A|C) = 1 - P(A|C) = 0.01$$
$$P(\neg A|D) = 1 - P(A|D) = 0.1$$

A further assumption in using the noisy-$\vee$ function is that the causes of a high temperature are independent of each other and, similarly, that the noise parameters (whatever it is that stops each illness from causing a high temperature) are independent of each other.

The noisy-$\vee$ function for B, C, and D is defined as follows:

If B, C, and D are all false, then $P(A) = 0$. Otherwise, $P(\neg A)$ is equal to the product of the noise parameters for all the variables that are true. For example, if B is true and C and D are false, then $P(\neg A)$ is equal to the noise parameter for B, and so

$$P(A) = 1 - 0.2$$
$$= 0.8$$

If C and D are both true, and B is false, then $P(\neg A)$ is equal to the product of the noise parameters for C and D, and so

$$P(A) = 1 - (0.01 \times 0.1)$$
$$= 0.999$$

Now we can define the noisy-$\vee$ function for our diagnosis example:

B	C	D	P(A)	P($\neg$A)
false	false	false	0	1
false	false	true	0.9	0.1
false	true	false	0.99	0.01
false	true	true	0.999	$0.01 \times 0.1 = 0.001$
true	false	false	0.8	0.2
true	false	true	0.98	$0.2 \times 0.1 = 0.02$
true	true	false	0.998	$0.2 \times 0.01 = 0.002$
true	true	true	0.9998	$0.2 \times 0.01 \times 0.1 = 0.0002$

Note that this noisy logical function is defined by just three conditional probabilities, as opposed to needing to store eight values. For Bayesian belief networks used in the real world with hundreds or even thousands of nodes, this can make a significant difference.

12.8   Bayes' Optimal Classifier

It is possible to use Bayesian reasoning to build a system that learns to classify data.

For example, let us suppose that for a given piece of data, y, there are five possible hypotheses, $H_1 \ldots H_5$, each of which assigns a classification to y. The classification, c, can be any value from a set C. For this example, let us assume that C consists of the values true and false.

Our classifier knows the posterior probabilities of each of the five hypotheses to be the following:

$P(H_1|x_1, \ldots, x_n) = 0.2$
$P(H_2|x_1, \ldots, x_n) = 0.3$
$P(H_3|x_1, \ldots, x_n) = 0.1$
$P(H_4|x_1, \ldots, x_n) = 0.25$
$P(H_5|x_1, \ldots, x_n) = 0.15$

where x_1 to x_n are the training data.

The probability that the new item of data, y, should be classified with classification c_j is defined by the following:

$$P(c_j|x_1\ldots x_n) = \sum_{i=1}^{m} P(c_j|h_i) \cdot P(h_i|x_1\ldots x_n)$$

where m is the number of available hypotheses, which in this case is 5. The **optimal classification** for y is the classification c_j for which $P(c_j|x_1\ldots x_n)$ is the highest.

In our case, there are two classifications:

c_1 = true

c_2 = false

Let us suppose that hypotheses H_3 and H_5 each define y as true, while H_1, H_2, and H_4 define y as false.

Hence, we have the following posterior probabilities:

$P(\text{false}|H_1) = 0$ $P(\text{true}|H_1) = 1$

$P(\text{false}|H_2) = 0$ $P(\text{true}|H_2) = 1$

$P(\text{false}|H_3) = 1$ $P(\text{true}|H_3) = 0$

$P(\text{false}|H_4) = 0$ $P(\text{true}|H_4) = 1$

$P(\text{false}|H_5) = 1$ $P(\text{true}|H_5) = 0$

Thus we can calculate the posterior probabilities for each of the two possible classifications for y as follows:

$$P(\text{true}|x_1\ldots x_n) = \sum_{i=1}^{5} P(\text{true}|H_i) \cdot P(H_i|x_1\ldots x_n)$$

$$= 0.2 + 0.3 + 0.25$$

$$= 0.75$$

$$P(\text{false}|x_1\ldots x_n) = \sum_{i=1}^{5} P(\text{false}|H_i) \cdot P(H_i|x_1\ldots x_n)$$

$$= 0.1 + 0.15$$

$$= 0.25$$

Hence, the optimal classification for y is true.

This method is known as an optimal classifier because it provides the best possible classification system. Another classification system, given the same data, can only hope to classify unseen data as well as this method—it cannot do better than the optimal classifier, on average.

12.9   The Naïve Bayes Classifier

The **naïve Bayes classifier** is a simple but effective learning system. Each piece of data that is to be classified consists of a set of attributes, each of which can take on a number of possible values. The data are then classified into a single classification.

To identify the best classification for a particular instance of data $(d_1, \ldots, d_n)$, the posterior probability of each possible classification is calculated:

$$P(c_i \mid d_1, \ldots, d_n)$$

where c_i is the ith classification, from a set of $|c|$ classifications.

The classification whose posterior probability is highest is chosen as the correct classification for this set of data. The hypothesis that has the highest posterior probability is often known as the **maximum a posteriori**, or MAP hypothesis. In this case, we are looking for the MAP classification.

To calculate the posterior probability, we can use Bayes' theorem and rewrite it as

$$\frac{P\left(d_1, \ldots, d_n \mid c_i\right) \cdot P\left(c_i\right)}{P\left(d_1, \ldots, d_n\right)}$$

Because we are simply trying to find the highest probability, and because $P(d_1, \ldots, d_n)$ is a constant independent of c_i, we can eliminate it and simply aim to find the classification c_i, for which the following is maximized:

$$P(d_1, \ldots, d_n \mid c_i) \cdot P(c_i)$$

The naïve Bayes classifier now assumes that each of the attributes in the data item is independent of the others, in which case $P(d_1, \ldots, d_n \mid c_i)$ can be rewritten and the following value obtained:

$$P\left(c_i\right) \cdot \prod_{j=1}^{n} P\left(d_j \mid c_i\right)$$

The naïve Bayes classifier selects a classification for a data set by finding the classification c_i for which the above calculation is a maximum.

For example, let us suppose that each data item consists of the attributes x, y, and z, where x, y, and z are each integers in the range 1 to 4.

The available classifications are A, B, and C.

The example training data are as follows:

x	y	z	Classification
2	3	2	A
4	1	4	B
1	3	2	A
2	4	3	A
4	2	4	B
2	1	3	C
1	2	4	A
2	3	3	B
2	2	4	A
3	3	3	C
3	2	1	A
1	2	1	B
2	1	4	A
4	3	4	C
2	2	4	A

Hence, we have 15 pieces of training data, each of which has been classified. Eight of the training data are classified as A, four as B, and three as C.

Now let us suppose that we are presented with a new piece of data, which is

$$(x = 2, y = 3, z = 4)$$

We need to obtain the posterior probability of each of the three classifications, given this piece of training data. Note that if we were to attempt to calculate $P(c_i|x = 2, y = 3, z = 4)$ without having made the simplifying step that we took above, in assuming that the attribute values are independent of each other, then we would need to have had many more items of training data to proceed. The naïve Bayes classifier requires far fewer items of training data.

We must now calculate each of the following:

$$P(A) \cdot P(x = 2|A) \cdot P(y = 3|A) \cdot P(z = 4|A)$$
$$P(B) \cdot P(x = 2|B) \cdot P(y = 3|B) \cdot P(z = 4|B)$$
$$P(C) \cdot P(x = 2|C) \cdot P(y = 3|C) \cdot P(z = 4|C)$$

Hence, for classification A, we obtain the following:

$$\frac{8}{15} \cdot \frac{5}{8} \cdot \frac{2}{8} \cdot \frac{4}{8} = 0.0417$$

This was calculated by observing that of the 15 items of training data, 8 were classified as A, and so $P(A) = 8/15$. Similarly, of the eight items of training data that were classified as A, five had $x = 2$, two had $y = 3$, and four had $z = 4$, and so $P(x = 2|A) = 5/8$, $P(y = 3 |A) = 2/8$, and $P(z = 4|A) = 4/8$.

Similarly, we obtain the posterior probability for category B:

$$\frac{4}{15} \cdot \frac{1}{4} \cdot \frac{1}{4} \cdot \frac{2}{4} = 0.0083$$

and for category C:

$$\frac{3}{15} \cdot \frac{1}{3} \cdot \frac{2}{3} \cdot \frac{1}{3} = 0.015$$

Hence, category A is chosen as the best category for this new piece of data, with category C as the second best choice.

Let us now suppose that we are to classify the following piece of unseen data:

$$(x = 1, y = 2, z = 2)$$

As before, we would calculate the posterior probability for A. However, in calculating the probabilities for B and C, we would have problems. In the case of category B, we would have

$$P(x = 1|B) = 1/5$$
$$P(y = 2|B) = 1/5$$
$$P(z = 2|B) = 0$$

Because there are no training examples with $z = 2$ that were classified as B, we have a posterior probability of 0. Similarly, for category C, we end up with

$$P(x = 1|C) = 0$$
$$P(y = 2|C) = 0$$
$$P(z = 2|C) = 0$$

In this case, we clearly must select category A as the best choice for the data, but it appears to be based on a fairly inadequate comparison because insufficient training data were available to properly compute posterior probabilities for the other categories.

This problem can be avoided by using the **m-estimate**, as follows:

We wish to determine the probability of a particular attribute value, given a particular classification, such as $P(x = 1|C)$. We will estimate this probability according to the following formula:

$$\frac{a + mp}{b + m}$$

where $a =$ the number of training examples that exactly match our requirements (e.g., for $P(x = 1|C)$, a is the number of training examples where $x = 1$ and that have been categorized as C. In this example, a is 0); $b =$ the number of training examples that were classified in the current classification (i.e., for $P(x = 1|C)$, b is the number of items of training data that were given classification C); $p =$ an estimate of the probability that we are trying to obtain (usually this is obtained by simply assuming that each possible value is equally likely—hence, in our example, for $P(x = 1|C)$, $p = 1/4 = 0.25$, as it would be for each of the other three possible values for x); m is a constant value, known as the **equivalent sample size**.

For example, let us use an equivalent sample size of 5 and determine the best classification for $(x = 1, y = 2, z = 2)$:

For category A, we first need to calculate the probability for each of the three attributes.

Hence, for $x = 1$:

$$\frac{2 + \frac{5}{4}}{8 + 5} = 0.25$$

For $y = 2$:

$$\frac{3 + \frac{5}{4}}{8 + 5} = 0.33$$

For $z = 2$:

$$\frac{1 + \frac{5}{4}}{8 + 5} = 0.17$$

Hence, the posterior probability estimate for A is

$$\frac{8}{15} \cdot 0.25 \cdot 0.33 \cdot 0.17 = 0.0076$$

Similarly, we can now obtain posterior probability estimates for categories B and C:

For category B, we obtain the following three probabilities:

$$\frac{1 + \frac{5}{4}}{5 + 5} = 0.225, \quad \frac{2 + \frac{5}{4}}{5 + 5} = 0.325, \quad \frac{0 + \frac{5}{4}}{5 + 5} = 0.125$$

This gives us a posterior probability for category B as follows:

$$\frac{5}{15} \cdot 0.225 \cdot 0.325 \cdot 0.125 = 0.0091$$

Finally, the posterior probability for category C can be obtained. We note first that each of the three probabilities is the same because none of the attribute values occur in the training data with category C. Hence, the probability we use will be

$$\frac{0 + \frac{5}{4}}{3 + 5} = 0.156$$

Hence, the posterior probability for category C is as follows:

$$\frac{3}{15} \cdot 0.156 \cdot 0.156 \cdot 0.156 = 0.0008$$

Hence, using this estimate for probability, we find that category B is the best match for the new data, and not category A as would have been obtained using the simpler probability estimates.

It is possible to further simplify the naïve Bayes classifier by considering the values to be positionless within each item of data. In other words, when considering a new item of data, rather than assigning values to three attributes, we can simply think of the data as consisting of three values, whose order is arbitrary.

For example, consider the piece of new data (2, 3, 4).

In this case, we use the same method as before, but rather than considering the probability that, for example, $x = 2$ when an item is classified as A, we simply consider the probability that any attribute has value 2.

This simplified version of the naïve Bayes classifier is often used in text classification applications. Here, the categories are often simply "relevant" and "irrelevant," and the data to be classified consist of the words contained within textual documents. For example, an item of data might be ("the," "cat," "sat," "on," "the," "mat"). Training data would be presented in the form of a set of documents that has been preclassified as relevant and a set that has been preclassified as irrelevant. This form of textual analysis is discussed in more detail in Chapter 20, which is concerned with information retrieval and natural language processing.

12.10 Collaborative Filtering

A further practical use for Bayesian reasoning is in **collaborative filtering**. Collaborative filtering is a technique that is increasingly used by online stores (such as Amazon.com) to provide plausible suggestions to customers based on their previous purchases. The idea behind collaborative filtering can be stated very simply: if we know that Anne and Bob both like items A, B, and C, and that Anne likes D, then it is reasonable to suppose that Bob would also like D.

Collaborative filtering can be implemented in a number of ways, and the Bayesian inference has proved to be a successful method. This involves working with posterior probabilities such as the following:

P(Bob Likes Z | Bob likes A, Bob likes B, . . ., Bob Likes Y)

Clearly, for this mechanism to work accurately, large amounts of data must be collected. Information about thousands of individuals is needed, and information is required about dozens or hundreds of items for each individual. In the case of commerce sites, this information can be collected on

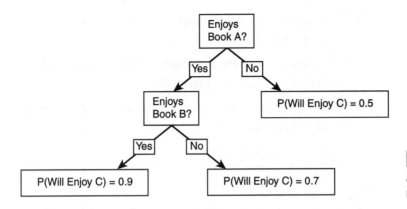

Figure 12.5

A decision tree for collaborative filtering

the basis of assuming that if a user buys a book or a CD, then he probably likes it. More accurate data can be collected by asking users to rate products.

To see how collaborative filtering works, consider the simple decision tree shown in Figure 12.5.

The decision tree in Figure 12.5 relates enjoyment of book C to information about enjoyment of books A and B. It states that if you did not enjoy book A, then you will only have a 0.5 probability of enjoying book C. On the other hand, if you did enjoy book A and also enjoyed book B, then you will have a 0.9 chance of enjoying book C.

A full collaborative filtering system would have one decision tree for each item. A full Bayesian belief network would then be built from these decision trees, which can be used to make inferences about a new person on the basis of their likes or dislikes.

12.11 Chapter Summary

- Probabilistic reasoning uses a notation similar to first-order predicate calculus, but with the addition of terms such as $P(A) = 0.5$, which states that the probability that A is true (or that A will occur) is 0.5.

- Conditional probability is defined as

$$P(B|A) = \frac{P(B \wedge A)}{P(A)}$$

- This means the probability that *B* will occur, given that we already know *A*.

- The joint probability distribution (or joint) is used to represent probabilities concerning more than one variable.

- Bayes' theorem can be used to determine the posterior (conditional) probability:

$$P(B|A) = \frac{P(A|B) \cdot P(B)}{P(A)}$$

- Bayesian concept learning involves selecting the most likely hypothesis to explain a piece of data, using Bayes' theorem to calculate posterior probabilities.

- A Bayesian belief network is an acyclic directed graph, where the nodes in the graph represent evidence or hypotheses, and where an arc that connects two nodes represents a dependence between those two nodes.

- Bayes' optimal classifier uses Bayes' theorem to learn to classify items of data. No other classifier can perform better than the optimal classifier, on average.

- The naïve Bayes classifier uses the simplifying assumption that all the variables used to represent data for classification are independent of each other.

- Collaborative filtering is used to guess an individual's likes or dislikes based on prior information about other interests. One very successful method for collaborative filtering is to build a Bayesian belief network, based on a set of decision trees.

12.12   Review Questions

12.1 Explain what is meant by the conditional probability of an event.

12.2 "Bayes' theorem uses a conditional probability and two prior probabilities to calculate just one conditional probability. That doesn't sound like it's very helpful." Discuss this comment.

12.3 Explain the purpose of the noisy-∨ function.

12.4 Explain how Bayes' theorem can be used to develop learning systems.

12.5 Explain how Bayes' optimal classifier and the naïve Bayes classifier work.

12.6 Explain why collaborative filtering is such a useful technique. How successful do you believe it can be? What might limit its efficacy?

12.13   Exercises

12.1 Implement a Bayesian belief network in the programming language of your choice to represent a subject in which you are interested (for example, you might use it to diagnose medical conditions from symptoms, or to deduce a band from a description of the band's music).

12.2 Implement the naïve Bayes classifier in the programming language of your choice, and use it to classify pages of text, based on which words appear on the page. To do this, you will first need to train the classifier with preclassified examples of pages. You should choose two classifications: interesting and not interesting, and try to make the interesting category fairly narrow: for example, it might be "pages about Bayesian reasoning." What happens if you make the category very broad (such as "pages I find interesting")?

12.3 Use the following facts to calculate normalized values for $P(B|A)$ and $P(\neg B|A)$:

$P(A) = 0.0025$

$P(B) = 0.015$

$P(A|B) = 0.6$

$P(A|\neg B) = 0.25$

12.4 Examine the collaborative filtering mechanism used by an online shopping system. How effective do you think it is? Might there be more effective methods to achieve the same goal? What kinds of mistakes does the mechanism make? In what situations does it perform well?

12.14   Further Reading

If you are interested in seeing the original proposal of Bayes' theorem by Thomas Bayes from 1763, you can find it in Swinburne (2002). You can read more about collaborative filtering by exploring the writings of Patti Maes. A less technical explanation can be found in Riedl and Konstan (2002).

Modeling the Internet and the Web: Probabilistic Methods and Algorithms by Pierre Baldi, Paolo Frasconi, and Padhraic Smyth (2003 – John Wiley & Sons)

Bayesian Theory by José M. Bernardo and Adrian F. M. Smith (2001 – John Wiley & Sons)

Empirical Analysis of Predictive Algorithms for Collaborative Filtering by John S. Breese, David Heckerman, and Carl Kadie (1998 – in *Proceedings of the Fourteenth Conference on Uncertainty in Artificial Intelligence*)

Expert Systems and Probabilistic Network Models by Enrique Castillo, Jose Manuel Gutierrez, and Ali S. Hadi (1997 – Springer Verlag)

Probabilistic Networks and Expert Systems edited by Robert G. Cowell (1999 – Springer Verlag)

Bayesian Methods for Nonlinear Classification and Regression by David G. T. Denison, Christopher C. Holmes, Bani K. Mallick, and Adrian F. M. Smith (2002 – John Wiley & Sons)

Bayesian Data Analysis by Andrew Gelman, Donald B. Rubin, and Hal S. Stern (2003 – CRC Press)

Probabilistic Theory of Pattern Recognition by Luc Devroye, Laszlo Gyorfi, and Gabor Lugosi (1998 – Springer Verlag)

Making Decisions by D. V. Lindley (1991 – John Wiley & Sons)

Learning Bayesian Networks by Richard E. Neapolitan (2003 – Prentice Hall)

Probabilistic Reasoning in Intelligent Systems: Networks of Plausible Inference by Judea Pearl (1997 – Morgan Kaufmann)

Word of Mouse: The Marketing Power of Collaborative Filtering by John Riedl and Joseph Konstan (2002–Warner Books)

The Bayesian Choice: From Decision-Theoretic Foundations to Computational Implementation by Christian P. Robert (2001 – Springer Verlag)

Monte Carlo Statistical Methods by Christian P. Robert and George Casella (1999 – Springer Verlag)

The Evidential Foundations of Probabilistic Reasoning by David A. Schum (2001 – Northwestern University Press)

Social Information Filtering: Algorithms for Automating "Word of Mouth by U. Shardanand and P. Maes (1995 – in *Proceedings of CHI'95—Human Factors in Computing Systems,* pp. 210–217)

Data Analysis: A Bayesian Tutorial by D. S. Sivia (1996 – Oxford University Press)

Bayes's Theorem (Proceedings of the British Academy, Vol. 113) edited by Richard Swinburne (2002 – British Academy)

CHAPTER 13

Artificial Life: Learning through Emergent Behavior

Natural Selection is the blind watchmaker, blind because it does not see ahead, does not plan consequences, has no purpose in view. Yet the living results of natural selection overwhelmingly impress us with the appearance of design as if by a master watchmaker, impress us with the illusion of design and planning.

—Richard Dawkins, *The Blind Watchmaker*

Agents can become more complex in two ways. First, a designer can identify a functionality that the agent needs to achieve, then investigate possible behaviors that could realize the functionality, and then introduce various mechanisms that give rise to the behavior. Second, existing behavior systems in interaction with each other and the environment can show side effects, in other words, emergent behavior.

—Luc Steels, *The Artificial Life Roots of Artificial Intelligence*

All things are artificial, for nature is the art of God.

—Sir Thomas Browne, *Religio Medici*

13.1   Introduction

This chapter provides a broad introduction to the subject of Artificial Life. Artificial Life techniques use methods modeled on the behavior of living systems in much the same way that Artificial Intelligence techniques use methods modeled on the way the human brain works. Many Artificial Life techniques (in particular, genetic algorithms) are an established part of the field of Artificial Intelligence.

This chapter starts by attempting to define "life"—a difficult problem, but one that needs to be discussed in order to consider Artificial Life. Emergent behavior is one of the most important concepts of Artificial Life—the idea that systems that are defined in a simple way can produce their own behavior, which can be remarkably complex.

The chapter introduces a number of Artificial Life techniques, many of which illustrate emergent behavior. Techniques such as cellular automata, genetic programming, evolutionary programming, and classifier systems are discussed. Discussion of classifier systems provides an introduction to the subject of genetic algorithms, which is covered in much more detail in Chapter 14.

The chapter also looks at the ways in which systems might be built that are self-reproducing, and a number of systems are explored that model evolution.

As you will see in this chapter and the next, Artificial Life (or A-Life) techniques build on a number of Artificial Intelligence techniques and provide ways in which systems can adapt (or *evolve*) to changing conditions. Classifier systems, which are explored in Section 13.12, show how the addition of evolutionary techniques to production systems (which are discussed in Chapter 9) can enable them to respond to changes in their environment and to learn to deal with unexpected situations.

13.2   What Is Life?

What does it mean to be alive? What differentiates living creatures from nonliving things? This is a question to which there is still no satisfactory answer. Aristotle, the Greek philosopher, said that a thing was alive if it could "nourish itself and decay." The following is a list of properties that are also often considered to be indicative of life:

- self-reproduction
- ability to evolve by Darwinian natural selection
- response to stimuli
- ability to die
- growth or expansion

Even this short list has problems. Mules are certainly alive, but they cannot reproduce. The question of whether viruses are alive is not universally agreed. Most lists of properties of life exclude some living creatures or include some things that may not be alive.

In other words, it is very difficult to define what life is. Hence, it is not necessarily easy to exclude artificial entities—even patterns of data or computer programs such as computer viruses. In this chapter, we examine systems that exhibit many properties of life, but we are not necessarily claiming that these systems are actually *alive*. The important thing is that we are building processes and systems modeled on the ways in which living organisms behave and evolve. In much the same way that Artificial Intelligence uses techniques modeled on the way in which the human brain works, so Artificial Life, a somewhat wider subject in some ways, uses techniques modeled on the way in which life works.

13.3   Emergent Behavior

The idea of **emergent behavior** is fundamental to the field of Artificial Life. By observing the ways in which patterns of sensible behavior emerge in real life, researchers have been able to develop systems that can produce their own behavior. We have seen this idea already: CYC, the system that has thousands of pieces of information, has been able to form its own analogies about the world by observing the patterns in the data that it sees.

Much of Artificial Life is based around a simple idea: Evolution works. The process or mechanism of evolution may not be fully understood, but the fact remains that complex creatures have evolved in such a way that they are able to survive, despite changing environments, lack of food or warmth, and other complications that are presented by nature.

The reason that evolution works is that creatures that are "successful" in some way survive and reproduce. If a creature survives and reproduces, then it will pass on its genetic structure to its offspring. Although this process takes place over hundreds of thousands of years, it is possible to use methods that are based on the same principle that can take place on a computer within hours, minutes, or even seconds.

One of the early principles of Artificial Life is that complex behavior can be generated (i.e., it **emerges**) from simple rules. An excellent example of this principle is the Boids system, developed by Craig Reynolds in 1987. The idea of this system was that it would model the flocking behavior of birds. Rather than having an overall mechanism for controlling the flock, his system had just a few simple rules that each individual bird obeyed.

One rule ensured that each boid would stay near to other boids by having each boid tend to move toward the center of gravity of the whole flock. Another rule ensured that boids did not collide with each other.

In running his simulation, Reynolds found that the boids moved in a way extremely similar to the way in which flocks of birds and shoals of fish move. This technique is now widely used in animation software and in producing computer graphics for movies.

One of the most interesting aspects of the boids was the way in which their behavior emerged from the rules. For example, no one told the system how to behave when the flock encountered obstacles. Reynolds found that when presented with a series of pillar-shaped obstacles, his computer-simulated boids split into two separate flocks to go around the pillars and then rejoined on the other side of the pillars.

Clearly, the boids knew that they could not fly through obstacles and that they should not collide with the obstacles, but the behavior that enabled the flock to navigate the obstacles was entirely emergent.

This shows how complex behavior can emerge from simple rules. As we will see later in this chapter, the introduction of evolutionary methods can produce even more startling results.

13.4   Finite State Automata

A finite state automaton (FSA) is a simple device that has a finite set of states and an input string (often thought of as being on a tape, running through a device that can read one symbol at a time). Each symbol that the FSA reads in is compared with a rule that dictates which state to move to from that state, with that input. After reading the entire input, the finite state machine is either in an **accepting state**, which means its answer is "yes" to some question, or it is in some other state, in which case the answer is "no." A finite state machine can be represented by a diagram such as the one in Figure 13.1.

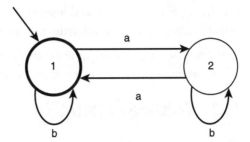

Figure 13.1
A finite state automaton

The FSA in Figure 13.1 determines whether an input string has an even number of a's or not. The two circles represent the two states, 1 and 2, which the FSA can be in. The possible input symbols are *a* and *b*. The arrow at the top left of the diagram shows where the FSA starts: in state 1. When the FSA is in state 1, it will stay there until it receives an *a*, which sends it to state 2. Similarly, when it is in state 2, it will stay there until it receives an *a*, which will send it back to state 1.

Hence, if the FSA receives an input with an even number of a's, it will finish in state 1, otherwise it will finish in state 2.

State 1 is an accepting state, which is shown by its having a thicker outline than state 2.

FSAs provide an extremely useful tool for Artificial Intelligence, and computer science in general. They also provide an interesting model for Artificial Life, as we see elsewhere in this chapter (Sections 13.5 and 13.10).

The FSA in Figure 13.1 has just two states, but in theory an FSA could have an extremely large number of states and a much larger vocabulary of input symbols.

A rather simplistic view of living entities might be to consider that each one is simply an FSA. In other words, place an entity in a particular situation and provide it with certain inputs from its environment, and its response will be deterministically decided by a set of rules. Of course, this is not how living creatures work at all, but it is possible to mimic certain behaviors of living creatures using FSAs. For example, boids can be thought of as FSAs. Each boid has a set of inputs (its own location and speeds, and information about where the other birds and obstacles are) and a state (which direction it is flying and how fast) and a set of rules that determine which state to move to from each state, according to the input data.

In the next section, we see how much simpler automata can be built, which when combined together can produce extremely interesting behavior.

13.5   Cellular Automata

13.5.1   Conway's Life

Conway's Life, also known as the Game of Life, is a system that uses a grid of squares and a set of simple rules. Conway's Life is an excellent illustration of the power of emergent behavior.

Conway's Life consists of a two-dimensional grid of squares (or **cells**), each of which can be either alive or dead. This could be considered to model a real-world terrain, where each square represented a piece of land, and a square would be considered alive if it had a living creature in it and dead (or empty) if it did not.

Any given configuration is changed into a successive configuration, or **generation**, by the application of a set of four rules. These rules determine what will happen to each cell on the basis of its eight neighbors (assuming an infinite grid). The rules can be defined as follows:

1.   If a dead cell has exactly three living neighbors in one generation, then those neighbors will reproduce in the next generation, and the empty cell will "come to life."

2.   If a living cell has two or three living neighbors, then that cell is "happy," and remains alive in the following generation.

3.   If a living cell has less than two living neighbors, then it dies of loneliness in the next generation.

4.   If a living cell has more than three living neighbors, then it dies of overcrowding in the next generation.

Figure 13.2 shows a set of configurations of Conway's Life, where each cell is either empty (dead) or contains an **O** (in which case it is alive). The first configuration shown in Figure 13.2 is transformed by the rules to the second configuration in the next generation. The second is transformed into the third, and so on. Hence, the five illustrations in Figure 13.2 show five successive generations of Conway's Life.

Figure 13.2

Five successive generations of Conway's Life

The most interesting aspect of this particular sequence is that the final configuration is almost exactly the same as the first configuration, except that it has been shifted across and down by one cell. Clearly, by applying the same rules again, the shape will continue to move in this way. This particular configuration is known as a **glider**.

Conway's Life becomes more interesting when played over a larger grid (for example, using a computer monitor with each pixel representing a cell) and with the starting configuration selected randomly. In some cases, after a number of generations, all the cells in the grid have died. In other cases, the system reaches a stable state where each generation is the same as the previous generation, or where the system oscillates between a few patterns.

One very interesting pattern is known as a **glider gun**. This configuration constantly spews out gliders, which then glide away from it. In this way, we can see a system that in a very simple way can be said to reproduce. Rather than just changing, or stagnating, the system is able to constantly produce new "entities," if we can consider a glider to be an entity. We will see how this concept can be more reasonably applied in other areas of Artificial Life.

Conway's Life is an example of a **cellular automaton**. A cellular automaton consists of a set of cells, each of which contains data (in this case, "alive" or "dead" or "empty" or "full" or 1 or 0). The system is an automaton, or computer, in the sense that it acts on a set of input data to produce an output.

Cellular automata can use more complex sets of rules, and cells can be allowed many more possible values than the two used in Conway's Life. John Von Neumann and Stanislaw Ulam invented the concept of Cellular automata in the 1950s. Ulam and Von Neumann considered each cell in the grid of the cellular automata to be a finite state automaton where each cell's state could be determined by applying a set of rules to its previous state. In their system, each cell could be in one of 29 possible states.

By applying the rules of the system to an initial configuration, cells would transform their neighbors into different kinds of cells.

Von Neumann's idea was that in this way, a machine could be created that could reproduce itself. This is a profound idea and is something that is still researched today, as we discuss in Section 13.6.

13.5.2 One-Dimensional Cellular Automata

The cellular automata that Von Neumann and Conway invented were two dimensional, so that each cell has eight neighbors. Much interesting research has been carried out on one-dimensional cellular automata, where cells are arranged in a line, rather than a grid, and each cell has two direct neighbors. It is usual in such systems for the rules to be based not just on the immediate neighbors, but on the cells one square away from those as well. So a cell is affected by a total of five values: its four neighbors (two on each side), as well as its own value.

For example, we could create a rule that says that if a living cell has at least two living neighbors on either side of it, then it will live, but if it has less than two neighbors, then it will die. We will further say that if a dead cell has at least three living neighbors, then it will come to life.

This kind of rule is known as a **legal** rule, in that if a cell is not alive, and has no living neighbors, then it will stay dead. It is also known as a totalistic rule, which means that the next state of a cell is determined solely by the total number of living cells there are in its vicinity. A totalistic rule does not take into account which side the living cells are on, for example.

Legal and totalistic rules for cellular automata can be expressed as a single five-bit number. Our rule above would be expressed as follows:

1	2	3	4	5
0	0	1	1	1

Figure 13.3 shows a cellular automaton in which this rule has been applied to produce five successive generations. The first line of the diagram shows the first generation. The second line shows the second generation, and so on.

Figure 13.3
Five generations of a one-dimensional cellular automaton

	O			O	O		O		O		O		O	O
			O		O	O	O		O		O	O	O	O
				O	O	O	O	O	O	O	O	O	O	O
			O	O	O	O	O	O	O	O	O	O	O	O
		O	O	O	O	O	O	O	O	O	O	O	O	O

Clearly, this particular cellular automaton is not going to produce very interesting behavior because it will eventually fill up the entire system with life and will reach a stable (or **stagnant**) configuration that will never change.

Because the rules consist of five bits, there are 32 possible rules for such cellular automata, some of which will produce much more interesting patterns than the one shown in Figure 13.3. Some sets of rules have been used to produce patterns that quite closely resemble the patterns that grow naturally on some sea shells.

Again, we are seeing how complexity can emerge from a simple set of rules.

Cellular automata have been applied in a number of fields, including pathology, where they are used to analyze blood smears. They have also been applied in the field of image processing, and it has been suggested that cellular automata rules resemble the manner in which the visual cortex is structured.

13.6   Self-Reproducing Systems

As we have already seen, Von Neumann postulated the idea of a self-reproducing system based on cellular automata in the 1950s. Another form of self-reproducing system was invented by Christopher Langton at the end of the 1970s. Langton's aim was to develop the simplest system that could reproduce itself.

His creations were called **loops**. Each loop consisted of just 94 cells, arranged in a shape rather like a lower-case letter q. Each cell could take one of eight possible values. Each loop contained all the information that was needed to produce another identical loop, which in turn could produce a further loop, and so on.

The loops' reproduction was carried out through the tail of the q shape, which contained cells that grew to produce a new loop, which then broke off once it had fully formed.

Of course, the loops were not real "living" creatures in any way, but they did exhibit one important property of life: reproduction. The loops only "existed" as data in a computer, or as images on a screen, but they represented a step forward—the first artificial system that was capable of self-reproducing.

Von Neumann's work predicted that it would be feasible to have a self-reproducing system in the real world: he imagined robots that could visit other planets, mine minerals from the planet, refine those minerals, and create new versions of themselves from the materials they found.

13.7   Evolution

Each change that occurs from one generation to the next in cellular automata such as Conway's Life is simple. By running a large number of generations of such a system, reasonably complex patterns can be observed. In his book, *The Blind Watchmaker*, Richard Dawkins (1991) describes such changes as **single-step selection**. By contrast, the process of evolution involves **cumulative selection**.

Cumulative selection means that at each step, existing entities or items of data "reproduce" to form new entities. Rather than each step being based on simple rules that define how one state will change to the next, the next state is based on the best features of the previous state and, in general, improves on that previous state.

In nature, natural selection is the process that chooses which entities will reproduce. Darwin's idea of "survival of the fittest" means that the creatures that manage to reproduce are probably the strongest, in some way, and so subsequent generations will tend to inherit stronger features from their parents.

In many Artificial Life systems, natural selection is replaced by artificial selection—for example, in some cases, a person chooses which entity should reproduce from a population of entities. In *The Blind Watchmaker*, Dawkins described **biomorphs**, a system of artificial selection that he originally designed to evolve tree-like shapes. The shape of any biomorph was determined by just nine variables, or **genes**. Each gene represented a feature of the biomorphs, such as the branching angle between branches or the length of branches.

The system produced a set of slightly different biomorphs, and the user could select one to reproduce. The next generation would consist of a set of biomorphs that were very similar to the one chosen by the user, but each one would differ slightly in one gene. This process of modification is known as **mutation**, and we see how it is applied in genetic algorithms in Chapter 14.

Although Dawkins had intended his biomorphs to resemble trees, after running just a few generations of his system, he found that the biomorphs were evolving into shapes that looked like insects. His system had produced creatures that he had never imagined it would be capable of generating. This is another example of emergent behavior: complex changes emerging from simple rules.

Dawkins' biomorphs exhibited artificial selection, where a human chose which entities could reproduce in each generation. Systems that more closely resemble natural selection are also possible. As we see in Chapter 14, genetic algorithms are evolved to solve particular problems by using a measure of fitness based on how close each algorithm comes to solving the problem.

13.8   Evolution Strategies

Evolution strategies were first developed in the 1960s by Ingo Rechenberg and Hans-Paul Schwefel as a way of solving engineering problems. The idea is similar to hill climbing, which we see in Chapter 4. A possible solution to the problem is represented as a set of parameters. The initial generation is a randomly selected set of parameters, and each subsequent generation is produced by adding a **normally distributed** value to each of the parameters.

(The normally distributed mutation values have a mean of zero, and smaller values are more likely than larger values. This is based on the fact that in nature, mutations tend to be small changes, rather than large changes).

If the new set of parameters (the **offspring**) gives a better solution than the previous set (the **parent**), then the process continues with the offspring. Otherwise, the offspring is rejected, and a new offspring is generated for the parent.

Note that in evolving evolution strategies, each offspring is produced from just one parent. In other words, the system uses **asexual reproduction**. We will see how **sexual reproduction** can be used to develop artificial evolution systems where offspring are produced from more than one parent, often combining good features of each parent to produce offspring that are "better," by some **metric**.

The idea of metrics is an important one, when applying artificial natural selection. To have a system that evolves entities without human intervention, a metric is needed that can be used to determine **fitness**. A fitter entity is one that is "better" by some criteria: better able to solve a particular problem, stronger, or more beautiful, for example.

Selecting a suitable metric is usually the first hurdle when developing an evolutionary solution to a problem. For example, to evolve a solution to the problem of sorting a set of numbers, a metric could count how many numbers were in the correct locations. A more sophisticated metric might count how many numbers were in the correct order, even if not in the right locations.

13.9   Genetic Programming

Genetic programming was developed by John Koza in the early 1990s. Koza used genetic programming to evolve solutions to problems in the form of LISP programs, or **S-expressions** (symbolic expressions). LISP programs and the data manipulated by LISP programs are both S-expressions, and so LISP programs can manipulate each other, or even themselves.

Genetic programming can be thought of as a way to search through the space of possible S-expressions for the one that best solves a given problem.

Each S-expression can be represented as a tree, with the operators and values in the expression at nodes in the tree. For example, Figure 13.4 shows the tree for the expression $2x + \log y$, which in LISP would be expressed as $+(*(2x) (\log (y)))$.

To apply genetic programming, the following five steps must first be taken:

1. *Select a set of terminals.*

   The terminals are the variables to be used in expressions. In the example above, the terminals are x and y.

2. *Select a set of primitive functions.*

   The primitive functions are the functions that are allowed in our expressions. In the expression above, we have used the primitive functions *, +, and log. We could allow other primitive functions, depending on the nature of the problem that is to be solved.

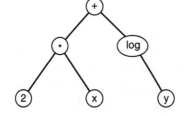

Figure 13.4

Tree representation of
$2x + \log y$

3.   *Select a fitness function.*

The fitness function is a way of determining how successful or fit any given expression is. Typically, this will involve applying the S-expression as a program to a set of sample data and seeing how close to the correct solutions the results are.

4.   *Select parameters for the system.*

The parameters to be chosen include the **population size** (that is, how many entities will exist in each generation) and the number of generations to run the system for.

5.   *Select a method for determining the result of a run.*

Each run of the system will produce a new generation. A method needs to be chosen that will determine which program that has been generated so far is the best. Similarly, a termination condition is often chosen that enables the system to stop when it has found a perfect solution.

To produce a new generation, mutation and **crossover** are applied to the current generation. Mutation simply involves making small changes to an S-expression (such as replacing the "+" operator with the "−" operator, or increasing the value of a constant from 2 to 2.1).

Crossover involves taking two entities from the population and combining features of each to produce a new offspring. In Chapter 14, we see how crossover is an important aspect of genetic algorithms.

13.10   Evolutionary Programming

Evolutionary programming (EP) was invented by Lawrence Fogel in 1966. EP was used to evolve solutions to the problem of working out what the next symbol would be in a finite sequence of symbols: $a_1, a_2, a_3, a_4, a_5, \ldots, a_n$. The method works by evolving FSAs. In the first generation, a set of random FSAs is generated. The next generation is evolved by producing one offspring from each FSA in the previous generation. Reproduction involves applying one of five mutation operators:

1.   changing an output symbol

2.   changing a state transition

3. adding a state

4. deleting a state

5. changing the initial state

To determine the fitness of an FSA, it is run against each initial subset of the list of symbols that exists so far and its prediction compared with the actual next values.

Hence, if the existing sequence is 1,2,3,4,5,6,7,8,9, then the FSA would first be run just with the number 1, and its output compared with 2. Next, it would be run with the sequence 1,2 and the output compared with 3. Finally, it would be run with 1,2,3,4,5,6,7,8 and its output compared with 9. A successful FSA would probably generate 10 as the next number in the complete sequence.

Each generation contains the parents from the previous generation and each parent's offspring. Half of these FSAs are allowed to survive—the ones that make the most correct guesses on the subsequences. These FSAs are then allowed to reproduce to generate the next generation, and so on.

13.11 L-Systems

In the late 1960s, a biologist, Aristid Lindenmayer, developed a set of rules to describe the growth patterns of plants. His "plants" consisted of cells, each of which could take on one of two values—*a* or *b*. These represented the two types of cells seen in the early growth stages of a particular type of algae. The rules Lindenmayer applied to the cells were as follows:

Rule 1:   a -> ab

Rule 2:   b -> a

Hence, if we start out with *a* in the first step, then on the next step this will become *ab*. On the next step, this will become *aba*, followed by *abaab* and then *abaababa*. This pattern of growth fairly closely matched the growth patterns of the plants that Lindenmayer was studying.

These sets of rules were called L-systems, and it turned out that L-systems could be used to produce images of remarkably lifelike artificial plants. By applying the L-system rules, strings of thousands of cells could be generated, and by interpreting the symbols in those strings as branching patterns, images of plant-like structures could be created. By using graphic rendering techniques, images can be generated from L-systems that are indistinguishable from real plants. These images are often used in computer games and films.

Perhaps more usefully, L-systems can also be used to model biological systems, such as the development processes involved in the growth of plants, thus making it possible to study the workings of life itself, by simulating it in a virtual laboratory.

13.12 Classifier Systems

Classifier systems, based on the expert systems we saw in Chapter 9, were invented by John Holland in 1986. As with expert systems, a classifier system consists of a set of rules that tell the system how to behave in particular circumstances—how to respond to features in its environment.

A classifier system, though, also has the ability to generate better responses and to learn to respond to unfamiliar situations by treating its rules as a population to be evolved.

The classifier system consists of the following components:

- detectors that receive inputs from the environment
- effectors that send outputs to the environment, and carry out actions
- a rule system, which consists of a population of classifiers; a variable measure of fitness is associated with each rule
- detectors that receive feedback from the environment concerning how well the system is performing
- a **bucket-brigade algorithm** for assigning credit and blame to classifiers
- a procedure for reproducing classifiers by application of a set of genetic operators
- a set of message lists—for input, output, and internal messages

The operation of the classifier system is as follows:

First, the environment sends the system an input message, which is received by the input detector.

This message tells the system about some feature of the environment, or about some event that has occurred (such as a move that has been made in a game).

This message is placed on the input message list and translated into a set of internal messages that the system can interpret, using its classifier rules.

These internal messages cause some of the classifiers to fire—the choice of which classifier rules fire is based on the relative fitness of the rules, and also on how well their antecedents match the internal messages. This is known as a **bidding system**, where the classifiers that generate the highest bid (based on fitness and closeness of match) get to fire.

The effect of the classifiers firing is either to generate further internal messages, which may cause further classifiers to fire, or to generate output messages, which are passed back to the environment.

The environment then evaluates the system's actions and provides feedback on how successful they were.

At this point, the system uses a **bucket-brigade algorithm** to assign credit or blame to the various classifiers in the system. This involves increasing the fitness of the classifiers that contributed most to a successful outcome and decreasing the fitness of those that contributed most to an unsuccessful outcome.

Finally, successful rules are allowed to reproduce using **crossover** and **mutation** operators to produce new rules, whereas unsuccessful rules are dropped from the system altogether.

Each classifier consists of three parts:

- a condition (the antecedent of the rule)
- a message (the action of the rule)
- a fitness measure

We can represent classifier rules in the form $(c_1, c_2, c_3, c_4, c_5)$ -> M, f. Here c_1 to c_5 are the variables that make up the input to the system, and M is the output message that results from firing this classifier rule, which represents an action or a classification. f is the fitness of the classifier rule.

For example, we can assume that the inputs to the system are numeric variables that can take on values from 1 to 10 and that the classification or action that results from each classification is one of five possible actions: A_1, A_2, A_3, A_4, or A_5. Classifier rules do not need to specify a value for each variable and can specify * to indicate that any value can match that variable. Hence, possible classifier rules might be:

$(1, 2, 3, 4, 5) \rightarrow A1, 0.7$

$(1, *, *, *, *) \rightarrow A3, 2.4$

$(4, 2, *, 1, *) \rightarrow A2, 9.1$

$(*, 9, *, 6, 2) \rightarrow A3, 7.2$

$(3, 4, 5, *, *) \rightarrow A4, 4.5$

$(1, 2, *, *, *) \rightarrow A5, 6.2$

Rule 1, for example, specifies that the string $(1, 2, 3, 4, 5)$ is classified as classification $A1$, with a fitness of 0.7.

Now let us imagine that an input message arrives from the environment, which is (1, 2, 3, 4, 5). This will match classifiers 1, 2, and 6. These three classifiers now bid. The value of a classifier's bid is a function of that classifier's fitness and how closely its antecedent matches the input message. This measure of closeness is determined by adding 1 for each exact match and 0.5 for each * (which matches any input symbol). These values are summed and divided by the length of the message. This number is then multiplied by the classifier's fitness to produce its total bid.

Hence, the bids for the three matching classifiers in our example are as follows:

For classifier 1:

$$bid = ((1 + 1 + 1 + 1 + 1) / 5) * 0.7 = 0.7$$

For classifier 2:

$$bid = ((1 + 0.5 + 0.5 + 0.5 + 0.5) / 5) * 2.4 = 0.96$$

For classifier 6:

$$bid = ((1 + 1 + 0.5 + 0.5 + 0.5) / 5) * 6.2 = 4.34$$

The classifier with the highest bid is successful, and fires, providing a classification of A5. This is fed back to the environment as an output message, and the environment evaluates it to determine if this is correct or not.

If the classifier has made a correct assessment, its fitness is increased, which is determined by subtracting the bid value from a positive reward score. If it made an incorrect assessment, the reward will be negative (or lower than the bid value) and so its fitness level will decrease.

In fact, in most classifier systems, the bidding process is far more complex, and more than one classifier can be successful by forming joint bids. This is where the bucket-brigade algorithm becomes important for determining which classifiers to reward and to what extent, based on how much they contributed to the success (or failure) of the system as a whole. Holland based this bidding system on economic processes, with individual classifiers acting like businesses bidding for contracts.

Finally, reproduction occurs. Let us examine how this happens, by assuming that the system has decided to reproduce from the two fittest classifiers, 3 and 4.

These classifiers are defined as follows:

3. (4, 2, *, 1, *) -> A2, 9.1
4. (*, 9, *, 6, 2) -> A3, 7.2

First, a position is chosen randomly from within the antecedent. This point is called the **crossover position**. For our example, we will assume that the system has chosen the position between the third and fourth variables as its crossover position, as follows:

3. (4, 2, *, | 1, *) -> A2, 9.1
4. (*, 9, *, | 6, 2) -> A3, 7.2

Now crossover is applied as follows: the first half of classifier 3, before the crossover position, is joined to the second half of classifier 4, after the crossover position. This produces an offspring classifier, which we will call classifier 7:

7. (4, 2, *, 6, 2) -> A2, 8.4

Note that the output message for this new classifier is chosen to be A2, because this is the output classifier of the parent classifier that contributed the larger part to the offspring (3 variables).

The fitness of the offspring is determined by taking proportionally from the parents—three-fifths of the fitness of classifier 3 (because it contributed three of the five variables) and two-fifths of the fitness of classifier 4. Hence the fitness of classifier 7 is defined as

$$(3 / 5) * 9.1 + (2 / 5) * 7.2 = 8.4$$

Similarly, crossover is applied in the other proportions by attaching the first part of classifier 4 to the second part of classifier 3, to produce

8. (*, 9, *, 1, *) -> A3, 7.96

The final part of the reproduction process involves the optional application of a mutation operator. This simply involves changing one of the parts of the offspring after it has been produced. For example, a variable value might change to another value, or to *. Typically, as we see in Chapter 14, mutation is applied sparingly, so that not too much of the parents' genetic information is lost. Hence, we might apply mutation to one of the symbols in offspring 7 to produce

    7. (4, 2, *, 6, *) -> A2, 8.4

The description of classifier systems so far has been rather abstract. We can imagine classifier systems being used, for example, to play a game such as chess, where a static evaluation function is used to determine whether a move was good or bad, and where the inputs are the positions of the pieces on the board.

In the 1980s, Stewart Wilson, a researcher at Polaroid, used classifier systems to build an artificial creature he called "*". * was placed in a world consisting of rocks and food. Over a period of time, * learned to deal with its world more and more efficiently. For example, it learned that food was often near a rock, but that banging into a rock was painful. Hence, when it encountered a rock, it would stop and then walk around the rock to see if any food was present. This artificial creature had learned to survive in its own environment without anyone needing to teach it how. Its survival emerged from a combination of its environment and its reasonably simple classifier system "brain."

Of course, this did not take place in the real world but, like most Artificial Life, took place inside a computer in the form of binary data.

13.13   Artificial Immune Systems

Artificial immune systems (AIS) are a relatively recent innovation. The idea behind AIS is to build systems based on the immune system in human beings and other animals. The biological immune system is a massively parallel system that is able to deal with changes in individual bodies, changes in environment, and even to adapt to rapidly evolving viruses and other attackers.

One of the first uses for AIS was to build a system that could defend computers against viruses. Early antivirus systems based on this technique relied on people reporting a new virus to the "immune system," which would then make attempts to analyze the virus to determine ways to identify and block it.

More advanced methods are now applied using artificial immune systems to solve combinatorial search problems and are also applied in computer security, machine learning, and fault diagnosis.

13.14   Chapter Summary

- A definition of life is not easy to produce. Counterexamples can be found for most definitions.

- Artificial Life is modeled on life in the same way that Artificial Intelligence is modeled on the human brain.

- Complex behavior tends to emerge from simple systems when using techniques modeled on life. Such behaviors are *emergent*.

- Cellular automata such as Conway's life show how life can be simulated in an extremely simple system based on finite state automata.

- Langton's loops were an example of a simple self-reproducing system. Von Neumann postulated an entity that could physically reproduce itself.

- Evolution strategies use asexual reproduction to search for solutions to engineering problems.

- Genetic programming methods evolve S-expressions or LISP programs to solve problems.

- Evolutionary programming involves evolving finite state automata to predict the next item in a sequence of symbols.

- L-systems use simple rules to build complex plant-like structures.

- Classifier systems combine evolutionary methods (genetic algorithm) with a production system to build a system that is able to adapt to changes in its environment.

13.15   Review Questions

13.1   What is life?

13.2   What is Artificial Life? How does it relate to Artificial Intelligence? Is one an alternative to the other, or are they complementary?

13.3   Explain what is meant by emergent behavior.

13.4 Explain how Conway's Life is modeled on life. What interesting properties does it exhibit? Why do you think it has fascinated people for so long?

13.5 Explain how a system might be built that could reproduce itself. Would such a system be alive?

13.6 Explain how genetic programming could be used to solve problems.

13.7 What is evolutionary programming? How does it differ from genetic programming?

13.8 Explain why L-systems are of interest to Artificial Life researchers.

13.9 Explain the relationship between classifier systems and production systems. How are classifier systems built? What advantages do they have over production systems?

13.10 Explain how systems modeled on the human immune system might provide a solution to the problem of computer viruses or of unsolicited bulk e-mails ("spam").

13.16   Further Reading

There is a great deal of literature on the subject of Artificial Life. A good introduction to the subject from a relatively nontechnical point of view can be found in Levy (1993) and Kelly (1994). Adami (1997) is a more advanced text on the subject.

Langton (1995) provides a number of interesting articles on Artificial Life, including philosophic and sociologic perspectives.

Classifier systems and genetic algorithms are covered by many of the main Artificial Intelligence texts, but few of them cover any other aspects of Artificial Life.

Information on artificial immune systems can be found in de Castro and Timmis (2002) and Dasgupta (1999).

Dawkins (1991) gives an excellent view of the subject from the biologic evolutionary perspective.

A fictional account of the potentials of Artificial Life can be found in *Prey* by Michael Crichton.

Introduction to Artificial Life, by Christoph Adami (1997 – Telos)

Genetic Programming: An Introduction: On the Automatic Evolution of Computer Programs and Its Applications, by Wolfgang Banzhaf, Peter Nordin, Robert E. Keller, and Frank D. Francone (1997 – Morgan Kaufmann)

Digital Biology, by Peter Bentley (2002 – Simon & Schuster)

The Philosophy of Artificial Life, by Margaret A. Boden (1996 – Oxford University Press)

Swarm Intelligence: From Natural to Artificial Systems, by Eric Bonabeau, Marco Dorigo, and Guy Theraulaz (1999 – Oxford University Press)

Artificial Immune Systems and Their Applications, edited by Dipankar Dasgupta (1999 – Springer Verlag)

The Blind Watchmaker, by Richard Dawkins (1996 – W. W. Norton & Company)

Artificial Immune Systems: A New Computational Intelligence Paradigm, by Leandro N. de Castro and Jonathan Timmis (2002 – Springer Verlag)

Evolutionary Computation in Bioinformatics, edited by Gary B. Fogel and David W. Corne (2002 – Morgan Kaufmann)

Creation: Life and How to Make It, by Steve Grand (2001 – Harvard University Press)

From Animals to Animats 7: Proceedings of the Seventh International Conference on Simulation of Adaptive Behavior, edited by Bridget Hallam, Dario Floreano, John Hallam, Gillian Hayes, and Jean-Arcady Meyer (2002 – MIT Press ; also available are the proceedings from the first to sixth conferences)

Silicon Second Nature: Culturing Artificial Life in a Digital World, by Stefan Helmreich (2000 – University of California Press)

Emergence: The Connected Lives of Ants, Brains, Cities, and Software, by Steven Johnson (2001 – Scribner)

Out of Control: The New Biology of Machines, by Kevin Kelly (1994 – Fourth Estate)

Swarm Intelligence by James Kennedy, Russell C. Eberhart, and Yuhui Shi (2001 – Morgan Kaufmann)

Genetic Programming: On the Programming of Computers by Means of Natural Selection, by John R. Koza (1992 – MIT Press)

Genetic Programming II: Automatic Discovery of Reusable Programs, by John R. Koza (1994 – MIT Press)

Artificial Life: An Overview, edited by Christopher Langton (1995 – MIT Press)

Artificial Life: A Report from the Frontier Where Computers Meet Biology, by Steven Levy (1993 – Vintage Books)

Evolutionary Algorithms for Single and Multicriteria Design Optimization, by Andrzej Osyczka (2001 – Physica Verlag)

Artificial Life VIII: Proceedings of the Eighth International Conference on Artificial Life, edited by Russell Standish, Mark A. Bedau, and Hussein A. Abbass (2003 – MIT Press; also available are the proceedings from the first through the seventh conferences)

Evolutionary Art and Computers, by Stephen Todd and William Latham (1992 – Academic Press)

Virtual Organisms: The Startling World of Artificial Life, by Mark Ward (2000 – St Martin's Press)

CHAPTER 14

Genetic Algorithms

Some call it evolution,
And others call it God.

—William Herbert Carruth, *Each in His Own Tongue*

The first technical descriptions and definitions of adaptation come from biology. In that context adaptation designates any process whereby a structure is progressively modified to give better performance in its environment. The structures may range from a protein molecule to a horse's foot or a human brain or, even, to an interacting group of organisms such as the wildlife of the African veldt.

—John H. Holland, *Adaptation in Natural and Artificial Systems*

14.1 Introduction

The idea of local search is introduced in Chapter 5. Local search methods involve making small changes to potential solutions to a problem until an optimal solution is identified. Genetic algorithms are a form of local search that use methods based on evolution to make small changes to a population of chromosomes in an attempt to identify an optimal solution.

In this chapter, the representations used for genetic algorithms are discussed, including the idea of schemata. The genetic operators, crossover and mutation, are explained, as is the idea of fitness.

The procedures used to run genetic algorithms are also discussed, and an attempt is made to explain why genetic algorithms work.

An example is given of how genetic algorithms might be used to evolve a strategy for playing a simple game (Prisoner's Dilemma), and the idea of allowing humans to input into the process in order to evolve images of "creatures" is also explored.

14.2   Representations

We have seen a number of different representations that can be used in evolutionary techniques like genetic algorithms. Genetic programming is used to evolve S-expressions, which can be used as LISP programs to solve problems. Classifier systems use a string of numbers that represent properties of the environment and symbols that represent responses to those properties.

The simplest representation for genetic algorithms is the one that was used by John Holland: a string of bits. A string of bits is known as a **chromosome**, and each bit is known as a **gene**. Both of these terms are directly borrowed from genetics and illustrate the close manner in which genetic algorithms mirror biological processes.

For most of this chapter, we discuss genetic algorithms using this representation, but it is worth remembering that many other representations are possible, and different representations will be more appropriate for particular problems.

The **population** consists of a set of chromosomes, each of which, as we have seen, is made up of genes. A chromosome is usually taken to represent a complete "individual" within the population—in other words, a complete representation of a solution, or a classification. It is also possible to combine chromosomes together to form **creatures**, which more closely mirrors real genetics because each individual in the real world has a number of chromosomes. For now, we will continue with Holland's approach, where a chromosome represents an entire individual.

Each gene in the chromosome represents some facet of that individual's genetic makeup. For example, the genes could be entirely independent and represent the presence or otherwise of certain body parts in an animal. More usually, the genes are combined together in a less transparent way. For example, we will see how genetic algorithms can be used to solve mathematical problems, where the bits of a chromosome are usually treated as the bits of a binary number that represents a solution to the problem.

14.3 The Algorithm

The process for running a genetic algorithm is as follows. Note that this process is largely independent of the representation that is being used.

1. Generate a random population of chromosomes (this is the first generation).

2. If the termination criteria are satisfied, stop. Otherwise, continue with step 3.

3. Determine the fitness of each chromosome.

4. Apply crossover and mutation to selected chromosomes from the current generation to generate a new population of chromosomes—the next generation.

5. Return to step 2.

Note that the evolutionary part of the classifier system process that we saw in Chapter 13 is in fact a genetic algorithm.

The size of the population should be determined in advance. Usually, the population size remains constant from one generation to the next. In some situations, it can be useful to have a population that changes size.

The size of each chromosome must remain the same for crossover to be applied. It is possible to run genetic algorithms with variable chromosome sizes, but this is unusual.

Typically, the fittest chromosomes are selected in each generation to mate with each other, and each pair of chromosomes is allowed to produce two offspring. The resultant set of offspring chromosomes then replaces the previous generation.

It is also possible to allow particularly fit parents to produce relatively more offspring and to allow certain members of a generation to survive to the next generation. For most of this chapter, we will assume that each pair of parents produces two offspring and that those offspring replace the parents.

14.4   Fitness

Richard Dawkins' biomorph world, which is discussed in Chapter 13, is a form of genetic algorithm. Rather than applying an objective fitness level, fitness was determined subjectively by a human operator. Additionally, each generation was the offspring of just one parent, to which mutation was applied.

With more traditional genetic algorithms, a metric is needed whereby the fitness of a chromosome can be objectively determined. For example, in using genetic algorithms to sort numbers into numeric order, a suitable fitness measure might be determined by running the algorithm and counting how many numbers it places in the correct position. A more sophisticated measure of fitness could be obtained by measuring how far from its correct place each incorrectly placed number is.

Karl Sims evolved "creatures" that were bred according to their abilities to perform simple tasks, such as walking, jumping, and swimming (Sims 1994). Sims used a representation and a set of rules that determined how the various body parts of his creatures interacted with each other and with their environment. In this case, then, the fitness measure was based on the extent to which the physical form (**phenotype**) represented by the genetic information (**genotype**) met certain criteria.

14.5   Crossover

In Chapter 13, we see how crossover is used in classifier systems. The crossover operator is applied to two chromosomes of the same length as follows:

1.   Select a random crossover point.

2.   Break each chromosome into two parts, splitting at the crossover point.

3.   Recombine the broken chromosomes by combining the front of one with the back of the other, and vice versa, to produce two new chromosomes.

For example, consider the following two chromosomes:

110100110001001
010101000111101

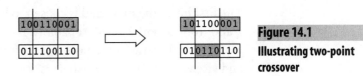

Figure 14.1

Illustrating two-point crossover

A crossover point might be chosen between the sixth and seventh genes:

```
110100 | 110001001
010101 | 000111101
```

Now the chromosome parts are recombined as follows:

```
110100 | 000111101    =>    110100000111101
010101 | 110001001    =>    010101110001001
```

This process is based on the way in which DNA strands recombine with each other in human reproduction to combine features of each parent in a child.

Single-point crossover is the most commonly used form, but it is also possible to apply crossover with two or more crossover positions.

In two-point crossover, two points are chosen that divide the chromosomes into two sections, with the outer sections considered to be joined together to turn the chromosome into a ring. The two sections are swapped with each other, as shown in Figure 14.1.

In Figure 14.1, the genes from parent 1 are shaded in grey, while the genes from parent 2 are not shaded.

Another form of crossover is **uniform crossover**. Here, a probability, p, is used to determine whether a given bit from parent 1 will be used, or from parent 2. In other words, a child can receive any random bits from each of its parents. For example, let us assume we have the following two parents:

```
Parent 1: 10001101
Parent 2: 00110110
```

The offspring of these two chromosomes might be determined as shown in Figure 14.2.

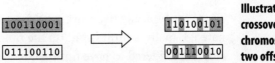

Figure 14.2

Illustrating uniform crossover of two-parent chromosomes to produce two offspring

The first bit of the first child is chosen to be from parent 1 with probability p and from parent 2 with probability $1 - p$. If a bit from parent 1 is chosen for child 1, then the corresponding bit from parent 2 is chosen for child 2, and vice versa. Uniform crossover is also often used to produce just one offspring from each pair of parents, unlike traditional one- or two-point crossover, which usually produces two offspring from each pair of parents.

Uniform crossover does mix up the genes of the gene pool substantially, and in some cases it can be sensible to use a very high (or very low) value of p to ensure that most of the genes come from one parent or the other.

In some cases, **cloning** can be applied, whereby crossover is not applied at all, and a new offspring is produced that is identical to its single parent. Dawkins' biomorph system can be thought of as a genetic algorithm with cloning and mutation, where fitness is determined subjectively.

14.6 Mutation

You may recognize genetic algorithms as being rather similar to the hill-climbing methods we see in Chapter 4. Hill-climbing involves generating a possible solution to the problem and moving toward a better solution than the current one until a solution is found from which no better solution can be found. Hill climbing does not perform well with problems where there are local maxima. To enable genetic algorithms to avoid this problem, the mutation operator was introduced.

Mutation is a **unary operator** (i.e., it is applied to just one argument—a single gene) that is usually applied with a low probability, such as 0.01 or 0.001. Mutation simply involves reversing the value of a bit in a chromosome. For example, with a mutation rate of 0.01, it might be expected that one gene in a chromosome of 100 genes might be reversed. Here we see mutation applied to one of the offspring from our example above:

010101110001001
⇓
010101110**1**01001

14.7 Termination Criteria

There are typically two ways in which a **run** of a genetic algorithm is terminated. Usually, a limit is put on the number of generations, after which the run is considered to have finished.

With some problems, the run can stop when a particular solution has been reached, or when the highest fitness level in the population has reached a particular value. For example, we see in the following section how a genetic algorithm can be used to solve a mathematical function. In this case, it is clear that the run can stop when the correct solution has been reached, which can be easily tested for.

In the case of Dawkins' biomorph world, no such termination conditions exist. It does not make sense to impose an artificial limit on the number of generations in the run, and because no objective measure of fitness is involved, the system cannot determine when to stop on that basis.

This is an important distinction. In many cases, genetic algorithms are used to solve problems that have an objective solution, in which case the algorithm can stop when it reaches that solution. In other cases, they are used for more abstract purposes, such as to generate interesting pictures. In these cases, human judgment must be used to determine when to terminate.

14.8   Optimization of a Mathematic Function

We will see how a genetic algorithm can be used to find a maximum value of a mathematic function.

We will attempt to maximize the following function:

$$f(x) = \sin(x)$$

over the range of x from 1 to 15, where x is in radians.

Each chromosome represents a possible value of x using four bits.

Figure 14.3 shows the discrete graph for this function.

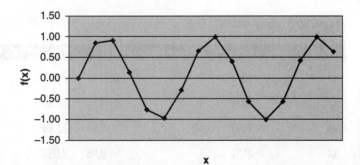

Figure 14.3

Discrete graph for the function $f(x) = \sin(x)$, where x ranges from 0 to 15.

We will use a population size of four chromosomes. The first step is to generate a random population, which is our first generation:

c1 = 1001

c2 = 0011

c3 = 1010

c4 = 0101

To calculate the fitness of a chromosome, we need to first convert it to a decimal integer and then calculate $f(x)$ for this integer.

We will assign fitness as a numeric value from 0 to 100, where 0 is the least fit and 100 is the most fit.

$f(x)$ generates real numbers between -1 and 1. We will assign a fitness of 100 to $f(x) = 1$ and fitness of 0 to $f(x) = -1$. Fitness of 50 will be assigned to $f(x) = 0$. Hence, fitness of x, $f'(x)$ is defined as follows:

$$f'(x) = 50(f(x) + 1)$$
$$= 50(\sin(x) + 1)$$

The fitness ratio of a chromosome is that chromosome's fitness as a percentage of the total fitness of the population. We will see later why this is a useful calculation.

Table 14.1 shows the calculations that are used to calculate the fitness values for our first generation.

Now we need to run a single step of our genetic algorithm to produce the next generation. The first step is to select which chromosomes will reproduce. **Roulette-wheel selection** involves using the fitness ratio to randomly select chromosomes to reproduce. This is done as follows:

Table 14.1   Generation 1

Chromosome	Genes	Integer value	$f(x)$	Fitness $f'(x)$	Fitness ratio
c1	1001	9	0.41	70.61	46.3%
c2	0011	3	0.14	57.06	37.4%
c3	1010	10	-0.54	22.80	14.9%
c4	0101	5	-0.96	2.05	1.34%

The range of real numbers from 0 to 100 is divided up between the chromosomes proportionally to each chromosome's fitness. Hence, in our first generation, c1 will have 46.3% of the range (i.e., from 0 to 46.3), c2 will have 37.4% of the range (i.e., from 46.3 to 83.7), and so on.

A random number is now generated between 0 and 100. This number will fall in the range of one of the chromosomes, and this chromosome has been selected for reproduction. The next random number is used to select this chromosome's mate. Hence, fitter chromosomes will tend to produce more offspring than less fit chromosomes.

It is important that this method does not stop less fit chromosomes from reproducing at all, though, because this helps to ensure that populations do not **stagnate**, by constantly breeding from the same parents.

In our example, though, chromosome c4 will be very unlikely to reproduce because this would only occur if the random number fell in the narrow range between 98.6 and 100.

We will need to generate four random numbers to find the four parents that will produce the next generation. Our first random number is 56.7, which means that c2 has been chosen as the first parent. Next, 38.2 is chosen, so its mate is c1.

We now need to combine c1 and c2 to produce two new offspring. First, we need to randomly select a crossover point. We will choose the point between the second and third bits (genes):

```
10 | 01
00 | 11
```

Crossover is now applied to produce two offspring, c5 and c6:

```
c5 = 1011
c6 = 0001
```

In a similar way, c1 and c3 are chosen to produce offspring c7 and c8, using a crossover point between the third and fourth bits:

```
c7 = 1000
c8 = 1011
```

The population c1 to c4 is now replaced by the second generation, c5 to c8. c4 did not have a chance to reproduce, and so its genes will be lost. c1,

Table 14.2   Generation 2

Chromosome	Genes	Integer value	$f(x)$	Fitness $f'(x)$	Fitness ratio
c5	1011	11	−1	0	0%
c6	0001	1	0.84	92.07	48.1%
c7	1000	8	0.99	99.47	51.9%
c8	1011	11	−1	0	0%

which was the fittest chromosome in the first generation, was able to reproduce twice, thus passing on its highly fit genes to all members of the next generation.

The fitness values for the second generation are shown in Table 14.2.

This generation has produced two extremely fit chromosomes and two very unfit chromosomes. In fact, one of the chromosomes, c7, is the optimal solution. At this point, the termination criteria would probably determine that the run could stop. Otherwise, the algorithm will continue to run but will not find any better solutions. It has taken just one step to get from a random configuration to the optimal solution.

Clearly, this was a very simplistic example. Real problems are likely to be much harder to solve. They are also likely to involve much larger population sizes (typically population sizes of between 100 and 500 are used), and chromosomes are likely to contain far greater numbers of bits.

In many cases, genetic algorithms quickly produce optimal or near-optimal solutions to combinatorial problems that would otherwise be impractical to solve. This raises an interesting question: Why do genetic algorithms work? We will now address this question.

14.9   Why Genetic Algorithms Work

Genetic algorithms are a local search method (see Chapter 5), in some ways similar to simulated annealing and hill-climbing methods.

It is possible to explain genetic algorithms by comparison with natural evolution: small changes that occur on a selective basis combined with reproduction will tend to improve the fitness of the population over time. This argument is not very convincing, and John Holland (1975) invented **schemata** (the plural of **schema**) to provide an explanation for genetic algorithms that is more rigorous.

14.9.1   Schemata

In Chapter 13, we see how strings of numbers are used to represent input patterns in classifier systems. In these patterns, * is used to represent "any value" or "don't care," so that the following string:

1011*001*0

matches the following four strings:

1011**000**100
1011**000**110
1011**100**100
1011**100**110

(The bits which have matched * are shown in bold).

A schema is a string of bits that represents a possible chromosome, using * to represent "any value." A schema is said to match a chromosome if the bit string that represents the chromosome matches the schema in the way shown above. For example, the following schema:

11

matches the following four chromosomes:

0110
0111
1110
1111

Note that a schema with n *'s will match a total of 2^n chromosomes.

Each chromosome of r bits will match 2^r different schemata. For example, the following chromosome:

101

matches the following eight schemata:

101
10*
1*1
1**
*01
0

```
**1
***
```

Because schemata are made up of three different values (0, 1, and *), there are 3^m different schemata of length m. For example, there are nine possible schemata of just two bits:

```
00
01
0*
10
*0
11
*1
1*
**
```

The **defining length** of a schema is defined as the distance between the first and last defined bits (bits that are not *) in the schema. For example, the defining length of each of the following schemata is 4:

```
**10111*
1*0*1**
11111
1***1
***********10**1***************
```

Note that a schema's defining length is not dependent on the number of bits it has, except that its defining length must be less than or equal to its length. We write this as

$$d_L(S) \leq L(S)$$

where $d_L(S)$ is the defining length of schema S, and $L(S)$ is the length of schema S.

The order of a schema is defined as the number of defined bits (i.e., the number of bits that are not *) in the schema. Hence, the following schemata all have order 4:

```
**10*11*
1*0*1**1
1111
1***1***1***1
1***********10**1***************
```

We will write the order of a schema S as $O(S)$. The order of a schema tells us how **specific** it is. A schema with a high order is more specific than one with a lower order.

14.9.2   How Reproduction Affects Schemata

We can think of genetic algorithms as a way of manipulating schemata. This will help us to reason about why genetic algorithms work.

First of all, we consider what it means for a schema to be present in a population. Let us consider the following population of 10 chromosomes, each of length 32:

C_1 = 01000100101010010001010100101010
C_2 = 10100010100100001001010111010101
C_3 = 01010101011110101010100101010101
C_4 = 11010101010101001101111010100101
C_5 = 11010010101010010010100100001010
C_6 = 00101001010100101010010101111010
C_7 = 00101010100101010010101001010011
C_8 = 11111010010101010100101001010101
C_9 = 01010101010111101010001010101011
C_{10} = 11010100100101010011110010100001

Let us consider the following schema:

S_0 = 11010************************

This schema is matched by three chromosomes in our population: c_4, c_5, and c_{10}. We say that schema S_0 matches three chromosomes in generation i and write this as follows:

   $m(S_0, i) = 3$

It is useful now to consider the concept of fitness as it applies to schemata. The fitness of a schema, S, in generation i is written as follows:

   $f(S, i)$

The fitness of a schema is defined as the average fitness of the chromosomes in the population that match the schema. Hence if we define the fitness of c_4, c_5, and c_{10} as follows:

   $f(C_4, i) = 10$
   $f(C_5, i) = 22$
   $f(C_{10}, i) = 40$

hence, the fitness of the schema S_0 is defined as the average of these three values:

$$f(S_0, i) = (10 + 22 + 40) / 3$$

$$= 24$$

We will now investigate which factors affect the likelihood of a particular schema surviving from one generation to the next. In other words, what probability is there that a given schema that is present in the parent generation will be in the subsequent generation?

First, let us consider the process whereby chromosomes reproduce, without introducing crossover or mutation.

First, let us assume that there is a chromosome that matches a schema, S, in the population at time i.

The number of occurrences of S in the population at time i is

$$m(S, i)$$

and the number of occurrences of S in the population in the subsequent generation is:

$$m(S, i+1)$$

The fitness of S in generation i is

$$f(S, i)$$

Now we will calculate the probability that a given chromosome, c, which matches the schema S at time i, will reproduce and thus its genes will be present in the population at time $i + 1$. The probability that a chromosome will reproduce is proportional to its fitness, so the expected number of offspring of chromosome c is

$$m(c, \ i+1) = \frac{f(c, \ i)}{a(i)}$$

where $a(i)$ is the average fitness of the chromosomes in the population at time i.

Because chromosome c is an instance of schema S, we can thus deduce

$$m(S, \ i+1) = \frac{f(c_1, \ i) + \ldots + f(c_n, \ i)}{a(i)} \qquad (1)$$

where c_1 to c_n are the chromosomes in the population at time i that match the schema S.

Let us compare this with the definition of the fitness of schema S, $f(S, i)$, which is defined as follows:

$$f(S, i) = \frac{f(c_1, i) + \ldots + f(c_n, i)}{m(S, i)} \qquad (2)$$

By combining formula 1 with formula 2 above, we obtain:

$$m(S, i+1) = \frac{f(S, i) \cdot m(S, i)}{a(i)}$$

This tells us that the more fit a schema is compared with the average fitness of the current population, the more likely it is that that schema will appear in a subsequent population of chromosomes. A schema whose fitness is the same as the average fitness of the population will likely maintain the same number of occurrences from one generation to the next. In contrast, there will be fewer occurrences of a given schema whose fitness is lower than the average fitness of the population and more occurrences of a given schema whose fitness is higher than the average.

14.9.3 How Mutation and Crossover Affect Schemata

The above calculations have not taken into account mutation or crossover. Both mutation and crossover can destroy the presence of a schema. In other words, mutation and crossover are both capable of reducing the number of occurrences of a particular schema in a population of chromosomes. They are also capable of increasing the number of occurrences of a given schema.

A given schema can be said to have **survived** crossover, if the crossover operation produces a new chromosome that matches the schema from a parent that also matches the schema.

If the crossover point is chosen so that it is within the defining length of a schema, S, then that schema will be destroyed by the crossover operation. For a schema to survive crossover, the crossover point must be outside the defining length. Hence, the probability that a schema S of defining length $d_L(S)$ and of length $L(S)$ will survive crossover is

$$p_s(S) = 1 - \frac{d_L(S)}{L(S) - 1}$$

Hence, a shorter schema is more likely to survive from one generation to the next than a longer schema. In practical terms, this means that a feature of the chromosomes that is expressed by relatively few bits is more likely to be passed on from a parent to its offspring than a feature that is expressed by a large number of bits.

The above formula assumes that crossover is applied to each pair of parents that reproduce. In fact, it is usually the case that some chromosomes are able to reproduce asexually (by cloning). Hence, if the crossover operator is applied with probability p_c, then the above formula can be modified as follows:

$$p_s(S) = 1 - p_c \cdot \frac{d_L(S)}{L(S) - 1}$$

Hence, the less likely crossover is, the more likely any given schema is to survive from one generation to the next.

In fact, even if the crossover point is chosen within the defining length, it is still possible for a schemata to survive crossover, as in the following example.

Let us apply crossover to the following two chromosomes:

10111101
01001110

The schema **0011** is matched by the second of these chromosomes. If a crossover point is chosen between the fourth and fifth bits, then the offspring will be

10111110
01001101

In this generation, the second chromosome also matches the schema **0011**, despite the fact that the crossover point was chosen within the defining length of the schema. Hence, we can modify our formula to allow for this (fairly unlikely) occurrence:

$$p_s(S) \geq 1 - p_c \cdot \frac{d_L(S)}{L(S) - 1}$$

Now let us consider the effect of mutation on schemata. The probability that mutation will be applied to any given bit in a chromosome is p_m. Hence, a schema will survive mutation if mutation is not applied to any of the defined bits of the schema. Because a schema S has $O(S)$ defined bits, the probability of survival can be defined as

$$p_s(S) = (1 - p_m)^{O(S)}$$

Hence, a schema is more likely to survive mutation if it has a lower order.

We can combine the three equations we have to give one equation that defines the likelihood of a schema surviving reproduction using crossover and mutation. This formula defines the expected number of chromosomes that match a schema, S, in a generation at time $i + 1$:

$$m(S, \ i+1) \geq \frac{f(S, \ i) \cdot m(S, \ i)}{a(i)} \cdot \left(1 - p_c \cdot \frac{d_L(S)}{L(S) - 1} \cdot \left((1 - p_m)^{O(S)}\right)\right)$$

This rather daunting formula represents the **schema theorem**, developed by Holland, which can be stated as "Short, low order schemata which are fitter than the average fitness of the population will appear with exponentially increasing regularity in subsequent generations".

The above analysis provides a way to understand the behavior of genetic algorithms and goes some way toward explaining why they work, but it does not really provide a full answer to that question.

Although genetic algorithms have been widely studied, and there is good empirical evidence that they work, there is yet no theoretical proof that use of crossover provides better solutions than other local search techniques.

14.9.4   The Building-Block Hypothesis

The building-block hypothesis is a consequence of the schema theorem, which can be stated as "Genetic algorithms manipulate short, low-order, high fitness schemata in order to find optimal solutions to problems." These short, low-order, high-fitness schemata are known as building blocks.

In other words, genetic algorithms work well when a small group of genes that are close together represent a feature that contributes to the fitness of a chromosome. Hence, the representation that is chosen for genetic algorithms is very important. Randomly selecting bits to represent particular features of a solution is not good enough. Bits should be chosen in such a way that they group naturally together into building blocks, which genetic algorithms are designed to manipulate.

14.9.5   Deception

One problem faced by genetic algorithms is known as **deception**. Let us assume a population of chromosomes of 8 bits. We will consider four schemata and their fitness levels:

$$S_1 = 11\text{******} \qquad f(S_1) = 50$$
$$S_2 = \text{******}11 \qquad f(S_2) = 40$$
$$S_3 = 11\text{****}11 \qquad f(S_3) = 5$$
$$S_4 = 00\text{****}00 \qquad f(S_4) = 65$$

Note that S_1 and S_2 are two building blocks, which combine together to give S_3, but that S_3 is much less fit than S_1 or S_2.

Let us now assume that the optimal solution in this problem is

$$S_5 = 11111111 \qquad f(S_5) = 100$$

The genetic algorithm will find it hard to reach this optimal solution because it will prefer to match the most fit building blocks with chromosomes such as

00111100

Hence, genetic algorithms can be misled or deceived by some building blocks into heading toward suboptimal solutions.

One way to minimize the effects of deception is to use **inversion**, which is a unary operator that reverses the order of a subset of the bits within a chromosome. For example, inversion applied to the following chromosome:

1010011100

between the fourth and eighth bits would produce the following chromosome:

1011110000

Like mutation, inversion is applied with a low probability (such as one in a thousand) and can help to avoid converging on incorrect solutions.

Another way to avoid deception is to use **messy genetic algorithms**, which are described in the next section.

14.10   Messy Genetic Algorithms

Messy genetic algorithms were developed as an alternative to standard genetic algorithms.

With messy genetic algorithms (mGAs), each bit is labeled with its position. A chromosome does not have to contain a value for each position, and, in fact, a given position in a chromosome can have more than one value.

Each bit in a chromosome is represented by a pair of numbers: the first number represents the position within the chromosome, and the second number is the bit value (0 or 1).

Hence, the following chromosome:

((1,0), (2,1), (4,0))

could be a chromosome with four bit positions, where the third bit position is not specified. The following chromosome, in contrast, has two values specified for the third position:

((1,0), (2,1), (3,1), (3,0), (4,0))

Goldberg (1989) specifies methods for dealing with chromosomes that are **underspecified** (i.e., where a bit position is not defined) or that are **overspecified** (where a bit position is defined twice).

Underspecified bits are filled in by copying bits from a **template** chromosome that is usually chosen as the best-performing chromosome from the previous generation.

A method is needed to deal with overspecified chromosomes: the most usual method is simply to work on a left-to-right basis and use the first value that is assigned to a given bit position. Hence, for example, the following chromosome:

((1, 0), (3, 0), (2, 1), (1,1))

would be modified to

((1, 0), (3, 0), (2, 1))

Because bit 1 is overspecified. The first occurrence, working from left to right, is used, and any other occurrences are discarded.

mGAs use the mutation operator as with standard genetic algorithms. Instead of crossover, mGAs use the **splice** and **cut** operators.

Two chromosomes can be spliced together by simply joining one to the end of the other. Hence the following two chromosomes:

((1,0), (3,0), (4,1), (6,1))
((2,1), (3,1), (5,0), (7,0), (8,0))

can be spliced to produce the following chromosome:

((1,0), (3,0), (4,1), (6,1), (2,1), (3,1), (5,0), (7,0), (8,0))

Note that the genes do not need to be in any particular order because each one has its position specified as part of its representation.

The cut operator splits one chromosome into two smaller chromosomes. Hence, the result of the above splice operation could be cut to produce the following two chromosomes:

((1,0), (3,0), (4,1))
((6,1), (2,1), (3,1), (5,0), (7,0), (8,0))

MGAs are more immune to deception than standard genetic algorithms and have been shown to converge on optimal solutions with extremely deceptive functions (Goldberg 1989).

14.11   Prisoner's Dilemma

We will now see how genetic algorithms can be used to evolve strategies for playing a simple game: **the Prisoner's Dilemma.**

The background of the game is as follows:

Two prisoners have been arrested on suspicion of committing a crime. They are kept in separate cells, and each is told that if he betrays his friend he will receive a reward. If his friend does not betray him, then he will go free, and receive a reward, while his friend is tortured. If both betray each other, they will both be tortured, and if neither betrays the other, they will be set free.

The dilemma for each prisoner is whether to **defect** and betray his friend, or whether to **cooperate** with his friend and keep silent. Defection always brings a greater reward than cooperation, but the best overall result is obtained if both prisoners cooperate.

The game of Prisoner's Dilemma is played over a number of turns, where on each turn each player can choose whether to defect or to cooperate, and points are awarded to each player according to the outcome, as defined in Table 14.3.

Table 14.3   Point allocation in Prisoner's Dilemma

Player 1	Player 2	S_1	S_2	Notes
defects	defects	1	1	Penalty for mutual defection
defects	cooperates	5	0	Player 1 has been tempted to defect. Player 2 is the "sucker."
cooperates	defects	0	5	Player 1 is the "sucker." Player 2 has been tempted to defect.
cooperates	cooperates	3	3	Reward for mutual cooperation

In Table 14.3, S_1 and S_2 are the number of points received by player 1 and player 2, respectively, in each given situation.

14.11.1   Strategy Representation

We will choose a representation that represents the strategy of a given "player" or chromosome in the population. For our system, we will allow each player to determine its move on a given turn in the game based on the results of the previous three turns.

Each turn in the game can have one of four outcomes, as shown in Table 14.3. We shall represent each of these outcomes by a number from 0 to 3:

>   0: reward (both players have cooperated)
>
>   1: sucker (the player cooperates, and the opponent defects)
>
>   2: penalty (both players defected)
>
>   3: temptation (the player defects and the opponent cooperates)

Now, by using 0 to represent defection and 1 to represent cooperation, a three-dimensional array of binary values can be used to represent a strategy. Because there are four possible choices for each turn, and our strategies will be based on the previous three turns, our array will need to be $4 \times 4 \times 4 = 64$ bits. We will also include three bits that represent the player's behavior on the first three turns, so each chromosome will be represented by 67 bits. (We will place the three bits that represent the first three turns at the end of the chromosome.)

Hence, a chromosome that consists of 67 1s would cooperate on every go, regardless of the behavior of its opponent. Similarly, 67 0s would mean that the chromosome defected on every turn.

Hence, the following chromosome:

10000000000000000000000000000000000000000000000000000000000000000111

represents the following rather simple strategy:

Cooperate on the first three turns, and thereafter, only cooperate in the event that both players have cooperated on the previous three turns. (The first bit represents the [0,0,0] position in the array, which corresponds to three consecutive occurrences of "reward.")

The following chromosome represents a slightly more sophisticated strategy:

1001000000001001000000000000000000000000000000000010010000000001001111

The last three chromosomes represent the first three decisions: this chromosome will cooperate on the first three turns. Thereafter, this chromosome will cooperate only if the opponent has cooperated on the previous three turns. If the opponent cooperates, then the possible results are either reward or temptation. Hence, there are eight possible combinations of three moves in which the opponent has cooperated. These are represented by the eight 1's in the chromosome above at positions 0, 3, 12, 15, 48, 51, 60, and 63.

Bit position 0 represents the decision when the previous three outcomes have all been value 0 - reward (i.e., both players have cooperated on the previous three turns). Position three represents (0, 0, 3) or (reward, reward, temptation)—in other words, the opponent has cooperated on each of the three turns, and the player cooperated on the first two turns and defected on the third turn.

Each chromosome represents a complete strategy for how to play Prisoner's Dilemma over an arbitrary number of turns, basing each decision on the outcome of the previous three turns, and with the first three decisions hard-coded. Clearly, there are an astronomical number of possible chromosomes ($2^{67} \cong 15 \times 10^{19}$) and therefore a correspondingly large number of possible strategies.

14.11.2   Possible Strategies

The simplest strategies for playing Prisoner's Dilemma are "always defect" and "always cooperate," whose chromosomes consist of 67 0s and 67 1s, respectively.

Each of these strategies is a reasonable way to play Prisoner's Dilemma. "Always defect" ensures that the opponent's score is minimized, whereas "always cooperate" ensures a maximum possible combined score, in the event that the opponent also always cooperates. Of course, "always cooperate" does not do well against "always defect." In fact, no strategy does well against "always defect," being able to achieve a maximum score of only 1 out of a possible 5 for each turn. Conversely, the player using the "always defect" strategy can achieve the full 5 points if its opponent cooperates but gets just 1 point if the opponent also defects.

One very successful strategy is called **tit-for-tat**. Tit-for-tat involves cooperating to begin with and thereafter doing whatever the opponent did on the previous turn.

This strategy only uses information about the previous turn, so much of the data of the chromosome that plays tit-for-tat is redundant. Our hope is that chromosomes whose strategies are based on the previous three turns, rather than just one turn, can perform better overall than tit-for-tat.

We will assume that a game consists of 100 turns of Prisoner's Dilemma, and that the total score for a chromosome for a game is the sum of the points awarded to it in those 100 turns.

Hence, playing tit-for-tat against tit-for-tat or against "always cooperate" would achieve a total of 300 points. Playing "always defect" can achieve a total of 500 points when playing against "always cooperate." Table 14.4 shows the six possible total scores for these three strategies played against each other over 100 turns.

Table 14.4 Total scores for three strategies played over 100 turns

Player1	Player2	S1	S2
Always cooperate	Always cooperate	300	300
Always cooperate	Always defect	0	500
Always cooperate	Tit-for-tat	300	300
Always defect	Always defect	100	100
Always defect	Tit-for-tat	104	99
Tit-for-tat	Tit-for-tat	300	300

Clearly, the scores for a game can vary between 0 and 500, depending on the strategy chosen and the strategy of the opponent.

14.11.3   Evolution of Strategies

The process for running this genetic algorithm is as follows:

1. Produce a random population of chromosomes. We will start with a population of just 100 chromosomes.

2. Determine a score for each chromosome by playing its strategy against a number of opponents.

3. Select a number of chromosomes from the population to reproduce, applying crossover and mutation according to appropriate probabilities.

4. Replace the previous generation with the new population produced by reproduction.

5. Return to step 2.

A method must be applied to determine for how many generations to run the genetic algorithm. We will use 100 runs of the genetic algorithm. A termination condition could be applied that determined when an optimal solution has been reached, but as we will see, it is not necessarily clear how to identify such a strategy.

14.11.4   Choice of Opponents

As a simple example, we will start by considering playing the chromosomes against a fixed strategy.

First, we will determine each chromosome's fitness by playing its strategy against "always defect" over 100 turns.

Clearly, the best strategy against "always defect" is also "always defect." In our experiments, a population of 100 chromosomes evolved such that the average score of the 100 chromosomes reached the maximum of 100 after just two generations, as shown in Figure 14.4.

Similar results were found when playing the chromosomes against "always cooperate": the best strategy here is to play "always defect." After just a few generations, the average score of the population converged on the maximum of 500 points.

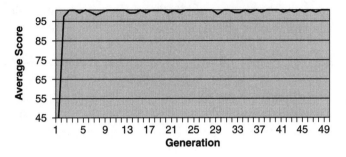

**average score over 50 generations
against "always defect"**

Figure 14.4

Average scores of a
population of 100
chromosomes playing
against "always defect"
over 50 generations

When playing against tit-for-tat, the genetic algorithms converged after just a few generations to play "always cooperate," which is the best strategy to play against tit-for-tat. In fact, the best strategy to play against tit-for-tat is to cooperate on every turn except the last turn, but our representation does not allow this strategy.

More interesting results were obtained when the chromosomes were able to play against each other, rather than against fixed strategies. This genetic algorithm was found to evolve strategies that were as successful as the best heuristic methods developed by humans (Axelrod 1987).

Playing the chromosomes against each other is similar to the idea of introducing predators into a population, which is discussed in Section 14.14.

14.12   Diversity

One problem with the genetic algorithm we have described above for playing Prisoner's Dilemma is that the populations tend to **stagnate**. That is, once a chromosome evolves that achieves a very high score, chromosomes that are different and score less well than this one will tend to die out, and the population will end up with all chromosomes playing the same strategy. In other words, the population lacks **diversity**.

Diversity is a useful measure that is often used in genetic algorithms to avoid stagnation. Like mutation, it also helps to avoid local maxima.

Hence, it is often a good idea to incorporate a measure of diversity into a genetic algorithm's fitness metric.

For example, a diversity score of a chromosome could be calculated by comparing that chromosome with the highest scoring chromosome and counting the number of bits that differ. This count could then be added to the fitness score (Winston 1992).

14.13   Evolving Pictures

In many genetic algorithm systems, the fitness of an individual chromosome is determined by treating the data that is contained in its genes as a representation of a possible solution to the problem or, in some cases, a strategy for dealing with particular situations.

In the case of Dawkins' biomorphs, the fitness was determined by user choice. In this case, the genes contained in each chromosome were not interpreted as a strategy or a solution to a problem, but as a visual representation of an image that resembled a living creature—a biomorph.

Similar work was done by Todd and Latham (1992), who used complex chromosomes and human determination of fitness to evolve extremely complex, rendered creatures. Their book includes pictures of surprisingly beautiful creatures that appear to have been designed by an extremely imaginative artist.

In biological terms, the chromosome is the **genotype** of the creature, and the physical (or visual) manifestation of the genotype is the **phenotype**.

Using this model, in most genetic algorithm systems, the phenotype is a kind of behavior, or a solution to a problem. It is possible to have the phenotype of a chromosome be interpreted in more than one way. For example, a genetic algorithm could be used to evolve strategies for playing a game such as Prisoner's Dilemma and where each chromosome is also interpreted as a visual representation of a creature. In this way, creatures would be evolved whose appearance was dependent in some nontransparent way on their behavior. By adding human intervention in determining fitness, a system can be developed that automatically evolves creatures, but where humans can override a creature's fitness in order to bias evolution toward particular kinds of images.

Using evolutionary techniques for drawing pictures has other applications. In principle, a person who has an idea of what he or she wants to draw can produce a picture using crossover and mutation without having any artistic ability. For example, police are able to use this technique to allow a witness to produce a picture of a suspect in a crime, by repeatedly selecting the face that looks most like the person they are thinking of.

Evolutionary techniques can also be used to evolve behaviors. Karl Sims evolved creatures whose genes were used to represent not only a physical body but a set of rules to determine how those body parts would behave. His aim was to evolve creatures that could perform simple tasks such as walking, swimming, and jumping.

14.14   Predators and Co-evolution

In Section 14.11 we see that when genetic algorithms were evolved to play Prisoner's Dilemma against each other, they developed much more complex strategies than they did when they were evolved to play against fixed opponents.

There is strong empirical evidence to suggest that one of the key driving factors behind the evolution of most complex behaviors and abilities in real-world organisms is the existence of predators. In a world without predators, there is less pressure to perform well and less need to develop sophisticated behaviors in order to survive. This principle also applies in artificial evolution.

In the 1980s, Danny Hillis used evolutionary methods to evolve algorithms for sorting a sequence of numbers. He called the entities he was evolving "**ramps**." He found that when he introduced "parasites," which generated increasingly complex sets of numbers to sort, his ramps were able to perform far better than they had without the parasites.

When the evolution of two or more species are intertwined in this way, the process is known as **co-evolution**. This phenomenon was first observed by Charles Darwin (1859). Coevolution can be thought of as an arms race: when one country develops the bow and arrow, its enemies need to develop a similarly powerful weapon or an appropriate defense. In doing so, this country might stumble upon explosives and thus force their enemies to develop suitable defenses to this. In much the same way that the development of one country's military might causes other countries to develop similar capabilities, coevolution in animals means that if one predator develops the ability to run faster, its prey must match its speed, or develop another defense, or it will be wiped out.

Of course, this process does not happen quickly: at first, the prey will do badly, and a great many of them will be wiped out. This fact will ensure that the stronger, faster, better-defended individuals will be more likely to survive and produce offspring. In this way, over a period of many generations, the species will gradually become better able to survive.

As a result, of course, the predator will need to become faster or develop new abilities that enable it to catch enough prey. In some cases the cycle is broken as one species dies out or a new species supersedes it.

Co-evolution is a vital element of biological evolutionary processes and can also be taken advantage of in genetic algorithms and other processes that involve artificial evolution.

14.15   Other Problems

Genetic algorithms have been successfully applied to a number of problems in computer science. Most combinatorial search problems (described in more detail in Chapter 5) can be successfully solved using genetic algorithms. A great deal of work has been done on applying genetic algorithms to the traveling salesman problem, for example, but also to a number of other problems, including the following:

- The Knight's Tour (moving a knight over a chess board using valid moves, such that it lands on each square exactly once)
- The CNF-satisfiability problem
- Robot navigation
- The knapsack problem
- The timetable problem (assigning teachers to pupils and classrooms)

14.16   Chapter Summary

- A genetic algorithm consists of a population of chromosomes, each of which contains a number of genes. The genetic algorithm manipulates these chromosomes using crossover and mutation to produce a new, superior generation of chromosomes. This operation is repeated, until an optimal solution is obtained.

- A fitness metric is essential if a problem is to be solved using genetic algorithms.

- Mathematical functions can be readily solved using genetic algorithms.

- Genetic algorithms manipulate schemata. A schema consists of a set of 1s, 0s, and *, where a * represents "don't care".

- The schema theory states: *Short, low order schemata which are fitter than the average fitness of the population will appear with exponentially increasing regularity in subsequent generations.*

- The building-block hypothesis states that genetic algorithms solve problems using discrete building blocks.

- Genetic algorithms are susceptible to deception—a problem whereby inadequate building blocks appear in highly fit entities.

- Genetic algorithms can be used to evolve strategies for playing the Prisoner's Dilemma.

- When playing against fixed strategies, the genetic algorithms quickly converge on the optimal strategy. When playing against each other, more complex strategies emerge.

- Diversity can be as important as fitness in evaluating chromosomes for genetic algorithms.

- Pictures can be evolved using strategies similar to genetic algorithms, but with a degree of human intervention.

- Coevolution is the process whereby the development of one species affects the evolutionary path taken by another species. Coevolution has been used successfully to improve the performance of systems developed using artificial evolution.

14.17   Review Questions

13.1 Explain the meaning of the following terms in the context of genetic algorithms:

- fitness
- chromosome
- gene
- population
- generation
- crossover

- mutation

- deception

13.2   Explain how crossover, mutation, and reproduction affect schemata.

13.3   Explain how schemata help us to understand why genetic algorithms work. What does the schema theorem tell us?

13.4   Explain why genetic algorithms are susceptible to deception. Why do messy genetic algorithms help avoid this problem?

13.5   Explain why diversity is important when using genetic algorithms to solve problems.

13.6   Explain why introducing predators can help in systems that use artificial evolutionary techniques.

13.7   Describe three problems that might be solved using genetic algorithms that were not described in this chapter.

13.8   Could genetic algorithms be used to play complex games such as chess and checkers? Explain your answer.

13.9   "Once you've chosen a good representation for your problem you might as well solve the problem using traditional means—genetic algorithms are a waste of effort". Discuss.

14.18   Exercises

13.1   Using pen and paper and a die as a random number generator, work through five generations of evolution starting from the following five chromosomes. You will need to select a mutation rate, and determine a strategy for crossover.

1100110011

0001111010

1010100001

0000101000

0111000101

13.2   Write a program in the programming language of your choice that uses a genetic algorithm to evolve strategies for playing Prisoner's Dilemma. Start out by having your chromosomes play against a fixed strategy, and observe the behavior of the system. Now have the chromosomes play against each other. How does this affect their performance?

14.19   Further Reading

For a detailed description of messy genetic algorithms, see Goldberg (1989). The original text on genetic algorithms is Holland (1992). More introductory coverage is available in the standard Artificial Intelligence texts. For a discussion of the connection between computer viruses and Artificial Life, see Spafford (1989). The best modern discussions of coevolution can be found in Kelly (1994) and Dawkins (1996).

Work carried out by Forrest and Mitchell (1992) on **Royal Road** functions has shown that in fact the schema theory does not model the real behavior of genetic algorithms as accurately as one would hope.

Genetic Algorithm for the Prisoner Dilemma Problem, by R. Axelrod (1987 - in *Genetic Algorithms and Simulated Annealing*, edited by L. Davis – Hyperion Books)

Efficient and Accurate Parallel Genetic Algorithms, by Erick Cantu-Paz (2002 – Kluwer Academic Publishers)

Practical Handbook of Genetic Algorithms, by Lance Chambers (1995 – CRC Press)

Genetic Algorithms and Genetic Programming in Computational Finance, edited by Shu-Heng Chen (2002 – Kluwer Academic Publishers)

An Introduction to Genetic Algorithms for Scientists and Engineers, by David A. Coley (1999 – World Scientific Publishing Company)

The Origin of Species, by Charles Darwin (1859 – reprinted by Penguin)

Adaptive Learning by Genetic Algorithms: Analytical Results and Applications to Economic Models, by Herbert Dawid (1999 – Springer Verlag)

The Blind Watchmaker, by Richard Dawkins (1996 – W. W. Norton & Company)

Genetic Algorithms and Engineering Optimization, by Mitsuo Gen and Runwei Cheng (1991 – Wiley Interscience)

Genetic Algorithms in Search, Optimization and Machine Learning, by David E. Goldberg (1989 – Addison Wesley)

Messy Genetic Algorithms: Motivation, Analysis and First Results by D.E. Goldberg (1989 - in Complex Systems, Vol. 3, pp. 493–530)

Rapid, Accurate Optimization of Difficult Problems Using Fast Messy Genetic Algorithms, by David E. Goldberg, Kalyanmoy Deb, Hillol Kargupta, and Georges Harik (1993 – in *Proceedings of the Fifth International Conference on Genetic Algorithms*, pp. 56–64)

Practical Genetic Algorithms, by Randy L. Haupt and Sue Ellen Haupt (1998 – Wiley Interscience)

Adaptation in Natural and Artificial Systems: An Introductory Analysis with Applications to Biology, Control, and Artificial Intelligence, by John H. Holland (1992 – MIT Press)

Genetic Algorithms + Data Structures = Evolution Programs, by Zbigniew Michalewicz (1999 – Springer)

An Introduction to Genetic Algorithms, by Melanie Mitchell (1998 – MIT Press)

The Royal Road for Genetic Algorithms: Fitness Landscapes and GA Performance, by Melanie Mitchell, Stephanie Forrest, and John H. Holland (1992 - In *Towards a Practice of Autonomous Systems: Proceedings of the First European Conference on Artificial Life*, edited by Francisco J. Varela and Paul Bourgine, pp. 245–254, MIT Press)

Prisoner's Dilemma: John Von Neumann, Game Theory and the Puzzle of the Bomb, by William Poundstone (1994 – MIT Press)

Representations for Genetic and Evolutionary Algorithms, by Franz Rothlauf and David E. Goldberg (2002 – Springer Verlag)

Artificial Evolution for Computer Graphics by Karl Sims (1991 –Siggraph '91 - Annual Conference Proceedings, 1991, pp. 319–328).

Evolving Virtual Creatures, by Karl Sims (1994 - Siggraph '94 - Annual Conference Proceedings, 1994, pp. 43–50)

Computer Viruses as Artificial Life, by Eugene Spafford (1989 – in *Artificial Life, An Overview*, edited by Christopher G. Langton, 1995, MIT Press, pp. 249–265)

The Simple Genetic Algorithm: Foundations and Theory, by Michael D. Vose (1999 – MIT Press)

Planning

Introduction To Part 5

Part 5 is divided into two chapters.

CHAPTER 15

Introduction to Planning

This chapter introduces the ideas behind planning. It starts by explaining the relationship between search and planning, and explains why in many real-world problems, planning is preferable to search. It also explains situation calculus, which is an extension to first-order predicate calculus used in planning systems, to represent the way the world changes over time.

This chapter explains the frame problem and introduces ways to overcome the problem. It also explains means–ends analysis, which is covered in more detail in Chapter 16.

CHAPTER 16

Planning Methods

Chapter 16 expands on the ideas introduced in Chapter 15. It presents a number of representations and methods that are used in planning, starting with STRIPS. It presents a number of examples to illustrate how STRIPS is able to solve planning problems and also discusses the kinds of problems that might be difficult to solve using STRIPS. A number of other representations such as planning graphs and ADL are also explored, as well as some more advanced planning methods such as probabilistic planning and dynamic world planning.

PART 5

CHAPTER 15

Introduction to Planning

The best laid schemes o' mice an' men gang aft a-gley.

—Robert Burns, *To a Mouse*

You can never plan the future by the past.

—Edmunde Burke, *Letter to a Member of the National Assembly*

Grow old along with me!
The best is yet to be,
The last of life, for which the first was made:
Our times are in His hand
Who saith 'A whole I planned,
Youth shows but half; trust God: see all nor be afraid!'

—Robert Browning, *Rabbi Ben Ezra*

In preparing for battle I have always found that plans are useless, but that planning is indispensable.

—Dwight D. Eisenhower

15.1 Introduction

Planning has recently become a very exciting area of research in Artificial Intelligence. Much of the work of Artificial Intelligence is concerned with problem solving. As we will see, planning is no exception. Planning is a very simple concept: a **planner** starts in an initial state and has a particular goal it needs to achieve. To reach the goal state, the planner develops a plan and then **executes** that plan.

The planner might be a robot arm, or a mobile robot, but in many cases it exists purely in software and is designed to plan solutions to virtual problems.

A planner has a set of possible actions it can take, and as we will see, these actions are usually limited, depending on the current state of the planner. For example, a robot cannot open a door if the door is already open, or if it is nowhere near the door, or if its hands are full.

The actions that a planner can take are its **atomic actions**—these actions are usually described in terms of the effect they have on the planner and on the world. For example, a planning system might use actions such as "pick up object X" or "close door" or "go to supermarket."

Note that thus far we have assumed that the planner is the same entity as the entity that will execute the plan. This is not necessarily the case because a planner may be intended to develop plans for another entity. In this book, though, we tend to continue with the assumption that the system that develops the plans is the same system that executes the plans.

A plan can usually be considered as a set of subgoals, much like the goal trees we see in Chapter 3. In this chapter and in Chapter 16, we see some of the representations that are used to describe the state of a planner and its actions. We also examine the methods used by planners to efficiently design and execute plans.

In this chapter, the ideas behind planning are introduced, starting with using search as a way of identifying a plan of actions.

This chapter also introduces situation calculus, which is a form of first-order predicate calculus, which enables us to reason about the way in which predicates change over time as the result of actions. **Effect axioms** and **frame axioms** are introduced, and we discuss the **frame problem** and how it can be solved by using **successor state axioms**.

This chapter also introduces the idea of **means–ends analysis**, an idea that is extensively illustrated in Chapter 16 in a discussion of STRIPS. To illustrate means–ends analysis, this chapter introduces the General Problem Solver, or GPS.

15.2   Planning as Search

One approach to planning is to use search techniques, as described in Part 2 of this book. For example, a robotic planning agent might have a state that is described by the following variables:

> Room the robot is in
>
> Room the cheese is in
>
> Is the robot holding the cheese?

Let us further suppose that there are just three rooms—room 1, room 2, and room 3—and that these rooms are arranged such that there is a door from each room to each other room. The robot starts out in room 1, and the cheese starts in room 3. The robot's goal is to find the cheese.

The actions the robot can take are as follows:

> Move from room 1 to room 2
>
> Move from room 1 to room 3
>
> Move from room 2 to room 1
>
> Move from room 2 to room 3
>
> Move from room 3 to room 1
>
> Move from room 3 to room 2
>
> Pick up cheese

Note that each of these rules has a set of dependencies: to move from room 1 to room 2, the robot must currently be in room 1, in order to pick up the cheese, and the robot and the cheese must be in the same room, and so on. In this chapter, and in Chapter 16, we examine in more detail how these rules are expressed, but for this example we will assume that the actions can only be carried out in a way that makes sense in our world.

We will use a three-value vector to represent the current state:

> (room robot is in, room cheese is in, is robot holding cheese?)

So the initial state can be described as (1, 3, no), and the goal state can be described as (x, x, yes) where x is a variable that indicates the room in which both the cheese and the robot are located.

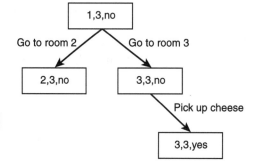

Figure 15.1

A highly simplistic search tree used to develop a plan

Note that there are 18 possible states that can be described by this vector, but that the following 6 states are not possible because they involve the robot holding the cheese, but with the cheese in a different room from the robot: (1, 2, yes), (1, 3, yes), (2, 1, yes), (2, 3, yes), (3, 1, yes), (3, 2, yes). Hence, there are actually only 12 valid states.

In each state where the robot and the cheese are in different rooms, there are two possible actions that can be taken. For example, in the state (1, 2, no), the robot can either move from room 1 to room 2, or can move from room 1 to room 3.

To develop a plan, the robot can simply produce a search tree, such as the one shown in Figure 15.1, which starts with the initial state and shows every state that can be achieved by applying each action from that state. A suitable plan is found when the goal state is reached. As with the search trees we built when examining the cannibals and missionaries problem in Chapter 3, we have excluded repeated states.

Note that in this simple problem, the search tree is very small, and finding a suitable plan is thus very easy.

In fact, in most real-world problems, and, indeed, in most Artificial Intelligence problems, there are many more possible states, many more actions that can be taken, and many more variables to consider.

For a robotic agent to be of any use in the real world, it would need to have hundreds or even thousands of possible actions it could take to be able to deal with the enormous complexities it would surely face. Similarly, for the robot to understand the world in sufficient detail, it would need to have a state representation that consisted of a very large number of variables. Given these factors, the search tree that would be produced for even a very simple problem would become prohibitively large.

The main problem with using search for planning is that it does not take any account of the effects of actions when considering which action to take. If the agent's goal is to find the cheese that is in the next room, then considering paths in the search tree that start with actions such as "phone the doctor," "look out of the window," "switch on the television set," and so on would be wasteful.

Additionally, as we will see, it does not necessarily make sense for a plan to be built starting from the initial state. As we have seen in Chapters 3 and 4, it often makes sense to approach a problem by starting from the goal state and working back toward the initial state. Search does not necessarily function well in such situations.

Another reason that search is not usually the best way to approach planning is that it does not take into account the independence of multiple goals. When a planner is presented with a goal that consists of several parts, such as "buy some eggs, feed the cat, and get little Johnny a haircut," it can consider each of these goals separately and solve each of them consecutively, rather than trying to solve them as a whole. Because a search-based approach would consider the three goals as a single problem, it would end up enormously overcomplicating the problem.

Of course, in some situations, the order in which subgoals are achieved can be very important. For example, the planner might have as a goal "feed the cat, and wash the cat's bowl." In this case, the planner might need to consider carefully the order in which it carries out its actions if it is to avoid making a simple error, such as putting food into the cat's bowl and then immediately washing it up, without waiting for the cat to eat.

Similarly, when solving problems such as the 8-puzzle, described in Chapter 4, each of the subgoals very much depends on the others. When taking actions to slide tile 5 into its square, it is very likely that all the other tiles will be moved about, and so independently placing each tile in its appropriate square will not do. Hence, search is a very good way to plan a solution to problems such as the 8-puzzle or the eight-queens problem.

15.3 Situation Calculus

In the example used above, we have used a very simple notation to indicate the current state of the planner. For most real problems this notation would not make sense because the number of variables to consider in each state would be prohibitively large.

One notation that is often used in discussing planning is **situation calculus**. Situation calculus is a form of first-order predicate calculus.

As we see in Chapter 7, first-order predicate calculus allows us to make assertions about objects but does not provide a very good way of expressing change, or temporal relationships. Situation calculus allows us to describe an object in one state, or situation, and then describe how that object will change when a given action is taken.

For example, the following situation calculus expression represents the assertion that in situation S_1, the robot is in the same room as the cheese:

$$\exists x \big(In\big(Robot, x, S_1\big) \wedge In\big(cheese, x, S_1\big)\big)$$

Here the predicate *In* is used to indicate which room a given entity is in. The predicate has been augmented with a third variable, which is the situation that is being described. This third variable, S_1, is known as a **situation variable**.

Of course, not all objects change over time, and so we can continue to use standard predicates without a situation variable. For example, we could use the following expression to assert that the robot's name is Robbie and that this will not change over time:

Name (Robot, Robbie)

To describe the effects that actions have on the world, we use the *Result* function. The *Result* function takes as arguments an action and a situation and returns the situation that occurs as a result of that action. For example,

Result (Move$_{i,j}$, S$_1$) = S$_2$

Here we are using the notation *Move$_{i,j}$* to indicate the action of moving from room i to room j. Hence, if the current situation is S_1, and the robot carries out the action of moving from room 1 to room 2, this will result in situation S_2.

A number of rules are needed to describe the effects of actions. These rules are known as **effect axioms**. For example, we might have the following effect axiom:

$$\forall x, y, s \; In\big(Robot, y, s\big) \wedge In\big(x, y, s\big) \Rightarrow Has\big(Robot, x, Result\big(Take, s\big)\big)$$

This effect axiom states the following rule:

If the robot is in a room, y, and an object x is also in that room, then if the robot carries out a *Take* action, this will result in a new situation in which the robot has object x. We might want to further refine this axiom, by ensuring that x is the kind of object that the robot can carry—for example, by stating that it must be light enough and small enough to carry and that it must not be fixed down.

15.4   The Frame Problem

As we have seen, when we carry out an action, the world changes. In fact, some aspects of the world change, but others stay the same. Determining which stay the same is known as the **frame problem**.

An effect axiom states what changes when the robot carries out a particular action in a particular situation. It does not make any statements about what does *not* change. For example, when the robot carries out a *Take* action, it does not find itself in a different room. This kind of rule can be expressed in a **frame axiom**, such as the following:

$$\forall y, s \; In\big(Robot, y, s\big) \Rightarrow In\big(Robot, y, Result\big(Take, s\big)\big)$$

Of course, most actions that we take do not have any effect on the vast majority of objects in the real world. This is likely to be true in the world of a robot or software planner. As a result, many of frame axioms are needed if we are to describe all of the effects that do *not* result from carrying out a particular action. The problem of having enormous numbers of frame axioms is known as the **representational frame problem**.

The representational frame problem can be solved by using **successor state axioms**, which effectively combine the effect axioms with the frame axioms. Successor state axioms describe the way in which a predicate changes over time. For example,

$$\forall a, x, y, s \; Has\big(Robot, x, Result(a, s)\big) \Leftrightarrow$$
$$\big(a = Take \wedge In(Robot, y, s) \wedge In(x, y, s)\big)$$
$$\big(Has(Robot, x, s) \wedge a \neq Drop\big)$$

The axiom states the following:

There are only two ways in which an action, a, can result in the robot holding object x. The first of these is if the action is *Take*, and the robot is in the same room (y) as the object. The second possibility (after the $\vee$ in the expression) is if the robot already has the object, and the action is *not Drop*.

Note that this axiom uses *iff* ($\Leftrightarrow$) rather than implies. $A \Leftrightarrow B$ means that A implies B, but that if B is not true, then A can also not be true. In other words, it is stating that if either the robot takes the object or it already has it, then it will have it, but that if neither of those is true, then it will not have it.

In this way, one successor state axiom is needed for each predicate whose value can change. Although these axioms may become very complex, they avoid the enormous number of unhelpful rules that a system based on effect axioms and frame axioms would have (such as "If I pick up the cheese, then the room's walls will not change color.")

15.5   Means–Ends Analysis

Typically, a planner needs to find a correct set of actions (a plan) that will take it from one state to another state—the goal state. One approach to planning is to consider the differences between the goal state and the current state, and select actions that aim to lessen those differences: this is called **means–ends analysis**.

Unlike search techniques, means–ends analysis can select an action even if it is not possible in the current state. If a planner selects an action that results in the goal state, but is not currently possible, then it will set as a new goal the conditions necessary for carrying out that action. For example, let us consider the **blocks world**, which is often used to illustrate planning problems.

The blocks world contains a number of blocks and a surface or table top. Blocks can be placed on top of each other or can be placed onto the table.

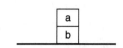

Figure 15.2

A start state in the blocks world

The planner is a robot arm that is able to pick blocks up and to move them around. Let us suppose that the world consists of two blocks, *a* and *b*, as shown in Figure 15.2.

Let us suppose that our robot's goal is to place block *b* on top of block *a*, with block *a* resting on the table. Using means–ends analysis, our planner starts by considering how the goal state differs from the current state. In this case, the differences are:

> Block *b* is not on top of block *a*.
>
> Block *a* is on top of block *b*.

Our planner could now consider the following two possible actions:

1.   Place block *b* on top of block *a*.
2.   Remove block *a* from on top of block *b*.

Each of these actions is interesting because it reduces the differences between the current state and the goal state. Our planner might start by selecting action 2 and removing block *a* from on top of block *b*. The differences between this new state and the goal state are now as follows:

> Block *b* is not on top of block *a*.
>
> Block *a* is not on the table.

The planner's next action might therefore be to place block *a* on the table. Now the difference between the current state and the goal state is as follows:

> Block *b* is not on top of block *a*.

The next action to consider is thus

3.   Place block *b* on top of block *a*.

Unfortunately, action 3 cannot be carried out because the robot arm is not currently holding block *b*. So we have a new goal state, which is

> Robot arm is holding block *b*.

Hence, before carrying out action 3, the planner must achieve this goal, which it does by carrying out the following action:

4.   Pick up block *b*.

Note that all of this planning is carried out before the robot starts to move. Hence, when it has completed building the plan, it is able to carry out the following actions:

>   Remove block *a* from on top of block *b*.
>
>   Place block *a* on the table.
>
>   Pick up block *b*.
>
>   Place block *b* on top of block *a*.

Hence, the goal has been achieved. As we will see, this approach can be used in much more complex planning systems to solve far more interesting problems.

The **General Problem Solver**, or **GPS**, was developed by Newell, Shaw, and Simon in the late 1950s (Newell et al. 1959, Newell and Simon 1963) as an attempt to simulate human thought, with the intention of using this approach to solve problems of a general nature.

GPS uses means–ends analysis to solve logic problems, such as showing the equivalence of the following two logical expressions:

$$(R \rightarrow \neg P) \wedge (R \rightarrow Q)$$
$$\neg(\neg Q \wedge P)$$

In their 1963 paper, Newell and Simon explain how GPS examines the differences between these two expressions and use a set of three simple methods that can be used to transform expressions, based on the logical equivalence rules shown in Chapter 7 of this book.

For example, GPS might start by removing the $\rightarrow$ operators in the first expression, using the following rule:

$$A \rightarrow B \Leftrightarrow \neg A \vee B$$

As we see in Chapter 16, **STRIPS** is a planning system that uses means–ends analysis in a manner similar to that used by GPS to control the actions of a robot through a simple environment.

15.6   Chapter Summary

- One way to find a plan to solve a problem is to apply a search method and search through the search space of all possible plans. This works well for very simple problems, but is not efficient for complex problems or those involving many possible actions and variables.

- In solving problems where each action can undo the effects of other actions, it is necessary to use search.

- Situation calculus is an extension of first-order predicate calculus, which uses situation variables to express how objects change over time.

- Effect axioms for an action state what changes after that action takes place.

- Frame axioms state what variables do *not* change after carrying out an action.

- The frame problem is the problem of determining what does *not* change when an action is carried out. Using successor state axioms, which combine features of effect axioms and frame axioms, solves this problem.

- Means–ends analysis, as used by GPS, involves determining the differences between the current state and the goal state, and choosing actions that minimize those differences.

15.7   Review Questions

15.1   What is planning?

15.2   Explain why the search methods described in Chapter 4 can be used for planning.

15.3   Why can first-order predicate calculus not be used for planning without the addition of situation variables?

15.4   Explain what is meant by the frame problem. What is the representational frame problem? Why are these problems so important to the study of planning?

15.5   Explain the idea behind means–ends analysis. Compare it with search as a planning method. Which more closely matches the methods people use when formulating plans in everyday life?

15.8   Exercises

15.1   Write a program in the language of your choice that uses search to formulate plans for moving from one arrangement of three blocks to another. Assume that the available actions that can be taken are to move a block from one of three locations to another, and that if one block is placed into a location in which another block is already present, then the second block is placed on top of the first block.

15.2   Consider extending your program to work with larger numbers of blocks. How well do you think it will work?

15.9   Further Reading

Most of the standard texts provide good coverage of planning. Russell and Norvig provide a particularly thorough treatment, in the context of intelligent agents. Newell, Shaw, and Simon's papers on GPS and Fikes and Nilsson's paper on STRIPS provide good introductions to those systems. The Further Reading section of Chapter 16 contains more references on planning.

STRIPS: A New Approach to the Application of Theorem Proving to Problem Solving, by Richard E. Fikes and Nils J. Nilsson (1971 – in *Computation & Intelligence*, edited by George F. Luger, 1995 – MIT Press)

The Robots Dilemma Revisited: The Frame Problem in Artificial Intelligence, by Kenneth M. Ford and Zenon W. Pylyshyn (1996 – Ablex Publishing)

GPS, A Program That Simulates Human Thought, by Alan Newell and Herbert A. Simon (1963 – in *Computation & Intelligence*, edited by George F. Luger, 1995 – MIT Press)

Report on a General Problem Solving Program, by Alan Newell, J. C. Shaw, and Herbert A. Simon (1959 – in *Proceedings of the International Conference on Information Processing*, pp. 256–264)

The Robots Dilemma: The Frame Problem in Artificial Intelligence, by Zenon W. Pylyshyn (1987 – Ablex Publishing)

Choices, Values, and Frames, edited by Daniel Kahneman and Amos Tversky (2000 – Cambridge University Press)

Recent Advances in AI Planning, by Daniel S. Weld (1998 – appeared in *AI Magazine*, 1999)

CHAPTER 16

Planning Methods

I have a cunning plan...

—Baldrick *from Blackadder*

This very remarkable man
Commends a most practical plan:
You can do what you want
If you don't think you can't,
So don't think you can't – think you can.

—Charles Inge, '*On Monsieur Coué*'

Awake, my St John! Leave all meaner things
To low ambition, and the pride of kings.
Let us (since Life can little more supply
Than just to look about us and to die)
Expatiate free o'er all this scene of man;
A mighty maze! but not without a plan.

—Alexander Pope, *An Essay on Man*

16.1   Introduction

Planning methods are used to solve problems where a sequence of actions must be carried out to reach a goal. In this chapter, we often consider the blocks world, in which a robot arm must reorganize a set of blocks from one arrangement to another. Planning is also used a great deal in industry, for routing transportation, organizing allocation of machines in factories, and controlling robots and intelligent agents.

In Chapter 19, we see how intelligent agents can base their actions on beliefs, desires, and intentions. Agents have beliefs about the world and desires that must be fulfilled. To achieve these desires, an agent forms intentions, or plans, which specify in advance what it will do. An agent that does not plan is able only to respond to its environment as it encounters it and will often find itself falling into traps that a planning agent would have foreseen.

Planning is an extremely important part of Artificial Intelligence research.

This chapter explores a number of algorithms and representations that are used in planning and introduces some of the ideas that have been researched in the past 10 years.

We start by examining STRIPS, which was an early planning system based on the means–ends strategy discussed in Chapter 15. Although STRIPS has been superseded by a number of more sophisticated methods, the language it uses to represent planning problems is still widely used.

We then briefly explore partial order planning, in which plans are specified such that the order in which some actions are carried out is unimportant.

This chapter explores the ways in which propositional calculus can be used to represent and solve planning problems, including producing plans by examining the satisfiability of propositional sentences.

We then explore some other representations for planning problems including planning graphs (used by the GraphPlan algorithm) and ADL, which is an extension of the STRIPS language.

We also examine ways in which planning can be carried out in an uncertain world and ways in which planners can learn from their past actions and mistakes.

Finally, we briefly explore the relationship between planning and scheduling.

16.2   STRIPS

STRIPS (Stanford Research Institute Problem Solver) is an **operator-based** planning approach that was developed by Fikes and Nilsson in the 1970s (Fikes and Nilsson 1971). This is in contrast with the use of situation variables and frame axioms that we see in Chapter 15, when using the logic of situation calculus.

STRIPS uses a means–ends analysis strategy, which was described in Section 15.5. Means–ends analysis simply involves identifying the differences between the current state and the goal state, and selecting actions that reduce those differences.

STRIPS uses well-formed formulae (wffs) in first-order predicate calculus to describe the world, in much the same way that we see in Chapter 15. STRIPS was designed to provide planning for robotic agents to enable them to navigate through a world of blocks, but the approach can also be used in other planning problems.

For example, the following wff can be used to state the rule that if an object is in one location, then it cannot be in another:

$$\left(\forall o \forall x \forall y\right)\left(\left(AT(o, x) \wedge (x \neq y)\right) \Rightarrow \neg AT(o, y)\right)$$

This wff states that if an object, o, is in location x, where x is not the same location as y, then object o cannot be in location y.

Note that unlike the examples in Chapter 15, locations in STRIPS are expressed as vectors, rather than as entire rooms. In other words, in the above expression, x and y represent the physical coordinates of the robot, measured in some units of distance from a point that is considered to be the origin: (0,0).

16.2.1 Planning and Executing

STRIPS uses a set of operators, which represent the actions that can be taken, or the steps that can be included in a plan. For example, operator *Push* (o, x, y) enables the robot to push object o from location x to location y. Note that there is a distinct difference between considering the operator *Push* and actually carrying out the act of pushing. This is the difference between planning and executing. Most of this chapter is concerned with planning, which means selecting a suitable sequence of operators. Once the sequence has been chosen, the plan can be executed, which means carrying out the actions described. This has some important implications: if carrying out an action has an unexpected effect that was not planned for, the plan may not succeed. Should the robot continue with the plan regardless, or should it stop and develop a new plan based on the unexpected state it has found the world in? We consider these issues in Section 16.11.

16.2.2   Operators

Each operator that STRIPS uses is defined by two components. The first is the effect that the operator will have on the world, and the second is the preconditions that must be met for the action to be carried out.

The preconditions are specified as a set of wffs that must be proven to hold for the current state, or **world model**. The world model contains a list of wffs that are true of the world in the current state, such as $AT(r, x)$, which means that the robot is at position x, or $AT(o, y)$, which means that object o is at position y.

STRIPS includes information on two different types of effect that an operator can have: the statements (or wffs) that become true after carrying out the action and the statements that are no longer true. Each operator can thus be defined by a list of wffs that must be added to the world model and a list of wffs that must be deleted. These lists are often called the **add list** and the **delete list**.

Hence, the *Push* (o, x, y) operator could be fully defined as in the following example:

Precondition: $AT(r, x)$

$\land AT(o, x)$

Delete: $AT(r, x)$

$AT(o, x)$

Add: $AT(r, y)$

$AT(o, y)$

In other words, to push object o from position x to position y, the robot and the object must both start out in position x. As a result of this action, neither the robot nor the object will still be in position x: both will be in position y.

This definition defines an **operator schema**, which means that it does not define an actual action, but rather a type of action. A real action is an **instance** of the schema, in which the variables are **instantiated** with actual objects. Hence, for example, we could describe pushing object o_1 from position with coordinates (2,3) to position (1,4) by the following operator instance:

$$Push\,(o_1, (2,3), (1,4))$$

When the world model includes statements that can be used to instantiate the preconditions of a particular operator, then we say that this operator is **applicable**.

The final element of STRIPS is the goal state, which is described by a wff, or a set of wffs, that define the state that the robot wants to reach. Once the planner finds a way to reach this goal state, it has successfully solved its problem and is ready to execute the plan.

16.2.3 Implementation of STRIPS

The algorithm used by the original STRIPS program to develop plans was as follows:

First, the current world model is compared with the wffs that define the goal state. If the goal can be satisfied by the current world model, then the problem is solved, and the planning can terminate.

In fact, STRIPS used the method explained in Chapter 8 for proving theorems using resolution. This method involves assuming the negation of the goal, and then showing that this is inconsistent with the current world state, by using the method of **unification** to instantiate variables in the schemata with real-world objects. If this method successfully shows an inconsistency, then the goal is consistent with the world state.

If this is not the case, then a plan must be developed.

To select a suitable operator (or action) to apply, STRIPS used the same method as GPS (which is described in Chapter 15), which means determining the differences between the current state and the goal state and selecting an operator that lessens those differences.

Having applied unification and resolution, the original STRIPS program used the resulting partial proof as a representation of these differences. Hence, the running of STRIPS involved alternately applying resolution (theorem proving) and means–ends analysis.

STRIPS solves the frame problem by making what is known as the **STRIPS assumption**: that any statement that is true before applying an operator is

Figure 16.1

Start state for the blocks world problem

also true after applying the operator, unless it is included in the operator's delete list.

16.2.4 Example: STRIPS

We will now examine a simple example of STRIPS in action, in the blocks world, which consists of a table, three blocks (a, b, and c) and a robot arm that can move blocks around.

The initial state of the world is shown in Figure 16.1. Block *a* is on the table, and block *b* is on top of block *c*, which is in turn placed directly on the table.

We will use two predicates to describe the world:

On (x, y) means that block *x* is on top of block *y*.

Clear (x) means that block *x* has no block on top of it.

We will also use *t* to represent the table. Hence, *On* (a, t) means that block *a* is on the table. *Clear* (t) will always be true because we assume that the table is large enough to hold at least three blocks at once.

Our goal is to place block *c* on top of block *a*, which can be stated as

On (c, a)

Our start state can be described as

On (a, t)

On (b, c)

On (c, t)

Clear (b)

Clear (a)

Clear (t)

We have one available operator schema: *MoveOnto* (x,y), which means "move object *x* from wherever it is, and place it on top of object *y*."

MoveOnto (*x,y*) is defined as

Preconditions: *On* (x, z) ∧ *Clear* (x) ∧ *Clear* (y)

Delete: *On* (x, z)

Clear (y)

Add: *On* (x, y)

Clear (z)

In fact, this is not quite correct because if we move object *b* from on top of object *c* and place it on the table, *Clear* (*t*) is still true. We could address this by including an additional operator schema *MoveOntoTable* (*x*), which is defined as follows:

Preconditions: *On* (x, y) ∧ *Clear* (x)

Delete: *On* (x, y)

Add: *On* (x, t)

Clear (y)

A number of approaches can be used to build the plan. The first approach we will consider is to use forward chaining. In other words, we will simply search through the space of possible plans until we find a suitable one. This will involve constructing a tree where the root node represents the start state, and other nodes represent other possible states that can be obtained by applying operators.

For example, from the initial state, there are three operators we could apply:

MoveOnto (a, b)

MoveOnto (b, a)

MoveOntoTable (b)

Other operators, such as *MoveOntoTable* (c) are not possible because their preconditions are not met by the current world state.

Let us suppose that we choose to apply *MoveOntoTable* (b). This has precondition

On (b, y) ∧ *Clear* (b)

which is matched by instantiating *y* with *c*. Hence, after using the operator, we will need to apply the following add and delete lists to our current state:

Delete: *On* (b, c)

Add: *On* (b, t)

Clear (c)

Hence, our state description becomes

On (a, t)

On (b, t)

On (c, t)

Clear (b)

Clear (a)

Clear (c)

Clear (t)

From this position we could apply any of the following operators:

MoveOnto (a, b)

MoveOnto (a, c)

MoveOnto (b, a)

MoveOnto (b, c)

MoveOnto (c, a)

MoveOnto (c, b)

Using the blind search method, we would simply try each of these and add a new node to the tree for each resulting state. In fact, by applying *MoveOnto* (*c, a*), we produce a state that matches the goal state, and so a suitable plan has been found.

This method did not use means–ends analysis, and although it would be feasible for a problem of this scale, it would not work at all for real-world problems involving hundreds of operators and objects.

The means–ends analysis approach would start by noticing the differences between the start state and the goal state: block *c* is not on block *a* and is in fact under block *b*. The fact that block *c* is not clear does not matter because this is not mentioned explicitly in the goal.

To reduce this difference, we could apply the operator *MoveOnto* (*c, a*). However, this operator's preconditions are not currently met because it requires that c be clear. We note that operator *MoveOntoTable* (b) has the desired effect of clearing c. Hence, we have arrived at a suitable plan by using a form of backward chaining—starting at the goal and identifying steps that could lead to the goal.

Of course, we were lucky in our second choice. We might equally have chosen *MoveOnto* (b, a) because this also has the effect of clearing c. In this case, we would then find ourselves in a position where we had further difficulties. At this point, the planner would likely backtrack and try a different choice because it clearly made the problem harder, rather than moving closer to a solution.

16.2.5 Example: STRIPS and Resolution

Let us now consider in more detail the mechanics of STRIPS and, in particular, how the original program used resolution and unification. We will consider a slightly different version of the blocks world, as designed by Fikes and Nilsson in their original description of STRIPS. The robot (named Shakey, due to his unstable gait) starts out in position x, and his task is to bring two objects, a and b, together. The two objects start out in positions y and z. We will assume that two objects are together when they are both at the same position, and we will further assume that the robot can push two objects together, ignoring the difficulties that this would pose in the real world.

Hence, the initial world state is described by

$$AT(r, x)$$

$$AT(a, y)$$

$$AT(b, z)$$

The goal can be described by the following wff:

$$(\exists p)(AT(a, p) \wedge AT(b, p))$$

The operators available to the planner are the following:

Push (o, x, y)

Precondition: $AT(r, x) \wedge AT(o, x)$

Delete: $AT(r, x)$

           $AT(o, x)$

Add:	$AT(r, y)$
	$AT(o, y)$

<u>Go (x, y)</u>

Precondition:	$AT(r, x)$
Delete:	$AT(r, x)$
Add:	$AT(r, y)$

The first stage is to negate the wff that describes the goal:

$$(\forall p)\bigl(\neg AT(a, p) \vee \neg AT(b, p)\bigr)$$

(Note that we have used the equivalence between $\neg(\exists x)e$ and $(\forall x)\neg e$ and have then applied DeMorgan's law to obtain this expression.)

For the purposes of resolution, we can consider this to be the set of clauses:

$\{(\neg AT(a,p), \neg AT(b, p))\}$

We now attempt to prove by using resolution that this expression is inconsistent with the current world state. In fact, this will not be possible, and we will obtain only a partial proof, which can then be used to describe the difference between the initial state and the goal state.

The first stage of this resolution would be to unify the following sets of clauses:

$\{(\neg AT(a,p), \neg AT(b,p))\}$

$\{(AT(r,x)), (AT(a, y)), (AT(b,z))\}$

We will apply the unifier $\{y/p\}$ and obtain the following set of clauses:

$\{(\neg AT(a,y), \neg AT(b,y)), (AT(r,x)), (AT(a,y)), (AT(b,z))\}$

This resolves to give the following set of clauses:

$\{(\neg AT(b,y)), (AT(r,x)), (AT(b,z))\}$

Clearly, a difference that needs to be rectified is that object b is not at location y, but is at location z. Hence, STRIPS will see if it can apply operator *Push* (b, z, y).

To determine whether this operator's preconditions are met, the preconditions are negated and added to the set of clauses. The preconditions for the push operator are

AT(r, z) ∧ AT(b, z)

We negate this and apply DeMorgan's law to give

¬AT (r,z) ∨ ¬AT (b,z)

We add these to the clauses and obtain

{(¬AT(b,y)), (AT(r,x)), (AT(b,z)), (¬AT(r,z), ¬AT(b,z))}

This resolves to give the following partial proof:

{(¬AT(b,y)), (AT(r,x)), (¬AT(r,z))}

Again, a complete proof was not possible, and we are left with a partial resolution proof. This shows that a further difference that needs to be rectified
is that the robot is at position *x*, whereas it should be in position *z*, in order
to carry out the *Push (b,z,y)* operator. Hence, the *Go (x,z)* operator is
attempted.

In this case, the precondition when negated is

¬AT(r, x)

This is now added to the set of clauses that are to be resolved, and the
process continues.

Eventually, a set of operators is found that enables the clauses to resolve to
falsum, meaning that the goal state has been reached.

16.3   The Sussman Anomaly

We return now to the blocks world of the example in Section 16.2.4.

Consider the start state shown in Figure 16.2. Our goal now is to place
block *c* on top of block *b*, and block *a* on top of block *b*. This is the second
state shown in Figure 16.2.

The STRIPS approach to this problem would start by either moving *b* onto
the table, and then placing *c* on *a*, or by moving *a* on top of *b* without first
removing *b* from *c*. In either of these cases, the solution cannot be reached
without undoing this first move. Many early planning systems could not

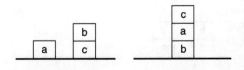

Figure 16.2

The start and goal states
for the Sussman anomaly
problem

solve problems of this nature, in which the two aspects of the goal have dependencies on each other. The correct solution, of course, is to first move *b* onto the table, then place *a* on top of *b*, and finally move *c* on top of *a*, but this involves interleaving the solutions to the two components of the goal, which is not easily achieved using STRIPS in its original form. Later in this chapter, we see methods that are able to deal with Sussman's anomaly more elegantly.

16.4   Partial Order Planning

The plans that we have considered so far are known as **total order plans** because they dictate the order in which each action must be carried out. In some cases, a **partial order plan** can be used, in which actions that are dependent on each other are ordered in relation to each other but not necessarily in relation to other independent actions.

For example, let us consider the blocks world problem with the start and goal states as shown in Figure 16.3.

A total order plan for this problem might be described as follows:

> *MoveOntoTable* (b)
>
> *MoveOntoTable* (d)
>
> *MoveOnto* (a, b)
>
> *MoveOnto* (c, d)

To place *a* on top of *b*, it is important that *b* is moved onto the table first. It does not matter whether *c* or *d* have moved yet.

Hence, a partial order plan can be described as shown in Figure 16.4.

This partial order plan shows that before *MoveOnto* (*a,b*) can be carried out, *MoveOntoTable* (*b*) must be applied; similarly, it shows that *MoveOntoTable* (*c*) must be applied before *MoveOnto* (*a,b*) can be carried out.

To finish, or reach the goal state, the robot must have carried out all four actions.

Figure 16.3

Start and goal states for a partial order planning problem

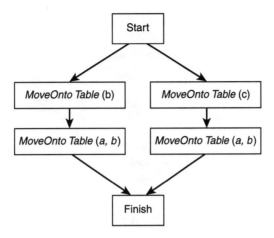

Figure 16.4
A partial order plan

This representation for a plan enables the planner to consider a number of different plans, without worrying about ordering actions that are not dependent on each other. At the time of execution, the robot can select any ordering that matches this partial order. Note that the partial plans can be interleaved. Hence, a suitable total plan might be

MoveOntoTable (b)

MoveOnto (a, b)

MoveOntoTable (d)

MoveOnto (c, d)

The idea behind partial order planning is to develop a partial order plan that ends with the goal state and where each transition in the plan is legal, according to the definitions of the available operators.

To see how this works, let us consider the blocks world problem shown in Figure 16.3. We will examine how the planning system might build up a partial order plan.

At first, the system has a start state and a goal state, as shown in Figure 16.5.

```
Start
```

Figure 16.5
The initial stage in build-ing a partial order plan

```
Goal
```

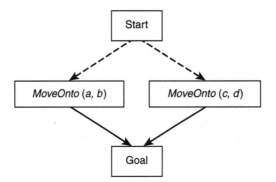

Figure 16.6

The next stage in building the partial order plan

Our task is now to build a plan that gets us from the start state to the goal state.

The first step is to add in operators that achieve the conditions set in the definition of the goal state. As we saw above, these operators are *MoveOnto* (*a*,*b*) and *MoveOnto* (*c*,*d*). In Figure 16.6, we have added these operators to the partial plan (it is a partial order plan, but it is also a partial plan, in the sense that it is not yet complete).

In Figure 16.6, the solid arrows represent **causal links** or **establishes links**, which show how an action causes or establishes a set of conditions that match the criteria for the goal state. The dashed arrows are not yet causal links because they do not explain how one gets from the start state to the next states. These dashed arrows simply show the order in which actions must occur, so in this case, the two operators shown must occur after the start state.

Next we must find operators that will enable us to satisfy the preconditions of the operators we have just added. These preconditions are met by *MoveOntoTable* (*b*) and *MoveOntoTable* (*d*).

Adding these operators to the partial plan shown in Figure 16.6 leads to the partial order plan (which is no longer a partial plan because it gives all the steps necessary to get from the start to the goal) shown in Figure 16.4.

In building a partial order plan, there is a potential problem to consider, which is that one action might undo the effects of another action, in which case the order in which those actions are carried out can be important. A causal link is said to be **protected** when it is needed to establish the preconditions of an operator below it in the plan. If another operator has the

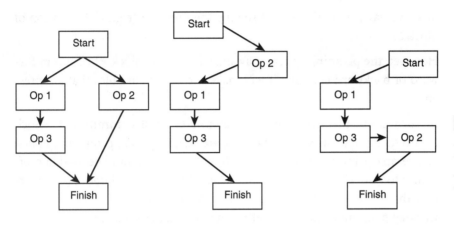

Figure 16.7
An example of a causal link being threatened by another operator and two ways in which this problem can be rectified

effect of deleting some necessary part of that precondition, then the protected link is said to be **threatened** by this second operator. This is shown in the first part of Figure 16.7.

Let us suppose that one of the preconditions of Op 3 is x, and that Op 1 has x in its add list. In other words, x is one effect of carrying out the action Op 1. Unfortunately, Op 2 has x in its delete list, meaning that one effect of carrying out Op 2 is to *undo x* or to set $\neg x$ to be true. Hence, the partial order plan shown in the first part of Figure 16.7 does not work because the nature of the partial order is such that Op 2 might be carried out between Op 1 and Op 3, thus ruining the plan. Hence, the second and third parts of Figure 16.7 show ways in which the plan can be rearranged to ensure that this problem is avoided.

In the second part of Figure 16.7, Op 2 has been **demoted**, which means that the plan ensures that it must occur before Op 1. In the final part of Figure 16.7, Op 2 has been **promoted**, meaning it must be carried out *after* Op 3. The partial order already dictated that Op 3 must take place after Op 1, so this also ensures that Op 2 must take place after Op 1.

16.5   The Principle of Least Commitment

In many planning problems, a number of additional variables exist that are not relevant to the problem nor need to be modified to solve it. For example, suppose that in solving the problem shown in Figure 16.3 there was actually another block, block e, on the table. Because the goal does not state anything about this block, it does not matter and can be left alone, unless it in some way gets in the way of solving the problem (e.g., if it is on top of block *b*).

However, the planning system may still want to use block *e* because in forward or backward chaining it will make use of the variables that are present.

In such cases, planners use the **principle of least commitment**, which means that as few variables as possible are instantiated in producing a plan. Hence, an operator schema such as *MoveOnto* (a, y) should be used in preference to one where *y* has been instantiated [e.g., *MoveOnto* (a, b)], wherever that is possible. In that way, the planner works with an accurate and working plan but does so in as efficient a manner as possible.

For example, if the solution involved moving block *a* onto block *b* via the table or another block, the planner could consider this without deciding whether to move it via a block or the table.

16.6   Propositional Planning

Many planning problems can be expressed purely in propositional logic notation. In fact, plans expressed in STRIPS notation can always be converted to propositional notation, although this will often involve increasing the number of variables required enormously.

For example, if we consider a blocks world problem in which there are two blocks, *A* and *B*, we might represent the various possible states in STRIPS notation using the following predicates:

Clear (x)

On (x, y)

In propositional notation, we will use one propositional variable for each possible state variable; hence:

X_1 is equivalent to *Clear* (A)

X_2 is equivalent to *Clear* (B)

X_3 is equivalent to *On* (A, B)

X_4 is equivalent to *On* (B, A)

In this case, we can represent any state by the use of just four propositional variables. Of course, if there were four blocks instead of two, then we would require 4 variables to represent *Clear* and 12 variables to represent *On*, and, in general, for *n* blocks, we will require n^2 propositional variables. Of course, in most planning problems we will have more than just blocks to consider, and so the number of propositional variables required will increase accordingly.

A state can be represented by an assignment of truth values to each of the available variables; hence, in our simple blocks world we could have a state represented by the following sentence:

$$X_1 \wedge \neg X_2 \wedge X_3 \wedge \neg X_4$$

This state can be represented in STRIPS notation as

$$Clear\,(A) \wedge \neg Clear\,(B) \wedge On\,(A, B) \wedge \neg On\,(B, A)$$

Of course, a propositional logic sentence can also represent a number of states. For example, the following sentence represents all states in which *A* is clear and *B* is not clear:

$$X_1 \wedge \neg X_2$$

In fact, due to the simplicity of this example, there is only one such state, but if we allow additional blocks, then $\neg X_2$ (*B* is not clear) could be caused by a block other than A, and so $X_1 \wedge \neg X_2$ represents a set of states, rather than a single state.

Actions can also be represented using propositional sentences. To do this, we use a new notation to represent the state that results from an action. If we use X_1 to represent the fact that *A* is clear before an action is taken, then we use $\neg X_1'$ to represent that *A* is no longer clear after the action. Hence, the action *MoveOnto* (*A, B*) can be represented by the following propositional sentence:

$$X_1 \wedge X_2 \wedge \neg X_3 \wedge \neg X_4 \wedge X_1' \wedge \neg X_2' \wedge X_3' \wedge \neg X_4'$$

This sentence states that the preconditions for the action are $X_1 \wedge X_2 \wedge \neg X_3 \wedge \neg X_4$, and that after the action is taken the state can be described as $X_1' \wedge \neg X_2' \wedge X_3' \wedge \neg X_4'$.

In this case, there is only one state in which the *MoveOnto* (*A, B*) action can be carried out. In most real problems, there will be several states from which a given action can be applied. If we assume that it is possible to move block *A* onto block *B* even if *A* is not clear (i.e., if some other object is on top of *A*), then we would express the action *MoveOnto* (*A*, *B*) by the following sentence, in disjunctive normal form:

$$(X_1 \wedge X_2 \wedge \neg X_3 \wedge \neg X_4 \wedge X_1' \wedge \neg X_2' \wedge X_3' \wedge \neg X_4') \vee$$

$$(\neg X_1 \wedge X_2 \wedge \neg X_3 \wedge \neg X_4 \wedge \neg X_1' \wedge \neg X_2' \wedge X_3' \wedge \neg X_4')$$

The reason that this propositional notation is useful for planning is that a number of techniques exist for manipulating propositional expressions, and these techniques can, in theory, be applied to planning, as we will see in the next section.

16.7   SAT Planning

One way in which propositional notation can be used in planning is to determine the satisfiability of a set of sentences that express the problem.

As explained in Chapter 7, a sentence is satisfiable if some assignment of truth values to the variables in the sentence makes the sentence true. The satisfiability problem (also known as SAT) in general is NP-complete, which means that in the worst case, solving a SAT problem for *n* variables will involve testing m^n possible assignments of variables, where *n* is the number of variables in the expression, and *m* is the number of values each variable can take.

During the 1990s, a number of techniques were developed that improved the performance of systems designed to solve the satisfiability problem. GSAT is an example of such a system, which is explained in detail in Selman et al. (1992).

There are two main approaches to SAT. One class of solutions uses a **systematic** approach, meaning that each possible assignment of truth values is tested until a solution is found. These methods are guaranteed to find a solution if one exists, but in the worst case can be very inefficient. **Stochastic** methods involve randomly testing assignments. One such method is **Walksat**, which operates in a similar way to the exchanging heuristics seen in Chapter 5. Walksat involves repeatedly changing the value of variables in unsatisfied clauses until a solution is found (Selman et al. 1994).

SAT planning involves encoding the start state, goal state, and operators (frame axioms and effect axioms) in conjunctive or disjunctive normal form and then using a method such as GSAT to show whether the sentences are satisfiable or not. If they are, then a suitable plan can be formulated.

16.8   Planning Graphs

A **planning graph** can be used to develop plans for problems that can be represented using propositional logic. GraphPlan is an example of an algorithm that uses planning graphs to develop plans for problems that are expressed in STRIPS notation (and can, therefore, as we saw above, be converted to propositional form).

A planning graph consists of a number of levels. This is illustrated in Figure 16.8. The first level (usually called the zeroth level) contains the propositions that are true in the start state for the problem. The next level of the graph contains the actions that can be carried out in this state. The level after that contains the states that can be led to by carrying out these actions. Hence, each even-numbered level in the plan represents a state, and each odd-numbered level represents actions. The final state in the graph represents the goal state.

The links between level 0 and level 1 show how the preconditions of the actions in level 1 are met by the propositions in level 0. Similarly, the links from level 1 to level 2 show how the actions in level 1 produce the state contained in level 3 (state 1).

It is useful to be able to show which propositions do not change as a result of a given action. These are shown by **persistence actions**, which are equivalent to the frame axioms discussed in Section 15.4. A persistence action is

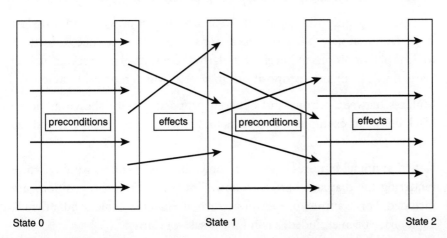

State 0   State 1   State 2

Figure 16.8

A stylized illustration of a planning graph

Figure 16.9

A blocks world problem, showing start state and goal state

usually shown on a planning graph as an arrow with a clear box on it (see Figure 16.10).

Planning graphs form a very compact representation: because the graph only shows actions that are possible in each state, it reduces significantly the number of actions that must be considered in constructing a plan.

A final feature of the planning graphs is the inclusion of **mutual exclusion** information, or **mutexes**. A mutex exists between two effects or actions that are mutually exclusive. For example, in our blocks work, *Clear* (*B*) is mutually exclusive with *On* (*A*, *B*) because the two statements cannot be true at the same time. At each level of the planning graph, lines are drawn between actions or propositions that are mutually exclusive with each other.

Let us examine the planning graph for the problem illustrated in Figure 16.9.

The available actions are *MoveOnto* and *MoveOntoTable*, as defined above in Section 16.2.4. We will continue to use the STRIPS notation predicates *On* (*x*, *y*) and *Clear* (*x*).

An incomplete planning graph for this problem is shown in Figure 16.10.

The planning graph in Figure 16.10 shows the actions that are possible from the initial state (State 0). The actions in level 1 are connected by links to their preconditions in Level 0. Similarly, the results of the actions in level 1 are shown by links to propositions in level 2 (which represents state 1).

Mutexes between actions and between propositions are shown as heavy black lines. For example, *Clear* (*A*) is mutex with both ¬*Clear* (*A*) and *On* (*B*, *A*).

Note that not all mutexes have been shown because to do so would involve rendering the diagram hard to follow. Similarly, not all propositions are included. For example, propositions such as ¬*On* (*A*, Table) and ¬*On* (*B*, Table) have been excluded, again for the sake of clarity.

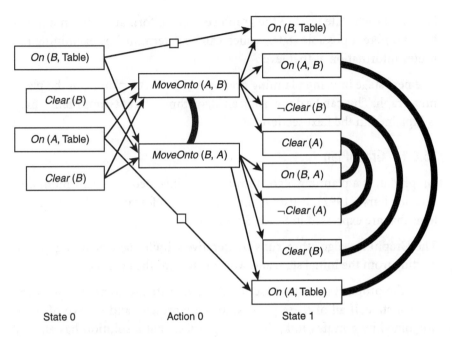

Figure 16.10
Partial planning graph for
the blocks world problem
shown in Figure 16.9

The graph shows persistence actions as lines with squares on them. These represent the possibility that a proposition might not change from one state to the next.

Note that for even an extremely simple problem, the planning graph can appear very complex. In fact, planning graphs produce a much more compact representation than many other methods.

The planning graph shows at each state every proposition that could possibly be true in that state, as a result of the actions that are in the previous level.

Having produced the planning graph, it is possible to determine immediately whether it is possible to formulate a plan that will solve the problem. If any of the literal propositions that are included in the goal state definition are *not* included in the final level of the planning graph, then it is not possible to formulate a plan to reach the goal state. On the other hand, if all the goal propositions are included in the final level, then it may be possible to formulate a suitable plan. This will depend on the mutexes in the final level, which restrict which states can be achieved.

Note that each state level in the graph contains information about a number of different possible states, which can be determined by examining the mutex information at that level.

The next stage in using planning graphs is to extract a plan from the planning graph. This can be done using an algorithm such as **GraphPlan**, which is explained in the next section.

16.8.1   GraphPlan

GraphPlan is a planning algorithm that was invented by Avrim Blum and Merrick Furst (1997). It uses planning graphs to formulate plans to problems that are expressed in STRIPS notation.

The GraphPlan algorithm runs by iteratively building a planning graph, starting from the initial state and working toward the goal state.

First, the propositions that describe the goal state are compared with the current state. If all of these propositions are present, and no two of them are joined by a mutex link, then it is possible that a solution has already been reached. At this stage, a second phase of the algorithm is run to try to extract a plan from the current graph plan.

If the current state does not contain all the necessary propositions, then the next level of the planning graph is produced by applying all applicable operators, and determining all possible propositions that can be made true by these operators.

This algorithm repeats until a suitable plan is found, or until it can be shown that no plan exists.

GraphPlan has the desirable property that if a plan exists, it is guaranteed to find it, and it is guaranteed to find the shortest possible plan due to the iterative way in which it builds the planning graph. It is also guaranteed to terminate in the case where no plan exists. In such cases, the planning graph will reach a state where each new level that is added is the same. At this stage, the graph is said to have **leveled off**. If the graph levels off, and the final level does not have all of the desired propositions or some of them are connected to each other by mutex links, then no suitable plan exists.

When a state is found in which all goal propositions are present and are not mutex, the method for finding a plan is applied, which works as follows: Starting from the final level in the planning graph and working backward, operators are selected at each level that are not mutex and that provide all of the conditions required at each level, either to meet the goal conditions or to meet the preconditions of the actions in the next level.

The plan that GraphPlan produces is a partial order plan, in which no ordering constraint is placed on actions that are at the same level.

16.8.2 Mutex Conditions

There are a number of reasons that a pair of actions or propositions are mutually exclusive, or mutex, to each other:

1. Two actions that have effects inconsistent with each other are mutex. For example, *MoveOnto* (A, B) and *MoveOntoTable* (A) are mutex because one has the effect of adding *On* (A, B) and the other adds *On* (A, Table).

2. If the effect of one action interferes with the precondition of another, then the two actions are mutex. For example, *MoveOnto* (A, B) has the effect of deleting *Clear* (B) and so is mutex with *MoveOnto* (B, A), which has the precondition *Clear* (B).

3. If one action has proposition *P* as its precondition, and another action has precondition ¬*P*, then the two actions are mutex.

4. If one proposition is inconsistent with, or the negation of, another proposition, then the two are mutex. For example, in our simple blocks world, *On* (A, B) is mutex with *On* (A, Table) and is also mutex with ¬*On* (A, B).

16.9 ADL and PDDL

A number of alternative representations exist for expressing planning problems, in addition to STRIPS. **ADL** (Action Description Language) is a more expressive language than STRIPS, which can be used to represent a number of problems that cannot be adequately represented in STRIPS. Unlike STRIPS, which can only represent unquantified expressions such as $A \land B$, goals in ADL can be quantified, allowing expressions such as $\exists x$. $P(x) \land \neg Q(x)$.

Preconditions in STRIPS must be expressed as conjunctions (such as $A \land B \land \neg C$), but preconditions in ADL can be expressed as disjunctions (such as $A \lor B$). Additionally, ADL allows for **conditional effects**, which state effects that will occur as a result of carrying out a particular action depending on certain conditions.

For example, in a more complex blocks world, it might be that block *A* is twice as big as blocks *B* and *C*, and so the action *MoveOnto* (*B*, *A*) might only have the effect of negating *Clear* (*A*) if *On* (*C*, *A*) is already true. This type of conditional effect would be hard to express in STRIPS notation.

Another feature of ADL is that it enables types to be attached to variables. This means that in many situations, fewer rules need to be expressed than with STRIPS because rules can be set up that ensure that objects involved in actions have the correct type.

PDDL (Planning Domain Definition Language) is a standardized syntax for expressing planning problems, which was developed for the AIPS (Artificial Intelligence Planning Systems) planning competition. PDDL can be used to represent STRIPS and ADL, and was introduced to provide a common notation that could be used by all planning systems.

16.10   Probabilistic Planning

In all of our discussion of planning so far, we have assumed that actions are deterministic. That is, we have assumed that if you apply action *A* in state *S*, then we can state with certainty what the resulting state will be. Of course, this is unrealistic for many real-world planning situations, and probabilistic planners have been developed that aim to deal with this uncertainty.

In some systems, it is possible to consider nondeterministic actions, where an action applied in a particular state will nondeterministically lead to one of several possible states.

Situation calculus can be extended to express probabilistic relationships (Mateus et al. 2001). This enables the language to express the various effects that can occur as a result of a particular action and how probable each of those effects are. Deterministic actions are a special case of probabilistic actions in which the probability of the effect is 1.

16.11   Dynamic World Planning

In addition to assuming that the actions our planner takes are deterministic, we have also assumed in this discussion that the world itself is static. Of course, the real world is dynamic, and in many situations there are other agents that can also affect the world.

It has been said that planning in a dynamic world is pointless because the world may change in such a way that the plan becomes useless. In spite of this difficulty, there are methods that can be applied to planning in dynamic environments.

One principle that is often applied is **execution monitoring**. Once a planner has produced a plan, let us say for a robot, that robot is usually expected to simply carry out, or execute, the plan. A planner that uses execution monitoring checks the preconditions of each action as it executes it. If the preconditions are no longer met, because something has changed, then the planner may need to start again and devise a new plan.

This process of devising a new plan when something has gone wrong is known as **replanning**.

Similarly, the planner checks the goal conditions at each step, in case it has accidentally solved the problem. For example, while executing a plan for a blocks world problem, another robot may have arrived and solved the rest of the problem, in which case our robot can stop executing its plan.

An alternative method for dealing with dynamic environments, or uncertainty, is to use **conditional planning**. Conditional planning assumes that at each step of the plan, one of several different possible situations could result. In other words, the planner does not have complete information about the problem domain before it starts planning.

The conditional planning approach involves developing a plan that covers every possible eventuality. This is a good way to guarantee that a plan will not fail, but in the real world, there may be far too many possibilities to plan for.

16.12   Case-Based Planning Systems

A traditional planning system must reformulate its plan every time it is presented with a new problem. Of course, in some situations it will be presented with a problem it has seen before, or a problem that shares elements with previous problems.

A **case-based planning system** stores each plan it formulates in memory and is able to reuse these plans to help it solve new problems.

CHEF is an example of a case-based planning system, which was designed to produce recipes for Chinese food based on a given set of ingredients.

When CHEF is presented with a set of ingredients that it has not encountered before, such as chicken and carrots, it is able to formulate a recipe based on an existing recipe, such as stir-fried beef and onions.

In situations where CHEF's plan has not been successful, it is able to learn from its errors, in order to avoid making such errors again. If for example it overcooks the chicken, it will learn that in future plans it should not cook chicken for as long as it might cook beef.

One important aspect of case-based planning systems is the memory that is used to store plans. Clearly it must be possible to look up a variety of items in this memory to find the plan or plans that best suit the current situation.

16.13   Planning and Scheduling

The planning techniques we have discussed in this chapter are extremely useful for solving a range of problems. We have mainly considered problems in the toy blocks world, which involve selecting the right sequence of actions to rearrange a collection of blocks from one configuration to another. Planning can also be helpful in solving problems such as the traveling salesman problem, which was discussed in Chapter 3, along with a range of other similar problems that involve selecting a suitable course of travel that meets a set of constraints, and enable the traveler to move from one location to another in a desired time frame.

A rather different kind of problem is **job shop scheduling**, which is used to plan a sensible allocation of machinery to a set of jobs. Each job consists of a set of tasks that must be carried out, usually specified as a partial order (hence, some tasks must be done sequentially, but other tasks can be carried out in parallel). Each machine can perform a subset of the available tasks, and the problem of job shop scheduling is to allocate tasks to machines such that no machine is being used for two tasks at the same time and so that all the tasks get carried out. In some cases, it is desirable to find the most efficient such arrangement, so that the jobs are completed as quickly as possible.

The problem of scheduling a number of tasks among a set of machines is very similar in many ways to the planning problems we have examined already. The main difference is that a schedule must specify *when* each task is carried out and how long it will take, whereas the plans we have examined simply specify a sequence of actions, with no concern about how long each action takes or when it should be done.

One approach to scheduling is to treat it as a straightforward planning problem. This results in a plan that describes the order in which actions should be carried out. A human operator can then augment this plan with information about when to perform each task.

Alternatively, scheduling can be seen as a constraint satisfaction problem (see Chapter 5), where the constraints specify how long each task will take and that one machine cannot be used for two tasks at a time.

In practice, a combination of approaches is usually used. Planning techniques such as the ones we have discussed in this chapter are applied in conjunction with search methods suitable for solving constraint satisfaction problems.

16.14   Chapter Summary

- STRIPS is an operator-based planning approach based on means–ends analysis.

- An operator can be defined by an operator schema that describes a number of possible operators, using variables that are instantiated to provide an operator.

- The Sussman anomaly occurs in problems in which a planner needs to be able to consider two aspects of the problem independently. Such problems cannot be readily solved using the traditional STRIPS approach.

- A total order plan specifies the order in which all actions must be carried out. A partial order plan allows some operators to be specified in parallel, such that the order is determined at execution time.

- The principle of least commitment states that it is a good idea at each stage of planning to commit to as few decisions as possible.

- Most plans (and in particular, all plans that can be represented using the STRIPS language) can be represented in propositional logic notation, meaning that plans can be developed using methods that solve the satisfiability problem for a set of propositions.

- A planning graph represents states and actions at alternate levels, and shows all possible states and all possible actions at each point by using mutex relationships to show which combinations are not allowed.

- GraphPlan is an algorithm that uses planning graphs to extract plans.

- ADL is an alternative planning representation that is more expressive than the STRIPS language.

- Probabilistic planning involves working with operators where the outcome of a given operator is not certain. Similarly, planning in many situations needs to function in a dynamic environment in which the world can change from one time-step to the next. Dynamic world planners often use replanning to cope when such changes interfere with their plans.

- Case-based planning involves storing plans in a searchable memory and reusing them to solve new problems.

- Planning means selecting which operators to apply; scheduling is used to determine at what time to carry out the actions in order to meet a set of constraints.

16.15   Review Questions

16.1   Explain the difference between the STRIPS language and the ADL language. Why is ADL described as being more expressive than STRIPS? What kinds of problems might ADL be used to solve for which STRIPS might not be adequate?

16.2   Explain what is meant by the principle of least commitment. How do you think it might relate to the generation of partial order plans?

16.3   Explain how the satisfiability problem relates to planning. How efficient do you think this method might be compared with STRIPS planning or using GraphPlan?

16.4   Explain what is meant by dynamic world planning. What is meant by probabilistic planning? What is the difference between probabilistic planning and nondeterministic planning?

16.5   What is meant by replanning?

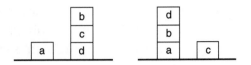

Figure 16.11

Start and goal state for Exercise 16.1

16.6 Explain why case-based planning can be used to produce a planning system that is able to learn.

16.7 Compare and contrast planning and scheduling.

16.16 Exercises

16.1 Use the operators described in Section 16.2.4 and the STRIPS method to solve the blocks world planning problem shown in Figure 16.11. The first state shown is the start state, and the second state is the goal state.

16.2 Produce a planning graph for the blocks world problem shown in Figure 16.11.

16.3 Use resolution and unification to solve the blocks world problem shown in Figure 16.11. How does this plan compare with the one you generated in exercises 16.1 and 16.2?

16.17 Further Reading

Planning has increased in prominence in the Artificial Intelligence world in the past decade, and as a result, better coverage can be found in the more recent textbooks. Russell and Norvig (1995) provide the fullest coverage of the standard texts.

Reasoning About Plans, by James F. Allen, Henry A. Kautz, Josh Tenenberg, and Richard Pelavin (1991 – Morgan Kaufmann)

Recent Advances in AI Planning, by Susanne Biundo and Maria Fox (2000 – Springer Verlag)

Fast Planning Through Planning Graph Analysis, by A. Blum and M. Furst (1997 – in *Artificial Intelligence*, Vol. 90, pp. 281–300).

Robot Motion: Planning and Control, edited by Michael Brady, John Hollerbach, Timothy Johnson, Tomás Lozano-Pérez, and Matthew T. Mason (1983 – MIT Press)

STRIPS: A New Approach to the Application of Theorem Proving to Problem Solving, by Richard E. Fikes and Nils J. Nilsson (1971 – in *Computation & Intelligence*, edited by George F. Luger, 1995, MIT Press)

Artificial Intelligence & Manufacturing Research Planning Workshop, edited by George F. Luger (1998 – AAAI)

Probabilistic Situation Calculus, by Paulo Mateus, António Pacheco, Javier Pinto, Amílear Sernadas, and Cristina Sernadas (2001 – in *Annals of Mathematics and Artificial Intelligence*)

A New Method for Solving Hard Satisfiability Problems, by B. Selman, H. Levesque, and D. Mitchell (1992 – in AAAI, Vol. 92, pp. 440–446)

Noise Strategies for Improving Local Search, by B. Selman, H. A. Kautz, and B. Cohen (1994 – in AAAI, Vol. 94, pp. 337–343)

Planning and Learning by Analogical Reasoning, by Manuela M. Veloso (1994 – Springer Verlag Telos)

Recent Advances in AI Planning, by Daniel S. Weld (in *AI Magazine*, Summer 1999)

Practical Planning: Extending the Classical AI Planning Paradigm, by David E. Wilkins (1989 – Morgan Kaufman)

Intelligent Scheduling, edited by Monte Zweben and Mark S. Fox (1998 – Morgan Kaufmann)

Intelligent Planning: A Decomposition and Abstraction Based Approach, by Qiang Yang (1998 – Springer Verlag)

Advanced Topics

Introduction to Part 6

Part 6 is divided into five chapters.

CHAPTER 17

Advanced Knowledge Representation

This chapter builds on the ideas presented in several of the earlier chapters in this book, in particular Chapters 7, 9, 15, and 16. It presents a number of more sophisticated knowledge representation methods, including the blackboard architecture, scripts, and the Copycat architecture.

It also presents more material on nonmonotonic reasoning and reasoning about change. Finally, this chapter expands on topics introduced elsewhere in this book by discussing case-based reasoning and knowledge engineering.

CHAPTER 18

Fuzzy Reasoning

This chapter introduces the subject of fuzzy logic. It discusses fuzzy sets and explains how they are used in fuzzy systems. It also explains how fuzzy logic provides an alternative to the traditional logic presented in Chapters 7 and 8 of this book. It also discusses the ideas of fuzzy expert systems and neuro-fuzzy systems.

CHAPTER 19

Intelligent Agents

Chapter 19 introduces the concept of software agents and, in particular, intelligent agents, which are able to independently carry out tasks on behalf of a user. The chapter discusses a number of properties that agents can have such as

intelligence, autonomy, benevolence, the ability to learn, and the ability to move about through a network, such as the Internet. The chapter introduces a number of types of agents, such as interface agents, reactive agents, collaborative agents, and mobile agents. It also discusses architectures and methods that can be used to build agents. The chapter also discusses robotic agents, such as the Braitenberg vehicles.

CHAPTER 20

Understanding Language

This chapter discusses a number of techniques that are used by computer systems to understand written or spoken human language. In particular, it focuses on natural language processing (NLP) and information retrieval (IR). It presents the methods used to parse sentences and explains how semantic and pragmatic analysis are used to derive meaning from sentences while avoiding being confused by the ambiguity inherent in human language.

CHAPTER 21

Machine Vision

This chapter presents a range of methods that are used to enable computers to analyze visual data. It discusses edge detection and explains how convolution can be used to detect edges in images. It also explains how images are segmented, and how the edges of three-dimensional line drawings can be labeled. It discusses texture and explains how important it is for computer vision systems to use information derived from texture.

This chapter also briefly discusses one method that is used for face recognition.

CHAPTER 17

Advanced Knowledge Representation

Let knowledge grow from more to more,
But more of reverence in us dwell;
That mind and soul, according well,
May make one music as before.

— Alfred Lord Tennyson, *In Memoriam*

Whether there be knowledge, it shall vanish away.

— The first epistle of Paul the apostle to the Corinthians, Chapter 13

What is all knowledge too but recorded experience,
and a product of history; of which therefore,
reasoning and belief, no less than action and passion,
are essential materials?

— Thomas Carlyle, *Critical and Miscellaneous Essays*

So it is in travelling; a man must carry knowledge with him, if he would bring
home knowledge.

— Samuel Johnson

17.1   Introduction

Human beings use representations for the world around them all the time.
One example is the use of language. Consider the following sentence:

The cat sat on the mat.

This sentence may seem trite, but it has real meaning to us. The word "cat" represents a four-legged feline creature. The word "sat" represents an action and tells us something about when that action took place. The word "mat" represents another object, and the word "on" represents a relationship between objects. What the word "the" represents is hard to define, but clearly each word in a sentence, taken individually and grouped with other words, conveys meaning to a person who reads, hears, or speaks the words.

Another representation we use regularly is that of images, or signs. Note that there is a significant difference between the audible representation of a word when it is spoken compared with the visible representation when it is written down. We use a vast number of signs, symbols, and images in our everyday lives, including the following:

- letters and numbers
- mathematical equations
- road signs
- photographs of people, places, and things
- caricatures and cartoons
- alarms and other audible signals

The list is endless.

The human mind uses some form of representation for all concepts, which enables us to understand such abstract ideas as "happiness," "lateness," and "common sense." In this way, even a human baby is able to understand the connection between the sound "woof!," the cartoon character Snoopy, and a dog. We use some kind of internal representation for a dog that allows us to associate those three different concepts together in some way.

Clearly this internal representation has a lot to do with our ability to think, to understand, and to reason, and it is no surprise, therefore, that much of Artificial Intelligence research is concerned with finding suitable representations for problems.

Throughout this book, we have considered representations and how they can be manipulated to solve problems. Representations we have considered include:

- propositional and predicate calculus
- semantic nets
- search trees
- frames

Most of the methods we have examined are dependent on a suitable representation being chosen. It is impossible to solve a problem using genetic algorithms, planning, or classifier systems without first selecting an appropriate representation for the problem.

In this chapter, we consider a number of methods of representing knowledge, as well as exploring extensions to some of the representations we have explored elsewhere.

A number of the sections in this chapter build on ideas presented in earlier chapters—in particular, Chapter 7 on logic, Chapter 9 on rules and expert systems, and Chapters 15 and 16 on planning.

The chapter starts by discussing the ideas of representation, semantics, and interpretations and tries to explain why these are so important to Artificial Intelligence.

It then introduces a number of specific representational methods—the blackboard architecture, scripts, and the Copycat architecture—and illustrates how each of them is used.

This chapter then concentrates on nonclassical logics, starting with a detailed discussion of nonmonotonic logics and nonmonotonic reasoning methods. The methods explained in this discussion include default reasoning, truth maintenance systems, the closed world assumption, circumscription, and abductive reasoning. This chapter also examines two methods for dealing with uncertainty: the Dempster–Shafer theory and certainty factors.

This chapter also expands on the discussion of situation calculus from Chapter 15 by explaining event calculus, temporal logic, and mental situation calculus, all of which are used to represent data in worlds that are subject to change.

This chapter has a brief discussion of the important steps in knowledge engineering, an idea that was first introduced in Chapter 9, and also briefly explains why case-based reasoning (introduced in Chapter 16) is useful.

17.2 Representations and Semantics

Many representations involve some kind of language. We have seen, for example, propositional calculus and predicate calculus in Chapter 7, which are languages used to represent and reason with logical statements; the language of mathematics enables us to represent complex numeric relationships; programming languages such as Java and C++ use objects, arrays, and other data structures to represent ideas, things, and numbers.

Human beings use languages such as English to represent objects and more complex notions. Human language is rather different from the languages usually used in Artificial Intelligence, as we shall see in Chapter 20. In particular, although human languages are able to express an extremely wide range of concepts, they tend to be ambiguous—a sentence can have more than one meaning, depending on the time and place it is spoken, who said it, and what was said before it. Human languages are also very efficient: it is possible to express in a few words ideas that took thousands of years for humans to develop (for example, the words existentialism, solipsism, and mathematics).

When considering any representational language, it is vital to consider the semantics of the language (i.e., what expressions in the language mean or what they represent).

In some ways, despite its tendency for ambiguity, human language is very explicit—each sentence has a meaning that can be determined without any external information. The sentence "the cat sat on the mat," for example, has a fairly specific meaning (although, it does not specify *which* cat or *which* mat).

In contrast, sentences in a language such as predicate calculus need to have an **interpretation** provided. For example, we might write

$$\forall x\, P(x) \rightarrow Q(x)$$

This sentence might have a number of interpretations, depending on our choice of meaning for P and Q. For example, we could interpret it as meaning "all men are mortal." An inference engine that manipulates such sentences does not need to know the meanings of the sentences, but if the sentences are being used to reason about the real world and to form plans, then of course the interpretations must be carefully chosen.

17.3 The Blackboard Architecture

The **blackboard architecture** is a method for **structured knowledge representation** that was invented in the 1970s by H. Penny Nii (Nii 1986) for a system called HEARSAY-II. HEARSAY-II contained an index of computer science papers, about which it was able to retrieve information in response to spoken queries by users.

In Chapters 3 and 9, we saw the difference between reasoning forward from a start state, applying rules or actions until a goal is reached, and working backward from a goal, seeing which rules or actions could lead to the goal state, and then selecting additional actions that satisfy the preconditions of those rules, and so on, until the start state is reached.

Each of these approaches has its advantages and is particularly useful when applied to certain problems. In other situations, it is more appropriate to use an **opportunistic reasoning model**, where rules can be applied forward or backward at different times, in whatever order most effectively solves the current problem. Opportunistic reasoning applies well to planning (which was discussed in Part 5 of this book), but in this section we are going to examine how it is used by blackboard systems to effectively represent and use specific domain knowledge.

In Chapters 3 and 9, we examined a structured knowledge representation system based on frames. Each frame contains information about an object, and frames are linked to other frames by relations that express the ways in which the objects relate to each other. As we saw, this representation uses the idea of inheritance to provide an efficient way to represent the ways in which one object shares properties with another object.

Also in Chapter 9, we examined production systems, which use rules to represent expert knowledge about a domain. Similarly, blackboard systems are also used to represent and manipulate expert domain knowledge. The idea behind blackboard systems is that disparate knowledge from different expert sources can be combined by providing a central database—the **blackboard**—on which the experts (known as **knowledge sources**) can "write" information. Because the blackboard is shared, one knowledge source can see facts appear as another knowledge source puts them there, and it can thus deduce new facts and add them to the blackboard. In this

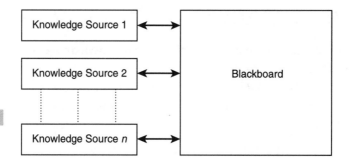

Figure 17.1

A simple blackboard architecture

way, a number of knowledge sources can be used together to solve a complex problem, but each knowledge expert does not need to know from where the data on the blackboard came.

A simple blackboard architecture is illustrated in Figure 17.1.

Because the blackboard system uses opportunistic reasoning, the various knowledge sources do not need to take turns to act. Each knowledge source can proactively examine the blackboard and add new data to it when it feels that it has something useful to contribute to the solution of the problem. In practice, there is usually a central control mechanism that determines when each knowledge source can interact with the blackboard, but it would be equally possible to have each knowledge source an independent agent, allowed to make its own decisions about when to act.

Nii (1986) compared this approach with a group of people solving a jigsaw puzzle on a large blackboard. Each person has a number of pieces of the puzzle, and when a person notices an opportunity to place one of his or her pieces on the board, he or she does so. The people involved do not need to communicate with each other, and no one needs to tell the individuals when to place their pieces on the board—they can each act independently and autonomously.

Nii extends the analogy by supposing that the room has a **monitor**, who is a person able to control who is allowed to visit the blackboard and when. Now only one person is allowed to place a piece on the blackboard at a time, and the monitor has complete authority to decide who can do so.

The jigsaw puzzle analogy is helpful, but it does not quite describe the real use of blackboard systems. Each person solving the jigsaw puzzle has different pieces of the puzzle, but they all have the same kind of domain knowledge. The idea behind blackboard systems is that experts with entirely different types of knowledge can work together to solve a single problem. In the next section, we explore in more detail the architecture of the blackboard system, and in the section after that we see how the blackboard system works in practice by considering the HEARSAY-II system.

17.3.1   Implementation

As has already been suggested, the particular implementation of blackboard system that is used can depend on the problem that is being solved, and also on the computer systems that are available. We will now look at some of the key elements of real implementations of blackboard systems.

The knowledge sources used in a blackboard system are entirely independent. This means that by use of appropriate interfaces, a blackboard system can use a number of different representations for its knowledge sources. Typically, knowledge sources are represented as rules or procedures. It is also possible to represent the information in a language such as first-order predicate calculus.

The only interaction that occurs between the different knowledge sources is through the blackboard data structure. The blackboard can contain items of data, partial solutions to the problem, and finally, a complete solution. These data are usually arranged hierarchically, so that each level in the hierarchy represents a different level of abstraction of the problem. In HEARSAY, for example, the levels represent aspects such as

1.   the digital audio signal

2.   the phonemes that make up the entire signal

3.   the syllables that can be constructed from the phonemes

4.   the words that can be constructed from the syllables

5.   the complete sentence

Each knowledge source looks at data in the level(s) that are appropriate for it and places data onto levels that are appropriate. For example, one knowledge source might have the ability to extract phonemes from an audio signal, in which case it would need only to examine data at Level 1 and would need only to add data at Level 2.

Typically, the blackboard system has a control mechanism that determines which knowledge source should act next, based on the most recent changes that have occurred in the database. Hence, if in the example given above a new set of phonemes has been determined, the control module might select a knowledge source that has the ability to analyze phonemes to act next. In making this choice, the control module is said to be choosing the **focus of attention** of the system. At any one time, the system's focus of attention is directed at one knowledge source, or one piece of data, or a pair that consists of a knowledge source and a piece of data.

The overall strategy of the blackboard system is determined by the control module and which ordering it uses when choosing the point of focus. Hence, this choice is clearly of particular importance.

17.3.2 HEARSAY

HEARSAY was designed as a system that would combine phonology, syntax, semantics, and a contextual understanding of words in order to understand human speech. In Chapter 20, we learn more about systems that understand spoken words, but in this section we will briefly examine how the blackboard architecture was applied to the problem.

In the HEARSAY-II architecture, there were a number of knowledge sources, each of which understood a different aspect of the sounds generated when a human user would speak into the system's microphone. The context knowledge source has knowledge about the world, which it is able to use to disambiguate words such as "their" and "there." This problem is discussed in more detail in Chapter 20.

One advantage of using the blackboard architecture for this problem is that a number of different knowledge sources could in fact be applied at each stage—in particular, for example, in determining which word is being spoken, a number of different possible solutions might be generated by different modules at one level, and a higher level would later disambiguate (using context, for example) and select the correct word. In this way, the sound can be analyzed in a number of different ways in parallel to ensure that the best solution is obtained.

17.4 Scripts

A **script** (also known as a **schema**) is a data structure that is used as a structured representation for a situation that can be broken down into a sequence of events. Scripts are often used in natural language processing, which is discussed in more detail in Chapter 20.

The idea behind scripts is that for a given situation (such as buying food in a supermarket or attending a job interview) there is a finite set of knowledge that is needed to understand what is said, and thus to determine how to act and what to say. A script is a data structure that represents a very specific situation (such as buying apples from a fruit market).

The script contains knowledge about the situation (such as the fact that in order to buy an apple, one must pay the market seller, and that apples are good to eat unless they are rotten). A script has a set of **entry conditions**, which state the preconditions necessary for a script to be used (e.g., to use the apples script, the story must start with someone near a fruit market), and **results**, which occur as a result of running through the situation described by the script.

A script also encodes **reasons**: that is, why one engages in the situation described by the script. This enables a script-based system to understand motivations (e.g., why a person would want to buy an apple).

A story can be understood by matching elements in the story to appropriate parts of the script. In this way, the script-based system can answer questions whose answers are not explicitly stated in the story.

Schank (1975) proposes a script for understanding stories about restaurants. His script includes a number of **roles**, or types of people that might be involved, including customer, waitress, and chef. The script includes information about reasons or why a customer might want to eat at a restaurant (clearly, hunger has something to do with this, as does money).

The script is then broken down into a set of episodes, such as "entering," "ordering," "eating," and "leaving."

Each episode is represented in the script data structure by a number of related actions that the various people might perform.

Let us consider the following short story:

> Fred went to his favorite restaurant. The food was not as good as usual. On his way home, he realized he had left his wallet behind.

The script system is able to match entities described in the story with its roles (Fred is the customer, for example). Although the story does not mention a waitress or a chef, the script system knows that they would have been involved.

The script system would also be able to answer questions such as "did Fred eat at the restaurant?" even though the answer is not explicitly stated in the story.

A script is necessarily extremely specific. As we see in Chapter 20, more general systems for understanding language are extremely complex. However, in many situations it is possible to use scripts to understand natural language, provided the available scenarios are sufficiently restricted.

17.5   Copycat Architecture

The Copycat architecture was invented by Melanie Mitchell in 1993. The motivation behind the Copycat system was an interest in solving problems by analogy, such as the following problem:

> hat is to head as glove is to what?

Of course, the answer to this problem is obvious, but for computer programs to make such analogies is not easy. The Copycat system invented by Mitchell works on textual analogies, such as the following:

> $abc \rightarrow abd$

Hence,

> $tuv \rightarrow ?$

In fact, there are a number of possible answers to this problem, depending on the approach you choose to take. The answer most people will give would be "tuw" because they will have noted that in the first line, the third letter in the group of three has been replaced by the letter that comes immediately after it in the alphabet (its successor, in other words). However, the following might also be a reasonable answer:

> tud

To solve such problems, the Copycat system uses a nondeterministic method, such that when run repeatedly with the same problem it generates different answers.

The architecture of the Copycat system consists of the following components:

- the **Workspace**
- the **Slipnet**
- the **Coderack**

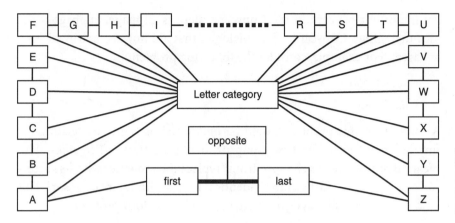

Figure 17.2
A simplified diagram of
the slipnet in the Copycat
system

The workspace is a data structure similar to a blackboard or to the message lists used in classifier systems (see Chapter 13). It contains the input data (such as "abc," "abd," and "tuv," for the problem given above) and is used as a working memory when solving problems. Eventually, it contains the answer that has been found.

The slipnet is a network that contains a number of concepts. Each letter is represented as a concept, as are ideas such as "opposite," "predecessor," "sameness," "right," and "left." Each concept in the slipnet has an **activation level** that indicates how relevant the concept is to the current problem. As a problem is being solved, the activation levels change.

The slipnet can be thought of as the system's long-term memory. It stores information that the system has built up about the nature of objects and concepts, and the relationships between those concepts. The slipnet can change over time, as the system solves problems.

Figure 17.2 shows a simplified version of the slipnet used by the Copycat system. Label nodes are included in the network that show, for example, which concepts are "opposite" to each other. In other words, concepts are used to show the relationship between concepts within the slipnet.

The coderack contains a number of agents, or **codelets**. Each codelet embodies a relationship between objects—such as "the b in abc is the successor of a." The higher a concept's activation level is, the more codelets will be assigned to working with that concept.

An important concept in the Copycat system is **slippage**. Slippage is the idea that allows Copycat to find analogies that are not necessarily directly apparent. For example, consider the following problem:

$abc \rightarrow abd$

$iijjkk \rightarrow ?$

A solution to this problem would be *iijjll*, which is found by relating the first letter in *abc* to the first group of identical letters (*ii*) in *iijjkk*. This means that the rule has changed from "replace the last letter with its successor" to "replace the last group of identical letters with their successor." This kind of change is slippage and is vital to solving analogy problems.

The final part of the Copycat architecture is the idea of **temperature**. As with simulated annealing (Chapter 5), temperature represents the degree of disorder in the system. The greater the temperature, the further from a solution the system is, and the more random its codelets are allowed to be.

The Copycat system starts with the problem representation in its workspace and with a reasonably high temperature.

As it works, it builds up relationships in its workspace, such as "the letters *abc* form a group where each letter is the successor of the letter to its left." It then tries to form **correspondences** between objects. For example, it might form a correspondence between the entire group of letters *abc* and the group *ijk* because they have a similar structure.

Copycat works by forming a rule that explains how to transform one object into another. For example, its rule might be "replace the rightmost letter by its successor." This rule is adapted as Copycat works, in order to produce a rule that will work with the problem object.

As the system runs, the temperature lowers until it falls below a probabilistic threshold, at which point it has reached a solution and can stop.

To fully understand the Copycat system, it is well worth trying the online demonstration system.

17.6   Nonmonotonic Reasoning

As was explained in Section 7.18, propositional logic and predicate logic are **monotonic** reasoning systems. This means that if a conclusion *C* can be derived from a set of expressions, *S*, then any number of additional expressions being added to S cannot change the truth value of C, provided the expressions in S remain consistent.

In other words, a monotonic reasoning system that stores facts about the world can deduce new facts from its existing facts but would never have cause to delete or modify an existing fact (unless the world changed). Hence, the number of facts the system stores will increase monotonically.

In real life, reasoning tends not to be so straightforward. For example, you might know that dogs like to eat meat, and that Fido is a dog. Hence, you conclude that Fido will like to eat meat. If you are later informed that Fido is a vegetarian dog, you will need to change your conclusion. This kind of reasoning is called **nonmonotonic reasoning**.

A nonmonotonic reasoning system needs to be able to deal with the fact that conclusions change as new facts are introduced and, hence, that its knowledge is not always certain because later facts may contradict it. In this context, we often use the word "belief" rather than "fact" to describe items of data that the system stores or deduces about the world.

In this section, we introduce a number of systems and principles that are used to deal with nonmonotonic reasoning situations.

17.6.1 Nonmonotonic Logic with the Modal Operator, *M*

One way to reason in nonmonotonic situations is to use nonmonotonic logic. This involves augmenting the predicate calculus with a modal operator, *M*, which is used to represent the idea that a statement is consistent with all our beliefs. Hence, we might write

$$\forall x \, bird \, (x) \wedge M \, flies \, (x) \rightarrow flies \, (x)$$

This can be read as follows: "for all *x*, if *x* is a bird and it is consistent with our beliefs to believe that *x* can fly, then *x* can fly." In other words, most birds can fly.

We would consider *M flies* (x) to be false if we already knew that the bird was dead and, in addition, we knew that dead birds could not fly. Note that we have just described a nonmonotonic logic, which is used for nonmonotonic reasoning.

17.6.2 Default Reasoning

Default reasoning is another form of nonmonotonic reasoning that involves assuming certain statements to be true, unless there is some clear evidence to the contrary. This is a form of reasoning that people employ all the time. For example, a car might drive past you too fast for you to see whether it has a driver or not. It would be reasonable for you to assume that the car has a driver, unless you happen to know that it is a remote-controlled car, or you saw the driver jump out previously. This is default reasoning, as it assumes certain facts by default, unless they are disproved by some other facts.

A notation similar to that described in Section 17.6.1 is used for default logic:

$$Car\ (x) \land :Has\_Driver\ (x) \rightarrow Has\_Driver\ (x)$$

This is a **default rule**, which states, in default logic notation, that if x is a car, and it is consistent with our beliefs to believe that x has a driver, then we can conclude that x does indeed have a driver.

Similarly, the sentence above could be read as "if x is a car and there's no reason to suppose that x does not have a driver, then conclude that x does have a driver."

17.6.3   Truth Maintenance Systems

A truth maintenance system (or TMS) stores information about how each belief was derived, as well as the beliefs themselves.

Truth maintenance systems are used in situations where **belief revision** is important. In other words, situations in which the system's beliefs need to change over time, as new facts come to light.

The justification-based truth maintenance system (JTMS) was proposed by Jon Doyle in 1979.

The JTMS stores **reasons** or **justifications** for beliefs, where a reason consists of a pair of sets, such that the belief is true if the statements in the first set (known as the **in** set) are all true, and the statements in the second set (known as the **out** set) are all false. For example, the belief Q might have the following reason:

$$(\{P, R\}, \{\neg S\})$$

This means that if P and R are both true, and $\neg S$ is false, then we can deduce that Q is true. If we use this reason to conclude that Q is true, and later discover that $\neg S$ is true, then we must **retract** our earlier conclusion.

The JTMS uses a network of nodes, where each node represents a belief (which can either be a simple statement such as "Fido is a dog" or a rule such as modus ponens, or "all dogs like to eat meat"). The JTMS also stores justifications for each belief.

The JTMS does not carry out logical operations on beliefs (such as ∧, ∨, and →) because these operations can be carried out by a problem-solving system external to the JTMS. Similarly, the JTMS does not need to understand the meanings of its beliefs. This kind of logical interpretation is carried out by the problem-solving system. The JTMS simply ensures that as new beliefs are added to the system, the existing beliefs remain consistent.

The JTMS is able to create new nodes, to add or retract justifications for nodes, and can mark a node as a contradiction if it is informed by the problem solver that that is the case.

The system either believes or does not believe in the statement represented by each node, and so a node is described as being either **in** (the system believes in it) or **out** (if the system does not believe in it). Of course, these beliefs can change, as new information is presented to the system and as it makes new arguments.

A node is considered to be contradictory if it represents a belief that is now believed to be untrue. When such a contradiction is determined, the JTMS must use this information to retract beliefs that it had formed based (directly or indirectly) on the incorrect belief. This retraction is done using **dependency-directed backtracking** (also called **nonchronological backtracking**— see Section 5.17). Dependency-directed backtracking in this case simply means working back from the contradictory node to find assumptions that led to the contradiction. These assumptions are retracted, until a minimal combination of retractions is found to ensure that the contradiction disappears.

An alternative to the JTMS is the assumption-based truth maintenance system, or ATMS. An ATMS is very similar to a JTMS, but rather than representing a complete statement of the system's beliefs at any given time, it includes information about all possible beliefs, or all possible worlds. Each node has associated with it a set of premises or assumptions that can be used to make the node true. Hence, a node might have the following assumptions associated with it:

$$(\{P\}, \{Q\})$$

This would mean that the node would be true if P is true, or it would be true if Q is true. A node that has an empty set associated with it is **necessarily true**, which means that it does not depend on other assumptions.

17.6.4   Closed-World Assumption

The **closed-world assumption** (also known as **negation by failure**, particularly as used by PROLOG) is an assumption used by systems that any fact not specifically known to be true is not true. For example, if a system uses a database of facts, and a particular fact is not included in the database, then that fact is assumed to be false.

The open-world assumption is the inverse of this: that any fact not explicitly contained within the database is assumed to be true. Note that one significant difference between STRIPS and ADL, two planning methods described in Chapter 16, is that STRIPS uses the closed-world assumption, whereas ADL uses the open-world assumption.

Clearly, systems that use the closed-world assumption (or the open-world assumption) must use nonmonotonic reasoning because they make assumptions that may later prove to be false.

PROLOG uses the closed-world assumption, which means that if a fact is not contained within its database, then it is assumed to be false.

17.6.5   The Ramification Problem

The **ramification problem** is similar to the frame problem, described in Chapter 15, which concerns the difficulty of needing to define all facts that do not change when an action is performed. The ramification problem concerns the additional consequences of actions that might not be immediately obvious. For example, if a robot picks up a block, and a fly has landed on the block, then the robot will also be picking up the fly. The ramification problem is the problem of determining how to deal with such potentially highly complex consequences.

17.6.6   Circumscription

McCarthy (1980) proposed a form of nonmonotonic reasoning, which he called **circumscription**. Circumscription was designed to deal, like the closed-world assumption, with situations in which not every possible fact is stated or denied.

McCarthy imagined someone attempting to solve the missionaries and cannibals problem (see Section 3.9.1), which involves having a group of missionaries and cannibals cross a river without the cannibals eating the missionaries. McCarthy imagined a person trying to solve this question by asking questions such as "Does the boat leak?" or "Is there a bridge?"

Circumscription allows us to modify a first-order predicate calculus expression to show that no facts are true other than those stated in the expression.

By applying circumscription in the problem of the cannibals and missionaries, we can conclude that any facts not explicitly stated in the problem specification are not true.

The circumscription of predicate P in an expression E is written

$$E(\phi) \wedge \forall x\,(\phi(x) \rightarrow P(x)) \rightarrow \forall x\,(P(x) \rightarrow \phi(x))$$

where $\phi(x)$ is the result of substituting all occurrences of P with ϕ in E.

Let us consider a simple example from the blocks world:

$$E = \text{IsBlock (A)} \wedge \text{IsBlock (B)} \wedge \text{IsBlock (C)}$$

Here the predicate IsBlock is used to indicate that an object is a block.

We can circumscribe the predicate IsBlock in E as follows:

First, we note that $E(\phi)$ is the following expression:

$$\phi(A) \wedge \phi(B) \wedge \phi(C)$$

Hence, the circumscription of IsBlock in E is

$$\phi(A) \wedge \phi(B) \wedge \phi(C) \wedge \forall x\,(\phi(x) \rightarrow \text{IsBlock}(x)) \rightarrow$$
$$\forall x\,(\text{IsBlock }(x) \rightarrow \phi(x))$$

Now to see what this really means, let us make the following substitution:

$$\phi(x) \equiv (x = A \vee x = B \vee x = C)$$

Clearly, $\phi(A)$ will become $(A = A \vee A = B \vee A = C)$, which is true, and similarly for $\phi(B)$ and $\phi(C)$. Hence, these parts can be eliminated from the expression (since TRUE $\wedge$ $A = A$).

This results in the following expression:

$$\forall x\,((x = A \vee x = B \vee x = C) \rightarrow \text{IsBlock}(x)) \rightarrow \forall x\,(\text{IsBlock }(x) \rightarrow$$
$$(x = A \vee x = B \vee x = c))$$

Now, we can use our original expression:

$$E = \text{IsBlock }(A) \wedge \text{IsBlock }(B) \wedge \text{IsBlock }(C)$$

Hence, $(x = A \vee x = B \vee x = C) \rightarrow$ IsBlock (x) is clearly true. Since

$$\text{TRUE} \rightarrow A = A$$

We can thus eliminate the left-hand side of the first implication, to give the following expression:

$$\forall x\, (\text{IsBlock}\, (x) \rightarrow (x = A \vee x = B \vee x = C))$$

In other words, not only are A, B, and C blocks, but there is nothing else in the world that can be called a block.

Note that if we now add an additional expression to E,

IsBlock (D)

the circumscribed expression we derived above is no longer true. We can instead, derive the following new circumscribed expression:

$$\forall x\, (\text{IsBlock}\, (x) \rightarrow (x = A \vee x = B \vee x = C \vee x = D))$$

This is a property of a nonmonotonic reasoning system: adding a new fact negates conclusions that have been logically deduced.

17.6.7   Abductive Reasoning

Recall the modus ponens rule from Section 7.11.4, which is written as follows:

$$\frac{A \quad A \rightarrow B}{B}$$

This tells us that if A is true, and we know that A implies B, then we can deduce B.

Abductive reasoning is based on a modified version of modus ponens, which while not logically sound, is nevertheless extremely useful:

$$\frac{B \quad A \rightarrow B}{A}$$

This tells us that if we observe that B is true, and we know that A implies B, then it is sensible to see A as a possible explanation for B.

For example, consider the case where B represents "Fred is not at work" and A represents "Fred is sick." If we know that when Fred is sick he does not come to work, and we also know that Fred is not at work, then we use abductive reasoning to conclude that Fred is sick. This might not be the case, as he may be on holiday or at a conference, but the point of abductive reasoning is that it provides a "good-enough" explanation for a phenomenon, which can be retracted later, if a preferable explanation is determined. In other words, abductive reasoning is nonmonotonic.

17.6.8   The Dempster–Shafer Theory

The **Dempster–Shafer theory** of evidence is used to discuss the degree of belief in a statement. A degree of belief is subtly different from probability. For example, suppose that a barometer tells you that it is raining outside and that you have no other way to determine whether this is the case or not and no knowledge about the reliability of the barometer.

Using probability theory, we might suppose that there is a 0.5 chance that the barometer is right, in which case the probability that it is raining would be 0.5.

However, using the Dempster–Shafer theory, we would start by stating that in fact we have no knowledge about whether it is raining or not, and so we write

$Bel\,(\text{Raining}) = 0$

Since we also have no knowledge about whether it is *not* raining, we can also write

$Bel\,(\neg\text{Raining}) = 0$

Note that $Bel\,(A)$ and $Bel\,(\neg A)$ do not need to sum to 1.

Now let us further suppose that we have determined that the barometer is 80% accurate.

Hence, we can modify our belief as follows:

$Bel\,(\text{Raining}) = 0.8$

This tells us that because the barometer says it is raining, we have a belief of 0.8 that it is in fact raining. At this point, we still have the following:

$Bel\,(\neg\text{Raining}) = 0$

Because the barometer is telling us that it is raining, we do not have any reason to believe that it is not raining. Note again the difference between this notation and normal probabilistic notation, where $P(\text{Raining})$ and $P(\neg\text{Raining})$ must sum to 1.

We also define the **plausibility** of a statement, X, as follows:

$Pl\,(X) = 1 - Bel\,(\neg X)$

Hence, we can define a range for X, which is $[Bel\ (X), Pl\ (X)]$. For the example above, our range is

$$[0.8, 1]$$

The narrower this range is, the more evidence we have, and the more certain we are about our belief. That is to say, if we have a belief range of $[0, 1]$, then we really do not know anything. If we have a belief range of $[0.5, 0.5]$, then we are certain that the probability of the proposition is 0.5. Hence, if we have a wide range, then we know that we need to seek more evidence.

Let us now suppose that we have a second barometer, which is 75% accurate, and which is also saying that it is raining outside. How does this affect our belief? Dempster (1968) proposed a rule for combining beliefs of this kind, which is applied as follows.

The probability that both barometers are reliable is

$$0.75 \times 0.8$$
$$= 0.6$$

The probability that both are unreliable is

$$0.25 \times 0.2$$
$$= 0.05$$

Hence the probability that at least one of the barometers is reliable is

$$1 - 0.05$$
$$= 0.95$$

Thus, we can assign the following belief range to the belief that it is raining:

$$[0.95, 1]$$

Once again, we have no reason to believe that it is not raining, and so the plausibility of the statement "it is raining" is 1. If we receive some evidence that it is not raining (e.g., if we cannot hear any rain), then we might modify this value.

Let us now suppose that the second barometer says that it is not raining, while the first barometer continues to say that it is raining.

Now, it cannot be the case that both barometers are reliable because they disagree with each other. The probability that the first barometer is reliable and that the second is unreliable is

$$0.8 \times 0.25$$

$$= 0.2$$

Similarly, the probability that the second is reliable and the first unreliable is

$$0.75 \times 0.2$$

$$= 0.15$$

The probability that neither is reliable is

$$0.2 \times 0.25$$

$$= 0.05$$

Dempster's rule now lets us calculate the belief that it is raining. We can calculate the posterior probability that it is raining, given that at least one of the barometers is unreliable as follows:

$$\frac{0.2}{0.2 + 0.15 + 0.05}$$

$$= \frac{0.2}{0.4}$$

$$= 0.5$$

Similarly, the probability that it is not raining, given that at least one of the barometers is unreliable is

$$\frac{0.15}{0.2 + 0.15 + 0.05}$$

$$= \frac{0.15}{0.4}$$

$$= 0.375$$

Hence, our belief that it is raining is Bel (Raining) = 0.5, and the plausibility of this belief is $1 - Bel(\neg\text{Raining}) = 1 - 0.375 = 0.625$. Hence, our belief can be expressed as the range

$$[0.5, 0.625]$$

17.6.9   MYCIN and Certainty Factors

In Chapter 9, we introduced expert systems or production systems and briefly mentioned MYCIN, which was a system developed at Stanford University in the 1980s for medical diagnosis. MYCIN was designed to help doctors select the correct antimicrobial agent to treat a patient, based on information about the patient's symptoms.

MYCIN uses abductive reasoning and backward chaining to estimate, based on a set of evidence concerning the patient's symptoms, which bacteria is most likely to be causing the illness.

MYCIN uses **certainty factors** to represent degrees of belief: much as the Dempster–Shafer theory uses the *Bel* notation, certainty factors represent the degree of belief or disbelief, where the two do not necessarily sum to 1, as they would in classical logic.

We use $M_B(H|E)$ to represent the measure of belief of hypothesis H, given evidence E, and $M_D(H|E)$ to represent the measure of disbelief of hypothesis H, given evidence E.

Because a particular piece of evidence either supports or contradicts a hypothesis, either $M_B(H|E)$ or $M_D(H|E)$ must be zero for any H and E.

We now define the certainty factor, $CF(H|E)$ as follows:

$$CF(H|E) = M_B(H|E) - M_D(H|E)$$

This value ranges from -1 to 1, where a high negative value indicates that the evidence gives a strong confidence that the hypothesis is false, and a high positive value indicates that the evidence gives a strong confidence that the hypothesis is true.

Each production rule used by MYCIN has a certainty factor associated with it. The following is a simplified example of one of MYCIN's rules:

```
IF: The patient has meningitis
AND: The patient has no serious skin infection
AND: The infection is bacterial
THEN: The infection could be caused by staphylococcus-coag-pos (0.75)
OR: streptococcus-group-a (0.5)
```

This rule is of the form

$$\text{IF } A \wedge B \wedge C \wedge \ldots N \text{ THEN } H_1\,(P_1) \vee H_2\,(P_2) \vee \ldots \vee H_n\,(P_n)$$

where $A \ldots N$ are the observed evidence, $H_1 \ldots Hn$ are the possible hypotheses to explain the evidence, and P_i is the certainty factor associated with H_i.

Certainty factor algebra is used to combine the certainty factors of rules with the certainty factors of the evidence to determine how certain the hypotheses are.

When a rule has a conjunction of premises, as in the example rule above, the minimum of the certainty factors of the premises is used as the certainty factor. If the rule has a disjunction of premises, then the maximum of the certainty factors is used.

17.7   Reasoning about Change

As we saw in Chapter 7, the classical propositional and predicate calculi provide us with a way to reason about an unchanging world. Most real-world problems involve a dynamic world, in which other people (or agents) effect changes, where the world itself changes, and where robotic agents can move themselves and thus change their environment proactively.

In Chapter 15, we briefly introduced the situation calculus that enables us to use a notation such as the following:

$$\exists x (In(Robot,x,S_1) \land In(cheese,x,S_1))$$

This sentence says that in situation S_1, the robot is in the same room as the cheese.

In this section we will explore two alternatives to the situation calculus: event calculus and temporal logic.

17.7.1   Temporal Logic

An early system for dealing with change was **temporal logic**, a form of modal logic. Temporal logic extends predicate calculus with a set of modal operators, which are usually defined as follows:

$\Box P$ means from now on, P will be true

$\Diamond P$ means that at some point in the future, P will be true

Compare these with the modal operators presented in Chapter 7, where the same symbols were used to indicate "necessarily" and "possibly." In temporal logic, the symbols are read as "henceforth" and "eventually."

Linear time temporal logic defines two other operators: "until" and "in the next time interval," which are usually written

$Q\mu P$ means that Q is true until P is true

$°P$ means that P will be true in the next time interval

A number of other operators are also sometimes used, including

P awaits Q	means that Q is true until P is true, or if P is never true, then Q is true forever (this contrasts with "*until*," which implicitly assumes that P will at some point be true)
Sofar P	means that P has been true until now
Once P	means that P was true at some time in the past
P precedes Q	means that P occurred before Q

These temporal operators implicitly assume that there is a concept of time, which is broken down into intervals. In particular, the $°$ operator indicates that some expression will be true in the next time interval. Temporal logic does not require the lengths of these time intervals to be defined, although clearly for it to be applied to real-world problems a mapping needs to be defined. In linear time temporal logic there is a finite set of states, such that each state has a unique successor. Hence, the logic cannot reason about multiple possible futures. This is possible with an alternative form of temporal logic: **computation tree logic** (CTL—also known as **branching time temporal logic**), which reasons about time in the form of a tree, with states represented by nodes in the tree. Because each state can have more than one successor, it is possible in this logical system to reason about several possible future outcomes.

CTL provides methods for reasoning about paths through the tree. For example, it is possible to create expressions such as "a path exists in which P is true" or "a path exists in which eventually P is true for all successor states." There also exist modal operators similar to the "necessarily" and "possibly" operators presented in Chapter 7, which state, for example, "P is true in all possible future states" or "P is true in at least one possible future state."

17.7.2 Using Temporal Logic

Temporal logic can be used in a number of applications. It is used, for example, in specification and verification of software programs and can also be used to verify the behavior of other systems, such as elevators. It can also be used to reason about problems that cannot otherwise be reasoned about using classical logics.

A system being defined by temporal logic has three main sets of conditions that define its behavior:

1. Safety conditions define behaviors that should never occur (such as the elevator being on two floors at once).

2. Liveness conditions specify what the system should do—for example, if someone pushes the button on the first floor, then the elevator should move toward that floor.

3. Fairness conditions define the behavior of the system in nondeterministic situations. For example, if the elevator is stationary on the second floor, and someone pushes the button on the first floor at the same time that someone else pushes the button on the third floor, the system must decide which direction to move the elevator.

We will now examine an example of temporal logic being used to specify a problem. The dining philosophers problem is defined as follows:

A number of philosophers are sitting around a round table, eating spaghetti and cogitating. There are six philosophers, six plates, and six forks. Each philosopher has a plate in front of him or her, and there is a fork between each pair of philosophers. For a philosopher to eat spaghetti, he or she must use two forks. Hence, only three philosophers can be eating at any one time. When a philosopher is not eating, he or she is thinking.

We will use the notation *eating*(i) to indicate that philosopher *i* is eating and *thinking*(i) to indicate that philosopher *i* is thinking.

The safety properties for this problem are defined as follows:

Each philosopher cannot be eating and thinking at the same time:

$$\Box \neg (eating\,(i) \land thinking\,(i))$$

Each philosopher is always either eating or thinking:

$$\Box \,(eating\,(i) \lor thinking\,(i))$$

If one philosopher is eating, then the next philosopher cannot be eating:

$$\Box \neg(eating\,(i) \wedge eating\,(i+1))$$

We can also define the liveness properties of the system as follows:

If a philosopher is eating now, then at some point in the future he or she will be thinking:

$$\Box\,(eating\,(i) \rightarrow \Diamond\, thinking\,(i))$$

Similarly, if a philosopher is thinking now, then at some point in the future he or she will be eating:

$$\Box\,(thinking\,(i) \rightarrow \Diamond\, eating\,(i))$$

Note that in this notation, unlike situation calculus, there is no mention of explicit states. This is not necessary with temporal logic, which is one reason for using it in preference to situation calculus.

17.7.3   Event Calculus

An alternative method for reasoning about properties that vary over time is the **event calculus**. Event calculus is concerned mainly with **fluents**. A fluent is a function that varies with time. For example, if a ball is dropped from a first-story window, then the ball's speed and height are both fluents.

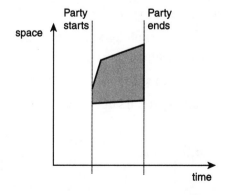

Figure 17.3

The space–time event that is a party at Tom's house

The event calculus also uses the notion of an **event**, which is a period of time bounded by a start and a finish point. Events can also be thought of as taking place in the real world and so have a space dimension as well as a time dimension. For example, the event called "the party at Tom's house" has a start and stop time, and takes place in a finite space, as shown in Figure 17.3.

The event calculus uses a number of predicates:

> *Happens* (*e, t*)
>
> *Starts* (*e, f, t*)
>
> *Ends* (*e, f, t*)

where *f* is a fluent, *e* is an event, and *t* is a variable of time.

Happens (*e, t*) means that event *e* happens at time *t*. In fact, *t* can be a function of time, and thus this predicate can be used to express the fact that an event (*e*) takes place over a period of time, defined by the function *t*.

Starts (*e, f, t*) means that the event *e* causes fluent *f* to hold immediately after time *t*, and similarly, *Ends* (*e, f, t*) means that event *e* stops fluent *f* at time *t*.

A further predicate lets us state that fluent *f* was beginning at the start of the time period we are considering:

> *Initially* (*f*)

For example, let us consider the event in which a ball drops from a height of 10 meters to the ground. For this example, we will assume that time starts at the moment the ball is dropped, and we will consider the following fluents:

> f_1 means the ball is motionless
>
> f_2 means the ball is falling
>
> f_3 means the ball is on the floor

We will also consider the following events:

> e_1 is the event that the ball is dropped
>
> e_2 is the event that the ball hits the floor

Hence, we can start with the following expression:

> *Initially* (f_1)

because the ball starts out motionless.

Next we can say

$$Happens\,(e_1, t_1)$$

which tells us that the ball is dropped at time t_1.

We can also define the causal relationships involved in this scenario, by saying the following:

$$Starts\,(e_1, f_2, t_1)$$
$$Ends\,(e_1, f_1, t_1)$$

Finally, we can define the consequences of the ball hitting the floor:

$$Happens\,(e_2, t_2)$$
$$Ends\,(e_2, f_2, t_2)$$
$$Starts\,(e_2, f_3, t_2)$$
$$Starts\,(e_2, f_1, t_2)$$

An additional predicate is used to express a period of time over which something occurs:

$$T\,(e, i)$$

This means that event e took place throughout the interval defined by i. For example, we might say

$$T\,(Dropping\,(\text{Ball}), \text{Today})$$

which would mean that the ball started dropping on or before the stroke of midnight this morning and continued to drop for the entire day.

It might be more useful to express the idea that the ball was dropping at some time today, for which we use the E predicate:

$$E\,(Dropping\,(\text{Ball}), \text{Today})$$

17.7.4 Mental Situation Calculus

The situation calculus and event calculus are used to describe events and their effects on the world. It is also useful to consider the effects that events have on an agent's beliefs about the world. For this, we use **mental situation calculus.**

The following functions are used:

> *Holds* (*P*, *S*)   means that proposition *P* holds in situation *S*
>
> *Believes* (*P*)   means that the agent believes proposition *P*

Hence, we might write:

> *Holds* (*Believes* (*Fly* (Pigs)), *S*)

This means that it is true in situation *S* that the agent believes that pigs can fly.

We also use a number of functions based around the idea of knowledge. It is convenient to write all of these using the same symbol:

> *Knows* (*P*)

In fact, this can have a number of different meanings depending on the nature of *P*.

For example,

> *Holds* (*Knows* (¬*Knows* (*P*)), *S*)

means that it is true in situation *S* that the agent knows that it does not know *P*, where *P* is some individual concept (such as the whereabouts of the piece of cheese for which the robot is searching, or Tom's telephone number).

Additionally, the *Knows* function can be used to refer to knowledge about propositions:

> *Holds* (*Knows* (*Fly* (Pigs)), *S*)

This means that it is true in situation *S* that the agent knows that pigs can fly. Note that in this notation we are treating *Fly* (Pigs) as a fluent, which may vary over time: It may be true at the moment that pigs can fly, but tomorrow they may forget how.

We can extend the *Believes* function to allow it to express the idea that a belief exists for an interval of time:

> *Believes* (*P*, *i*)

which means that the agent believes proposition *P* during the entirety of the interval defined by *i*.

We can also treat knowledge and beliefs as fluents. For example, we might want to say

> *T*(*Believes* (*Fly* (Pigs), Yesterday), Today)

which means it is true (for the whole of) today that throughout yesterday the agent believed that pigs could fly.

Events can occur that change an agent's beliefs. For this purpose, we define a **point fluent** as defining the fact that an event takes place at some moment in time. We write

$$Occurs\,(e, S)$$

to state that event e occurs in situation S.

We can then define a new function:

$$Learns\,(P)$$

which means that the agent learns proposition P.

Hence,

$$Occurs\,(Learns\,(P), S) \rightarrow Holds\,(F\,(Knows\,(P)), S)$$

$F\,(P)$ means that P will be true in the future. Hence, this sentence means that if in situation S the agent learns proposition P, then it is true that the agent will know proposition P at some future time.

17.8   Knowledge Engineering

Knowledge engineering was introduced in Chapter 9, in the context of expert systems. In fact, knowledge engineering is an essential part of many Artificial Intelligence systems.

All systems that are based on propositional calculus, predicate calculus, situation calculus, event calculus, temporal logic, and other such languages are primarily designed to manipulate knowledge. For those systems to perform useful tasks, knowledge needs to be gathered that can be entered into the system. Of course, in some systems, knowledge is gathered by an autonomous agent, and no knowledge engineering is necessary. In many Artificial Intelligence systems today, this is not the case, and a knowledge engineer is an essential component of the system.

The knowledge engineer's task is to gather knowledge (**knowledge acquisition**) about the problem space and to convert this knowledge into a form usable by the system (e.g., into first-order predicate calculus). The knowledge engineer must also consider the level of detail to use. For example, in defining the properties of a building, it might be considered sufficient to simply say *Building* (*P*) to define *P* as representing a building. It might also be more useful to include details such as *HasWindows* (*P*, 6), *HasFloors* (*P*, 2), and *HasRoof* (*P*). Alternatively, it might make more sense to define these properties for all buildings:

$$\forall x \; Building \,(x) \rightarrow HasWindows \,(x) \wedge HasFloors \,(x) \wedge HasRoof \,(x)$$

The knowledge engineer might then choose to include detail about the nature of buildings in terms of bricks, wood, and steel, and might further include details about the physical nature of these materials. In some cases, this detail might be superfluous. In other words, it is important for the knowledge engineer to select the correct level of detail to include in the knowledge base that is being built.

The important principle is to select predicates, functions, and constants that match the problem to be solved. If a system is being designed to determine the best layout of windows in a building, where the desired answer is simply the number of windows to include on each wall, then having a constant to represent each brick in the building would be unnecessary.

17.9   Case-Based Reasoning

Case-based reasoning was briefly introduced in Chapter 16, where it was discussed in the context of planning. Case-based reasoning involves reusing previously identified solutions to solve new problems and is often used in expert systems, as well as in other types of systems, such as the checkers-playing system developed by Samuel (see Chapter 6).

A case-based reasoning system uses a memory that can store solutions to past problems, along with information about whether each solution was successful or not. Such a system must therefore have the ability to look up a new problem, in order to find a previous case that was similar or identical to the current problem. Once such a case is found, the solution that was applied is modified in order to apply it directly to the current problem. This solution is then stored in the memory, along with information about whether it succeeded or failed.

For a case-based system to function adequately, the representation of cases must be carefully considered. The details that are used to index each case need to be relevant and also must be able to distinguish the case from other, dissimilar cases. The notion of *similarity* is important: what features mark two cases as similar? This is not always obvious, and the features that are used to define each case must be carefully selected.

Case-based systems make the task of knowledge acquisition relatively straightforward: the knowledge engineer simply needs to obtain examples of problems and their solutions (cases), which are entered into the system's memory.

Cases can be stored in a number of formats. For example, each case can be defined simply as a vector of the features that define the case and its solution. Alternatively, each case can be stored as a set of situated action rules (as used in Brooks' subsumption architecture, which is described in Chapter 19), each of which represents a solution to a particular situation (problem).

Case-based reasoning can be a very efficient way for a system to learn to solve problems, by examining its performance at solving past problems. As the system encounters more cases, it becomes better able to solve new problems. Of course, as the database of cases becomes larger, it becomes slower at retrieving cases from the database, and so there is a trade-off between performance and efficiency. It is possible to avoid this problem by only storing the most successful solutions and "forgetting" solutions that were less successful. Samuel's checkers program used this idea to remember only the "best" positions.

17.10   Chapter Summary

- Knowledge representation is vital to Artificial Intelligence and has been used extensively throughout this book.

- The blackboard architecture is a structured knowledge representation that uses opportunistic reasoning to combine inputs from a number of knowledge sources.

- Scripts are used to represent situations (such as going to a restaurant) that often conform to a particular pattern.

- The Copycat architecture is used to solve analogy problems of the form "A is to B as C is to what?"

- Classical logic is monotonic, which means that as new facts are added to a database, old conclusions are never contradicted. Many real-life situations require nonmonotonic reasoning.

- The modal operator M is used to represent the idea that a proposition is consistent with our current beliefs.

- Default reasoning uses assumptions about default values for certain variables, unless evidence to the contrary is found.

- Truth maintenance systems are used to ensure that the facts contained in a system's database are consistent, in a nonmonotonic reasoning environment.

- The closed-world assumption is the assumption that any statement not explicitly known to be true is false.

- The ramification problem is an extension of the frame problem. The ramification problem is the problem of dealing with small but potentially significant side effects of actions.

- Circumscription is a form of nonmonotonic reasoning that enables us to deduce which facts are false, based on a limited set of statements.

- Abductive reasoning involves determining a possible explanation for an observed phenomenon and is widely used by people and Artificial Intelligence systems.

- The Dempster–Shafer theory provides a way to reason about degrees of belief.

- MYCIN uses certainty factors to reason about degrees of certainty.

- Temporal logic is an extension of first-order predicate calculus, which uses a set of modal operators to reason about change.

- Event calculus is similar to situation calculus, but reasons about finite events.

- Mental situation calculus allows us to reason about beliefs and knowledge, and how they change over time.

- Knowledge engineering is a vital element of many Artificial Intelligence systems.

- Case-based reasoning allows a system to learn from previous solutions to problems, in order to solve new problems.

17.11   Review Questions

17.1 Explain why the blackboard architecture is an effective way to combine information from a number of knowledge sources. Describe the main components of the blackboard architecture.

17.2 Explain what kinds of problems the Copycat architecture can solve.

17.3 Explain what is meant by *nonmonotonic* reasoning, and explain why it is so important in Artificial Intelligence. Explain the difference between the terms *nonmonotonic reasoning* and *nonmonotonic logic.*

17.4 Explain the purpose of a truth maintenance system.

17.5 Explain what is meant by abductive reasoning. Explain your views on its usefulness in solving the following types of problems:

a. solving logical puzzles

b. medical diagnosis

c. controlling the behavior of a robotic agent

d. understanding spoken human language

17.6 Compare and contrast the Dempster–Shafer theory and certainty factors.

17.7 Explain the idea behind temporal logic. What kinds of problems is it useful for solving? Give three examples.

17.8 Can semantic networks be used to represent anything that can be represented using temporal logic? Explain your answer.

17.9 Explain what is meant by knowledge engineering, and why it is useful for systems other than expert systems.

17.10 What is case-based reasoning? From which attributes of human intelligence do you think it is derived? Describe the last time you used case-based reasoning in your normal life.

17.12   Exercises

17.1 Download the Copycat demonstration applet, the details for which can be found on the Internet using any search engine. Examine the following problems, and observe how the Copycat system solves them. In each case, produce three suitable solutions yourself before you see what solutions Copycat comes up with. How often does it find the same solutions as you do?

a. AABB is to AACC as JJKK is to what?

b. ABB is to ABCC as JKK is to what?

c. AABC is to AABD as IJKK is to what?

    d.   BCD is to BCE as JFFWWW is to what?

    e.   A is to Z as EFG is to what?

    f.   FSF is to SFS as ABBBC is to what?

17.2   Use temporal logic to describe the following situation:

There are three barbers in the shop. Each barber can shave either of the other two barbers but cannot shave himself. If a barber is not shaving, then he sits and reads the newspaper. If a customer arrives and a barber is free, then he will shave that customer. If a customer arrives and no barber is free, then the customer will sit and read the paper until a barber is free. Each barber needs to be shaved once a day.

17.3   Devise a representation for the following statement:

Yesterday, Bob went to the cinema, and he saw the film Titanic. *Afterward, he went straight home, with thoughts of the film going through his head. Angela went to the cinema at the same time and saw the film* The Lord of the Rings. *After the film, Angela went for a swim.*

Now add sufficient facts to the knowledge base you have created to enable an Artificial Intelligence system to answer the following questions:

    Did Bob meet Angela yesterday?

    Did Bob and Angela leave the cinema at the same time?

    Did Bob and Angela spend time together after the films?

    Did Bob enjoy the film?

You will need to add basic facts to the knowledge base such as:

    Lord of the Rings is longer than *Titanic.*

    Lord of the Rings started at the same time as *Titanic.*

Some of these facts will be common sense, and others you will need to invent to give reasonable answers to the questions.

How do you use the facts in the knowledge base to derive answers to the questions?

17.13   Further Reading

Luger (1995) provides an excellent range of papers on the subject of Artificial Intelligence in general, and in particular it has a number of papers that are relevant to this chapter. Russell and Norvig (1995) have a great deal of coverage of knowledge representation and knowledge engineering, primarily in the context of intelligent agents.

Additional references for MYCIN are contained in the Further Reading section of Chapter 9 of this book.

Nonmonotonic Reasoning, by Grigoris Antoniou (1997 – MIT Press)

A Logical Theory of Nonmonotonic Inference and Belief Change, by Alexander Bochman (2001 – Springer Verlag)

Nonmonotonic Reasoning : An Overview, by Gerhard Brewka, Jürgen Dix, and Kurt Konolige (1995 – Cambridge University Press)

Nonmonotonic Reasoning : From Theoretical Foundation to Efficient Computation, by G. Brewka (1991 – Cambridge University Press)

A Generalization of Bayesian Inference, by A. P. Dempster (1968 - in *Journal of the Royal Statistical Society*)

A Truth Maintenance System, by Jon Doyle (1979 – in *Computation & Intelligence – Collected Readings*, edited by George F. Luger, The MIT Press)

Probabilistic Interpretations for Mycin's Certainty Factors, by O. Heckerman (1986 – in *Uncertainty in Artificial Intelligence*, edited by L. N. Kanal and J. F. Lemmer, Elsevier Science Ltd., pp. 167–196)

Handbook of Logic in Artificial Intelligence and Logic Programming: Nonmonotonic Reasoning and Uncertain Reasoning, edited by Dov M. Gabbay, J. A. Robinson, and Christopher John Hogger (1994 – Oxford University Press)

Case-Based Reasoning, by Janet Kolodner (1993 – Morgan Kaufmann)

Case-Based Reasoning: Experiences, Lessons, and Future Directions, edited by David B. Leake (1996 –AAAI Press)

For the Sake of the Argument : Ramsey Test Conditionals, Inductive Inference and Nonmonotonic Reasoning, by Isaac Levi (1996 – Cambridge University Press)

Nonmonotonic Logic: Context-Dependent Reasoning, by V. W. Marek and M. Truszczynski (1993 – Springer Verlag)

Circumscription: A Form of Non-Monotonic Reasoning, by John McCarthy (1980 – in *Computation & Intelligence – Collected Readings*, edited by George F. Luger, The MIT Press)

A Production System Version of the Hearsay-II Speech Understanding System, by Donald McCracken (1981 - UMI Research)

Blackboard Systems: The Blackboard Model of Problem Solving and the Evolution of Blackboard Architectures, by H. Penny Nii (1986 – in *Computation & Intelligence – Collected Readings*, edited by George F. Luger, The MIT Press)

Soft Computing in Case Based Reasoning, edited by Sankar K. Pal, Tharam S. Dillon, and Daniel S. Yeung (2000 – Springer Verlag)

Inside Case-Based Reasoning, by Christopher K. Riesbeck and Roger C. Schank (1989 – Lawrence Erlbaum)

Change, Choice and Inference: A Study of Belief Revision and Nonmonotonic Reasoning, by Hans Rott (2002 – Oxford University Press)

The Structure of Episodes in Memory, by Roger C. Schank (1975 – in *Computation & Intelligence – Collected Readings*, edited by George F. Luger, The MIT Press)

CHAPTER 18

Fuzzy Reasoning

And new philosophy calls all in doubt,
The element of fire is quite put out;
The sun is lost, and th'earth, and no man's wit
Can well direct him, where to look for it.

—John Donne, *An Anatomy of the World*

To be, or not to be: that is the question.

—William Shakespeare, *Hamlet*

I used to love mathematics for its own sake, and I still do, because it allows for no hypocrisy and no vagueness, my two bêtes noires.

—Henri Beyle Stendahl, *La Vie d'Henri Brulard*

18.1 Introduction

This chapter introduces the idea of fuzzy sets and fuzzy logic. The chapter explains how fuzzy sets are defined and explains how linguistic variables, fuzzy operators, and hedges are applied. It also explains the concepts of fuzzy logic and how they can be applied in solving real-world problems.

This chapter explains how fuzzy expert systems can be built, as well as neuro-fuzzy systems, which are a cross between neural networks and fuzzy systems.

18.2   Bivalent and Multivalent Logics

In classical logic, which is often described as Aristotelian logic, there are two possible truth values: propositions are either true or false. Such systems are known as **bivalent logics** because they involve two logical values.

The logic employed in Bayesian reasoning and other probabilistic models is also bivalent: each fact is either true or false, but it is often unclear whether a given fact is true or false. Probability is used to express the likelihood that a particular proposition will turn out to be true.

One early multivalent logic was used to reason about the Uncertainty Principle, used in quantum physics. This logic had three values: true, false, and undetermined.

An extension of this three-valued logic is to consider 0 to represent false, 1 to represent true, and to use real numbers between 0 and 1 to represent degrees of truth.

Note that this is not the same as probability: if a fact has a probability value of 0.5, then it is as likely to be true as it is to be false, but in fact it will only be either true or false. If in a multivalent logic we have a proposition that has a logical value of 0.5, we are saying something about the degree to which that statement is true. In probability theory we are dealing with uncertainty (at the moment we don't know whether the proposition will be true or false, but it will definitely either be true or false—not both, not neither, and not something in between), but with multivalent logic we are certain of the truth value of the proposition; it is just **vague**—it is neither true nor false, or it is both true and false.

Although this kind of logic may sound absurd, in this chapter we will see how it can be put to practical use and indeed how multivalent logics, and in particular **fuzzy logic**, have become an extremely important part of Artificial Intelligence.

18.3   Linguistic Variables

In fuzzy set theory and fuzzy logic, we make great use of **linguistic variables**. A linguistic variable is a concept such as "height," which can have a value from a range of fuzzy values including "tall," "short," and "medium." The linguistic variable "height" may be defined over the **universe of dis-**

course from 2 feet up to 8 feet. As we will see, the values "tall," "short," and "medium" define subsets of this universe of discourse.

18.4 Fuzzy Sets

Fuzzy logic is used to reason about **fuzzy sets**. Fuzzy sets contrast with the sets used in traditional set theory, which are sometimes known as **crisp sets**. A crisp set can be defined by the values that are contained within it. A value is either within the crisp set, or it is not. For example, the set of natural numbers is a crisp set: 1, 2, 3, 4, and so on are natural numbers and so are definitely members of the set of natural numbers. Numbers such as 0.2, 101.101, and π are definitely not members of the set of natural numbers.

On the other hand, let us consider the set of tall people. Bill is 7 feet tall, and so it is pretty clear that he is included in the set of tall people. John is only 4 feet tall, and so most would say that he is not included in the set. What about Jane, who is 5 feet 10 inches tall? Some would certainly say she is tall, but others would say she is not.

The fuzzy set of tall people contains Bill, and it also contains Jane, and it even contains John. Each is a member of the set to some degree and is not a member of the set to some degree. This can be seen in the chart in Figure 18.1, which shows the degree of membership that a person of a given height has in the fuzzy set of tall people.

This definition of a fuzzy set is extremely natural and fits much better with the way people really talk about things. It is very common to say of someone that she is "fairly tall" or "not very tall" but actually quite unusual to use the unqualified descriptions "tall" or "not tall." This is because each person

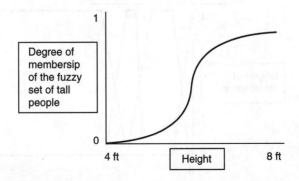

Figure 18.1

Chart showing the membership function for the fuzzy set of tall people

has his or her own idea of what tall means, and in fact our definitions of tall are not precise—if we were asked to define a group of people as either tall or not tall, and then asked to repeat the exercise, we might well classify one person as tall on the first occasion and as not tall on the second occasion. This is modeled very clearly in the fuzzy set, which defines each person as being both tall and not tall, to some extent.

You may recall from Section 7.20 that we defined the law of the excluded middle, which is a fundamental rule of classical logic, and which states that a proposition must either be true or false: it cannot be both true and false, and it is not possible for a statement to be neither true nor false. This is the basis of Aristotelian logic, but as we will see, in fuzzy logic, a statement can be both true and false, and also can be neither true nor false. Whereas in classical logic we can state axioms such as

$$A \lor \neg A = \text{TRUE}$$

$$A \land \neg A = \text{FALSE}$$

in fuzzy logic these do not hold—$A \lor \neg A$ can be, to some extent, false, and $A \land \neg A$ can to some extent be true: the law of the excluded middle does not hold in fuzzy logic.

The idea of the intersection between crisp sets is easy to understand: if an item is in set A and is also in set B, then it is in the intersection of sets A and B. Similarly, we can define an intersection between fuzzy sets. Consider the fuzzy sets whose membership functions are shown in Figure 18.2.

Figure 18.2 shows the membership functions for the fuzzy sets baby, child, teenager, and adult. Note that there are intersections between baby and

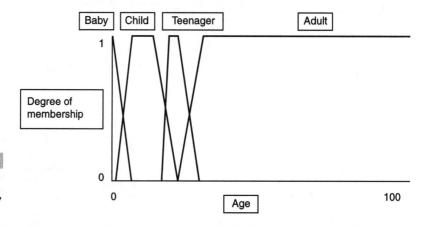

Figure 18.2

Graph showing membership of the fuzzy sets baby, child, teenager, and adult

child, between child and teenager, and between teenager and adult. Note that at some age, let us say 12, a person might be defined as all of the following: a child, not a child, a teenager, *and* not a teenager. Our definitions of the sets do not allow a person to be a child and an adult at the same time, but we could easily redefine the sets such that a person could be to some extent a child and at the same time to some extent an adult.

18.4.1   Fuzzy Set Membership Functions

A fuzzy set A is defined by its membership function, M_A.

For example, we might define the membership functions for the fuzzy sets B and C (baby and child) as follows:

$$M_B(x) = \begin{cases} 1 - \dfrac{x}{2} & \text{for } x \le 2 \\ 0 & \text{for } x > 2 \end{cases}$$

$$M_C(x) = \begin{cases} \dfrac{x-1}{6} & \text{for } x \le 7 \\ 1 & \text{for } x > 7 \text{ and } x \le 8 \\ \dfrac{14-x}{6} & \text{for } x > 8 \end{cases}$$

Similarly, we could define membership functions for fuzzy sets T (teenager) and A (adult). Note that there is nothing special about these functions—they have been chosen entirely arbitrarily and reflect a subjective view on the part of the author. Different functions could very well be chosen for $M_B(x)$ and $M_C(x)$, which would equally reasonably define those sets.

To represent a fuzzy set in a computer, we use a list of pairs, where each pair represents a value and the fuzzy membership value for that value. Hence, we write the fuzzy set A as

$$A = \{(x_1, M_A(x_1)), \ldots, (x_n, M_A(x_n))\}$$

For example, we might define B, the fuzzy set of babies as follows:

$$B = \{(0, 1), (2, 0)\}$$

This can also be thought of as representing the x and y coordinates of two points on the line, which represents the set membership function, as shown in Figure 18.2. Similarly, we could define the fuzzy set of children, C, as follows:

$$C = \{(1, 0), (7, 1), (8, 1), (14, 0)\}$$

18.4.2   Fuzzy Set Operators

Traditional set theory (developed by Georg Cantor in the 19th century) uses a number of operators that can be applied to sets A and B:

Not A the complement of A, which contains the elements that are not contained in A

$A \cap B$ the intersection of A and B, which contains those elements that are contained in both A and B

$A \cup B$ the union of A and B, which contains all the elements of A and all the elements of B

We can think of these as being related to the logical operators, $\neg$, $\wedge$, and $\vee$. Naturally, the set "Not A" is the same as $\neg A$. The intersection of A and B is the same as the conjunction of A and B: $A \wedge B$. Similarly, the union of A and B is the same as the disjunction of A and B: $A \vee B$.

As a result, the set operators are commutative, associative, and distributive, as we would expect, and they obey DeMorgan's laws:

$$\neg(A \cup B) = \neg A \cap \neg B$$
$$\neg(A \cap B) = \neg A \cup \neg B$$

We can define similar operators for fuzzy sets. The complement of fuzzy set A, whose membership function is M_A is defined as

$$M_{\neg A}(x) = 1 - M_A(x)$$

Thus, we could define the set of not-babies, $\neg B$, as follows:

$$M_{\neg B}(x) = 1 - M_B(x)$$

So,

$$\neg B = \{(0, 0), (2, 1)$$

Similarly, we can define $\neg C$:

$$\neg C = \{\{(1, 1), (7, 0), (8, 0), (14, 1)\}$$

For each x, we have defined $M_{\neg C}(x)$ as being $1 - M_C(x)$.

We can now define fuzzy intersection of two sets as being the minimum of the fuzzy membership functions for the sets. That is,

$$M_{A \cap B}(x) = \text{MIN}(M_A(x), M_B(x))$$

So, for example, let us determine the intersection of B and C, babies and children:

Recall that we define B and C as follows:

$B = \{(0, 1), (2, 0)\}$

$C = \{(1, 0), (7, 1), (8, 1), (14, 0)\}$

To determine the intersection, we need to have the sets defined over the same values; hence, we augment set B:

$B = \{(0, 1), (1, 0.5), (2, 0), (7, 0), (8, 0), (14, 0)\}$

Similarly, we augment C:

$C = \{(0, 0), (1, 0), (2, 0.166), (7, 1), (8, 1), (14, 0)\}$

Now we can find the intersection, by using

$M_{B \cap C}(x) = \text{MIN}\,(M_B(x), M_C(x))$

$\therefore\ B \cap C = \{(0, 0), (1, 0), (2, 0), (7, 0), (8, 0), (14, 0)\}$

But this has not worked! Clearly we need to define the set using values that will correctly define the ranges. In other words, we can correctly define $B \cap C$ as follows:

$B \cap C = \{(1, 0), (1.75, 0.125), (2, 0)\}$

where 1.75 was used as the value for x. This was determined by calculating the value of x for which $M_B(x) = M_C(x)$.

Let us consider for a moment what the intersection of two fuzzy sets actually means. As we said previously, $B \cap C$ can be thought of as being similar to $B \wedge C$. If a person is in the set $B \cap C$, then she is *both* a baby *And* a child. So the intersection of two sets is the set of elements that belong to both those two sets, or the elements that belong to the conjunction of the two sets.

Similarly, we can define the union of two fuzzy sets A and B as follows:

$M_{A \cup B}(x) = \text{MAX}\,(M_A(x), M_B(x))$

Hence, the union of the fuzzy sets of babies and children is as follows:

$B \cup C = \{(0, 1), (1.75, 0.25), (7, 1), (8, 1), (14, 0)\}$

Again, recall that the union $B \cup C$ is similar to the disjunction $B \vee C$. A person who belongs to the set $B \cup C$ is *either* a baby *Or* a child.

Let us consider one final fuzzy set operator—**containment**.

In traditional set theory, if crisp set A **contains** crisp set B, then this means that all elements of set B are also elements of set A. In other words, the

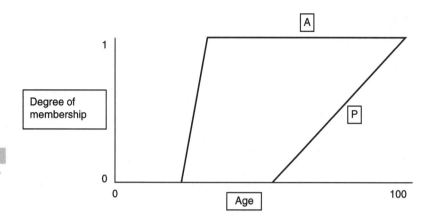

Figure 18.3

Membership functions for the fuzzy sets adults (A) and pensioners (P)

union $A \cup B = A$ and the intersection $A \cap B = B$. In this case, B is said to be a **subset** of A, which is written $A \subset B$.

To see how fuzzy subsets work, let us consider a new fuzzy set, P, which is the fuzzy set of pensioners. We will define this set by the following membership function:

$$M_p(x) = \begin{cases} 0 & \text{for } x \leq 55 \\ \dfrac{x - 55}{45} & \text{for } x > 55 \end{cases}$$

Let us suppose in this case that we are considering the universe of people to range over the ages between 0 and 100 (not to exclude people over the age of 100, but simply to make the mathematics a little simpler).

In Figure 18.3 we can see the membership functions for A and P.

The intersection of A and P, $A \cap P$, can be seen clearly from this diagram to be P. Hence, P is a subset of A, or $A \subset P$.

The definition of fuzzy containment is as follows:

$$B \subset A \text{ iff } \forall x \, (M_B(x) \leq M_A(x))$$

In other words, B is a fuzzy subset of A if B's membership function is always smaller than (or equal to) the membership function for A.

18.4.3   Hedges

A **hedge** is a fuzzy set qualifier, such as "very," "quite," "extremely," or "somewhat." When one of these qualifiers is applied to a fuzzy set, such as "tall people," we produce a new set. For example, by applying the "very" hedge to "tall people," we produce a subset of "tall people" called "very tall people." Similarly we can produce a new subset of "quite tall people" or "somewhat tall people."

The meanings of these hedges are fairly subjective, as are the meanings of fuzzy sets themselves. However, it is usual to use a systematic mathematic definition for the hedges so that they can be applied logically.

Often a hedge is applied by raising the set's membership function to an appropriate power. For example, it is common to consider the "very" hedge to square the value of the membership function. For example, if M_A is the membership function for fuzzy set A of tall people, then the membership function for VA, the fuzzy set of very tall people is

$$M_{VA}(x) = (M_A(x))^2$$

Similarly, we can define hedges such as "quite," "somewhat," and "extremely," as raising the membership function to powers of 1.3, 0.5, and 4, respectively.

Hence, if Jane has a fuzzy membership value of the "tall people" set of 0.6, then she has a membership value of "very tall people" of $0.6^2 = 0.36$; a membership value of "quite tall people" of $0.6^{1.3} = 0.515$; a membership value of "somewhat tall people" of $0.6^{0.5} = 0.775$; and a membership value of "extremely tall people" of $0.6^4 = 0.1296$.

Note that while hedges such as "very," "extremely," and "quite" define a subset of a fuzzy set, hedges such as "somewhat" or "more or less" expand the set to which they are applied. A person who is not at all tall, for example, might be defined as being, to some extent, "somewhat tall."

18.5 Fuzzy Logic

Fuzzy logic is a form of logic that applies to fuzzy variables. Fuzzy logic is non-monotonic, in the sense that if a new fuzzy fact is added to a database, this fact may contradict conclusions that were previously derived from the database.

We have already seen that the functions MAX and MIN can be used with fuzzy sets to calculate the intersection and union of two fuzzy sets. Similarly, the same functions can be used in fuzzy logic to calculate the disjunction or conjunction of two fuzzy variables.

Each fuzzy variable can take a value from 0 (not at all true) to 1 (entirely true) but can also take on real values in between. Hence, 0.5 might indicate "somewhat true," or "about as true as it is false."

If A and B are fuzzy logical values, then we can define the logical connectives $\wedge$ and $\vee$ as follows:

$$A \vee B \equiv \text{MAX} (A, B)$$
$$A \wedge B \equiv \text{MIN} (A, B)$$

Similarly, we can define negation as follows:

$$\neg A \equiv 1 - A$$

Recall from Chapter 7 that we can define any binary logical connective using just $\neg$ and $\wedge$. Hence, we can define any fuzzy logic connective using just MIN and the function $f(x) = 1 - x$.

Clearly, we cannot write a complete truth table for a fuzzy logical connective because it would have an infinite number of entries. We can, however, produce a fuzzy truth table for a finite set of input values. For example, we could consider the set $\{0, 0.5, 1\}$, which would be used in a multivalent logic that had three logical values. Hence,

A	B	A ∨ B
0	0	0
0	0.5	0.5
0	1	1
0.5	0	0.5
0.5	0.5	0.5
0.5	1	1
1	0	1
1	0.5	1
1	1	1

We could similarly draw up truth tables for $\wedge$ and the other logical connectives. Consider the following, which is the three-valued truth table for $\neg$:

A	¬A
0	1
0.5	0.5
1	0

Note in particular that if $A = 0.5$, then $A = \neg A$. The extent to which A is true is the same as the extent to which it is false. This is a fundamental aspect of fuzzy logic and is a feature that would be entirely anathema to the thinking of most classical logicians.

Now let us look at defining fuzzy logical implication, or $\rightarrow$. Recall from Chapter 7 that in classical logic $\rightarrow$ is defined by the following:

$$A \rightarrow B \equiv \neg A \lor B$$

Hence, it would seem natural to define fuzzy implication as follows:

$$A \rightarrow B \equiv \text{MAX} \left((1 - A), B \right)$$

Let us now examine the truth table for this function:

A	B	A → B
0	0	1
0	0.5	1
0	1	1
0.5	0	0.5
0.5	0.5	0.5
0.5	1	1
1	0	0
1	0.5	0.5
1	1	1

It is interesting to note that using this definition of implication, $0.5 \rightarrow 0 = 0.5$. This is somewhat counterintuitive because we would expect $0.5 \rightarrow 0 = 0$. Also, we have the counterintuitive statement that $0.5 \rightarrow 0.5 = 0.5$, whereas we would expect $0.5 \rightarrow 0.5 = 1$.

As a result of this, a number of alternative definitions for fuzzy implication have been proposed. One such definition is known as **Gödel implication**, which is defined as follows:

$$A \rightarrow B \equiv (A \leq B) \lor B$$

Using this definition, we can draw up an alternative fuzzy truth table for $\rightarrow$ over three logical values as follows:

A	B	A → B
0	0	1
0	0.5	1
0	1	1
0.5	0	0
0.5	0.5	1
0.5	1	1
1	0	0
1	0.5	0.5
1	1	1

This table seems more intuitive.

Now let us consider modus ponens, the logical rule we saw in Section 7.11.4:

$$\frac{A \qquad A \to B}{B}$$

In fuzzy logic this rule also holds. We will now examine, by drawing up a truth table, whether it also holds for three-valued fuzzy logic.

A	B	A → B	(A ∧ (A → B)) → B
0	0	1	1
0	0.5	1	1
0	1	1	1
0.5	0	0	1
0.5	0.5	1	0.5
0.5	1	1	1
1	0	0	1
1	0.5	0.5	1
1	1	1	1

We have drawn up this truth table using our original, less satisfactory definition of $\rightarrow$, and as a result, we have found that modus ponens does not quite hold. If $A = 0.5$ and $B = 0.5$, then we have

$$(A \wedge (A \rightarrow B)) \rightarrow B = 0.5$$

Assuming we want modus ponens to hold, then this is not satisfactory because we would want to obtain

$$(A \wedge (A \rightarrow B)) \rightarrow B = 1$$

If we draw up the equivalent truth table but use Gödel implication, then we find that each row in the truth table has a final value of 1, as we would expect, and thus modus ponens holds.

18.6 Fuzzy Logic as Applied to Traditional Logical Paradoxes

There are a number of well-known paradoxes in classical logic: problems that cannot be solved using propositional logic because they lead to a conclusion that contradicts one or more of the premises. For example, **Russell's paradox** can be stated as follows:

A barber, who himself has a beard, shaves all men who do not shave themselves. He does not shave men who shave themselves.

We now ask the following question: Who shaves the barber? If he shaves himself, then according to the second sentence in the statement above, he cannot shave himself. But if he does not shave himself, then the first sentence above tells us that he does shave himself.

This paradox exemplifies the law of the excluded middle—the problem arises due to the fact that we cannot have $A \wedge \neg A$. In fuzzy logic, this problem does not exist, and Russell's paradox is not a paradox: the barber both shaves himself and does not shave himself.

Similarly, consider another commonly discussed paradox:

"All Cretans are liars," said the Cretan.

If the Cretan is a liar, as his claim would suggest, then his claim cannot be believed, and so he is not a liar. But if he is not a liar, then he is telling the truth, and all Cretans are liars. But because he is a Cretan, he must therefore be a liar. Again, this is a paradox that can be resolved by using fuzzy logical values, instead of the two logical values "true" and "false." The Cretan's statement is true and false, to some extent, at the same time.

This makes perfect sense: when the Cretan says that all Cretans are liars, it is unlikely that he is really speaking of every single Cretan. It is also unlikely that he really means that every Cretan lies every time he opens his mouth. Hence, his statement has a fuzzy truth value somewhere below 1, but somewhere above 0.

18.7 Fuzzy Rules

We will now consider fuzzy rules, which are the fuzzy equivalent of the rules we used in Chapter 9, when we considered expert systems.

The rules we saw in Chapter 9 had the following form:

IF A THEN B

A fuzzy rule has the form

IF $A = x$ then $B = y$

In fact, to be more precise, a fuzzy rule can take the following form:

IF A op x then $B = y$

Where op is some mathematical operator (such as =, >, or <)

Hence, we might have fuzzy rules such as the following:

IF temperature > 50 then fan speed = fast

IF height = tall then trouser length = long

IF study time = short then grades = poor

By using fuzzy inference, which is explained in the next section, an expert system can be built based around fuzzy rules such as these.

18.8 Fuzzy Inference

An alternative to Gödel implication called **Mamdani implication** (or **Mamdani inference**) is often used in fuzzy systems. Mamdani inference allows a system to take in a set of crisp input values (from a set of sensors or inputs from a human operator, for example) and apply a set of fuzzy rules to those values, in order to derive a single, crisp, output value or action recommendation. Mamdani inference was invented by Professor Ebrahim Mamdani in the 1970s and was used by him to control a steam engine and boiler.

We will now examine a simple example to see how this form of reasoning works.

Let us suppose that we are designing a simple braking system for a car, which is designed to cope when the roads are icy and the wheels lock.

The rules for our system might be as follows:

Rule 1 IF pressure on brake pedal is medium

THEN apply the brake

Rule 2 IF pressure on brake pedal is high

AND car speed is fast

AND wheel speed is fast

THEN apply the brake

Rule 3 IF pressure on brake pedal is high

AND car speed is fast

AND wheel speed is slow

THEN release the brake

Rule 4 IF pressure on brake pedal is low

THEN release the brake

To apply these rules, using Mamdani inference, the first step is to **fuzzify** the crisp input values.

To do this, we need first to define the fuzzy sets for the various linguistic variables we are using.

For this simple example, we will assume that brake pressure is measured from 0 (no pressure) to 100 (brake fully applied). We will define brake pressure as having three linguistic values: high (H), medium (M), and low (L), which we will define as follows:

$H = \{(50, 0), (100, 1)\}$

$M = \{(30, 0), (50, 1), (70, 0)\}$

$L = \{(0, 1), (50, 0)\}$

Figure 18.4 shows the membership functions for these three fuzzy sets.

Let us suppose that the pressure value in a given situation is in fact 60. This corresponds to fuzzy membership values for the three sets of

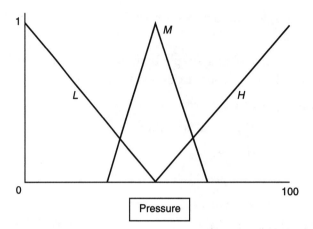

Figure 18.4

Graph showing member-ship functions for fuzzy variable pressure

$$M_L(60) = 0$$
$$M_M(60) = 0.5$$
$$M_H(60) = 0.2$$

Similarly, we must consider the wheel speed. We will define the wheel speed as also having three linguistic values: slow, medium, and fast. We will define the membership functions for these values for a universe of discourse of values from 0 to 100:

$$S = \{(0, 1), (60, 0)\}$$
$$M = \{(20, 0), (50, 1), (80, 0)\}$$
$$F = \{(40, 0), (100, 1)\}$$

If the wheel speed is in fact 55, then this gives us membership values as follows:

$$M_S(55) = 0.083$$
$$M_M(55) = 0.833$$
$$M_F(55) = 0.25$$

For the sake of simplicity, we will define the linguistic variable *car speed* using the same linguistic values (*S*, *M*, and *F* for slow, medium, and fast), using the same membership functions. Clearly, in a real system, the two would be entirely independent of each other.

Let us suppose now that the car speed is 80, which gives us the following membership values:

$$M_S(80) = 0$$

$$M_M(80) = 0$$
$$M_F(80) = 0.667$$

We now need to apply these fuzzy values to the antecedents of the system's rules.

Rule 1, taken on its own, tells us that the degree to which we should apply the brake is the same as the degree to which the pressure on the brake pedal can be described as "medium."

We saw above that the pressure is 60 and that $M_M(60) = 0.5$. Hence, Rule 1 gives us a value of 0.5 for the instruction "Apply the brake."

Rule 2 uses an AND:

IF pressure on brake pedal is high

AND car speed is fast

AND wheel speed is fast

THEN apply the brake

The membership functions for the three parts of the antecedent are

$$M_H(60) = 0.2$$
$$M_F(80) = 0.667$$
$$M_F(55) = 0.25$$

Usually, the conjunction of two or more fuzzy variables is taken to be the minimum of the various membership values. Hence, the antecedent for Rule 2 in this case has the value 0.2. Thus, Rule 2 is giving us a fuzzy value of 0.2 for "Apply the brake."

Similarly, we evaluate Rules 3 and 4:

Rule 3 $M_H(60) = 0.2$

$M_F(80) = 0.667$

$M_S(55) = 0.083$

Hence, Rule 3 gives a value of 0.083 for "Release the brake."

Rule 4 $M_L(60) = 0$

Hence, Rule 4 gives us a fuzzy value of 0 for "Release the brake."

Now we have four fuzzy values: 0.5 and 0.2 for "Apply the brake" and 0.083 and 0 for "Release the brake."

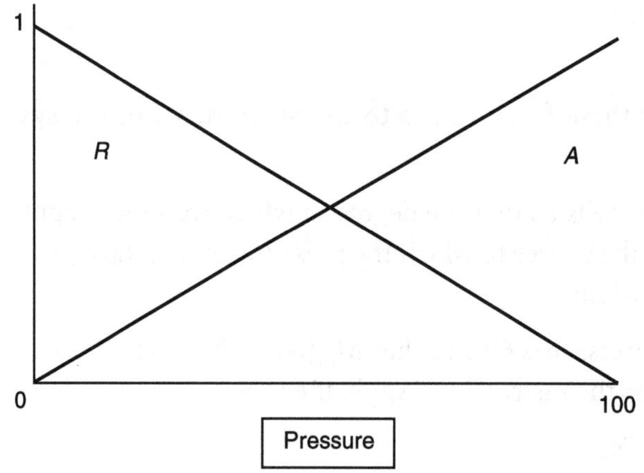

Figure 18.5
Membership functions for "Apply the brake" (A) and "Release the brake" (R)

We now need to combine these values together.

First, let us see what we mean by "Apply the brake" and "Release the brake." Figure 18.5 shows fuzzy membership functions for "Apply the brake" (A) and "Release the brake" (R), which show the degree of pressure the brake should apply to the wheel for each value of these variables.

To put that another way, the x-axis of the graph in Figure 18.5 shows the pressure applied by the brake to the wheel, and the y-axis shows the degree to which "Apply the brake" and "Release the brake" are true ($M[A]$ and $M[R]$).

To apply the rules, we first need to decide how to combine the differing values for each of the two fuzzy variables. We have 0.2 and 0.5 for "Apply the brake" and 0.083 and 0 for "Release the brake." We could sum the values or take the minimum or take the maximum. The appropriate combination will depend on the nature of the problem being solved. In this case it makes sense to sum the values because the separate rules are giving different reasons for applying or releasing the brakes, and those reasons should combine together cumulatively.

Hence, we end up with a value of 0.7 for "Apply the brake" and 0.083 for "Release the brake."

The next step is to **clip** the membership functions of the two variables to these values, as is shown in Figure 18.6.

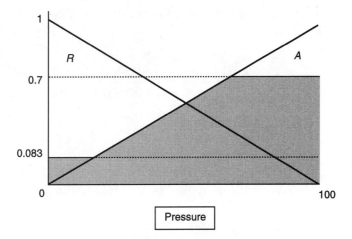

Figure 18.6

Showing how the fuzzy values for the antecedents of the rules are applied to the consequents

In Figure 18.6, the membership function for *A* has been clipped at 0.7, and the membership function for *R* has been clipped at 0.083. The resulting shape is the shaded area under the two clipped lines and shows the combined fuzzy output of the four rules.

To use this fuzzy output, a crisp output value must now be determined from the fuzzy values. This process of obtaining a crisp value from a set of fuzzy variables is known as **defuzzification**. This can be done by obtaining the **center of gravity** (or **centroid**) of the shaded shape shown in Figure 18.6.

The formula for the center of gravity, *C*, is as follows:

$$C = \frac{\sum M_A(x)x}{\sum M_A(x)}$$

where $M_A(x)$ is the membership function illustrated by the shaded area in Figure 18.6.

In fact, the center of gravity should really be calculated as a continuous integral, but if we use a discrete sum over a reasonable selection of values, we can obtain an answer that is close enough. In fuzzy systems it is not usually necessary to be accurate to several decimal places, but rather to obtain a value in the right range.

Hence, we can calculate the center of gravity of the shaded shape in Figure 18.6 as follows:

$$C = \frac{(5 \times 0.83) + (10 \times 0.1) + (15 \times 0.15) + (20 \times 0.2) + \ldots + (100 \times 1)}{0.083 + 0.1 + 0.15 + 0.2 + \ldots + 1}$$

$$= \frac{717.666}{10.533} = 68.13$$

Hence, the crisp output value for this system is 68.13, which can be translated into the pressure applied by the brake to the wheel in the car.

18.9   Fuzzy Expert Systems

Expert systems, or production systems, are described in more detail in Chapter 9. An expert system consists of a set of rules that are developed in collaboration with an expert. Expert systems are used, for example, for medical diagnosis. Traditional expert systems use crisp logical values to determine a diagnosis or a recommendation based on a set of evidence. In many ways, this is a fine way to apply the expert's knowledge. On the other hand, most expert decisions are not black and white. An expert who is presented with a patient with one set of symptoms will not usually be able to provide a diagnosis with absolute certainty but will have a strong feeling about a diagnosis based on the weight of evidence.

Hence, applying fuzzy logic to these rules seems like a natural way to progress.

The fuzzy expert system can be built by choosing a set of linguistic variables appropriate to the problem and defining membership functions for those variables. Rules are then generated based on the expert's knowledge and using the linguistic variables. The fuzzy rules can then be applied as described above using Mamdani inference.

Let us now look at a simple example of how a fuzzy expert system can be built from an expert's knowledge.

We will consider an imaginary medical system designed to recommend a dose of quinine to a patient or doctor based on the likelihood that that patient might catch malaria while on vacation.

Creating the fuzzy expert system will involve the following steps:

1. Obtain information from one or more experts.

2. Define the fuzzy sets.

3. Define the fuzzy rules.

To use the fuzzy expert system, we will use the following steps:

1. Relate observations to the fuzzy sets.

2. Evaluate each case for all fuzzy rules.

3. Combine information from the rules.

4. Defuzzify the results.

18.9.1 Defining the Fuzzy Sets

Having obtained suitable information from our experts, we must start by defining the fuzzy sets.

In this case, we will use the following fuzzy sets, or linguistic variables:

- average temperature of destination (T)

- average humidity of destination (H)

- proximity to large bodies of water (P)

- industrialization of destination (I)

Note that this is a purely imaginary example for the purposes of illustration and explanation and has no real bearing on the way that malaria is prevented or treated!

As well as defining the linguistic variables, we need to give each one a range of possible values. For this example, we will assume that each has just two values: Temperature, humidity, and industrialization can be high (H) or low (L), and proximity to water can be near (N) or far (F).

To represent the fuzzy membership functions, we will use the notation M_{AB} (x), where A is the variable (T, H, P, or I) and B is the value (H, L, N, or F). For example, M_{HL} is the membership function for the fuzzy subset described as "humidity low."

The crisp values that we will allow as inputs will range from 0 to 100 for temperature, humidity, and industrialization, and from 0 to 50 for proximity to water.

We will define the membership functions for each of these fuzzy subsets using the following equations:

$$M_{TH}(x) = \begin{cases} \dfrac{x-25}{75} & \text{for } x \geq 25 \\ 0 & \text{for } x < 25 \end{cases}$$

$$M_{TL}(x) = \begin{cases} 1 - \dfrac{x}{75} & \text{for } x \leq 75 \\ 0 & \text{for } x > 75 \end{cases}$$

$$M_{HH}(x) = \dfrac{x}{100}$$

$$M_{HL}(x) = 1 - \dfrac{x}{100}$$

$$M_{PN}(x) = \begin{cases} 1 & \text{for } x < 10 \\ \dfrac{40-x}{30} & \text{for } 10 \leq x < 40 \\ 0 & \text{for } x \geq 40 \end{cases}$$

$$M_{PF}(x) = \begin{cases} 0 & \text{for } x < 10 \\ \dfrac{x-10}{30} & \text{for } 10 \leq x < 40 \\ 1 & \text{for } x \geq 40 \end{cases}$$

$$M_{IH}(x) = \begin{cases} 0 & \text{for } x < 10 \\ \dfrac{x-10}{10} & \text{for } 10 \leq x < 20 \\ 1 & \text{for } x \geq 20 \end{cases}$$

$$M_{IL}(x) = \begin{cases} 1 & \text{for } x < 10 \\ \dfrac{20-x}{10} & \text{for } 10 \leq x < 20 \\ 0 & \text{for } x \geq 20 \end{cases}$$

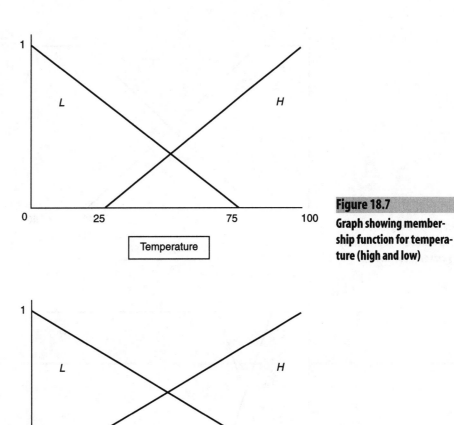

Figure 18.7

Graph showing member-
ship function for temperature (high and low)

Figure 18.8

Graph showing member-
ship function for humidity
(high and low)

Figures 18.7 to 18.10 show graphs for all of these fuzzy membership functions.

We need to define one more fuzzy set, which is the set used to describe the output of the system. In this case, our system will prescribe a dose of qui-nine which can take on one of three values:

very low dose (V)

low dose (L)

high dose (H)

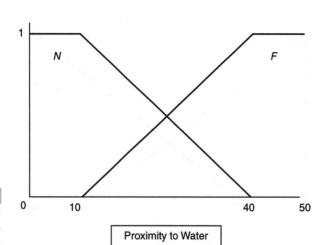

Figure 18.9

Graph showing membership function for proximity to water (near and far)

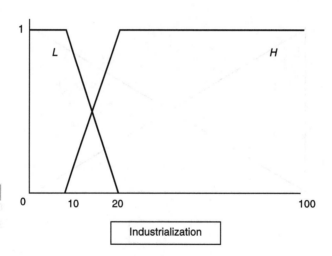

Figure 18.10

Graph showing membership function for industrialization (high and low)

We will define three membership functions for these three fuzzy sets as follows:

$$
M_{QV}(x) = \begin{cases} \dfrac{10 - x}{10} & \text{for } x \leq 10 \\ 0 & \text{for } x > 10 \end{cases}
$$

$$
M_{QL}(x) = \begin{cases} \dfrac{50 - x}{50} & \text{for } x \leq 50 \\ 0 & \text{for } x > 50 \end{cases}
$$

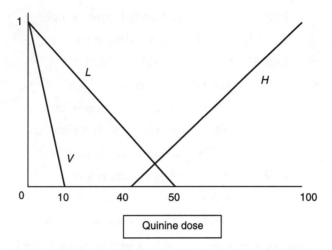

Figure 18.11

Membership functions for quinine dose values; V (very low), L (low), and H (high).

$$M_{QH}(x) = \begin{cases} 0 & \text{for } x \leq 40 \\ \dfrac{x-40}{60} & \text{for } x > 40 \end{cases}$$

Graphs for these three membership functions are shown in Figure 18.11.

18.9.2   Defining Fuzzy Rules

The second step in creating our fuzzy expert system is to define a set of fuzzy rules.

These rules, unlike those used by traditional expert systems, are expressed in vague English terms and do not define cut-off points or thresholds, but rather use subjective terms such as "high" and "low." This maps more naturally to the way an expert would express his or her knowledge and makes the process of converting that knowledge into rules far simpler and less prone to error.

Our rules are defined as follows:

Rule 1   IF   temperature is high
          AND   humidity is high
          AND   proximity to water is near
          AND   industrialization is low
          THEN   quinine dose is high

Rule 2:	IF	industrialization is high
	THEN	quinine dose is low
Rule 3:	IF	humidity is high
	AND	temperature is high
	AND	industrialization is low
	OR	proximity to water is near
	THEN	quinine dose is high
Rule 4:	IF	temperature is low
	AND	humidity is low
	THEN	quinine dose is very low

These rules may not be the best way to express this information, but they will suffice for this example.

18.9.3   Relating Observations to Fuzzy Sets

We are now ready to make use of our fuzzy expert system.

We will examine five sets of data, for five individuals, each of whom is traveling to a country that is at risk from malaria.

The crisp data are as follows:

temperature = {80, 40, 30, 90, 85}
humidity = {10, 90, 40, 80, 75}
proximity to water = {15, 45, 20, 5, 45}
industrialization = {90, 10, 15, 20, 10}

Hence, for example, person three is traveling to an area where the average temperature is 30, the humidity is 40, the distance to water is 20, and the level of industrialization is 25.

We must now convert these crisp values into fuzzy membership values. This can be done by simply applying the relevant fuzzy membership functions to each of the values. For example, let us look at some of the calculations for the first person:

Temperature = 80.

These membership functions were defined as:

$$M_{TH}(x) = \begin{cases} \dfrac{x-25}{75} & for \ x \geq 25 \\ 0 & for \ x < 25 \end{cases}$$

$$M_{TL}(x) = \begin{cases} 1 - \dfrac{x}{75} & for \ x \leq 75 \\ 0 & for \ x > 75 \end{cases}$$

So,

$M_{TH}(80) = (80 - 25) \ / \ 75 = 0.733$

$M_{TL}(80) = 0$

Similarly, we obtain the following membership function values:

$M_{HH}(10) = 10 \ / \ 100 = 0.1$

$M_{HL}(10) = 1 - (10 \ / \ 100) = 0.9$

$M_{PN}(15) = (40 - 15) \ / \ 30 = 0.833$

$M_{PF}(15) = (15 - 10) \ / \ 30 = 0.167$

$M_{IH}(90) = 1$

$M_{IL}(90) = 0$

In a similar fashion, we can obtain membership values for the other four travelers, which results in the following:

$M_{TH} = \{0.733, 0.2, 0.067, 0.867, 0.8\}$

$M_{TL} = \{0, 0.467, 0.6, 0, 0\}$

$M_{HH} = \{0.1, 0.9, 0.4, 0.8, 0.75\}$

$M_{HL} = \{0.9, 0.1, 0.6, 0.2, 0.25\}$

$M_{PN} = \{0.833, 0, 0.667, 1, 0\}$

$M_{PF} = \{0.167, 1, 0.333, 0, 1\}$

$M_{IH} = \{1, 0, 0.5, 1, 0\}$

$M_{IL} = \{0, 1, 0.5, 0, 1\}$

Note that for all of the fuzzy sets apart from temperature, the two possible values sum to 1 in every case. For example, for the third person, membership of "high humidity" is 0.4, and membership of "low humidity" is 0.6. This relationship does not always have to hold for fuzzy sets, and in this case it does not hold for temperature.

18.9.4   Evaluating Each Case for the Fuzzy Rules

We now have a set of fuzzy inputs that can be applied to the antecedents of the rules.

For example, let us examine traveler number 1. The values are as follows:

$$M_{TH} = 0.733$$
$$M_{TL} = 0$$
$$M_{HH} = 0.1$$
$$M_{HL} = 0.9$$
$$M_{PN} = 0.833$$
$$M_{PF} = 0.167$$
$$M_{IH} = 1$$
$$M_{IL} = 0$$

Rule 1, written with the appropriate fuzzy membership values for person 1, is as follows:

IF	temperature is high	(0.733)
AND	humidity is high	(0.1)
AND	proximity to water is near	(0.833)
AND	industrialization is low	(0)
THEN	quinine dose is high	(0)

Recall that to apply the fuzzy AND operator, we take the minimum value of the antecedents. In this case, therefore, the rule fires with value 0, which means it does not fire at all.

We will now apply the remaining rules in the same way:

Rule 2	IF	industrialization is high	(1)
	THEN	quinine dose is low	(1)

In this case, the rule fires with fuzzy strength of 1.

Rule 3	IF	humidity is high	(0.1)
	AND	temperature is high	(0.733)
	AND	industrialization is low	(0)
	OR	proximity to water is near	(0.833)
	THEN	quinine dose is high	(0.1)

Note that in this case, the rule has an OR clause. This is calculated by taking the maximum value of its arguments, which in this case is 0.833. Hence, the overall result of the rule is the minimum of 0.1, 0.733, and 0.833, which is 0.1.

Rule 4	IF	temperature is low	(0)
	AND	humidity is low	(0.9)
	THEN	quinine dose is very low	(0)

We can use this method for all of the five sets of input data and obtain results as follows:

Rule 1 (high dose): {0, 0, 0.067, 0, 0}

Rule 2 (low dose): {1, 0, 0.5, 1, 0}

Rule 3 (high dose): {0.1, 0.2, 0.067, 0.8, 0.75}

Rule 4 (very low dose): {0, 0.1, 0.6, 0, 0}

In this case, to combine Rules 1 and 3, which each give values for the "high dose" fuzzy set, we will take the maximum value, thus obtaining the following values for "high dose" from these two rules:

high dose: {0.1, 0.2, 0.067, 0.8, 0.75}

18.9.5 Defuzzification

We now need to defuzzify the outputs to obtain a crisp dosage recommendation for each traveler.

Let us examine this process for traveler 1:

Traveler 1 obtained the following three fuzzy outputs:

very low dose (V): 0

low dose (L): 1

high dose (H): 0.1

To defuzzify this output, we use the clipping operation described in Section 18.8. This clipping is shown graphically in Figure 18.12.

In this case, we clip the V set to value 0, which means it is effectively not used at all. We clip the L set to value 1, which means it is not clipped, and we clip the H set to value 0.1. The shaded area in Figure 18.12 is the combined result of the three fuzzy sets, and obtaining the centroid of this shaded shape will give us the crisp output value, which is the recommendation for dosage for this traveler.

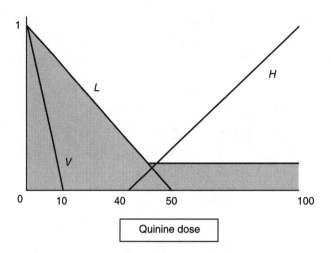

Figure 18.12

**Clipped fuzzy set for the
output for traveler 1**

Recall that we define the center of gravity as follows:

$$C = \frac{\sum M_A(x)x}{\sum M_A(x)}$$

We will sum over values of x, which increase in increments of 5. A more accurate result could be obtained using smaller increments, but for this example, increments of 5 will give sufficient accuracy.

Hence,

C = (0.9 × 5) + (0.8 × 10) + (0.7 × 15) + (0.6 × 20) + (0.5 × 25) + (0.4 × 30) +
(0.3 × 35) + (0.2 × 40) + (0.1 × 45) + (0.1 × 50) + (0.1 × 55) + (0.1 × 60) +
(0.1 × 65) + (0.1 × 70) + (0.1 × 75) + (0.1 × 80) + (0.1 × 85) + (0.1 × 90) +
(0.1 × 95) + (0.1 × 100)

0.9 + 0.8 + 0.7 + 0.6 + 0.5 + 0.4 + 0.3 + 0.2 + 0.1 + 0.1 + 0.1 + 0.1 + 0.1 + 0.1
+ 0.1 + 0.1 + 0.1 + 0.1 + 0.1

= 165 / 5.6

= 29.46

Thus, the recommended dose for traveler 1 is 29.46.

We will now defuzzify the results for traveler 3.

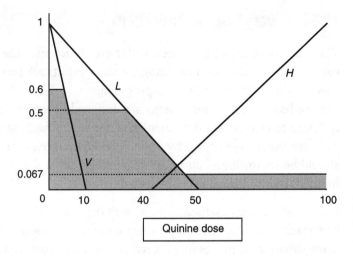

Figure 18.13

Clipped fuzzy set for the
output for traveler 3

Traveler 3 had the following results:

 very low dose (V): 0.6

 low dose (L): 0.5

 high dose (H): 0.067

Figure 18.13 shows the result of using these values to clip the three fuzzy
sets, H, L, and V.

The centroid of the shaded area shown in Figure 18.13 is calculated as follows:

C = (0.6 × 5) + (0.5 × 10) + (0.5 × 15) + (0.5 × 20) + (0.5 × 25) + (0.4 × 30) +
 (0.3 × 35) + (0.2 × 40) + (0.1 × 45) + (0.067 × 50) + (0.067 × 55) + (0.067 × 60) +
 (0.067 × 65) + (0.067 × 70) + (0.067 × 75) + (0.067 × 80) + (0.067 × 85) +
 (0.067 × 90) + (0.067 × 95) + (0.067 × 100)

0.6 + 0.5 + 0.5 + 0.5 + 0.5 + 0.4 + 0.3 + 0.2 + 0.1 + 0.067 + 0.067 + 0.067 + 0.067 + 0.067 +
0.067 + 0.067 + 0.067 + 0.067 + 0.067 + 0.067

= 128 / 4.3

= 29.58

Using this same method, dosages can also be calculated for the other four
travelers. This is left as an exercise for the reader.

18.10   Fuzzy Systems That Learn

The fuzzy systems we have seen so far are static: once the fuzzy sets and rules are set up, they do not change. As new inputs are presented to them, they do not learn from those inputs. This makes sense because the rules that we have given to the systems are designed by experts and, so, should not need to change. On the other hand, we have already said that the rules from the experts are subjective and vague. When one expert says that a dial should be set to "high," another expert might say it should be set to "very high," but mean the same crisp setting.

Fuzzy systems are designed to be able to cope with this kind of vagueness and inaccuracy, and tend to produce good results regardless. However, in some situations it makes more sense to allow the fuzzy system to adapt. In Chapter 11, we saw how neural networks use a system based on the neural structures in human brains to learn how to deal with new problems. These systems are able to adapt—to learn how to deal with situations that they have not previously encountered and, in extreme cases, are able to learn to survive when the environment in which they operate changes.

We will now look at how fuzzy logic can be used in combination with neural networks to produce fuzzy systems that are able to adapt and learn.

18.10.1   Neuro-fuzzy Systems

A **neuro-fuzzy system** is a neural network that learns to classify data using fuzzy rules and fuzzy classifications (fuzzy sets). A neuro-fuzzy system has advantages over fuzzy systems and traditional neural networks: A traditional neural network is often described as being like a "black box," in the sense that once it is trained, it is very hard to see why it gives a particular response to a set of inputs. This can be a disadvantage when neural networks are used in mission-critical tasks where it is important to know why a component fails.

Fuzzy systems and neuro-fuzzy systems do not have this disadvantage. Once a fuzzy system has been set up, it is very easy to see which rules fired and, thus, why it gave a particular answer to a set of inputs. Similarly, it is possible with a neuro-fuzzy system to see which rules have been developed by the system, and these rules can be examined by experts to ensure that they correctly address the problem.

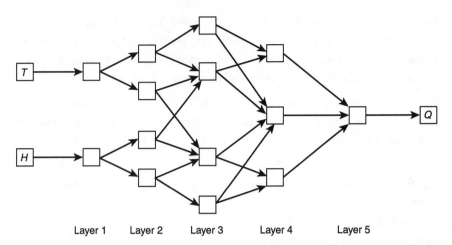

Figure 18.14
Typical layout of a five-layer neuro-fuzzy network

Typically, a fuzzy neural network is a five-layer feed-forward network. The five layers are as follows:

1. input layer—receives crisp inputs
2. fuzzy input membership functions
3. fuzzy rules
4. fuzzy output membership functions
5. output layer—outputs crisp values

Figure 18.14 shows the typical layout of such a network.

The network in Figure 18.14 has two crisp inputs, T and H, and produces one crisp output, Q. It has five layers, whose functions are as follows:

The first layer, the input layer, simply passes its crisp input values to the next layer in the network.

The second layer contains information about the various fuzzy sets that are being used to map the crisp inputs. In other words, it fuzzifies the inputs in the same way that we fuzzified our inputs in the examples in Section 18.9.3.

Typically, the neurons used in this second layer have triangular activation functions, which represent the triangular membership functions of the fuzzy sets, although any functions can be used.

The third layer represents the fuzzy rules of the system. Each neuron in this layer represents a single fuzzy rule.

Typically, the system would be set up with initial fuzzy rules built in, and the network would develop suitable weightings to give the best possible responses. In some cases, it is possible to start the system with no built-in rules, in which case the system learns its own rules and develops weights for them.

The fourth layer in the network contains the neurons that represent the membership functions of the various possible outputs of the fuzzy rules (in this case there are three possible outputs, and so three neurons in the fourth layer).

The fifth and final layer is the layer that combines and defuzzifies the various outputs to produce one single crisp output for the network in response to a given set of inputs. In this case, the network has just one final output, but it is possible to have a fuzzy neural network that produces a number of outputs.

The connections between the layers have weights associated with them, and using the methods such as back-propagation, which are described in Chapter 11, the system is able to learn.

Let us now examine in detail the behavior of each of the levels of neurons in the network to see how the entire network behaves.

We will use the network shown in Figure 18.14 to learn a simple version of the fuzzy rules used in Section 18.9.2 for prescribing quinine. We will use just two input variables: temperature (T) and humidity (H).

18.10.2   Layer 1: The Input Layer

This layer simply passes the input values it receives (T and H in our example) to each of the neurons in the second layer. In fact, in our example this layer is set up so that input T is passed to the top two neurons of Layer 2, and input H is passed to the bottom two neurons. This is because in this example each of the inputs has two possible values, which have different membership functions.

18.10.3   Layer 2: The Fuzzification Layer

The neurons in Layer 2 represent the fuzzy membership functions for the two inputs to the system. The top two neurons in this layer represent the membership functions for "high temperature" and "low temperature," whereas the bottom two represent "high humidity" and "low humidity." If the membership functions for "high humidity" and "high temperature" were the same, then these could be combined into one neuron.

Each neuron in this layer has an activation function (defined in Chapter 11) that is identical to the membership function it is representing. In this case, the activation functions will be the membership functions shown in Figures 18.7 and 18.8.

Hence, the output of each neuron (or the extent to which it fires) in this layer is determined by applying the appropriate membership function to its inputs.

18.10.4 Layer 3: The Fuzzy Rule Layer

The outputs of Layer 2 are the values that represent the extent to which each of the inputs belongs to each of the fuzzy sets "high humidity," "low humidity," "high temperature," and "low temperature."

The way in which this layer usually works is that the various input values are multiplied together to give the **fuzzy intersection** of the inputs. This single input is then used as the antecedent of the rule, which determines the extent to which the neuron fires.

The network in this example will be using rules such as these:

IF T_H THEN Q_H AND Q_L

IF T_H AND T_L AND H_H THEN Q_H AND Q_L

IF T_L AND H_H AND H_L THEN Q_L AND Q_V

IF H_L THEN Q_L AND Q_V

(These can be seen by examining the network shown in Figure 18.14 and assuming that the neurons in Layer 2 are ordered from the top—T_H, T_L, H_H, H_L—and that the neurons in Layer 4 are ordered from the top—Q_H, Q_L, Q_V).

These rules will also be modified by the weights of the network. In cases where the system is initially set up so that each rule uses each of the inputs, the weights adapt so that inputs that are not relevant to a given rule fade to zero.

18.10.5 Layer 4: The Output Membership Function Layer

Each neuron in Layer 4 represents the membership function of one of the fuzzy outputs of the rules in Layer 3. In our example, the neurons thus represent the membership functions for "high quinine dose," "low quinine dose," and "very low quinine dose." The activation functions for these neurons thus match the membership functions shown in Figure 18.11.

18.10.6   Layer 5: The Defuzzification Layer

Each output of the system has a neuron in the fifth layer. In our case, the system outputs just one value—the dose of quinine to prescribe to the traveler. The single node in Layer 5 takes inputs from each of the output nodes in Layer 4 and combines them together to form one crisp output. This is calculated, as explained in Section 18.8, by combining the clipped fuzzy membership sets and determining the centroid of the shape that this combined function describes. This centroid is the output value of the system.

18.10.7   How the System Learns

The neuro-fuzzy system learns using the same techniques used by traditional neural networks. Learning is done by adjusting the weights of the connections between neurons in the network.

For example, using back-propagation, a set of input training data is applied to the system and the outputs compared with the correct outputs. The error between the outputs and the correct outputs is then fed back through the network to adjust the weights to improve the network's performance with that set of training data. When this process is repeated, the network eventually converges on an optimal set of weights.

The system can start with a set of rules that are a "blank canvas"—where all nodes in one layer are connected to all nodes in the next layer. In this case, the system learns its own rules from the training data and eliminates unnecessary inputs and outputs from nodes by setting their weights to zero.

Alternatively, the system can be set up using input from an expert or experts. This information can be used to create suitable rules in much the same way as for a traditional fuzzy system, and the network will determine the optimal weights to use with those rules. Such systems are very robust and can usually detect rules that have been entered erroneously. For example, if one expert gave the following rule:

IF T_H and H_H then Q_H

and another expert gave the following rule:

IF T_H and H_H then Q_V

clearly, one of these experts is incorrect. The system would show this by setting all the weights for the wrong rule to zero because the training data would match the correct rule but would not match the incorrect rule (assuming the training data are correct).

18.11   Chapter Summary

- Bivalent logics are based on two truth values (true and false, usually).

- Multivalent logics allow a range of possible values.

- A linguistic variable is a word such as "height" that can be used to represent a variable that can take a number of possible fuzzy values.

- A fuzzy set is defined by its membership function.

- A number of fuzzy operators can be applied to fuzzy sets, including fuzzy intersection, fuzzy union, and fuzzy inverse.

- A hedge such as "very" or "extremely" can be applied to linguistic variables.

- Fuzzy logic defines how we reason about fuzzy variables.

- Fuzzy rules can be defined that tell a fuzzy system how to behave based on the value of certain fuzzy inputs.

- Fuzzy inference (such as Mamdani inference) allows a fuzzy system to convert crisp input values into fuzzy variables and then to reason about those variables, resulting in a single crisp output.

- Fuzzy expert systems have several advantages over traditional, nonfuzzy expert systems.

- Neuro-fuzzy systems are fuzzy systems that use techniques from neural networks in order to learn.

18.12   Review Questions

18.1   Explain the difference between bivalent and multivalent logics. Which type of logic are you more familiar with?

18.2   What is the law of the excluded middle? Argue against the need for this law.

18.3   What is a linguistic variable? Give 10 examples of linguistic variables that you might use to describe a building.

18.4   What are hedges? Give five hedges that apply to the linguistic variables you gave in answer to question 18.3.

18.5   How do fuzzy sets differ from traditional sets? What is the connection between linguistic variables and fuzzy sets?

18.6   What is the connection between fuzzy sets and fuzzy logic?

18.7   Explain carefully how fuzzy logic differs from traditional Aristotelian logic.

18.8   Explain how Mamdani inference works.

18.9   Explain what is meant by Defuzzification. How is it performed?

18.10   What advantages would fuzzy expert systems have over traditional expert systems. Would they have any disadvantages?

18.11   What is a neuro-fuzzy system? How does it learn? Compare and contrast neuro-fuzzy systems with traditional neural networks.

18.13   Exercises

18.1   Develop fuzzy rules to control a set of traffic lights at a four-way junction. Assume that there are sensors at each junction that determine how many cars are waiting and how long they have been waiting. The fuzzy rules should control the lights to minimize delay to all cars. Each junction has a traffic light that can be red (stop) or green (go). You can add additional lights to each junction to control traffic moving in different directions: in other words, you could allow traffic turning right to go, while traffic going straight or turning left is required to stop. You can allow more than one light to be green, as long as it cannot cause any accidents. Implement the fuzzy rules in a fuzzy system in the programming language of your choice.

18.2   Prove the following expressions using fuzzy logic:

$A \wedge B \to A$

$A \wedge B \to \neg A$

$A \wedge B \to A \vee B$

18.14   Further Reading

Kosko (1993) provides a nontechnical introduction to the subjects covered in this chapter. Of the main texts, Negnevitsky (2002) provides the greatest coverage of fuzzy logic and fuzzy systems, providing some excellent concrete examples of how fuzzy systems work and how fuzzy techniques can be combined with other Artificial Intelligence methods, such as neural networks and expert systems.

The Fuzzy Systems Handbook: A Practitioner's Guide to Building, Using, & Maintaining Fuzzy Systems, by Earl Cox (1999 – Morgan Kaufmann)

Fuzzy Logic for Business and Industry, by Earl Cox (2000 – Charles River Media)

An Introduction to Fuzzy Control, by Dimiter Driankov, Hans Hellendoorn, and M. Reinfrank (1996 – Springer Verlag)

Computational Intelligence: An Introduction, by Andries P. Engelbrecht (2003 – John Wiley & Sons)

Fuzzy Control: Synthesis and Analysis, edited by Shehu S. Farinwata, Dimitar P. Filev, and Reza Langari (2000 – John Wiley & Sons)

Fuzzy and Neural Approaches in Engineering, by J. Wesley Hines (1997 – Wiley Interscience)

Applications of Fuzzy Logic: Towards High Machine Intelligence Quotient Systems, edited by Mohammad Jamshidi, Andre Titli, Lotfi Zadeh, and Serge Boverie (1997 – Prentice Hall)

Neuro-Fuzzy and Soft Computing: A Computational Approach to Learning and Machine Intelligence, by Jyh-Shing Roger Jang, Chuen-Tsai Sun, and Eiji Mizutani (1996 – Prentice Hall)

Multistage Fuzzy Control: A Model-Based Approach to Fuzzy Control and Decision Making, by Janusz Kacprzyk (1997 – John Wiley & Sons)

Fuzzy Thinking: The New Science of Fuzzy Logic, by Bart Kosko (1994 – Hyperion)

Fuzzy Logic: The Revolutionary Computer Technology That Is Changing Our World, by Daniel Mcneill (1994 – Simon & Schuster)

Uncertain Rule-Based Fuzzy Logic Systems: Introduction and New Directions, by Jerry M. Mendel (2000 – Prentice Hall)

An Introduction to Fuzzy Sets: Analysis and Design, by Witold Pedrycz and Fernando Gomide (1998 – MIT Press)

The Importance of Being Fuzzy, by Arturo Sangalli (1998 – Princeton University Press)

CHAPTER 19

Intelligent Agents

An active line on a walk, moving freely without a goal. A walk for a walk's sake. The agent is a point that shifts position.

—Paul Klee, *Pedagogical Sketchbook*

My team had written a number of programs to control swarms of agents. These programs were modeled on behavior of bees. The programs had many useful characteristics. Because swarms were composed of many agents, the swarm could respond to the environment in a robust way. Faced with new and unexpected conditions, the swarm programs didn't crash; they just sort of flowed around the obstacles, and kept going.

—Michael Crichton, *Prey*

For I also am a man set under authority, having under me soldiers, and I say unto one, Go, and he goeth; and to another, Come, and he cometh; and to my servant, Do this, and he doeth it.

—The Gospel according to St Luke, Chapter 7, Verse 8

19.1 Introduction

An **agent** is an entity that is able to carry out some task, usually to help a human user. Agents can be biologic (people or animals, for example), robotic, or computational. This chapter is primarily concerned with the latter type, in particular with **software agents**. A software agent is a computer program designed to carry out some task on behalf of a user.

As we will see, there are a number of ways in which software agents can be built and a number of properties that they can have. One property with which we are particularly concerned is **intelligence**. We will discuss in more detail what is meant by intelligence, in the context of agents, in Section 19.2.1.

This chapter also introduces other important properties that agents may or may not have, including **autonomy**, **benevolence**, the ability to **collaborate** (with other agents, for example), and the ability to learn.

A number of architectures that can be used to build agents are discussed.

This chapter also introduces a number of types of agents, such as **reactive agents**, **interface agents**, **information agents**, and **multiagent systems**, which use a number of agents together to solve a single problem.

Finally, the chapter briefly introduces the ideas behind robotic agents and discusses a particular type of robot, known as a Braitenberg vehicle, which is used to discuss the nature of intelligence and our interpretation of behavior.

In many ways, the field of Artificial Intelligence as a whole can be seen as the study of methods that can be used to build intelligent agents. For example, the techniques discussed in Chapters 3 through 6 can be thought of as methods that intelligent agents can use to enable them to search or to play games. Each of the methods explained in this book can be used by an intelligent agent or to build intelligent agent systems.

19.2   Properties of Agents

19.2.1   Intelligence

An agent is a tool that carries out some task or tasks on behalf of a human. For example, a simple agent might be set up to buy a particular stock when its price fell below a particular level. A simple Internet search agent might be designed to send queries to a number of search engines and collate the results.

Intelligent agents have additional domain knowledge that enables them to carry out their tasks even when the parameters of the task change or when unexpected situations arise. For example, an intelligent agent might be designed to buy books for a user on the Internet at the lowest possible price. The agent would need to be able to interact with a set of online bookstores but would also need to be able to learn how to deal with new bookstores or with individuals who were offering secondhand books. These kinds of agents that perform tasks on behalf of people are called **interface agents**, which are discussed in Section 19.5.

Many intelligent agents are able to learn, from their own performance, from other agents, from the user, or from the environment in which they are situated. The ways in which agents can learn have been covered in some detail in Part 4 of this book, and the way in which some of these ideas can be applied by intelligent agents are introduced in Section 19.12.

19.2.2   Autonomy

In addition to intelligence, an important feature of many intelligent agents is **autonomy**—the ability to act and make decisions independently of the programmer or user of the agent. For example, an intelligent buying agent that is designed to buy goods on behalf of a user needs to be able to make decisions about what items to purchase without checking back with the user. This autonomy is what sets intelligent agents aside from many other Artificial Intelligence techniques.

19.2.3   Ability to Learn

Many agents have an ability to learn. In other words, when presented with new information, such an agent is able to store that new information in a useful form. For example, agents can learn from a user by observing actions or by being given instruction. We see how interface agents use these kinds of learning in Section 19.5. Agents can also learn from other agents in **multiagent systems**, which are described in Section 19.8.

Learning allows agents to improve their performance at carrying out a particular task over time. If a human user tells an agent that it has carried out a task poorly, it is useful for that agent to be able to learn from this experience to avoid making the same mistakes in the future.

19.2.4   Cooperation

In multiagent systems, agents usually **cooperate** with each other. This cooperation implies some form of **social interaction** between agents. For example, a buying agent may negotiate with selling agents to make purchases. As has been mentioned, agents can also learn from each other. To use the buying agent example again, a buying agent may be informed by another buying agent of a new shopping portal that the agent may find useful.

Of course, it is also useful for agents to cooperate with the humans who use them. Although in most agent systems, this cooperation is in the form of simple inputs and instructions, the manner in which agents cooperate with people can be very important, as we see in Section 19.5 when we discuss interface agents.

19.2.5   Other Agent Properties

Agents can have a number of other properties. A **versatile** agent is one that is able to carry out many different tasks. Most agents are **benevolent**, but some can be **competitive** or **nonhelpful**. Similarly, agents may be **altruistic** or **antagonistic**. Some agents can have the ability to lie to other agents, or to users, whereas other agents are always truthful (this property is known as **veracity**).

Other properties of agents include the extent to which they can be trusted with delegated tasks and whether or not they **degrade gracefully** (i.e., when the agent encounters a new problem that it is unable to solve, does it fail completely, or is it able to make some progress?).

An agent's **mobility** is defined by its ability to move about on the Internet or another network.

19.3   Agent Classifications

As has been discussed in Section 19.2, agents can be classified according to a number of parameters. We will now discuss a variety of types of agents that are classified according to these, and other, parameters.

The types of agents that we will look at are not mutually exclusive: an interface agent can be reactive or utility based. It can also be versatile or nonversatile.

The main classes of agents are defined as follows:

- reactive agents
- collaborative agents
- interface agents
- mobile agents
- information-gathering agents

We also look at the difference between reactive agents and goal-based and utility-based agents, which are defined by the ways in which they are motivated. Reactive agents simply respond to inputs they receive, whereas goal-based and utility-based agents have an ability to reason about their positions and make decisions on the basis of that reasoning.

Some agents are **hybrids,** which exhibit properties of more than one of the categories listed above. The eventual aim of most intelligent agent research is to develop **smart agents,** which would be fully autonomous and able to learn and cooperate with other agents. Smart agents do not yet exist and are not covered by this book.

19.4   Reactive Agents

A simple **reactive agent** (also known as a **reflex agent**) is a production system where inputs from the environment are compared with rules to determine which actions to carry out. In other words, reactive agents simply react to events in their environment according to predetermined rules.

A simple example of a reactive agent is the automatic mail filter that many e-mail systems now possess. This mail filter examines each e-mail as it arrives and compares it against a set of rules, or templates, and classifies it accordingly. A common use for such systems is to reject so-called "junk mail" or "spam." More complex systems are used to route e-mails within an organization, so that a consumer can send an e-mail to a central mail address, and the system will determine to which department within the company to send the mail, based on its contents.

In the case of the e-mail–filtering agent, the environment is simply an e-mail inbox and the contents of that inbox.

A reactive agent does not tend to perform well when its environment changes or when something happens that it has not been told about. For example, an e-mail–filtering system might have problems when it receives an e-mail that is entirely in Chinese. New rules can of course be written to deal with such situations, but it might be more desirable to have an agent that can learn to adapt to new situations.

A more complex reactive agent can be developed that combines inputs from its environment with information about the state of the world and information about how its actions affect the world.

Hence, a scheduling system might be based on the e-mail–filtering agent system, which assigns tasks to employees based on the content of e-mails as they arrive.

For example, when an e-mail arrives from a customer, reporting a bug in the company's software system, the agent might assign a task to the engineering department to fix the bug. The agent would then wait for further information from the engineering department. If it did not receive assurance that the bug had been fixed within a reasonable amount of time, it might contact the engineering department again. The agent's ability to do this derives from the fact that it is able to store information about the state of the world (such as "engineering department working to fix bug number 36,234,120") and about how its actions affect the state of the world (such as "when I send this e-mail to engineering, they will start to work on fixing the bug").

If a subsequent e-mail arrives from a different customer, reporting the same bug, the agent would not need to report the bug again because it knows that it has already reported it. Instead, it might reply to the customer saying something like

> *Thank you for your email—we are already aware of this problem, and our engineers are working to fix it now.*

19.4.1   Goal-based Agents

Goal-based agents are more complex than reactive agents. Rather than following a predetermined set of rules, a goal-based agent acts to try to achieve a goal. This is often done by using **search** (see Part 2) or **planning** (see Part 5).

A goal-based agent might, for example, be given the goal of finding pages on the Internet that are of interest to an Artificial Intelligence researcher. The agent will be designed so that it is capable of carrying out actions (such as loading a web page, examining it, and following links from one web page to another). It is also able to identify when it has reached a goal (for example, by matching the pages it finds against a set of keywords whose presence indicates relevance to Artificial Intelligence).

This goal based agent would search the Internet looking for pages that matched its criteria and would presumably report those pages to its owner or to a client. This kind of agent does not take into account how efficiently it is searching or how relevant the pages are that it is finding. In other words, its aim is simply to satisfy its goal; it does not take into account how *well* it has satisfied the goal or how *efficiently*. **Utility-based agents**, which are described in the next section, use these concepts to attempt to provide better results and in a more efficient manner.

19.4.2   Utility-based Agents

A **utility-based agent** is similar to a goal-based agent, but in addition to attempting to achieve a set of goals, the utility-based agent is also trying to maximize some **utility value**. The utility value can be thought of as the happiness of the agent, or how successful it is being. It may also take into account how much work the agent needs to do to achieve its goals.

Let us return to our example from the previous section of an agent that searches for pages on the Internet that are of interest to Artificial Intelligence researchers.

The utility-based agent can use knowledge about the Internet to follow the most worthwhile paths from one page to another. In other words, it can use heuristic-based search techniques to minimize the amount of time it spends examining pages that are not of interest and to maximize the likelihood that if an interesting page exists, it will be found (this combines search concepts from Chapters 4 and 5 with information retrieval techniques, which are discussed in Chapter 20).

The techniques we saw in Chapter 6 for game-playing systems can also be used as part of a utility-based agent. In this case, the agent's utility function is based on how successful it is at playing the game, and its goal is to maximize this utility function by winning the game.

19.4.3   Utility Functions

A utility function maps a set of states to the set of real numbers. In other words, given a particular state of the world, an agent is able to use its utility function to derive a score, or utility value, that tells it how "happy" it is in that state or how successful it has been if it reaches that state.

The static board evaluators that we saw in Chapter 6 are an example of a utility function that is used to evaluate a single position in a board game.

By searching through a tree of possible future states, based on available actions, and selecting a path that maximizes the utility function throughout the tree, a utility-based agent is able to achieve its goals effectively and efficiently.

For example, our Artificial Intelligence research agent might assign a high utility value to pages that are written in English and that appear to be written by a reliable source.

The idea of utility is closely related to the idea of **rationality**. An agent that behaves rationally is one that attempts to maximize its utility function. This utility function may not seem rational to all observers, although a rational agent might be programmed to lose at chess as spectacularly as possible. By losing a game, this agent maximizes its utility function and so, contrary to appearance, it is behaving rationally.

This model of utility is based on economics theory. One utility function for people is money. In general, people tend to prefer to have more money rather than less money. It is not as simple as this though. We might assume that the utility function for a human relating to money (ignoring other aspects of life) is simply based on the amount of money that that person had. This is contradicted by an experiment carried out in 1982 by psychologists, Tversky and Kahneman. In their experiment, they offered subjects two consecutive choices:

1. A or B:

    A = 80% chance of winning $4000

    B = 100% chance of winning $3000

2. C or D:

    C = 20% chance of winning $4000

    D = 25% chance of winning $3000

Most subjects choose A, rather than B; and C, rather than D. Let us consider the utility of these choices. In the choice between A and B, we have an 80% chance of winning $4000 or a 100% chance of winning $3000. The expected values of these two choices are

$$E(A) = 0.8 \times 4000 = 3200$$
$$E(B) = 1.0 \times 3000 = 3000$$

Hence, the most rational choice, using a simple utility function, would be to select A rather than B. For the choice between C and D, the expected values are

$$E(C) = 0.2 \times 4000 = 800$$
$$E(D) = 0.25 \times 3000 = 750$$

So in this choice, most people make the more rational decision on the basis of the simple utility function. What this experiment tells us is that people have much more complex utility functions than we might assume.

Similarly, utility-based intelligent agents usually need sophisticated utility functions. In the case of a chess playing agent, for example, a utility function based solely on the number of pieces each player has would not be sufficient. A utility function based on which player wins is fine, but as we saw in Chapter 6, this does not help the agent to play the game because the search tree is usually too large for the agent to reach a position where one player has won.

19.5   Interface Agents

An interface agent can be thought of as a personal assistant. Interface agents are typically autonomous agents, capable of learning in order to carry out tasks on behalf of a human user. Typically, interface agents collaborate with the user, but do not need to collaborate with other agents; although in some cases, interface agents can learn by seeking advice from other agents.

A typical example of an interface agent is a tool that is used to help a user learn to use a new software package. Such an agent has the ability to observe what the user does and make suggestions for better ways to perform those tasks. It is also able to assist the user in carrying out complex tasks, possibly learning as it does so. Interface agents can thus take instructions from users and can also learn from feedback from users about whether they are doing a good job or not, in order to perform better in future.

It is often useful for repetitive tasks to be delegated to an interface agent. The interface agent can learn how to carry out the task by observing the user and then is able to repeat the task as required.

Kozierok and Maes (1993) describe an interface agent that is able to assist a user with scheduling meetings on a calendar. The agent is able to arrange meetings with other people and is also able to accept, reject, and rearrange meetings on behalf of the user. By observing the user's behavior, it is able to learn, for example, that the user does not like to book meetings on Friday afternoons and so is able to avoid such meetings.

A number of tools exist that filter Usenet postings and new articles for a user. These tools can typically be trained by example: a user can show examples of interesting articles, and examples of uninteresting articles and the agent can learn to identify interesting articles and present those to the user, while avoiding uninteresting ones.

19.6   Mobile Agents

Mobile agents are those capable of "moving" from one place to another. In the case of mobile robots, this literally means moving in physical space. In the case of mobile software agents, this mobility usually refers to the Internet or other network. An agent that is not mobile is **static**.

Mobile agents travel from one computer to another, gathering information and performing actions as needed on the basis of that information. A computer virus can be thought of as a form of mobile agent, although most viruses are not intelligent, merely autonomous. That is, they are able to act without being given direct instruction from a human, but they do not adapt intelligently to their surroundings—they simply follow a fixed set of rules that tells them how to infect a computer and how to reproduce.

For mobile agents to run on remote computers, a suitable environment must of course be provided that allows the agent to run on that machine. An example of a system that provides such an environment is Telescript, developed by General Magic. The Java programming language, developed by Sun, can also be used for developing mobile agents.

The idea that a mobile agent can be sent from one computer across the Internet to run on another computer raises many security questions.

The main advantages of mobile agents are in efficiency. An agent that has to communicate with a number of remote servers and request large quantities of information in order to make a decision uses a large amount of bandwidth, which can be avoided if the agent is able to physically move to the remote server and query it locally.

Similarly, the mobile agent may be able to take advantage of superior computing power or the existence of particular functional abilities at the remote machine that are not present locally.

In this way, mobile agents can be used to generate a **distributed computing architecture**, where computation takes place on multiple computers at arbitrary locations.

A further advantage of mobile agents is that they can carry out their tasks asynchronously: the user can set a mobile agent off on a particular task and can then get on with other work, or maybe even switch the computer off. When the user is ready to receive the results, the agent can be recalled.

19.7   Information Agents

Information agents, also known as **information-gathering agents**, are usually used on the Internet and so are also sometimes called **Internet agents**. An information agent is used to help a user find, filter, and classify information from the vast array of sources available on the Internet.

Information agents may be static or mobile. Some information agents are capable of learning, whereas the behavior of others is fixed. Additionally, information agents can be collaborative or can work independently of other agents. The distinctive feature of an information agent is the function that it provides, rather than the way it works.

There is an overlap between information agents and other kinds of agents described in this chapter. The interface agents described in Section 19.5, which monitor Usenet postings or online news articles, are examples of information agents.

Information agents know how to search the Internet, usually using a number of search tools. In this way, they are able to cover as much content as possible and thus maximize their **recall** (see Chapter 20). The real challenge is usually **precision**. This is heavily dependent on the ability of the agent to receive input instructions from the user. Some agents learn by example: the user shows the agent examples of pages that are relevant and pages that are not relevant, and the system learns to differentiate the two groups. Other agents are directed by keywords or more sophisticated information retrieval techniques (see Chapter 20) to identify relevant material for the user.

The Internet provides some unique challenges to these agents. Internet data is very **dirty**: most of the information on the Internet is not organized in any way; much of it includes misspellings, incorrect grammar, and incorrect facts. Additionally, the Internet is global in nature, and so material is available in almost every language.

The sheer quantity of the data and the dirty nature of the data make it very difficult for many information agent systems to provide adequate precision in identifying relevant documents.

Of course, this is one of the reasons that information agents are so useful. It is even harder for humans to locate the data they want than it is for the agents. Agents have the advantage of speed and of being able to examine pages asynchronously, delivering results to a user, perhaps by e-mail, once they are available.

More sophisticated information agents are able to monitor the browsing habits of users to identify the kinds of material they are interested in and to use that information to improve the performance of future searches.

19.8   Multiagent Systems

In many situations, simple reactive agents are sufficient. The fact that they do not have the ability to learn means that they are not suited to operating in complex, dynamic environments. Also, because such an agent is based on a set of rules, the number of tasks and situations that it can deal with is limited by the number of rules it has. In fact, most agents do not exist in isolation.

Multiagent systems are a common way of exploiting the potential power of agents by combining many agents in one system. Each agent in a multiagent system has incomplete information and is incapable of solving the entire problem on its own, but combined together, the agents form a system that has sufficient information and ability to solve the problem. The system does not have a centralized control mechanism for solving the problem.

An example of how many simple agents can combine together to produce complex behavior can be seen by examining the way that ant colonies function. Each ant has very little intelligence and very little ability to learn. Taken as a whole, however, the ant colony is able to deal with complex situations and in some ways behaves as a single living entity.

In much the same way, many "dumb" agents can be combined together to produce a more intelligent system. For example, the legs of a robot might be controlled by a set of agents. Each leg is controlled by a simple reactive robot that has instructions for how to move the leg according to what the leg encounters.

Communication and **collaboration** are desirable properties of multiagent systems. Communication means, for example, that agents can inform each other of changes in the environment or of new discoveries they have made. Collaboration means that agents can work together to solve a common goal.

In fact, multiagent systems often involve relatively simple interactions between agents, and as we have seen with systems like Reynolds' Boids (Chapter 13), the system as a whole is able to solve complex problems without the individual agents necessarily knowing anything about the overall problem. Such emergent behavior is a valuable property of multiagent systems.

Multiagent systems can be given the ability to learn to solve new problems using genetic algorithms (see Chapter 14). In this way, robots have been successfully developed whose limbs are controlled by individual agents, each of which has been developed using a genetic algorithm. The robots are able to walk in a way that mimics the locomotion of insects (Gary Parker 1997, 1998).

Agents in a multiagent system can be collaborative or competitive. Agents designed to play chess against other agents would clearly be competitive, whereas agents that traverse the Internet searching for specific material may find it advantageous to cooperate with other similar agents.

An **agent team** is a group of agents that collaborate together to achieve some common goal. It is often the case that an agent team consists of agents that operate in different ways and have different goals to accomplish. For example, a team of agents might be used to arrange travel for a businessman: one agent might book flights, another agent arranges hotel accommodation, a third agent arranges meetings with business associates, while a fourth agent arranges meals and entertainments.

In some situations, these agents will be competing with other agents, bidding for purchases, but the agents within the team will cooperate with each other (e.g., the meal-booking agent will inform the meeting booking agent if it changes its restaurant bookings, which might affect a meeting that has been arranged in that restaurant).

19.9   Collaborative Agents

Collaborative agent systems are multiagent systems in which the agents collaborate with each other to accomplish goals. This property, of cooperating to achieve a common goal, is known as **benevolence**.

Collaborative agents typically do not have the ability to learn, although some have simple learning abilities. As with multiagent systems, the idea is that a combination of many simple agents can solve a problem that each agent individually would not be able to solve.

Collaborative agent systems are able to take advantage of their parallel nature in order to solve problems faster than would otherwise be possible. They are also more reliable than traditional systems because additional agents can be added to provide redundancy: if one agent fails, or provides incorrect information, this will not affect the overall performance of the system because other agents will provide corrective information.

19.10   Agent Architectures

In this section, we will look at a number of **architectures** that can be used to build intelligent agents. The architecture of an agent is the way in which its various processing modules are connected together and the way in which those modules are connected to the environment in which the agent operates.

19.10.1   Subsumption Architecture

There are a number of architectures suitable for reactive agents. One of the most commonly used is Brooks' **subsumption architecture** (Brooks 1985). The subsumption architecture is a layered architecture that was designed for implementing physical robots, which does not involve any centralized intelligence or control mechanism.

The agent in this architecture has a set of inputs, a possible set of actions, and a layered set of modules, each of which is designed to control some aspect of the agent's behavior. Each layer is able to inhibit the behavior of layers below it.

The modules are **augmented finite state machines** (AFSMs), which are similar to the finite state automata we saw in Chapter 13. AFSMs are often based on production rules, as used by expert systems, which take the form

```
input → action
```

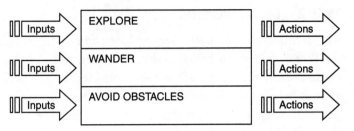

Figure 19.1
A three-layer subsumption architecture

These rules are called **situated action rules** or **situation action rules** because they map situations to actions. An agent that uses such rules is said to be **situated**, in that it is affected by where it is in its environment.

An AFSM is triggered when its inputs exceed a threshold. Each AFSM also has inhibitor inputs that can prevent it from triggering.

Rather than having a centralized representation, the subsumption architecture relies on lower-level modules that combine together. From these combined modules emerges intelligent behavior.

A simple subsumption architecture is shown in Figure 19.1.

This architecture was proposed by Brooks as a control mechanism for a robot. Each layer in the architecture is designed to handle one type of behavior: exploring, wandering, or avoiding obstacles. The modules act **asynchronously**, but each module can affect the behavior of the other modules.

The WANDER module will take into account the instructions generated by the AVOID OBSTACLES module, but it is also able to suppress the instructions generated by the AVOID OBSTACLES module, in order to ensure that while avoiding collisions, the robot still wanders around. This is to ensure that the robot does not simply focus on avoiding obstacles to the exclusion of everything else.

More important than wandering, for this robot, is exploration. Hence, the EXPLORE module is able to suppress instructions from the WANDER module to ensure that the robot continues to explore new territory, rather than simply wandering aimlessly.

Further layers can be added to the architecture to generate more sophisticated behavior—for example, Brooks describes a system that is able to wander around among desks in an office, looking for empty drink cans. This system has an architecture with additional layers for identifying drink cans, identifying desks, and so on (Brooks 1993).

19.10.2   BDI Architectures

BDI architectures, or **Belief Desire Intention** architectures, are based on the three concepts of belief, desire, and intention. A belief is a statement about the environment that the agent considers to be true. BDI agents have a set of beliefs that are similar to the set of facts contained in a rule-based production system. A desire is a goal state that the agent would like to reach, and the agent's intentions are the plans it has for how to behave in order to achieve its desires.

An agent can have an intention to carry out a particular action, in which case it will probably do so. Alternatively, an agent can have an intention to bring about a particular state.

When an agent **commits** to carrying out a particular action, or achieving a particular goal, it 'promises' that it will do so. Hence, a BDI agent has a set of beliefs that lead it to establish a set of desires. To achieve its desires, the BDI agent considers a number of **options** and commits to one or more of them. These options now become the agent's intentions.

Intentions persist until the goals are achieved, or until it becomes unreasonable to continue to attempt to achieve them (e.g., if it becomes obvious that the goals can never be achieved or if new beliefs are developed that lead the agent to change its desires).

A **bold** agent is one that establishes a set of intentions and then aims to carry them out without ever stopping to consider whether it should change its intentions. A **cautious** agent is one that considers its intentions continually. Kinny and Georgeff (1991) found that bold agents perform better than cautious agents in worlds where the environment does not change very frequently and that cautious agents perform better than bold agents in worlds that change quickly.

19.10.3   Other Architectures

A number of other agent architectures exist. Logic-based agents apply rules of logical deduction to a **symbolic representation** of their environment. The state of such an agent is usually represented using first-order predicates, and its behavior is determined by a set of deduction rules, usually expressed in first-order predicate logic.

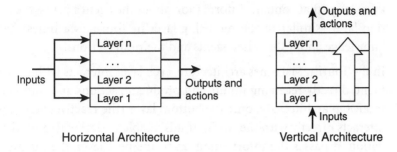

Figure 19.2
**Horizontal and vertical
agent architectures
compared**

In contrast to logic-based architectures, purely reactive agents do not perform any symbol manipulation and rely on a simple mapping from inputs to actions.

A number of layered architectures exist other than the subsumption architecture. The subsumption architecture is an example of a **horizontal layered architecture**, where each layer receives inputs and contributes to the actions and outputs of the agent. In a **vertical layered architecture**, input is passed to one layer, which then passes information on to a further layer. Actions and outputs are eventually produced by the final layer. These two architecture types are illustrated in Figure 19.2.

TouringMachines is an example of a horizontal architecture, which is based on three layers:

- *Reactive layer:* This layer uses situation rules to react to changes in the agent's environment.

- *Planning layer:* This layer uses a library of plans (called **schemas**) to determine the behavior of the agent, in order to achieve particular goals. In most situations, this is the layer that decides the main behavior of the agent.

- *Modeling layer:* This layer contains a model of the agent and any other agents in the world, in order to avoid conflicts with other agents.

InteRRaP is an example of a vertical layered architecture, which has three layers with very similar functions to the layers of the TouringMachines architecture. Each layer in the InteRRap architecture has a database of relevant knowledge: the reactive layer has a database of knowledge about the world the agent inhabits; the planning layer has a database of planning knowledge that contains information about the agent's plans; the cooperation layer (similar to the modeling layer in TouringMachines) has social knowledge about the other agents and their interactions.

In the TouringMachines architecture, each layer interacts with the environment, directly receiving inputs and producing actions and outputs. In the InteRRap architecture, only the bottom layer (the reactive, behavior layer) interacts directly with the world. If it is unable to deal with a particular situation, it passes the information on to the next layer, the planning layer. Similarly, if this layer cannot deal with the current situation, it passes the information on to the final layer, the cooperation layer. Outputs are passed back to the behavior layer, which turns them into actions or outputs.

19.11   Accessibility

When playing a game such as chess, each player knows what position he will be in after making any given move. What he does not usually know is what move his opponent will make and, thus, what position he will reach after his opponent's move.

In some cases an agent's state after carrying out a particular action can be deterministically predicted. In many situations, however, this is not the case, and the outcome is unpredictable, or **stochastic**. Given that an agent usually has a certain degree of knowledge about the world and the way its actions affect its state, we can make certain predictions. For example, an agent can say that if it is in state S_1 and it takes action A, then it will move into state S_2 with probability p. These probabilities are contained within a **transition model**, which enables the agent to make predictions about what effect its actions will have on it and its environment.

If an agent is able to determine all relevant facts about the environment in which it operates, then that environment is described as being **accessible**. If it is **inaccessible**, then certain facts are hidden from the agent, although it may be able to deduce them by maintaining internal information about the state of the environment. For example, if an agent is in an environment in which it is unable to determine the temperature, it may have a rule that says "if you turn up the heating, the temperature will increase."

We could consider two types of agents that play chess. One agent might have the ability to examine the board at each move of the game and make decisions about what move to make from that point. The agent does not have the ability to remember moves that have been made in the past, and thus the only way it can determine the current position is by examining the board.

This agent acts in an accessible environment because, at any given point, it has access to all the information it needs to be able to play the game. If we imagine that this agent is playing a game where half of the board is covered up, and it is unable to see what happens there, then we can see that the agent would have great difficulties because it would have no way of determining what was happening on that side of the board apart from a few limited facts it could deduce, such as "my king is on this side of the board, so I know I do not have a king on the other side of the board."

A different type of agent might play the game without any direct access to the board at all. This agent stores information about the moves that have been made in the past and is able to use this information to determine the current position of the board. This agent would play equally well whether the board were entirely visible or entirely covered up.

This agent operates in an inaccessible environment, but, in fact, because the environment it operates in is entirely deterministic, it is able to derive complete knowledge about the board at all times.

An agent that played a game such as poker would need to be able to act in an inaccessible, stochastic environment because the cards the opponent has are neither visible nor deterministically allocated.

In an accessible, stochastic environment, agents use **Markov decision processes** (MDPs) to determine the best course of action. In an inaccessible, stochastic environment, agents use **partially observable Markov decision processes** (POMDPs). Clearly, POMDPs must operate with far less information and so tend to be more complex than MDPs.

19.12   Learning Agents

Machine learning is covered in more detail in Part 4 of this book. An agent that is capable of **learning** (a **learning agent**) is able to acquire new knowledge and skills and is able to use the new knowledge and skills to improve its performance.

One common way to provide agents with the ability to learn is to use neural networks, which are covered in more detail in Chapter 11. A neural network is designed to learn in a similar manner to the way a human brain learns. Another method for enabling agents to learn is to use genetic algorithms. One way to use genetic algorithms in this way is to have the genetic algorithm breed populations of agents, with the aim of breeding a highly successful agent. Another way is to have each agent use a genetic algorithm to develop suitable strategies for dealing with particular problems.

19.12.1   Multiagent Learning

Multiagent systems are often required to solve problems in dynamic and unpredictable environments. In these circumstances, a learning ability is particularly important because the environment can change too quickly for predetermined behaviors to be effective.

Multiagent learning can in many ways be more impressive than the learning carried out by individual agents. Each agent in a learning multiagent system can learn independently of the other agents and can also learn from the other agents.

In this way, the agents can explore multiple potential strategies in parallel, and when one agent discovers a particularly effective strategy, it can pass this knowledge on to other agents. For this reason, when the environment changes, multiagent learning systems are able to adapt much more quickly than nonlearning systems, or even individual learning agents.

In **centralized learning**, the agents learn on an individual and distinct basis, whereas in **decentralized learning**, the actions of the individual agents lead to the whole system learning. The classifier systems described in Chapter 13 are an example of a decentralized multiagent learning system, where each rule can be thought of as a separate agent, and where the whole system learns by experience how best to solve a problem.

19.13   Robotic Agents

The agents described in this chapter so far have been software agents—they exist only in a virtual world. **Robotic agents**, or **robots**, are artificial agents that exist physically in the real world.

Mobile robotic agents controlled by Brooks' subsumption architecture have been briefly described in Section 19.10.1.

Robotic agents operate in an inaccessible, stochastic environment. The real world has many properties that make the tasks of robotic agents much harder than those of many software agents. An ability to deal with **uncertainty** is clearly important, as is robustness in the face of extremely unpredictable and potentially dangerous environments.

Robots have been designed that build cars, using robotic arms and conveyer belts.

More sophisticated are the robots that are designed to explore other planets and collect samples for scientific analysis. Such robots, of course, require autonomy: they cannot be controlled directly by human input because they would be too far away from the earth. One important aspect of such robots is their ability to walk: this involves not just knowing how to move legs in such a way as to move forward, but also how to navigate over hills and rocks, around pot-holes and through valleys. Agents such as Atilla and Genghis, designed by the MIT Mobot Lab (Mobot means "mobile robot"), have these abilities and are modeled on insects.

Genghis has six legs and a number of sensors that enable it to determine certain facts about its inaccessible environment. The interesting thing about Genghis is that nobody ever told it how to walk or steer around obstacles. Its brain consists of 57 augmented finite state machines, each of which is responsible for a simple piece of behavior, such as lifting a leg or wandering. Using these AFSMs and feedback from its sensors, Genghis was able to learn to walk from the experience of trying and failing to do so.

19.14   Braitenberg Vehicles

Braitenberg vehicles were invented by a neuroscientist, Valentino Braitenberg, in the 1980s. Braitenberg vehicles are imaginary robots used by Braitenberg in thought experiments on the nature of intelligence. There are 14 different classes of vehicles, ranging from extremely simple to fairly complex. We will consider just the six simplest types.

Even the simplest of his vehicles can exhibit interesting behaviors and tell us a great deal about our assumptions concerning intelligence and thought.

The simplest type of Braitenberg vehicle, known as vehicle 1, simply has one motor and a sensor. The sensor is wired directly to the motor, such that the more of whatever the sensor is designed to sense there is, the faster the motor turns. For example, if the sensor were a light sensor, then the motor would turn faster when the sensor could detect more light.

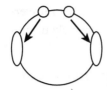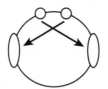

Figure 19.3

Two varieties of Braitenberg vehicles type 2, seen from above

The behavior of this vehicle is very simple: the more light there is, the faster it moves. It would normally move in a straight line, although imperfections in its environment (such as friction and obstacles) might cause it to deviate.

The second type of Braitenberg vehicle has two sensors and two motors. The motors and sensors are placed symmetrically around the vehicle, as shown in Figure 19.3.

In the first vehicle shown in Figure 19.3, the left-hand sensor (the sensors are on the front of the vehicle) is connected to the left-hand motor, and the right-hand sensor to the right-hand motor. In the second vehicle shown, the sensors and motors are connected the other way around. The first vehicle will tend to move away from the source that its sensors detect, whereas the second vehicle will move toward it.

These vehicles can be thought of as **timid** (the one that moves away from the source) and **bold** (the one that moves toward the source).

Let us now consider a type of the timid vehicle, which has a sensor for proximity and where its motors have a built-in tendency to move even without any stimulation to the sensors. When placed in a simple maze, this vehicle will navigate through the maze without bumping into the walls. Clearly, apparently complex behavior can emerge from very simple concepts. This timid vehicle was certainly not designed to traverse a maze, and it does not have any knowledge of mazes or the world. An observer who did not know how the vehicle worked might conclude that it relied on a very sophisticated form of Artificial Intelligence.

It is interesting to note at this point some of the words that we have been using to describe agents: *timid, bold, cautious,* and so on. There is a tendency to anthropomorphize the behaviors of agents, which is at least partly due to the impression that agents can give of having almost human-like intelligence.

The third type of vehicle is similar to the second type except that the sensors are wired in such a way that they inhibit the motors: the more stimulation they receive, the slower the motors turn. These types of vehicles will tend to move toward a source of stimulation but will end up near the source, either facing it or turned away from it, depending on which way its sensors are wired to the motors.

Braitenberg vehicles can have more than one type of sensor—for example, a vehicle might have light sensors and proximity detectors for objects. These sensors can be connected to motors in different ways, producing more and more complex behaviors.

The fourth type of Braitenberg vehicle has a nonlinear relationship between input to the sensors and the speed of the motors. For example, one of these vehicles might move slowly toward a light source and speed up as it gets closer, then slow down again as it gets very close to the source.

The fifth type of vehicle has a primitive memory that can be used to store information about events that happened in the past.

The sixth type of Braitenberg vehicle is evolved using artificial evolution, as described in Chapters 13 and 14.

Braitenberg vehicles teach us the following principle, which Braitenberg called the principle of "Uphill Analysis and Downhill Invention": It is easier to invent something than to analyze it. Fully functioning Braitenberg vehicles can be built using easily available components, and yet their behavior can be extremely complex and, in some cases, impossible to analyze or explain.

19.15 Chapter Summary

- An agent is an entity that carries out a task on behalf of a human user.

- A software agent is an agent that exists solely as a computer program.

- Intelligent agents have more knowledge or understanding of their environment than simple agents and are able to use this intelligence to carry out their tasks more effectively.

- Autonomous agents are able to carry out their tasks without direct input from a human.

- Some agents are able to learn from their user, from other agents, from the environment, or by observing the consequences of their own actions.

- Reactive agents simply react to the environment they are in, using situated action rules, which provide an action for each situation.

- Goal-based agents seek to achieve some goal, whereas utility-based agents seek to maximize some utility function.

- Interface agents are automated personal assistants.

- Mobile agents are able to travel over a network, such as the Internet.

- An information agent collects information (often from the Internet) on behalf of its owner.

- Multiagent systems use a number of agents that usually collaborate together to achieve some common goal.

- The subsumption architecture is an example of a vertically layered architecture for controlling robots.

- BDI architectures use beliefs, desires, and intentions to control agents.

- An accessible environment is one in which all necessary facts are available to the agent. Many agents must be able to operate in inaccessible environments and often in stochastic ones, where the changes in the environment are unpredictable.

- Robotic agents operate in the real world.

19.16   Review Questions

19.1 "A computer virus is a kind of intelligent agent." Discuss this statement. Consider the various agent properties that have been discussed in this chapter. Which of these properties do computer viruses have?

19.2 Explain what is meant by the following terms in the context of agents:

- intelligence
- autonomy
- learning
- collaboration
- utility

19.3 Explain the idea behind the BDI architecture. Why do you think this architecture is particularly appealing to human researchers?

19.4   Explain the nature of the first six types of Braitenberg vehicles. Discuss how these vehicles can help us to understand the nature of intelligence.

19.5   Think of a real-world interface agent. Discuss to what extent this agent has autonomy, learning abilities, and intelligence.

19.6   What do Braitenberg vehicles teach us about intelligence? Do you think the intelligence given to Braitenberg vehicles could be put to some practical use?

19.7   In Michael Crichton's novel, *Prey*, he postulates a multiagent system consisting of millions of tiny robotic agents. The system evolves over a period of days to develop human-like intelligence, and a belligerent desire to destroy life. Discuss how plausible you think this idea is, in the context of the subjects introduced in this chapter.

19.17   Exercises

19.1   Implement an intelligent agent system to carry out a simple task for you in the programming language of your choice.

19.2   Investigate a software agent that comes with your computer, or find one that you can download for free. Explore its limitations and its capabilities. To what extent would you describe it as "intelligent"? What simple improvements would you suggest for the agent? Which of the following properties does the agent exhibit:

- intelligence
- autonomy
- ability to learn
- cooperation
- benevolence
- veracity

To what extent would it still be useful if it did not have the properties that it does have? Which of the above properties might be given to the agent to improve it? How would it be improved?

19.18   Further Reading

Several texts cover the subject of Artificial Intelligence from the perspective of Artificial Agents—in particular, Russell and Norvig (1995) and Pfeifer and Scheier (1999). Weiss (1999) provides an excellent exploration of multiagent systems.

Brooks' subsumption architecture was introduced in *A Robust Layered Control System For a Mobile Robot* (from *IEEE Journal of Robotics and Automation, RA-2, April,* pp. 14–23), and was also published as *MIT AI Memo 864* (1985).

Braitenberg (1986) provides a fascinating description of his vehicles, as well as providing an absorbing philosophical argument. A good practical explanation of Braitenberg's vehicles is also found in Pfeifer and Scheier (2000)

Behavior-Based Robotics, by Ronald C. Arkin (1998 – MIT Press)

Software Agents, edited by Jeffrey M. Bradshaw (1997 – AAAI Press)

Vehicles: Experiments in Synthetic Psychology, by Valentino Braitenberg (1986 – MIT Press)

Intelligent Agents for Mobile and Virtual Media, edited by Rae Earnshaw, John Vince, and Margaret A. Arden (2002 – Springer Verlag)

Commitment and Effectiveness of Situated Agents, by D. Kinny and M. Georgeff (1991 – in *Proceedings of the Twelfth International Joint Conference on Artificial Intelligence,* pp. 82–88)

Braitenberg Creatures, by David W. Hogg, Fred Martin, and Mitchel Resnick (1991 – originally published as *Epistemology and Learning Memo #13*)

A Learning Interface Agent for Scheduling Meetings, by R. Kozierok and P. Maes (1993 – in *Proceedings of the ACM-SIGCHI International Workshop on Intelligent User Interfaces*)

Evolutionary Robotics: The Biology, Intelligence, and Technology of Self-Organizing Machines, by Stefano Nolfi and Dario Floreano (2000 – MIT Press)

Evolving Hexapod Gaits Using a Cyclic Genetic Algorithm, by Gary Parker (1997 – in *Proceedings of the IASTED International Conference on Artificial Intelligence and Soft Computing,* pp. 141–144)

Generating Arachnid Robot Gaits with Cyclic Genetic Algorithms, by Gary Parker (1998 - in Genetic Programming III, pp. 576–583)

Metachronal Wave Gait Generation for Hexapod Robots, by Gary Parker (1998 – in *Proceedings of the Seventh International Symposium on Robotics with Applications*)

Understanding Intelligence, by Rolf Pfeifer and Christian Scheier (2000 – MIT Press)

Layered Learning in Multiagent Systems: A Winning Approach to Robotic Soccer, by Peter Stone (2000 – MIT Press)

Multiagent Systems: A Modern Approach to Distributed Artificial Intelligence, edited by Gerhard Weiss (1999 – MIT Press)

Introduction to MultiAgent Systems, by Michael Wooldridge (2002 – John Wiley & Sons)

Strategic Negotiation in Multiagent Environments, by Sarit Kraus (2001 – MIT Press)

Intelligent Information Agents: The Agentlink Perspective (Lecture Notes in Computer Science, 2586), edited by Matthias Klusch, Sonia Bergamaschi, and Pete Edwards (2003 – Springer Verlag)

An Introduction to AI Robotics, by Robin R. Murphy (2000 – MIT Press)

Real-Time and Multi-Agent Systems, by Ammar Attoui (2000 – Springer Verlag)

Understanding Agent Systems, edited by Mark D'Inverno and Michael Luck (2001 – Springer Verlag)

Agent Technology: Foundations, Applications, and Markets, edited by Nicholas R. Jennings and Michael J. Wooldridge (1998 – Springer Verlag)

Socially Intelligent Agents - Creating Relationships with Computers and Robots, edited by Kerstin Dautenhahn, Alan H. Bond, Lola Canamero, and Bruce Edmonds (2002 – Kluwer Academic Publishers)

CHAPTER 20

Understanding Language

Philosophy is a battle against the bewitchment of our intelligence by means of language.

—Ludwig Wittgenstein, *Philosophische Untersuchungen*

Language is a form of human reason, and has its reasons which are unknown to man.

—Claude Lévi-Strauss, *La Pensée Sauvage*

I linger yet with nature, for the night
Hath been to me a more familiar face
Than that of man; and in her starry shade
Of dim and solitary loveliness
I learned the language of another world.

—Lord Byron, *Manfred*

20.1   Introduction

This chapter explores several techniques that are used to enable humans to interact with computers via natural **human languages**.

Natural languages are the languages used by humans for communication (among other functions). They are distinctly different from **formal languages**, such as C++, Java, and PROLOG. One of the main differences, which we will examine in some detail in this chapter, is that natural languages are **ambiguous**, meaning that a given sentence can have more than one possible meaning, and in some cases the correct meaning can be very hard to determine. Formal languages are almost always designed to ensure that ambiguity cannot occur. Hence, a given program written in C++ can have only one interpretation. This is clearly desirable because otherwise the computer would have to make an arbitrary decision as to which interpretation to work with.

It is becoming increasingly important for computers to be able to understand natural languages. Telephone systems are now widespread that are able to understand a narrow range of commands and questions to assist callers to large call centers, without needing to use human resources.

Additionally, the quantity of unstructured textual data that exists in the world (and in particular, on the Internet) has reached unmanageable proportions. For humans to search through these data using traditional techniques such as Boolean queries or the database query language SQL is impractical. The idea that people should be able to pose questions in their own language, or something similar to it, is an increasingly popular one.

Of course, English is not the only natural language. A great deal of research in natural language processing and information retrieval is carried out in English, but many human languages differ enormously from English. Languages such as Chinese, Finnish, and Navajo have almost nothing in common with English (although of course Finnish uses the same alphabet). Hence, a system that can work with one human language cannot necessarily deal with any other human language.

In this section we will explore two main topics. First, we will examine natural language processing, which is a collection of techniques used to enable computers to "understand" human language. In general, they are concerned with extracting grammatical information as well as meaning from human utterances but they are also concerned with understanding those utterances, and performing useful tasks as a result.

Two of the earliest goals of natural language processing were automated translation (which is explored in this chapter) and database access. The idea here was that if a user wanted to find some information from a database, it would make much more sense if he or she could query the database in her language, rather than needing to learn a new formal language such as SQL.

Information retrieval is a collection of techniques used to try to match a query (or a command) to a set of documents from an existing **corpus** of documents. Systems such as the search engines that we use to find data on the Internet use information retrieval (albeit of a fairly simple nature).

20.2 Natural Language Processing

In dealing with natural language, a computer system needs to be able to process and manipulate language at a number of levels.

1. *Phonology.* This is needed only if the computer is required to understand spoken language. Phonology is the study of the sounds that make up words and is used to identify words from sounds. We will explore this in a little more detail later, when we look at the ways in which computers can understand speech.

2. *Morphology.* This is the first stage of analysis that is applied to words, once they have been identified from speech, or input into the system. Morphology looks at the ways in which words break down into components and how that affects their grammatical status. For example, the letter "s" on the end of a word can often either indicate that it is a plural noun or a third-person present-tense verb.

3. *Syntax.* This stage involves applying the rules of the grammar from the language being used. Syntax determines the role of each word in a sentence and, thus, enables a computer system to convert sentences into a structure that can be more easily manipulated.

4. *Semantics.* This involves the examination of the meaning of words and sentences. As we will see, it is possible for a sentence to be syntactically correct but to be semantically meaningless. Conversely, it is desirable that a computer system be able to understand sentences with incorrect syntax but that still convey useful information semantically.

5. *Pragmatics.* This is the application of human-like understanding to sentences and discourse to determine meanings that are not immediately clear from the semantics. For example, if someone says, "Can you tell me the time?", most people know that "yes" is not a suitable answer. Pragmatics enables a computer system to give a sensible answer to questions like this.

In addition to these levels of analysis, natural language processing systems must apply some kind of world knowledge. In most real-world systems, this world knowledge is limited to a specific domain (e.g., a system might have detailed knowledge about the Blocks World and be able to answer questions about this world). The ultimate goal of natural language processing would be to have a system with enough world knowledge to be able to engage a human in discussion on any subject. This goal is still a long way off.

We will now look at the individual stages of analysis that are involved in natural language processing.

20.2.1   Morphological Analysis

In studying the English language, morphology is relatively simple. We have endings such as *-ing, -s,* and *-ed,* which are applied to verbs; endings such as *-s* and *-es,* which are applied to nouns; we also have the ending *-ly,* which usually indicates that a word is an adverb. We also have prefixes such as *anti-, non-, un-,* and *in-,* which tend to indicate negation, or opposition. We also have a number of other prefixes and suffixes that provide a variety of semantic and syntactic information.

In practice, however, morphologic analysis for the English language is not terribly complex, particularly when compared with agglutinative languages such as German, which tend to combine words together into single words to indicate combinations of meaning.

Morphologic analysis is mainly useful in natural language processing for identifying parts of speech (nouns, verbs, etc.) and for identifying which words belong together. In English, word order tends to provide more of this information than morphology, however. In languages such as Latin, word order was almost entirely superficial, and the morphology was extremely important. Languages such as French, Italian, and Spanish lie somewhere between these two extremes.

As we will see in the following sections, being able to identify the part of speech for each word is essential to understanding a sentence. This can partly be achieved by simply looking up each word in a dictionary, which might contain for example the following entries:

> (swims, verb, present, singular, third person)
>
> (swimmer, noun, singular)
>
> (swim, verb, present, singular, first and second persons)

(swim, verb, present plural, first, second, and third persons)

(swimming, participle)

(swimmingly, adverb)

(swam, verb, past)

Clearly, a complete dictionary of this kind would be unfeasibly large. A more practical approach is to include information about standard endings, such as:

(*-ly*, adverb)

(*-ed*, verb, past)

(*-s*, noun, plural)

This works fine for regular verbs, such as *walk*, but for all natural languages (except Esperanto, the human-invented language) there are large numbers of irregular verbs, which do not follow these rules. Verbs such as *to be* and *to do* are particularly difficult in English as they do not seem to follow any morphologic rules.

The most sensible approach to morphologic analysis is thus to include a set of rules that work for most regular words and then a list of irregular words. For a system that was designed to converse on any subject, this second list would be extremely long. Most natural language systems currently are designed to discuss fairly limited domains and so do not need to include over-large look-up tables.

In most natural languages, as well as the problem posed by the fact that word order tends to have more importance than morphology, there is also the difficulty of ambiguity at a word level. This kind of ambiguity can be seen in particular in words such as *trains*, which could be a plural noun or a singular verb, and *set*, which can be a noun, verb, or adjective. We will see later how parsers are designed to overcome these difficulties.

20.2.2   BNF

In Section 20.2.4, we look at the methods that are available for **parsing** a piece of text. Parsing involves mapping a linear piece of text onto a hierarchy that represents the way the various words interact with each other syntactically.

First, we will look at **grammars**, which are used to represent the rules that define how a specific language is built up.

Most natural languages are made up of a number of parts of speech, mainly the following:

- verb
- noun
- adjective
- adverb
- conjunction
- pronoun
- article

In fact it is useful when parsing to combine words together to form syntactic groups. Hence, the words, *a dog*, which consist of an article and a noun, can also be described as a **noun phrase**. A noun phrase is one or more words that combine together to represent an object or thing (material or otherwise) that can be described by a noun. Hence, the following are valid noun phrases:

- *Christmas*
- *the dog*
- *that packet of chips*
- *the boy who had measles last year and nearly died*
- *my favorite color*

Note that a noun phrase is not a sentence—it is part of a sentence.

Similarly, we have **verb phrases**. A verb phrase is one or more words that represent an action. The following are valid verb phrases:

- *swim*
- *eat that packet of chips*
- *walking*

A simple way to describe a sentence is to say that it consists of a noun phrase and a verb phrase. Hence, for example:

> *That dog is eating my packet of chips.*

In this sentence, *that dog* is a noun phrase, and *is eating my packet of chips* is a verb phrase. Note that the verb phrase is in fact made up of a verb phrase, *is eating*, and a noun phrase, *my packet of chips*. In the next section, we will explore this idea in more detail and see how it enables us to build a parse tree to identify the syntactic structure of a sentence.

A language is defined partly by its grammar. The rules of grammar for a language such as English can be written out in full, although it would be a complex process to do so. To allow a natural language processing system to parse sentences, it needs to have knowledge of the rules that describe how a valid sentence can be constructed.

These rules are often written in what is known as **Backus–Naur form** (also known as Backus normal form—both names are abbreviated as BNF).

BNF is widely used by computer scientists to define formal languages such as C++ and Java. We can also use it to define the grammar of a natural language.

A grammar specified in BNF consists of the following components:

1. **Terminal symbols.** Each terminal symbol is a symbol or word that appears in the language itself. In English, for example, the terminal symbols are our dictionary words such as *the, cat, dog*, and so on. In formal languages, the terminal symbols include variable names such as *x, y*, and so on, but for our purposes we will consider the terminal symbols to be the words in the language.

2. **Nonterminal symbols.** These are the symbols such as *noun, verb phrase*, and *conjunction* that are used to define words and phrases of the language. A nonterminal symbol is so-named because it is used to represent one or more terminal symbols.

3. **The start symbol.** The start symbol is used to represent a complete sentence in the language. In our case, the start symbol is simply *sentence*, but in first-order predicate logic, for example, the start symbol would be *expression*.

4. **Rewrite rules.** The rewrite rules define the structure of the grammar. Each rewrite rule details what symbols (terminal or nonterminal) can be used to make up each nonterminal symbol.

Let us now look at rewrite rules in more detail.

We saw above that a sentence could take the following form:

noun phrase verb phrase

We thus write the following rewrite rule:

Sentence → NounPhrase VerbPhrase

This does not mean that every sentence must be of this form, but simply that a string of symbols that takes on the form of the right-hand side can be **rewritten** in the form of the left-hand side. Hence, if we see the words

The cat sat on the mat

we might identify that *the cat* is a noun phrase and that *sat on the mat* is a verb phrase. We can thus conclude that this string forms a sentence.

We can also use BNF to define a number of possible noun phrases. Note how we use the "|" symbol to separate the possible right-hand sides in BNF:

NounPhrase → Noun

| *Article Noun*

| *Adjective Noun*

| *Article Adjective Noun*

Similarly, we can define a verb phrase:

VerbPhrase → Verb

| *Verb NounPhrase*

| *Adverb Verb NounPhrase*

The structure of human languages varies considerably. Hence, a set of rules like this will be valid for one language, but not necessarily for any other language. For example, in English it is usual to place the adjective before the noun (*black cat, stale bread*), whereas in French, it is often the case that the adjective comes after the noun (*moulin rouge*).

Thus far, the rewrite rules we have written consist solely of nonterminal symbols. Rewrite rules are also used to describe the parts of speech of individual words (or terminal symbols):

Noun → cat

| *dog*

| *Mount Rushmore*

| *chickens*

Verb → *swims*

　　　| *eats*

　　　| *climbs*

Article → *the*

　　　| *a*

Adjective → *black*

　　　| *brown*

　　　| *green*

　　　| *stale*

These rules form a **lexicon** of the language, which details which words are available and which parts of speech they are.

20.2.3　Grammars

We have briefly looked at the ways in which grammars can be described. Let us now examine the types of grammars that exist.

Noam Chomsky invented a hierarchy of grammars. The hierarchy consists of four main types of grammars.

The simplest grammars are used to define **regular languages**. A regular language is one that can be described or understood by a finite state automaton. Such languages are very simplistic and allow sentences such as "aaaaabbbbbb." Recall that a finite state automaton consists of a finite number of states, and rules that define how the automaton can transition from one state to another.

A finite state automaton could be designed that defined the language that consisted of a string of one or more occurrences of the letter *a*. Hence, the following strings would be valid strings in this language:

aaa

a

aaaaaaaaaaaaaaaa

Regular languages are of interest to computer scientists, but are not of great interest to the field of natural language processing because they are not powerful enough to represent even simple formal languages, let alone the more complex natural languages. Sentences defined by a regular grammar are often known as **regular expressions**.

The grammar that we defined above using rewrite rules is a **context-free grammar**. It is context free because it defines the grammar simply in terms of which word types can go together—it does not specify the way that words should agree with each. For example, the grammar defined in Section 20.2.2 allows the following sentence, which is grammatically correct (although not necessarily semantically):

> *A stale dog climbs Mount Rushmore.*

It also, however, allows the following sentence, which is not grammatically correct:

> *Chickens eats.*

A context-free grammar can have only at most one terminal symbol on the right-hand side of its rewrite rules. Rewrite rules for a **context-sensitive grammar**, in contrast, can have more than one terminal symbol on the right-hand side. This enables the grammar to specify number, case, tense, and gender agreement. Each context-sensitive rewrite rule must have at least as many symbols on the right-hand side as it does on the left-hand side.

Rewrite rules for context-sensitive grammars have the following form:

$$A \, X \, B \rightarrow A \, Y \, B$$

which means that in the context of A and B, X can be rewritten as Y. Each of A, B, X, and Y can be either a terminal or a nonterminal symbol.

Context-sensitive grammars are most usually used for natural language processing because they are powerful enough to define the kinds of grammars that natural languages use. Unfortunately, they tend to involve a much larger number of rules and are a much less natural way to describe language, making them harder for human developers to design than context-free grammars.

The final class of grammars in Chomsky's hierarchy consists of **recursively enumerable grammars** (also known as **unrestricted grammars**). A recursively enumerable grammar can define any language and has no restrictions on the structure of its rewrite rules. Such grammars are of interest to computer scientists but are not of great use in the study of natural language processing.

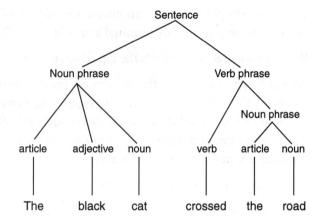

Figure 20.1
Parse tree for the sentence "the black cat crossed the road"

20.2.4   Parsing: Syntactic Analysis

As we have seen, morphologic analysis can be used to determine to which part of speech each word in a sentence belongs. We will now examine how this information is used to determine the syntactic structure of a sentence. This process, in which we convert a sentence into a tree that represents the sentence's syntactic structure, is known as **parsing**.

Parsing a sentence tells us whether it is a valid sentence, as defined by our grammar (for this section, we will assume that we are working with the English language and that the grammar we are using is English grammar). If a sentence is not a valid sentence, then it cannot be parsed.

Parsing a sentence involves producing a tree, such as that shown in Figure 20.1, which shows the parse tree for the following sentence:

> The black cat crossed the road.

This tree shows how the sentence is made up of a noun phrase and a verb phrase. The noun phrase consists of an article, an adjective, and a noun. The verb phrase consists of a verb and a further noun phrase, which in turn consists of an article and a noun.

Parse trees can be built in a bottom-up fashion or in a top-down fashion. Building a parse tree from the top down involves starting from a sentence and determining which of the possible rewrites for *Sentence* can be applied to the sentence that is being parsed. Hence, in this case, *Sentence* would be rewritten using the following rule:

> *Sentence → NounPhrase VerbPhrase*

Then the verb phrase and noun phrase would be broken down recursively in the same way, until only terminal symbols were left.

When a parse tree is built from the top down, it is known as a **derivation tree**.

To build a parse tree from the bottom up, the terminal symbols of the sentence are first replaced by their corresponding nonterminals (e.g., *cat* is replaced by *noun*), and then these nonterminals are combined to match the right-hand sides of rewrite rules. For example, *the* and *road* would be combined using the following rewrite rule:

NounPhrase → Article Noun

In the next section we examine a practical example of a parser and see how it works.

20.2.5   Transition Networks

A **transition network** is a finite state automaton that is used to represent a part of a grammar. A transition network parser uses a number of these transition networks to represent its entire grammar. Each network represents one nonterminal symbol in the grammar. Hence, in the grammar for the English language, we would have one transition network for *Sentence*, one for *Noun Phrase*, one for *Verb Phrase*, one for *Verb*, and so on.

Figure 20.2 shows the transition network equivalents for three production rules.

In each transition network, S1 is the start state, and the accepting state, or final state, is denoted by a heavy border. When a phrase is applied to a transition network, the first word is compared against one of the arcs leading from the first state. If this word matches one of those arcs, the network moves into the state to which that arc points. Hence, the first network shown in Figure 20.2, when presented with a *Noun Phrase*, will move from state S1 to state S2.

If a phrase is presented to a transition network and no match is found from the current state, then that network cannot be used and another network must be tried. Hence, when starting with the phrase *the cat sat on the mat*, none of the networks shown in Figure 20.2 will be used because they all have only nonterminal symbols, whereas all the symbols in *the cat sat on the mat* are terminal. Hence, we need further networks, such as the ones shown in Figure 20.3, which deal with terminal symbols.

Production Rule   **Transition Network**

Sentence → NounPhrase VerbPhrase

Sentence

VerbPhrase → Verb
     | Verb Noun

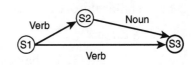

VerbPhrase

NounPhrase → Noun
     | Article Noun
     | Article Adjective Noun

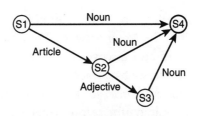

NounPhrase

Figure 20.2

Transition network equivalents for three rewrite rules

Production Rule   **Transition Network**

Noun → cat
    | mat

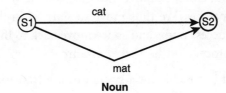

Noun

Article → the
    | a

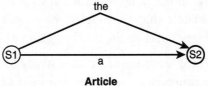

Article

Verb → sat

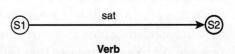

Verb

Figure 20.3

Transition network equivalents for three rewrite rules that represent terminal symbols

Transition networks can be used to determine whether a sentence is grammatically correct, at least according to the rules of the grammar the networks represent.

Parsing using transition networks involves exploring a search space of possible parses in a depth-first fashion.

Let us examine the parse of the following simple sentence:

> *A cat sat.*

We begin in state S1 in the *Sentence* transition network. To proceed, we must follow the arc that is labeled *NounPhrase*. We thus move out of the *Sentence* network and into the *NounPhrase* network.

The first arc of the *NounPhrase* network is labeled *Noun*. We thus move into the *Noun* network. We now follow each of the arcs in the *Noun* network and discover that our first word, *A*, does not match any of them. Hence, we backtrack to the next arc in the *NounPhrase* network. This arc is labeled *Article*, so we move on to the *Article* transition network. Here, on examining the second label, we find that the first word is matched by the terminal symbol on this arc. We therefore **consume** the word, *A*, and move on to state S2 in the *Article* network. Because this is a success node, we are able to return to the *NounPhrase* network and move on to state S2 in this network. We now have an arc labeled *Noun*.

As before, we move into the *Noun* network and find that our next word, *cat*, matches. We thus move to state S4 in the *NounPhrase* network. This is a success node, and so we move back to the *Sentence* network and repeat the process for the *VerbPhrase* arc.

It is possible for a system to use transition networks to generate a derivation tree for a sentence, so that as well as determining whether the sentence is grammatically valid, it parses it fully to obtain further information by semantic analysis from the sentence. This can be done by simply having the system build up the tree by noting which arcs it successfully followed.

When, for example, it successfully follows the *NounPhrase* arc in the *Sentence* network, the system generates a root node labeled *Sentence* and an arc leading from that node to a new node labeled *NounPhrase*. When the system follows the *NounPhrase* network and identifies an article and a noun, these are similarly added to the tree. In this way, the full parse tree for the sentence can be generated using transition networks.

Parsing using transition networks is simple to understand, but is not necessarily as efficient or as effective as we might hope for. In particular, it does not pay any attention to potential ambiguities or the need for words to agree with each other in case, gender, or number. In the next section, we examine augmented transition networks, which are a more sophisticated parsing tool.

20.2.6   Augmented Transition Networks

An **augmented transition network**, or ATN, is an extended version of a transition network. ATNs have the ability to apply tests to arcs, for example, to ensure agreement with number. Thus, an ATN for *Sentence* would be as shown in Figure 20.2, but the arc from node S2 to S3 would be conditional on the number of the verb being the same as the number for the noun. Hence, if the noun phrase were *three dogs* and the verb phrase were *is blue*, the ATN would not be able to follow the arc from node S2 to S3 because the number of the noun phrase (plural) does not match the number of the verb phrase (singular). In languages such as French, checks for gender would also be necessary.

The conditions on the arcs are calculated by procedures that are attached to the arcs. The procedure attached to an arc is called when the network reaches that arc. These procedures, as well as carrying out checks on agreement, are able to form a parse tree from the sentence that is being analyzed.

20.2.7   Chart Parsing

Parsing using transition networks is effective, but not the most efficient way to parse natural language. One problem can be seen in examining the following two sentences:

1. *Have all the fish been fed?*
2. *Have all the fish.*

Clearly these are very different sentences—the first is a question, and the second is an instruction. In spite of this, the first three words of each sentence are the same. When a parser is examining one of these sentences, it is quite likely to have to backtrack to the beginning if it makes the wrong choice in the first case for the structure of the sentence. In longer sentences, this can be a much greater problem, particularly as it involves examining the same words more than once, without using the fact that the words have already been analyzed.

Figure 20.4

The initial chart for the sentence The cat eats a big fish

(0) The   (1) cat   (2) eats   (3) a   (4) big   (5) fish   (6)

Another method that is sometimes used for parsing natural language is **chart parsing**. In the worst case, chart parsing will parse a sentence of n words in $O(n^3)$ time. In many cases it will perform better than this and will parse most sentences in $O(n^2)$ or even $O(n)$ time.

In examining sentence 1 above, the chart parser would note that the words *two children* form a noun phrase. It would note this on its first pass through the sentence and would store this information in a **chart**, meaning it would not need to examine those words again on a subsequent pass, after backtracking.

The initial chart for the sentence *The cat eats a big fish* is shown in Figure 20.4.

Figure 20.4 shows the chart that the chart parse algorithm would start with for parsing the sentence. The chart consists of seven **vertices**, which will become connected to each other by **edges**. The edges will show how the constituents of the sentence combine together.

The chart parser starts by adding the following edge to the chart:

[0, 0, *Target* → • *Sentence*]

This notation means that the edge connects vertex 0 to itself (the first two numbers in the square brackets show which vertices the edge connects). *Target* is the target that we want to find, which is really just a placeholder to enable us to have an edge that requires us to find a whole sentence. The arrow indicates that in order to make what is on its left-hand side (*Target*) we need to find what is on its right-hand side (*Sentence*). The dot (•) shows what has been found already, on its left-hand side, and what is yet to be found, on its right-hand side. This is perhaps best explained by examining an example.

Consider the following edge, which is shown in the chart in Figure 20.5:

[0, 2, *Sentence* → *NounPhrase* • *VerbPhrase*]

This means that an edge exists connecting nodes 0 and 2. The dot shows us that we have already found a *NounPhrase* (*the cat*) and that we are looking

Figure 20.5

Partial chart for the sentence The cat eats a big fish, showing the edge [0, 2, Sentence → NounPhrase • VerbPhrase]

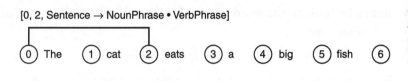

[0, 2, Sentence → NounPhrase • VerbPhrase]

(0) The   (1) cat   (2) eats   (3) a   (4) big   (5) fish   (6)

for a *VerbPhrase*. Once we have found the *VerbPhrase*, we will have what is on the left-hand side of the arrow—that is, a *Sentence*.

The chart parser can add edges to the chart using the following three rules:

1. If we have an edge [*x, y, A* → *B* • *C*], which needs to find a *C*, then an edge can be added that supplies that *C* (i.e., the edge [*x, y, C* → • *E*]), where *E* is some sequence of terminals or nonterminals which can be replaced by a *C*).

2. If we have two edges, [*x, y, A* → *B* • *C D*] and [*y, z, C* → *E* •}, then these two edges can be combined together to form a new edge: [*x, z, A* → *B C* • *D*].

3. If we have an edge [*x, y, A* → *B* • *C*], and the word at vertex *y* is of type *C*, then we have found a suitable word for this edge, and so we extend the edge along to the next vertex by adding the following edge: [*y, y* + 1, *A* → *B C* •].

Let us now see how this works, by examining the example of the sentence shown in Figure 20.4: *The cat eats a big fish.*

We start with the edge [0, 0, *Target* → • *Sentence*], which means that to find our target, we must first find a sentence.

Using rule 1 above, we can add the following edge to the chart:

[0, 0, *Sentence* → • *NounPhrase VerbPhrase*]

This means we must now find a *NounPhrase* and a *VerbPhrase*.

We now apply rule 1 again, to try to find a suitable *NounPhrase*, which involves adding the following edge:

[0, 0, *NounPhrase* → • *Article NounPhrase*]

Now we are able to apply rule 3 because the word at the end of this edge (from vertex 0 to vertex 0) is *the*, which is an *Article*. (This would be determined by looking the word up in a lexicon.) Hence, we can now add the following edge:

[0, 1, *NounPhrase* → *Article* • *NounPhrase*]

Now we are looking for another *NounPhrase*, so we use rule 1 again to add the following edge:

[0, 1, *Noun Phrase* → • *Noun*]

We can now use rule 3 again because the next word is indeed a *Noun*, to add the following edge to the chart:

[0, 2, *NounPhrase* → *Noun* •}

This process now continues, until we have reached an edge in which we have found everything we need. In this example, the final edge will be

[0, 6, *Sentence* → *NounPhrase VerbPhrase* •}

To build a parse tree from the chart, we modify rule 2 so that when it combines two edges together, it stores in the new edge information about the two edges that were combined to form it (the **children edges**). Then when the parse has completed, we can obtain the parse tree directly from the edges of the tree by starting from the first edge and recursively examining the children edges of each node.

20.2.8   Semantic Analysis

Having determined the syntactic structure of a sentence, the next task of natural language processing is to determine the meaning of the sentence. Semantics is the study of the meaning of words, and semantic analysis is the analysis we use to extract meaning from utterances.

Semantic analysis involves building up a representation of the objects and actions that a sentence is describing, including details provided by adjectives, adverbs, and prepositions. Hence, after analyzing the sentence *The black cat sat on the mat*, the system would use a semantic net such as the one shown in Figure 20.6 to represent the objects and the relationships between them.

Figure 20.6

A semantic net representation for the sentence The black cat sat on the mat

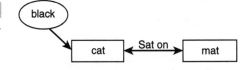

A more sophisticated semantic network is likely to be formed, which includes information about the nature of a cat (a cat is an object, an animal, a quadruped, etc.) that can be used to deduce facts about the cat (e.g., that it likes to drink milk).

In fact, semantic analysis is most useful in disambiguating sentences, as we see in the next section.

20.2.9   Ambiguity and Pragmatic Analysis

One of the main differences between natural languages and formal languages like C++ is that a sentence in a natural language can have more than one meaning. This is **ambiguity**—the fact that a sentence can be interpreted in different ways depending on who is speaking, the context in which it is spoken, and a number of other factors.

We will briefly examine some of the more common forms of ambiguity and look at ways in which a natural language processing system can make sensible decisions about how to **disambiguate** them.

Lexical ambiguity occurs when a word has more than one possible meaning. For example, a bat can be a flying mammal or a piece of sporting equipment. The word *set* is an interesting example of this because it can be used as a verb, a noun, an adjective, or an adverb. Determining which part of speech is intended can often be achieved by a parser in cases where only one analysis is possible, but in other cases semantic disambiguation is needed to determine which meaning is intended.

Syntactic ambiguity occurs when there is more than one possible parse of a sentence. The sentence *Jane carried the girl with the spade* could be interpreted in two different ways, as is shown in the two parse trees in Figure 20.7.

In the first of the two parse trees in Figure 20.7, the prepositional phrase *with the spade* is applied to the noun phrase *the girl*, indicating that it was the girl who had a spade that Jane carried. In the second sentence, the prepositional phrase has been attached to the verb phrase *carried the girl*, indicating that Jane somehow used the spade to carry the girl.

Semantic ambiguity occurs when a sentence has more than one possible meaning—often as a result of a syntactic ambiguity. In the example shown in Figure 20.7 for example, the sentence *Jane carried the girl with the spade*, the sentence has two different parses, which correspond to two possible meanings for the sentence. The significance of this becomes clearer for practical systems if we imagine a robot that receives vocal instructions from a human.

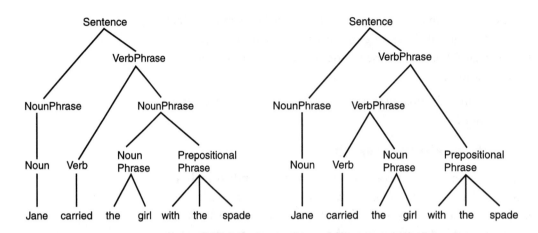

Figure 20.7

Two possible parse trees for the sentence Jane carried the girl with the spade

Referential ambiguity occurs when we use **anaphoric** expressions, or pronouns to refer to objects that have already been discussed. An anaphora occurs when a word or phrase is used to refer to something without naming it. The problem of ambiguity occurs where it is not immediately clear which object is being referred to. For example, consider the following sentences:

John gave Bob the sandwich. He smiled.

It is not at all clear from this *who* smiled—it could have been John or Bob. In general, English speakers or writers avoid constructions such as this to avoid humans becoming confused by the ambiguity. In spite of this, ambiguity can also occur in a similar way where a human would not have a problem, such as

John gave the dog the sandwich. It wagged its tail.

In this case, a human listener would know very well that it was the dog that wagged its tail, and not the sandwich. Without specific world knowledge, the natural language processing system might not find it so obvious.

A **local ambiguity** occurs when a part of a sentence is ambiguous; however, when the whole sentence is examined, the ambiguity is resolved. For example, in the sentence *There are longer rivers than the Thames*, the phrase *longer rivers* is ambiguous until we read the rest of the sentence, *than the Thames*.

Another cause of ambiguity in human language is **vagueness**. As we saw in Chapter 18, when we examined fuzzy logic, words such as *tall*, *high*, and *fast* are vague and do not have precise numeric meanings. A natural language processing system may have no problem syntactically analyzing the sentence *The car is very fast*, but it needs a good deal of world knowledge to understand exactly what this sentence means. Of course, it will have different meanings to different people and in different circumstances: a normal American driver might interpret it as meaning that the car is traveling (or can travel) faster than 70 miles per hour. A German, used to traveling on the Autobahn, might consider 70 miles per hour to be very slow and might interpret the sentence as meaning that the car could travel over 130 mph.

Humans use a number of other constructions, such as metaphor (as in *he ran like the wind*) and metonymy (using a part of an object to describe the whole, as in *the suit sat next to me*). We tend to take these forms of speech for granted and do not need to carry out much additional thought to understand what is meant by them. Clearly, for a computer system this is not so easy.

The process by which a natural language processing system determines which meaning is intended by an ambiguous utterance is known as **disambiguation**. Disambiguation can be done in a number of ways. One of the most effective ways to overcome many forms of ambiguity is to use probability. This can be done using prior probabilities or conditional probabilities. Prior probability might be used to tell the system that the word *bat* nearly always means a piece of sporting equipment. Conditional probability would tell it that when the word *bat* is used by a sports fan, this is likely to be the case, but that when it is spoken by a naturalist it is more likely to be a winged mammal.

Context is also an extremely important tool in disambiguation. Consider the following sentences:

> *I went into the cave. It was full of bats.*
>
> *I looked in the locker. It was full of bats.*

In each case, the second sentence is the same, but the context provided by the first sentence helps us to choose the correct meaning of the word "bat" in each case.

Disambiguation thus requires a good **world model**, which contains knowledge about the world that can be used to determine the most likely meaning of a given word or sentence. The world model would help the system to understand that the sentence *Jane carried the girl with the spade* is unlikely to mean that Jane used the spade to carry the girl because spades are usually used to carry smaller things than girls. The challenge, of course, is to encode this knowledge in a way that can be used effectively and efficiently by the system.

The world model needs to be as broad as the sentences the system is likely to hear. For example, a natural language processing system devoted to answering sports questions might not need to know how to disambiguate the sporting bat from the winged mammal, but a system designed to answer any type of question would.

20.3   Machine Translation

One of the early goals of natural language processing was to build a system that could translate text from one human language to another. Behind this attempt is an implicit assumption that human languages are like codes: in other words, a word in one language is simply a code for a real-world object, emotion, action, place, etc., and can therefore be exchanged for the code in another language for the same thing. Clearly this works to some extent: translating the world *cheval* from French into English can be achieved by simply looking it up in a dictionary.

It is much harder to translate entire sentences, for many of the reasons that have been given above for the difficulty of natural language processing in general. In particular, machine translation is not possible simply using syntactic and lexical analysis: a knowledge of the world that is being discussed is also essential, in order to disambiguate the text that is being translated. It may be, in some cases, that the text can be translated directly, ignoring the ambiguity, and creating a similarly ambiguous sentence in the target language. This does not always work, however: the word *bat* in English has (at least) two meanings, but there is no single word in French that has both of those meanings. Hence, for a system to translate that word from English to French, it must first determine which of the meanings is intended.

Machine translation systems have been developed, but at present the best results they can achieve are inadequate for most uses. One way in which they can be used is in combination with a human translator. The machine is able to provide a rough translation, and the human then tidies up the resultant text, ensuring that ambiguities have been handled correctly and that the translated text sounds natural, as well as being grammatically correct.

20.3.1   Language Identification

A similar, but easier problem to machine translation is that of language identification. There are many thousands of human languages in the world, and several hundred that are widely used today. Many of these are related to each other, and so can be easily confused. For an English speaker who knows no Italian or Spanish, those two languages can sometimes appear similar, for example. A system that can identify which language is being used in a piece of text is thus very useful. It is also particularly useful in applying textual analysis of all kinds to documents that appear on the Internet. Because pages on the Internet often have no indication of which language is being used, an automated system that is analyzing such documents needs to have the ability first to determine which language is being used.

One way to determine the language of a piece of text would be to have a complete lexicon of all words in all languages. This would clearly provide accurate results, but is likely to be impractical to develop for a number of reasons. The lexicon would be enormous, of course, and it would be very difficult to ensure that all words were really included.

The **acquaintance algorithm** is a commonly used method for language identification that uses ***n*-grams**. An *n*-gram is simply a collection of *n* letters, but detailed statistics exist that indicate the likelihood of a particular set of letters occurring in any given language. Hence, for example, the trigrams *ing, and, the, ent,* and *ant* probably indicate that a document is in English. When the acquaintance algorithm is presented with sufficient text (usually a few hundred to a thousand words is sufficient), it is able to identify the language with a surprisingly high degree of accuracy.

The acquaintance algorithm is trained by being presented with text in each language that it is expected to identify. The system then calculates a vector for each language based on the training data. This vector stores information about how many times each *n*-gram occurs in that language. When a document in an unknown language is presented to the algorithm, it calculates a similar vector for this document and compares it with the vectors it has calculated for the training data. The vector that is closest indicates which language is being used in the document.

One advantage of this approach is that it is easy to tell how certain the algorithm is about a particular document. A score is calculated for a document for each possible language, and the language with the highest score is selected. If the highest score is very much higher than the second highest score, this indicates a high degree of certainty. Conversely, if the top two or three scores are similar, then the algorithm is less certain, and there are one or more other possibilities that might need to be examined.

20.4   Information Retrieval

Information retrieval involves matching the text contained in a query or a document to a set of other documents. Often, the task involves finding the documents from a corpus of documents that are relevant to a user's query. Information retrieval was briefly introduced in Chapter 12, where we saw how Bayes' theorem can be used to produce a system that is effective at matching documents to a query and thus retrieving relevant documents from a corpus in response to a user request.

The idea behind information retrieval is that if a user enters a query such as *what is the capital of Sri Lanka?*, then a good approach to finding the answer is to find a document that contains all (or some) of the words contained in the query. In fact, words such as *what, is, the,* and of would normally be stripped from the query (using a **stop list**, which contains words that are to be stripped from all queries) before processing, and the information retrieval system would locate the documents that contained the words *capital, Sri,* and *Lanka.*

The corpus of documents is clearly very important. As has already been discussed, ambiguities in the query text can be avoided if the corpus is a very specific one. Information retrieval systems tend not to deal well with ambiguity because they are usually not given any world knowledge but are simply designed to perform statistical analysis of words in order to pick out suitable responses to a query.

As well as providing responses to a query, information retrieval can be used to find other documents that are similar to a given document. This provides a "more like this" function that many search engines use, which enables a user to say "I like this web site—find me other ones that are similar."

The main concept used in information retrieval is known as **TF-IDF**, (Term Frequency – Inverse Document Frequency).

Usually, a TF-IDF value is calculated for each of a set of words, and the resultant values are placed in a vector, which represents a document or piece of text (such as a query).

The inverse document frequency (IDF) of a word W is calculated as follows:

$$IDF(W) = \log \frac{|D|}{DF(W)}$$

Where $|D|$ is the number of documents in the corpus; $DF(W)$ is the **document frequency** of W, which is the number of documents in the corpus that contain the word W.

The term frequency of word W in document D is written $TF(W, D)$ and represents the number of times the word W occurs in document D.

The TF-IDF vector is the product of the TF and IDF values for a set of words for a particular document:

$$TF\text{-}IDF(D, W_i) = TF(W_i, D) \times IDF(W_i)$$

Let us now consider why this calculation makes sense. The inverse document frequency is designed to give a large value for infrequent words and a low value for frequent words. It is important that this calculation is done using the number of occurrences in the appropriate corpus. In some cases, the corpus can be representative of the English language as a whole, in which case no assumptions are being made about the nature of the subjects being searched for.

In many other cases, however, the corpus should be representative of a particular subject area. Hence, if the corpus were a set of documents about New York City, then the word *elephant* would be relatively infrequent and would thus produce a relatively high IDF value. Conversely, words such as *taxi, building, New York,* and *streets* would be relatively common and so would receive relatively low IDF values.

Let us consider the following query that is put to an information retrieval system using a corpus of documents about New York City:

When did an elephant walk through the streets of New York?

First, the stop words would be stripped, leaving the following words:

Elephant walk through streets New York

An IDF value would now be calculated for each word in the query. The word *elephant* would certainly receive the highest score, and the words *through, streets, New,* and *York* would all obtain very low scores.

Now, an index of the corpus of documents is consulted to obtain all documents that contain all (or some) of the words contained in the query. One technique here would be to require the least common word (*elephant*) to be in all documents, but to allow documents to have some combination of one or more of the other query words. Hence, the user would effectively be making the following Boolean query:

"Elephant" and ("walk" or "through" or "streets" or "New" or "York")

At this point, the TF part of TF-TDF comes into play. For each document that is retrieved, a TF-IDF value is calculated for the words in the query, producing a vector of six values for each document.

The idea behind the TF calculation is that if a document mentions the word *elephant* 10 times, then it is much more likely to be relevant to this query than a document that mentions it just once. On the other hand, a document that mentions the word *elephant* just once is still more likely to be relevant than a document that does not mention the word *elephant* at all, even if it has all the other words in the query several times.

The most common behavior for an information retrieval system in response to a query such as this is to return one or more of the most relevant documents that were obtained from the corpus. The relevance of a document can be obtained by obtaining the magnitude of its TF-IDF vector.

It is also possible to show a document to a corpus and ask it to find the most similar documents in the corpus. In some cases, queries are considered to be documents and are treated in this way. In this case, a TF-IDF vector is calculated for the query document and is also calculated for each document in the corpus. The most relevant documents are deemed to be those whose TF-IDF vectors are closest to the vector of the query document.

20.4.1 Stemming

If a user enters the query "where are elephants?", it would clearly be foolish for the system to reject a document that contains several occurrences of the word *elephant* simply because it does not contain the word *elephants* exactly as used in the query.

Stemming is often applied in information retrieval systems to avoid this problem. Stemming simply involves removing common stems such as *-ing*, *-s*, and *-ed* from words. In this way, the word *swimming* will be stemmed to *swim* and will match *swims*, *swimmers*, and so on. It will not usually be able to match *swam* or *swum* because these are irregular forms.

The most commonly used stemmer is **Porter's stemmer**, which is an extremely simple algorithm that has in some cases been shown to improve the performance of information retrieval systems.

Porter's stemmer is explained in detail in Spärck Jones and Willett (1997). The following is a brief description of the algorithm. Each step is carried out in turn on each word. The algorithm also includes conditions relating to word length so that words such as *sing* are not stemmed, whereas words such as *hissing* are. The algorithm is also careful to differentiate between single and double letters, ensuring that *hopping* is stemmed to *hop*, and *hissing* is stemmed to *hiss*.

1. *-s* is removed, and *-sses* is converted to *ss* (hence, *caresses* is stemmed to *caress*).

2. *-ed*, *-ing* are removed. After *-ed* is removed, an *-e* is added if the word now ends in *-at*, *-bl*, or *-iz*, ensuring that *grated*, *disabled*, and *realized* are correctly stemmed to *grate*, *disable*, and *realize* rather than *grat*, *disabl*, and *realiz*.

3. *-y* is converted to *-i*. This seems like a strange step, but ensures that *fly* and *flies* are considered to be the same word because they are both stemmed to *fli*.

4. A number of specific rules are now applied such as:

    -ATIONAL → ATE

    -IVENESS → IVE

    -BILITI → BLE

5. Endings such as *-ative*, *-ful*, *-ness*, *-able*, and *-er* are removed, and endings such as *-icative*, *-iciti*, and *-ical* are converted to *-ic*.

6. *-e* is removed.

7. Double letters at the end of some words (based on length) are converted to single letters—for example, *controll* is converted to *control*. This ensures that the following words are all considered to be the same: *controlling, control, controlled, controllable.*

The aim of stemming is to ensure that a query word will match other words with the same meaning that differ only in endings in the corpus. Hence, it is desirable not necessarily that the stemmed words are real words, but that when two words are stemmed they become the same if they really are the same word. Hence, the words *flying, fly,* and *flies* all stem to the nonword *fli.* The fact that *fli* is not a word does not matter because the aim is to match these words together in query and documents, not to show the stemmed words to the user.

20.4.2   Precision and Recall

The success of an information retrieval system can be measured using two metrics: **precision** and **recall**. If a system has 100% precision, it means that when it says that a particular document is relevant, then it is guaranteed to be correct. Lower precision means that it will wrongly classify some documents as being relevant (**false positives**).

For a system to have 100% recall, it must be guaranteed to find all relevant documents within a corpus in response to a particular query. Lower recall means that the system will fail to identify some documents as being relevant (**false negatives**).

In general, for most information retrieval techniques, precision and recall are in opposition to each other, meaning that when the system's precision increases it does so at the expense of recall, and vice-versa. This is intuitive: the only way to get 100% recall in most real-world situations is to be very relaxed about which documents are classified. In other words, a great deal of documents must be classified as being relevant to ensure that all relevant documents are found. Inevitably, this will mean that some irrelevant documents will be found as well.

Similarly, to obtain 100% precision it is necessary to return very few documents, meaning that some documents that are in fact relevant will not be returned.

A perfect information retrieval system would be one that achieved 100% recall and 100% precision over a given corpus and a given set of queries.

Such an information retrieval system is highly unlikely to ever be developed for most reasonable problems. One of the main causes of this difficulty is the complexity of human language, and the ambiguities it presents, as discussed above.

Information retrieval systems, unlike natural language processing systems, do not tend to take into account grammatical structures and thus are poor at, for example, noticing that "*the city that used to be the capital of Sri Lanka*" is no longer the capital of Sri Lanka.

20.5   Chapter Summary

- Morphologic analysis involves examining the structure of individual words.

- BNF (Backus–Naur form or Backus normal form) is used to define the rules that make up a grammar for a language.

- Grammars define the syntactic rules and structures of a language.

- Parsing (or syntactic analysis) uses the grammar of a language to determine the structure of a sentence or utterance, in order to derive further information (such as meaning) from the words.

- Semantic analysis involves examining the meaning of words and phrases.

- Ambiguity is a common problem with natural language processing systems. It can be dealt with to some extent by pragmatic analysis.

- Machine translation involves presenting a piece of text in one human language, which a computer program is then expected to translate into another human language. Although a great deal of work has been carried out in this field, the success predicted in the 1950s has yet to be achieved.

- Determining the language of a piece of text can be done by examining the occurrence of particular trigrams within the text.

- Information retrieval (IR) involves producing a response to a user query by selecting relevant documents from a corpus of documents (such as the Internet).

- An IR system that achieves 100% precision can guarantee that any document it returns is relevant to the query.

- An IR system that achieves 100% recall can guarantee that if a relevant document exists for a query, then it will find it.

- Achieving 100% recall and 100% precision is the goal of most information retrieval systems and one that has not yet been achieved.

20.6   Review Questions

20.1   Explain what is meant by *Natural Language Processing*. Why is it such a difficult subject?

20.2   Explain the role of each of the following in Natural Language Processing:

morphology

syntax

semantics

pragmatics

grammars

20.3   What is BNF? Why is it used to describe grammars?

20.4   How are transition networks used to represent a grammar?

20.5   Explain the difficulties involved in machine translation.

20.6   What is information retrieval? How does it differ from natural language processing?

20.7   What are precision and recall? How are they related? Explain why it is not usually possible to have 100% precision and 100% recall in the same system. Can you imagine a scenario in which it would be possible to achieve 100% precision and 100% recall?

20.7   Exercises

20.1   Examine the BNF definition of the syntax of a programming language such as C++, BASIC, or Java. What differences are immediately obvious compared with the BNF for a human language grammar? Are there any similarities?

20.2   Implement Porter's stemming algorithm in the programming language of your choice. You will need to find a full description of the algorithm. You can find this in Porter (1980), Spärck Jones (1997), or online. Apply the algorithm to a dictionary of words, such as the one that comes with most UNIX implementations. Then allow a user to enter a word, and have the system look this word up and say "yes" if it is present in its stemmed form in the dictionary or "no" if it is not. For example, if the dictionary contains *swim*, *fish*, and *cheese*, then it should say "yes" to *swimming*, *fishing*, and *cheeses* but no to *chocolate* and *swam*.

20.3 Find a book or web site that defines a set of rules for English grammar or the grammar of another human language. Express all of the rules in BNF and as transition networks. What problems do you encounter? Are there any rules that you cannot represent in either system or in both systems?

20.4 Find a machine translation service online. Have it translate a piece of text in a language with which you are not familiar into English. What errors does the translator introduce? Can you determine any sophisticated features based on the translation it produces?

20.5 Implement a language identification system in the programming language of your choice. You should start by selecting a number of languages (four or five should do). You should have a suitable quantity of typical material in each language—about 1000 words in each language would be plenty. First, write an algorithm that determines the most common 100 trigrams in each language. Now build these data into a program that uses it to determine the language of unseen text. Produce an alternative version of the software that calculates a frequency vector using all (26 * 26 * 26) trigrams. How does this system perform compared with the first one you produced in terms of accuracy and efficiency?

20.8 Further Reading

Natural language processing is briefly covered by most of the standard texts; information retrieval is less well covered. Spärck Jones and Willett (1997) provide an excellent coverage of the topics of information retrieval, with papers from a number of researchers in the field.

Natural Language Understanding, by James Allen (1995 – Addison Wesley)

Modern Information Retrieval, by Ricardo Baeza-Yates and Berthier Ribeiro-Neto (1999 – Addison Wesley)

Plan Recognition in Natural Language Dialogue, by Sandra Carberry (1990 – MIT Press)

Cross-Language Information Retrieval, edited by Gregory Grefenstette (1998 – Kluwer Academic Publishing)

Foundations of Computational Linguistics: Human-Computer Communication in Natural Language, by Roland R. Hausser (2001 – Springer Verlag)

Information Retrieval, by William R. Hersh (2002 – Springer Verlag)

Spoken Language Processing: A Guide to Theory, Algorithm and System Development, by Xuedong Huang, Alex Acero, Hsiao-Wuen Hon, and Raj Reddy (2001 – Prentice Hall)

Natural Language Processing and Knowledge Representation: Language for Knowledge and Knowledge for Language, edited by Lucja M. Iwanska and Stuart C. Shapiro (2000 – AAAI Press)

Text-Based Intelligent Systems: Current Research and Practice in Information Extraction and Retrieval, edited by Paul Schafran Jacobs (1992 – Lawrence Erlbaum Assoc.)

Speech and Language Processing: An Introduction to Natural Language Processing, Computational Linguistics and Speech Recognition, by Dan Jurafsky, James H. Martin, Keith Vander Linden, and Nigel Ward (2000 – Prentice Hall)

Intelligent Multimedia Information Retrieval, edited by Mark T. Maybury (1997 – AAAI Press)

Computational Linguistics, by Tony McEnery (1992 – Coronet Books – out of print)

Text Information Retrieval Systems, by Charles T. Meadow, Bert R. Boyce, and Donald H. Kraft (2000 – Academic Press)

Natural Language Processing for Online Applications: Text Retrieval, Extraction, and Categorization, by Peter Jackson and Isabelle Moulinier (2002 – John Benjamins Publishing Company)

Spotting and Discovering Terms through Natural Language Processing, by Christian Jacquemin (2001 – MIT Press)

Foundations of Statistical Natural Language Processing, by Christopher D. Manning and Hinrich Schütze (1999 – MIT Press)

Readings in Machine Translation, edited by Sergei Nirenburg, Harold L. Somers, and Yorick A. Wilks (2002 – MIT Press)

Natural Language Processing, by Fernando C. N. Pereira and Barbara J. Grosz (1994 – MIT Press)

An Algorithm for Suffix Stripping, by M. F. Porter (1980 – in Spärck Jones and Willett 1997)

Fundamentals of Speech Recognition, by Lawrence Rabiner and Biing-Hwang Juang (1993 – Pearson Education)

Evolutionary Language Understanding, by Geoffrey Sampson (1996 – Continuum)

Evaluating Natural Language Processing Systems: An Analysis and Review, by Karen Spärck Jones, Julia R. Galliers (1996 – Springer Verlag)

Readings in Information Retrieval, edited by Karen Spärck Jones and Peter Willett (1997 – Morgan Kaufmann)

Translation Engines: Techniques for Machine Translation, by Arturo Trujillo (1999 – Springer Verlag)

CHAPTER 21

Machine Vision

The Lord looseth men out of prison: the Lord giveth sight to the blind.

—Psalm 146, Verse 7

You see, but you do not observe.

—Sir Arthur Conan Doyle, *The Adventures of Sherlock Holmes*

All the mighty world
Of eye and ear, both what they half create,
And what they perceive.

—Sir William Wordsworth

21.1   Introduction

The vision system in mammals (such as human beings) is one of the most remarkable systems in the natural world. Without vision, it can be argued that human beings would not have reached their current levels of technical achievement, and indeed that none of the creatures alive today would have been able to evolve successfully without vision.

Providing the ability for computer systems, agents, or robots to perceive the world visually is clearly highly desirable.

In this chapter, we look at the techniques that are used to enable computers to "see" the real world, in much the same way that we do.

This chapter explains how the Canny method uses convolution to detect edges in images. It also explains how an image recognition system can then go on to segment the image and thus determine what objects are being viewed. This chapter presents a popular method that is used for face recognition and also discusses the importance of textures in computer vision systems.

21.2   Human Vision

In this section, we briefly describe the structure and function of the components that make up the mammalian visual system and, in particular, the human visual system. Understanding how humans see is vital to understanding how it can be possible to enable computers to perceive in a similar way.

Figure 21.1 shows a simplified diagram of the human vision system.

The most important parts of the human visual system are the eyes and the brain—in particular, the part of the brain that is associated with vision is the visual cortex.

The eye is the device that captures light that has bounced off nearby objects. This is achieved by a lens that focuses the light onto the retina, which is a screen at the back of the eye containing millions of photoreceptors. Photoreceptors are cells that are sensitive to light. There are two types of photoreceptors: **rods** and **cones**.

Rod cells are highly sensitive and so respond well in situations where there is little light, but they have a low level of acuity, meaning that the images they transmit to the brain are less detailed and "fuzzier" than those transmitted by the cones. Additionally, rods do not have the ability to recognize differences in color.

Cones, on the other hand, are relatively insensitive and so only respond well when presented with high levels of light, but they have a high level of acuity and are able to recognize differences in colors. The cone cells are mainly situated in the center of the retina, whereas the cones are mainly situated around the edges. This explains why most of our vision in normal, well-lit circumstances takes place in the center of our field of vision (the corresponding area of the retina is called the **fovea**), whereas at night, our peripheral vision is more important. You will notice, for example, that on a dark night, you can often see stars out of the corner of your eye, but if you turn your eye to look at those stars, they seem to disappear.

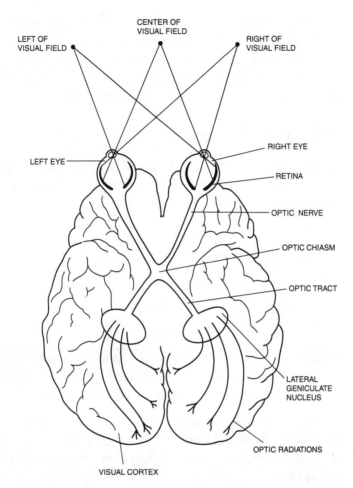

Figure 21.1

A diagram of the human brain, showing the mammalian vision system

Signals from the photoreceptors in the retina are passed via the **optic nerve** to the **lateral geniculate nucleus** (LGN) and also to the **superior colliculus**. The main pathway is the one to the LGN.

The nerves that travel from the right eye go to the left-hand side of the brain, and the nerves from the left eye go to the right-hand side of the brain. The point where the optic nerves cross over each other is the **optic chiasm**.

From the LGN, the signals are carried to the visual cortex by the **optic radiations**. This is done in such a way that if both eyes can see a point in the field of view, then the signals corresponding to this point from the two eyes will arrive at the same part of the brain. It is as a result of this that we are able to perceive a three-dimensional depth to the world that we see. If you shut one eye you will find that it is much harder to accurately perceive depth. For example, if you hold out a pen in one hand, shut one eye, and then try to place the cap on the pen with the other hand, you will find it much harder to do than if you have both eyes open. This is due to the fact that we have binocular ("two eyes"), **stereoscopic** vision.

21.3   Image Processing

In this section, we introduce the main techniques that are used in computer vision systems to process images. The process of image recognition can be broken down into the following main stages:

- image capture
- edge detection
- segmentation
- three-dimensional segmentation
- recognition and analysis

Image capture can be performed by a simple camera (or pair of cameras, to give stereoscopic vision), which converts light signals from a scene to electrical signals, much as the human visual system does.

Having obtained these light signals, which are simply a set of 1s and 0s (assuming a black and white system—if color is being used then each **pixel**, or picture element, would be represented by a number indicating that pixel's color).

For example, look at the images shown in Figure 21.2.

Figure 21.2

A picture of a plant and a magnified view of a rectangular region of this same photograph. The magnified region has been taken from the area highlighted in the lower right-hand side of the photograph.

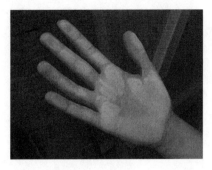

Figure 21.3
A photograph of a hand

In the second image in Figure 21.2, you can see the individual grey-scale pixels that made up a portion of the original photograph. Each pixel takes on one of a number of possible grey-scale values, often from 0 to 255. Color images are broken down in the same way, but with varying colors instead of grey scales. When a computer receives an image from an image sensor (such as a camera), this is the form it receives—a set of pixels. We see in this chapter how these pixels can be interpreted to give the computer an under-standing of what it is perceiving.

21.3.1 Edge Detection

The first stage of analysis, once an image has been obtained, is to determine where the edges are in the image. This idea has a sound biological basis, and there is evidence that edge detection is an important part of the mam-malian visual system. Because objects in the real world almost all have solid edges of one kind or another, detecting those images is the first stage in the process of determining which objects are present in a scene.

Consider the photograph shown in Figure 21.3 and the image shown in Figure 21.4, which shows the edges detected from this photograph.

Note that in Figure 21.4, the edges of the hand have been clearly picked out because these are the highest contrast edges in the photograph. Less clear are the edges of the fencing from the background, although these are also visible.

The reason that edge detection is useful in mammalian vision is that in most situations a predator (or prey) can be seen to be contrasted sharply with its background. Hence, noting the edges in the field of vision will enable an animal to quickly recognize other important animals near it. This, of course, explains why camouflage is such a popular technique in the animal kingdom. A photo of a brown moth sitting on the brown bark of a

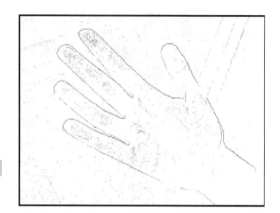

Figure 21.4

The edges from the photograph in Figure 21.3

tree will have very few edges, and they will not be easy to detect, compared with the edges in an image such as the photograph in Figure 21.3.

There are a number of types of edges that can appear in a visual scene. The edges we can see in Figure 21.4 are mostly **depth discontinuities**, which are edges that represent the differences in depths between parts of the image. In this case, most of the edges represent the difference in depth between the hand and the fencing behind it.

When viewing a three-dimension object such as a block on a table (as shown in Figure 21.5) there are **surface orientation discontinuities** (marked in bold lines in Figure 21.5), which represent edges between faces of the same object—in other words, such an edge appears because the objects on either side of the edge are facing different directions.

There are two other types of edges, which are caused by differences in color (or texture) on a single surface (**surface reflectance discontinuities**) and by shadows cast by objects (**illumination discontinuities**).

All of these types of edges can be (and are) used in image recognition systems to determine the position and nature of objects within a visual field.

Figure 21.5

An object illustrating surface orientation discontinuities (edges between faces of an object) (These edges are shown in bold.)

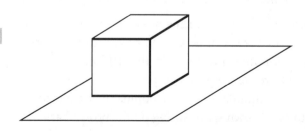

21.3.2   Convolution and the Canny Edge Detector

The simplest way to find edges in an image is to differentiate the image. Areas of consistent color will produce low differentials, and edges that are areas of greatest change will produce greater differentials.

Unfortunately, because real images contain a great deal of noise, differentiation does not work well as an edge detection method because the noise produces extremely high differentials in areas where there is really no edge.

A more effective method of edge detection is to use **convolution**.

The convolution of two discrete functions $f(a, b)$ and $g(a, b)$ is defined as follows:

$$f(a, b) * g(a, b) = \sum_{u=-\infty}^{\infty} \sum_{v=-\infty}^{\infty} f(a, b)g(a - u, b - v)$$

The convolution of continuous functions $f(a, b)$ and $g(a, b)$ is defined as follows:

$$f(a, b) * g(a, b) = \int_{-\infty}^{\infty} \int_{-\infty}^{\infty} f(a, b)g(a - u, b - v)\, du\, dv$$

The idea of using convolution is to eliminate the effects of noise by **smoothing** the image. One way to smooth an image is to convolve it with the following Gaussian function:

$$G_\sigma(x) = \frac{1}{\sqrt{2\pi\sigma}} e^{-x^2/2\sigma^2}$$

After convolving the image with the Gaussian function, the resultant can be differentiated to determine where the edges are. In fact, it is possible to eliminate a step from this process because it can be shown that convolution with $G_\sigma(x)$ and then differentiating the result is the same as convolution with the differential of $G_\sigma(x)$, which is defined as follows:

$$G'_\sigma(x) = \frac{-x}{\sqrt{2\pi\sigma}^3} e^{-x^2/2\sigma^2}$$

Hence, to detect edges in an image, we can convolve the image with $G'_\sigma(x)$ and obtain the peaks in the resultant. The peaks will correspond to the edges in the image. In doing so, we are using $G'_\sigma(x)$ as a **filter** because we are filtering out everything except the edges in the image.

Unfortunately, this method only works for one-dimensional strips of an image. It will detect an edge in a single line of pixels taken from an image, which is useful, but not enough for detecting edges in real images.

To detect edges that might be at any angle in an image, we need to convolve the image with two filters:

> Filter 1: $G'_\sigma(x)\ G_\sigma(y)$
>
> Filter 2: $G'_\sigma(y)\ G_\sigma(x)$

The image is convolved with each of these filters, and the results are squared and added together:

$$(I(x, y) * G'_\sigma(x)\ G_\sigma(y))^2 + (I(x, y) * G'_\sigma(y)\ G_\sigma(x))^2$$

where $I(x, y)$ is the value of the pixel at location (x, y) in the image.

Peaks in the resultant then correspond to edges in the image. Pixels that are considered to be edges are joined with adjacent pixels that are also edges in order to determine the shape and location of the entire edge. This method, known as the **Canny edge detector**, produces edges such as the ones shown in Figure 21.4.

21.3.3   Segmentation

Once the edges have been detected in an image, this information can be used to **segment** the image into homogeneous areas. In this case, when we say that an area of an image is homogeneous, we mean that its color or intensity of shading does not vary dramatically—in other words, there are no edges within the area.

There are other methods available for segmenting an image, apart from using edge detection. One simple method is **thresholding**. Thresholding involves finding the color of each pixel in an image and then considering adjacent pixels to be in the same area as long as their color is similar enough. This is very similar to edge detection but is used to segment the image, rather than just to find the edges in the image. This is different because edge detection will not necessarily produce continuous edges and will, therefore, not necessarily divide the image into more than one area. In the photograph shown in Figure 21.3, there are clearly a number of distinct

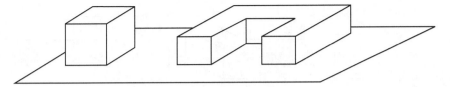

Figure 21.6
A line drawing of a simple blocks world

segments, but the edges detected in Figure 21.4 divide the image into only one or two segments.

A similar method for segmenting images is **splitting and merging**. Splitting involves taking an area that is not homogeneous and splitting it into two or more smaller areas, each of which is homogeneous. Merging involves taking two areas (e.g., two individual pixels) that are the same as each other, and adjacent to each other, and combining them together into a larger area. This provides a sophisticated iterative approach to segmenting an image that is often far more reliable than simple thresholding.

21.3.4 Classifying Edges in Line Drawings

Once a computer vision system has extracted the edges from an image, it has something that is rather similar to a line drawing. The line drawings in Figure 21.6 are illustrative of the kind of representations a system might have in observing a simple blocks world.

Such illustrations are easy for us to interpret. For a computer system to understand what it is observing, it needs to first classify the edges in the diagram it has produced.

There are three types of edges:

- A **convex** edge is an edge between two faces that are at an angle of more than 180° from each other.

- A **concave** edge is an edge between two faces that are at an angle of less than 180° from each other.

- Where only one of the two faces that are joined by an edge is visible in the image, the edge is an **occluding** edge. (An occluding edge is a depth discontinuity.)

In Figure 21.7, the edges have been labeled as convex, concave, or occluding using the traditional notation of + for a convex edge, − for a concave edge, and an arrow for an occluding edge. The direction of the arrow on an

Figure 21.7

Simple blocks world line
drawing with edges
labeled as convex (+),
concave (−), and
occluding (arrow)

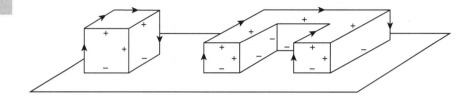

occluding edge is such that the visible surface is on the right of the direction of the arrow.

Having determined which type each edge in the image is, the system can make further assessments about the nature, shape, and relative position of the objects in the picture. Now we need a method for determining which type each edge is.

First, if we assume that all objects in our image are polyhedral (i.e., all the edges are straight and all surfaces are flat), then we can make the following assumption: A single line will have the same type (convex, concave, or occluding) for its entire length. If you look carefully at Figure 21.7, you will see that this is the case. No line starts out as concave and ends up convex, or any other combination. This is because the type of an edge is determined by the angle of the faces that the edge joins, and if all lines are straight and all faces flat, then this angle cannot change. (To see that this is true, try to imagine a polyhedral object where the angle between two faces varies over the edge that joins them).

In the 1970s, Huffman (1971) showed that further assumptions could be made that would help in the analysis of line drawings of polyhedral shapes. If one considers a vertex at which a number of edges meet, it can be shown that there are only a few possible combinations of edges that can make up that vertex.

Most vertices form a point of connection for three flat faces. Such vertices are called **trihedral** vertices. There are only 16 possible arrangements of edges that can make up trihedral vertices in the real world, and these are shown in Figure 21.8.

As you can see from Figure 21.8, there are a number of labelings of a trihedral vertex that are simply not possible.

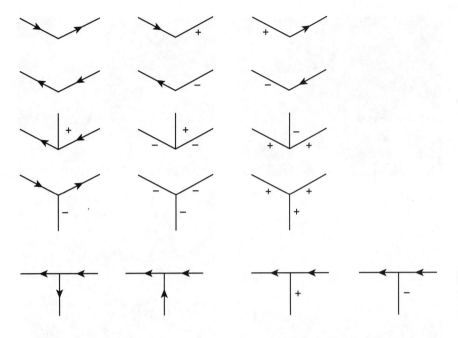

Figure 21.8
Figure 21.8
The 16 possible ways to label trihedral vertices

As a result, in analyzing a scene such as the one shown in Figure 21.6, a computer vision system can use Huffman's 16 trihedral vertices as constraints to limit the possible labelings for the diagram.

The Waltz algorithm does so by selecting a possible label for one junction, from the list shown in Figure 21.8, and then moving onto an adjacent junction and attempting to apply a labeling to this junction. If none is possible, the algorithm backtracks and tries a different labeling for a previous junction. Hence, the method applies depth-first search to the structure until a labeling is found that ensures that all junctions have valid labelings.

In some cases, there will be more than one possible labeling. In other words, the image is ambiguous. In such cases, additional information must be used. Often shading information can be used to provide additional constraints.

21.4 Using Texture

Texture is a vital aspect of the visual world. It helps us to identify a wide range of facets of what we see—it does not just tell us the materials that things are made of; it also gives us information about movement and shapes.

Figure 21.9
Four different textures

Texture, in the visual sense, can be defined as the pattern that we perceive on the surface of an object or in an area. The photos in Figure 21.9 show a variety of textures.

Clearly, the textures of the images in Figure 21.9 show us that we are looking at grass, pebbles, clouds, and roofing tiles. As we will see, the textures also tell us a great deal more than this.

21.4.1   Identifying Textures

To make use of texture information from an image, a computer system must first analyze the image and determine the nature of its texture or textures.

The simplest type of texture is the texture we usually expect to find on blocks in the simple blocks world—this is a completely plain, vanilla texture, which could be described as textureless, or smooth. In dealing with the blocks world, we tend to assume that our blocks are textureless and therefore pay no attention to texture. In fact, of course, in a real blocks world, the blocks must be made of something (wood, metal, plastic) and must therefore have a texture.

In examining a blocks world scene, texture usually is not terribly important because the shapes are so simple that determining their position, orientation, and so on can be done using edge detection and simple mathematical algorithms. In more complex environments, a system must make use of texture to make these kinds of analyses.

There are a number of statistical methods that can be used to categorize a particular texture in an image. We will now examine one such method, based on the use of **cooccurrence matrices**.

The idea of this method is to determine the relationships between pixels in the image of particular intensities. We will represent our image as a matrix of pixel values, which for this example will range from 0 to 4. Let us define a matrix P, which we will use for this example as the matrix representing the intensity values of the grey pixels in our image:

$$P = \begin{bmatrix} 1 & 0 & 3 & 2 \\ 2 & 3 & 0 & 1 \\ 1 & 4 & 1 & 3 \\ 3 & 2 & 2 & 4 \end{bmatrix}$$

Clearly, P defines a rather uninteresting image, but for a real image the matrix would be significantly larger and would have a greater range of values. P will suffice for us to illustrate this statistical method for analyzing textures.

Each pixel in P is defined as $P(x, y)$, so that for example:

$P(0, 0) = 1$

$P(1, 1) = 3$

$P(3, 2) = 3$

We will now define a new matrix, D, which is defined as follows:

$D(m, n)$ is the number of pairs of pixels in P for which

$P(i, j) = m$

$P(i + \delta i, j + \delta j) = n$

where i and j are any pixels in P, and δi and δj are small increments defined for this particular matrix D.

In other words, D defines how likely it is that any two pixels a particular distance apart (δi and δj) will have a particular pair of values.

We will see how this works for our matrix.

Let us first define $(\delta i, \delta j) = (1, 1)$. In other words, we are interested in pairs of pixels that are diagonally one pixel apart.

We can now define the matrix D.

$D(0, 0)$ is equal to the number of pairs of pixels in P that are $(1, 1)$ apart, and which are both valued 0. Looking at P, we can see that there is one such pair:

$$P(1, 0) = 0$$
$$P(2, 1) = 0$$

Hence, $D(0, 0) = 1$.

$D(1, 0)$ is equal to the number of pairs of pixels in P that are $(1, 1)$ apart and which are values 1 and 0, respectively. You should be able to see that no such pairs exist in P. Hence, $D(1, 0) = 0$.

We can define the whole of matrix D in the same way. D is a 5×5 matrix because there are five possible pixel values in P:

$$D = \begin{bmatrix} 1 & 0 & 0 & 1 & 0 \\ 0 & 0 & 1 & 1 & 1 \\ 0 & 0 & 0 & 0 & 1 \\ 0 & 1 & 0 & 0 & 0 \\ 0 & 0 & 1 & 0 & 0 \end{bmatrix}$$

Let us see now the difference when we apply this method to a different matrix:

$$P_1 = \begin{bmatrix} 1 & 0 & 4 & 3 \\ 2 & 1 & 0 & 4 \\ 3 & 2 & 1 & 0 \\ 4 & 3 & 2 & 1 \end{bmatrix}$$

Clearly this matrix represents an image where the texture is far more noticeable than in the previous matrix, P. We should expect to see this represented in the corresponding matrix D_1, which is defined as follows:

$$D_1 = \begin{bmatrix} 2 & 0 & 0 & 0 & 0 \\ 0 & 3 & 0 & 0 & 0 \\ 0 & 0 & 2 & 0 & 0 \\ 0 & 0 & 0 & 1 & 0 \\ 0 & 0 & 0 & 0 & 1 \end{bmatrix}$$

Finally, let us examine the following matrix:

$$P_2 = \begin{bmatrix} 3 & 4 & 0 & 1 \\ 4 & 0 & 1 & 2 \\ 0 & 1 & 2 & 3 \\ 1 & 2 & 3 & 4 \end{bmatrix}$$

This matrix, P_2, is clearly similar to P_1, but reflected about the Y-axis. Let us see how D_2 turns out:

$$D_2 = \begin{bmatrix} 0 & 0 & 3 & 0 & 0 \\ 0 & 0 & 0 & 2 & 0 \\ 0 & 0 & 0 & 0 & 1 \\ 1 & 0 & 0 & 0 & 0 \\ 0 & 2 & 0 & 0 & 0 \end{bmatrix}$$

The difference between D_2 and D_1 is as we would expect. The values in D_1 are on the main diagonal, whereas in D_2 they are on two minor diagonals. This reflects the relationship between the vector $(\delta i, \delta j) = (1, 1)$ and the textures in the images.

One extension to this method is to assume that we should not distinguish between $D(m, n)$ and $D(n, m)$. Hence, we produce the cooccurrence matrix, C, which is defined as follows:

$$C = D + D^T$$

Where D^T is the transposition of matrix D.

C has the property that $C(m, n) = C(n, m)$ because

$$\begin{aligned} C(m, n) &= D(m, n) + D(n, m) \\ &= D(n, m) + D(m, n) \\ &= C(n, m) \end{aligned}$$

This matrix, C, gives us a useful statistical analysis of the texture contained within the image, relative to the vector $(\delta i, \delta j)$ that we have chosen. By using a number of different $(\delta i, \delta j)$ vectors, we can determine more information about the texture.

21.4.2 Structural Texture Analysis

An alternative to the statistical approach is to analyze textures using a structural approach, based on units of texture called **texels**. A texel is a single texture element or a piece of image that is repeated throughout the image to produce the texture. Looking at the final photo in Figure 21.9, of roofing tiles, we can see that this texture is made up of a single tile, repeated over the image. This tile is the texel. Note that in fact, due to perspective and other distortions, the texels will not all be identical (e.g., perspective will cause them to have different shapes and sizes, and distortions will also be caused by mapping the texture onto a curved surface).

Texel analysis thus involves searching for repeated components within an image, taking into account distortions such as elongation, rotation, compression, and so on. As we see in the next sections, once the texture has been determined in this way, this information can be used to determine a number of useful properties about the object whose texture we are looking at.

21.4.3 Determining Shape and Orientation from Texture

Usually, when examining a texture, we are able to use information gained from the texture to determine the shape of the surface. This assumes, of course, that the picture involves a surface. This is certainly the case for three of the images in Figure 21.9 (the pebbles, the grass, and the tiles are all placed on some surface). For the fourth image, of clouds, the texture tells us something about the "surface" of the clouds, although this is somewhat illusory because the clouds are not solid. Still, the techniques used by computer vision systems will draw mostly the same conclusions about the shape and the "surface" of the clouds that we would when examining that picture.

Notice how the variation of the shape of the bricks in the photo in Figure 21.10 enables us to see, without any external help, that the wall in the picture is curved. The main reason that we can tell that the wall is curved is the foreshortening of the bricks on the right-hand side of the picture, suggest-

Figure 21.10
A section of curved wall, showing how surface shape can be determined, to some extent, from the texture

ing that they are further away, and seen from a sharper angle, than those on the left-hand side of the picture.

In a similar way, a photograph of a golf ball can be used to determine the shape of the golf ball, by examining the way in which the small circular indentations on the surface of the ball vary in apparent shape. See the illustration in Figure 21.11, for example.

These circles on the surface of the ball, and the bricks in Figure 21.10, are the texels that make up the texture, which we use to determine the shape of the object in the picture.

Although the image in Figure 21.11 is flat, it is translated in our minds into a sphere because that is the simplest explanation for the way the circles distort as they get farther from the center of the image.

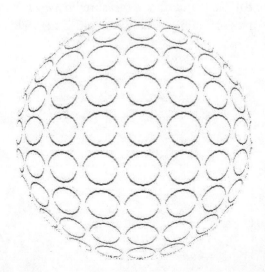

Figure 21.11
An illustration showing how the texture on the surface of a golf ball helps us to understand the shape of the ball

Figure 21.12

A photograph of a section of wall. The angle between the perpendicular to this wall and the camera can be determined by examining the distortion of the texels (in this case, the individual bricks).

A simple way to extract shape from a texture of this kind is to assume that each texel is flat (which with a curved surface is probably not true but is a reasonable approximation). By determining the extent and direction of distortion of a given texel, the slant of the texel can be determined and a perpendicular line projected from it. Once perpendiculars have been determined for all the texels in an image, the surface shape has been determined.

In the same way, the orientation of a flat surface, such as the section of wall shown in Figure 21.12, can be determined.

A similar, though less obviously intuitive, method can be applied to textures such as those shown in Figure 21.9. In these cases, the orientation of the surfaces beneath the grass, pebbles, and roofing tiles would be determined, as would the apparent shape of the clouds.

When determining orientation, we are interested in two factors: **slant** and **tilt**. Slant and tilt are measured between a vector perpendicular to the surface of an object and the z- and x-axes. This is illustrated in Figure 21.13.

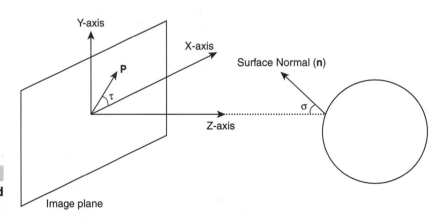

Figure 21.13

Showing how slant (σ) and tilt (τ) are measured.

Slant, which is usually written as the Greek letter sigma—σ, is measured between the surface normal (the vector n, in Figure 21.13), which is perpendicular to the object we are observing at the point we are interested in, and the z-axis. This is shown in Figure 21.13.

We measure tilt (often written as the Greek letter tau—τ) as the angle between the x-axis and the projection, p, of the normal vector n onto the plane of the image. In other words, the tilt is an apparent angle, determined by the position and orientation of the viewer.

In the diagram in Figure 21.13, we are measuring slant and tilt of a specific point on the surface of a sphere. This point is the point on the surface from which the normal vector, n, has been measured.

21.5   Interpreting Motion

One of the most important aspects of mammalian vision is the ability to detect (and thus react to) motion. For hunters, it is important to be able to spot prey and follow it as it attempts to flee, and for the prey, it is important to detect the hunter as quickly as possible. In a world full of confusing visual information, most animals (including humans) use motion to provide additional information about what is being seen.

Similarly, for an agent that has the ability of vision, it is important to be able to detect motion.

There are two main types of motion that an observer is interested in—motion of other objects and the apparent motion of the environment caused by the observer's own motion.

We will start with the latter type of motion—the apparent motion caused by the movement of the camera or other image capture device.

The photograph in Figure 21.14, for example, was taken using a camera on a moving train. A subsequent photo, taken a second later, would show that the buildings, trees, and other objects in the photograph had apparently moved. Of course, this is in fact due to the fact that the train, and therefore the camera, has moved. This apparent motion in an image is known as **optical flow**, and the vectors that define the apparent motion make up what is known as the **motion field**. Some of these vectors have been drawn onto the photograph in Figure 21.14. The photograph was taken from the

Figure 21.14

A photograph taken from a train, illustrating the idea of the motion field. Some of the motion field vectors have been drawn in as arrows, moving away from the camera.

back of the train, so the vectors show that the objects are apparently moving away from the camera.

The direction of the motion field will clearly depend on the direction in which the camera is moving. If the photograph in Figure 21.14 had been taken from a car crossing a level crossing, the arrows would have gone horizontally across the image, for example, instead of heading toward the **vanishing point**, the point toward which perspective causes all parallel lines in the image to converge.

Hence, by examining a sequence of images taken from a moving camera, if the direction and speed of the optical flow can be determined, then this can provide information about the direction and speed of travel of the camera, relative to the background.

It is possible to estimate the nature of the motion field, and thus the optical flow, in a sequence of images by comparing the features of the images. First, we assume that the objects in a sequence of images will not themselves change, and so any changes that occur to them are caused by the movement of the camera. This will clearly not apply if there are moving objects (e.g., cars, people, animals) in the image, but it will still apply to the majority of the features within most images, and the anomalies can be dealt with separately.

By computing common points in a sequence of images, we can thus calculate the optical flow vectors and thus determine the speed of motion of the camera. This technique can also be applied in cases where the camera is still and is capturing a sequence of images of a moving or rotating object.

21.6   Making Use of Vision

We have thus far described techniques that can enable a computer system to extract information from a visual scene that has been recorded on a device such as a camera. We will now look at ways in which this information can be used for practical purposes.

Images such as the one shown in Figure 21.14 might be used to control the motion of a vehicle. In this case, the visual information could be used to control the speed of travel of the train. If another train or other obstacle appeared on the tracks in front of the train, the brakes could be applied, for example. A more complex system could control the motion of a car, which could be designed to negotiate traffic, stop at traffic lights, and avoid pedestrians, other vehicles, and the sidewalk.

One of the most common uses of machine vision in robotic agents is to identify objects in the agent's path. In simple cases, these objects will be limited to blocks of various shapes and sizes, but in real-world systems, the objects could be almost anything.

The main task is therefore to map the image that has been received to an internal representation of an object. The method that is usually used depends on the principle that there are some properties of any object that are **invariant**. In other words, whatever angle you view the object from, whatever lighting conditions it is in, whatever changes occur to its shape, the invariant properties will remain constant.

In the case of a sphere, this is fairly simple: the sphere will appear in a two-dimensional image as a circle under almost any conditions. This is of course complicated by the possibility of other objects obscuring the object we are looking at and also by the complications of texture. A sphere with a checkerboard pattern on it might look rather different when placed against a checkerboard background than if it were placed against a plain background.

The method that is usually used to identify objects is known as the **parts decomposition method**, which involves breaking an object into its constituent parts and then attempting to identify those parts in the image. For example, a cat could be broken down into a head, eyes, mouth, tail, legs, fur, etc.

Another method, which does not work so well with cats, but works well with more rigid objects, is to assume that an object will look the same once a set of transformations (e.g., rotation, translation, and increase or decrease in size) are applied. Hence, if an image is found that looks somewhat like a cube, but not exactly the same as the image of a cube that the system has been trained with, the image can be transformed using rotation, translation, and resizing, until it matches more closely the training image. This method is known as the **alignment** method. This method thus involves finding an object whose internal representation matches that being seen in the image after applying one or more allowable transformations.

Having identified an object, the agent can use its behavior model (defined perhaps using the subsumption architecture—see Chapter 19) to determine what to do—it may need to move toward the object to examine it in more detail, it may want to avoid the object, or it may want to pick it up. If the agent cannot detect objects using vision, then it can be very difficult for it to decide what to do. Hence, agents that need to interact with objects in the real world in any way more complex than simply moving past them need to be able to receive some kind of visual input from the world and then to analyze that visual information.

21.7   Face Recognition

One very popular area of computer vision at present is the study of automatic face recognition. This problem is an excellent example of the kinds of problems that Artificial Intelligence techniques are usually applied to: it is a problem that humans find so simple that we take it for granted, yet it is a problem that traditional computer science has found almost impossible to solve.

The difficulties with automatic face recognition are numerous. First of all, the conditions in which a face can be seen, such as lighting, distance from camera to face, and angle, can dramatically alter the appearance of the face. This problem is faced with most object recognition systems. Face recognition is further complicated by the fact that human faces are so flexible and so capable of being altered. Facial expressions are one complexity, but people also are able to grow beards; cut or grow their hair; wear glasses, sunglasses, hats, and earrings; and grow older, all of which can significantly affect the appearance of a face.

As a result, identifying invariant properties of a given face is an important first step in automating the process of face recognition. These properties need to be invariant regardless of distance, angle, orientation, and lighting, but also regardless of what has happened to the face—whether it is wearing glasses, whether it has its eyes shut or open, and so on.

One early approach to face recognition was to identify particular facial features, such as eyes, nose, mouth, eyebrows, and so on, and to store information about the relative positions of those features. These features could be compared in a new face to determine if it is one that has been seen before. This method works in some circumstances, but is not particularly robust. One problem with this method is that it assumes that the best way to tell the difference between two faces is to note the locations of the features such as eyes, mouth, and so on. This might not be the case.

This observation led to another face recognition method that uses **eigenfaces**. Eigenfaces are based on the idea of **principle component analysis**. Principle component analysis is an important idea in computer science. The idea is that to learn to recognize any type of items of data, the best way is to determine the features of the data that vary most from one item to another. This idea was applied, for example, in Chapter 20, when we saw that the way in which a system could search for responses to a query from a corpus of text was to treat the words that are most infrequent within the corpus as being the most important in queries. In the same way, if we look at a selection of ten faces and note that the position of the tip of the nose relative to the end of the chin is the feature that varies the most, then this is a principle component and should be treated as an important feature for identifying faces. This is the idea behind eigenfaces.

The eigenfaces are the components chosen to represent the faces in the training set. These features are chosen as being the features that provide the greatest differentiation between the faces in the training set and thus provide the greatest likelihood of giving a correct match when presented with a new face.

The eigenfaces can be viewed graphically and tend to look like morphed images of several faces, which is indeed what they are. When attempting to match a single face, a number of these eigenfaces are combined together, and it is the manner in which these faces are combined together that is used to identify which face is being viewed.

This method can also be thought of in terms of vectors. The eigenfaces are the vectors (or eigenvectors) that form the principle components of the training data, and thus define the **face space**. When a new face is examined, it is constructed as a sum of some combination of the eigenvectors, and this vector is compared with the vectors that were already calculated for the faces in the training data. The face with the closest vector is the match.

Usually a number of faces are used for each person in the training set, with a variety of expressions and with different additional elements such as hats, glasses, and so on. In this way, the eigenfaces method provides a very robust way of recognizing faces. In experimentation, this method has given an accuracy of over 90% at matching faces from a small database of training images (around 50 images).

21.8 Chapter Summary

- The mammalian vision system is a remarkably sophisticated system, and most computer vision systems are based to some extent on it.

- Edge detection is often the first stage in image-processing systems. Edge detection involves determining the location of high-frequency areas of an image, which usually correspond to edges or changes in depth in the image.

- Convolution is used by the Canny edge detector to find edges in images.

- Once edges have been detected in an image, the image is usually segmented into homogeneous areas, which correspond roughly to particular objects or textures.

- Edges in a three-dimensional line drawing can be classified using the Waltz algorithm.

- Texture can be used to provide a great deal of information about a scene, such as shape and orientation.

- Detecting and interpreting motion is an important part of the mammalian vision system and is also useful in many computer image recognition systems (particularly in robotic agents that need to navigate in the real world).

- Face recognition is one of the hardest problems of image recognition, but one in which a great deal of success has already been achieved. One popular method is to use eigenfaces, which are based on the idea of principle component analysis.

21.9 Review Questions

21.1 Why does it make sense to model computer vision systems on the human vision system? Can you think of any suitable alternative models?

21.2 Why is edge detection used as an early stage of computer vision? Can you think of any situations in which edge detection methods would fail completely?

21.3 Explain how convolution is used to detect edges in images.

21.4 What is the purpose of segmentation?

21.5 Explain the purpose of the Waltz algorithm. Describe in detail how it works.

21.6 Why is texture so important for computer vision systems? What differences would there be if the world had no texture and all objects were smooth and uniformly colored? Would this make it easier or harder for machine vision systems? What if there were no shadows and everything was uniformly illuminated from all sides as well?

21.7 How do computer vision systems make use of motion?

21.8 Explain the way that eigenfaces are used in face recognition systems.

21.10 Exercises

21.1 Apply the Waltz algorithm using pen and paper to the three-dimensional scene shown in Figure 21.6. Is it possible that you will end up with a different labeling from that shown in Figure 21.7? If your answer was yes, how could this happen? If your answer was no, why not, and can you imagine any situation in which there is more than one possible labeling for such an image?

21.2   Implement an edge detection system in the programming language of your choice. You will need first to find a way to obtain pixel data from an image and convert this into a two-dimensional array of pixels. Your edge detection system should be capable of outputting an image showing the edges.

21.11   Further Reading

There are many books available on the subject of image recognition, computer vision, face recognition, and other related subjects. Shapiro (2001) and Forsyth (2002) both provide excellent coverage of the subject. Nalwa (1993) provides a very readable introduction. Hoffman (1998) provides a different perspective, with a cognitive scientist's view of human vision.

2D Object Detection and Recognition: Models, Algorithms, and Networks, by Yali Amit (2002 – MIT Press)

Intelligent Machine Vision: Techniques, Implementations and Applications, by Bruce G. Batchelor and Frederick M. Waltz (2001 – Springer Verlag)

Advances in Image Understanding: A Festschrift for Azriel Rosenfeld, edited by Kevin W. Bowyer and Narendra Ahuja (1996 – Wiley IEEE Press)

Neural Networks for Vision and Image Processing, edited by Gail A. Carpenter and Stephen Grossberg (1992 – MIT Press)

Machine Vision: Theory, Algorithms, Practicalities, by E. R. Davies (1996 – Academic Press)

Three-Dimensional Computer Vision, by Olivier Faugeras (1993 – MIT Press)

Computer Vision: A Modern Approach, by David A. Forsyth and Jean Ponce (2002 – Prentice Hall)

Dynamic Vision: From Images to Face Recognition, by Shaogang Gong and Stephen J. McKenna (2000 – Imperial College Press)

Computer and Robot Vision (Volume II), by Robert M. Haralick and Linda G. Shapiro (2002 – Pearson Education)

Visual Intelligence: How We Create What We See, by Donald D. Hoffman (1998 – W. W. Norton & Company)

Robot Vision, by Berthold K. Horn (1986 – McGraw Hill Higher Education)

Machine Vision, by Ramesh Jain, Rangachar Kasturi, and Brian G. Schunck (1995 –McGraw Hill)

Computer Vision and Fuzzy Neural Systems, by Arun D. Kulkarni (2001 – Prentice Hall)

A Guided Tour of Computer Vision, by Vishvjit S. Nalwa (1993 – Addison Wesley)

Feature Extraction in Computer Vision and Image Processing, by Mark S. Nixon and Alberto Aguado (2002 – Butterworth-Heinemann)

Algorithms for Image Processing and Computer Vision, by J. R. Parker (1996 – John Wiley & Sons)

Learning-Based Robot Vision, edited by Josef Pauli (2001 – Springer Verlag)

Computer Vision, by Linda G. Shapiro and George C. Stockman (2001 – Prentice Hall)

Image Processing: Analysis and Machine Vision, by Milan Sonka, Vaclav Hlavac, and Roger Boyle (1998 – Brooks Cole)

Introductory Techniques for 3-D Computer Vision, by Emanuele Trucco and Alessandro Verri (1998 – Prentice Hall)

Human Face Recognition Using Third-Order Synthetic Neural Networks, by Okechukwu A. Uwechue and Abhijit S. Pandya (1997 – Kluwer Academic Publishers)

Face Recognition: From Theory to Applications, by Harry Wechsler (1998 – Springer Verlag)

Glossary

This glossary includes definitions and descriptions of the most important terms used in this book.

A

Abduction

A *nonmonotonic form of reasoning that helps us to find plausible explanations for observed phenomena.

Accepting state

A *state in a *finite state machine that represents a "yes" response.

Acquaintance algorithm

A vector-based approach to identifying languages using *n-grams.

Action description language (ADL)

A more expressive variation of the *STRIPS planning language.

Activation function

The function applied to the inputs of a *neuron in a *neural network. The output of this function is compared with the *activation level to determine if the neuron fires.

Activation level

The level of output that a *neuron must reach in order to fire.

Activity product rule

The rule used in *neural networks that use *Hebbian learning to determine how the *weights between *neurons change.

Admissibility

A *heuristic method is defined as admissible if it never overestimates the cost of getting from a given *state to a *goal state.

Adversarial methods

Methods used by game-playing systems to search a *game tree for a *path that will lead to a win over an opponent.

Agent

An entity (usually a software entity) that exists to assist humans in carrying out some task or solving some problem. Types of agents include *software agents, *interface agents, *mobile agents, and *information agents.

Agent team

A group of *agents that collaborate together to reach a common goal.

Alphabet

The set of symbols available for a logical system.

Alpha–beta pruning

A method used to make searching a *game tree more efficient. It relies on the principle that if a part of a game tree is going to give a bad result, it is not worth further examining that part of the tree.

Ambiguity

The problem that an *utterance in a *human language can have more than one possible meaning. Types of ambiguity include lexical, semantic, syntactic, referential, and local.

Ancestor

An ancestor, a, of a *node, n, in a *tree is a node that is further up a *path in the tree than n. n is a *descendant of a.

And-goal

And-goals are *subgoals in a *goal tree that must all be satisfied in order to satisfy the goal tree.

And-node

A *node that represents an *and-goal.

And–or tree

See *goal tree.

Antecedent

The part of the *rule that comes before the *implication. In the rule $A \rightarrow B$, A is the antecedent. See *consequent.

Artificial Intelligence

The subject of this book. See Chapters 1 to 21 for more information. See also *weak AI, *strong AI.

Artificial Life

Methods modeled on life that often use *emergent behavior to find better solutions to problems than can be found using traditional methods.

Artificial neural network

See *neural network.

Associativity

A property of mathematical and logical operators. Operator o is associative if $A \text{ o } (B \text{ o } C) \equiv (A \text{ o } B) \text{ o } C$.

Atomic action

Individual actions used by *planning systems. An atomic action can consist of a number of smaller actions, but it is treated as one indivisible action for the purpose of constructing a plan.

Atomic formula

A *well-formed formula of the form $P(x1, x2, x3, \ldots, xn)$.

Attractor network

See *recurrent network.

Augmented finite state machine (AFSM)

A type of *finite state machine that uses *situated action rules. AFSMs are used in Brooks's *subsumption architecture.

Augmented transition network (ATN)

A type of *transition network that is used for *parsing sentences. An ATN has *procedures and tests that are attached to its arcs.

Autoassociative memory

A type of memory that can recognize an object but cannot associate one object or piece of data with another. A *Hopfield network is an autoassociative memory. See *heteroassociative memory.

Autonomy

A property of *agents. An autonomous agent has the ability to act independently to some extent of its owner or programmer. This is often a desired property for *intelligent agents.

Axon

The part of a *neuron in the human brain that provides output to other neurons via a *synapse.

B

Backpropagation

A method used to modify the *weights in a multilayer *neural network. Errors at the output layer are fed back through the network, correcting the weights. Over a number of iterations, this usually leads to a network that gives mostly correct responses to the *training data.

Backus–Naur form (BNF)

A language used to define the grammar of *formal and *informal languages. BNF uses *terminal and *nonterminal symbols, and *rewrite rules that express how sentences can be legally built up out of terminal symbols.

Backward chaining

See *goal-driven search.

Bayesian belief network

An acyclic directed *graph, where the *nodes in the graph represent evidence or hypotheses, and where an edge that connects two nodes represents a dependence between those two nodes. Each node is labeled with a set of probabilities that express how that node depends on other nodes.

Bayes' optimal classifier

A system that uses *Bayes' theorem to learn to classify data. It can be shown that this classifier is optimal, which means that it provides the best possible mechanism for classifying data.

Bayes' theorem

Bayes' theorem can be used to calculate the probability that a certain event will occur or that a certain proposition is true, given that we already know a related piece of information. It is written as follows:

$$P(B|A) = \frac{P(A|B) \cdot P(B)}{P(A)}$$

Belief desire intention architecture (BDI)

An architecture used by *agents that uses beliefs about the world and desires to develop intentions about how the agent should behave.

Bidirectional associative memory (BAM)

A *neural network used to associate items from one set with items in another set.

Binary operator

A logical or mathematical operator that takes two arguments, such as logical and ($\wedge$) and logical or ($\vee$). See *unary operator.

Bivalent logic

A logical system that has two *truth values. Classical logic is bivalent because a logical expression can either be true or false. See *multivalent logic and *fuzzy logic.

Blackboard architecture

A method for structure knowledge representation that combines information from a number of knowledge sources (such as human experts) in order to solve a problem.

Blind search method

A *search method that does not use *heuristics. Also known as *uninformed search. *Depth-first search and *breadth-first search are blind search methods.

Blocks world

A scenario that is used to explain planning techniques. The blocks world consists of a table with a number of blocks, which are usually cubes. The blocks world has very simple properties, and there are usually a limited set of actions that can be taken to interact with the world, such as "pick up" and "put on."

Bottom up

An approach to solving problems that involves first solving the smaller sub-problems, and repeatedly combining these solutions together until a complete solution is found. See *top down.

Bounded lookahead

A method used when searching *game trees that involves cutting off *search when a specified depth in the tree is reached. This is particularly useful in games such as chess or Go that have very deep search trees.

Bound variable

A bound variable in a logical expression is one that has been quantified within the same scope. For example, in the expression $\forall x(x \rightarrow y)$, x is bound because it is quantified by the $\forall$ *quantifier. See *free variable.

Braitenberg vehicle

A type of *robotic vehicle that is used in thought experiments to study the nature of intelligence. Braitenberg vehicles range from very simple robots that follow or avoid light to more complex systems. None of them have any real intelligence, but they often display behavior that appears intelligent.

Branch

A connection between two *nodes within a *tree.

Branching factor

A node within a tree has a branching factor of n if that node has n *children. In a tree that has a branching factor of n, all nodes (apart from *leaf nodes) have n children.

Breadth-first search

A *blind, *exhaustive search method that visits all *nodes at a given depth before moving on to the next depth in the *tree.

Brute-force search

A *search method that examines every *path in a *search tree until it finds a goal. See *exhaustive search.

Bucket-brigade algorithm

A method used by *classifier systems that assigns blame and credit to individual components within the system.

Building-block hypothesis

A consequence of the *schema theorem, which can be stated as: "*Genetic algorithms manipulate short, low-order, high-fitness *schemata in order to find optimal solutions to problems."

C

Candidate elimination

A *learning method that uses *version spaces to learn to classify data. The method uses two sets of hypotheses, which start out as the most general possible hypothesis and the most specific hypothesis. On successive iterations these hypotheses converge until a match is found.

Canny edge detector

An *edge detection method based on *convolution.

Case-based planning

A case-based planning system stores the *plans it formulates for solving problems and is able to reuse whole plans or parts of plans to solve similar problems in the future. Case-based planners use *case-based reasoning to solve problems.

Case-based reasoning

See *case-based planning.

Causal link

In *partial order planning, a causal link is a link between an action and one or more conditions, which shows that that action causes the conditions to become true. See *protected link.

Cellular automaton

A set of cells that live or die according to a set of rules. A cellular automaton of sufficient complexity can reproduce itself. See *Conway's Life.

Center of gravity

See *centroid.

Centroid

The point in a two-dimensional shape that has equal area on all sides of it. This is the *center of gravity of the shape.

Certainty factor

A representation of the degree of belief in a hypothesis. Used by *MYCIN.

Chart parser

An efficient method of *parsing natural language sentences that uses a chart to store information about the sentence being parsed.

Chinese room

A thought experiment that is used to claim that a computer is not capable of thought in the same way that a human is. The experiment consists of a room with a person inside it who does not speak or understand any Chinese. This person has a set of symbols and a set of rules for how to manipulate the symbols. A question in Chinese is passed into the room, and the human uses the rules to construct an answer in Chinese. Although the human clearly does not understand Chinese, the room as a whole appears to have understood the question and given a sensible answer, thus displaying the kinds of behavior that a computer might display when answering questions using Artificial Intelligence.

Chomsky's hierarchy

A hierarchy of *grammars invented by Noam Chomsky, which includes *regular grammars, *context-free grammars, *context-sensitive grammars, and *recursively enumerable grammars.

Chromosome

A representation of a single solution to a problem as used by a *genetic algorithm. A chromosome is also a structure contained in biological cells that contains genetic information.

Chronological backtracking

A method of backtracking (used by depth-first search) that backtracks to the next available *path that has not yet been taken. This contrasts with *nonchronological backtracking, which can often be more efficient.

Circumscription

A form of *nonmonotonic reasoning that is designed to deal with situations in which not all facts are either stated or denied. See *closed-world assumption.

Class

A group of objects that is defined by some shared property. For example, we might consider the class of humans or the class of things with three sides. An *object is an instantiation of a class.

Class frame

A *frame within a *frame system that represents a *class.

Classical logic

The logical system based on that proposed by Aristotle. This system contrasts with nonclassical logics such as *nonmonotonic logics and *modal logics.

Classifier system

An *expert system that uses *genetic algorithms and a *bucket-brigade algorithm to improve its ability to solve problems.

Clause

A *sentence in *conjunctive normal form consists of a *conjunction of clauses, where each clause is of the following form:

$$B_1 \lor B_2 \lor B_3 \lor \ldots \lor B_n$$

CLIPS (C Language Integrated Production System)

An *expert system shell.

Cloning

A reproductive method in *genetic algorithms that does not use *crossover. A cloned offspring is an exact replica of its parent, apart from any effects of *mutation.

Closed-world assumption

The assumption that any fact not specifically known to be true must be false. Also known as *negation by failure. The closed-world assumption is used by *PROLOG.

Coevolution

The process whereby the evolution of two species is tightly connected. Usually this applies to a predator species and a prey species. As the predator species becomes better at catching the prey, the prey must evolve techniques to enable it to escape. In turn this causes the predator to evolve new abilities. Coevolution can often cause species to evolve much faster than they otherwise would and to reach levels of sophistication that would not otherwise be possible. This was used successfully by Danny Hillis in developing his ramps to solve problems.

Cognitive psychology

A branch of psychology that studies the way in which the human brain processes knowledge or data to solve problems.

Collaborative agent

An *agent that is part of a *multiagent system and that cooperates with other agents to achieve a common goal.

Collaborative filtering

A method used to determine an individual's likes or dislikes by comparing his or her past behavior with that of other individuals.

Combinatorial explosion

The problem encountered when computers attempt to solve problems whose complexity grows *exponentially.

Combinatorial problem

A problem that involves assigning values to a number of variables in order to find some optimal solution. The eight-queens problem is an example of a combinatorial problem.

Commutativity

A property of mathematical and logical operators. Operator o is commutative if $a \mathbin{o} b \equiv b \mathbin{o} a$.

Competitive learning

A form of *unsupervised learning used by *Kohonen maps.

Completeness

A property of *search methods. A search method is complete if it guarantees that it will find a solution if one exists. Completeness is also a property of logical systems: A logical system is complete if every *valid statement in the logic can be proved by applying the rules of deduction to the axioms. Both *propositional logic and *first-order predicate logic are complete. See *soundness.

Complete path

A *path in a *tree that leads from the *root node to a *goal node.

Composition

An operator that can be combined to two *substitutions to produce a new *substitution that is the same as applying the two original substitutions consecutively.

Computation tree logic (CTL)

A form of *temporal logic that uses a *tree to represent time.

Concave edge

An edge in a two-dimensional line drawing that is between two faces that are at an angle of less than 180° from each other.

Concept learning

Concept learning involves learning to map from a set of input variables to a Boolean value. Concept-learning systems can thus learn to determine whether or not an object meets a particular criterion based on a number of that object's attributes.

Conditional planning

A *planning method that does not start with complete information about the problem, so it allows for several possible results of each action.

Conditional probability

The *probability that one fact will be true given that another fact is known to be true. This is written $P(A|B)$, which is read "the probability of A given B". See *posterior probability, *prior probability.

Conditional probability table

A table that shows the probabilities that one variable will be true given the possible values of other variables on which it depends.

Conflict

A situation that arises in multiple inheritance or in *rule-based systems in which two contradictory pieces of data arise. For example, two *rules in a rule-based system fire that recommend contradictory actions.

Conflict resolution

The methods used in a *rule-based system to decide which *rule to use when a *conflict occurs. See *expert system, *metarule.

Conjunction

The conjunction of two logical variables is the logical and ($\land$) of those two variables, written $A \land B$. $A \land B$ is true if and only if A and B are both true. See *disjunction.

Conjunctive normal form

An expression is in conjunctive normal form if it consists of a *conjunction of a set of *clauses. See *disjunctive normal form.

Consequent

The part of a rule that comes after the implication. The consequent of a rule in an *expert system represents the diagnosis or recommended action that is the consequence of the *antecedent.

Constant

A symbol in *first-order predicate calculus that names a specific object. A constant cannot be quantified as a variable can.

Constraint

A rule that dictates limitations on the possible values variables can take in solving a problem.

Constraint satisfaction problem

A problem in which a set of *constraints dictate possible values for variables. The eight-queens problem is an example of a constraint satisfaction problem. In this case, the constraint is that no two queens can be on the same row, column, or diagonal.

Context-free grammar

A *grammar with *rewrite rules that can have at most one *terminal symbol on the right-hand side. This type of grammar does not specify how words should agree with each other in case, number, or gender. See *context-sensitive grammar, *Chomsky's hierarchy.

Context-sensitive grammar

A *grammar with *rewrite rules that can have more than one *terminal symbol on the right-hand side, and which can therefore specify rules concerning the agreement of case, number, and gender. Context-sensitive grammars are often used for *natural language processing. See *context-free grammar, *Chomsky's hierarchy.

Contingent

A logical statement whose *truth value is not fixed, but varies depending on circumstances, is contingent. For example, $A \wedge B$ is true if and only if both A and B are true. See *noncontingent, *interpretation.

Contradiction

If a logical system has two facts that disagree with each other, there is a contradiction. For example, it would be a contradiction, in *classical logic, to believe both A and $\neg A$.

Convex edge

An edge between two faces that are at an angle of more than $180°$ from each other.

Convolution

A mathematical operator used in *edge detection. The convolution of two discrete functions $f(a, b)$ and $g(a, b)$ is defined as follows:

$$f(a, b) * g(a, b) = \sum_{u=-\infty}^{\infty} \sum_{v=-\infty}^{\infty} f(a, b) g(a - u, b - v)$$

The convolution of continuous functions $f(a, b)$ and $g(a, b)$ is defined as follows:

$$f(a, b) * g(a, b) = \int_{-\infty}^{\infty} \int_{-\infty}^{\infty} f(a, b) g(a - u, b - v) \, du \, dv$$

Applying convolution to an image is one way to *smooth an image.

Conway's Life

A two-dimensional *cellular automaton that consists of a grid of cells. Each cell can be either alive or dead, and rules are used to determine from one generation to the next which cells will live, which will die, and which will come to life.

Co-occurrence matrix

A matrix used in *image recognition. The co-occurrence matrix, C, is defined as follows:

$$C = D + D^T$$

Where D^T is the transposition of the matrix D.

Copycat architecture

A system designed to solve analogy problems such as "*ABC* is to *CBA* as *DEF* is to *???.*"

Corpus

A body of text, usually used in *information retrieval problems.

Credit assignment

The technique used to decide which parts of a system contributed to its success. This method is used by *classifier systems and other systems that use a *bucket-brigade algorithm. See *reinforcement learning, *winner takes all algorithm.

Crisp set

An ordinary, nonfuzzy set. Each item in the world either is or is not a member of a given crisp set. There is no idea of "degree of membership" of a crisp set. See *fuzzy set.

Crossover

An operator used in *genetic algorithms that combines genetic information from two *chromosomes to produce one or two offspring.

CYC

A *frame-based knowledge representation system that uses a database of millions of facts and *rules to make common-sense deductions about the world.

Cycle

A *path through a *semantic net or other *graph that visits the same *node twice. A *tree is a net that does not have any cycles.

D

Data-driven search

A *search method that works from a start *state toward a goal state. See *goal-driven search.

Deception

A problem that arises in *genetic algorithms, due to the use of building blocks. Deception can be avoided by using *inversion or *messy genetic algorithms.

Decidability

A logical system is decidable if it is possible to produce an algorithm that will determine whether any *well-formed formula is a *theorem. In other words, if a logical system is decidable, then a computer can be used to determine whether logical expressions in that system are *valid or not.

Decision tree

A *tree in which each *node represents a question and the answers to the question determine which *path is to be followed from that *node. *Leaf nodes represent classifications determined by the decision tree. See *ID3, *decision-tree induction.

Decision-tree induction

A method that learns to classify data by building a *decision tree based on the *training data.

Deduction

A process that applies a set of inference rules to a set of assumptions to lead logically to a conclusion. We write

$$\{A_1, A_2, \ldots, A_n\} \vdash C$$

where $A_1, A_2, \ldots, A_n$ are the assumptions, and C is the conclusion that can be deduced from them.

Default reasoning

A form of *nonmonotonic reasoning that uses default rules to assume that certain facts are true unless there is evidence to contradict them. See *closed-world assumption.

Default value

The value that is assigned to a *slot in a *frame-based system unless it is overridden.

Defining length

The defining length of a *genetic algorithm *schema is defined as the distance between the first and last defined bits (bits that are not) in the schema.

Defuzzification

The process whereby a crisp value can be obtained from the *fuzzy sets derived by a *fuzzy system.

Demon

A *procedure in a *frame-based system that is run automatically when the value in a particular *slot is changed.

DeMorgan's laws

A pair of complementary logical rules that can be expressed as follows:

$$A \wedge B \equiv \neg(\neg A \vee \neg B)$$
$$A \vee B \equiv \neg(\neg A \wedge \neg B)$$

Dempster–Shafer theory

A method that is used to reason about degrees of belief in a theory.

Depth-first search

A *blind search method that follows one *path to its first *leaf node before *backtracking chronologically to the next deepest choice. See *breadth-first search.

Depth threshold

A limit that is applied in *depth-first search that cuts search off at a specified depth. This avoids the problem that occurs when a *tree has a *path that is of infinite length, meaning that the search might never find a *goal.

Derivation tree

A *parse tree that is built from the *top down.

Descendant

A descendant, d, of a *node, n, in a *tree is a node that is further down a *path in the tree than n. n is an *ancestor of a.

Describe and match

A method that uses a *decision tree to identify an object, by asking questions about the object.

Diagnosis

A process of explaining the cause of some observed phenomenon. Often used in medicine to explain the cause of a patient's symptoms.

Directed graph

A graph in which directions are attached to the edges between *nodes, meaning that if one edge exists between two nodes, it is only possible to travel in one direction between those nodes, but if two edges exist between two nodes, it is possible to travel in both directions between those nodes.

Discontinuity

A line in a two-dimensional line drawing that has one plane on one side and another plane on its other side. Discontinuities can be caused by two faces meeting, by perception of depth, by lighting, shadows, or *texture.

Disjunction

The disjunction of two logical variables is the logical or ($\vee$) of those two variables, written $A \vee B$. $A \vee B$ is true if either A or B is true. See *conjunction.

Disjunctive normal form

An expression is in disjunctive normal form if it consists of a *disjunction of a set of *clauses. See *conjunctive normal form.

Diversity

A measure of the difference between chromosomes in a population.

Domain expert

A human expert who provides domain knowledge to an *expert system. For example, a medical expert system would have input from a number of domain experts, most of whom would probably be doctors.

Dualism

The philosophical idea that mind and matter are the two distinct constituents of the universe.

Dynamic planning

*Planning methods that take account of unforeseen circumstances by allowing the execution of the plan to change in reaction to events and changes in the environment.

E

Edge

A line in a *graph that directly connects two *nodes. In *image recognition, an edge is a perceived line that exists between two areas of different depth, *texture, orientation, or color.

Edge detection

A method in *image recognition that locates the *edges in an image, often by looking for areas of high frequency, which indicate a change in color or *texture.

Effect axiom

In *situation calculus, a rule that describes the effect of an action.

Effective branching factor

If a search method expands n *nodes of a *search tree when solving a particular problem, then the effective *branching factor (b) of the *search is the branching factor of a *uniform tree that contains n nodes.

Emergent behavior

Complex behavior that emerges from an apparently simple system. Emergent behavior usually involves a system developing some useful behavior that was not built in by its designer.

Entropy

The extent to which a system is disordered. See *information gain, *ID3.

Epoch

A complete iteration of the training cycle of a *perceptron.

Equivalence

Two logical expressions that must always have the same *truth value for all interpretations are equivalent. This is written $A \equiv B$. For example, $A \wedge B \equiv B \wedge A$ because whatever truth values are assigned to A and B, $A \wedge B$ must have the same truth value as $B \wedge A$.

Error gradient

A measure that *neural networks employ in *backpropagation. The error gradient for an output node k is defined as the *error value for this node multiplied by the derivative of the *activation function:

$$\delta_k = \frac{\partial y_k}{\partial x_k} \cdot e_k$$

x_k is the weighted sum of the input values to the node k.

Error value

The difference between the expected output of a *node in a *neural network and the actual output.

Event calculus

A method for reasoning about entities that vary over time. See *situation calculus.

Evolution

The biologic process by which species change over a number of generations. Evolution is modeled in many *Artificial Life methods, particularly in *genetic algorithms.

Evolutionary programming

A method that evolves *finite state automata to find a solution to the problem of determining the next symbol in a finite sequence of symbols, $a_1, a_2, a_3, a_4, a_5, \ldots, a_n$. See *genetic algorithm, *Artificial Life.

Excluded middle, law of

A law from Aristotelian logic that says that it is not possible to assert both A and $\neg A$. Similarly, it states that either A must be true, or $\neg A$ is true. These can be written as the two logically *equivalent statements:

$\neg(A \wedge \neg A)$

$A \vee \neg A$

See *fuzzy logic, *classical logic.

Execution

The process of carrying out the steps determined by a *planner for solving a problem.

Execution monitoring

A method that is used during the *execution of a *plan to ensure that the plan is still a sensible solution to the problem, by checking that the *preconditions of the planned actions still hold.

Exhaustive search

See *brute-force search.

Existential quantifier

The existential quantifier ∃ is read as "there exists," and is used to refer to some variable of which at least one must exist, but which is not explicitly defined. For example, we can write $\exists x \, (P(x))$, which can be read as "there exists an x for which $P(x)$ is true." See *universal quantifier, *first-order predicate calculus.

Expectiminimax

A version of the *minimax algorithm that works with games of chance, by taking into account the *probability that each *path through the game tree will be taken.

Expert system

A system, usually built using a set of *rules, that uses expert knowledge to solve problems and explain phenomena such as symptoms. See *expert system shell, *production system.

Expert system shell

A toolkit that can be used to build *expert systems. *CLIPS is an example of an expert system shell.

Exponential growth

A function grows exponentially if its output grows as a function of some value raised to the power of its input. For example, $f(x) = 2^x$ is an exponential function. A problem whose complexity grows exponentially as the problem grows is usually very hard to solve. See *NP-Complete, *combinatorial explosion.

F

Face recognition

Methods used to identify an individual by examining his or her face.

Fact

A *clause in *PROLOG that has no negative *literals and thus has nothing on the right-hand side of the implication, as in the following example:

A :-

Failure node

An *or-node in a *goal tree that is also a *leaf node and is thus impossible to solve.

False negative

In *information retrieval, a result that is classified as *not* being of interest but which in fact is interesting is a false negative. The fewer false negatives an information retrieval system gives, the higher its *recall. See *false positive, *precision.

False positive

In *information retrieval, a result that is classified as being of interest but which in fact is not interesting is a false positive. The fewer false positives an information retrieval system gives, the higher its *precision. See *false negative, *recall.

Falsum

The symbol $\perp$ is called **falsum**, which is used to indicate an absurdity, or a *contradiction.

Feasible region

The part of a *search space that contains possible solutions to the problem.

Feed-forward network

A *multilayer neural network with an input layer, an output layer, and one or more hidden layers.

Filter

A function that, when applied to an image, removes all undesired parts of the image. For example, a filter might remove all non-edge regions from an image.

Finite state automaton (FSA)

A finite state automaton is a simple device that has a finite set of states and an input string (often thought of as being on a tape, running through a device that can read one symbol at a time). Each symbol that the finite state automaton reads in is compared with a rule that dictates to which state to move from that state, with that input. After reading the entire input, the finite state machine is either in an **accepting state**, which means its answer is "yes" to some question, or it is in some other state, in which case the answer is "no."

First-order predicate logic

A logical system in which *quantifiers can be applied to terms but not to functions or predicates. See *propositional calculus, *propositional logic, *classical logic, *monotonic logic, *nonmonotonic logic.

Fitness

A *metric that is used to measure how successful a given *chromosome is at solving the *genetic algorithm's problem. It is usually the case that a chromosome with higher fitness will produce more offspring or have a greater chance of reproducing than a chromosome with lower fitness.

Fluent

A function that varies with time.

Foothill

A *local maximum.

Forgetting factor

A value used in *Hebbian learning systems to reduce the *weights of *nodes.

Formal language

A language such as PROLOG or C++, as compared with a *natural language.

Forward chaining

See *data-driven search.

Forward pruning

A method used by game-playing systems that involves cutting off examination of the *game tree at a point where the position has become unacceptably poor for the computer.

Frame

In a *frame system, a frame defines either a *class or an *instance of a class and contains one or more *slots that hold values for attributes of that class or instance.

Frame axiom

A rule that states what aspects of the world do not change when an action takes place. See *effect axiom, *frame problem.

Frame problem

The problem that it is usually easy to determine the effects of an action but often very difficult to work out what does *not* change as a result of the action. See *frame axiom, *ramification problem.

Frame system

A *semantic network that consists of a set of *frames, connected together by relations.

Free variable

A free variable in a logical expression is one that has not been quantified within the same scope. For example, in the expression $\forall x(x \rightarrow y)$, y is free because it is not quantified by the $\forall$ *quantifier. See *bound variable.

Fundamental memory

One of the stable values of a *recurrent network.

Fuzzification

The process of converting a crisp input value into a fuzzy value.

Fuzzy expert system

An *expert system that uses *fuzzy logic rules.

Fuzzy inference

The process by which a fuzzy system applies fuzzy rules to a set of crisp input values to derive a single crisp value. See *Mamdani inference.

Fuzzy logic

An alternative to *classical logic in which the *law of the excluded middle does not apply and in which logical variables can take on any real number value between 0 and 1. See *multivalent logic.

Fuzzy reasoning

The process of reasoning using fuzzy logic.

Fuzzy rule

A rule used by a *fuzzy expert system that takes the form

> IF A op x then $B = y$

where op is some mathematical operator (such as "=," ">," or "<").

Fuzzy set

A set with a membership function that determines the extent to which any item is a member. See *crisp set.

G

Game tree

A *tree that represents the moves in a game. The *root node represents the state before any moves have been made, the *nodes in the tree represent possible states of the game (or positions), and *edges in the tree represent moves in the game.

Gene

A single unit of *genetic algorithm contained within a *chromosome.

General problem solver (GPS)

A computer program invented in the 1950s that uses *means–ends analysis to solve logical problems.

Generalization

The act of moving from an *instance of a *class to the class itself. Also known as the "is–a" relationship. For example, one can generalize from Ronald Reagan to the class of presidents of the United States.

Generate and test

A *search method that involves examining every *node in the *search space until one is found that matches some criteria that describe the *goal state.

Genetic algorithm

A system that uses methods modeled on natural *evolution to solve complex problems. See *chromosome, *gene.

Genetic programming

A method that evolves *LISP programs or *S-expressions. The method searches through the *search space of possible S-expressions until it finds one that best solves the current problem.

Genotype

The genetic information represented by a set of *genes that make up an individual person or other biologic creature. See *phenotype.

Geometric progression

A sequence of numbers where each number in the progression is obtained by multiplying the previous number by some constant.

Global maximum

The best possible solution in a *search space. When the search space is represented as a curved surface, the global maximum is the highest peak in the surface. See *foothill, *plateau, *ridge.

Goal

The solution to a problem. See *goal node.

Goal-based agent

An *agent that uses *search or *planning to achieve some *goal.

Goal-driven search

A search method that works from a goal state toward the start state. See *data-driven search.

Goal node

The *node (of which there may be more than one) in a *search tree that represents the solution of the problem that is being solved. The aim of all *search methods is to find a goal node. See *goal.

Goal reduction

See *problem reduction, *goal tree.

Goal tree

A *tree that is used to represent the way in which a problem can be broken down into subgoals. Each *node in the tree represents a subgoal. See *and–or tree, *and-node, *or-node, *success node, *failure node.

Gödel implication

A form of logical *implication that is used in *fuzzy logic. It is defined as follows:

$$A \rightarrow B \equiv (A \leq B) \vee B$$

Gradient descent

A method used in training *backpropagation neural networks, which involves descending the steepest part of the *error gradient.

Grammar

A set of rules that define the syntax and structure of a language. See *Backus–Naur form, *context-sensitive grammar, *context-free grammar.

Graph

A data structure that consists of *nodes connected by *edges. See *tree, *semantic net, *cycle.

GraphPlan

A *planning method that uses *planning graphs to solve problems that are expressed in *STRIPS notation.

Ground instance

A ground instance of a *clause is a version of that clause in which any variables it contains have been replaced by *ground terms from the *Herbrand universe.

Ground term

A *constant or *function that does not contain any *variables.

H

Halting Problem

The problem of determining whether a given computer program will ever halt. It can be proved that no computer program can ever be written that can solve the Halting problem. The proof is as follows: Imagine a program H, which when given an argument P, which is another program, determines whether P halts or not. If H determines that P does halt, then H enters an infinite loop and therefore never halts. If H determines that P does not halt, then it reports a positive response and exits. Now further imagine that H is applied to itself. Let us suppose that H determines that H does halt. In that case, it will enter an infinite loop and never halt. Hence, its assessment was wrong. Similarly, if it decides that H does not halt, then it halts, disproving its own assessment again.

Hamming distance

The Hamming distance measures the number of elements of two vectors that differ. The Hamming distance between two vectors, X and Y, is written $||X, Y||$. For example, $||(1,0,0,1),(1,0,1,1)|| = 1$ because there is only one element of the vectors that differs.

HEARSAY II

A system that used a *blackboard architecture and an index of computer science papers to answer spoken questions on the subject.

Hebbian learning

A method of *unsupervised learning used in *neural networks. Hebbian learning is based on the idea that if two *neurons in a neural network are connected together, and they fire at the same time when a particular input is given to the network, then the connection between those two neurons should be strengthened.

Hedge

A fuzzy set qualifier, such as *very, quite, extremely*, or *somewhat*.

Herbrand base

The Herbrand base of a set of *clauses, S, is defined as the set of *ground atoms that can be obtained by replacing variables in S by members of the *Herbrand universe for S. The Herbrand base of S is written $H_S(S)$.

Herbrand interpretation

A Herbrand Interpretation for a set of *clauses, S, is defined as a set of assignments of true and false to the elements of the *Herbrand base, $H_S(S)$.

Herbrand universe

For a set of *clauses, S, the Herbrand universe, H_S, is defined as being the set of constants that are contained within S and the set of functions in S applied to those constants. See *ground term.

Heteroassociative memory

A type of memory that can associate one object or piece of data with another.

Heuristic

A rule or piece of information that is used to make *search or another problem-solving method more effective or more efficient.

Heuristic evaluation function

A function that when applied to a *node gives a value that represents a good estimate of the distance of the node from the *goal.

Heuristic repair

A method of solving *combinatorial problems that involves generating a random solution to the problem and iterating toward a better solution by making simple changes that reduce the number of errors.

Hidden layer

A layer of *neurons within a *neural network that is between an input layer and an output layer. The hidden layer usually carries out the calculations of the network.

Hill climbing

An *informed search method that acts by always moving toward a better solution one step at a time, ensuring that every step improves the current state. Hill climbing is very susceptible to problems such as *ridges, *foothills, and *plateaus.

Hopfield network

A *recurrent neural network that usually uses the sign activation function:

$$Sign(X) = \begin{cases} +1 & for \ x > 0 \\ -1 & for \ x < 0 \end{cases}$$

Horizon problem

This problem involves an extremely long sequence of moves in a game that clearly lead to a strong advantage for one player, but where the sequence of moves, although potentially obvious to a human player, takes more moves than can be examined by a computer using *bounded lookahead. Hence, the significant end of the sequence has been pushed over the horizon.

Horn clause

A *clause that has at most one positive *literal.

Human language

One of the many hundreds of languages spoken and written by human beings around the world, such as English, Japanese, Russian, Swahili, and French. See *formal language, *natural language.

Hybrid agent

An *agent that exhibits properties of more than one agent type.

Hypothesis

A possible explanation for a set of observed phenomena.

I

ID3

A *decision tree induction algorithm that builds a decision tree from the top down. The nodes in the decision tree are selected by choosing features of the *training data set that provide the most information about the data and turning those features into questions.

Image capture

The process of obtaining an image from a real-world scene so that some kind of image processing can be carried out on the image.

Image recognition

The process of identifying features and making informed decisions about a scene by examining an image of the scene. See *edge detection, *segmentation.

Implication

A logical operator that is defined by the following *truth table:

A	B	A → B
false	false	true
false	true	true
true	false	false
true	true	true

Independence

If the value of one variable does not in any way affect the value of another, then the two variables are said to be independent. Hence, for example, the color of the sky is independent of my name, but the color of the sky is not independent of the time of day.

Inductive bias

Restrictions imposed on a *learning method by its assumptions.

Inductive reasoning

Reasoning about what will happen in the future based on evidence from the past. See *deduction, *abduction.

Inference engine

The part of an *expert system that controls the process of deriving conclusions and recommended actions from a set of rules and facts.

Inference rule

A rule that is used in the process of logical *deduction.

Information agent

An *agent that gathers information on behalf of a human user. Usually information agents are used to gather information from the Internet and so are also called *internet agents.

Information gain

The reduction in *entropy caused by some change in a system.

Information retrieval

Information retrieval involves matching the text contained in a query or a document to a set of other documents. Often, the task involves finding the documents from a *corpus of documents that are relevant to a user's query.

Informed search method

A *search method that uses a *heuristic to ensure that it searches the *search space as efficiently as it can.

Inheritance

The way in which one *class or *object can derive features from a *superclass from which it is itself derived.

Initial state

The *state in which a problem-solving system starts to solve its problem.

Instance

An instance of a *class is an *object that has properties of that class.

Instance constructor

A *procedure that creates an *instance of a *class.

Instance frame

A *frame within a *frame system that represents an *instance of a *class.

Intelligent agent

*Software agents are often referred to as intelligent agents, but an intelligent agent is really an agent that has the particular property of intelligence. This means, for example, that it has the ability to reason independently about data. Many intelligent agents have the ability to learn. Another important property of most intelligent agents is *autonomy.

Interface agent

An *autonomous *intelligent agent that acts as a personal assistant for a user.

Internet agent

See *information agent.

Interpretation

An interpretation is a specific choice of assignment of values to a set of variables. A logical expression can be true under one interpretation and false under another.

Inversion

A *unary operator that reverses the order of a subset of the bits within a *chromosome. Inversion is used to avoid the problem of *deception.

Irrevocability

A *search method is irrevocable if it does not employ *backtracking—in other words, it explores just one *path through a *search tree. *Hill climbing is an example of an irrevocable search method.

Iterated local search

A *local search method that is repeated iteratively using different starting points in order to avoid the problem of *local maxima.

J

Joint probability distribution (joint)

The distribution of *probabilities of a combination of two logical variables. For example, we could refer to the joint probability distribution of $A \land B$, which would be represented by a table such as the following:

	A	¬A
B	0.11	0.09
¬B	0.63	0.17

K

Knowledge base

The database of *rules used by an *expert system. The knowledge base contains the data that represent the system's knowledge about the domain.

Knowledge engineer

The human being who is responsible for a large part of the creation of an *expert system. Specifically the knowledge engineer is responsible for inputting *metaknowledge into the system.

Kohonen map

An *unsupervised learning *neural network. A Kohonen map is capable of classifying data into a set of classifications without being given the specific classifications in advance. This kind of classification is also known as automatic clustering.

L

Leaf node

A *node in a *tree that has no *successors. All *goal nodes are leaf nodes, but not all leaf nodes are goal nodes. In other words, it is possible to reach a leaf node at the end of a path in a tree without successfully finding a goal node.

Learning agent

An *agent that is capable of *learning and is therefore able to acquire new knowledge and skills and is able to use the new knowledge and skills to improve its performance. This learning is often carried out using a *neural network.

Lexicon

A dictionary of words and other linguistic units that make up a language.

Life, game of

See *Conway's life.

Likelihood

The *probability that a given piece of evidence (E) would occur, given that a particular hypothesis (H) were true:

$$P(E \mid H)$$

This is the likelihood of E, given H, as compared with the probability of H given E, which would be written $P(H \mid E)$.

Linear threshold function

A step function used as an *activation function by artificial *neurons. The linear threshold function gives a value of 0 for inputs below a threshold (t) and a value of 1 for inputs above t.

Linearly separable function

A function that can be drawn in a two-dimensional graph such that a straight line can be drawn between the values so that inputs that are classified into one classification are on one side of the line, and inputs that are classified into the other are on the other side of the line. Logical-OR is a linearly separable function, but exclusive-OR is not. *Perceptrons can only be used to learn linearly separable functions.

Linguistic variable

A fuzzy variable such as *height* or *age* that is defined not in objective numerical terms but in terms of fuzzy values such as *tall, short, old*, and *young*.

LISP

(LISt Programming). A programming language widely used in Artificial Intelligence research.

Literal

One of the basic symbols of *propositional logic. For example, in the following expression

$$\neg A \wedge (B \vee C)$$

the literals are $\neg A$, B, and C.

Local maximum

A peak within a *search space that is higher than all the points immediately around it but is lower than the global maximum, which is the highest point in the entire search space and the most desirable goal. Many search methods are prone to identifying local maxima rather than *global maxima.

Techniques such as *simulated annealing and *iterated local search are designed to avoid this problem. See *local optimization.

Local optimization

A method of solving *combinatorial problems that involves finding a *local maximum by moving toward a better solution in the *search space. See *hill climbing.

Local search

Local search methods work by starting from some initial configuration (usually random) and making small changes to the configuration until a state is reached from which no better state can be achieved. See *meta-heuristic, *local optimization, *hill climbing, *simulated annealing.

L-systems

A system that describes the way a set of artificial "trees" grow using a set of simple rules:

$$\text{Rule 1:} \quad a \rightarrow ab$$
$$\text{Rule 2:} \quad b \rightarrow a$$

M

Machine translation

The use of computer software to translate text from one *human language to another.

Mamdani inference

A form of *fuzzy inference that allows a system to take in a set of *crisp input values (from a set of sensors or inputs from a human operator, for example) and apply a set of *fuzzy rules to those values in order to derive a single, crisp, output value or action recommendation.

Map coloring

The problem of finding a way to color the countries in a map so that no two adjoining countries are the same color. It can be shown that any normal two-dimensional map can be colored using at most 5 colors.

Maximum a posteriori hypothesis (MAP)

The *hypothesis that has the greatest *posterior probability for explaining an observed piece of evidence. The MAP classification for a piece of data is the classification that is the most likely one for the data.

Means–ends analysis

An approach to *planning that involves identifying the differences between the goal state and the current state, and selecting actions that aim to lessen those differences.

Membership function

A function that defines the membership of a *fuzzy set. Membership of fuzzy sets is defined as a value between 0 and 1, where 1 means complete membership of the fuzzy set, and 0 means nonmembership. For example, the following membership function:

$$M_B(x) = \begin{cases} 1 - \dfrac{x}{2} & for\ x \leq 2 \\ 0 & for\ x > 2 \end{cases}$$

defines a membership function for a fuzzy set, B. Input values above 2 are not members of B at all. The number 0 is completely a member of B, with a membership value of 1.

Memory

A property of *recurrent neural networks that enables it to change its *weights as new inputs are presented to it.

Mental situation calculus

A form of *situation calculus that allows an agent to reason about the effects that events have on an its beliefs about the world.

Messy genetic algorithm (MGA)

An alternative to a standard *genetic algorithm. Each bit in a messy genetic algorithm *chromosome is represented by a pair of numbers: the first number represents the position within the chromosome, and the second number is the bit value (0 or 1). A chromosome in a messy genetic algorithm can be *overspecified (a bit is defined more than once) or *underspecified (a bit is not defined at all). See *schema.

Metaheuristic

A *heuristic used by a *local search method. See *simulated annealing, *tabu search, *local optimization.

Metaknowledge

Knowledge about knowledge. See *metarule.

Metarule

Rules that define how *conflict resolution and other aspects of an *expert system work.

Metric

A measure that is used to quantify the performance of a system. See *fitness.

Minimax

An algorithm that is used by game-playing software to determine the best move to make. The algorithm assumes that it is playing against a *rational opponent and uses a *static evaluator at *leaf nodes. See *alpha–beta pruning, *expectiminimax.

Mobile agent

An *agent that is capable of moving, either in the physical world or across networks such as the Internet.

Modal logic

An extended version of a *classical logic that allows reasoning about certainty and possibility.

Modal operator, M

A logical operator that indicates that an expression is consistent with an agent's beliefs. See *modal logic, *nonmonotonic logic.

Modus ponens

A logical rule that is used in *deduction, which states that if A implies B, and we know that A is true, then we can deduce that B is true:

$$\frac{A \quad A \to B}{B}$$

Monotonicity

1. A search method is described as **monotone** if it always reaches a given node by the shortest possible path.

2. A function that increases monotonically is one that never decreases if its argument increases.

3. A logical system is described as being monotonic if a valid proof in the system cannot be made invalid by adding additional premises

or assumptions. In other words, if we find that we can prove a conclusion C by applying rules of deduction to a premise B with assumptions A, then adding additional assumptions A' and B' will not stop us from being able to deduce C.

See *nonmonotonic.

Morphologic analysis

Analysis of the structure of individual words within an *utterance in a *human language. See *natural language processing, *semantic analysis, *syntactic analysis, *pragmatic analysis.

Most general hypothesis

The most general hypothesis is defined as a vector such as $<?, ?, ?, ?, ?, ?>$, which allows for any set of data values. See *most specific hypothesis, *hypothesis.

Most general unifier (mgu)

A *unifier, u_1, is called a most general unifier if any other unifier, u_2, can be expressed as the composition of u_1 with some other substitution (i.e., $u_2 = u_1 \text{ o } u_3$).

A most general unifier is a unique unifier that provides the most general set of *substitutions to unify a set of *clauses.

Most specific hypothesis

The most specific hypothesis is defined as a vector such as $<\emptyset, \emptyset, \emptyset, \emptyset, \emptyset, \emptyset>$, which does not allow for any set of data values. See *most general hypothesis, *hypothesis.

Motion field

The vectors that define the apparent motion in a still photograph. See *optical flow.

Multiagent system

A system that uses a number of *agents to solve a single problem. See *agent team, *collaboration, *intelligent agent.

Multilayer neural network

An artificial *neural network that has more than one layer of *neurons. See *perceptron, *Hebbian learning, *Kohonen map, *Hopfield network.

Multiple inheritance

The *inheritance of properties from more than one *frame or *class.

Multivalent logic

A logical system that has more than two logical values. See *bivalent logic, *fuzzy logic.

Mutation

A *unary operator that flips a single bit within a *chromosome from zero to one or from one to zero. See *crossover, *genetic algorithm.

Mutual exclusion (mutex)

In a *planning graph, a mutex exists between two actions or effects that are mutually exclusive—in other words, they cannot both exist at the same time. Hence, if a mutex exists between two actions and one action is taken, then the other action cannot be taken.

MYCIN

A medical *expert system that uses *certainty factors to diagnose symptoms.

N

N-gram

A grouping of *n* letters (Some examples of trigrams that occur commonly in English are *ing*, *the*, *ant*, and *ize*). *N*-grams are used to identify a language from a piece of text, using the *acquaintance algorithm.

Naïve Bayes classifier

A system that uses *Bayes' theorem to learn to classify data.

Natural language

See *human language.

Natural language processing (NLP)

The analysis of the *syntax, *semantics, *morphology, *phonology, and *pragmatics of *utterances in *human languages. Natural language processing is used to enable a computer system to "hear" spoken human language, interpret the words, and carry out some action (such as a database query) on the basis of the words.

Nearest neighbor algorithm

An instance-based learning method. See *Shepard's method.

Nearest neighbor heuristic

A *heuristic used to solve problems such as the traveling salesman problem, which functions by extending the *path to the nearest unvisited city.

Negation by failure

See *closed-world assumption, *PROLOG.

Neural network

A network of simple processing *nodes (*neurons), which is roughly modeled on the human brain. See also *backpropagation, *bidirectional associative memory, *Hebbian learning, *activation function, *hidden layer, *Hopfield network, *linear threshold function, *multilayer neural network.

Neuro-fuzzy system

A *neural network that learns to classify data using *fuzzy rules and *fuzzy sets.

Neuron

The individual computation devices that make up the human brain. Neurons are also the building blocks of artificial *neural networks. A neuron generally takes in one or more inputs to which an *activation function is applied. The result of this function is compared with the *activation level to determine if the neuron should fire.

Node

1. A *neuron within an artificial *neural network.

2. The building block of *graphs, *nets, and *trees. A graph consists of a set of nodes, which are connected by *edges. Each node represents a decision or a piece of data within the graph. See *leaf node, *goal node, *and-node, *or-node.

Nonchronological backtracking

A form of *backtracking that involves using additional information about the search problem to backtrack to a more helpful *node than the last one in the *tree. See *chronological backtracking.

Noncontingent

A logical statement whose *truth value is fixed and does not vary with circumstances is noncontingent. For example, $A \wedge \neg A$ is always false, regardless of the value of A. See *contingent, *interpretation.

Nondirected graph

A *graph in which an *edge between two *nodes goes in both directions. See *directed graph.

Nonmonotonic

In a nonmonotonic logical system, a valid proof can be made invalid by adding additional premises or assumptions. See *monotonic, *abduction, *circumscription, *classical logic, *default reasoning, *modal operator M, *truth maintenance system.

Nonterminal symbol

A symbol in a *grammar that is used to represent a number of *terminal symbols or nonterminal symbols.

Normal distribution

Also known as the Gaussian distribution or bell curve, the normal distribution is defined as follows:

$$P(-\infty, x) = \frac{1}{\sqrt{2\pi}} \int_{-\infty}^{\infty} e^{-t^2/2} \, dt$$

Normalization

Normalization is the process whereby the *posterior probabilities of a pair of variables are divided by the normalizing constant to ensure that they sum to 1. The normalizing constant is defined as follows:

$$\alpha = \frac{1}{P(A|B) \cdot P(B) + P(A|\neg B) \cdot P(\neg B)}$$

Noun

A word in a *human language that is used to define a thing, a person, a place, or an abstract thing such as "happiness." See *noun phrase, *verb.

Noun phrase

A phrase that has the same properties within a *grammar as a noun and can thus be used interchangeably with a noun, at least as far as the syntactic rules of the grammar are concerned. For example, the following are all noun phrases: *America, a big green dog, the house that I lived in when I was younger.*

NP-complete

A problem that is NP can be solved nondeterministically in polynomial time. This means that if a possible solution to the problem is presented to the computer, it will be able to determine whether it is a solution or not in polynomial time. The hardest NP problems are termed NP-complete. All NP-complete problems can be mapped directly onto the satisfiability problem.

O

Occam's razor

The assertion that the simplest possible solution to a problem should always be selected. See *inductive bias.

Occluding edge

A depth *discontinuity within a two-dimensional line drawing.

Opening book

A database of opening moves for use in playing games such as chess and checkers.

Operator schema

A template that defines a number of operators within a *planning system.

Optical flow

The apparent motion within a still photograph. See *motion field.

Optimality

An optimal *search method is one that will find the solution that involves taking the least number of steps to a *goal node, if such a solution exists.

Optimal path

The shortest *path from the *root node in a *search tree to a *goal node.

Or-goal

A *goal that can be solved by solving any one of its *subgoals. Represented in a *goal tree by an *or-node. See *problem reduction.

Or-node

A *node in a *goal tree that represents an *or-goal.

Overfitting

A problem that affects *learning systems, whereby the system performs well at classifying the *training data but, due to fitting its model of the data too closely to inaccurate training data, does not perform well at classifying unseen data.

Overriding

The act of assigning a new value to an inherited default value.

Overspecified chromosome

A *chromosome where one or more bits have more than one value assigned to them. See *messy genetic algorithm, *underspecified chromosome.

P

Parallel search

*Search methods that are designed to take advantage of multiple processor computers by running parts of the search in parallel with each other.

Parser

A tool that breaks down a *sentence in a *human language to its component parts by matching the sentence with the structure imposed by the language's *grammar.

Partial order

A relation on a set that is reflexive, transitive, and antisymmetric. For example, $\leq$ defines a partial order on the set of integers. This can be proved as follows:

$a \leq a$ for all integers. Hence, $\leq$ is reflexive.

$a \leq b \wedge b \leq c \rightarrow a \leq c$. Hence, $\leq$ is transitive.

$a \leq b \wedge b \leq a \Leftrightarrow a = b$. Hence, $\leq$ is antisymmetric.

Partial order planning

A *planning method in which the order of actions that are not dependent on each other is not necessarily defined.

Partial path

A *path in a *tree that leads from the *root node to a *leaf node that is not a *goal node.

Path

A route through a *tree or *graph. The shortest path consists of just one *node. Normally, a path consists of more than one node, connected together by one or more edges.

Pattern matching

The identification of patterns in images, text, or other data by comparing the data with a set of templates or regular expressions.

Perceptron

A simple *neuron that is used to classify input data into one of two categories. See *linearly separable function.

Phenotype

The physical characteristics of a creature, as determined by the creature's *genotype and its environment.

Pixel

A picture element. A single unit of light and color as displayed on a computer screen.

Plan

A sequence of actions that has been determined by the act of *planning to be a way to solve a particular problem.

Planning

The act of taking a starting state and a goal state and building a *plan that consists of a sequence of actions that when carried out should lead from the start state to the goal state. See *partial order planning, *case-based planning, *atomic action, *STRIPS.

Planning Domain Definition Language (PDDL)

A planning language that can be used to represent problems expressed in *STRIPS or *ADL.

Planning graph

A *graph that contains a number of levels that represent states and actions that is used by algorithms such as *GraphPlan to devise plans for solving problems. See *GraphPlan, *mutual exclusion.

Plateau

A flat region in the *search space, where moving in any direction leads to an area at the same height as the current height. See *hill climbing, *local maximum, *global maximum.

Ply

One level in a *game tree.

Population

The complete collection of *chromosomes that a *genetic algorithm has developed in a given generation.

Possible world

A universe that could logically exist but is not necessarily the same as the one we live in now.

Posterior probability

The *probability of a variable given that we know that another variable is true. The posterior probability of B is written $P(B \mid A)$. See *prior probability, *conditional probability.

Pragmatic analysis

The analysis of the real meaning of an *utterance in a human language, by disambiguating and contextualizing the utterance. See *semantic analysis, *syntactic analysis, *morphologic analysis, *natural language processing.

Precision

A measure of the success of an *information retrieval system. A system that gives no *false positives has 100% precision. See *recall, *false negative.

Precondition

A requirement that must be met for a particular action to be carried out by a *planning system.

Predecessor

The *node immediately above a given node in a *tree. Each node has exactly one predecessor, except for the root node, which has no predecessors. See *ancestor, *descendant, *successor.

Predicate calculus

See *first-order predicate calculus.

Premises

A set of logical statements from which a conclusion is drawn using logical *deduction.

Prenex normal form

An expression that is in *conjunctive normal form and in which all *quantifiers are at the beginning is in prenex normal form.

Principle component analysis

Analysis of data by determining the features of the data that vary the most greatly from one item to another.

Prior probability

The *probability of a variable, regardless of any other variables. The prior probability of B is written $P(B)$. See *posterior probability, *conditional probability.

Prisoner's Dilemma

A two-player game based on the following scenario:

Two prisoners have been arrested on suspicion of committing a crime. They are kept in separate cells, and each is told that if he betrays his friend he will receive a reward. If his friend does not betray him, then he will go free, and receive a reward, while his friend is tortured. If both betray each other, they will both be tortured, and if neither betrays the other, they will be set free.

Probabilistic planning

*Planning in nondeterministic environments, in which an action will cause an effect with a given probability.

Probabilistic reasoning

Reasoning about the probabilities of events or attributes.

Probability

The probability of A is a measure of how likely it is that A will occur under ordinary circumstances. This is written $P(A)$. See *conditional probability, *joint probability distribution, *posterior probability, *prior probability.

Problem reduction

A method of solving problems by breaking each problem down into a number of subproblems, each of which may in turn be further broken down. By solving all of the subproblems and combining the results correctly, the original problem can be solved. See *goal reduction, *goal tree.

Procedural attachment

A *procedure that is associated with a *frame.

Procedure

A method that is associated with a *frame. Each procedure is a set of instructions that can be executed on request. Some procedures are executed automatically when particular events occur, such as upon creation. See *demon, *procedural attachment.

Product rule

The rule used in *Hebbian learning to determine the extent to which the weights attached to each *node are increased or decreased during learning.

Production rule

1. A rule used by an *expert system. Each rule has the form input -> action or input -> diagnosis.

2. A rule used to define a part of a grammar. Each rule explains how one *nonterminal symbol is made up of one or more terminal or nonterminal symbols. See *rewrite rule.

Production system

See *expert system.

PROLOG

(PROgramming in LOGic). A language that is widely used in Artificial Intelligence research. PROLOG programs are based around a database of facts and rules.

Propositional calculus

The language that is used to express the concepts of *propositional logic.

Propositional logic

A *monotonic logical system based around logical operators (such as, ∧, ∨, and ¬) and proposition terms. See *classical logic, *first-order predicate calculus, *propositional calculus.

Propositional planning

A *planning system that models plans purely using *propositional calculus.

Protected link

A *causal link is said to be protected when it is needed to establish the *pre-conditions of an operator below it in the plan that is being developed.

Pruning

Cutting off sections of a *search tree that are (probably) not worth examining. See *alpha–beta pruning.

Pure AND-OR tree

A *goal tree that has the following properties: the *tree has an *or-node at the top, each or-node has *and-nodes as its direct *successors, and each and-node has or-nodes as its direct successors. Another condition of a pure AND-OR tree is that it does not have any *constraints that affect which choices can be made. A *game tree is a pure AND-OR tree.

Q

Quantifier

See *universal quantifier, *existential quantifier, *first-order predicate logic.

R

Ramification problem

The problem of identifying all consequences of an action including trivial ones or ones that are hard to foresee. See *frame problem.

Rationality

An *agent or other computer program that behaves rationally is one that acts to maximize some *utility function. In playing games, for example, a rational opponent is one that is attempting to win. An irrational opponent would be one that wanted to win but did not always play its best move.

Reactive agent

An *agent that simply responds to inputs from its environment. A reactive agent has a set of rules (like an *expert system) that instruct it how it should behave based on any given input from the environment.

Recall

A measure of the success of an *information retrieval system. A system that gives no *false negatives has 100% recall. See *precision, *false negative.

Recurrent network

A *multilayer neural network that is able to feed information back from its outputs to its inputs, and thus is able to act as a *memory.

Recursively enumerable

A class of *grammars that has no restrictions on the *rewrite rules that can be used to define the grammar. Recursively enumerable grammars are also known as unrestricted grammars. See *context-sensitive grammar, *context-free grammar.

Reductio ad absurdum

A rule that states that if we assume that some expression E is false, and by a process of logical deduction starting from this assumption can deduce falsum, then E must in fact be true. See *refutation proof.

Reflex agent

See *reactive agent.

Refutation proof

A method that proves a logical *deduction is valid by first negating the conclusion and then using the resulting *clauses to deduce falsum. See *resolution, *reductio ad absurdum.

Regular expression

A *sentence defined by a *regular grammar.

Regular grammar

A *grammar that defines the syntax of a *regular language.

Regular language

The simplest *grammar from *Chomsky's hierarchy of grammars. A simple language is one that can be described by a *finite state automaton.

Reinforcement learning

A *learning system that uses positive reinforcement when it succeeds and negative reinforcement when it fails. See *bucket-brigade algorithm, *credit assignment.

Relative likelihood

The relative likelihood of two hypotheses, H_1 and H_2, given evidence E is defined as follows:

$$\frac{P(H_1|E)}{P(H_2|E)}$$

The relative likelihood thus tells us how much more likely one explanation is than another for a piece of observed evidence.

Relaxed problem

A version of a *combinatorial problem that has fewer *constraints.

Replanning

The process of devising a new *plan during *execution when circumstances have changed such that the existing plan is no longer suitable—for example, because one of the *preconditions of the next planned action is no longer satisfied.

Representation

A model used by a computer to represent a real-world situation or to store some data that are used in solving a problem.

Representational adequacy

The ability of a representational system to represent different situations is measured by representational adequacy. If representational system A can model more situations than representational system B, then A has a higher representational adequacy than B.

Resolution

A method used in *propositional logic and *first-order predicate logic to prove theorems by *contradiction. See *unification, *skolemization, *skolem normal form, *most general unifier, *substitution.

Rete

A directed, acyclic *graph or *tree used by *expert systems to make the process of modifying stored facts in the database efficient.

Rewrite rule

See *production rule.

Ridge

A narrow high region in a *search space that can cause problems for search methods such as *hill climbing.

Robot

A physical *agent. A robot can take many forms, such as an arm, an insect, or a bucket on wheels.

Robotic agent

See *robot, *software agent.

Root goal

The overall *goal of a problem that is being solved by *problem reduction. The root goal is represented by the *root node of the *goal tree.

Root node

The only *node in a *tree that has no predecessor. The top node in the tree.

Rote learning

*Learning by simply storing each piece of *training data and its classification.

Roulette-wheel selection

A method that is used to make a random selection in which some items are more likely to be selected than others. Roulette-wheel selection is used, for example, to select *chromosomes to reproduce in *genetic algorithms.

Rule

A method of *representing the *knowledge used by a *rule-based system. Each rule has an *antecedent and a *consequent. A rule can be written $A \rightarrow B$ or IF A THEN B, which are equivalent.

Rule-based system

A system whose behavior in a given situation is defined by a set of rules. See *production system, *expert system.

S

Satisfiability

An expression is satisfiable if it true under some *interpretation.

SAT planning

A method of determining whether a suitable *plan exists to solve a given problem. The problem is represented as a set of expressions, and if those expressions can be shown to be *satisfiable, then a plan can be devised to solve the problem.

Scheduling

A method for allocating resources to machines (or other agents). Scheduling takes account of the time each task takes, which can be compared with *planning in which the time taken to carry out each task is usually ignored.

Schema

A template used to represent a set of *chromosomes, using the symbol * to represent any value. See *messy genetic algorithm, *genetic algorithm.

Schema theorem

A theorem that states that short, low-order schemata that are fitter than the average fitness of the population will appear with exponentially increasing regularity in subsequent generations. See *genetic algorithm, *schema.

Script

A structured *representation for a scenario that involves a sequence of events, such as buying a house or going to a restaurant.

Search

The process of locating a solution to a problem by systematically looking at nodes in a *search tree or *search space until a *goal node is located. See *heuristic, *blind search method, *informed search method.

Search space

The set of possible permutations that can be examined by a *search method in order to find a solution. The search space represents every possible solution and all the arrangements that do not satisfy the problem's *constraints.

Search tree

A *tree that is used to represent a *search problem and is examined by a search method to search for a solution.

Segmentation

The process of breaking an image down into homogeneous areas. See *edge detection, *image recognition.

Semantic analysis

The analysis of the meaning of words in an *utterance in a human language. See *syntactic analysis, morphologic analysis, *pragmatic analysis, *natural language processing.

Semantic net

A *graph in which the *nodes represent objects and the *edges between nodes represent relationships between the objects. See *semantic tree.

Semantic tree

A *semantic net in which each *node has exactly one *predecessor, apart from the *root node, which has none.

Sentence

See *well-formed formula.

S-expression

A symbolic expression used by *LISP as either data or as a program to be executed.

Shepard's method

A variant of the *nearest neighbor algorithm in which the contribution of each neighbor is determined by its distance from the point that is being classified.

Sigmoid function

A mathematical function that is defined as follows:

$$\sigma(x) = \frac{1}{1 + e^{-x}}$$

The sigmoid function is often used as the *activation function in *backpropagation *neural networks because it is easy to differentiate.

Sign activation function

A mathematical function that is usually used as the *activation function in *Hopfield networks:

$$Sign(X) = \begin{cases} +1 & for\ X > 0 \\ -1 & for\ X < 0 \end{cases}$$

Simulated annealing

A *local search method based on the way in which metal or glass can be made very strong by being heated and then cooled very slowly.

Situated action rule

A *rule used by an *augmented finite state automaton that takes the form *input -> action.*

Situation calculus

A form of *first-order predicate calculus that is able to represent change and the way in which variables relate to each other over time.

Situation variable

A variable used in a *situation calculus expression that represents the situation that that expression represents. For example, in the following expression, S_1 is the situation variable:

$$\exists x(In(Robot, x, S_1) \wedge In(cheese, x, S_1))$$

Skolem constant

A variable that is used to replace an *existentially quantified variable when *skolemizing an expression.

For example, the expression $\exists x.x \rightarrow b$ would be skolemized as $x \rightarrow c$, where c is the skolem constant.

Skolem function

A function that is used to replace an *existentially quantified variable that comes after a *universal quantification when *skolemizing an expression.

For example, $\forall x \exists y (x \wedge y) \rightarrow b$ would be skolemized as $\forall x (x \wedge f(x)) \rightarrow b)$, where $f(x)$ is the skolem function.

Skolemization

The process of replacing an *existentially quantified variable in an expression with a *skolem constant or *skolem function. Skolemization is a part of the process of *resolution and results in an expression that is in *skolem normal form.

Skolem normal form

The normal form produced by applying the process of *skolemization to an expression.

Slipnet

A structure that represents the long-term memory of the *copycat architecture.

Slot

A named variable that is used in a *frame system to store an item of data.

Slot reader

A *procedure that returns the value that is stored in a *slot.

Slot value

The item of data that is stored in a *slot in a *frame system.

Slot writer

A *procedure that inserts a value into a *slot.

Smart agent

A fully *autonomous, *intelligent, cooperative *agent. Smart agents are the ultimate goal of *agent research.

Smoothing

The process of removing noise from an image. See *convolution.

Software agent

An *agent that exists only as a computer program, as compared with a *robotic agent.

Soundness

A logical system is sound if every *theorem is a *tautology. See *completeness.

Spidering

The process of retrieving documents from the Internet by following hypertext links from one page to another. Spidering systems usually follow some search strategy such as *depth-first or *breadth-first search.

Stack

A data structure that stores its data sequentially and has just two operators: "push," which places a new item onto the top of the stack, and "pop," which removes the top item from the stack. A stack is a "LIFO" or last-in-first-out data structure.

State

The set of variables that define the current situation in a *world model.

State space

See *search space.

Static evaluator

A function used to evaluate a single position in a game, such as chess.

Stemming

The process of removing suffixes from words to render words with a common stem into the same form. For example, the following words would all be stemmed to *swim*: *swimmer, swimming, swimmers, swims*. Most stemmers would not successfully convert *swam* or *swum* into *swim*. Stemmers are used in *information retrieval systems to increase *recall.

Stop list

A list of words that an *information retrieval system is instructed to ignore in queries and in the corpus it is searching against. The stop list usually contains extremely common words such as *and, the,* and *of*.

STRIPS

An operator-based *planning approach and the corresponding planning language that uses *well-formed formulae to represent the *state of the world.

STRIPS assumption

The assumption used by *STRIPS *planning systems that any statement that is true before applying an operator is also true after applying the operator, unless it is included in the operator's delete list.

Strong AI

The belief that a computer system that is given sufficient processing power and sufficiently powerful artificial intelligence would actually be capable of having mental states in the way that humans are. See *weak AI.

Strong methods

Artificial Intelligence methods that rely on systems with a great deal of knowledge built in. See *expert system, *weak methods.

Subclass

The *class that *inherits the properties of a *superclass.

Subgoal

See *subproblem.

Subproblem

One of the smaller problems into which a large problem is broken down by the process of *problem reduction. By achieving all of the subproblems of a problem, the complete problem can be solved.

Subset

Set A is a subset of set B if A is wholly contained by B. For example, the set of all men is a subset of the set of all humans.

Substitution

The process of replacing a *free variable in an expression with another free variable in order to facilitate the process of *unification. See *resolution.

Subsumption architecture

A layered architecture designed for the control of reactive *robotic agents.

Success node

An *and-node in a *goal tree that is a *leaf node.

Successor

The *node immediately below a given node in a *tree. Each node has one or more successors, except for leaf nodes, which have no successors. See *ancestor, *descendant, *predecessor.

Superclass

The *class from which a subclass *inherits certain properties.

Supervised learning

A form of *learning method in which the learning system is presented with a set of preclassified data before being expected to classify unseen data. See *backpropagation, *competitive learning, *unsupervised learning.

Syllogism

A logical argument that contains a set of statements (premises) from which is logically derived a conclusion. An example of a syllogism is:

All cats have two ears.

Mavis is a cat.

Therefore, Mavis has two ears.

Synapse

A connection between two *neurons in the human brain.

Syntactic analysis

The analysis of the grammatical or syntactic structure of an *utterance in a *human language. See *parser.

T

Tabu search

A *metaheuristic that uses a list of states that have already been visited to attempt to avoid repeating *paths.

Tautology

An expression that is true under all *interpretations.

Temporal logic

A form of *modal logic that was designed to reason about change and the effects of time.

Term

A *constant, a variable, or a function of terms in *first-order predicate calculus.

Term frequency - Inverse document frequency (TF-IDF)

A method used in *information retrieval to identify words that occur rarely in a *corpus of text, but frequently in a particular document.

Terminal symbol

A symbol used in expressing a *grammar for a language that represents a real word that appears in the language. See *nonterminal symbol.

Texel

A single *texture element that is repeated in an image to produce an area of a particular texture.

Texture

A perceived pattern on the surface of an object in an image. See *texel, *image recognition.

Theorem

A theorem of a logical system is a statement that can be proved by applying the rules of *deduction to the axioms in the system.

Three-coloring problem

See *map coloring.

Tit for tat

A strategy employed when playing the *Prisoner's Dilemma game. The strategy involves cooperating on the first iteration of the game, and then for each subsequent iteration, doing what the opponent did in the previous iteration.

Top down

An approach to solving problems that involves recursively breaking a problem down into smaller *subproblems until trivial problems are obtained and the whole problem can be solved. See *bottom up, *problem reduction.

Towers of Hanoi

A problem that involves moving a number of discs from one peg to another. The *constraints that are applied are that no disc can ever be placed on top of a smaller disc and that a disc cannot be moved if it has another disc on top of it.

Training

The process of teaching a *learning system to classify data by showing it preclassified *training data.

Training data

The preclassified data that is shown to a *learning system in the *training phase.

Transition network

A *finite state automaton used to represent a part of a *grammar.

Trihedral vertex

A vertex at which three faces meet.

Truth maintenance system (TMS)

A system that stores a set of beliefs along with information about how those beliefs were derived. The TMS is able to use this information to retract beliefs if conflicting information later arrives. See *nonmonotonic reasoning.

Truth table

A table that represents the behavior of a logical operator by showing the possible input *truth values for the operator and the corresponding output truth values.

Truth value

A representation of whether an expression is correct or not. In *classical logic, the truth values are *true* and *false*. In *multivalent logics, there are more truth values. *Fuzzy logic has an infinite range of truth values from 0 to 1.

Turing Test

A test devised by Alan Turing to determine whether an attempt to create a truly intelligent computer has been successful or not, by seeing whether the computer can fool a human into thinking that it might actually be human too. See *strong AI.

U

Unary operator

A logical or mathematical operator that takes just one argument, such as ¬ (logical negation).

Uncertainty

A lack of knowledge about the world. Most real-world problems are full of uncertainty, but many Artificial Intelligence techniques deal very poorly with uncertainty.

Underspecified chromosome

A *chromosome in which one or more bits do not have any value assigned to them. See *messy genetic algorithm, *Overspecified chromosome.

Unification

The process of applying a *substitution to a set of *clauses that enables those clauses to be *resolved.

Unifier

A *substitution that is applied to a set of clauses to enable those clauses to be resolved.

Uniform crossover

A form of *crossover in which a probability, p, is used to determine whether a given bit from parent 1 will be used or from parent 2.

Uniform tree

A *tree in which each non-leaf *node has the same *branching factor.

Uninformed Search

A *search method that does not use *heuristics.

Universal quantifier

The quantifier ∀, which can be read "for all" and indicates that a property holds for all possible values of the quantified variable. Hence, $\forall x.P(x)$ can be read as "for all values of x, $P(x)$ is true." See *existential quantifier, *first-order predicate calculus.

Universe of discourse

The range of possible values for a *linguistic variable.

Unsupervised learning

A form of *learning method that does not require training or any other human intervention. See *Hebbian learning, *Kohonen map, *supervised learning.

Utility-based agent

An *agent that seeks to maximize some *utility function.

Utility function

A function that defines for any state how successful an *agent has been. A high utility function is the goal of any *rational agent.

Utterance

A *sentence or partial sentence in a *human language that is spoken or written by a human being or by an agent.

V

Validity

A logical *deduction is valid if its conclusions follow logically from its premises.

Vanishing point

The point to which perspective causes all parallel lines to appear to vanish.

Verb

A word in a *human language that is used to define an action. See *verb phrase, *noun.

Verb phrase

A phrase that has the same properties within a *grammar as a *verb and can thus be used interchangeably with a verb, at least as far as the syntactic rules of the grammar are concerned. For example, the following are all verb phrases: *jump, jump over the moon, jumping over the table which is next to the door.*

Version space

The set of *hypotheses that correctly map each of a set of *training data to its classification.

W

Weak AI

The view that intelligent behavior can be modeled and used by computers to solve complex problems. See *strong AI.

Weak methods

Artificial Intelligence methods that use logic or other representational systems to solve problems but do not rely on any real-world knowledge. See *strong methods.

Weight

A value associated with each connection between *neurons in an artificial *neural network that indicates how important that connection is and how much of a role in the learning process that connection plays.

Weighted linear function

A function that takes the form $ax + by + cz + \ldots$, where a number of variables (in this case $x, y, z \ldots$) are each multiplied by a weight (in this case $a, b, c \ldots$) and the results summed.

Weight vector

A vector that represents the *weights of all connections from a given *neuron in an artificial *neural network.

Well-formed formula (wff)

An expression that is correctly constructed according to the syntactic rules of *propositional calculus or *first-order predicate calculus.

WHEN-CHANGED procedure

A *procedure that is run automatically whenever the value of a *slot is changed.

WHEN-NEEDED procedure

A *procedure that is run automatically when the value of a given *slot needs to be determined.

WHEN-READ procedure

A *procedure that is run automatically whenever the value of a *slot is read.

WHEN-WRITTEN procedure

See *WHEN-CHANGED procedure.

Winner takes all algorithm

The algorithm used by *Kohonen maps to assign credit to nodes in the network. See *competitive learning, *credit assignment.

Workspace

A data structure similar to a *blackboard that is used by the *copycat architecture.

World model

A representation of the state of the world or environment as it affects an *agent.

Z

Zero sum game

A game in which if one player wins, the other player loses.

Bibliography

A

Introduction to Artificial Life, by Christoph Adami (1997 – Telos)

Natural Language Understanding, by James Allen (1995 – Addison Wesley)

Reasoning About Plans, by James F. Allen, Henry A. Kautz, Josh Tenenberg, and Richard Pelavin (1991 – Morgan Kaufmann)

2D Object Detection and Recognition: Models, Algorithms, and Networks, by Yali Amit (2002 – MIT Press)

Nonmonotonic Reasoning, by Grigoris Antoniou (1997 – MIT Press)

The Handbook of Brain Theory and Neural Networks: Second Edition, edited by Michael A. Arbib (2002 – MIT Press)

Behavior-Based Robotics, by Ronald C. Arkin (1998 – MIT Press)

Real-Time and Multi-Agent Systems, by Ammar Attoui (2000 – Springer Verlag)

Genetic Algorithm for the Prisoner Dilemma Problem, by R. Axelrod (1987 - in *Genetic Algorithms and Simulated Annealing*, edited by L. Davis – Hyperion Books)

B

Handbook of Evolutionary Computation, edited by T. Bäck, D. B. Fogel, and Z. Michalewicz (1997- Institute of Physics Publishing)

Francis Bacon: The New Organon, by Francis Bacon; edited by Lisa Jardine and Michael Silverthorne (2002 – Cambridge University Press)

Modern Information Retrieval, by Ricardo Baeza-Yates and Berthier Ribeiro-Neto (1999 – Addison Wesley)

Modeling the Internet and the Web: Probabilistic Methods and Algorithms, by Pierre Baldi, Paolo Frasconi, and Padhraic Smyth (2003 – John Wiley & Sons)

Genetic Programming: An Introduction: On the Automatic Evolution of Computer Programs and Its Applications, by Wolfgang Banzhaf, Peter Nordin, Robert E. Keller, and Frank D. Francone (1997 – Morgan Kaufmann)

Knowledge Representation, Reasoning and Declarative Problem Solving, by Chitta Baral (2003 – Cambridge University Press)

The Handbook of Artificial Intelligence, edited by A. Barr and E. Feigenbaum (1989 – William Kaufman)

Intelligent Machine Vision: Techniques, Implementations and Applications, by Bruce G. Batchelor and Frederick M. Waltz (2001 – Springer Verlag)

Digital Biology, by Peter Bentley (2002 – Simon & Schuster)

Bayesian Theory, by José M. Bernardo and Adrian F. M. Smith (2001 – John Wiley & Sons)

Neural Networks for Pattern Recognition, by Christopher M. Bishop (1996 – Oxford University Press)

Fundamentals of Expert System Technology: Principles and Concepts, by Samuel J. Biondo (1990 – Intellect)

Recent Advances in AI Planning, by Susanne Biundo and Maria Fox (2000 – Springer Verlag)

Fast Planning Through Planning Graph Analysis, by A. Blum and M. Furst (1997 – in *Artificial Intelligence,* Vol. 90, pp. 281–300)

A Logical Theory of Nonmonotonic Inference and Belief Change, by Alexander Bochman (2001 – Springer Verlag)

The Philosophy of Artificial Life, by Margaret A. Boden (1996 – Oxford University Press)

Swarm Intelligence: From Natural to Artificial Systems, by Eric Bonabeau, Marco Dorigo, and Guy Theraulaz (1999 – Oxford University Press)

Understanding 99% of Artificial Neural Networks: Introduction & Tricks, by Marcelo Bosque (2002 – Writers Club Press)

Advances in Image Understanding: A Festschrift for Azriel Rosenfeld, edited by Kevin W. Bowyer and Narendra Ahuja (1996 – Wiley IEEE Press)

Software Agents, edited by Jeffrey M. Bradshaw (1997 – AAAI Press)

Robot Motion: Planning and Control, edited by Michael Brady, John Hollerbach, Timothy Johnson, Tomás Lozano-Pérez, and Matthew T. Mason (1983 – MIT Press)

Empirical Analysis of Predictive Algorithms for Collaborative Filtering, by John S. Breese, David Heckerman, and Carl Kadie (1998 – in *Proceedings of the Fourteenth Conference on Uncertainty in Artificial Intelligence*, Morgan Kaufmann)

Nonmonotonic Reasoning: An Overview, by Gerhard Brewka, Jürgen Dix, and Kurt Konolige (1995 – Cambridge University Press)

Nonmonotonic Reasoning: From Theoretical Foundation to Efficient Computation, by G. Brewka (1991 – Cambridge University Press)

Cambrian Intelligence: The Early History of the New AI, by Rodney A. Brooks (1999 – MIT Press)

Rule-Based Expert Systems: The MYCIN Experiments of the Stanford Heuristic Programming Project, by B. G. Buchanan and E. H. Shortliffe (1984 – Addison Wesley)

Propositional Logic: Deduction and Algorithms, by Hans Kleine Büning and Theodor Lettmann (1999 – Cambridge University Press)

A Resolution Principle for a Logic with Restricted Quantifiers, by H. J. Burckert (1992 – Springer Verlag)

C

The Essence of Neural Networks, by Robert Callan (1999 – Prentice Hall)

Prolog Programming for Students: With Expert Systems and Artificial Intelligence Topics, by David Callear (2001 – Continuum)

Efficient and Accurate Parallel Genetic Algorithms, by Erick Cantu-Paz (2002 – Kluwer Academic Publishers)

Plan Recognition in Natural Language Dialogue, by Sandra Carberry (1990 – MIT Press)

Neural Networks for Vision and Image Processing, edited by Gail A. Carpenter and Stephen Grossberg (1992 – MIT Press)

Symbolic Logic and *Game of Logic*, by Lewis Carroll (Published in one volume – 1958 – Dover Books)

Expert Systems and Probabilistic Network Models, by Enrique Castillo, Jose Manuel Gutierrez, and Ali S. Hadi (1997 – Springer Verlag)

The Essence of Artificial Intelligence, by Alison Cawsey (1998 – Prentice Hall)

Artificial Intelligence, by Jack Challoner (2002 – Dorling Kindersley, Essential Science)

Practical Handbook of Genetic Algorithms, by Lance Chambers (1995 – CRC Press)

Symbolic Logic and Mechanical Theorem Proving, by Chin-Liang Chang and Richard Char-Tung Lee (1973 – Academic Press)

Introduction to Artificial Intelligence, by Eugene Charniak and Drew McDermott (1985 – Addison Wesley; out of print)

Genetic Algorithms and Genetic Programming in Computational Finance, edited by Shu-Heng Chen (2002 – Kluwer Academic Publishers)

Learning from Data: Concepts, Theory, and Methods, by Vladimir Cherkassky and Filip Mulier (1998 – Wiley Interscience)

The Computational Brain, by Patricia S. Churchland and Terrence J. Sejnowski (1992 – The MIT Press)

An Introduction to Genetic Algorithms for Scientists and Engineers, by David A. Coley (1999 – World Scientific Publishing Company)

Adaptive Parallel Iterative Deepening Search, by Diane J. Cook and R. Craig Varnell (1998 – in *Journal of Artificial Intelligence Research*, Vol. 9, pp. 139–166)

Introduction to Algorithms, by Thomas H. Cormen, Charles E. Leiserson, Ronald L. Rivest, and Clifford Stein (2001 – MIT Press)

Probabilistic Networks and Expert Systems, edited by Robert G. Cowell (1999 – Springer Verlag)

The Fuzzy Systems Handbook: A Practitioner's Guide to Building, Using, & Maintaining Fuzzy Systems, by Earl Cox (1999 – Morgan Kaufmann)

Fuzzy Logic for Business and Industry, by Earl Cox (2000 – Charles River Media)

AI: The Tumultuous History of the Search for Artificial Intelligence, by Daniel Crevier (1999 – Basic Books)

The Turing Test and the Frame Problem: AI's Mistaken Understanding of Intelligence, by Larry J. Crockett (1994 – Intellect)

D

The Origin of Species, by Charles Darwin (1859 – reprinted, by Penguin)

Artificial Immune Systems and Their Applications, edited by Dipankar Dasgupta (1999 – Springer Verlag)

Multiobjective Heuristic Search: An Introduction to Intelligent Search Methods for Multicriteria Optimization, by Pallab Dasgupta, P. P. Chakrabarti, and S. C. Desarkar (1999 - Friedrich Vieweg & Sohn)

Socially Intelligent Agents - Creating Relationships with Computers and Robots, edited by Kerstin Dautenhahn, Alan H. Bond, Lola Canamero, and Bruce Edmonds (2002 – Kluwer Academic Publishers)

Machine Vision: Theory, Algorithms, Practicalities, by E. R. Davies (1996 – Academic Press)

Adaptive Learning, by *Genetic Algorithms: Analytical Results and Applications to Economic Models*, by Herbert Dawid (1999 – Springer Verlag)

The Blind Watchmaker, by Richard Dawkins (1996 – W. W. Norton & Company)

Artificial Immune Systems: A New Computational Intelligence Paradigm, by Leandro N. de Castro and Jonathan Timmis (2002 – Springer Verlag)

A Generalization of Bayesian Inference, by A. P. Dempster (1968 - in *Journal of the Royal Statistical Society* Vol. 30 (pp. 205–217))

Bayesian Methods for Nonlinear Classification and Regression, by David G. T. Denison, Christopher C. Holmes, Bani K. Mallick, and Adrian F. M. Smith (2002 – John Wiley & Sons)

Brainstorms: Philosophical Essays on Mind and Psychology, by Daniel Dennett (1978 – Bradford)

Consciousness Explained, by Daniel Dennett (1992 – Little, Brown & Co.)

Probabilistic Theory of Pattern Recognition, by Luc Devroye, Laszlo Gyorfi, and Gabor Lugosi (1998 – Springer Verlag)

Understanding Agent Systems, edited by Mark D'Inverno and Michael Luck (2001 – Springer Verlag)

A Truth Maintenance System, by Jon Doyle (1979 – in *Computation & Intelligence – Collected Readings*, edited by George F. Luger, The MIT Press)

What Computers Still Can't Do, by Hubert L. Dreyfus (1999 – The MIT Press)

An Introduction to Fuzzy Control, by Dimiter Driankov, Hans Hellendoorn and M. Reinfrank (1996 – Springer Verlag)

How to Solve it, by Computer, by R. G. Dromey (1982 – out of print)

Artificial Intelligence: Strategies, Applications, and Models Through Search, by Benedict Du Boulay and Christopher James Thornton (1999 – AMACOM)

E

Intelligent Agents for Mobile and Virtual Media, edited by Rae Earnshaw, John Vince, and Margaret A. Arden (2002 – Springer Verlag)

Neural Darwinism: The Theory of Neuronal Group Selection, by Gerald M. Edelman (1990 – Oxford University Press)

Computational Intelligence: An Introduction, by Andries P. Engelbrecht (2003 – John Wiley & Sons)

Predicate Logic: The Semantic Foundations of Logic, by Richard L. Epstein (2000 – Wadsworth Publishing)

Propositional Logics: The Semantic Foundations of Logic, by Richard L. Epstein (2000 – Wadsworth Publishing)

F

Fuzzy Control: Synthesis and Analysis, edited by Shehu S. Farinwata, Dimitar P. Filev, and Reza Langari (2000 – John Wiley & Sons)

Three-Dimensional Computer Vision, by Olivier Faugeras (1993 – MIT Press)

Fundamentals of Neural Networks, by Laurene V. Fausett (1994 – Prentice Hall)

STRIPS: A New Approach to the Application of Theorem Proving to Problem Solving, by Richard E. Fikes and Nils J. Nilsson (1971 – in *Computation & Intelligence*, edited by George F. Luger, 1995, MIT Press)

Artificial Intelligence: A Knowledge-Based Approach, by Morris W. Firebaugh (1988 – Boyd & Fraser Publishing Company – out of print)

The Anatomy of Programming Languages, by Alice E. Fischer and Frances S. Grodzinsky (1993 – Prentice Hall)

Blondie 24: Playing at the Edge of AI, by David B. Fogel (2001 – Morgan Kaufmann)

Evolutionary Computation in Bioinformatics, edited by Gary B. Fogel and David W. Corne (2002 – Morgan Kaufmann)

The Robots Dilemma Revisited: The Frame Problem in Artificial Intelligence, by Kenneth M. Ford and Zenon W. Pylyshyn (1996 – Ablex Publishing)

Computer Vision: A Modern Approach, by David A. Forsyth and Jean Ponce (2002 – Prentice Hall)

Parallel Computing Works, by G. C. Fox, R. D. Williams, and P. C. Messina (1994 – Morgan Kaufmann)

Understanding Artificial Intelligence (Science Made Accessible), compiled by Sandy Fritz (2002 – Warner Books)

G

Handbook of Logic in Artificial Intelligence and Logic Programming: Nonmonotonic Reasoning and Uncertain Reasoning, edited by Dov M. Gabbay, J. A. Robinson, and Christopher John Hogger (1994 – Oxford University Press)

Bayesian Data Analysis, by Andrew Gelman, Donald B. Rubin, and Hal S. Stern (2003 – CRC Press)

Genetic Algorithms and Engineering Optimization, by Mitsuo Gen and Runwei Cheng (1991 – Wiley Interscience)

Expert Systems: Principles and Programming, by Joseph C. Giarratano (1998 – Brooks Cole)

Tabu Search, by Fred W. Glover and Manuel Laguna (1998 – Kluwer Academic Publishers)

Genetic Algorithms in Search, Optimization and Machine Learning, by David E. Goldberg (1989 – Addison Wesley)

Messy Genetic Algorithms: Motivation, Analysis and First Results, by D. E. Goldberg (1989 - in *Complex Systems*, Vol. 3, pp. 493–530)

Rapid, Accurate Optimization of Difficult Problems Using Fast Messy Genetic Algorithms, by David E. Goldberg, Kalyanmoy Deb, Hillol Kargupta, and Georges Harik (1993 – in *Proceedings of the Fifth International Conference on Genetic Algorithms*, pp. 56–64, Morgan Kaufmann)

Dynamic Vision: From Images to Face Recognition, by Shaogang Gong, Stephen J. McKenna, and Stephen J. McKenna (2000 – Imperial College Press)

Creation: Life and How to Make It, by Steve Grand (2001 – Harvard University Press)

Cross-Language Information Retrieval, edited by Gregory Grefenstette (1998 – Kluwer Academic Publishing)

Managing Uncertainty in Expert Systems, by Jerzy W. Grzymala-Busse (1991 – Kluwer Academic Publishers)

An Introduction to Neural Networks, by Kevin Gurney (1997 – UCL Press)

H

From Animals to Animats 7: Proceedings of the Seventh International Conference on Simulation of Adaptive Behavior, edited by Bridget Hallam, Dario Floreano, John Hallam, Gillian Hayes, and Jean-Arcady Meyer (2002 – MIT Press; also available are the proceedings from the first to sixth conferences)

Computer and Robot Vision (Volume II), by Robert M. Haralick and Linda G. Shapiro (2002 – Pearson Education)

Algorithmics: The Spirit of Computing, by David Harel (1987 – Addison Wesley)

Expert Systems: Artificial Intelligence in Business, by Paul Harmon (1985 – John Wiley & Sons – out of print)

Artificial Intelligence: The Very Idea, by J. Haugeland (1985 – The MIT Press)

Practical Genetic Algorithms, by Randy L. Haupt and Sue Ellen Haupt (1998 – Wiley Interscience)

Foundations of Computational Linguistics: Human-Computer Communication in Natural Language, by Roland R. Hausser (2001 – Springer Verlag)

Neural Networks: A Comprehensive Foundation, by Simon S. Haykin (1998 – Prentice Hall)

The Organisation of Behavior: A Neuropsychological Theory, by D. O. Hebb (1949 – republished in 2002, by Lawrence Erlbaum Assoc.)

Probabilistic Interpretations for Mycin's Certainty Factors, by O. Heckerman (1986 – in *Uncertainty in Artificial Intelligence,* edited by L. N. Kanal and J. F. Lemmer, Elsevier Science, pp. 167–196)

Silicon Second Nature: Culturing Artificial Life in a Digital World, by Stefan Helmreich (2000 – University of California Press)

Information Retrieval, by William R. Hersh (2002 – Springer Verlag)

Fuzzy and Neural Approaches in Engineering, by J. Wesley Hines (1997 – Wiley Interscience)

Visual Intelligence: How We Create What We See, by Donald D. Hoffman (1998 – W. W. Norton & Company)

Braitenberg Creatures, by David W. Hogg, Fred Martin, and Mitchel Resnick (1991 - originally published as *Epistemology and Learning Memo #13*)

Adaptation in Natural and Artificial Systems: An Introductory Analysis with Applications to Biology, Control, and Artificial Intelligence, by John H. Holland (1992 – MIT Press)

Robot Vision, by Berthold K. Horn (1986 – McGraw Hill Higher Education)

Behind Deep Blue: Building the Computer That Defeated the World Chess Champion, by Feng-Hsiung Hsu (2002 – Princeton University Press)

Spoken Language Processing: A Guide to Theory, Algorithm and System Development, by Xuedong Huang, Alex Acero, Hsiao-Wuen Hon, and Raj Reddy (2001 – Prentice Hall)

I

Natural Language Processing and Knowledge Representation: Language for Knowledge and Knowledge for Language, edited by Lucja M. Iwanska and Stuart C. Shapiro (2000 – AAAI Press)

J

Introduction to Expert Systems, by Peter Jackson (1999 – Addison Wesley)

Introduction to Artificial Intelligence, by Philip C. Jackson (1985 – Dover Publications)

Natural Language Processing for Online Applications: Text Retrieval, Extraction, and Categorization, by Peter Jackson and Isabelle Moulinier (2002 – John Benjamins Publishing Company)

Text-Based Intelligent Systems: Current Research and Practice in Information Extraction and Retrieval, edited by Paul Schafran Jacobs (1992 – Lawrence Erlbaum Assoc.)

Increased Rates of Convergence Through Learning Rate Adaptation, by R. A. Jacobs (1987 - in *Neural Networks,* Vol. 1, pp. 295–307)

Spotting and Discovering Terms through Natural Language Processing, by Christian Jacquemin (2001 – MIT Press)

Machine Vision, by Ramesh Jain, Rangachar Kasturi, and Brian G. Schunck (1995 –McGraw Hill)

Applications of Fuzzy Logic: Towards High Machine Intelligence Quotient Systems, edited by Mohammad Jamshidi, Andre Titli, Lotfi Zadeh, and Serge Boverie (1997 – Prentice Hall)

Neuro-Fuzzy and Soft Computing: A Computational Approach to Learning and Machine Intelligence, by Jyh-Shing Roger Jang, Chuen-Tsai Sun, and Eiji Mizutani (1996 – Prentice Hall)

Simulated Annealing for Query Results ranking, by B. J. Jansen (1997 – in *ACM Computer Science Education Conference,* ACM Press)

Agent Technology: Foundations, Applications, and Markets, edited by Nicholas R. Jennings and Michael J. Wooldridge (1998 – Springer Verlag)

Emergence: The Connected Lives of Ants, Brains, Cities, and Software, by Steven Johnson (2001 – Scribner)

AI Application Programming, by M. Tim Jones (2003 – Charles River Media)

Speech and Language Processing: An Introduction to Natural Language Processing, Computational Linguistics and Speech Recognition, by Dan Jurafsky, James H. Martin, Keith Vander Linden, and Nigel Ward (2000 – Prentice Hall)

K

Multistage Fuzzy Control: A Model-Based Approach to Fuzzy Control and Decision Making, by Janusz Kacprzyk (1997 – John Wiley & Sons)

Choices, Values, and Frames, by Daniel Kahneman (Editor) and Amos Tversky (2000 – Cambridge University Press)

An Introduction to Computational Learning Theory, by Michael J. Kearns and Umesh V. Vazirani (1994 – MIT Press)

Learning and Soft Computing: Support Vector Machines, Neural Networks, and Fuzzy Logic Models (Complex Adaptive Systems), by Vojislav Kecman (2001 – MIT Press)

The Essence of Logic, by John Kelly (1997 – Prentice Hall)

Out of Control: The New Biology of Machines, by Kevin Kelly (1994 – Fourth Estate)

Swarm Intelligence, by James Kennedy, Russell C. Eberhart, and Yuhui Shi (2001 – Morgan Kaufmann)

Knowledge Acquisition for Expert Systems: A Practical Handbook, by Alison L. Kidd (1987 – Plenum Publishing Corporation)

Commitment and Effectiveness of Situated Agents, by D. Kinny and M. Georgeff (1991 – in *Proceedings of the Twelfth International Joint Conference on Artificial Intelligence*, pp. 82–88, Morgan Kaufmann)

Intelligent Information Agents: The Agentlink Perspective (Lecture Notes in Computer Science, 2586), edited by Matthias Klusch, Sonia Bergamaschi, and Pete Edwards (2003 – Springer Verlag)

An Analysis of Alpha Beta Pruning, by Donald Knuth and R. W. Moore (1975 - in *Artificial Intelligence*, Vol. 6 (4), pp. 293–326)

Art of Computer Programming: Sorting and Searching, by Donald Knuth (1973 – Pearson Addison Wesley)

Self-Organizing Maps, by Teuvo Kohonen (2000 – Springer Verlag)

Case-Based Reasoning, by Janet Kolodner (1993 – Morgan Kaufmann)

Learning to Solve Problems, by Searching for Macro-Operators (Research Notes in Artificial Intelligence, Vol. 5), by Richard E. Korf (1985 – Longman Group United Kingdom)

Search, by Richard E. Korf (1987 – in *Encyclopedia of Artificial Intelligence*, edited by E. Shapiro – Wiley)

Bidirectional Associative Memories, by Bart Kosko (1988 - in *IEEE Transactions Systems, Man & Cybernetics*, Vol. 18, pp. 49–60)

Fuzzy Thinking: The New Science of Fuzzy Logic, by Bart Kosko (1994 – Hyperion)

Genetic Programming: On the Programming of Computers, by *Means of Natural Selection,* by John R. Koza (1992 – MIT Press)

Genetic Programming II: Automatic Discovery of Reusable Programs, by John R. Koza (1994 – MIT Press)

A Learning Interface Agent for Scheduling Meetings, by R. Kozierok and P. Maes (1993 – in *Proceedings of the ACM-SIGCHI International Workshop on Intelligent User Interfaces,* ACM Press)

Strategic Negotiation in Multiagent Environments, by Sarit Kraus (2001 – MIT Press)

Computer Vision and Fuzzy Neural Systems, by Arun D. Kulkarni (2001 – Prentice Hall)

The Age of Spiritual Machines, by Ray Kurzweil (1999 – Viking Penguin)

L

Artificial Life: An Overview, edited by Christopher Langton (1995 – MIT Press)

Case-Based Reasoning: Experiences, Lessons, and Future Directions, edited by David B. Leake (1996 –AAAI Press)

The Resolution Calculus, by Alexander Leitsch (1997 – Springer Verlag)

Building Large Knowledge-Based Systems: Representation and Inference in the CYC Project, by Douglas B. Lenat and R. V. Guha (1990 – Addison Wesley)

The Logic of Knowledge Bases, by Hector J. Levesque and Gerhard Lakemeyer (2001 – MIT Press)

For the Sake of the Argument: Ramsey Test Conditionals, Inductive Inference and Nonmonotonic Reasoning, by Isaac Levi (1996 – Cambridge University Press)

Artificial Life: A Report from the Frontier Where Computers Meet Biology, by Steven Levy (1993 – Vintage Books)

Making Decisions, by D. V. Lindley (1991 – John Wiley & Sons)

Knowledge Representation and Defeasible Reasoning (Studies in Cognitive Systems, Vol. 5), edited by Ronald P. Loui and Greg N. Carlson (1990 – Kluwer Academic Publishers)

Automated Theorem Proving: A Logical Basis, by Donald W. Loveland (1978 – Elsevier Science – Out of Print)

Artificial Intelligence & Manufacturing Research Planning Workshop, edited by George F. Luger (1998 – AAAI)

Artificial Intelligence: Structures and Strategies for Complex Problem-Solving, by George F. Luger (2002 – Addison Wesley)

Computation & Intelligence: Collected Readings, edited by George F. Luger (1995 – The AAAI Press / The MIT Press)

M

Foundations of Statistical Natural Language Processing, by Christopher D. Manning and Hinrich Schütze (1999 – MIT Press)

Nonmonotonic Logic: Context-Dependent Reasoning, by V. W. Marek and M. Truszczynski (1993 – Springer Verlag)

Probabilistic Situation Calculus, by Paulo Mateus, António Pacheco, Javier Pinto, Amílear Sernadas, and Cristina Sernadas (2001 – in *Annals of Mathematics and Artificial Intelligence*)

Intelligent Multimedia Information Retrieval, edited by Mark T. Maybury (1997 – AAAI Press)

Circumscription: A Form of Non-Monotonic Reasoning, by John McCarthy (1980 – in *Computation & Intelligence – Collected Readings*, edited by George F. Luger, The MIT Press)

Some Expert Systems Need Common Sense, by John McCarthy (1983 – in *Computer Culture: The Scientific, Intellectual and Social Impact of the Computer*, edited by Heinz Pagels, Vol. 426)

A Production System Version of the Hearsay-II Speech Understanding System, by Donald McCracken (1981 - UMI Research)

A Logical Calculus of the Ideas Immanent in Nervous Activity, by W. S. McCulloch and W. Pitts (1943 - in *Bulletin of Mathematical Biophysics*, Vol. 5, pp. 115–137)

Computational Linguistics, by Tony McEnery (1992 – Coronet Books – out of print)

Fuzzy Logic: The Revolutionary Computer Technology That Is Changing Our World, by Daniel McNeill (1994 – Simon & Schuster)

Text Information Retrieval Systems, by Charles T. Meadow, Bert R. Boyce, and Donald H. Kraft (2000 – Academic Press)

Uncertain Rule-Based Fuzzy Logic Systems: Introduction and New Directions, by Jerry M. Mendel (2000 – Prentice Hall)

Building Expert Systems in Prolog, by Dennis Merritt (1995 – Springer Verlag)

Genetic Algorithms + Data Structures = Evolution Programs, by Zbigniew Michalewicz (1999 - Springer)

How to Solve It: Modern Heuristics, by Zbigniew Michalewicz and David B. Fogel (1999 – Springer Verlag)

A Framework for Representing Knowledge, by Marvin Minsky (1975 – in *Computation & Intelligence – Collected Readings*, edited by George F. Luger, The MIT Press)

Perceptrons, by Marvin Minsky and Seymour A. Papert (1969 – now available in an extended edition: *Perceptrons - Expanded Edition: An Introduction to Computational Geometry*, 1987 – MIT Press)

The Society of Mind, by Marvin Minsky (1988 – Simon & Schuster)

Steps towards Artificial Intelligence, by Marvin Minsky (1961 – in *Computation & Intelligence – Collected Readings*, edited by George F. Luger, MIT Press)

Learning Search Control Knowledge: An Explanation Based Approach, by Stephen Minton (1988 – Kluwer Academic Publishers)

Minimizing Conflicts: A Heuristic Repair Method for Constraint Satisfaction and Scheduling Problems, by S.Minton, M. D. Johnson, A. B. Philips, and P. Laird (1992 – *Artificial Intelligence, Vol. 58*)

An Introduction to Genetic Algorithms, by Melanie Mitchell (1998 – MIT Press)

The Royal Road for Genetic Algorithms: Fitness Landscapes and GA Performance, by Melanie Mitchell, Stephanie Forrest, and John H. Holland (1992 - In *Towards a Practice of Autonomous Systems: Proceedings of the First European Conference on Artificial Life*, edited by Francisco J. Varela and Paul Bourgine, pp. 245–254, MIT Press)

Machine Learning, by Tom M. Mitchell (1997 – McGraw Hill)

The Turing Test: The Elusive Standard of Artificial Intelligence, edited by James H. Moor (2003 – Kluwer Academic Publishers)

Robot: Mere Machine to Transcendent Mind, by Hans P. Moravec (2000 – Oxford University Press)

An Introduction to AI Robotics, by Robin R. Murphy (2000 – MIT Press)

N

A Guided Tour of Computer Vision, by Vishvjit S. Nalwa (1993 – Addison Wesley)

Local Search for Planning and Scheduling: Ecai 2000 Workshop, Berlin, Germany, August 21, 2000: Revised Papers (Lecture Notes in Computer Science, 2148), edited by Alexander Nareyek (2001 – Springer Verlag)

Machine Learning: A Theoretical Approach, by Balas K. Natarajan (1991 – Morgan Kaufmann)

Learning Bayesian Networks, by Richard E. Neapolitan (2003 – Prentice Hall)

Artificial Intelligence: A Guide to Intelligent Systems, by Michael Negnevitsky (2002 – Addison Wesley)

Automated Theorem Proving: Theory and Practice, by Monty Newborn (2001 – Springer Verlag)

Deep Blue: An Artificial Intelligence Milestone, by Monty Newborn (2003 – Springer Verlag)

Kasparov Versus Deep Blue: Computer Chess Comes of Age, by Monty Newborn (1997 – Springer Verlag)

Computer Science as Empirical Enquiry: Symbols and Search, by Allen Newell and Herbert A. Simon (1976 - in *Computation & Intelligence – Collected Readings,* edited by George F. Luger, MIT Press)

GPS, A Program That Simulates Human Thought, by Alan Newell and Herbert A. Simon (1963 – in *Computation & Intelligence,* edited by George F. Luger 1995 – MIT Press)

Report on a General Problem Solving Program, by Alan Newell, J. C. Shaw, and Herbert A. Simon (1959 – in *Proceedings of the International Conference on Information Processing,* pp. 256–264, UNESCO)

Blackboard Systems: The Blackboard Model of Problem Solving and the Evolution of Blackboard Architectures, by H. Penny Nii (1986 – in *Computation & Intelligence – Collected Readings*, edited by George F. Luger, The MIT Press)

Artificial Intelligence: A New Synthesis, by N. J. Nilsson (1998 – Morgan Kauffman)

Readings in Machine Translation, edited by Sergei Nirenburg, Harold L. Somers, and Yorick A. Wilks (2002 – MIT Press)

Feature Extraction in Computer Vision and Image Processing, by Mark S. Nixon and Alberto Aguado (2002 – Butterworth-Heinemann)

Evolutionary Robotics: The Biology, Intelligence, and Technology of Self-Organizing Machines, by Stefano Nolfi and Dario Floreano (2000 – MIT Press)

O

Computational Explorations in Cognitive Neuroscience: Understanding the Mind, by Simulating the Brain, by Randall C. O'Reilly (Author) and Yuko Munakata (2000 – MIT Press)

Evolutionary Algorithms for Single and Multicriteria Design Optimization, by Andrzej Osyczka (2001 – Physica Verlag)

P

Soft Computing in Case Based Reasoning, edited by Sankar K. Pal, Tharam S. Dillon, and Daniel S. Yeung (2000 – Springer Verlag)

Kasparov and Deep Blue, by Bruce Pandolfini (1997 – Fireside)

Combinatorial Optimization: Algorithms and Complexity, by Christos H. Papadimitriou and Kenneth Steiglitz (1998 – Dover Publications)

Evolving Hexapod Gaits Using a Cyclic Genetic Algorithm, by Gary Parker (1997 – in *Proceedings of the IASTED International Conference on Artificial Intelligence and Soft Computing*, pp. 141–144, IASTED/ACTA Press)

Generating Arachnid Robot Gaits with Cyclic Genetic Algorithms, by Gary Parker (1998 - in *Genetic Programming III*, pp. 576–583)

Metachronal Wave Gait Generation for Hexapod Robots, by Gary Parker (1998 – in *Proceedings of the Seventh International Symposium on Robotics with Applications*, ISORA)

Algorithms for Image Processing and Computer Vision, by J. R. Parker (1996 – John Wiley & Sons)

Learning-Based Robot Vision, edited by Josef Pauli (2001 – Springer Verlag)

Heuristics: Intelligent Search Strategies for Computer Problem Solving, by Judea Pearl (1984 – Addison Wesley)

Probabilistic Reasoning in Intelligent Systems: Networks of Plausible Inference, by Judea Pearl (1997 – Morgan Kaufmann)

An Introduction to Fuzzy Sets: Analysis and Design, by Witold Pedrycz and Fernando Gomide (1998 – MIT Press)

The Emperor's New Mind: Concerning Computers, Minds, and the Laws of Physics, by Roger Penrose (1989 – Oxford University Press)

Natural Language Processing, by Fernando C. N. Pereira and Barbara J. Grosz (1994 – MIT Press)

Understanding Intelligence, by Rolf Pfeiffer and Christian Scheier (2000 – ISBN: The MIT Press)

An Algorithm for Suffix Stripping, by M. F. Porter (1980 - in Spärck Jones and Willett, 1997)

Introduction to Logic: Propositional Logic, by Howard Pospesel (1999 – Prentice Hall)

Prisoner's Dilemma: John Von Neumann, Game Theory and the Puzzle of the Bomb, by William Poundstone (1994 – MIT Press)

Views into the Chinese Room: New Essays on Searle and Artificial Intelligence, edited by John Preston and Mark Bishop (2002 – Oxford University Press)

The Robots Dilemma: The Frame Problem in Artificial Intelligence, by Zenon W. Pylyshyn (1987 – Ablex Publishing)

Q

Induction of Decision Trees, by J. R. Quinlan (1986 – from *Machine Learning*, Vol. 1 (1), pp. 81–106)

R

Fundamentals of Speech Recognition, by Lawrence Rabiner and Biing-Hwang Juang (1993 – Pearson Education)

Modern Heuristic Search Methods, edited by V. J. Rayward-Smith, I. H. Osman, Colin R. Reeves, and G. D. Smith (1996 – John Wiley & Sons)

Logic for Computer Science, by Steve Reeves and Michael Clarke (1993 – Addison Wesley)

Are We Spiritual Machines?: Ray Kurzweil vs. the Critics of Strong A.I., edited by Jay W. Richards (2002 – Discovery Institute)

Word of Mouse: The Marketing Power of Collaborative Filtering, by John Riedl and Joseph Konstan (2002 – Warner Books)

Inside Case-Based Reasoning, by Christopher K. Riesbeck and Roger C. Schank (1989 – Lawrence Erlbaum)

The Bayesian Choice: From Decision-Theoretic Foundations to Computational Implementation, by Christian P. Robert (2001 – Springer Verlag)

Monte Carlo Statistical Methods, by Christian P. Robert and George Casella (1999 – Springer Verlag)

Logic, Form and Function: The Mechanization of Deductive Reasoning, by John Alan Robinson (1980 – Elsevier Science)

The Perceptron: A Probabilistic Model for Information Storage and Organization in the Brain, by F. Rosenblatt (1958 - in *Psychological Review*, Vol. 65, pp. 386–408)

Representations for Genetic and Evolutionary Algorithms, by Franz Rothlauf and David E. Goldberg (2002 – Springer Verlag)

Change, Choice and Inference: A Study of Belief Revision and Nonmonotonic Reasoning, by Hans Rott (2002 – Oxford University Press)

Artificial Intelligence: A Modern Approach, by Stuart Russell and Peter Norvig (1995 – Prentice Hall)

S

Logical Forms: An Introduction to Philosophical Logic, by Mark Sainsbury (1991 – Blackwell)

Evolutionary Language Understanding, by Geoffrey Sampson (1996 – Continuum)

Some Studies in Machine Learning Using the Game of Checkers, by Arthur Samuel (1959 - in *Computation & Intelligence* – Collected Readings, edited by George F. Luger - MIT Press)

Using Sophisticated Models in Resolution Theorem Proving (Lecture Notes in Computer Science, Vol. 90), by David M. Sandford (1981 – Springer Verlag)

The Importance of Being Fuzzy, by Arturo Sangalli (1998 – Princeton University Press)

One Jump Ahead: Challenging Human Supremacy in Checkers, by Jonathan Schaeffer (1997 – Springer Verlag)

A Re-examination of Brute-force Search, by Jonathan Schaeffer, Paul Lu, Duane Szafron, and Robert Lake (1993 – in *Games: Planning and Learning*, AAAI 1993 Fall Symposium, Report FS9302, pp. 51–58)

A World Championship Caliber Checkers Program, by Jonathan Schaeffer, Joseph Culberson, Norman Treloar, Brent Knight, Paul Lu, and Duane Szafron (1992 – in *Artificial Intelligence*, Vol. 53 (2–3), pp. 273–290)

Artificial Intelligence: An Engineering Approach, by Robert J. Schalkoff (1990 – McGraw Hill)

The Structure of Episodes in Memory, by Roger C. Schank (1975 – in *Computation & Intelligence – Collected Readings*, edited by George F. Luger, The MIT Press)

The Evidential Foundations of Probabilistic Reasoning, by David A. Schum (2001 – Northwestern University Press)

Minds, Brains, and Programs, by John R. Searle (1980 – in *The Behavioral and Brain Sciences*, Vol. 3, Cambridge University Press)

Minds, Brains and Science, by John R. Searle (1986 – Harvard University Press)

Algorithms, by Robert Sedgewick (1988 – Addison Wesley)

A New Method for Solving Hard Satisfiability Problems, by B. Selman, H. Levesque, and D. Mitchell (1992 – in Proceedings of the Tenth National Conference on Artificial Intelligence, pp. 440–446, AAAI)

Noise Strategies for Improving Local Search, by B. Selman, H.A. Kautz, and B. Cohen (1994 – Proceedings of the Tenth National Conference on Artificial Intelligence, pp. 337–343, AAAI)

Computer Vision, by Linda G. Shapiro and George C. Stockman (2001 – Prentice Hall)

The Encylopedia of Artificial Intelligence, edited by S. C. Shapiro (1992 – Wiley)

Social Information Filtering: Algorithms for Automating "Word of Mouth," by U. Shardanand and P. Maes (1995 – in *Proceedings of CHI'95 - Human Factors in Computing Systems*, pp. 210–217)

A Two Dimensional Interpolation Function for Irregularly Spaced Data, by D. Shepard (1968 - *Proceedings of the 23rd National Conference of the ACM*, pp. 517–523, ACM Press)

Computer Based Medical Consultations: Mycin, by Edward Shortliffe (1976 – Elsevier Science, out of print)

Artificial Evolution for Computer Graphics, by Karl Sims (1991 – *Siggraph '91 - Annual Conference Proceedings*, 1991, pp. 319–328, Eurographics Association)

Evolving Virtual Creatures, by Karl Sims (1994 - Siggraph '94 - Annual Conference Proceedings, 1994, pp. 43–50, Eurographics Association)

The Algorithm Design Manual, by Steven S. Skiena (1997 – Telos)

Data Analysis: A Bayesian Tutorial, by D. S. Sivia (1996 – Oxford University Press)

Image Processing: Analysis and Machine Vision, by Milan Sonka, Vaclav Hlavac, and Roger Boyle (1998 – Brooks Cole)

Knowledge Representation: Logical, Philosophical, and Computational Foundations, by John F. Sowa and David Dietz (1999 – Brooks Cole)

Computer Viruses as Artificial Life, by Eugene Spafford (1989 – in *Artificial Life An Overview*, edited by Christopher G. Langton, 1995, MIT Press, pp. 249–265)

Evaluating Natural Language Processing Systems: An Analysis and Review, by Karen Spärck Jones and Julia R. Galliers (1996 – Springer Verlag)

Readings in Information Retrieval, edited by Karen Spärck Jones and Peter Willett (1997 – Morgan Kaufmann)

Logic and Prolog, by Richard Spencer-Smith (1991 – Harvester Wheatsheaf)

Resolution Proof Systems: An Algebraic Theory (Automated Reasoning Series, Vol. 4), by Zbigniew Stachniak (1996 – Kluwer Academic Publishers)

Artificial Life VIII: Proceedings of the Eighth International Conference on Artificial Life, edited by Russell Standish, Mark A. Bedau, and Hussein A. Abbass (2003 – MIT Press; also available are the proceedings from the first through the seventh conferences)

Layered Learning in Multiagent Systems: A Winning Approach to Robotic Soccer, by Peter Stone (2000 – MIT Press)

Reinforcement Learning: An Introduction (Adaptive Computation and Machine Learning), by Richard S. Sutton and Andrew G. Barto (1998 – MIT Press)

Bayes's Theorem (Proceedings of the British Academy, Vol. 113), edited by Richard Swinburne (2002 – British Academy)

T

Evolutionary Art and Computers, by Stephen Todd and William Latham (1992 – Academic Press)

Introductory Techniques for 3-D Computer Vision, by Emanuele Trucco and Alessandro Verri (1998 – Prentice Hall)

Translation Engines: Techniques for Machine Translation, by Arturo Trujillo (1999 – Springer Verlag)

Managing Expert Systems, edited by Efraim Turban and Jay Liebowitz (1992 – Idea Group Publishing)

U

Human Face Recognition Using Third-Order Synthetic Neural Networks, by Okechukwu A. Uwechue and Abhijit S. Pandya (1997 – Kluwer Academic Publishers)

V

Simulated Annealing: Theory and Applications, by P. J. M. Van Laarhoven and E. H. L. Aarts (1987 - D Reidel Publishing Company – out of Print)

Statistical Learning Theory, by Vladimir N. Vapnik (1998 – Wiley Interscience)

Planning and Learning, by *Analogical Reasoning*, by Manuela M. Veloso (1994 – Springer Verlag Telos)

Learning and Generalization: With Applications to Neural Networks, by Mathukumalli Vidyasagar (2002 – Springer Verlag)

The Simple Genetic Algorithm: Foundations and Theory, by Michael D. Vose (1999 – MIT Press)

W

Virtual Organisms: The Startling World of Artificial Life, by Mark Ward (2000 – St Martin's Press)

In the Mind of the Machine: The Breakthrough in Artificial Intelligence, by Kevin Warwick (1998 – Random House)

Face Recognition: From Theory to Applications, by Harry Wechsler (1998 – Springer Verlag)

Multiagent Systems: A Modern Approach to Distributed Artificial Intelligence, edited by Gerhard Weiss (1999 – MIT Press)

Recent Advances in AI Planning, by Daniel S. Weld in *AI Magazine*, Summer 1999

Practical Planning: Extending the Classical AI Planning Paradigm, by David E. Wilkins (1989 – Morgan Kaufman)

Arguing A. I.: The Battle for Twenty-First Century Science, by Sam Williams (2002 – Random House)

Artificial Intelligence, by Patrick Henry Winston (1992 – Addison Wesley)

Introduction to MultiAgent Systems, by Michael Wooldridge (2002 – John Wiley & Sons)

X

Y

Intelligent Planning: A Decomposition and Abstraction Based Approach, by Qiang Yang (1998 – Springer Verlag)

Z

Intelligent Scheduling, edited by Monte Zweben and Mark S. Fox (1998 – Morgan Kaufmann)

Index

Outstanding New Titles:

 Computer Science Illuminated, Second Edition
Nell Dale and John Lewis
ISBN: 0-7637-0799-6
©2004

 Programming and Problem Solving with Java
Nell Dale, Chip Weems,
and Mark R. Headington
ISBN: 0-7637-0490-3
©2003

 Databases Illuminated
Catherine Ricardo
ISBN: 0-7637-3314-8
©2004

 Foundations of Algorithms Using Java Pseudocode
Richard Neapolitan and Kumarss Naimipour
ISBN: 0-7637-2129-8
©2004

 Artificial Intelligence Illuminated
Ben Coppin
ISBN: 0-7637-3230-3
©2004

 The Essentials of Computer Organization and Architecture
Linda Null and Julia Lobur
ISBN: 0-7637-0444-X
©2003

 A Complete Guide to C#
David Bishop
ISBN: 0-7637-2249-9
©2004

 A First Course in Complex Analysis with Applications
Dennis G. Zill and Patrick Shanahan
ISBN: 0-7637-1437-2
©2003

 Programming and Problem Solving with C++, Fourth Edition
Nell Dale and Chip Weems
ISBN: 0-7637-0798-8
©2004

 C++ Plus Data Structures, Third Edition
Nell Dale
ISBN: 0-7637-0481-4
©2003

 Applied Data Structures with C++
Peter Smith
ISBN: 0-7637-2562-5
©2004

 Foundations of Algorithms Using C++ Pseudocode, Third Edition
Richard Neapolitan and Kumarss Naimipour
ISBN: 0-7637-2387-8
©2004

 Managing Software Projects
Frank Tsui
ISBN: 0-7637-2546-3
©2004

 Readings in CyberEthics, Second Edition
Richard Spinello and Herman Tavani
ISBN: 0-7637-2410-6
©2004

 C#.NET Illuminated
Art Gittleman
ISBN: 0-7637-2593-5
©2004

Discrete Mathematics, Second Edition
James L. Hein
ISBN: 0-7637-2210-3
©2003

Take Your Courses to the Next Level

Turn the page to preview new and forthcoming titles in Computer Science and Math from Jones and Bartlett...

Providing solutions for students and educators in the following disciplines:

- Introductory Computer Science
- Java
- C++
- Databases
- C#
- Data Structures

- Algorithms
- Network Security
- Software Engineering
- Discrete Mathematics
- Engineering Mathematics
- Complex Analysis

Please visit http://computerscience.jbpub.com/ and http://math.jbpub.com/ to learn more about our exciting publishing programs in these disciplines.

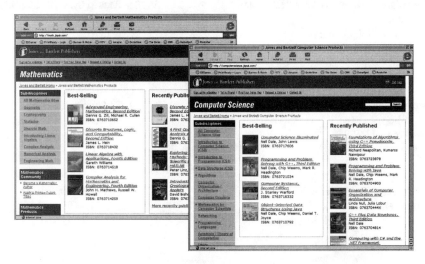

http://www.jbpub.com/   JONES AND BARTLETT PUBLISHERS   1.800.832.0034
BOSTON   TORONTO   LONDON   SINGAPORE